SEMUT

Christine Helliwell is an anthropologist, author and academic, currently Emeritus Professor at the Australian National University in Canberra. She has been carrying out research on Borneo's indigenous Dayak peoples – including living with them in their communities for months at a time – for almost forty years and has published widely on Dayak social and cultural life. In recent years she has begun to look into the secret operations conducted by SRD (popularly known as Z Special Unit) in Borneo during World War II, and in 2018 co-curated an Australian War Memorial exhibition about them. This is her first book for a general readership.

SEMUT

The untold story of a
**SECRET AUSTRALIAN
OPERATION IN WWII BORNEO**

Christine Helliwell

MICHAEL JOSEPH
an imprint of
PENGUIN BOOKS

MICHAEL JOSEPH

UK | USA | Canada | Ireland | Australia
India | New Zealand | South Africa | China

Michael Joseph is part of the Penguin Random House group of companies whose
addresses can be found at global.penguinrandomhouse.com.

Penguin
Random House
Australia

First published by Michael Joseph, 2021

Cover design by James Rendall © Penguin Random House Australia
Front cover portrait of Dita Bala and Major Gordon Senior 'Toby' Carter from the
Australian War Memorial National Collection (ref P01806.010); Japanese sun by
pisoieh/Shutterstock.com; beige background texture by chainarong06/Shutterstock.com;
black and white background by Yurlick/Shutterstock.com
Maps by Alicia Freile, Tango Media Pty Ltd, 2021
Longhouse illustrations on pp 145 & 321 by Guy Holt
Longhouse diagrams on pp 145 & 321 by James Rendall © Penguin Random House Australia
Text design by Midland Typesetters, Australia
Typeset in Sabon by Midland Typesetters, Australia

Every effort has been made to trace creators and copyright holders of quoted
and photographic material included in this book. The publisher welcomes
hearing from anyone not correctly acknowledged.

Printed and bound in Australia by Griffin Press, part of Ovato, an accredited
ISO ANZ/NZS 14001 Environmental Management Systems printer

 A catalogue record for this
book is available from the
NATIONAL
LIBRARY National Library of Australia
OF AUSTRALIA

ISBN 978 0 14379 002 0

penguin.com.au

For the operatives of Semut

and the many Dayaks who worked and fought beside them

And for

Jack Tredrea (1920–2018)

Barry Hindess (1939–2018)

'Going up that river was like travelling back to the earliest beginnings of the world, when vegetation rioted on the earth and the big trees were kings.'
Joseph Conrad, *Heart of Darkness*

'The Dayaks were our saviours, really.'
Bob Long, Operation Semut veteran, September 2014

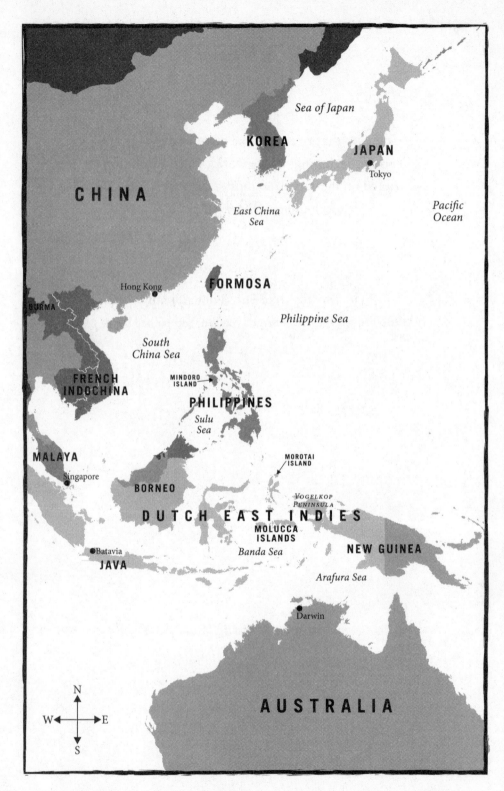

Eastern Asia and the western Pacific Ocean immediately prior to WWII.

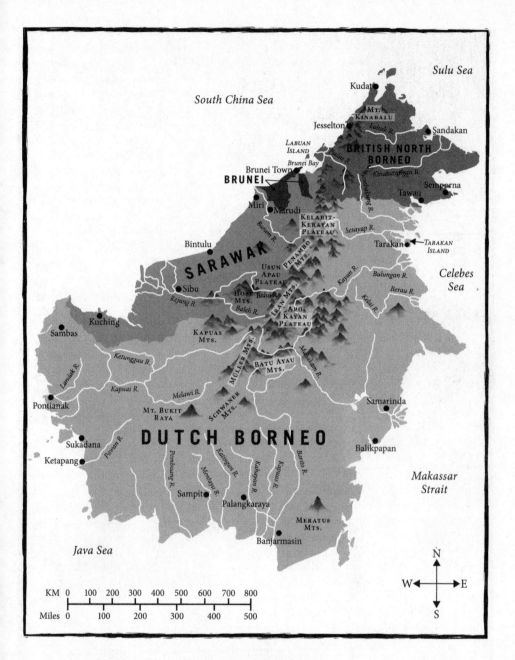

Borneo immediately prior to the Japanese occupation.

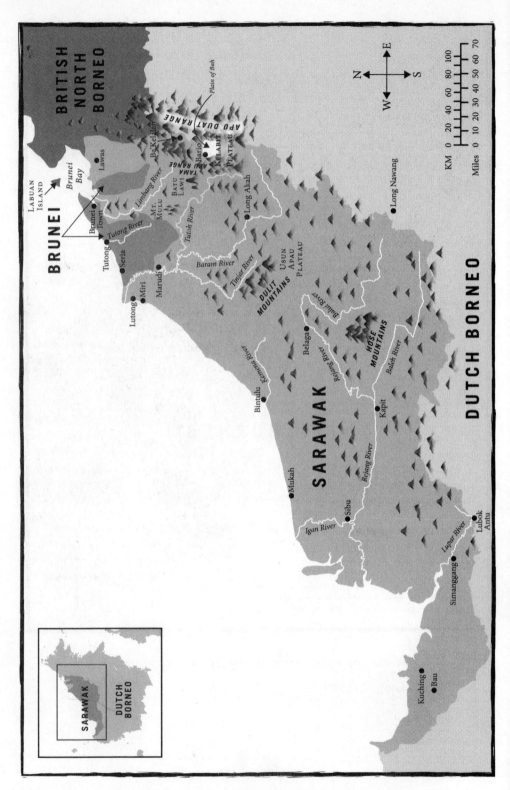

Sarawak immediately prior to the Japanese occupation.

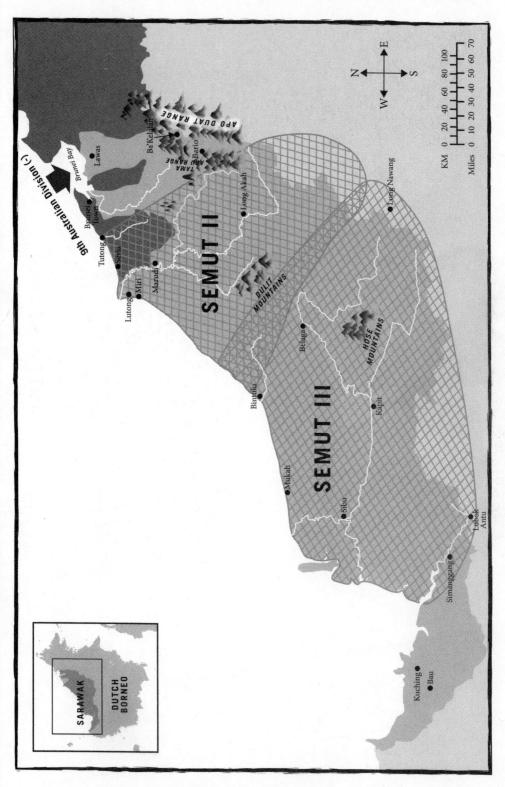

Sarawak showing Semut II and Semut III approximate operational areas.

CONTENTS

MAPS

PREFACE

AN OLD MAN, HIS arm around a woman, smiles from a photograph at the top of my computer screen. His thin white hair and neat cardigan somehow speak of his lifelong vocation as a tailor: a gentle profession also reflected in the shyness of his gaze. However, in 1945 this man, then aged just twenty-four, led a troop of local Dayak tribesmen through Borneo's jungles in a secret war against the Japanese. His name is Jack Tredrea and in the photo he is ninety-four years old. And the woman he is hugging is me.

I first met Jack in 2014 when I visited his home in Adelaide to interview him after learning he had taken part in a World War II (hereafter WWII) Allied special operation in Borneo. Although I had been carrying out research on WWII in Borneo for some time, Jack was the first Allied soldier I interviewed. I flew to Adelaide in September of that year, accompanied by a videographer from the Australian War Memorial (AWM). I was thrilled to be meeting someone who had travelled through Borneo's astonishing jungles in the 1940s, long before the terrible destruction inflicted on them in later years by rampant logging and the establishment of vast palm oil plantations. I had first gone to Borneo in the 1980s – forty years after Jack – as a young woman looking to conduct research for a PhD in anthropology, and had lived for twenty months in a long-house in the jungle, studying the social and cultural life of its Dayak inhabitants. Like Jack it had been my first time outside Australasia. I have spent a lot of time on the island in the years since, but never forgotten my first few months there.

As we settled down in Jack's immaculate living room under the eye of the video camera and his family photos, I asked him about the Borneo jungle. 'I thought,' he said, 'that it was the most beautiful place on earth.' And so began our friendship, forged over a shared love for a tragically disappearing place.

In early 2016 Jack and I joined forces to lobby the AWM to install a plaque on its grounds honouring Z Special Unit, the name by which Jack knew the Australian secret military organisation with which he had fought during WWII. Like all Z Special Unit personnel, he had signed secrecy provisions, and during his postwar debriefing he was ordered to remain silent for the next thirty years about his activities with the organisation. Other, although by no means all, Z Special men received similar orders – some even being sworn to secrecy for life. Many obeyed and, as a result, in large parts of Australia there were no Z Special Unit veterans' associations until the 1970s; in the absence of a Z Special banner, Jack marched with the 1st Australian Parachute Battalion each Anzac Day. The organisation's lack of visibility meant that it was one of very few from WWII never to have been honoured with a dedicated plaque at the Memorial.

Memorial approval for the plaque was quickly received and I began a search throughout Australia and overseas for Z Special personnel and their families, hoping that many would travel to Canberra for the dedication ceremony. This was a crazily ambitious undertaking since the organisation's recruits had come from several countries and few up-to-date contact details were available. In addition, those who remained would now be very elderly and likely to find travel difficult. But finally on 1 August 2016, after seventy years of waiting, more than twenty aged veterans and around one thousand family members gathered opposite the AWM sculpture garden (a group even having crossed the Tasman Sea from New Zealand) to honour and remember. Many of those who attended had lost husbands, fathers, grandfathers, brothers, uncles and friends to the organisation's notoriously perilous operations, and had made the trip to lay their grief to rest. As the Ode was read and the melancholy strains of the Last Post sounded across the Memorial's sweeping lawns under a sombre winter sky, it was impossible not to weep.

Jack was one of two veterans who unveiled the plaque that day in front of assembled dignitaries including the Chief of the Australian Defence Force. I sat with him on the stage before the ceremony and held his hand in the biting Canberra cold.

'How are you feeling?' I asked.

'Good,' he replied. 'No worries. I'll be fine.'

And he was. Back ramrod straight, he played his part to perfection. Afterwards he whispered to me quietly: 'It was the best day of my life.'

As well as producing ongoing friendships with veterans and their families, the day yielded an unexpected sequel. Not long after, a literary agent got in touch. She had seen Jack and me on TV during the numerous interviews we had done together and wondered whether I might like to write a book for a popular audience on Jack's WWII Borneo operation: Operation Semut. It was a breathtaking suggestion. I had been collecting material for a book on WWII in Borneo. But as an academic anthropologist, the book I'd planned was very different from the one dangled before me.

I spoke to Jack. 'There's never been a detailed book written about the whole of Semut,' he said wistfully. But I had no need for that gentle prod. Within a day I had decided. And so I, unlikeliest of military historians – an anti-war activist for much of my life – found myself writing a book about a secret military operation in the heart of Borneo.

Much has happened in the ensuing four and a half years. I began collecting archival and personal material for the book, interviewing the remaining operatives, talking to operatives' families, and revisiting the many interviews I had conducted in Borneo about the war. Jack and I developed a habit of speaking on the phone every Sunday afternoon: a weekly pause for laughter and shared confidences. I visited him in Adelaide in October 2016, staying in his little house in the suburbs where he cooked me porridge for breakfast and his daughter Lynnette brought us comforting evening meals. We pottered around in his garden, watched AFL on television and drank countless cups of tea. But mostly we talked about the war, Jack working back through his prodigious, remarkably accurate memories.

In the meantime I co-curated an exhibition at the Australian War Memorial on Australian WWII special operations in Borneo. Four of the five surviving operatives from those operations, including Jack, made it to Canberra for the opening in April 2018: all now looking unbearably frail. Jack and I slogged through more media rounds. But 2018 was a bitter year. In May my life partner Barry Hindess died. In July Jack followed him. I travelled back to Borneo a month later, nursing my sense of loss as I trekked to longhouses and communities, following in the footsteps of Jack and his comrades more than seventy years earlier.

And curiously, in the grip of profound grief, the story of Operation Semut sustained me. The hardships and joys experienced by its men became my own; I dreamed about them at night and sweated with them during the intensely humid days. Gradually, the book turned into two as I realised the operation was too large and sprawling to be confined within the pages of a single volume. My publisher kindly granted me extra time to get it finished.

Jack gave me carte blanche to write about the operation exactly as it happened, joking on several occasions: 'There's nothing they can do to me now.' So I have scrupulously set down the truth while, at the same time, trying to do him and his fellow operatives justice through the use of additional material to contextualise their experiences. His only stipulation was that the role of Borneo's indigenous Dayak peoples should be properly acknowledged: 'You have to tell them how important the Dayaks were.' This accorded with my own instincts as a student of Dayak peoples, and I have done what he asked. I hope the result would have made him proud.

NOTE ON Z SPECIAL UNIT AND SRD

The organisation to which Jack belonged – which he called Z Special Unit – had the formal name Special Operations Australia (hereafter SOA). SOA took the cover name Services Reconnaissance Department (hereafter SRD), and this latter name is the one by which it is more commonly known. Australian Army personnel who joined SRD – the majority of those in the organisation – were posted to and administered by Z Special Unit, and this was the name usually recorded on their service records, secrecy declarations and discharge papers. This name was also recorded on the documents of many other SRD personnel, even those who had not joined from the Australian Army.

As a result, Z Special Unit was the only name many SRD recruits knew for the unit they served with, some not discovering until long after the war that the larger SRD organisation existed. Many saw themselves, both during and after the war, simply as members of Z Special Unit.

SRD is the name I generally use for the organisation throughout this book. I use the terms Z Special Unit and SOA only when the particular context requires it.

NOTE ON SOURCES, ORTHOGRAPHY, LANGUAGE AND ABBREVIATIONS

Had I realised in advance how challenging it would be to write an accurate history of Operation Semut I might not have started – and so would have missed the experience of a lifetime. The project's difficulties have been due not least to the absence of detailed military accounts of the operation from the time. Most SRD files appear to have been destroyed at the end of the war, and those remaining were culled by official agencies in the following years. Similarly, personnel files for individuals who served with SRD are often missing from both the Australian and British archives. The unpublished history of SOA, produced after the war by the body's official historian, is partisan and, with reference to Operation Semut at least, full of inaccuracies – partly because it uncritically accepts information provided in operational reports that were themselves often incorrect. Unit war diaries were not kept for SRD, as they were for many other military units. And even when official accounts are available, details can vary markedly from report to report. As a result, I have struggled to pin down dates, places, personnel and even what happened for any particular event.

This means I have been heavily reliant at times on personal accounts, from both operatives and local peoples. Not only has it been difficult to locate such accounts – almost all of them are unpublished – but they are also notoriously inaccurate. All of the operatives were required to sign secrecy provisions when they were recruited to SRD; as a result, many did not begin recording their experiences until long after the war. Like the official reports, these accounts have had to be handled with great care.

To complicate matters further, both official and unofficial accounts from the operative side are full of mistakes with respect to local names (of both people and places) and local detail, including locations and distances. Sometimes it has taken weeks of sustained research to accurately identify a longhouse the operatives visited, a river where an important action took place, or a local leader they met. In this I was often reliant on local Borneo memories – as well as the fieldnotes of an older generation of anthropologists and the always invaluable *Sarawak Gazette*.

The arrival of COVID-19 on the world stage in early 2020, and subsequent closure of archives in Australia and the UK, created additional complexity. From this time it became impossible to access certain crucial documents. As a result I was required, very late in the piece, to reshape elements of the book.

But the research's rewards have far outweighed its tribulations. I have spent a great deal of time poking around archives, including the Australian War Memorial, the National Archives of Australia, the National Archives (UK), the Imperial War Museum (UK) and the Australian Special Air Service Regiment Historical Archives. A number of very generous individuals also allowed me to dig through their private collections of papers.

As well as foraging in both official and unofficial written records, I have fossicked in oral ones. In 2015 and 2018 I travelled throughout the northwestern part of the island of Borneo (the Malaysian state of Sarawak), largely to the areas where Semut had operated, and recorded – the majority of them on video-camera – around one hundred and twenty lengthy interviews with locals, mostly Dayaks who were alive during the war. I also interviewed – several of them a number of times – most of the surviving SRD operatives who had been on WWII operations in Borneo, including all three who had taken part in Operation Semut. I was lucky enough to have additional casual telephone conversations with two of these Semut operatives (Jack Tredrea and Bob Long), during which Operation Semut was often discussed. The information gained from these encounters was key to filling many of the gaps in the Semut record.

Perhaps most importantly, since 1985 I have had the privilege of conducting years of ethnographic fieldwork in Borneo: from this I have learned a great deal about its peoples – especially its Dayak peoples – and places. During this time I have taken part, using local languages as much as possible, in hundreds of informal conversations with Dayaks – and others – about WWII. This has provided the ballast for my account.

The Borneo fieldwork and interviews presented their own suite of difficulties. Travelling throughout remote Borneo even today can be gruelling, which possibly accounts for the note of sympathy the reader may detect when I describe operatives' 1945 jungle journeys. Many Dayaks are highly mobile; entire communities will up sticks and move to a new place for a variety of reasons. On two occasions I went to considerable effort to reach remote communities mentioned in operatives' accounts, only to discover that the people who were now there were not the same as those who had been there seventy years earlier. In addition, I was required to work across a large number of different Dayak languages, which entailed its own logistical challenges.

Since this book is intended for a general readership rather than an academic one, I have not provided exhaustive footnotes. Rather I have detailed sources of quotations and other key information in endnotes at the ends of paragraphs.

Unless stated otherwise I have used modern spellings throughout – these are generally much closer to the local terms than the largely Europeanised spellings of 1945. For example, the Rajang River of the 1945 accounts is spelled Rejang River here. In the original accounts it is not uncommon to have three or four spellings for one place or person – e.g. Long Beruang on the Tutoh River is variously spelled Long Bruang, Long Beruang, Long Berawan and Long Briang. Again, unless indicated otherwise, I have reduced them all to one common spelling: the one conventional in 2021 when this book was finalised. Similarly, many of the old accounts spell Dayak as 'Dyak', and some readers may be familiar with that spelling. However, it is now considered archaic, and I have spelled it as 'Dayak' throughout, except in direct quotes.

As an anthropologist, I have wanted to convey something of the lifeworlds of those who took part in Operation Semut, and to that end have included many direct quotes from participants in the text. Readers should be aware that, as a result, they may be confronted with terms acceptable to an earlier generation – such as 'boys' for Borneo locals and 'Jap' or 'Nip' for Japanese – that many now consider inappropriate or disrespectful.

One of the most difficult aspects of writing this book has been getting on top of the multitude of acronyms afflicting military literature. I have tried to protect my readers from this disease, and have used acronyms as little as possible. However, some were unavoidable; they are mostly found in Chapter 3, on operational planning. They are given below.

AIF	Australian Imperial Force
BBCAU	British Borneo Civil Affairs Unit
HQ	headquarters
LMG	light machine gun
OR	other ranks
POW	prisoner of war
SOA	Special Operations Australia
SOE	Special Operations Executive
SRD	Services Reconnaissance Department
SWPA	South-West Pacific Area
WWII	World War Two

Christine Helliwell
February 2021

GLOSSARY

The following local Borneo terms each occur more than once within the text.

arak	distilled liquor, usually made from fermented rice mash
borak	fermented rice wine (also called *tuak*)
damar	local resin burned in lamps
kampung	village, town precinct
kebal	invulnerability, especially to weapons
kepala kampung	village head
kuala	river mouth, estuary
kubu	timber fort
orang puteh	white person, European
parang	sword, bush knife; also machete
penghulu	regional leader sanctioned by the government
prahu/perahu	boat, canoe
raja/rajah	sultan, king, sovereign
sama kulit	lit: 'same skin', referring to skin colour
sirat	loincloth
sumpit	blowpipe
sungai/sungei	river
Temenggong	noble title conferred by the ruler
towkay	Chinese business owner, usually shopkeeper or trader
tuak	fermented rice wine (also called *borak*)
tuan	European male, 'Mr'

1

'THIS EDEN OF MIXED BLESSINGS'

25 March 1945

IT WAS LATE IN the rainy season, close to harvesting time, when Keling Langit first heard the sound: a deep, reverberating roar, coming from above the clouds that so often blanketed her valley high on Borneo's remote Kelabit Plateau. It seemed to circle the valley, louder, softer, then louder again. The young Kelabit woman was terrified: could it be spirit beings? She grasped her younger sister's hand and ran for her home in the nearby longhouse.

Early the next morning the sound came again, thrumming far above, eerie in its back-and-forth resonance. But this time, as she looked skyward, Keling Langit saw something emerge through the morning's low cloud. Seventy years later she described it to me as a 'white umbrella'. The first was joined by more umbrellas drifting down towards the bright green padi fields in which she stood. Keling Langit was so frightened she began to weep.

Above the cloud, twenty-four-year-old Jack Tredrea, a tailor in civilian life, was up from his seat in the gloomy belly of the aircraft that had transported his small party from the Philippines island of Mindoro. He was stretching, adjusting his parachute harness, doing a final mental check of his weaponry. Mostly he was trying not to think of what might be waiting on the ground below. Japanese soldiers and a slow agonising death under torture? Headhunting Dayaks looking to decapitate him? His tongue found the latex covering of the cyanide capsule secreted in his cheek.

Now he and his three companions were moving to the bomb bay out of which they would jump, Jack second in line behind the party leader. One of the Liberator crew joked to ease the tension: 'Lovely day for a jungle picnic, boys!' The man behind Jack tried for a cheeky retort but his voice failed halfway through. As the bomb doors opened Jack became aware of his heart's furious beating: he was sure he could hear it above the throb of the aircraft engine. Then his party leader was gone and the empty slide yawned in front. He thought fleetingly of his wife back in Adelaide. And he jumped.[1]

◌◌

Borneo 1945. The Japanese had occupied the island from late 1941 and now lived in garrisons scattered mostly around its coastal edge. The island's vast heart, shadowed with mountains and dense tropical jungle, remained largely beyond their reach. Here, in the tops of giant trees, gibbons floated their haunting songs at grey dawn and the macabre hornbill birds – seemingly more beak than body – hung in ponderous flight. Here, too, lived most of Borneo's indigenous Dayak peoples: carving clearings for their longhouses and rice fields, hunting game and gathering jungle products for a dizzying array of uses.

This book is the first of a planned pair that together set out the story of Operation Semut, a secret Australian military operation that took place behind Japanese lines in Sarawak and immediate surrounds, in the northern part of Borneo in 1945. The operation is regarded by some as one of the most successful of the Australian secret operations launched in the Pacific during WWII, by others as 'consistently over-glamorised [. . .] puerile and [. . .] unnecessary', and by others again as illustrating the 'lack of control and accountability' of Australian special operations at the time.[2]

The book tells of how several parties of SRD operatives were covertly inserted by parachute and seaplane into the rugged northern interior of Borneo starting in March 1945. Their orders included establishing local intelligence and guerrilla networks that could be used in support of the Australian invasion at Labuan Island and Brunei Bay, on Borneo's north coast, planned for June 1945. My aim is not only to describe and assess the operation, but also to convey something of how it felt for the operatives – and also sometimes the Dayaks – who took part. This has meant writing Borneo itself, in all its colour and life, into the heart of the narrative.

The operatives were mostly very young Australians, although they also included British, New Zealanders, Malayans and Canadians, among others. For many it was their first direct experience of war. The operation's success depended entirely on winning the support of local Dayak peoples and persuading them to participate in a secret campaign against the Japanese. Yet the loyalties of Dayak groups in the area were uncertain: it could be that they supported the Japanese and welcomed the ousting of the previous European colonial regimes. In addition, Japanese ferocity towards local people who opposed them was well known in Borneo as elsewhere; Dayaks might well decide that the risk of supporting the operation was too great. In either case the operatives would almost inevitably end up in Japanese hands if they were not killed first by Dayaks.

Theirs is a remarkable story on both sides. It was the time of the White Australia policy, and many of the operatives had barely encountered Asian or indigenous people of any kind, let alone been to Asia or even outside Australia. For their part, some of the Dayaks had never before seen a white face. Dayaks were baffled at the European preoccupation with solitude and privacy, while most of the operatives had never before eaten rice – the local staple – except as a gluey substance in sweet puddings.

Operatives were apprehensive when told they were going to Borneo, and not only because of its Japanese occupiers. The name 'Borneo' has long conjured up fearful images in the European mythos: of monstrous fetid jungles teeming with perilous wildlife and headhunting savages. Unhelpfully, headhunting was described as a Dayak 'sport' in a booklet distributed by the Australian Military Forces for use in Borneo during the war, and an accompanying cartoon showed a near-naked dark-skinned man – several white heads scattered around his feet – cheerfully slicing off the head of a khaki-clad white man. It is not surprising that for the operatives being sent there, as one of their number told me seventy years later: 'It was hard to know which to be more worried about: the Japs or the Dayaks.'[3]

೦ೲ

Today almost all of Borneo's mighty jungles are gone, hostage to the greedy pursuit of profit for those who choose to live elsewhere, but in 1945 they covered the island. For most of the young men who took part in Semut – accustomed as they were to more arid, more domesticated landscapes – the jungles came as a shock. This is clear from portrayals in their personal accounts – both verbal and written – as well as from the vivid stories they brought back home. Almost without exception, their families were able to repeat parts of those stories to me seventy years later.

It is not surprising the jungles left such an indelible mark. Massive trees, often hundreds of years old, blanketed vast areas, their huge symmetrical trunks rising like sculpted pillars before proliferating far overhead into a canopy of green, broken only here and there by patches of light torn by those that had fallen. Climbers such as lianas and rattans used the trees as supports, twining themselves round and round trunks and trailing from branches in endless matted webs, in some cases – as with the aptly named strangling fig – choking their hosts to eventual death in a tremendous efflorescence of sun-seeking foliage and aerial roots.

Ferns dotted the ground as well as tree trunks and the canopy itself, creating their own miraculous hanging gardens extending up to several metres in diameter. Mushrooms and other fungi grew in profusion among the rotting vegetation and undergrowth of the forest floor, often displaying a vivid, almost incandescent beauty. And everything was forever wet, captive to the frequent downpours and incomparable humidity that characterise this equatorial region.

In spite of the shadows cast by the giant trees, the jungles were places of interminable sound and movement. Birds flashed and darted overhead, monkeys swung themselves from branch to branch with astonishing agility, and butterflies – sometimes huge and brilliantly coloured – fluttered in murky glades. Not all life here was benevolent: crocodiles skulked around rivers, streams and the frequent marshy areas and snakes – including the deadly king cobra, which can 'stand' to a height of a metre or two – lurked out of sight. Add to these various species of deer, wild pigs, sun bears, the beautiful secretive clouded leopards, orangutans and their relatives the gibbons, and you gain some sense of the bewildering abundance of life the jungles sheltered. Sadly, many of these creatures are now critically endangered.

And the noise! Birds squawked and twittered and monkeys screeched. Perhaps best of all, gibbons constructed glorious whooping songs to welcome the dawn. But outdoing all else was the sibilant resonating thrum – often so loud as to be deafening – created by thousands of cicadas basking in the sun on the forest's canopy: the iconic sound of a Borneo jungle.

Some of the operatives embraced this overwhelming size, this profusion, this sensory battering; others loathed and feared it. Jack Tredrea was one of the former, telling me the first time I met him in 2014 that the Borneo jungle was 'the most beautiful place on earth'. For many operatives, however, the jungle was a hellish place with which they struggled to come to terms. Thus Roland Griffiths-Marsh, of Semut I, writes of the 'horrifying conditions' in which he fought.

> The energy-sapping heat, accompanied by intense humid-ity, incessant rains and inadequate medication, brought with it the black Anopheles malarial mosquito with its often fatal dose of malignancy. Dengue was the norm, bacillary or amoe-bic dysentery was inevitable. [The skin infection] yaws, with its huge craters of rotten flesh sometimes so deep the bone could be seen as a grain of rice, and scrub typhus were, if possible, lesser evils to the hookworm which burrowed through the bloodstream, to make its home in the intestines. The infested swamps were hellish places, where leeches weaved from side-to-side in response to body heat, before dropping on their victim, where glands in groin and armpits swelled to the size of golf balls, in reaction to some unknown tropical malignancy.[4]

For these men the jungle could appear as an alien presence, recalling Joseph Conrad's vengeful 'implacable force'. This 'jun-gle fever', as it came to be known, could afflict operatives to such a degree that they dreaded being there on their own, especially at night. Tom Harrisson, commanding officer of Semut I, appears to have suffered from this frightening malaise:

The nastiest noise of the jungle night is the one that isn't. I mean
the suspicion or expectation or feeling of something moving;
but you cannot be sure whether what moves is a thing more
than pure imagination. [. . .] Can a centipede not be silently
crawling along the hammock rope? That microswitch must
be a bat; and about to tear into the netting? [. . .] I developed
the absurd fantasy of a large Sambhur deer stalking through the
forest and accidentally pronging me with its antlers from underneath. [. . .]

Waking, half, from jungle sleep, it was fearfully easy to feel
suddenly surrounded by *human* noise, by the breath of man.
And who else would this be but Japanese?[5]

All wars are cruel, but the war against the Japanese throughout
the jungles of the Pacific – including in Borneo – was especially so.
The Pacific War was deeply racialised on both sides, intensifying its
ferocity. The Japanese deliberately cast the Allies as white-skinned
colonisers out to exploit darker-skinned Asian peoples, and contrasted pure Japanese with monstrous, demonic Americans and
British. For their part, the Allies reached back into ancient arche-
types of the Asian 'Yellow Peril' to characterise Japanese as more
animal than human, with propaganda and press reports referring to
them as 'mad dogs', 'yellow vermin', 'living snarling rats', monkeys,
insects and reptiles: sub-human creatures with a seemingly infinite
capacity for cruelty, strange suicidal tendencies and an inhuman
talent for jungle warfare. The Allies hated and feared the Japanese
much more than the Germans.[6]

As a result, the level of savagery witnessed in the Pacific theatre
was shocking, far worse than that seen in the European theatre.

Kill or be killed. No quarter, no surrender. Take no prisoners. Fight to the bitter end. These were everyday words in the

combat areas [. . .] As World War Two recedes in time and scholars dig at the formal documents, it is easy to forget the visceral emotions and sheer race hate that gripped all participants.

In fact, many of those who took part did not forget. When I interviewed aged SRD veterans more than seventy years after the war's end, most alluded to the hatred of the Japanese that had driven them to volunteer for secret missions, a hatred that still led some to cross the road to avoid someone who appeared Japanese. Their voices still shook when they talked of the Japanese enemy.[7]

And they spoke of the fear they felt towards this seemingly inhuman foe: a fear that crept unbidden into their thoughts both before and during operations. Indeed, hatred and fear were so intertwined it was difficult to see where one started and the other ended. Roland Griffiths-Marsh again:

Capture [by the Japanese] [. . .] at best meant disembowelling by bayonet, or more often the obscenity of torture; perhaps a sliver of bamboo thrust down the urethra, or immolation by petrol, or some equally bestial death. For these frontline soldiers the only expectation of life was death.[8]

For Allied operatives in Borneo, the jungles – in which they spent most of their time – potentially harboured Japanese, spectral companions on every journey. As a result, for many, jungle merged with Japanese into a single ominous enemy, heightening the unrelenting sense of threat. As Brian Walpole of Semut III wrote later with reference to jungle warfare against the Japanese:

There's no backup behind enemy lines – if you get into trouble you're on your own. There's no front line either. They can come at you from anywhere.[9]

Frederick Spencer Chapman, who famously operated behind Japanese lines in WWII Malaya – a short hop from Sarawak across the South China Sea – describes well this apprehension of the equatorial jungle as a dark enemy. As he tells it, most British soldiers feared the Malayan jungle so much that, cut off from their units and left alone in it, they expected to die before long. And so they did. Spencer Chapman attributed his own survival, operating completely on his own under dreadful conditions for several years, to his acceptance of the cardinal rule: 'the jungle is neutral.'[10]

By no means did all Semut operatives see the jungle as unremittingly malign. Some, while alive to its terrors, were touched by its sublime beauty; for Bill Sochon, commanding officer of Semut III, both jungle and the island it enfolded were 'this Eden of mixed blessings'. But none were left unmoved, and learning to accept it as neutral or even friend was imperative. Yet in most official accounts of the operation the jungle appears – if at all – as a pallid version of itself far removed from the vivid living world of operative experience. This account will be different.[11]

෨෨

The same is true of the Dayaks. Operative memoirs are suffused with the strangeness of these people beside whom they ate, slept, slogged their way across the forested terrain, and fought for months: with their physical appearance, their behaviour, their unimaginable jungle skills, their noisy cavernous longhouses. Yet, like the jungle in which they were so mesmerisingly at home, the Dayaks appear – if they appear at all – as strangely disembodied in the operation's official accounts.

Many scholars have pointed out that official records and histories of the war in the Pacific tend to overlook the role played by local peoples. Nevertheless, I was unprepared for the degree of Dayak invisibility I encountered when I first began reading official reports and documents relating to Operation Semut. Here, for example, is the report of an action carried out on the lower Baram River on 23 June 1945 by Robert Wilson, then second-in-command of Semut II.

> Following a couple of successful actions at Lobok [Lubok] Nibong on 23 June in which the enemy lost 1 officer and 8 ORs killed and a Kiki (LMG) captured, I decided to withdraw up river rather than accept battle under what I appreciated to be unfavourable circumstances.[12]

Taken at face value, this description is patently absurd. Wilson had at this point been in Borneo exactly a week and had no knowledge of the local language. It is impossible that he could be operating by himself. How had he travelled downriver to Lubok Nibong in the first place? How did he know the best place to set up his ambushes? How did he know where to retreat to?

In fact, as further digging in the archives and conversations with local Baram peoples made clear, Wilson had not been alone at Lubok Nibong. He had with him not only another operative (mentioned earlier in the report), but a force of around fifteen to twenty local guerrillas, both Dayak and Chinese (unmentioned in the report). One of the guerrillas had died during the action, yet this is also not mentioned in the report. And in this respect Wilson is no better and no worse than any other Semut commander: local contribution is routinely absent from their official accounts.

I am not suggesting this stems from a deliberate intention on the part of Semut officers to exclude locals from their reports: it is in the nature of military reports to provide only the bare, necessary facts. But the invisibility of locals reflects a tendency to see the presence of Europeans as noteworthy in a way that the presence of locals was not. There is no doubt that the death of a White operative would have counted for much more in the official reckoning than did the death of the unnamed local.

In fact, Dayak guerrillas were the backbone and mainstay of the operation. Dayak warfare has rarely taken the form of conventional Western warfare – in which armies face off against one another in open displays of military might – since this is useless in the close confines of a Borneo jungle. Consequently, in contrast to many of the operatives, most guerrillas had a sure grasp of the techniques necessary for jungle warfare, in which guile, sabotage, and rapid raids when the enemy least expect them are the order of the day. It is no accident that many of the most demanding aspects of this kind of warfare – scouting out and invisibly shadowing enemy forces, effecting unexpected rapid strikes, luring the enemy into false moves – were carried out on Operation Semut by Dayaks. The European operatives, by their own admission, lacked the necessary skills.

In contrast to the operatives, Dayaks also understood the weather, the terrain, the movements of the rivers, the local flora and fauna – all critical to tactical and strategic planning. Many of Semut's most effective actions against the Japanese – ambushes, hit-and-run raids, unexpected attacks – were proposed in the first instance by guerrillas, whose knowledge of place meant they saw possibilities invisible to operatives.

If Dayak guerrillas earn only occasional mention in official documents, those who performed the mundane work of guiding, bearing, paddling and so on – not to mention finding food, cooking, erecting overnight shelters – are almost completely absent. Yet these people, both men and women, enabled the operatives to function. An account by Charles Hardy of Semut I conveys something of the difficulties of Semut jungle journeys:

July 10th (Tuesday) – I left Long Malada for Long Beruan at 0700 hours, and I arrived Long Beruan at 1530 hours, travelling very slowly. I now have an abscess on the same leg as the large ulcer; I will probably take five to six days to reach Long Berang. Persistent downpours, it is extremely heavy going, icy winds on the mountain tops, burning humidity in the valleys and padi fields; constant thirst, sometimes the water running into my mouth is salty perspiration, sometimes very welcome rainwater. Last trip took only three days, but this is vastly different weather and now there is much less food in the villages along the way.

Looking closely at Hardy's account we discover that he had at least thirty-five local Dayaks with him: fifteen to twenty warriors to protect him and twenty bearers to carry equipment and supplies. Without these people – not to mention those in the longhouses along the way who provided him with food and shelter – he could not have survived.[13]

Even this does not tell the full story. When I began to trawl through memoirs written by operatives, I discovered that many – perhaps even most – kept what are usually referred to as 'personal boys' or 'right-hand boys': young men employed to take care of mundane day-to-day matters such as carrying one's kit and obtaining and preparing food. Inevitably, given that most of the operatives had extremely poor local language skills and little knowledge of the local situation, these young men also acted as go-betweens with locals to organise boatmen, porters, guides, scouts and so on. But again, they are largely missing from the official accounts.

Gradually I came to realise that when the operatives wrote of their activities in the first person – as in the Wilson and Hardy examples above – most of the time at least one Dayak, their 'personal boy', had been with them. Often, again as in these two examples, there had been many more.

There is no shame, and no lessening of the honour due these brave men, in this fact of Dayak support. All five of the SRD operatives I interviewed who had served in Borneo were at pains to emphasise a fundamental truth: 'None of us would have survived more than a day in that environment on our own.' Ironically, Dayak invisibility in the official accounts makes a mockery of a basic tenet of special operations' philosophy: the critical need to cultivate local support if an operation is to be successful.[14]

Dayaks are not the only ones to have been overlooked in official accounts of the operation. Other groups – including Chinese, Malays, Eurasians and men from throughout the then Dutch East Indies – also contributed to it, often in very significant ways. But the operation was planned from the start to be located in Dayak areas and to seek recruits primarily from Dayak groups. And this is what happened. In areas closer to the coast, more Chinese and Malays came on board, but throughout the remote inland areas where the operation had its bases, support came largely from Dayaks. Consequently this book focuses on the Dayak contribution. Additional books will hopefully be written that look more closely at the contributions of others.

The search for historical accuracy has thus involved moving Dayaks forward to assume their rightful roles as equal and sometimes leading participants in most aspects of the operation. However, tragically, I have been unable to achieve my key aim of including in the book a list of all the local guerrillas who participated in the operation. For the parts I focus on in this volume at least, it has proved impossible to identify more than a handful of guerrillas, in spite of scouring all the archives in Australia and the UK where I expected to find their names. And yet there is also something horribly apt about this, highlighting as it does our failure of recognition. Instead I have left several pages blank at the end of the book to remind us of where their names should be.

I discussed in the Preface the exhaustive (and exhausting) research I have undertaken to return locals to their rightful place in the operation. Nevertheless, sadly, the record remains scanty: I lack detailed information about Dayak contribution to every – even most – activities and actions that occurred as part of it. As a result I have often been unable to include this contribution in my account, even though every instinct tells me that I should. I have done what I can. In return I ask you, the reader, to keep yourself constantly open, as you read this book, to the possibility of Dayak presence. Even if not mentioned, they were probably there.

∽

So who were – or rather are – the Dayaks? It is imperative that we know something about these people if we are to understand Operation Semut. The name 'Dayak' is itself a confusing one, used differently in different parts of Borneo. In this book I use it as the operatives did, and as many scholars now do: as an umbrella term to refer to the indigenous pagan (now mostly Christian) peoples of Borneo. When used in this way, Dayaks stand in contrast to Malays, who are the indigenous Muslim peoples of Borneo, although the distinction between the two groups is by no means as cut-and-dried as this suggests. Many Dayaks have now moved to coastal towns, but in the 1940s most lived in inland jungled regions, while Malays tended to live closer to the coast.

There is a baffling array of Dayak groups, most with their own distinct languages, although any Dayak individual is likely to speak the languages of several neighbouring groups. In this book we will encounter the Berawan, Bukit, Iban, Kayan, Kejaman, Kelabit, Kenyah, Lahanan, Long Kiput, Lun Dayeh/Lun Bawang, Murik, Murut, Penan, Punan, Punan Bah, Rejang, Sa'ban, Sebop, Sekapan, Seping, Tagal and Ukit/Bukat, since these are the groups that inhabited the territories where the Semut operation took place.

Most of those who have ruled them – Malay sultanates, European colonial regimes, Japanese occupiers, and post-colonial governments of Malaysia, Brunei and Indonesia – have seen these peoples as primitive. But this view inevitably tells us more about the rulers than the ruled, and fails to recognise the complexities of Dayak belief systems, the astounding intricacy and beauty of their carvings, weavings and paintings – which now sell for staggering prices in the galleries of the West – and the genius of their environmental adaptations. It also overlooks the respect and affection Dayaks tend to inspire in outsiders who take the trouble to spend time with them.

Most Dayak peoples now live in free-standing houses. But at the time of WWII, apart from nomadic groups like the Penan, they largely lived in magnificent sprawling longhouses usually located along the banks of rivers. A longhouse was essentially an entire village raised several metres off the ground on massive ironwood piles (which were resistant to humidity and termites), and covered with a single roof of sago palm leaf thatch or handmade wooden shingles. Entry was gained via a notched wooden log at each end, which Dayaks were able to scramble up with conspicuous agility, but which Europeans – including the operatives – invariably found a challenge (especially after a cup or two of rice wine) and were reduced to inching up on all fours. Chickens, pigs and even cattle were often penned beneath the longhouse, a remarkably efficient arrangement that enabled families to drop food scraps directly to their animals.

Longhouses varied greatly from group to group in both architectural style and length. The smallest were no more than 20 yards (18m) long and contained only three or four households, while the largest stretched for 500 yards (460m) and included hundreds of households. However, whatever its style, in general a longhouse was divided into two distinct areas: an outer open gallery, and an inner area comprised of separate household apartments. Each apartment had its own door opening onto the gallery; as a result, in most local languages apartments were referred to as 'doors' and the size of a longhouse was measured by the number of doors it contained.

In the outer gallery neighbours came together to smoke, chew betel nut, share the gossip of the day or simply stroll in the breeze. The inner apartment area, on the other hand, was the place where the members of each household slept and usually cooked and ate together. Visitors to a longhouse rarely entered the inner apartments: they slept and ate on the gallery.

Dayak longhouses of the 1940s were companionable, bustling and usually very noisy. Indeed, to the Westerner, perhaps the most unforgettable feature of longhouse life was the bewildering cacophony of sound found within. During the day the entire structure reverberated and shook to the *boom, boom, boom* of women pounding rice to release the milky edible grain from its husk. Children screamed and ran in play while adults called and chatted to one another, and the wooden planks of the floor shivered and rattled to the rhythm of people moving across them. The swish and clatter of women's rice-winnowing trays, wielded with sinuous grace, added background accompaniment. Roosters crowed from beneath with a disturbing frequency rarely, it seemed, waiting – as they should – for the dawn.

Longhouse smells were also distinctive. The sour reek rising from the pig pens pervaded the entire structure, and mingled with the welcoming aromas of roasting coffee and cooking meat. In sweetcorn season the smoky scent of blackened baby cobs, caramelised over the embers, quickened the appetite. At durian time the sultry pong of this most delectable of fruits gladdened the heart with anticipation. In the evenings the aromatic perfume of burning *damar* lamps (made from local resin) mingled with the musky fragrance of burning resinous wood. From dusk until dawn smoke, from fires lit underneath in an effort to deter mosquitos, often filled every nook and cranny, leading to streaming eyes and running noses.

When they were not at their longhouses, most Dayak peoples of the time were at their rice fields. Rice was literally the stuff of life for almost all Dayak groups, in a way that many of us now find difficult to imagine. There were no supermarkets or government assistance in 1940s Borneo, and so the failure of the rice crop could mean starvation. Most groups grew rice not in the irrigated 'paddy fields' of Western imagination, but rather in annual plots cleared on the sunny, non-irrigated slopes of hills – in much the same way as Westerners grow wheat or corn.

People also cultivated cassava, eating both tubers and leaves, a range of condiments such as chillies and turmeric, and sometimes sago, as well as fruit trees: bananas, durian, mangos, oranges, rambutan, coconuts and papaya, among others. They hunted for game and foraged for bamboo shoots, fern fronds and other edible plant products in the jungles, and fished in the rivers. Nevertheless, rice was the staple food and its cultivation the overwhelmingly important occupation for most Dayaks of the time. Daily life in a longhouse danced to its insistent tune.

Most Dayak peoples have since converted to Christianity, but at the time of Operation Semut almost all were pagan, with different groups sharing similar religious beliefs and practices. Dayaks at the time believed in a form of animism whereby the world around them was full of spirits, both malign and benign: they could harm humans if offended, and aid them if appeased. Spirits could make their wishes known to humans using animals or birds as omens. Omens were also deliberately sought when people needed guidance from the spirits: most commonly, a pig was slaughtered and its organs, especially the liver, read by an omen specialist. The presence of spirits and omens animated the Dayak world in ways the operatives often found baffling and frustrating.

Jack Tredrea from Semut I describes how if a certain kind of bird flew across the jungle path in front as he and his troop of Dayak guerrillas were setting out on a march, the guerrillas would often refuse to go any further. 'I just learned to sit down where we were and wait,' he told me. 'No point in getting impatient or annoyed.' For his Dayak companions the bird was a sign from the spirits that misfortune would befall them if they proceeded on their journey that day.[15]

∽

And so to headhunting – a subject of dark fascination for Europeans – which plays a crucial role in this narrative. Headhunting by Dayaks was actively encouraged by operatives during the Semut campaign. As a result, many of the grinning human skulls, stained dark with smoke, that were still common in Dayak longhouses when I first went to Borneo in the 1980s, were Japanese in origin. They stood as a last reminder of what Dayaks term the Japanese war.

Headhunting was an important religious ritual, performed by many – although by no means all – Dayak groups in the past. Up until the twentieth century, taking a human head and escorting it back to one's own village was a means by which men of those groups could increase both their own potency, fertility and invulnerability, and those of their communities. Contrary to popular belief, Dayak headhunters did not set out to kill simply for killing's sake, or remove heads in some kind of barbaric frenzy. Rather, bringing heads home, performing the appropriate rituals with them, and hanging them (usually) from the longhouse rafters, increased the spiritual and bodily health of individual and community, leading to increased wealth and good rice harvests. As the early twentieth-century Dutch explorer Hendrik Tillema noted:

> I do not in any way wish to justify the custom, but I must say
> that it was in no way founded on cruelty or lust of blood, and
> it seems to me regrettable that when this custom, which was to

a certain extent based upon ethical conceptions, was abolished, we did not attempt to replace it by some other conception of spiritual value.[16]

Similarly, a group of US airmen, who spent several months with the Lun Bawang during WWII after their plane was shot down, were surprised by the headhunting ceremony they witnessed after their hosts had beheaded a group of Japanese soldiers:

> Neither he nor the other Yanks felt disgust at such treatment of the *heitais*' [Japanese soldiers'] corpses. [. . .] What they were seeing was clearly not an act of disrespect. On the contrary, the Dayaks were performing a sacred rite; the airmen felt privileged to be witnessing it.[17]

For most groups, headhunting involved the incorporation of the victim's spirit into the head-taker's family and community. For the Iban, for instance,

> The victim died to old relationships but was born into new ones. The ritual activities associated with headhunting illustrate how enmity was transformed into friendship. After the head of an enemy had been taken, it was ceremonially received at the foot of the longhouse ladder, just as is a guest at a festival. [. . .] After the skull had been cleaned, it was hung in a wicker casing in a place of prominence on the verandah of the head-taker's family, as testimony to the courage of the hunter and in honour of the spirit of the skull.

The arrival of fresh heads at their new home was an event of great joy – women would welcome the warriors carrying the heads with much ceremony. Once home, the head would usually be treated – either boiled and skinned or smoked – to preserve it, and then hung from the rafters of the longhouse or in special head houses.[18]

In spite of the richness and complexity of Dayak lives, the single thing most Semut operatives knew about Dayaks before they went to Borneo was that they had once been – and perhaps still were – headhunters. This alone was enough to fill many with a dread otherwise reserved for the Japanese, even though headhunting was by then largely extinct on the island.

Similarly, throughout their later lives many Semut operatives had persistent nightmares featuring vivid images of newly taken Japanese heads dangling from the bloody hands of Dayak warriors. Roland Griffiths-Marsh wrote in 1990:

I wanted to retch, but could not. The heads were close-cropped, reminding me of bloodless pigs' heads displayed in Australian butcher shops; pasty yellow, glazed, non-seeing eyes behind drooping lids, colourless lips puckered in terror, while bits of sinew and marrow dangled from the base of the skull.

He adds: 'my nightmares that night were ghastly.' Similarly, Bill Sochon commented years later:

The atavistic scene burned its way into my brain and even today I am still unable to restrain a physical shudder as I recall the sight of the glassy eyes and gaping, distorted mouths of the decapitated heads.[19]

None of this is surprising. Europeans have for centuries placed great value on the integrity of the human body, and on the need to maintain bodily unity after death. For this reason, medieval English torturers were forbidden to sever or divide the body – they were restricted to squeezing, twisting or stretching it – and quartering, or cutting the body into four pieces, was used to punish only the most heinous of crimes, especially high treason. It is because parts break off the leper's body that leprosy still inspires such revulsion and terror among many Westerners, and discomfort with the idea of dividing the body after death helps to explain our low rates of organ donation.[20]

And in the pantheon of body parts, heads carry particular weight: removal of the head from the body after death is especially shocking. Modern terrorists understand this, and so often use beheading to terrorise and disgust European audiences.

However, not all peoples place such value on bodily unity after death, and it is clear that Dayaks of the time were among them. This meant that for Dayaks, as for some other peoples, the sight of a severed head did not incite the dismay it does in a European. Indeed, we can speculate that for Dayaks of the time the idea of leaving dead bodies with heads intact – as routinely happens on European battlefields – was not only astounding, but distressing. Instead of being carried home and incorporated into the social fabric of the killer's longhouse, heads were left literally out in the cold: abandoned, unwanted. This perhaps appeared as gratuitous killing: done for its own sake rather than to increase the wellbeing of family and community.

I have no desire to celebrate headhunting: it was violent and cruel, creating ongoing misery for groups that were its recurrent victims. But it was no more so – and in many respects much less so – than other forms of warfare we find acceptable. All warfare is, of necessity, a shockingly brutal business: it involves blood, gore and death whether carried out using modern weapons or headhunters' swords. Given this, there is much to recommend headhunting over other forms. Compared with the use of mortars, grenades or bombs, for instance, headhunting – performed hand-to-hand – is highly discriminating in its targets, producing few casualties and, paradoxically, often leaving bodies much more intact.

But European horror at Dayak headhunting is shadowed by even more excruciating ironies. Many Allied soldiers – mostly American – themselves collected the heads of dead Japanese to send or take home during the Pacific war. This reflects the other side of Western repugnance with severed heads: a simultaneous dark attraction to them. Thus European travellers and administrators collected human heads from throughout the world during the eighteenth and nine-teenth centuries, and transported them back to Europe where they were often put on public display. Even today, crowds come to gawk at the human heads exhibited in museums around the world, includ-ing at the Pitt Rivers Museum at Oxford University. When it was rumoured in 2007 that the Pitt Rivers exhibit might be withdrawn, a public outcry ensued.[21]

Another – and perhaps more significant – irony involves the long-term willingness of Europeans to enlist other peoples to engage in headhunting when it is to European advantage. Thus the European colonial regimes in both Sarawak and Dutch Borneo – following on from the identical practice of the Malay sultans who had preceded them as rulers of Borneo – employed Dayak mercenaries, usually Ibans, in their punitive expeditions against Dayak groups that had persisted with headhunting against govern-ment decree. The explicit understanding was that not only would rebel longhouses be sacked and plundered but, yes, rebel heads would be taken.[22]

Put simply, for much of the period of European rule in Borneo, headhunting was actively sponsored by those who condemned and outlawed it, in order to punish those who practiced it. The moral tor-tuousness of this position has stalked relations between Europeans and Dayaks throughout Borneo's history. It continued to do so during Operation Semut when the operatives' sheer hatred of the

Japanese – the urge to kill or be killed, as they saw it – impelled them not only to license the practice but, indeed, to pay some Dayaks to engage in it.

Yet, again, almost no mention of this was made in any of the official reports, presumably because the operation's commanding officers were aware that desecration of enemy bodies during war was potentially a violation of the 1929 Geneva Convention. But herein lies an oddity: why should removing the head from a dead body in order to honour it, as Dayaks did, be seen as any more of a crime than shattering a live body into thousands of unrecognisable pieces with a grenade? The answer of course is that European sensibilities, not Dayak ones, carry the most sway when it comes to formulating legal codes pertaining to war.

 ∽

There have been a number of accounts of Semut published over the years, but all have been based on a limited range of source materials with the result that none has told anything like the full story. In particular, to date there has been no detailed published account covering all four parts of the operation (Semut I, II, III and IV): the different parts have mostly been treated separately, and piecemeal, by different authors. This has precluded an understanding not only of the operation in its entirety, but also of any individual part, since each part was planned in relation to the larger whole. When I began this book several years ago, it was with the intention of covering the entire operation. However, part-way into it I realised that if I were to do the operation justice, I would need to divide my account into two volumes.[23]

This first volume briefly outlines the Japanese occupation of Borneo and the operation's planning and first operative entries, before focusing on Semut II and III, which took place along Sarawak's two great rivers: the Baram and Rejang respectively. Semut I and Semut IV will be treated in the planned second volume.

Elevating Semut II and Semut III above Semut I may seem counter-intuitive – surely a book should start with the number 1? However, there are good reasons to start elsewhere in this case. What eventually became Semut II was originally intended as the core Semut operation, with what became Semut I and Semut III both planned as side operations (Semut IV was a later addition). The shape and character of the overall operation thus cannot be understood without some familiarity with Semut II. Semut III was a direct offshoot of – and had its origins in – Semut II, so the narrative moves most naturally from Semut II to Semut III.

Although Semut II was intended as the core operation, very little is known about it. The official records relating to it are sparse, and there are few operative personal accounts available. A short article about its commanding officer, Toby Carter, published in a New Zealand surveyors' magazine is the only firsthand published narrative of it we have. While there are more detailed personal accounts available for Semut III, overall it is no better served than Semut II. Almost no official records pertaining to it now remain: its final party report, for instance, is found only in one very obscure archive.[24]

Semut I, on the other hand, is well furnished with respect to both official and unofficial records. Its commanding officer, Tom Harrisson, wrote the bestselling book *World Within* about this part of the operation, and many of its operatives produced personal accounts, including twenty – of varying quality and length – collected into a single published volume. In addition, Harrisson left a large and invaluable corpus of papers relating to Semut I to various libraries and archives, including the Australian War Memorial.[25]

Harrisson possessed an extraordinary appetite for self-promotion which saw him take every opportunity after the war to publicise his own role – and that of Semut I – in relation to the larger operation. As one of his postwar colleagues acidly commented:

About the only thing [Harrisson's extensive writings] have in common is an almost invariable reference to the fact that the author had been parachuted into Borneo. [. . .] The SRD operation was, I think, the emotional climax of his career.

As a result, many secondary accounts of the operation have focused largely, or even exclusively, on Semut I, drawn not simply by its more extensive – and more readily available – resources, but also by the flamboyant figure of Harrisson himself, which continues today to exert a strange fascination over many. A sad effect of this is that Semut I is often treated as almost coterminous with the entire operation. Yet it cannot easily be claimed that Semut I was more important than Semut II or Semut III; arguably it was less so.[26]

In addition, many secondary accounts of the operation rely heavily on Harrisson's writings, especially *World Within*. But these writings tend to be profoundly self-serving, often containing inaccuracies that are then repeated in the later accounts. An added benefit of starting my own story with Semut II is that it serves to shift the focus away from Harrisson and Semut I, enabling us to look at the overall operation through fresh eyes.

Peter Stanley writes powerfully of the insights to be gained from 'sniffing the ground' of any wartime site before one writes about it. As an anthropologist, I knew little about military history – including that of Borneo – when I began this book; it has been a steep learning curve. But I had one great advantage: I had lived and worked with Dayak peoples in Borneo since the mid-1980s. As a result, I have certainly done my share of ground-sniffing.[27]

I have been to almost all the places described in this account, and spoken to the people there, including many who were alive in 1945. Equally as important, I was lucky enough to travel extensively in Borneo in the 1980s, when most Dayak peoples were still living in longhouses and the great jungles remained largely intact, before wanton logging and other atrocities left their bleak scars across the landscape. So I write from a deep sense of familiarity with Borneo as it was when the men of Semut came calling.

2

THE JAPANESE OCCUPATION

BORNEO, THIRD LARGEST ISLAND in the world. Resting languidly across the equator between mainland Southeast Asia to the west, the Philippines to the north, and the meandering flotilla of Indonesia to the south, west and southeast. The backbone of the island, running from the northeast to its centre and beyond, is a succession of rugged mountain ranges from whence a clutch of rivers – the Kapuas, Mahakam, Barito and Rejang, among others – begin their sinuous journeys to the sea, birthing along the way hundreds of tributaries. The island is rich in natural resources including timber and oil, making it an attractive prize to outsiders.

Japanese forces arrived here at dawn on 16 December 1941, just nine days after the bombing of Pearl Harbor. Around five thousand troops landed in Miri, a town on the island's north coast, and took it, along with the nearby oilfields and refinery at Seria and Lutong, largely unopposed. A local Malay schoolboy, Safri Awang bin Zaidell, later recalled looking towards the sea out the window of his home and seeing 'flags – red ball on white – fluttering on landing crafts'.[1]

The main opposition to the invasion came from the weather: a severe storm caused a number of landing crafts to be swamped, leading to the drowning of some Japanese soldiers. Despite local expectation of an impending Japanese invasion, the arrival was so sudden that confidential government documents, codes and cyphers had not yet been destroyed.[2]

Responsibility for British Borneo in the north of the island, where the blow first fell, lay with the British Far East Command based in Singapore. With its eyes turned to Malaya and Singapore, defence of Borneo rated low on its list of priorities. In any case, the British War Office had decided, in the words of one of its officials, it was

> unlikely that the Japanese would stage a major attack on North Borneo, and [. . .] impossible for them to undertake two major offensives in Southeast Asia, e.g. North Borneo and Malaya concurrently.

The same logic that led to the disaster of Singapore – one of the most humiliating defeats in British military history – paved the way for the occupation of Borneo. As a result, British Borneo was shamefully underprepared to deal with an attack. No air or sea forces were stationed there, and there was no basic defence equipment such as anti-aircraft guns. As with Singapore, the lack of air power in particular made defeat inevitable.[3]

The efficiency with which the invasion at Miri was effected and the key town of Kuching taken on 24 December made it clear that occupation of the remainder of the island could not be far off. Agnes Keith, the American wife of a British colonial officer based at Sandakan, in the northeast of the island, perfectly captured this sense of inevitability:

The Japs took Kuching, Sarawak, Borneo on Christmas Day.
We smelled smoke and saw flames. Then they went north [. . .]
They didn't get tired at all, just kept going, and walked into
Jesselton, North Borneo, our own state, in early January.

Indeed, the time that elapsed between the invasion of Miri on the
north coast of British Borneo and the capture of Banjarmasin in the
southernmost part of Dutch Borneo – and complete occupation of
the island – on 10 February 1942, was less than two months.[4]

∞

The Japanese occupation was by no means the first invasion of
Borneo by foreign powers. In the mid-nineteenth century the Dutch
as well as the British adventurer James Brooke – both driven by the
seemingly insatiable European appetite for new territories to exploit
and new peoples to conquer – each claimed a section of the island:
in the south and northwest respectively. Later, in the 1880s, the
remaining two sections of the island, both in the northeast, became
protectorates of Great Britain.

When the Japanese arrived, Borneo was thus politically
divided into a northern British domain and a much larger southern Dutch domain. The British section included the protectorates of
Sarawak (ruled by the Brooke family) in the west, the tiny sultan-
ate of Brunei (ruled by its Malay *raja*) on the north coast and British
North Borneo (administered by the British North Borneo Chartered
Company) in the east. Dutch Borneo was one piece in the cornuco-
pia of islands that was the Dutch East Indies, extending across what
is now Indonesia and governed as a colony of the Netherlands.

This book is chiefly concerned with Sarawak in the northwest of
the island. Here, in 1841, James Brooke had replaced the previous
ruler – the Sultan or *Raja* of Brunei – and established himself as the
'White Rajah'. He founded a Brooke ruling dynasty that endured

for a century, ending only with the Japanese invasion. The dynasty progressively eradicated warfare and headhunting among Dayak groups through a series of brutal so-called 'punitive expeditions' – involving indiscriminate killing, burning of longhouses, destruction of crops and looting of valuables – against Dayak groups it deemed rebellious.[5]

In a remarkable irony, the expeditions also involved head-taking by Iban members of the government forces, who were not formally 'paid' for their services but instead recompensed through permission to take plunder and heads. This proved a marvellously efficient means of recruiting Iban warriors – hungry for heads to enhance their potency – and often served more to perpetuate headhunting than to eradicate it. However, by the early 1900s headhunting and warfare had been wiped out in most areas – although intermittent rebellions continued into the 1930s – and a system of civil administration and taxation extended throughout the territory.[6]

Nevertheless, when the Japanese invaded in 1941 Sarawak remained a sleepy outpost in the backwaters of Asia. Contact with the world beyond the island was largely limited to weekly services of mail and passengers between Singapore and Kuching as well as Singapore and Sibu. The Kuching airfield – the first airfield in Sarawak, completed in 1938 – was almost never used. A second airfield opening planned for Lutong (site of Sarawak's major oil refinery) in 1939 had failed to materialise.[7]

The territory's coastal towns and major rivers boasted a handful of administrative centres – many including small wooden forts – where District Officers and Native Officers lived alongside clusters of *towkays* or Chinese traders. Otherwise, apart from a very few large-scale foreign enterprises – including the oilfields at Miri and Lutong on the northeast coast – operating mostly in coastal areas, not much had changed from a hundred years earlier.

∽

For centuries the two main populations of Sarawak – as elsewhere in Borneo – have been the (mostly) Muslim Malays and the (mostly) pagan, later Christian, Dayaks. For the peoples of Borneo, the distinction between Malay and Dayak is crucial, determining such things as the god(s) one worships, the foods one eats, the clothes one wears, the place one lives and the language one speaks. Each of these populations – especially the second – can be further divided into a host of subgroups, many with their own distinct languages and traditions.

There is also a plethora of immigrant groups. Most important of these is the Chinese, whose traders have visited for centuries but who, encouraged by local Malay rulers, migrated in large numbers from the mid-eighteenth century to work the goldfields of northwest Dutch Borneo. From there, many moved to other parts of the island, including Sarawak, in subsequent years as the gold deposits ran out.[8]

These pre-existing populations notwithstanding, at the time of the Japanese invasion Sarawak – like most of the rest of Borneo – was ruled by a minuscule European elite who lived in large timbered houses usually in the coastal towns. They pursued existences of relative luxury supported by Malay and Chinese servants and porters, and their social lives revolved mainly around Whites-only institutions and activities. As Agnes Keith, who lived in Sandakan, the capital of British North Borneo, in the early 1940s wrote:

Here British Colonial life lived itself placidly and without confusion as British life should, on the edge of the Borneo jungles, by the blue tepid waters of Sulu and China Seas. Here Social Club, Golf Club, Tennis Club, Squash Club, Bridge Club, rugger and polo and soccer, made British the day.

At the time, Keith tells us, Sandakan contained 70 Europeans and 15,000 'Asiatics'.[9]

Below the Europeans in the Sarawak pre-war caste hierarchy were the Chinese, who controlled medium- and small-scale trade as shopkeepers, traders, moneylenders, miners and sawmill operators. Like the Europeans they resided mostly in the towns, although some had penetrated far inland and established trading centres along major rivers. On the eve of WWII, the Chinese were probably the most pro-European of the Sarawak populations. Many were Christian, and had forged comfortable accommodations with colonial European society. In addition, many were deeply engaged with the ongoing Sino-Japanese war and concerned about Japanese expansion in the region.

Under the Chinese were the Malays, especially those from elite families living in urban areas, many of whom were employed in the colonial civil service. However, most Malays were still small-scale farmers, producing rice for subsistence and a variety of cash crops such as rubber and pepper. Malays were more neutral in their attitudes towards European rule than the Chinese. They were divided from the Europeans through their adherence to the Muslim faith, and many in the elite clung to the memory of Malay rule and harboured resentment about lack of advancement under the Europeans. Indeed, at war's end many Malays – along with many Dayaks – in Dutch Borneo agitated against the return of the Dutch and pushed instead for Dutch Borneo to become part of an independent Indonesia.

At the bottom of the heap were the Dayaks. The vast majority still lived in the jungles and along the rivers of the island's largely unexplored interior, supporting themselves through rice farming as well as hunting and collecting, and maintaining only sporadic contact with areas downriver and the coastal towns. Very few Dayak children attended school, and almost none outside of urban areas. Some Christian missionisation of Dayak groups had occurred, but large parts of the island – including most of the areas with which this book is primarily concerned – did not receive missionaries until the 1930s or later. Most of these peoples still adhered to their traditional religious beliefs, and were guided in their everyday behaviours by the omens they detected in the world around them.

Responses to the European rulers varied across the different Dayak groups. Many – perhaps most – were favourably disposed towards the Europeans, largely because of their success in putting a stop to headhunting and warfare. Even among those Dayaks who had previously embraced these practices, there were many who welcomed the greater mobility and freedom from perpetual fear of attack resulting from the new laws.

However, for others – Ibans in particular – the requirement to pay government taxes was an ongoing source of resentment, while members of the tiny mission-educated urban Dayak elite shared Malay frustration at the lack of possibilities for promotion. Indeed, while many Dayaks came to the aid of fleeing Europeans in the wake of the Japanese invasion, others seized the opportunity to take revenge on their erstwhile rulers. When Sarawak's then White Rajah sounded out the possibility of an anti-Japanese rebellion among the Iban, he was advised that they would be unlikely to risk their lives on such a mission.[10]

By the 1940s most travel within Sarawak was still, as it always had been, by river and jungle track. There were no roads outside the towns (themselves very small) and coastal areas: in 1941, when the Japanese invaded, Sarawak had only 30 miles (48 km) of continuous road. The rugged inland terrain, a network of densely-forested mountains and fast-flowing rivers studded with rapids, repelled all but the most intrepid outsiders, and few Europeans ventured far beyond the towns. When they did travel upriver, the fetid steaminess of the jungle and its active populations of leeches, mosquitoes and stinging ants, reinforced their sense of the island's savage heart.

After a century of colonial rule, many Dayaks had still to encounter a white face.

၈၃

The Japanese move on Borneo so soon after Pearl Harbor was linked to the island's wealth in oil and other natural resources, chiefly rubber and timber. It also owed much to Borneo's strategic location equidistant between the twin lures of Singapore and Java. It is no accident that within weeks of the Japanese invasion of Borneo, Singapore (5 February 1942) and Batavia (now Jakarta, 1 March 1942) had also fallen. By early March the Japanese had taken Lae and Salamaua in New Guinea, within spitting distance of Australia, and commenced regular bombing of Darwin, on the Australian north coast.[11]

Japanese invaders encountered little opposition in either the northern British or the southern Dutch parts of the island. In response to ongoing appeals from the government of Sarawak, a British Indian Army infantry unit, the 2nd Battalion, 15th Punjabi Regiment, had been sent to Sarawak from Singapore, with the last of its companies arriving in May 1941. However, reflecting the shambolic character of defence preparations, its men had no experience of jungle warfare and the ferret scout cars they brought were useless in a country effectively without roads.[12]

A field force known as the Sarawak Rangers, mostly comprised of Ibans, had been established within the Sarawak Constabulary in September 1941 with the intended role of harassing enemy invaders. But by December its men were still largely untrained. European members of the civil administration and the Sarawak Constabulary had also been recruited into the defence forces along with volunteers: in all (including the 1050 Punjabis), Sarawak defence totalled 2565 men. No troops had been stationed in neighbouring British North Borneo, and defence forces there were limited to the constabulary and a small group of volunteers.[13]

While some European administrators were left in place in the immediate wake of the invasion, by May 1942 all had been either interned or executed. Many were treated harshly by their Japanese captors, partly as a propaganda move designed to demonstrate that it was possible for Asians to overthrow and subordinate Europeans.

∽

For the purposes of government, the Japanese divided Borneo into two sections: Northern Borneo (*Kita Boruneo*) which comprised the former British northern part of the island, and Southern Borneo (*Minami Boruneo*) which comprised the former southern Dutch part of the island. Northern Borneo was administered by the Imperial Japanese Army and Southern Borneo by the Imperial Japanese Navy.

In Northern Borneo the 4th Independent Mixed Regiment took control in March 1942. In May of that year this regiment was absorbed into the Borneo Garrison Army, and in June its headquarters was established in Kuching, where the Brooke regime's seat of government had been. Over time the 4th Independent Mixed Regiment became the 40th and 41st Infantry Battalions, and the Borneo Garrison Army became the 37th Army. In Southern Borneo the 22nd Naval Base Force based at Balikpapan took responsibility for the maintenance of law and order while the 2nd Naval Garrison Unit based at Tarakan was in charge of military matters.[14]

Oil was vital to the Japanese war effort. Consequently, restoration of production from the Miri–Seria–Lutong oilfields and refinery on the north coast of Sarawak and neighbouring Brunei, as well as from the oilfields and refineries at Balikpapan and Tarakan on the east coast of Dutch Borneo, was perhaps the most urgent task facing the occupying force. In the build-up to the invasion British and Dutch workers at all oilfields and refineries had carried out the policy of 'denial' of oil plants and resources mandated by their governments. Heads had been blown off gas wells, plant and machinery destroyed, and storage tanks of oil fired.

In spite of the denial efforts, the Japanese rapidly brought all fields and refineries on the island back into production, and even managed to enlarge and extend some using Javanese forced labour. The output from Miri–Seria–Lutong was particularly impressive: a Japanese report of September 1944 stated that almost all crude oil shipped to Japan at the time was coming from here, most of it ships' oil. Japan was especially reliant on the Miri–Seria fields because of the vulnerability of Tarakan and Balikpapan – both located on the east side of the island – to Allied attack.[15]

‍§‍

Meanwhile, the Japanese needed to exercise order over potentially unruly populations. To this end, special police forces, the equivalent of the Nazis' Gestapo, were established in both Northern and Southern Borneo. In Northern Borneo the force in question was the notorious *Kempei Tai* (military police), whose name was synonymous with brutality throughout Asia and the Pacific by war's end. As a writer in the *Sarawak Tribune* put it in 1946: 'The very sight of a KP man was enough to make the more nervous of us tremble in our shoes.' In Southern Borneo the *Kempei Tai*'s no less cruel cousin, the *Tokkei Tai* (special naval police), adopted the same role.[16]

Radios were confiscated and reliable information about events inside, let alone outside, Borneo became almost unobtainable. In keeping with their dreary aims, both the *Kempei Tai* and the *Tokkei Tai* recruited networks of informers and agents, including children, from all ethnic groups: their brief was to report on members of their communities. People informed on neighbours out of malice or to settle petty grudges, and arrests often seemed capricious. Lives were shadowed with fear.

Maarof bin Abdullah, a Malay teacher, was arrested in Beaufort, in the former British North Borneo, in April 1944 after a number of people informed against him. Below is an excerpt from the original transcript of the signed testimony he gave to Major Hardwick of the Australian Imperial Force (hereafter AIF) at the end of the war:

[O]n 2nd April 1944 [. . .] I was called by the Japanese Govt. in BEAUFORT. I went there with a clear conscience because I was guilty of no wrong. [. . .]

The next day I reached BEAUFORT at 2.30 P.M. and was taken to the Military Police and locked up in spite of being innocent. There I was detained one week without any rice, only a pot of water in a rusty tin which I was compelled to drink. By ALLAH I hope it won't happen twice – better dead than alive.[17]

Among the crimes of which Maarof bin Abdullah was accused were keeping a map of the world, keeping a Grand Life Insurance Policy (taken to mean he was anxious for Europeans to return), and teaching the geography of Borneo including its rivers, mountains, islands and minerals. Tried on 9 April 1944 he was not permitted to speak or defend himself, and was sentenced to death.[18]

Maarof bin Abdullah was one of the lucky ones: after being imprisoned for four-and-a-half months he was released. Few others accused and found guilty of anti-Japanese activity lived to tell the tale.

If someone was reported, the *Kempei Tai* or *Tokkei Tai* usually assumed them to be guilty, and took as their function the extraction of a confession. Suspects were routinely beaten and tortured during interrogation, the horror amplified by the everyday banality of many of the buildings in which interrogations occurred. For those found guilty after the subsequent trial, execution by beheading, or a slow death through starvation and misuse in prison, loomed.

∾

Even in the midst of such violence the everyday routines of government must grind on as normal: surely one of the great incongruities of enemy occupation. To this end, many Malays and Dayaks who had held positions in the civil administration under the colonial regimes stayed on in their roles under the Japanese. Some of these embraced opportunities for promotion and higher salaries not available to them under the employment policies of the previous governments.

Malay and Dayak administrators in inland areas, including Native Officers, were largely left in place, at least in the early days of the occupation. The Japanese regarded Dayak people as uncivilised but were, at the same time, wary of their warriorship, and so deemed it sensible to adopt a laissez-faire policy towards them. For the most part they retained the Dayak leaders formally recognised under European rule, and took the prudent step in many cases of raising their salaries.[19]

Malay and Dayak members of the colonial police forces were also largely retained and new recruits, especially Ibans, added. Some held positions of considerable responsibility, including that of Inspector. Dayaks, again especially Ibans, were also recruited into the Japanese militia – serving in inland garrisons in some areas, and even fighting against the Allies during the 1945 landings of the Allied forces in British North Borneo.[20]

If some Malays and Dayaks made the decision to suspend judgement on – or even to support – the Japanese takeover, who can blame them? Marginalised under European colonialism, many locals may well have felt as Sukarno – later to be the founding President of an independent Indonesia – did when the Japanese released him from Dutch detention after taking Java in 1942: 'For the first time in my life I saw myself reflected in an Asian mirror.' Indeed, local resentment towards European rule made it difficult for the British to mount special operations in Southeast Asia during WWII: for local indigenous peoples 'there was often doubt as to who *was* the real enemy – the invading Japanese, or the colonial power they had thrown out'.[21]

In addition, this was a war about which most Dayaks and Malays knew little, and to which they had not been formal signatories. Sarawak's reigning White Rajah, Charles Vyner Brooke, had departed for a holiday in Malaya and Australia six weeks before the Japanese invasion – in the face of widespread expectation that it was imminent – and never returned. Some European administrators and residents had fled almost as soon as the Japanese arrived, and even those who waited longer to capitulate or flee had generally failed to discuss the situation with locals or provide any explanation. The result was confusion and strong anti-European sentiment among locals in some areas.[22]

As with the previous European regimes, many Dayaks and Malays had little choice but to accommodate in order to survive. The Sarawak Iban leader Tun Jugah put it succinctly in a radio interview from 1979:

[We] were asked by the Japanese whether we supported the British. We answered that we supported the British because they had administered the government. 'But now you Japanese administer the government,' we replied, 'so we follow you.'[23]

Among Chinese the response to the Japanese was often rather different. The ongoing Sino-Japanese war with its horrific legacy of unbridled Japanese brutality towards Chinese civilians at Nanjing (Nanking) and elsewhere, had left a pall of revulsion and fear over

Chinese nationals throughout the region, including in Borneo. The Japanese, for their part, were suspicious of the local Chinese, especially those who had actively contributed to funds assisting the Chinese war effort, and at pains to portray Chinese to the indigenous population as exploitative colonisers on a par with Europeans. Throughout the island the Chinese mostly bore the brunt of the interrogations and violence inflicted by the *Kempei Tai* and *Tokkei Tai*, although this varied markedly from place to place.[24]

⟨∞⟩

For most people who lived through it, the experience of the occupation is best summarised today by the local Malay word *kurang*: 'not enough'. The Allied blockade on shipping led to scarcities of imported essential goods such as salt, rice (in which Borneo was not self-sufficient), sugar, cloth, cooking oil, matches and medications, which worsened as the war turned against the Japanese and fewer and fewer supply ships reached the island. Control over the sale and distribution of commodities had been taken from the Chinese and handed over to Japanese business organisations and companies, with Chinese often required to work for them as middle men. This produced a notoriously inefficient system and rampant inflation.

Across the island Japanese troops routinely requisitioned rice and other foodstuffs from farmers, sometimes at gunpoint and usually at the threat of a beating or worse for those who resisted. Many communities were left hungry. To make matters worse, the Japanese had made it illegal to trade rice or transport it from one area to another.[25]

As if this was not bad enough, the Japanese also demanded that people from all ethnic communities, especially young men, be sent to work on Japanese projects including rice fields, sawmills, oilfields and the construction of airfields and roads. Conscripted labourers were often treated harshly and provided with little food and no pay. Moreover, their families and communities lost their labour.

Everywhere people adapted in order to keep themselves alive: living on sago and cassava root, hiding stockpiles of rice in places where the Japanese would not find them, cutting up hessian sacks, beating bark or using locally produced rubber to make clothes, substituting white sugar for locally made red sugar, boiling water from salt springs to produce salt, and using stones and tinder to generate fire. But nothing can replace sufficient nourishment and effective medicines, so malnutrition was rife and people's health deteriorated alarmingly.

The other word local people still employ today when speaking of the occupation is *takut*: 'fearful'. Their fear was a response to the pervasive violence that characterised the period.

In attempting to capture this violence it would be misleading to focus exclusively on the *Kempei Tai* and *Tokkei Tai*, brutal though both these organisations undoubtedly were. The occupation was marked by a routine, almost casual, violence inflicted by regular Japanese soldiers. The cause of this everyday violence lay, most often, in failure to demonstrate the requisite respect towards all things Japanese.

Japanese expansion into Southeast Asia and the Pacific had as its ultimate objective the establishment of the 'Greater East Asia Co-Prosperity Sphere', in which territories would be occupied and their inhabitants encouraged to identify as Japanese. In this model Japan was to be the father of one big happy Asian family, with other peoples as the children. A key element of this program was the annihilation of the 'blue-eyed enemy and their black slaves' and the encouragement of local peoples to look into the mirror and identify themselves not as European, but as Asian.[26]

To advance this process, programs for the spread of Japanese values and culture were instituted, especially in schools. Japanese language classes were mandatory for everyone in the towns, clocks were put back an hour to align with Japanese time, and Japanese flags flew from available buildings. The Japanese also issued their own paper currency – referred to locally as 'banana money' because of the images of bananas printed on some of the notes – and issued a set of stamps.

All locals were expected to perform the *saikeirei*, the deep 90-degree bow from the waist, to any Japanese person they encountered, since he or she was understood as the local embodiment of the Emperor. Failure to perform this correctly could lead to slaps and blows about the face, head and body, and even to arrest. These attacks were often savage and completely arbitrary. As an elderly Dayak explained to me years later:

> If you didn't bow to a Japanese soldier, even if you hadn't seen him, he would grab you and hit you across the face. Hit you hard. First on one side, then on the other. You had to stand still while he did it, while he hit you again and again, PAK, PAK, PAK. You weren't allowed to move away, weren't allowed to fall down. You had to stand and take it.[27]

၅၀

Some of the violence involved an almost incomprehensible level of cruelty: that against Europeans, in particular, often seemed designed to subjugate and humiliate. The atrocities that took place at Long Nawang and Sandakan-Ranau are well known and relevant to the Semut story. At Long Nawang, in remote northernmost Dutch Borneo close to the Sarawak border, several different parties of fleeing Europeans – civilians, soldiers, airmen and missionaries – from both Sarawak and Dutch Borneo, had converged in 1942 and been sheltered by the local Kenyahs. The Japanese tracked them down and over several weeks in August and September 1942 killed forty-one European men, women and children after having raped the women. A Kenyah man wept as years later he recounted to me the story of this tragedy, told him by his parents who had lived in

Long Nawang at the time and witnessed it firsthand. He described how small children were forced to climb palm trees and were impaled on the points of soldiers' swords as, exhausted, they fell.[28]

One of the most notorious Japanese prisoner-of-war camps was located close to Sandakan in British North Borneo. There, more than 2400 Australian and British POWs were incarcerated from mid-1942. Many died of disease, starvation and misuse. Starting in January 1945 the remainder, already ill and emaciated, were forced to embark on a series of 'death marches' inland, over 160 miles (260 km) of rugged terrain, to Ranau. Few outlived the marches, and those who did died or were killed over the ensuing weeks – the last beheaded on 15 August 1945, the day of the Japanese surrender. Only six men, all Australians who had escaped into the jungle and were assisted by locals, survived.[29]

Yet, too often histories of war focus on the cruelty done to Europeans. In the case of the Japanese occupation of Borneo, Europeans were by no means the only ones killed or brutalised. The infamous 'Pontianak Affair' starting in October 1943 involved the arrest, torture and execution of prominent people from all ethnic communities around the coastal town of Pontianak in south-west Borneo. Half to two-thirds of those executed appear to have been Chinese, with one-third being 'native Indonesians', presumably including both Malays and, to a lesser degree, Dayaks. Around 1500 people were killed in all. While in general Malays appear to have been favoured by the Japanese, those executed included all twelve Malay sultans in Dutch West Borneo.[30]

Chinese, mistrusted by the Japanese, were a particular target. Throughout the former British North Borneo they were treated with special ferocity after the suicidal action known variously as the Jesselton/Kinabalu/Api/Double Tenth Uprising took place. On the night of 9 October 1943 several hundred people – around 100 Chinese, 200–300 inhabitants of offshore islands (Suluk, Udar,

Mantanani and Dinawan), plus Dayak and Indian members of the local police force – attacked Jesselton (now Kota Kinabalu) on the west coast of British North Borneo and ransacked police stations, Japanese administrative offices and warehouses before dispersing a day later. Fifty to ninety Japanese and Formosans (Taiwanese), mostly civilians, were killed.

Japanese reprisals were extreme: many Chinese living in the Jesselton-Tuaran area were executed, and extermination of all Suluk and Bajau males, along with the killing of many women and children, was carried out in the nearby islands: as a result, when the Allies reached these islands in 1945 there were no men left to greet them. On 21 January 1944, 175 alleged rebels were executed by beheading, and another 131 were imprisoned at Labuan, with only seven surviving the war. Entire villages along the British North Borneo coast were wiped out. Four thousand people in total are estimated to have been killed as part of the Japanese retaliation.[31]

British North Borneo – 'this broken land' as Paul Ham describes it – undoubtedly endured worse treatment from the Japanese than any other part of Borneo, and perhaps than any other British possession. In part this was simply because it had the heaviest Japanese presence in Borneo; but it was also the grim harvest of the Jesselton Uprising.[32]

Dayaks, at least in Sarawak and Dutch Borneo, appear to have endured less violence at Japanese hands than other groups. This is probably because most lived in remote inland areas where they were able to avoid contact with soldiers and police: many Japanese regarded Dayaks with contempt, but were also fearful of their martial – especially headhunting – skills, and so were reluctant to venture far into the interior. In British North Borneo however, where the high Japanese presence meant they penetrated inland to a much greater degree than elsewhere, Dayaks were subject to beatings, killings and the burning of villages.[33]

Conscripted Javanese labourers suffered especially badly. They were forced into hard physical work (the women among them often coerced into sexual servicing of Japanese soldiers), brutally treated, and mostly provided with little in the way of food or shelter. In Northern Borneo in the final months of the war they were abandoned by the Japanese, since their physical deterioration meant that they were no longer of use. Far from their homes, with little help at hand, they died in their thousands of disease, starvation and misuse.[34]

Nevertheless, not all locals suffered at Japanese hands. Indeed, as with any enemy occupation, some from all ethnic groups profited under Japanese rule, whether via the black market or as a result of inducements or promotions offered by the administration. In addition, by no means all Japanese were cruel or uncaring: as Braithwaite is at pains to tell us, there are monsters and angels on both sides in any war. Years later, elderly members of all Sarawak ethnic groups – including Chinese – recalled for me acts of kindness performed by Japanese soldiers.[35]

In the Betong area in southwest Sarawak, for instance, relations between Japanese and local Ibans were so warm that the occupation period was looked upon long afterwards with some nostalgia. In the war's final days, when several thousand Ibans from further inland were on their way to attack the Japanese in Betong, other Ibans along the route pleaded with them to spare particular Japanese individuals. Several weeks later, Japanese troops that had retreated inland walked back through this area to surrender to the Allies at the coast. They were starving and in tatters, and the local Iban responded by feeding them.[36]

Nor were such friendships confined to Dayaks. Lim Beng Hai – a Chinese who went on to become a Semut guerrilla – records the close relationship his family had with several Japanese soldiers in Kuching:

After the morning manoeuvre at the site of the Chinese cemetery opposite the General Hospital, Kishimoto and Matsuda complete with their gear [. . .] would come over with their packets of green beans and sugar which my mother cooked into soup for all to enjoy.

So trusting was this friendship that Lim showed the soldiers magazines he had illicitly kept (buried under his floorboards) recording the Sino-Japanese conflict: in the wrong hands these would have seen him executed. Still, in 2010, he grieved over the subsequent loss of contact. Other friendships survived the war: some Japanese returned again and again to visit friends in Sarawak, and some Sarawakians visited Japan.[37]

And indeed, some Japanese displayed heroic levels of compassion. A doctor in Sibu provided locals with medicine at great personal risk and at Sandakan POW camp some guards stole food for prisoners and suffered beatings for refusing to punish them severely enough. Many of those we lump together as 'Japanese' soldiers were, in fact, conscripted Koreans and Formosans who themselves were subject to abuse and maltreatment by their Japanese captors and superiors. Like almost all occupying forces, that in Borneo was composed of many different kinds of people and cannot easily be reduced to the monochrome figure of the brutal, dominating Japanese soldier.[38]

Nevertheless, my own travels throughout Borneo over the years have made it clear that many Japanese occupiers treated locals with callousness and disrespect, and a substantial number were cruel. I first began my research project on WWII in Borneo with the intention of shining a light on what I saw as Allied exaggeration of Japanese cruelty on the island. As the project progressed I was forced to accept, to my dismay, that – even allowing for inevitable exaggeration by locals – the Allied accounts were largely true. Hearing story after story of petty tortures, rapes and casual brutality firsthand from the wrinkled lips of aged Dayaks filled me with a profound grief at the sometimes unfathomable depths of human behaviour.

꩜

As the occupation dragged on, and particularly from early 1944, conditions worsened and the violence escalated. An unfortunate consequence of the Jesselton Uprising was a heightened level of Japanese paranoia and surveillance in the northern British part of the island. This was made worse by the capture of three Australian special operations agents – from the same secret organisation as the men of Operation Semut – in the area around Sandakan in the far northeast of the island early in 1944.

But the main driver of the black mood creeping across the Japanese was undoubtedly the turning of the tide in the Pacific War. By late 1944, the establishment of nearby American airbases allowed the Allies to bomb vessels at Labuan naval base on the north coast of Borneo, and harass craft around its coastline. As a result, Japanese shipping to the island was almost at a standstill. An Allied attempt to retake Borneo loomed more and more as a possibility.

In response the Japanese military presence on the island was massively increased. In Sarawak and British North Borneo alone, the number of Japanese soldiers jumped in September 1944 from a paltry 3000 or so to around 20,000; by May 1945 the total number on the island was approximately 31,000. This lifted demand for essential commodities at a time when Allied naval activities had made transportation of goods from Japan almost impossible and so led to the requisition of yet more food – especially rice – from local farmers to feed Japanese soldiers.[39]

Many of these soldiers were themselves now starving: by the end of the war in some areas of North Borneo they were each receiving only 100 grams of rice rations per day. As a result their health deteriorated. Allied reports show that in northern Borneo one-third to one-half of Japanese soldiers were confined to bed at the end of the war, many unable to walk. Field hospitals had completely disappeared. For Japanese soldiers on the ground the Borneo war had become one of bitter attrition, fought not only against the Allied enemy, but also against a hateful environment and an increasingly hostile population. The suffering of local people rose accordingly.[40]

At the same time the Japanese military increased surveillance over the population's activities, and troops were moved in to some inland areas, replacing local administrators and police in many places. Shotguns – valuable possessions among Dayaks – were confiscated.

On the rare occasions when goods requisitioned from local peoples were paid for, inflation had caused the 'banana money' issued by the Japanese to become almost worthless. This currency initially had the same value as pre-war Sarawak and Straits currency, but by January 1945 $1 in Sarawak (pre-Japanese) currency was worth $30 in Japanese currency; by August 1945 it was worth almost $90. In 2018 Borneo locals still spoke with contempt of the Japanese 'banana dollar', a contempt which increasingly extended to those who had introduced it.[41]

⌒⌒

T.E. Lawrence's activities in Arabia during WWI made clear the potentially fatal error an enemy occupier commits in failing to gain the support of the local population, or at least an influential sector of it. This was especially true for the Japanese during WWII. With troops spread from China throughout mainland Southeast Asia, and across Indonesia and the Philippines into the Pacific, Japanese military and administrative resources were stretched painfully thin.

Many Dayaks were not unsympathetic to the Japanese at the start of the occupation. This is hardly surprising. The war was not of Dayak making, and it is a peculiar idea of loyalty that expects people to love those Europeans who colonise them. The primary concern of most Dayaks, as generally for indigenous groups caught up in other people's wars, was to survive. If Japanese occupation had improved their quality of life, most would have had no cause to complain about it.

However, the unbearable ironies of a war embarked on ostensibly to liberate Asians, but which had resulted instead in the seizure of their food, their resources and their labour, as well as their subjection to astonishing levels of ill-treatment, were becoming plain for all to see. The main source of the growing resentment among Dayaks was the Japanese requisitioning of food, especially rice.

As Dayaks today describe it, a troop of Japanese soldiers would enter a village and demand its inhabitants hand over their rice. If there was a sign of protest, they would be clubbed or threatened with guns. The soldiers would sometimes also take eggs, chickens and occasionally larger animals such as pigs. The sense of grievance would be intensified by the use of villagers as porters to carry their own foodstuffs to the nearest Japanese camp or garrison.

For people living at subsistence level the loss of rice was potentially calamitous; it resulted in widespread hunger throughout the interior. As rice stocks ran out, people were forced to live off cassava root and/or sago, both considered by most Dayak people to lack the life-sustaining qualities of rice. As a result, many Dayaks hid both rice and fields. They made rice fields in deep jungle where the Japanese would not see them, and stored the grain in huts at the fields rather than in the village. Many also moved out of their longhouses to live in their farm huts or in makeshift shelters in the jungle, to escape Japanese demands. Consequently, many longhouses were eerily empty during this period.

But Dayaks suffered not only from the loss of rice. They also felt deeply the lack of sugar, salt and cloth, items they normally obtained via trade with downriver people, but which the Allied blockade on shipping had rendered unavailable. The ominous sense of injury was only intensified by the confiscation of shotguns, starting in late 1943. Many groups relied on shotguns to protect their rice crops from marauding animals, as well as to supplement the daily diet with jungle game. In some places, cartridges were in short supply so shotguns had become largely unusable by the later part of the occupation. But they were nevertheless symbols of status and manhood, and the resentment over their loss was profound.

As the occupation dragged on, the consumption of cassava and sago in place of rice, the substitution of red palm sugar for white sugar, the use of local herbs in place of salt, and the wearing of barkcloth, all served to produce a deep sense of humiliation. Dayaks everywhere felt degraded by lives that had become distressingly primitive, on the ragged edge of being human, as they saw it. Seventy years later, people still squirmed as they recalled the shame of wearing barkcloth – the itching, the lice, the way it fell apart when wet – as well as the mortification of grubbing for cassava root in place of eating rice each day.

Initially, the straitened circumstances were blamed on local behaviours that had offended Dayak spirits. But as time went by and the scale of the misfortune increased such explanations became manifestly inadequate. Dayaks today speak of the 'bad taste' that pervaded every sphere of life in the later days of the Japanese period, indicating the ascendancy of malign forces that had resulted in scourges of snails and rats among other signs of a world badly off-balance. Cosmic disturbance on such a scale suggested major spiritual inadequacy and dereliction stretching far beyond the transgressions committed in any one community. Increasingly the search for a cause narrowed in on the Japanese.

～

In 2015, in a house not far out of Lawas in the northeast corner of Sarawak, an ancient Tagal woman recalled for me her memories of WWII while the rain played steady percussion on the roof of her house. She talked, eyes alight in her brown wrinkled face, of how the members of her group had killed a Japanese soldier and taken his head. When I asked why they had decided to support the White soldiers rather than the Japanese, especially given that Tagals seemed to me more physically akin to Japanese than Europeans, she replied:

> Japanese may be small and brown, just like us. They may have brown skin like us. And Whites may be tall with fair hair and pale skin, like spirits or ghosts. But under the skin Australians and Dayaks are kindred. It is the Japanese who are alien.[42]

Wherever the Japanese went in Asia and the Pacific during WWII, they stressed their racial affinities with local people: 'we are *sama kulit* [same skin]' was the mantra as it was expressed in the Malay language throughout Borneo. At the same time, they drew attention to the physical difference – the white skin and blue eyes – of the former European rulers. In this way they hoped to tap into resentment towards European colonialism and win the support of the locals. But with respect to Dayaks at least, this was a seriously misjudged strategy.

Most Dayaks were little interested in any physical similarity to the Japanese, although many were impressed by certain *cultural* similarities. In particular, some Dayaks saw echoes of the martial aspects of their own cultures in the Japanese warrior ethos of *bushido*. Indeed, some greatly admired the Japanese practice of beheading criminals with swords, seeing in this a reflection of their own headhunting traditions.[43]

But it was not the colour of their skin or any cultural affinities they shared with Dayaks that established the Japanese right to rule in Dayak eyes. No – this right had been gained purely from the Japanese military success in so comprehensively vanquishing the previous European administrations. This success demonstrated the exceptional spiritual potency of the Japanese – a potency far beyond that of mere mortals – and their superhuman credentials. At the same time, the humiliating defeat and flight of the Europeans laid bare their spiritual weakness and ordinary humanity, undermining any right to rule they once may have possessed.

In contrast to the Japanese, for Europeans skin colour had always been an advantage in their dealings with Dayaks: most Dayak groups at the time admired pale skin, and identified it with spirits, even gods, and with superhuman feats. The Kelabit of the remote Sarawak highlands, for instance, sang stories in which 'shiningly moon-white men with bodies of steel' defeated everyone else in tests of warriorship and athleticism. The Gerai, in the southwest of the island, told ancient tales of tall, pale people living in the sky, who possessed powers far beyond those of earthly humans. Early European travellers on the island often describe how Dayaks touched and stroked their skin.[44]

In the mid-1980s I conducted PhD research in a Dayak longhouse in southwest Borneo. In my first few months there, mealtimes were confronting affairs, as dozens of people from neighbouring villages would line the walls of my longhouse apartment to watch me eat rice, the local staple. This was because as local Dayaks understood it, only humans ate rice: demons, spirits and gods (who might look human) did not. Europeans were highly ambiguous entities. Were they spirits? Were they gods? Were they simply peculiar human beings? My reactions when given rice to eat presented an opportunity to cast light on this puzzle.

Similarly, when the Dutch administrator Georg Müller crossed what we now call the Müller Mountains in central Borneo in 1825, he was captured by a group of Punan. Uncertain as to whether he was human or a spirit, they pricked his skin with a knife. On seeing him bleed they knew he was human. And so they cut his head off.[45]

The whiteness of European skin, in Dayak eyes, went along with an astonishing immunity to the supernatural forces – spirits, omens, taboos – that filled and shaped the lives of Dayak individuals. Europeans could, it seemed, offend spirits, ignore omens and break taboos without suffering the potentially devastating consequences resulting from similar behaviour by Dayaks. Europeans appeared, in fact, to possess the prized attribute of *kebal* – invulnerability – that Dayak warriors sought for themselves through the use of charms and magic. It was believed by many that Europeans held a special magic which conferred protection against the bad luck signalled by omens.[46]

In addition, Whites invariably travelled with hordes of aides and porters, the latter transporting large quantities of valuable goods. The Dutch explorer Anton Nieuwenhuis took two associates plus 110 porters and bodyguards when he crossed Borneo in 1897, while his compatriot Hendrik Tillema needed a convoy of eleven longboats to transport his goods and supplies along the Kayan River to Long Nawang in 1931. For inland Dayaks these must have seemed gigantic retinues and staggering amounts of property, marking the White leaders of the expeditions as beings of great influence and wealth. This in turn undoubtedly signalled that they were possessed of extraordinary, perhaps even superhuman, spiritual potency, a potency which could extend to those associated with them.[47]

White skin, then, was a boon for Europeans in their encounters with Dayaks: it marked precisely their difference from Dayaks and other mere mortals – in particular their greater potency – and so their right to rule. But that right had now been withdrawn, although not because of the colour of their skin. Rather it was due to the disappointing lack of spiritual potency they had revealed in fleeing so precipitously during the Japanese invasion.

However, by 1945 the legitimacy of Japanese rule had also come into question. A ruler's potency should bring with it increased prosperity and wellbeing for those living in its orbit. But Japanese rule had brought only a steady deterioration in the quality of life for most inland Dayaks. As the years went by this fuelled a growing sense of alienation from the Japanese, in spite of their brown faces. 'It's true we had the same skin,' an old Dayak man explained in southwest Borneo in 1986, vigorously chewing betel nut on his longhouse verandah, 'but we had different hearts.' This was a view repeated endlessly during my travels around Sarawak in 2015 and 2018: while Dayaks and Japanese may *look* similar, inside they are different.[48]

But disillusionment with Japanese rule did not mean Dayaks necessarily desired a return to European rule – many, probably most, did not. As Dayaks saw it, both Europeans and Japanese had been uninvited external rulers. Their orders were followed not out of the love or loyalty many Europeans fondly imagine to exist in those subject to European rule, but rather out of a straightforward recognition of superior potency and a corresponding pragmatics of power and survival. An Iban man put it succinctly years later:

> While the war was still on, the Japanese were fine because they were the ones who were the rulers.[49]

Or, as an elderly Murut headman explained, his people would have had little cause to turn against the Japanese if their hearts had been as straight as the roads they built.[50]

By early 1945 the Japanese mantra of *sama kulit*, proclaimed so optimistically at the start of the occupation, had become a dangerous liability. Ironically, the 'same skin' declaration now reinforced the growing belief that the Japanese were not superhuman, but rather ordinary humans: no more potent and no less vulnerable than

Dayaks themselves. As a result, local apprehension over the consequences of resisting Japanese rule had begun to abate. This was especially true in the inland areas where most Dayaks lived: here, Japanese oversight was at its weakest, and the threat of betrayal and discovery much slighter. In these areas people's thoughts began to turn to their weapons.

PART I
BEGINNINGS

3

PLANNING

BY EARLY 1944 THE war in the Pacific had turned decisively in favour of the Allies. In the South-West Pacific Area (hereafter SWPA) commanded by the American General Douglas MacArthur, they had won crucial victories against the Japanese in southeastern New Guinea and Guadalcanal in late 1942 and early 1943. These successes were followed by an Allied counteroffensive along the northern New Guinea coast, culminating in landings on the Vogelkop Peninsula, at the northwestern tip of the island, at the end of July 1944.

The New Guinea victories paved the way for movement westward towards the Philippines and Java. In mid-September 1944 US forces landed on the Japanese-held small island of Morotai, 700 miles (1125 km) east of Borneo, most northerly of the string of islands known as the Moluccas (now Maluku) in the then Dutch East Indies. Morotai was ideally located to provide a stepping-off point for further operations west.

MacArthur had little interest in Borneo for its own sake. His gaze was fixed firmly on the Philippines, a pre-war territory of the US now in the hands of the Japanese, as well as Japan itself. However, he had committed to the invasion of Java to conclude his SWPA offensive, and Borneo promised bases from which this could be launched. By October 1944 MacArthur – reluctant to include Australia in his triumphal advance through the Philippines – had begun to prepare for Australian landings at Brunei Bay and Kudat in the north of Borneo.[1]

With planning for the Brunei Bay landings underway, it was agreed that special operations parties should be sent into northern Borneo to gather intelligence and build guerrilla movements among local people prior to the assaults. One operation, given the code-name Agas, the Malay word for sandfly, would take place in British North Borneo. Another would be located in Sarawak, inland from the expected landings at Labuan and Brunei Bay. Its codename was the Malay word for ant: Semut.

৩৯

The Services Reconnaissance Department was an Australian covert operations and intelligence organisation which operated through-out the Pacific and parts of Southeast Asia during World War II. Its history had been brief but turbulent. The initial element was formed in May 1942 as the Inter-Allied Services Department, a combined British, Dutch and Australian special operations and intelligence agency guided to a large degree by the British secret operations organisation, Special Operations Executive (hereafter SOE).

By July 1942, with the maturation of MacArthur's General Headquarters and the massive build-up of US troops in the Pacific, it had become clear a more comprehensive organisation was needed to undertake clandestine and intelligence activities throughout the region. Thus the Allied Intelligence Bureau was formed within General Headquarters, and the Inter-Allied Services Department became one of its four sub-sections. In March 1943 the latter was renamed as Special Operations Australia (SOA), with the cover name Services Reconnaissance Department (SRD). By late 1944 it had gone through yet another evolution and was now directly responsible to General Thomas Blamey, Commander-in-Chief of the Australian Military Forces.[2]

All those recruited to SRD from the Australian Army – the majority of its members – were posted to Z Special Unit for administrative purposes, and this name was recorded throughout their military documents. Recruits to SRD who were not from the Australian Army – including those from the Royal Australian Navy, the Royal Australian Airforce and other national services – were not posted to Z Special Unit, even though its name was also often recorded on their documents. This has led to considerable confusion around the relationship between SRD and Z Special Unit. Some of the men who served in Operation Semut were recruited from units other than the Australian Army and, while members of SRD, were not posted to Z Special Unit. For this reason I have elected generally to use the name Services Reconnaissance Department (SRD) in this book.

SRD was a multinational organisation. Many of its officers were British, and most of its other ranks were Australians. However, New Zealanders, French and Canadians also served in considerable numbers, having been seconded from their own military forces. Men from Malaya (now West Malaysia), Dutch East Indies (now Indonesia), the Netherlands and Portugal were among others recruited to the organisation.

On joining, new recruits were immediately required to sign a document promising they would not

> [E]ither whilst you are a member of Z Special Unit or after you have ceased to be a member, disclose to any person [. . .] any information whatsoever concerning Z Special Unit, including [. . .] details of the personnel of the unit, the activities or

operational role of the unit and any operation which members
of the unit may have carried out in the past.

Australia did not at the time have an Official Secrets Act, so punishment for disobeying this order was threatened under the
Commonwealth Crimes Act and the National Security (General)
Regulations. Secrecy secured, recruits were then put through a rigor-
ous training program – usually on Fraser Island off the Queensland
coast – which included courses in fitness, junglecraft, small boats
operation, weaponry and intelligence.[3]

All those who joined SRD were volunteers for special service.
They weren't told when they signed up exactly what they would
be doing, but they were told it was dangerous – an effective means
of winnowing out those with less of a propensity for risk-taking.
Henry Fawkes was promised 'nothing but a wooden cross' and
Keith Barrie told his odds of survival were about fifty-fifty. Both
men nevertheless signed on. 'I reckoned I could not ask for better
odds than that,' Barrie commented later.[4]

Some joined the organisation after responding to written or spoken advertisements. Lloyd Campbell, serving with the Australian
Army in New Guinea, read the battalion order 'Applications are
requested for volunteers to operate behind enemy lines on long-
range patrols' and was elated at the thought of escaping from the
routines of normal army life. New Zealander Frank Wigzell served
as a signaller in the Pacific with the New Zealand Army before seeing a notice on his camp barracks board stating that eight men were
required for a special job. Others were tapped on the shoulder, often
after having engaged in actions for which they might otherwise have
been punished.[5]

And they were not just any soldiers. SRD recruited a special
breed, epitomised by a highly individualistic and even rebellious
spirit, what Australians like to term 'larrikins'. As the military

historian Alan Powell – who interviewed many of them in the
1990s – comments, these were men (SRD had almost no women in
operational roles) who were enterprising, impatient with conventional military life and eager for action.[6]

ೲ

By mid-1944 SRD had been pressing for some time to undertake
missions to the northern part of Borneo. There were several reasons
for this. With future military operations likely, there was a need for
reliable intelligence about the area. Further, information had been
received suggesting that a large number of Australian and British
prisoners-of-war (hereafter POWs) was being held at Sandakan in
the island's northeast. But SRD's interest also stemmed from British
concerns about the island.

While the Americans cared little for Borneo itself, this was not
the case for the British. The British viewed their former territories
in Borneo as 'lost property' they had a right to reclaim and were
anxious to establish the basis for a speedy resumption of colonial
government immediately after liberation. Information they had
received from British North Borneo suggesting the development
of anti-colonial sentiments in the territory added to their sense of
urgency. However, since Borneo fell within the American-led SWPA
command – with the closest British armed forces located in Burma –
the British had no direct input to Allied plans for the island.[7]

But the British had an indirect route to SWPA decision-making
via SRD. From the outset, SRD had been heavily influenced by
the British special operations organisation SOE. The Inter-Allied
Services Department, SRD's forerunner, had been set up by Blamey
at British suggestion, with SOE funds even used to pay its initial
salaries and expenses. SRD was headed by a British SOE officer,
Lieutenant Colonel P.J.F. Chapman-Walker, and those in command
positions were largely British, many having been recruited directly

by SOE in London. Of around 780 SRD personnel at the end of 1944, 214 were British, and most of those were in command roles.[8]

For many of these men SRD was simply 'a branch of SOE'. Tom Harrisson, for instance, recruited by SOE to participate in Operation Semut, was told at his recruitment interview in London that the British needed to find men who would go into Borneo to 'save some of the face' lost to the Japanese. Some British writers make no distinction between SRD and SOE, referring to both simply as 'SOE'.[9]

The Americans were not stupid. They were well aware of the British influence over SRD, viewing the organisation as 'a British trojan horse in the American backyard' despite its Australian garb. And the Americans were deeply suspicious of British special operations activities in the Pacific region, seeing them as driven by political rather than military interests. As far as the Americans were concerned, the primary objective of such activities was to maintain British control of its colonial territories once the war was over, rather than to advance the progress of the war itself. Indeed, Americans often derisively translated the initials of the British-led South East Asia Command – which abutted MacArthur's SWPA Command and was concerned mainly with mainland south and southeast Asia – as 'Save England's Asiatic Colonies'.[10]

Nor were these suspicions unfounded: the British officers running SRD maintained close contact with the British Colonial Office, whose main priority with respect to its Borneo territories was to establish a British presence there in readiness for a Japanese defeat. A letter from the British Secretary of State for the colonies to the British Prime Minister Winston Churchill in March 1945 sets out the role of SOE and SRD (here referred to as SOA) in that process.

> The Colonial Office has a major interest in the establishment
> of a recognised British military force both in Borneo and South

China. There are no British operational forces of the ordinary sort in either theatre and we have therefore to reply [sic] on para-military forces to show the flag in connection with the liberation of Borneo and Hongkong . . . I therefore attach the greatest importance to S.O.E. retaining a recognised role in areas suitable for their activities against the Japanese especially in South China and also (in association with their Australian counterpart S.O.A.) in Borneo.[11]

However, since Borneo fell within the SWPA command, special operations on the island could only be carried out with the permission of SWPA's American leadership. And there was little doubt it would be on the lookout for British 'political' manoeuvrings in any proposals it received. This meant that one of the biggest challenges confronting any attempt by SRD to mount an operation in Borneo would be selling it to the Americans.[12]

ↄ৩

In spite of the potential difficulties in gaining permission, preliminary planning for Operation Semut had been occurring for some time. The idea of inserting operatives into Sarawak had been bandied around the British and Australian intelligence community for several years.

A meeting headlined 'Project Semut' was held on 16 February 1944 between a number of ex-Sarawak officials and two members of the SRD directorate to discuss an operation to be located principally in Sarawak, with some possible overlap into neighbouring parts of Borneo. The operation would consist of three parties: the main party operating in the Bintulu area, and two sub-parties, one operating in the inland further southwest and one inland further to the northeast. Its objectives were initially to collect intelligence, and later to conduct clandestine operations against oilfields, shipping and so on, as well as to organise local resistance to the Japanese.[13]

Among other things the meeting compiled lists of potential operation personnel, many of them old Sarawak hands. SOE had been
actively recruiting men with firsthand knowledge of Sarawak and its
people for several months. John Fisher and William Ditmas, both
colonial officers in the pre-war Brooke administration, as well as
George Crowther and Toby Carter, who had both worked as surveyors for Shell's Sarawak Oilfields Ltd, had all been approached in
late 1943 and early 1944. SRD and SOE were determined to avoid
the problems that had bedevilled their previous forays into Borneo
by using men with experience of the island in both planning and
operational command roles.

SRD had inserted two earlier parties behind Japanese lines in
British North Borneo: Python 1 (inserted October 1943) and Python 2
(inserted January 1944). The first of these succeeded over several
months in establishing an intelligence network of local informants
stretching from Sandakan in the east of British North Borneo to
Tarakan on the east coast of northern Dutch Borneo.

However, the Python operations had ended in disaster, with
three operatives captured, tortured and eventually executed by
the Japanese in December 1944. The failure of Python had many
causes, not least the high Japanese presence, level of vigilance
and degree of maltreatment meted out to the local population in
British North Borneo – in part as a result of the Jesselton Uprising
in October 1943 – and a corresponding reluctance on the part of
terrified locals to assist the Python parties. But lack of knowledge
of the country, its peoples and its languages was undoubtedly a
contributing factor.[14]

Over the months following the first meeting, Project Semut's
planning personnel changed frequently as men were assigned to
other operations and tasks. But three men gradually emerged at its
nerve centre: clever, clear-headed Major – promoted in June 1944
to Lieutenant Colonel – Jack Finlay, at the time in charge of SRD's

Planning Directorate; commanding, enthusiastic Major – promoted late in 1944 to Lieutenant Colonel – G.B. 'Jumbo' Courtney,
appointed at the end of the year as overall commander of SRD operations in the northern islands of the Dutch East Indies, Borneo and
the China Seas; and kind, avuncular Captain George Crowther,
assessed at age fifty as too old to be a field operative, and instead put
in charge of SRD's Sarawak Country Section.

All three men were British, having been transferred into SRD
from SOE. Finlay and Courtney were both professional soldiers,
while Crowther had been Chief Surveyor in the Lands and Surveys
Department at Shell Oil in British Borneo for more than ten years
before the war.

During this period plans were drawn up and destroyed regularly, as the project was rethought and refined. One of the biggest
problems the planning group faced was lack of information
about the current situation in Sarawak, including the location of
Japanese garrisons. Thus an SRD report dated 3 March 1945 – a
year after planning for Operation Semut had begun – on conditions
in British Borneo contains fourteen pages on British North Borneo
and a measly one page on Sarawak. This gap in knowledge was
not helped by the gross inaccuracies littered throughout maps of
the area.[15]

By 9 June 1944 the project had been reconstituted with Captain
Toby Carter as its leader, and by mid-August an Outline Plan had
been submitted to the Directorate for approval. In this new plan the
operation's main headquarters (hereafter HQ) would be in remote
country northwest of Belaga at the top of the Rejang River, with
secondary 'sub-party' bases on the Kelabit Plateau and in Dutch
Borneo, the latter across the border from Lubok Antu in the far
southwest of Sarawak. The main objective of the operation was to
gather intelligence on shipping and air movements, enemy activities
and dispositions, and the local situation, including local reactions

to the Japanese. The party would also seek information on former Sarawak government employees still at large in the interior, and arrange for their evacuation to Australia. And it would identify possible drop zones for later air operations.[16]

Over the coming weeks this plan was workshopped further until by early September the mission's objectives had been considerably refined and expanded. Now the primary objective of the operation was to establish a central HQ in a safe area, from which all special operations activity in Sarawak could be organised. From here, operatives would:

1. reconnoitre other parts of the territory with an eye to later operational activities;
2. contact friendly locals to gather information about Japanese activities, troop dispositions and so on;
3. seek out former government employees and arrange for their evacuation;
4. identify possible drop zones, landing strips and seaplane landing sites;
5. establish observation posts manned by local coast watchers to report on air and shipping movements;
6. provide meteorological information;
7. make arrangements for the recruitment of suitable local personnel for training in Australia.[17]

No mention was made of the British government's more political objectives, aimed ultimately at returning Sarawak to Brooke or British government once the Japanese were ousted. However, these undoubtedly lurked beneath the anodyne goals set out in the formal proposal, carefully crafted as that was to appease the Americans. A note at the time from an SOE officer to the head of SOE spells out the level of duplicity contained in the equivalent proposal for

Semut's partner operation Agas, to be mounted in neighbouring British North Borneo at almost the same time.

> The real [. . .] objects of this mission, namely the softening of local inhabitants, the training of guerrillas, and the arrangements for ex-Government officials to resume government of the Colony as soon as it has been liberated, have not been mentioned to S.W.P.A. as they are matters in which they would have no interest.[18]

Courtney, who eventually became the overall controller of SRD's Borneo operations, including Agas and Semut, later freely acknowledged these veiled political goals. The Borneo operations, he explained, allowed the organisation to 'contribute effectively to the restoration of British rule in its Asian colonies and of its lost political influence in the Far East'.[19]

The mission had also been distilled to two parties: a main party led by Carter, which would establish the operation's HQ in the Belaga area, and a much smaller, later party to be located on the Kelabit Plateau. This second party would be led by Captain Tom Harrisson, a recent recruit via SOE.

Carter's party was to be inserted by submarine on the Sarawak coast northeast of Bintulu in mid-October. It was believed that in this area a submarine could get within 4 miles (6.4 km) of the coast and the men could go ashore in rubber boats. Harrisson's party would be inserted by Liberator aircraft sometime in December, after the expected Allied assault on Morotai had established an airbase there. If the Morotai airbase had not yet eventuated, the second party would also be inserted by submarine.[20]

The planning group was hopeful the proposal would receive rapid American support, especially given growing momentum among the Allies towards seizing part of Borneo from the Japanese.

They needed the approval by early October at the latest if Carter's party was to be inserted in mid-October as planned. But early October came and went without a response.

∽

SRD had learned hard lessons from previous operational disasters, including that of Python. The planners of Operation Semut decided early in the piece that the operation's leaders should have on-the-ground experience in Borneo, including fluency in the island's lingua franca, Malay. The operation's overall Commanding Officer, Captain G.S. 'Toby' Carter, a tall, lean 34-year-old New Zealander, met these prerequisites admirably.

Carter had spent several years in Sarawak before the war work-ing for Shell's Sarawak Oilfields Ltd as a surveyor, and had many contacts among locals and resident expatriates. He spoke not only fluent Malay, but also a smattering of several Dayak languages. He was serving in New Guinea with the AIF when he was sought out by Semut's original planning group to lead the operation. Underlining yet again British dominance of the operation, he was required to transfer to the British Army, and move from there to SRD, before he could take on the role of party leader.

Carter was a reserved, modest man with a strong sense of duty and a dislike of the limelight. He was a skilled diplomat, a tal-ent that had been put to good use during his travels throughout Sarawak on behalf of Shell. He liked and admired Dayak peoples, and had a sound knowledge of their cultures. This was combined with an attitude of paternalistic protectionism towards them – common among Europeans at the time – which he shared with the other two party leaders.

It is hard to think of a man less like the self-effacing Toby Carter than his second-in-command, and the second party leader, Captain Tom Harnett Harrisson. Harrisson was a 32-year-old Harrow- and

Cambridge-educated Englishman who had joined the planning group in June 1944. Before the war he had been a scholar, participating in various research projects including a four-month Oxford expedition to Sarawak in 1932 to explore the state's flora and fauna. The expedition was his only in-country experience of Sarawak and he had very little Malay when he joined the operation. After undertaking officer training with the British Army, Harrisson was recruited for Semut by SOE in March 1944 and flew to Australia in June.[21]

Harrisson tended to polarise people: while some adored him, others loathed him. Alastair Morrison, who worked with him in Sarawak after the war, comments: 'I never knew a man with such a capacity for quarrelling,' a personality trait also reflected in the title of Judith Heimann's biography: 'the most offending soul alive'. He was a narcissist (Heimann refers to his 'ravenous' ego), a bully – especially towards subordinates – and an endless self-promoter. But he was also highly intelligent and possessed of a tremendous appetite for life.[22]

The third senior party member, Captain W.L.P. 'Bill' Sochon, had arrived to join the group in early September. At almost 40, he was older than the other two, and much stouter, both of which made him the butt of repeated jibes from Harrisson. He had served in the British merchant navy for several years and also in the UK Prison Service before moving to Sarawak in 1929. He had spent nine years there working as a senior officer of the Police and Prison Services. As a result, like Carter, he possessed an impressive network of contacts across all ethnic groups, and spoke fluent Malay. At the outbreak of war he had joined the British Home Guard where he had risen to the rank of Major. He had been recruited directly from there by SOE for Operation Semut, accepting a demotion to the rank of captain in the process since there were no vacancies for Major available in SOE at the time.

Sochon was a down-to-earth, pragmatic man: less reserved ('a rougher diamond') than Carter, less theatrical and bumptious than Harrisson. He was gregarious and plain-speaking. This led one of the Australians who served under him to pay him the ultimate compliment of describing him as 'an "Englishman" – not a "pom"', at a time when the latter term was considered derogatory.[23]

Of the three, Carter was the only one to have already seen active military service overseas.

☙

Failure to gain approval for Semut by early October marked a turning point. The operation's planning group knew that once the northeast monsoon hit Sarawak in late October, submarine land-ing on the Sarawak coast would become impossible for three to four months. The operation as planned could not now be launched until the monsoon's end in February/March 1945.[24]

But as one window closed, another was opening. By early October the Americans had advanced across the Pacific and taken control of the island of Morotai. The airbase they established there drastically reduced the distance Allied planes needed to travel to reach Borneo. The Americans were now planning an assault on the island of Mindoro in the Philippines; if successful, this would decrease the distance even further. For the first time it became pos-sible to consider landing the initial Operation Semut party by air.[25]

The question of how to insert the operatives and their supplies had bedevilled planning from the start. It had been agreed early in the piece that the operation should be based in Sarawak's remote interior rather than its coastal areas. There were three reasons for this. Firstly, the scanty information available suggested that, as in British North Borneo, the Japanese in Sarawak were largely concentrated on the coastal strip and had failed to penetrate far inland. An absence of Japanese would mean that not only were the operatives unlikely to encounter Japanese soldiers on arrival, but locals would be less frightened about the repercussions of assisting them.

Secondly, inland Dayak groups were deemed potentially more loyal to the Brooke regime and the British than the largely Malay and Chinese inhabitants of coastal and urban areas. These latter groups, it was feared, may have been influenced by the Japanese to reject White rule. And thirdly, but by no means least importantly, many inland Dayak groups were known to have martial traditions, including headhunting. This should make it easier to train them for anti-Japanese guerrilla activities.

The problem, however, was how to get operatives, along with their supplies, through the dangers of the coastal strip and into inland areas. Initially there was little option other than insertion by sea: the nearest air bases in Australia were too far from Borneo for planes to make the round trip, heavily loaded as they would be with men and supplies. And submarine insertion had been used successfully by the Allies in both Europe and North America, so was initially favoured by Finlay and Courtney.

However, as a number of the old Borneo hands in the planning group explained, submarine insertion into Sarawak was an entirely different proposition from submarine insertion into Europe and North America. Sarawak's coastline was dotted with coral reefs and much of it was comprised of slow shelving mud which would make it difficult for a submarine to come close to land. The monsoon presented added difficulties.[26]

As if this was not bad enough, once the men had struggled several miles to shore over treacherous waters in rubber boats, they would confront the recurring problem of the Japanese-controlled coastal strip, containing not only Japanese soldiers but unreliable, terrorised locals. To make matters worse, they had to somehow get not only themselves across that strip, but also enough supplies to sustain them until they were established. And if the operation was to be reasonably long term, as hoped, they had to find a way to organise ongoing supply, probably using local porters operating across the same strip, under the noses of the Japanese – a profoundly perilous exercise. No wonder a number of the men, including all three operational leaders, had serious reservations about this strategy.[27]

But now Morotai – and possibly Mindoro before long – promised a base from which long-range aircraft could make the return flight to Borneo. This made air insertion of both operatives and supplies feasible, as well as opening up the possibility of a larger-scale, longer-term operation that could be provisioned via regular air-drops. Morotai was a game-changer.

∽

In the meantime, Sarawak had been confirmed as an area of importance for Allied military strategists more broadly. With the Australian Oboe landings at Brunei Bay now scheduled for June 1945, Semut's planning group sensed a golden opportunity to sell the operation to the Americans. They went back to the drawing board.

By 11 November the group had produced a revised plan. It included a proposal to have an efficient intelligence network – using sympathetic locals trained by SRD operatives with knowledge of the area – in place prior to the Allied invasion. In order to effect this, operatives would need to be in Borneo by the end of 1944, six months before the scheduled invasion date.

Other objectives of the previous proposal remained the same, although the emphasis had now shifted from locating and evacuating pre-war Sarawak government employees to organising escape routes for Allied Air Force personnel who were believed to have been shot down over the territory. This was another direct pitch to the Americans, who had lost several planes in the area.[28]

The operation's location had also changed. The Americans at General Headquarters had informed SRD that the landings scheduled for Brunei Bay meant Brunei now had a high priority for intelligence purposes. As a result, Belaga – many days journey from Brunei across rugged countryside – was no longer an ideal site for Operation Semut's HQ. Instead, encouraged by Toby Carter, the planning group turned its attention to the Baram River, which flows from headwaters high in the Kelabit Plateau to join the sea not far southwest from Brunei Bay, close to the oilfields at Seria and Lutong.

Carter had travelled extensively in the Baram River basin before the war and spoke a little of the languages of the Kayan and Kenyah, the dominant Dayak groups in the upper Baram region. In his view, Long Akah – a Chinese trading settlement high up the Baram River where the Brookes had built a fort – would provide the perfect location for the operation's HQ. Long Akah was close to the Kenyah community of Long San where the great chief Tama Weng Ajeng had his home.

Carter was confident the Kayan, Kenyah, and other Dayak groups living along the river would support the operation: he was well known in the area, and had developed close ties with some of its highest-ranking chiefs, including Tama Weng Ajeng himself. And the riverine and jungle skills of these peoples should mean that, with their cooperation, it would be possible to mount secret operations further down the river in Japanese-held territory.

The planning group agreed. The operation's main HQ was moved from Belaga at the top of the Rejang River to Long Akah in the upper reaches of the Baram River. Long Akah now became the focal point of the entire operation: the place from which all special operations activity in Northern Sarawak and Brunei would be organised.[29]

However, while Carter's main HQ had shifted from the Rejang River to the Baram River, the Rejang – the longest and most important waterway in Sarawak – nevertheless remained integral to the group's schemes. It was earmarked as the location for a future offshoot operation to be mounted, if everything went to plan, once the main party was established at Long Akah. This Rejang operation would focus on intelligence-gathering, with a special brief to recruit members of the Sarawak Rangers, an official paramilitary/constabulary force that had existed in the pre-war era, many of whose personnel were Iban from the Rejang River area.

Sochon was chosen to lead this offshoot operation. He had excellent contacts within the Rangers as a result of his lengthy experience in the Sarawak Constabulary. In fact, several years earlier he had submitted a proposal to the British military whereby he and a team would be landed on the Rejang River via flying boat, and would reform the Sarawak Rangers for anti-Japanese activities. While the proposal had disappeared into the maw of the British military machine, the plan itself might still see the light of day.[30]

൦ൟ

Attention was now focused on the key issue of insertion. While the planning group was coming round to the idea of insertion by parachute, this presented its own suite of difficulties. Chief among them was the location of a suitable drop zone. The interior of eastern Sarawak, including the upper Baram River where the party HQ would be located, is rugged and mountainous, and in 1945 almost all of it was covered by dense jungle reaching far up the sides of mountain peaks and down to the banks of rivers. Dropping paratroopers in to such terrain was hazardous – they might well be caught up in trees from which they could not climb to the ground, or be skewered on the sharp, partly-burned stumps left after the clearing of Dayak rice fields. And dropping stores risked huge losses: the slightest navigational error could see them disappear for good into dense jungle, a lesson already learned from RAAF resupply attempts along the Kokoda Trail in New Guinea.

Finally, Harrisson undertook research on the problem in the libraries of Sydney and Melbourne. He emerged with a solution. A great plain, the Plain of Bah, was located on the 2000–3000 feet (600–900 m) high Kelabit Plateau in the remote northeastern interior of Sarawak, close to the border with Dutch Borneo. The plain was bounded by mountain ranges on three sides, with the headwaters of the Baram River – whose upper reaches would host the operation's HQ – on the fourth. From the Plain of Bah it was a journey of eight or nine days to Long Akah on the upper Baram, where Carter intended to locate his HQ.

The plain's inaccessibility made it unlikely to have been reached by the Japanese, and it was home to a potentially friendly Dayak population: the Kelabit. The Kelabit grew rice in irrigated fields on their high plain, in contrast to most other Dayaks who cultivated rice in unirrigated slash-and-burn fields on the slopes of hills. Since wet rice cultivation requires the removal of most tree stumps, these fields would not present the same danger to incoming parachutists as unirrigated fields. In addition, the plain contained considerable areas of open grassland which would provide perfect drop zones.[31]

The planning group – containing as it did a number of men who had long experience in Borneo's interior – knew that such a drop zone would pose considerable challenges. The Plain of Bah is set on a narrow valley surrounded by mountains which rise to 4000–5000 feet (1200–1500 m) above the valley floor. The mountains were certain to be cloud-covered, and it was likely the high valley itself was also shrouded in cloud for much of the day. Flying conditions would be difficult and dangerous.

However, it was agreed that in the early morning, before clouds had begun to rise from the steaming jungles, it might be possible for a skilled pilot to get low enough to make the drop. Not for the last time during the operation a choice had to be made from a number of imperfect options. And so the insertion strategy was finally settled: the men and their supplies would parachute directly in to the Kelabit Plateau.[32]

꩜

Agreement on air insertion provoked a new question: was it wise to risk the party leader, Toby Carter, in a blind parachute drop into completely unknown territory? The planning group quickly decided this would be rash. A more sensible approach would be to first insert a reconnaissance party to spy out and prepare the land for the arrival of Carter's main party fourteen days later. Tom Harrisson – who, by his own admission, was determined to 'go in first' – was selected to lead the reconnaissance party. He would establish a sub-party HQ on the Kelabit Plateau and locate a suitable drop zone there for the insertion of the main party. From the Plateau the main party would trek across the rugged 5000-foot (1500-m) high Tama Abu mountains to the proposed HQ at Long Akah on the Baram River.[33]

However, it would be impossible to carry all the equipment and supplies the main party would need – weighing around two tons – from the drop zone on the Kelabit Plateau across the mountains. Accordingly, the reconnaissance party was tasked with itself crossing the mountains soon after its arrival, and identifying a suitable supplies drop zone at Long Lellang, a remote Kelabit longhouse in the headwaters of the Akah River. The Akah is a tributary of the Baram River, flowing into the larger river at Long Akah. Carter had journeyed up the Akah River to Long Lellang in the past, and knew that although it was studded with rapids, it was possible for local boatmen to transport supplies along it to Long Akah.

Once Harrisson had identified a drop zone on the Kelabit Plateau where the main party could be inserted, and a drop zone at Long Lellang where their supplies could be landed, he would provide the co-ordinates of both to SRD HQ in Darwin by radio. Two weeks after the insertion of the reconnaissance party, the personnel of the main party would be landed at the drop zone on the Kelabit Plateau, while their supplies would be dropped at the Long Lellang site.[34]

The new revised plan was submitted to General Headquarters for approval on 24 November 1944. It was approved early in December. After almost ten months of planning, Operation Semut was finally on its way.

∽

In the meantime, Harrisson had been charged, as leader of the reconnaissance party, with organising a preliminary flight over the Kelabit Plateau to confirm its suitability as both a drop zone and a preliminary base for his party. On 15 January 1945 he and Squadron Leader Cook of the RAAF hitched a ride from the American base on Morotai to the Brunei Bay area in a US Navy Liberator. On his return to base the pilot kindly detoured to the Baram River and Kelabit Plateau so that Harrisson and Cook could survey the area. Above the Kelabit Plateau the plane found its way into an interior valley in which Harrisson was able to identify 'several large clear places, *flat* [. . .] and clearly under extensive cultivation'. This must be the Plain of Bah.[35]

En route to this hidden valley they discovered an astonishing rock formation not then found on any map. Two giant white sandstone pillars joined by a saddle, around 6000 feet (1830 m) high, thrust up unexpectedly from the jungle north of the Plain of Bah. They were not to know it at the time, but this was the great peak – one of the highest in Sarawak – known to local Dayaks as Batu Lawi. Its twin pinnacles, representing male and female, still today resonate throughout the mythology of Dayak groups in its vicinity. For Harrisson and Cook it had a more prosaic function: it could serve as a guiding landmark for all subsequent flights to the valley.[36]

∽

By now it was late January 1945, too late for the operation's key objective of having an intelligence network set up well before the Oboe landings at Brunei Bay, scheduled for June. Instead, the planning group began to explore a more ambitious goal: the organisation of guerrilla operations in support of the invasion forces. Carter was now charged with investigating the possibility of establishing guerrilla groups, recruited from Dayak peoples, to be run under the supervision of European operatives.[37]

But this was not the only deviation to have occurred from the formal list of objectives put to the Americans in November. According to Carter's Party Report the operation was now also asked to

> Investigate the internal political situation and ascertain the feeling of the natives towards the pre-war Government and the possible return of the Rajah and/or British Government. In this connection should conditions prove favourable it was intended to set up spheres of influence on the lines of pre-war Govt. in order that the expected change over from active hostilities, to peace, could be carried out with a minimum of confusion.[38]

Courtney noted later that by the end of 1944, with the Americans almost exclusively focused on the Philippines and Japan, they had relinquished direct control over Borneo operations to the Australians. As a result, the British imperialist aims the Americans had resisted for so long in SRD's activities were able to feature explicitly in operational planning. For Operation Semut, as for many special operations since, winning the peace had now become almost as important as winning the war.[39]

With the start of the operation around the corner, early in February Carter and Harrisson were both promoted to Major. Unfortunately for Sochon – the only one of the three to have previously held that rank – he could not join them. There were only two vacancies available at Major level, and these went to Carter and Harrisson as the first and second to join the operation, and as party leader and second-in-command respectively. Sochon, to his annoyance, was forced to remain a captain.

By now details of the air insertion were being worked out. Late in 1944, after a period of intense lobbying, it had been decided that the Allied Intelligence Bureau would have its own flight of aircraft, No. 200 Flight RAAF. As one of the organisations sitting under the Bureau's umbrella, SRD was set to benefit from this decision: its Borneo operations, especially, were accorded a high priority with respect to the Flight's use. Semut's reconnaissance and main parties would both be inserted by 200 Flight. Indeed, the insertion of the reconnaissance party was to be its first operational mission.

The Flight began its formal existence on 15 February 1945 with six Liberator aircraft; this was later increased to eight aircraft with, eventually, twelve aircrew of twelve men each (including a third pilot). The Liberator was chosen not only because of its long range even when fully loaded with men and stores, but also because of its ability to defend itself while over enemy territories. Its crew of twelve men included no fewer than six gunners.

In the absence of 200 Flight, Operation Semut would very likely have been stillborn. Yet the Flight has, sadly, never received its due acknowledgement. It is too easy to forget those whose service lies primarily in preparing the way for others, even when that service is intensely hazardous. The dropping of parachutes in mountainous jungled territory was fraught with danger, requiring precision flying and exquisite judgement. In addition, the planes were mostly flying over enemy territory, at constant risk of being shot down. Of the twelve 200 Flight crews, three were lost.[40]

Seventy years after that first 200 Flight mission, Jack Tredrea, one of the members of the Semut reconnaissance party on the flight that day, spoke from the heart. 'They [200 Flight personnel] were our comrades in arms,' he told me, 'the bravest of the brave. Without them we were nothing.'[41]

m

Now the planning group knew how and where insertion would occur, all that remained was to finalise details of the operation. It had been decided that the reconnaissance party and the main party would each comprise eight men, including their leaders. The members of both parties had been selected months earlier and had been undergoing the necessary additional training – including in parachute jumping and Malay language – since at least late November 1944. The men from each party were kept strictly together during the training period and, as with all SRD operations, were forbidden from speaking about their operation with anyone outside the party.

The seven men to go with Harrisson in the reconnaissance party comprised six Australians and one New Zealander (who had enlisted in the Australian Army):

- Captain Eric 'Ric' Edmeades, the party's second-in-command, was a frighteningly fit, baby-faced 24-year-old New Zealander. A clerk in civilian life, he had served with the AIF – often as an instructor – before being transferred to SRD in May 1944.
- Warrant Officer Class 1 Roderick 'Rod' Cusack was a large, cheerful 24-year-old, one of only two in the party who had already seen operational service overseas with SRD. A bank clerk in civilian life, he had served as an Army instructor before being recruited into SRD in October 1943.
- Staff Sergeant Douglas 'Doug' Bower, one of two signallers in the party, was a bespectacled, tenacious 27-year-old, who had already seen operational service with the 3rd Australian Armoured Division and SRD in New Guinea. A career soldier

(he eventually reached the rank of Lieutenant Colonel), he was recruited into SRD in September 1943.

- Sergeant John 'Keith' Barrie, a wiry and resourceful 31-year-old, had already seen service with the AIF in both the Middle East and New Guinea. A surveyor in civilian life, he had been recruited to SRD by Toby Carter (with whom he had worked at Shell Oil before the war) in August 1944, specifically to take part in Operation Semut.
- Sergeant Kelvin 'Kel' Hallam, the second signaller, was a tall, easygoing 21-year-old, an accounts clerk in civilian life. He had served as an Army signals instructor and had a brief stint in New Guinea, before being recruited into SRD in July 1943.
- Sergeant Jonathan 'Jack' Tredrea (promoted to Warrant Officer Class 2 in July 1945), the party's medical orderly, was a snowy-haired, self-contained 24-year-old, a tailor in civilian life. He had previously served with the Army Medical Corps in Australia as an instructor, before being transferred to SRD in March 1944.
- Corporal Charles 'Fred' Sanderson (promoted to Sergeant in April 1945), was a small, tough 25-year-old; son of a Thai mother and an English father he had grown up in Southeast Asia and spoke several languages, including fluent Malay. He had served with the AIF in the Middle East and New Guinea before transferring to SRD in March 1944.

Apart from Harrisson and Barrie – both in their thirties – the average age of the group was a youthful 24 years old. Three of them (including Harrisson) had never served overseas. And in spite of the Malay classes – delivered by a Scotsman! – the Malay they possessed was (with the exception of Sanderson) rudimentary at best.

⟨∽

As the day of departure drew closer, the terrifying figure of the Japanese enemy stalked the thoughts and dreams of those in the reconnaissance party. They had no idea whether Japanese would be present in the drop zone vicinity: it was possible they were about to deliver themselves directly into the hands of an enemy they believed capable of unparalleled cruelty. As Sanderson later remembered:

> God only knew our fate; all I knew was that we were to be dropped into enemy occupied Borneo by parachute with no means of returning to our forces until an assault was made which would be months hence. Japanese occupied territory! And I had not been married very long.[42]

This was not all: the men were also tormented with worries about the Dayaks who inhabited the area around the drop zone. They had been assured by Carter and others from the planning group that Dayaks were generally well-disposed towards Europeans, and briefed on the courtesies they should follow to ensure they stayed that way. Nevertheless, the men knew the area was largely terra incognita, and that there was uncertainty about the reaction they could expect from its Dayak inhabitants. As Jack Tredrea told me years later:

> We knew very little about the local Dayaks before we went in. We knew that they'd had almost no contact with Europeans and that they were very primitive. And we were pretty sure they were headhunters. That was it.[43]

Bob Long, who was part of Toby Carter's main party to be inserted two weeks later, remarked:

It was like the frying pan and the fire. If the Japs didn't get you the Dayaks might. It was hard to know which to be more worried about.[44]

But fears must be subdued in deference to love of country and family, and hatred of the enemy. So finally, after months of planning and preparation, the moment of truth arrived. Just before midnight on 15 March 1945, the eight members of the reconnaissance party assembled at the Leyburn airfield, home of 200 Flight, on the Darling Downs in Queensland.

Each operative carried his own personal items in either his haversack or on his person. These included a change of clothes, waterproof matches, cigarette lighter, tobacco, cigarette papers, gum, a compass, water bottle, torch, signalling mirror, jungle hammock, maps, several days' worth of concentrated rations and a medicine kit, as well as his weapons: an Austen submachine gun or US carbine with spare magazines, a Colt .45 automatic pistol and/ or a Smith & Wesson .38 revolver and/or a Welrod pistol (different operatives preferred different weapons) plus a commando knife and ammunition.

Many operatives also carried grenades as a matter of course, and some had favourite weapons they had made for themselves during their training. While most of these were knives, Jack Tredrea had made himself what he called a 'waddy', named after the heavy wooden clubs used by some Australian indigenous peoples:

> I was able to procure a twelve-inch piece of white rubber hose; a cartridge in the business end was filled with lead pellets while the handle end was finished off with another cartridge and a leather thong for a wrist strap. Marvellous to belt anyone over the head! Very silent, too![45]

The men were forbidden from carrying dog tags or anything else that could identify or incriminate them: SRD had no colour patch – small patches of cloth, worn usually on the upper sleeve, that indicated the wearer's unit – for this reason. Cameras were also disallowed, although Toby Carter for one disobeyed this injunction – or perhaps, as party leader, it never applied to him. In any case, we can be grateful that he did, since many of the most significant images we now have from Semut were recorded on his camera.

At Leyburn, Toby Carter and the men of the main party – who would meet up with Harrisson's party in two weeks' time if all went to plan – were waiting, quiet and subdued. Carter shook hands with each member of the reconnaissance party and presented him with a silk map, a compass and a latex-covered cyanide capsule that could be bitten into in the event of capture by the Japanese: what the men came to call their 'L-pills' (L for 'lethal'). Different operatives secreted the capsules in different parts of their clothing or bodies.

It was not done to show fear at such times, but fear has a way of insinuating itself uninvited into one's being. Fred Sanderson wrote later that if Carter 'could only have known how my heart was thumping'. Elsewhere, he added: 'Departing from Leyburn at 3 am on a blind date with Fate in Japanese occupied Borneo with a one way ticket was grim.' Even calm, measured Jack Tredrea felt it. As he told me in 2017: 'I already had a sense of how dangerous the mission was, but the cyanide pill brought it home to me. It was a shock.'[46]

Finally, the eight men boarded two 200 Flight Liberators. Since this was 200 Flight's first mission its Squadron Leader, Graham Pockley DFC and Bar, commanded one of the planes; the other was commanded by Flight Lieutenant Frank Ball. Four operatives joined the crew in each of the aircraft and their more general supplies were packed into the bomb bays. The emotion was not confined to those in the planes. Sochon wrote later:

The feelings of us left on the ground watching the first party leave, definitely left a lump in the throat, knowing that they were going into unknown danger and possibly it would be the last we would see of them.[47]

Three days later, after pauses at Darwin and Morotai, the party arrived at McGuire Airfield on Mindoro Island in the Philippines. Their next stop was Sarawak's Kelabit Plateau.

෨

Over the next few days the Liberators, laden with operatives and supplies, made two trips from Mindoro to Sarawak in an effort to insert the reconnaissance party at its hidden valley high on the Kelabit Plateau. On both occasions heavy cloud cover across the valley made it impossible to see the drop zone and the flights had to be aborted.

The prolonged waiting was hard to bear – 'The strain on my nerves,' Sanderson records, 'was most damaging' – and the men were desperate for it to be over. To improve their chances on the next attempt, they decided to leave slightly earlier in the morning, in the hope that the cloud blanketing the valley for much of the day would not yet have risen from the jungles below.[48]

And so, on 25 March before dawn, the eight men assembled for the third time at McGuire Airfield. They filed into the Liberators, each man in the same plane, and with the same crew – whom by now he was beginning to know well – as on the previous two occasions.[49]

The Liberators crossed the coast of British North Borneo into enemy airspace around dawn, the rugged mountains of the interior directly ahead in the growing light. Reaching the sandstone and shale mass of Mt Mulu, second-highest summit in Sarawak, they turned southeast towards the great peaks of the Tama Abu Range.

And there, as expected, gleaming white in the morning sun, were the twin fingers of Batu Lawi.

As the nervous tension ratcheted up, the planes came over the range and into the air above the valley. And hallelujah, for the first time the pilots had clear sight of the drop zone. The Semut men were already up, stretching, adjusting their parachute harnesses, moving to the bomb bay out of which they would be despatched, the Liberator crew joshing them, as was customary in such times of tension.[50]

The plane commanded by Pockley stalled, with consummate skill, over a stretch of inviting open grassland below, and dropped its human cargo of four (Harrisson, Barrie, Bower and Sanderson) right on cue. Then, another circle, another stall, and it relinquished their supplies, suspended from their own blossoming parachutes. Meanwhile the second plane, commanded by Ball (carrying Edmeades, Cusack, Hallam and Tredrea), circled nearby in a holding pattern.[51]

However, by the time Ball's plane moved to position itself for the drop moments later, the weather had deteriorated. Cloud cover already made it impossible to see the drop zone below. Twice Ball prepared to run in for the stall and drop, but each time the cloud cover increased and he could see nothing.

Edmeades, in command of the operatives on the second plane, had the option of aborting. But with the men from the first plane having already jumped he could not countenance such a course. Instead he instructed Ball to take the plane to a point that he estimated to be over the drop zone. Here the men would jump 'blind'. Out they went, with Tredrea so close behind Edmeades in the slippery dispatch slide that his feet hit Edmeades' head. Another circle and moments later their supplies followed them.[52]

As the eight operatives hung in a silent world of cloud, the second plane roared away to join the first, following the two fingers of

Batu Lawi towards the coast. But only one made it back to Mindoro. The first plane, the 'Pockley plane' as it has since been known, disappeared without trace. It was the first casualty of the operation.

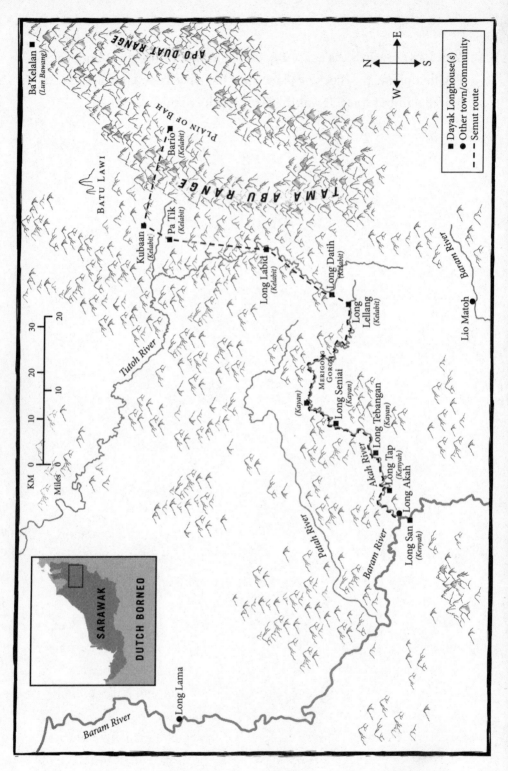

Semut route from Bario to Long Lellang and Long Akah.

4

ARRIVAL

IT WAS EARLY MORNING when Keling Langit heard the sound again. The young Kelabit woman paused at her work amid the cool slush of the rice field. Yesterday's eerie echo had returned, moving back and forth above the clouds that hung across her valley high on the Kelabit Plateau. It was like nothing she had ever heard before: quite different from the rhythmic whooshes of the hornbills' wings as they flew across the valley in the evenings, or the slowly climaxing whoops of the gibbons as they called to one another in the jungle trees at dawn. This was a strange reverberating roar that filled the valley, overwhelming all other sounds.

Peering skyward Keling Langit saw, to her horror, several giant white figures materialise through the cloud. They resembled the pale spirit beings said to have once inhabited the area, their superhuman exploits remembered in song during long evenings in her Bario long-house home. Closer and closer they came, descending slowly and silently like birds stooping in to land. Keling Langit felt such terror that she began to weep. Climbing out of the rice field, she ran for her home.[1]

Back at the longhouse – normally largely empty during the day as people went about their daily work – there was pandemonium as residents hurried in to report sightings of the pale figures. Some were fearful they were connected with the new rulers who had recently established themselves in Sarawak, convincingly demonstrating their spiritual potency by so easily ousting the previous White regime. Although the Japanese had not made it as far inland as Bario – halting at Ba'Kelalan, a day's walk away through the Apo Duat range – local Kelabits travelled regularly outside the valley and were aware of the Japanese reputation for mistreating local populations, including molesting women. It was agreed that if the arrivals should turn out to be Japanese, the women in the longhouse would run to the jungle and hide.[2]

However, most residents were of the view that the newcomers were spirit beings, their earlier presence in the area inscribed in many local landmarks including the great twin peaks of Batu Lawi. The longhouse head, Lawai Bisarai, was hopeful that they came in peace rather than to punish the longhouse for some kind of infraction. If the locals had committed a serious wrongdoing, he reasoned, *balio* – the process of petrification Kelabits understood to follow any major transgression – would surely already be occurring, and the Bario longhouse would have turned partly to stone.

Like most Dayaks, Lawai Bisarai was a pragmatic man. Accordingly, he decided on a sensible course of action: several young men would be sent to look for the beings and invite them back to the longhouse where they could be appropriately honoured with food and drink. Each young man took with him a small piece of white cloth, customarily used during spirit propitiation ceremonies. Tied to the end of his long, carved blowpipe, this would serve as a message of respect and welcome for the new arrivals.[3]

After the young men had gone, the remaining longhouse residents began to prepare food and drink. And they dressed in their best ceremonial regalia, as befitted an encounter with spirit beings.

⁐

As they emerged through the cloud, the four men from the first Liberator saw immediately below, to their relief, the soft ooze of a marsh. They fell in a series of splashes into deep brown mud that 'sogged and swooshed at the least movement' amid tussocks of rush and sedge. And all around them, shocking after the absolute silence of the clouds, that most distinctive of Borneo sounds: the ceaseless deafening throb of cicadas.[4]

Sanderson, the party's designated contact man, had managed to locate the local longhouse as he fell: perched on a rise at the base of the steep, jungle-covered mountains encircling the valley. He extricated himself from the mud as quickly as he could and set off in its general direction. The other three remained behind, wallowing through the swamp, searching for their stores, leaving him to do his work.

In the meantime, the four men from the second Liberator, jumping blind, had exited the cloud to the frightening sight of dense jungle immediately below: they had overshot the drop zone by around 3 miles (4.8 km). Tredrea, who had stored his L-pill in his mouth for the descent, panicked at the sight of the trees rushing towards him and spat it out: 'Bad luck if the Japs got me,' he told me years later. 'No way I was landing with that in my mouth.' Crash-landing in the trees, they ended up hooked high on rainforest foliage in a world filled – like the first party – with the sibilant pulsating thrum of cicadas. They cut their shroud lines and climbed or slid down the slippery moss-covered trunks to safety: 'I did an express trip down,' said Hallam later, 'finally hitting Borneo very hard with my backside.'[5]

It took the four men of the second party hours to find one another. The task was made more difficult by the fact that Edmeades' American carbine, which he carried in front of him with the safety catch off ready for immediate action, had discharged as he hit the trees. Fearing the worst – that Japanese soldiers were firing at one of their comrades – the others were reluctant to call out or use their whistles to attract each other's attention. But finally they were all located and Edmeades pulled out his compass, hoping to navigate his way to the drop zone. Progress was slow, however, as the terrain was uneven and they had to hack their way through dense, apparently trackless, jungle. They moved with extreme caution in case any Japanese in the vicinity had heard the gunshot and were on their way to investigate.[6]

Back at the swamp, as Harrisson, Barrie and Bower searched for their stores, there materialised suddenly, perched at the edge of the mud, a small brown-skinned man. He had long flowing black hair and wore a yellow bark loincloth. In his hand was a lengthy wooden blowpipe, and attached to its end was a piece of white fabric. Astonishingly, the Kelabit symbol of welcome to spirit beings and the European symbol of peace coalesced in that one remarkable moment. In their relief Barrie and Bower leapt forward with cigarettes, and the shared smoke – that near-universal ceremony of conciliation in those more innocent days – was soon underway.[7]

Meanwhile, Sanderson had arrived at the Bario longhouse. His job was a tricky one: to convince the local Kelabits, possibly in the absence of any shared language, that the newcomers intended them no harm. Sanderson was fluent in Malay, the Sarawak lingua franca, but Carter, Harrisson and others had warned him that the valley's remoteness might mean locals did not speak it. He could not trust language to convey his goodwill; he needed to signal it more directly.

Accordingly, as Sanderson approached the longhouse he took care to unhook his carbine from over his shoulder and trail it along the ground behind him. Locals told me seventy years later of the effect this had: they knew of guns and their potentially deadly effects. Some went outside to greet him, as he wended his way through the irrigation ditches and up the rise on which the long-house stood. Finally he was standing at the base of the structure, alongside the massive posts supporting the floor several metres above his head. Next to him was the tall notched log that served as a ladder up to that floor. And waiting for him in front of the log was an elderly man.[8]

Lawai Bisarai was resplendent in ceremonial regalia befitting his status as a high-ranking Kelabit chief: leopard-skin hat, hornbill feathers and a khaki coat (a relic of the Brooke era); he wore brass earrings in his long stretched earlobes and brass bangles on his calves, and he carried a long sword in an elaborately decorated sheath. He gestured for Sanderson to climb the ladder into the longhouse.[9]

❦

Bario longhouse was on the small side by Dayak standards: around 250 feet (76 m) from end to end and containing approximately one hundred inhabitants. At the top of the entry ladder a three-foot hole gave egress to the gallery. Members of the reconnaissance party had been briefed on longhouses, but nothing could possibly have prepared Sanderson for what confronted him as he climbed through the hole that morning.

Directly in front: an enormous gallery, dark and smoky, stretching the length of the building. A thatched palm-leaf roof soaring over-head, its ridgepole blackened from decades of smoke. Underfoot, a floor of worn handmade planks, slightly uneven, so they trembled and clattered as he moved across them. All around, a baffling array of objects – woven baskets of all sizes and shapes, traps, animal skins, woven mats, spears, blowpipes – some on the floor but most scattered on, or suspended from, a confusion of platforms and crossbeams not far above his head. Mangy dogs that yelped and skipped around his legs. And, perhaps most confronting of all, a tremendous babble of noise.[10]

Many of the inhabitants, men and women alike, had the extended earlobes common among the Kelabit and related groups at the time, some reaching far below the shoulder. Like our own various cosmetic surgeries, these were seen to enhance the attractiveness of the individual. Today they have almost disappeared, hostage to Western ideals of beauty.

From holes in the earlobes hung brass rings and other ornaments; many people also wore brass bangles on their arms and legs. Some of the men had small holes cut in the upper parts of their ears, from which protruded additional ornaments. Both men and women wore strings of beautiful ancient glass beads around their necks, and some of the women wore skull caps made of strung circles of larger beads. The women wore skirts and the men loincloths – most, in these straitened times, made from bark in place of the more usual fabric. All were barefoot.

Members of the reconnaissance party – as of the main party to follow – had received some rudimentary instruction on Dayak culture and how to behave towards Dayak people: be polite and friendly in demeanour and behaviour, never refuse offered food and drink (such a refusal potentially being read as a rejection of sociality itself), sit on the gallery floor when invited into a longhouse and never, ever touch the women. In fact, the last of these injunctions tells us more about prudish European attitudes than it does about Dayak ones of the time: few, if any, Dayaks – including the women – would have had any objection to operatives having sexual affairs with widows or unmarried Dayak women and, indeed, many were puzzled that they did not.

Carter had worked hard to instil a sense of respect for Dayak peoples into the men who would serve in Semut: Jack Tredrea and Bob Long both later remembered being told by him 'in no uncertain terms' before leaving Australia that any signs of disrespect towards locals would be punished. He had laid down a set of rules of behaviour in relation to Dayak (and other local) peoples that he expected his men to follow, including a ban on any derogatory terms of reference or address.[11]

However, the point repeated over and over during the men's training – reflecting both Carter's long acquaintance with Dayak peoples and the input of many old Borneo hands to the operation – was to 'never throw your weight around with them' as Jack Tredrea explained it later on. An SRD information summary prepared for the operation puts it succinctly:

> When dealing with natives, particularly Sea Dayaks [Ibans] and Kayans, there must be no attempt at browbeating. They are a most hospitable people, and are strictly honest. Behave as you would normally in a house in which you are a welcome guest. Eat with the Head of the house. Admire and make a fuss of the children.[12]

This was wise advice. Dayaks have always been known for their refusal to kowtow to Europeans or anyone else. Thus Barrie noted later that it was wrong to translate the term *tuan*, used by Dayaks to address European males, as 'master':

> [T]he word 'tuan' has often been interpreted to mean 'master' in the old colonial context, with its connotations of servility. Well, I never detected too much evidence of servile attitudes among the Borneo people [. . .] I had the impression from the start their approach was at least as an equal. I preferred to interpret the term 'tuan' as 'boss', in the same way as we used to consider the Surveyor in a survey party in the bush as 'the boss' and addressed him as such without any suggestion of touching the forelock.[13]

As an important visitor, Sanderson was ushered along the gallery to its central section, outside the inner apartment where Lawai Bisarai and his family lived. Here he sat down – a gratifying mark of respect, as the locals saw it – on the raised platform running the length of the gallery, and reached into his haversack. He pulled out the small gifts he had prepared for this moment – biscuits, cigarettes, sweets – and distributed them among those present. And he began to speak slowly in Malay.[14]

Here the party had its first stroke of luck. Lawai Bisarai had, in his youth, killed a man and been sentenced to two years' detention in Marudi. While there he had learned to speak some Malay, the only person in the longhouse to do so. His Malay was poor, but sufficient for limited communication. Sanderson began the laborious task of explaining that others of his party, plus a host of stores, were still to be located. However, he was soon interrupted by the arrival of Harrisson and Barrie, along with their new Kelabit acquaintance. Before long a large number of locals had been sent off with Barrie to join Bower in searching for the missing supplies.

ᕓ

Over the months of planning for the operation, immense thought had been given to the equipment and stores the men should take with them. The operatives themselves had carried out numerous tests to ensure these supplies could endure months of tough jungle conditions. Socks appear to have caused particular angst, with four different parties reporting adversely 'on the Army socks as currently issued to this Unit by Stores': 'One pair sprang a hole in 3 miles.'[15]

Endless lists of food, medical supplies, weaponry, equipment, trade items, personal items and clothing had been compiled and refined. Earlier schedules had included '2 lbs. Horlicks tablets', '4 lbs. curry powder' and '4 lbs. Vegemite', but these had all failed to make the final cut. Nevertheless some 'comforts' had been

included in the stores dropped with the reconnaissance party:
'12 lbs. Havelock Fine Cut Tobacco', '100 pkts. Cigarette Papers',
and '2 boxes Chewing Gum'. And money! A total of nine thousand
Sarawak one-shilling, five-shilling and ten-shilling notes (weighing
ten pounds) were included in the party's inventory, as well as gold
sterling to a total of twenty-seven pounds weight.[16]

With weight at a premium, everything was itemised down to the
finest detail. On the advice of a geologist who had previously visited
the Kelabit Highlands, Harrisson also took fifty thousand fish hooks
and a quarter of a million needles to use as currency with local
people. They turned out to be useless for this function – the
locals much preferring gold – but he found another use for them:
'Ingeniously arranged, set in bamboo, they made reassuring pali-
sades, hidden in the ground around jungle camps at night.'[17]

Supplies – apart from personal ones the operatives carried with
them – were packed into clever containers called 'storpedoes'. These
were cylinders around 6 feet (almost 2 m) long and 2 feet (around
60 cm) in diameter, made of very hard cardboard. The body was reinforced with metal bands and the hollow head was tapered to a point,
while the rear was fastened to a parachute. Supplies and equipment
were loaded inside the body. When the storpedo was ejected from
the plane, the parachute opened and swung round so the hollow
head was facing downwards. This hit the ground first and crumpled,
absorbing a great deal of the shock. It was a remarkably effective
way to insert supplies, and even fragile radio equipment was landed
in this way. However, Harrisson later estimated that around 20 per
cent of all storpedoes were lost, mostly in jungle and rivers.[18]

Barrie and Bower, later joined by Sanderson, worked hard for the
remainder of the day: searching with the Kelabits for the storpedoes,
helping to carry them – eight or nine people per storpedo –
to the area beside the longhouse, and then unpacking and sorting
their contents. By mid-afternoon Edmeades' party had arrived, and

the search was expanded to include their storpedoes. As evening fell most had been located, and all those from Harrisson's party carried to the longhouse.

In the process of gathering the supplies the parachutes themselves were also collected. Here the operatives made an unexpected discovery: the parachute silk was of more value than almost anything else they had with them. The shortage of cloth caused by the Allied blockade had bitten hard in Bario, as everywhere else in Borneo, and many locals – like the young man who had first appeared at the swamp – were reduced to the humiliation of wearing clothes made from bark cloth. In such circumstances the soft, supple parachute silk must have seemed like the most luxurious fabric on earth: everyone wanted a piece of it. It became a crucial form of currency for this – and, indeed, every later – Semut party.[19]

つ⁀

Back at the longhouse, Harrisson had settled down with Sanderson in the gallery to drink *borak*, the local rice wine, and establish friendly relations with Lawai Bisarai and the other inhabitants. It was the first time any of the locals except Lawai had seen Europeans, and they looked so unlike Kelabits that they found it almost impossible to believe they could be human. Harrisson and Sanderson worked hard, using simple Malay and hand signs, to convince them otherwise and to indicate that they needed their help. The fact that Sanderson spoke Malay – which the Kelabits knew was a human language, and which shared some similarities with the Kelabit language – made their claim to be human more convincing. But most important was the friendliness of their gestures and behaviours, the smiles on their faces, and their ready consumption of the food and drink provided.[20]

Harrisson and Sanderson also laboured to explain that they were in Bario to fight the Japanese in preparation for a mass return of

White people, and to request Lawai Bisarai's support. Lawai Bisarai was no fool. While Bario was sufficiently remote to have escaped the worst excesses of Japanese rule, he was nevertheless unhappy about the disappearance of goods such as cloth, sugar and medicines that had occurred under the Japanese aegis. However, he – along with everyone else at Bario, in spite of its remoteness – had heard about what was happening in areas with a stronger Japanese presence. He knew of the Japanese reputation for brutality and the potential repercussions of assisting Harrisson's party. Already at least a dozen Dayaks in neighbouring areas had been either taken prisoner or killed by the Japanese for helping shot-down US airmen.

Accordingly, in response to Harrisson's request, Lawai asked, very astutely, whether there would be guns available for his men to use. Harrisson assured him there would. Lawai Bisarai also asked how his people would be protected from Japanese reprisals. Harrisson explained that his own party of eight was simply the forerunner of large numbers of European soldiers who would soon be coming to liberate the island. Between them they would make sure that Bario and surrounding areas were kept safe. And, crucially, the Europeans would win the war.[21]

By late afternoon, after many cups of *borak*, the longhouse inhabitants had largely accepted the group's human credentials. And Lawai Bisarai – having received the assurances he needed – had pledged the support of not only himself, but all the Kelabits in the longhouse, to the Semut cause. Harrisson's first crucial task had been successfully accomplished. He had found the place to establish not only his preliminary HQ but also a drop zone for Carter's main party.

∽

After a day of high drama and dizzying success, Harrisson's men were exhausted. But the residents of Bario were only just getting started. As darkness fell and the lamps – fuelled by *damar*, an aromatic slow-burning resin – were lit along the gallery, they sat down in the flickering light to a welcome feast complete with dancing, singing and seemingly inexhaustible quantities of *borak*. Barrie later wrote:

> A huge earthenware vat appeared in the communal part of the longhouse containing what looked like some sort of milky dishwater, and to the accompaniment of some poetic rhetoric on the part of the headman [. . .] a scruffy half coconut shell was periodically dipped into the liquid and proceeded to be passed round the assembled company from which each of us in turn took a good swig, drinking a toast to sentiments expressed. As none of us had any experience with borak [. . .] and as its taste was quite sweet, like some primitive 'lolly water', it was considered to be innocuous. I guess it's the most deceptive alcoholic beverage I have ever drunk.[22]

Barrie's 'milky dishwater' was, at the time, one of the most important elements of the hospitality Dayaks throughout Borneo extended to longhouse visitors. Locally-made rice wine (known as *borak* in some areas, and *tuak* in others), at its best both sweet and deliciously tangy, was used to ease connection and lubricate friendship between hosts and guests. In many areas its consumption was almost compulsory for guests, and the operatives had already been advised that they should on no account refuse. Drinking often took the form of mild competitions, with the local aim being to render visitors as drunk as possible. It is easy to imagine the delight Lawai Bisarai and other Bario residents must have taken that night in plying the visiting Europeans – erstwhile masters of the region – with *borak*, and watching as their pretentions fell away and they steadily descended into revelry.

The result was a riotous evening, as Dayak welcoming parties of the time so often were. Perhaps most memorable was the praise-singing, practised in many Dayak longhouses as a way of welcoming guests. One of the hosts would perform a long improvised chant setting out the supposed virtues of the guest, with the general crowd joining in on a chorus at the end of each stanza. Guests were then expected to respond in similar vein. At the end of each song those praised were required to gulp down yet more rice wine.

Barrie later remembered:

The Penghulu's chanting was to express their happiness at our arrival which was poetically likened to the return of their mothers and fathers from heaven. It soon became obvious that some sort of response was expected and I must say Tom rose to the occasion magnificently. At the appropriate juncture he began to intone responses like an Anglican priest, to the effect that we were likewise happy to be the vanguard of the forces assembling to rid them of their despotic overlords etc. etc. [. . .]

The occasion developed into a full-blown mutual admiration ceremony which required a more specific gesture of goodwill and support from the new arrivals as a group. This took the form of a rousing chorus to supplement Tom's recitative [. . .]

So Tom led off, enthusiastically followed by the rest of us – 'Fuck 'em all, fuck 'em all. The long and the short and the tall etc. etc.' The whole unexpurgated version and with the aid of adequate borak lubrication the merriment continued with increasing gusto well into the night, the sounds of ribald celebration reverberating down the valley with increasing decibels, so that if there had been any Japs remotely within hearing distance the question of their proximity would have been well and truly settled in short order. All the pre-embarkation briefing about security went out the window.[23]

Halfway through the night Tredrea, at least, remembered his training:

I said to Keith Barrie, 'Hey Keith, do you know that we haven't even got a sentry out?' 'Who cares Tred, who cares.'

Edmeades later wrote:

All my security training seemed awash with 'borak' and I remember remarking to someone else in our party 'What a wonderful way to go to war.'[24]

Even when the party was over and the men had finally settled down on the gallery outside Lawai Bisarai's apartment, they discovered that sleep was not a given. They had not counted on the longhouse dogs.

This was our first experience of the appalling clamour with which Kelabit dogs decorate the gamut of darkness. If they are kept in the long-house, they spend the night dashing about in packs, scratching and fighting around and across the sleeping humans. If they are kept out, they yowl and shriek, bay the moon, bark the owl, chase the pigs, infuriate the buffaloes beneath your plank. This first night, they were left in. Several of us lost valued army boots in consequence. (Poor Cusack last saw his self-winding wrist-watch disappear with a dog chewing the strap).[25]

The next morning, the men woke feeling decidedly the worse for wear. 'After drinking their Borak,' Tredrea commented later, 'I knew what a hangover meant.' Nevertheless they got to work. While Harrisson was engaged full time in meeting the scores of Kelabits from surrounding areas flocking to the longhouse in response to messages sent out by Lawai Bisarai; Barrie, Cusack, Edmeades and Sanderson continued the work of collecting and sorting the stores.[26]

Soon Cusack began to unpack the guns. Rifles, carbines, Sten guns, Bren guns, hand grenades, submachine guns . . . The Kelabits, only some of whom had seen guns before but who all knew of their power, were entranced. Memories of the days before the European rulers had outlawed headhunting and warfare flooded back in a paroxysm of excitement, especially when told that they could use the weapons against the Japanese.

> The idea that white men might actually sanction a *return* to arms for murderous purposes seemed almost as marvellous as the para-facts of our appearance.[27]

There was a rush by able-bodied men to enlist in the operation. Harrisson suddenly found himself with as many runners, porters and fighters as he could possibly want. But he also found himself with a potential future problem.

> I began to realize that one of my big problems was going to be damping down over-enthusiasm and keeping control over the urge to kill. Not that this was a problem of tomorrow. There were nowhere near enough guns to go round even those present, yet. But, according to all reports, soon thousands of people would be swarming upon me. Every one of them would be asking for a gun.[28]

In this he was to prove remarkably prescient.

In the meantime, Tredrea, the medical orderly, opened a make-shift clinic in the longhouse gallery. This was the first shot fired in a campaign to win local support, recommended by Carter and other members of the planning group before the party left Australia.

They were confident that under the Japanese the supply of 'White people's' medicines would have dried up, and many locals would need medical attention.

For their part, the two radio operators, Bower and Hallam, began to work on the party's 'Boston' portable radio transmitter, powered by a hand generator, which had been packed in one of the storpedoes. The radio had been damaged in the drop and needed attention. Once repairs had been made they took it up the nearest mountain and, with the help of locals, cleared an area of jungle large enough to hold a small radio hut. Having erected an aerial, and taking it in turns with bemused Kelabits to crank the portable generator, they began transmitting the party's code sign over and over on the reserved frequency where they knew the signals station at Darwin would be keeping anxious watch.

And finally, as evening set in, their patience was rewarded. The dots and dashes of the SRD HQ code sign stuttered suddenly, almost unexpectedly, from the radio. For the Kelabits present this was extraordinary. For Bower and Hallam it must have seemed no less so; against all the odds, from a longhouse in the remote centre of Borneo, they were in contact with Australia.[29]

∞

Having successfully established radio contact with HQ, Harrisson was able to turn to his other tasks. On the following day, 27 March, he despatched Edmeades, Barrie and Hallam to reconnoitre the route from Bario to Long Lellang, northwest of Carter's proposed HQ site at Long Akah. On arrival at Long Lellang, they were to identify a drop zone where supplies – too heavy to be carried across the mountains – could be landed for Carter's main party. Since this was perhaps Harrisson's key task, his orders were to undertake it himself, along with three other members of his party. However, he decided instead to remain in Bario.[30]

Once the three men had reached Long Lellang and identified a suitable drop zone, Edmeades was to return to Bario. Barrie and Hallam, on the other hand, would remain at Long Lellang and await the supplies drop. When the plane arrived over the area they were to guide it to the drop zone with a smoke signal, and then collect the supplies it unloaded.

Hallam took his ATR-4 transceiver on the journey. The ATR-4 was smaller and lighter than the more powerful Boston – it weighed twenty pounds plus a five-pound battery pack – and was made to be carried in a backpack. With the Boston now in operation at Bario the ATR-4 would allow Hallam to remain in touch with base and receive vital information, including the expected arrival dates of the supplies drop and Carter's party. Once the latter had reached Long Lellang, Barrie and Hallam would return to Bario.[31]

The three men left Bario early in the morning. To get to Long Lellang they needed first to cross the 5000-foot (1500-m) high Tama Abu mountain range, which forms the western barrier to the long valley in which Bario is located. They would then trek southwards for several days across the hilly, pitted country to the west of the range. Recognising the impossibility of finding the route on their own, and needing help with carrying equipment, the group took with them a number of Kelabit guides and porters. Some of these were women since, in contrast to Western stereotypes of the time, most Dayak groups saw women as perfectly able to transport heavy burdens over long distances. The porters carried their loads using baskets supported by shoulder straps and a strap around the forehead, with the latter taking most of the weight.

The trip to Long Lellang was gruelling. On the first day they climbed up and over the Tama Abu (Tamabo) range – blessed witnesses to staggering views across the interior from its top – following in the footsteps of shining-white Kelabit ancestors still recalled in song:

Sirum lawé la'ih rayeh, la'ih kail uput,

Hear how he went, the giant jumper,

Liang langit doo' pelika peluun apad Tamabo,

Clear in the sky over every Tamabo,

Dita' lat ngan aping batuh tulud pelaliwah,

Higher than cliff or swiftlet soaring,

Buda' lat ngan laput lem uned tuped edto . . .

Whiter than cloud in the driest daylight.[32]

They arrived very late in the afternoon at the Kelabit community of Kubaan on the other side. After a night there they entered the hilly catchment zone of the Tutoh and Patah Rivers, which offered a tortuous landscape of endless ridges and crests, zigzagging here and there without any discernible logic. Although the Tutoh River cuts across the area, it is a shadow of the waterway it becomes closer to the coast, and largely unnavigable to those travelling upstream. Instead they were forced to travel overland. Several days' trek through this challenging terrain brought them to the catchment area of the Akah River, and finally, Long Lellang itself.

Most of the journey – save for the highest mountain slopes – was through dense, damp jungle. Almost all the Semut operatives had undergone jungle training in Queensland rainforests as part of their SRD program. Some, including Barrie and Hallam, had served already in New Guinea during the war. Nevertheless, few were prepared for the rigours of travel in a Borneo jungle.

Here, as they discovered, shadows cast by giant trees above made it difficult to see where they were going. Frequent downpours – sometimes so heavy they stung bare heads and hands – splashed up from the ground in misty veils that reduced visibility further and rendered walking a slog through thick mud, with the slightest misstep on slippery stones or logs potentially ending in disaster. The rain conspired with the unbearable humidity and the men's intense

perspiration, ensuring they were never dry. While it could be wonderfully refreshing on overheated bodies, it could also, especially in
mountainous areas, lead to a dismal cold.

And then there were the mosquitoes and leeches. The latter
found their way into boots and underwear as well as onto any
exposed parts of the body. Touching them with a lighted cigarette
was an effective way of removing them, with the result that many
Semut operatives became chain-smokers. Leech and mosquito bites
often turned to sores or ulcers, adding to the doleful legacies of these
jungle journeys.[33]

On the trip to Long Lellang, the everyday difficulties of jungle
travel were intensified by the steepness of the terrain. Up rocky outcrops and rock faces they climbed, stumbling on loose stones, vines
and huge tree roots in the shadows of the canopy high overhead.
Reaching the top of a ridge or crest, they were confronted with an
immediate steep descent followed by another ridge beyond. They
crossed and recrossed streams, struggling to maintain their balance
on the slippery stones. Vines hanging in surrealistic garlands from
trees and hugging rocks often promised the possibility of assistance
over difficult ground. But they quickly learned that many were covered with sharp thorns which lacerated clothes, faces and hands.

On reaching the Tutoh catchment area the party spent days
walking along the centres of steep mountain streams – fast-flowing
and slippery underfoot – since this was easier than pushing through
jungle. The going was so tough that after a few days Edmeades'
lightweight American rubber and canvas 'jungle boots' began
to fall apart. It was small comfort to see their bearers also struggling: their breath at the most difficult stretches coming in the long
gasping whistles with which Kelabits express physical discomfort.
Stumbling, sliding, falling, they made slow progress forward.[34]

High up the range, where the normal jungle vegetation quails
in the face of cloud and the unrelenting wet it imposes, they passed

through an astonishing moss forest, the like of which used to be found on the upper slopes of many Borneo mountains. Here, in this constantly dripping world, grotesquely stunted trees and roots were covered with thick spongy lichens as in a magician's enchanted forest, and all around them sprouted tiny vivid orchids and brightly coloured, seductive pitcher plants. Travel in this place was particularly treacherous since huge puffy mounds of moss concealed mats of roots 3 or 4 feet (0.9–1.2 m) above the ground, or even crevasses.[35]

To add to their woes, the area was thick with large black leeches – 'the tiger leeches in this country were plentiful and all empty,' Hallam commented drily years later – and the men were forced to stop every hour to 'de-leech' their legs. Even in longhouses they could not escape the challenges of the local fauna.

That night at Kubaan I still thought cleanliness was important so took my boots off to sleep and the Kelabit dogs ate the back out of the right boot making it very hard to wear [. . .] the dogs enjoyed my leech blood and salt from my sweat no doubt – slept with my 1½ boots on from then on.[36]

Thick mountainous jungle is probably the most difficult terrain in the world for a stranger to navigate. In part this is because visibility is limited to 50–100 yards (45–90 m), and even if the vegetation clears to allow sight beyond this, one hill looks exactly like another. It is also due to the difficulty of judging distance under such conditions: the amount of energy expended fools strangers into thinking they have travelled further than they have. But perhaps the biggest problem is that having decided on a direction, the hapless traveller is often unable to move that way because of the undergrowth, trees, swamps, rivers, outcrops of rock, banks, cliffs and so on, continually forcing him or her off course.[37]

Without their guides the trio would quickly have become hopelessly lost. Keith Barrie, a surveyor in civilian life, plotted their route assiduously for the later main party to follow, demanding that the group stop at every significant change of direction in order to use his sexton and take notes.[38]

They passed through the Kelabit communities of Kubaan, Pa Tik, Long Labid and Long Datih, receiving a warm welcome at each and, in several cases, staying the night. On other nights they slept in simple lean-tos constructed out of branches by their Kelabit guides. Finally on 2 April, after six days of hard slog, they arrived at Long Lellang.[39]

On the night of their arrival at the Long Lellang longhouse they were welcomed, as at Bario, with a great feast. And again as at Bario, once their mission was explained they received fervent promises of help and support. The next morning, secure in the knowledge that his mission was complete, Edmeades – astonishingly, given the rigours of the journey – left to return to Bario. He took with him the guides and porters as well as Barrie's maps for Carter to use later. As instructed by Harrisson, Barrie and Hallam stayed behind at Long Lellang, waiting to collect the stores drop for Carter's main party.[40]

෨෧

The feast the men had been treated to on arrival turned out to conceal a bitter truth: there was almost no food at Long Lellang. The rugged slopes to the west of the Tama Abu range were a far cry from the fertile valley to its east within which Bario was located, famous today for the rice it produces. From Kubaan through to Long Lellang, food was in much shorter supply, a situation exacerbated by the Japanese occupation, whose impact had been far greater here than on the Plain of Bah. Carter was later to describe Long Lellang as the most impoverished Kelabit town he had ever seen.[41]

Harrisson had adopted a policy whereby those serving under him were required to live like local people and off the land as far as possible. As a result, Barrie and Hallam had been given almost no rations to bring with them. They soon found themselves with little to eat; all the locals had was rice and, although they generously shared it, even this was in short supply: no fruit, no meat, not even salt or sugar cane. Before long the situation became desperate.

Initially they slept in the centre of the longhouse, on the gallery section of the chief's apartment, as honoured guests to the longhouse always did. However, embarrassed to be imposing on the locals during such straitened times, they soon moved out to a camp in the nearby jungle, setting up their jungle hammocks – ingenious inventions with a waterproof fly cover and mosquito nets around the sides – between friendly trees. Here they attempted to hunt and forage for food while they scouted out the area and located a suitable drop zone for Carter's stores. But they were inept provisioners in an environment unfamiliar to them; apart from a couple of fish and a pig they managed to kill late in the piece, they had almost nothing but rice, and not enough of that. They were lucky in their companionship as every food item they obtained they shared. Nevertheless, they came close to starving.[42]

Hallam attempted every day to contact Bario on his ATR-4 transceiver radio at the scheduled times. As soon as the party arrived at Long Lellang he had erected an aerial and commenced transmission. His output readings were good, but there was no response. Over the following days he and Barrie tried again and again: moving the aerial after each 'sked' (as the scheduled times were called) to the top of a new ridge. But in the face of Bario's obstinate silence Hallam was transmitting blind – with no way of knowing whether his messages were being received. He was later told that the ATR-4 was almost useless when there were tall mountains between transmitter and receiver, as there were between Long Lellang and Bario.[43]

In the absence of radio communication, the two men kept vigil every day; waiting, waiting, waiting for the sound of the aircraft engine signalling the stores drop. But as the days went by, they began to worry that the endless promises they had been making to locals – about large numbers of Europeans to follow with arms and ammunition, ready to retake Borneo from the Japanese – would be seen as untrue, and the locals would turn against them. Alone as they were in an alien environment, fearful about the proximity of the Japanese, increasingly weak from lack of food, and with little ability to communicate with the people around them on whom they were terrifyingly dependent, it is hardly surprising that their nerves began to fray:

> In such a situation the jungle is anything but silent so our listening [for the sound of aircraft] encompassed a large variety of strange sounds and the buzzing of insects, some of which in our state of tense expectancy often sounded like aircraft engines. Hence we lost count of the number of false alarms.[44]

So jumpy had they become that one morning they were awakened at first light in their jungle camp by what appeared to be a person at the edge of the trees. Fearing the worst – discovery by the Japanese – they leapt in such panic for their Brens that they damaged their hammocks. Only to see an orangutan disappear through the undergrowth.[45]

On another occasion they heard what sounded like a Liberator approaching and lit a smoke canister. But to their horror, a Japanese 'Betty' bomber soon came into view. Fortunately the plane flew off after circling briefly, presumably having decided that the smoke came from a Dayak fire. But it was a near escape, and a reminder of the enemy's presence.[46]

Finally, fuelled by both a pre-existing dislike of Harrisson and a sense of injury over his perceived ill-treatment of them, they wrote him at least two letters. In the first they listed a number of grievances, including Edmeades' behaviour during the journey to Long Lellang and the inadequacy of the supplies provided. In the second they complained bitterly about Harrisson's own conduct – especially his failure to furnish them with rations from the reconnaissance party's store – and requested a transfer from his party to Carter's when it arrived. Long Lellang locals were tasked with delivering these letters across the mountains to Bario.[47]

∾

Meanwhile in Bario, Harrisson was engaged in a protracted struggle with his own radio. After the initial success in contacting Darwin, communication had deteriorated, becoming haphazard and unreliable. Harrisson was convinced this was partly due to geography: the massive mountains encircling the valley in which Bario was located created a barrier through which the Boston's transmissions could not pass. The solution, as he saw it, was to move to higher ground from where signals could travel over the mountains. However, this could not be done before the arrival of Carter's main party.

But geography was not the only problem. The codes the men were required to use were fiendishly complicated.

> It was a major operation to encode or decode a message, involving two large volumes [. . .] This code was so arranged, in five-letter groups, that presumably no one in the world could ever crack it. By the same token, a trivial mistake in a message could readily make the whole thing meaningless. What with errors of cyphering, transmission atmospherics and the distances we were working (enormous on such simple, portable equipment) no wonder that at times we almost cracked up ourselves [. . .]
>
> [O]ur signals had to be repeated; and repeated in reply to queries already distorted. These were some of the worst

hours ever. Some nights I spent entirely with the code books
and a hurricane lamp.[48]

As a result, messages received in Darwin – if they were received
at all – were often so garbled that senior SRD officers in Australia
began to worry the operation had been compromised. While
Harrisson had managed to convey the news that he was ready to
receive the main party at Bario and that a supplies drop zone had
been prepared at Long Lellang, there were fears in Australia that he
had been captured and was broadcasting under duress. If this was
so, the main party was being led into a Japanese trap.

Partly for this reason, but also because of poor weather and the
disruption to 200 Flight caused by the loss of the Pockley plane, the
main party was forced to postpone its insertion, initially due around
8 April. Given the fears about the fate of the reconnaissance party,
there was pressure on Carter to cancel the insertion altogether. But
he refused. Instead, it was scheduled for 16 April and the date transmitted to Harrisson.[49]

And so several days before that date the main party of eight men
retraced the steps of the reconnaissance party: flying from Leyburn
to land eventually on 15 April at the US base on the island of
Mindoro. Stopping at Morotai on the way, they encountered some
SRD acquaintances recently returned from a raid in the Celebes
(now Sulawesi) during which they had lost two of their number,
including their leader. It was a sobering reminder of the dangers of
such operations: 'The war suddenly seemed to close in around us a
little more tightly,' Sochon commented later.[50]

On arrival at Mindoro, Carter received a message which, he
was told, had originated from Harrisson's radio in Bario: received
first in Darwin, relayed on to SRD HQ in Melbourne, and then
relayed again to the Philippines. The message was almost completely indecipherable, but the party's two signallers were able

to make out a single three-word phrase. It stated baldly: 'NOT COME IN.'

Carter's sobering conclusion was that Harrisson's party was either on the run or had been killed or captured. He was faced with a dilemma: should he stay or should he go? He consulted with his second-in-command, Bill Sochon, and the two agreed they could not abandon Harrisson's group: the operation would go ahead as planned. Having made their decision, Carter then gave every man in the party the option of withdrawing. He explained the situation and promised that there would be no adverse consequences for anyone who pulled out. No-one did.[51]

Early the next morning the eight men of the main party assembled at the airfield where their three 200 Flight Liberators were waiting: two to carry the men and the Long Lellang stores, and a third to carry additional stores for Harrisson. At 4 am (local time) they boarded – Carter and Sochon in separate planes – and headed southwest towards Sarawak.

5

TO THE BARAM

THE THREE LIBERATORS, IN open formation, crossed into Borneo airspace as the sun was rising. Reaching Mt Mulu, they turned not southeast towards Bario as the earlier flight had done, but due south towards Long Lellang.

Toby Carter, who knew the area well, went forward to assist the pilots in locating the drop zone. But it was quickly apparent that they had arrived too early in the day: thick blankets of mist still clung to the valley floors, making it almost impossible to identify landmarks. The plane swept in wide circles – terrifyingly close to the adjacent mountains – while Carter craned his neck this way and that. Then a momentary break in the cloud and he saw, as in a still photograph, the gleaming course of a river and tiny Dayak rice huts. Another opening and there, quite suddenly, was the agreed signal: a thick column of white smoke.[1]

Three times the pilot, now covered in perspiration, prepared to run in for the supplies drop. Each time the ground below disappeared under a layer of cloud. At last a break – but the signal could no longer be seen. Instead, they were looking at a clearing in the otherwise unbroken jungle, beside a bend in the river. Taking a gamble that it was close to the location of the smoke, they despatched the stores. Carter watched them floating downward through the cloud as the planes banked and turned east, heading for Bario.

Now they were crossing the Tama Abu range and the tension inside the planes was extreme. The cloud had begun to dissipate in places, but nevertheless remained frustratingly thick over Bario's secret valley. And then, again, a break, and Carter found himself looking at a line of smoke rising from near a longhouse in a wide grassy valley.[2]

But there was a problem. Weather conditions meant that the planes, currently at 3000 feet (900 m), could fly no lower. The normal height for dropping parachutists – the height at which the operatives had trained – was 800–1000 feet (250–300 m). There were two options: risk the jump at more than three times that height, or abort and return to Mindoro. Carter – who was facing his first ever parachute jump – chose to go ahead.[3]

Out they came, first Carter's group of four, then Sochon's: 'the sky seemed full of parachutes floating lazily down.' Sochon slipped through the silence of the clouds.

And then, quite clearly, I could see the valley below. The green of the padi planting; the meandering course of the stream; the longhouse, perched on the side of a low knoll, and many figures standing about it or running towards my probable point of landing.[4]

Clutching their guns with the safety catches off, and hoping the figures they could see were not Japanese, they fell, most landing on soft grass close to the longhouse. Their orders were to go immediately on the defensive and seek cover. But too late: Long reports that as he struggled to his feet there were already twenty people surrounding him. The local Kelabits had come to offer their assistance.[5]

∽

At Long Lellang, Barrie and Hallam were almost out of hope. And then, early in the morning of 16 April, they heard the distinctive throb of a Liberator. A thick canopy of cloud hid the skies above, but they took a punt and set off a smoke canister. However, to their bitter disappointment, no parachutes emerged through the cloud. After seeming to circle for a time, the plane finally flew away north.

The two men retired to their jungle camp to lick their wounds. They were still there, several hours later, when a group of Dayaks arrived. A number of objects had fallen from the sky some distance north of Long Lellang in the Tutoh River catchment area. Since the story of the Bario landings had spread throughout the region, people had come to identify the white umbrellas with the European soldiers. And so people from the Tutoh River had made the journey to Long Lellang to bring Barrie and Hallam the news.

Hurriedly mobilising as many locals and canoes as they could, Barrie and Hallam travelled to the area of the drop, about 4 miles (6.5 km) from Long Lellang. The goods had fallen into dense jungle, and it took several days of hard searching to retrieve them. Some – including a storpedo containing gold sovereigns and Sarawak currency – were not found (local Kelabits came across the hoard of coins after the war and delivered it to the District Office in Marudi). But finally most were safely back at Long Lellang. Carter's main party could not be far away.[6]

∽

The men inserted with Carter and Sochon had all transferred to SRD from the Australian Army. Those with Carter in the first plane were:

- Captain (Dr) Ian 'Doc' McCallum (promoted to Major in June 1945), the party's medical officer, a tall, straight-talking 28-year-old. A GP in civilian life, he had served in New Guinea with 19th Australian Field Ambulance before transferring to SRD in November 1944.
- Sergeant The Soen Hin, a tough, wiry 25-year-old Timor-born Chinese, and fluent Malay speaker. A seaman in civilian life, he had served with the 3 Australian Water Transport Company before eventually being recruited into SRD in March 1944.[7]
- Sergeant Charles 'Wally' Pare, one of two signallers in the party, a quiet blue-eyed 20-year-old Englishman, an apprentice fitter-and-turner in civilian life. After qualifying as a signaller he had transferred to SRD in July 1943, and already had operational experience in New Guinea.[8]

In the second plane with Sochon were:

- Warrant Officer Class 2 Donald 'Don' Horsnell, 23 years old, a store-hand in civilian life, small and intense. He had already seen extensive service with the AIF in the Middle East and New Guinea – he was wounded in the latter – before being transferred to SRD early in 1944.
- Sergeant Bertram 'Bob' Long (promoted to Warrant Officer Class 2 in July 1945), the second signaller, a reserved, slow-talking 23-year-old, a salesman in civilian life. He had served with various AIF signals units throughout Australia before transferring to SRD in March 1944.

- Corporal Abu Kassim (promoted to Sergeant on
  26 April 1945), a tiny, accommodating Malaya (now
  Peninsular Malaysia)-born Malay of around 28 years, who
  had arrived in Sydney after the fall of Singapore. A pearl
  diver in civilian life, he spoke fluent Malay and had served
  for a time with both the 3 Australian Water Transport
  Company and the 51 Australian Water Transport Company
  before eventually being recruited to SRD in March 1944.

Most of the eight landed close to the Bario longhouse and were
quickly reunited. However, Horsnell, the lead Bren gun opera-
tor, landed much further away. Large weapons and equipment,
including Brens, had their own parachutes and Horsnell – almost
inseparable from his Bren – was worried about what would become
of it during the drop. So after leaving the plane he guided his own
parachute along the haphazard, swirling course of the Bren, across
the windy valley. As a result he (and the Bren) landed more than a
mile (1.6 km) away from the drop zone. Sanderson was sent to find
him and later wrote in his report:

> We finally located [Horsnell]. He was in a bad mood. The first
> words he said was 'Where the hell have you bastards been? I've
> been blowing my lungs out with this whistle'. Don looked like
> a Chicago gangster, a Bren gun over his shoulder, a revolver
> strapped to his thigh and an automatic pistol under his armpit.[9]

Sochon was another whose landing was less than ideal;
indeed, he was lucky to survive. Given the high cost of parachutes,
Australian military policy at the time decreed that parachutes issued
to infiltrating groups – which would not be returned to base for
future use – should be old, well-used ones that would otherwise be
thrown out. Sochon almost paid for this scandalous policy with his

life. He was a heavy man and, as he came down, many of the worn
panels of his parachute simply fell apart at the seams: fourteen of
the total thirty-two panels blew out. Fortunately he was an experienced parachutist, and somehow managed to steer what remained
to an area of swampy ground which cushioned his fall.[10]

They were there. And best of all they now heard from Harrisson
that there were no Japanese in the vicinity.

∞

In a small hut that Harrisson had taken over as his operations
HQ – beside the Bario longhouse – Carter, Harrisson and Sochon
discussed progress to date and future plans. Harrisson reported
that no Japanese had so far crossed the mountains to the Plain of
Bah and, according to Edmeades, none had made it to Long Lellang
where the main party's stores had been dropped.

Carter was anxious to get to Long Lellang where Barrie and
Hallam were waiting, hopefully with the newly arrived stores,
as soon as possible. From there it was only several days journey
to Long Akah – close to the longhouse of the great Kenyah chief
Tama Weng Ajeng – where Carter hoped to establish his HQ. Tama
Weng was not only the paramount Kenyah chief in the Baram area;
he was also the highest-ranking chief among related groups the length
of the Baram River, and a *penghulu* – a regional leader sanctioned
by the Brooke government. As a result, his influence throughout the
entire Baram River basin – including among the powerful Kayan –
was immense. It was critical to obtain his early support for
the operation.

Carter was keen to begin the trek across the mountains to Long
Lellang the following day. However, for the sake of security – to
lessen the chance of ambush in the mountains – he decided that
the main party should split into two to make the trip. Sochon, Abu
Kassim and Horsnell would leave the next morning. Carter would

remain in Bario one additional night, and would depart with The Soen Hin and Pare the day after.

The men agreed that Harrisson's reconnaissance party would stay in the Bario area, consolidating the intelligence and guerrilla recruitment work it had begun, while Carter's party moved on to establish the operation's overall HQ in the Baram River valley. The delicate matter of the letters Harrisson had received from Barrie and Hallam was discussed, and it was agreed that both men would transfer from Harrisson's reconnaissance group to Carter's main party. In return for signaller Hallam, signaller Long would remain with Harrisson's party. Dr McCallum would also stay behind in Bario for the time being to treat sick people in the area, continuing the PR work already begun by Tredrea.[11]

Sochon's party – with Horsnell, to Sochon's awed amazement, carrying his beloved Bren gun in addition to his 70 lb (32 kg) pack – left for Long Lellang the next morning, 17 April. They took with them two Kelabit guides-cum-porters. Once they had gone Carter used part of his remaining day with Harrisson to chastise him for the unprofessional way, as he saw it, the Bario operation had been run to date. Harrisson wrote later that Carter was 'visibly displeased with the atmosphere of relaxed tension and aggressive exuberance which he fell into'. Sochon, for his part, commented on the 'unbusinesslike atmosphere' of Bario: 'there was an air of playing "secret agents"' and 'perhaps rather more accent on borak than battle'.[12]

Among other things Harrisson had taken to dressing like the locals, with bare feet and a sarong. He had also adopted the American style of wearing a Major's gold crown on his cap instead of the usual British pips on his shirt. Locals had begun to refer to him – and in certain respects to treat him – as Sarawak's White Rajah, and Harrisson, by his own admission, did nothing to deter them. This dismayed Carter, an infinitely more conventional man and a great admirer of the actual Rajah. It was thus with relief that

Harrisson saw him off to Long Lellang the following day, a sentiment almost certainly shared by Carter.[13]

On 23 April – six days after leaving Bario – Sochon, Horsnell and Abu Kassim crossed the open ground beside the Long Lellang longhouse to a delighted welcome from Barrie and Hallam. Carter arrived the following day with The Soen Hin and Pare. One of Carter's bearers for the trip was the husband of Keling Langit, the young Kelabit woman who had watched the reconnaissance party's descent on 25 March. Her husband liked Carter so much that they later named their first child – due at the time – after him: Kata/Carter.

Carter's introduction to the Long Lellang longhouse was memorable. Having had part of his boot eaten by a dog in the longhouse at Kubaan, it was Hallam's habit to kick any nearby dogs in the longhouse at Long Lellang. This terrorised them to such a degree that the moment Hallam appeared at either end of the longhouse gallery, the longhouse dogs – around fifty or sixty in all – would disappear in a small stampede out the other end: the luckiest or quickest down the notched entry log, the rest plunging, in their panic, the eight or so feet (two and a half metres) directly to the muddy ground below.

> Well I spotted Toby [Carter] coming down the slope towards the northeastern end of the longhouse and me being so damned pleased to see him I raced in the other end of the longhouse forgetting about my effect on the local canine population. And as my frame came in one door Toby was at about the foot of the notched pole at the other entrance. And [he was] about half way up the same pole as the dogs decided that he was a safer bet than me and literally swamped poor old Toby and flattened him on his back in the Long Lelang mud.[14]

☙

On 25 April, the day after his arrival at Long Lellang, Carter got to work. He knew from conversations with locals that no Japanese had yet reached the Long Lellang area, which was protected both by the surrounding rugged terrain and many dangerous rapids downstream on the Akah River. However, he was less certain of the situation at his destination, Long Akah.

Long Akah was located on the point where the Akah River flows into the much larger Baram River. The Baram was one of the two most important rivers in Sarawak, joining the sea very close to the oilfields of Seria and Lutong. There were certain to be many Japanese in its vicinity, at least some of whom would have penetrated upriver. Every step the men took away from the sheltering remoteness of the Kelabit Plateau towards the Baram River increased their peril.

Consequently, Carter's first move was to send a Kelabit scout down the Akah River to seek information about any Japanese in the area. The scout was also asked to organise boatmen from among the Kayan people living further downstream for the party's journey on to Long Akah.[15]

Meanwhile, the men began unpacking the storpedoes Barrie and Hallam had retrieved. There they made a disturbing discovery. The pedal generator for the Boston radio transmitter – the party's main radio, the only one capable of communicating with HQ in Darwin – had been lost in the stores drop, and the radio could not function without it. The only usable radios the party had were the ATR-4 transceivers. But their range was barely long enough for the party to contact Bario – indeed, Hallam had been unsuccessful in gaining any response from Bario to date – let alone Darwin.

The entire operation was to be managed and co-ordinated from Carter's HQ on the Baram River. From there Carter would maintain regular contact with Harrisson's and Sochon's parties on the Kelabit Plateau and Rejang River respectively, as well as with SRD HQ in Australia or Morotai. But he could not do this without a powerful radio like the Boston. Accordingly, he immediately sent a message to Harrisson by runner, asking him to send Carter his hand generator.[16]

In the meantime, Carter's scout had returned and reported, to the party's relief, an absence of Japanese along the route to the Baram River. So a day or two later Carter, Hallam, Horsnell, Pare and The departed down the Akah River to Long Akah. Carter and Sochon had agreed some time earlier that Barrie and Abu Kassim would join Sochon's Rejang River offshoot operation once it was formed, and Carter deemed it sensible for the three men of that operation to begin working together immediately. They stayed behind to finish unpacking and sorting the stores, with instructions to follow with them several days later. Despite the scout's assurances, Carter remained worried about Japanese ambushes. He believed it would be prudent for the party to make the journey down the Akah River in two stages.

⁓

The Akah River was then one of the most spectacular in Borneo, looping through a jungled landscape that was crazily intersected with crests and ravines, and enclosed on three sides by mountain peaks. Huge outcrops of rock broke here and there through the jungle canopy, repeated along the river itself. This flowed in some places between massive boulders – with barely enough room for a canoe to fit – and in others through gorges carved into rocky staircases, sometimes dropping several feet between each step. Of the scores of rapids down its length, four or five were considered to be among the most dangerous on the island.

Like almost all Dayak peoples living on Borneo's rivers, the Kayans who transported Carter's party down the Akah were supremely skilled boatmen. Poling, paddling and pushing their flimsy craft around rocks, jumping in and out of the water to wrestle them through the most treacherous passages and stopping periodically to bail out the water, they appeared in perfect harmony with their vessels. Their brown muscled bodies, sleek and wet from the flying spray, moved to the roared rhythm of their stirring boat songs. Carter's men were enthralled.

The boatmen entered rocky bottlenecks at terrifying speed and with every sign of relish. Sochon:

> Immediately ahead we could see the swirling, foaming waters, twisting and snaking round innumerable black rocks, jagged and awesome. Up forward the most experienced boatman in each prahu [boat] balanced with the ease of years of practice, and with skill and decision signalled back to the stern paddler, warning him of rocks and submerged dangers ahead. Now travelling hell-for-leather through the foaming water, the frail craft bucked and lurched as the paddlers slewed it first this way, then that, to answer the bow-guide's signals. Missing the great jagged teeth by less than inches they shot through the boiling waters with consummate proficiency and suddenly we were through, the surface of the river still running swift, but as calm as a mill pond. It was a wonderful sensation.[17]

In some places, including the dramatic Merigong Gorge marking the boundary between the Kelabit and Kayan peoples – where the river descends hundreds of feet over a distance of 1.5 miles (2.4 km) – even the boatmen had to admit defeat in the face of the water's frenzy. Here they pulled over to the bank and portaged the contents along paths above the swirling water. The boats themselves were eased through the rapids by means of rattan ropes attached to their sterns which were held by members of the crew braced against rocks, waist-deep in the maelstrom.[18]

Progress was slow as Carter deemed it politic to stop at every longhouse along the way, to solicit support for the operation and promise the imminent defeat of the Japanese. The Akah River is inhabited mostly by Kayans, some of whom were already known to Carter from before the war, and the closer the party came to the Baram River the more people they encountered who spoke Malay. At every longhouse they were welcomed and feted. Pigs were killed in their honour and rice wine flowed freely, for all the world as if there were no food shortages. It was difficult to refuse such effusive hospitality, and the men spent longer on these visits than anticipated.

They spent each night in a Kayan longhouse as a guest of the headman, with Carter and The Soen Hin, the two Malay speakers in the party, talking far into the night by the dim light of the *damar* lamps. As part of the policy of winning over locals, Horsnell, who had some rudimentary medical knowledge, held clinics in the galleries of the longhouses they passed through, and dispensed as much medical aid as he could. And like Harrisson before him, Carter distributed pieces of the precious parachute silk retrieved from his drops. He later described the silk as a 'godsend' in his negotiations with locals.[19]

In each longhouse, after the celebratory pig had been dispatched, the local omen specialist was called on to read its liver. Having made a long cut down the belly of the dead beast he extracted the liver and arranged it carefully on banana leaves laid on the ground. He then examined it minutely while locals and visitors alike waited anxiously for his prognosis. In each case he finally straightened and announced that the omens were good for the success of Carter's operation. Either the European or the Dayak gods were smiling on Semut; it felt to Carter as if the journey had taken on the semblance of a triumphal procession.[20]

Each evening, following the staging system used everywhere in Borneo for journeys of this type, Carter paid off the day's boatmen who then returned upstream to their own longhouse. He used pre-war Sarawak payment rates: fifty cents per man in Straits Dollars. This was a clever move as it drew an explicit contrast between his own party and the Japanese who, if they paid at all, paid only in the useless 'banana' currency. During the evening Carter would recruit new boatmen from the current longhouse for the next stage of the journey.

On 30 April the party finally arrived at Long Tap, a Kenyah settlement around 3–4 miles (6 km) upriver from Long Akah. Here they were met by some of Carter's pre-war Kenyah friends who had travelled up the Akah River in the large, elaborately decorated, ceremonial boat of the Kenyah chief Tama Weng Ajeng himself. Tama Weng had been apprised of their approach and had sent the boat – complete with traditional thatched covering over the central part to provide welcome relief from the sun – to convey them the last part of the journey.[21]

The Kenyahs also brought welcome confirmation that there were no Japanese in the Long Akah vicinity. In fact, a Japanese group had come to Tama Weng Ajeng's longhouse at Long San several days earlier looking for rice, but had since returned down the Baram River. As far as the Kenyahs knew, the Japanese had no inkling that there were Europeans in the area. Carter's luck had held.[22]

So it was that on 1 May the party swept down the final stretch of the Akah River to the point where that tempestuous tributary pours into the majestic Baram River, lifeblood of the region. At the confluence of the two rivers – around 130 miles (210 km), as the crow flies, from the mouth of the Baram in the South China Sea, but at least twice that distance if one follows the endlessly winding waterway itself – stood the tiny settlement of Long Akah: a row of six Chinese shophouses, set some distance back from the riverbank on the path running upstream towards Long San. On high ground overlooking the Baram, several hundred yards from the Chinese bazaar, the Brookes had deemed it judicious to build a tiny timber fort as a reminder of their rule in this far outpost of their realm. This was Carter's ultimate destination.

But first he had important business to attend to. The boat turned onto the Baram River, passing the fort and the bazaar at Long Akah, and continuing about 2 miles (3.2 km) further upstream to the opposite side of the river, paddlers straining against the current. Here at Long San, where the tiny San River mingles with the Baram, the latter became a seething mass of boulders, the air filled with the rushing murmur of water as it surged across the rapids. At the downriver edge of the rapids stood the longhouse of Tama Weng Ajeng.

Today, extensive logging around the Baram River has caused erosion along its criminally denuded banks, and silting of the river itself. But thankfully, plans for a massive hydro-electric dam, to have been constructed on the upper reaches of the river, were abandoned by the Sarawak government early in 2016. This narrow escape came only after years of activism, including blockades, by local Kayan, Kenyah, Penan and other Baram peoples, who had seen the pernicious effects of similar schemes elsewhere in Sarawak.[23]

As a result of this victory the upper Baram, including Long San and Long Akah, remains a beautiful area, the broad river set against the backdrop of imposing mountain ranges. But the great jungles are mostly gone and, visiting it today, one's heart grieves at their loss. In 1945, however, they were still in place, and both the Chinese village at Long Akah and the Kenyah longhouse at Long San were located in clearings cut from endless stretches of giant trees.

Tama Weng Ajeng was not simply the paramount Kenyah chief in the area. His mother was Kayan and he had tremendous influence among Kayan and other groups the entire length of the Baram. He was unquestionably the most powerful chief in the region and his support was crucial if the operation was to have any chance of success.[24]

As the party came up to the Long San longhouse he was waiting at the riverside to receive them: a solid block of a man, short in stature but broad and fleshy. He was then aged around fifty, although his unwrinkled complexion made him appear younger, with a round chubby face and the calm, deceptively passive countenance and demeanour Kayan, Kenyah and related groups value in their nobility. His head was shaved up the sides and back, and the remaining hair cropped at the top in the pudding-bowl style then favoured by the Kenyah, with central locks kept long, tumbling down his back. His earlobes were extended and decorated with rings, and through small holes cut in the tops of his ears he wore the teeth of an animal, probably a clouded leopard, while a bead necklace hung around his neck. All of these ornaments indicated his status.

Malcolm MacDonald, formerly British Governor-General of Malaya and British Borneo, describes Tama Weng Ajeng from visits to the Baram in 1947 and 1951:

[His] features, coupled with a serene, benign expression in his face, gave him a striking resemblance to the Buddha. His manner was in keeping with that character. Placid and contemplative, he talked little but thought much. His tranquillity was the calm of self-assurance, and his silence the quietude of strength. [...]

Born and bred [...] in the ancient tradition, Tama Weng rose above it and could see beyond it. [...] He was no ordinary, petty pagan chieftain, but a man of character, courage and vision who, in his small world, attained the stature of a statesman.

While the paternalism of the time is pronounced here, these passages nevertheless capture the aura surrounding Tama Weng, and his standing among both locals and Europeans. [25]

Carter had known Tama Weng well, before the war, when Carter was working for Shell Oil as a surveyor along the Baram River. He respected the great chief immensely, knowing him as a man who thought carefully but creatively about how to respond to events affecting his people. He was aware that Tama Weng would not accept lightly the terrible risk of Japanese reprisals that would result from any decision to ally himself to Carter's operation. Carter must have been readying himself – and his arguments – for this moment for days, even weeks. So it was with immense relief that he saw the obvious pleasure with which Tama Weng stepped forward to greet him.

∾

On an island already famous for its hospitality, the welcomes accorded visitors in the Baram River area were the stuff of legend. For the chiefly families of these longhouses, the provision of hospitality to travellers was both duty and prerogative, allowing them to display their standing as well as to create political alliances. Consequently, as the anthropologist Peter Metcalf notes, in this area 'every arrival took on the quality of a state visit'. This was certainly true of the arrival of Carter's group at Long San. [26]

Tama Weng Ajeng had known for days that the group was on its way and had made good use of the intervening time. He had summoned subordinate chiefs and allies from throughout the Baram River basin to his longhouse. When Carter's party paddled up in Tama Weng's own ceremonial canoe hundreds of people, many of whom Carter already knew, were lining the bank outside the longhouse to greet them. He was touched by the gesture. Alighting from the boat, he and his men were ushered by Tama Weng across the muddy ground in front of the longhouse and up the entry ladder to the gallery.[27]

For Laran Along, a ten-year-old Kenyah boy who had travelled from the nearby longhouse of Long Tepalit to be there that day, these were the first White people he had ever seen. He was both awed at their pale skins and afraid of the guns they carried.[28]

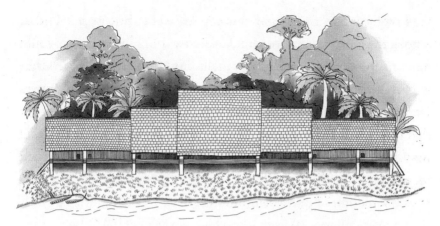

Top: As seen from the river.

Right: Cross-section (above) and floorplan (below).

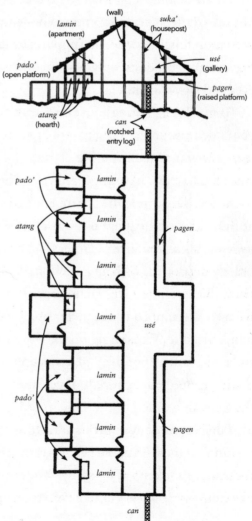

Longhouse apartment (*lamin*) size and position reflects social status. The chief's apartment is located in the centre of the longhouse and is flanked by those of other nobles. Commoners' apartments are located at the ends.

TYPICAL KENYAH LONGHOUSE[29]

Longhouses throughout this region were still, in the 1940s, among the most impressive found in Sarawak. This is in part because most of the groups found here, including the Kenyah, were stratified into three distinct social stations: chiefs/nobility, commoners and slaves. Longhouses were built around a chiefly core, and were in part a means by which noble families could display their power and wealth. Accordingly, they were often monumental in character: built far above the ground (partly for protection against marauding enemies), sometimes hundreds of metres long, and with pitched roofs stretching to almost 30 feet (10 m) high at their centres. Many of the houses sported carvings on the wooden posts holding them up, as well as on lintels, doors and supports for tables and platforms: carvings of mythical dogs, dragons and other fantastic figures with huge eyes and swirling tails.[30]

Tama Weng's longhouse at Long San was no exception: it contained twenty-seven separate apartments or 'doors' (*lamin*), so the gallery (*usé*) confronting Carter and his men at the top of the entry ladder must have appeared vast. The operatives were led along to the section outside the apartment of Tama Weng himself, located at the centre of the longhouse, as chief's apartments almost always were in this region. It was larger than its neighbours and more elaborately decorated, with an ancient garland of human heads hanging from the rafters above. Here, seated on woven mats, Carter and his men succumbed to the increasingly familiar noise and bustle of longhouse life. Welcoming *borak* was produced and women began to lay out tray upon tray of food up and down the length of the gallery, to feed the hundreds of guests.[31]

Kenyah women of the time, in addition to extended earlobes, also displayed dense, intricate tattoos on their arms and legs, as essential to their feminine beauty as the removal of body hair or the wearing of makeup is to many Western women. These markings, like blue-black woven mittens or stockings, covered the arms from the elbows to the fingers, while on the legs they extended from the toes or the calves to almost as far as the hips.

Men also displayed elaborate ornamentation. Sometimes this conveyed important information about those who wore it. As Hallam recorded later:

> We could always pick a man who had taken a head because instead of the usual Leopard teeth through the top of his ears he wore the yellow and red Hornbill beaks trimmed down to the same size as the white Leopard teeth and the usual bead ornamentation at the back of each ear. Needless to say many Hornbills [. . .] died in 1945.[32]

The feasting was lavish and extensive, as befitted a chief of Tama Weng's status. The usual praise-songs of welcome were sung and speeches made. As night came in, *damar* lamps were lit along the gallery, making the space appear – by a trick of the light – even vaster. And then, in the weird moving shadows cast by the lamps, the serious business of discussion and negotiation with Tama Weng and his lieutenants began.[33]

The list of chiefs assembled at Long San that night reads like a who's who of the Baram River area at the time. The great Kayan chief and *penghulu*, Kebing – 'extremely astute', Carter later wrote of him – had come from his longhouse at Long Pilah, further down the Baram. Tama Weng Ajeng's right-hand man, the Kenyah chief Gau (another *penghulu*) was also there, having travelled from his longhouse at Long Ikang, close to Marudi. Indeed, most of the chiefs and longhouse heads living on the Baram River itself were present: scores of Kayan and Kenyah leaders who had travelled upstream from longhouses close to Marudi and downstream from Lio Matoh and beyond. Many more had come from the Baram's tributaries, including Berawans, Bukits and Kayans from the Tutoh River, and representatives from various groups along the Tinjar River. If Carter could persuade this assembly to come onside, he would have the backing of most Dayaks throughout the Baram River basin.[34]

Carter detailed, in his fluent Malay, the purpose of his mission, emphasising that Allied forces were even now readying themselves to land in Sarawak and take back the territory. He explained that he was mounting an operation to not only seek intelligence about Japanese activities further down the Baram but also, all going well, engage in guerrilla warfare in support of the invading Allied forces. He pointed out the reasons why the assembled chiefs should support the operation: it would, after all, rid Sarawak – and the Baram – of rulers who had led the Kenyah and their allies into a state of miserable penury and hardship.

And he presented them with astounding news: this war was so important to the Europeans that they would make an exception to the ban on headhunting instituted by the Brookes. After a century of pro-scription, headhunting – 'Jap heads only' – would now be permitted. A shiver of excitement spread through the assembled throng.[35]

As Carter had expected, Tama Weng proved to be shrewd and well-informed about the course of the war. Like many other Dayak leaders he had been wooed by the Japanese; however, he had man-aged to maintain a careful neutrality, assisted by the distance of his longhouse from centres of Japanese authority downriver. He knew that joining Carter's operation would mean repudiating the safety of that neutrality and committing not only his own remote long-house, but longhouses under his chiefly authority up and down the river, to the dangers attendant on insurrection. The repercussions, should Carter's plan be faulty, were potentially catastrophic for many people in the region.

Accordingly, Tama Weng and his lieutenants came back again and again to the same questions: Were Carter's plans workable? Would the Japanese in fact be defeated? Would the people of the

Baram be protected from Japanese reprisals if things went wrong? Would arms be provided to locals who joined the operation? And, since five men did not seem a very imposing number, were more *orang puteh* (white people) and arms on the way?

The discussion continued over several days and nights, with Carter and The Soen Hin doing most of the work on the operatives' side, since they were the only two who spoke good Malay. On some nights the group slept in the longhouse gallery; on others the men returned wearily, early in the morning, to the fort at Long Akah for a few hours' sleep.[36]

While the talks were still in progress, Sochon's party arrived from Long Lellang, bringing with it boatloads of supplies. The arrival had been perfectly timed by Carter, since it validated his claim that his party was simply the vanguard of what would eventually become a much larger group. Sochon and Abu Kassim, both fluent Malay speakers, now added their voices to those of Carter and The Soen Hin during the negotiations. But the primary voices belonged to Carter and Tama Weng: chief to chief.

Finally, after several days, Tama Weng told Carter that he and his men now needed time to reflect on the proposal. Mindful of the need for speed, he promised to get back to Carter within a day. 'We were not unduly alarmed at this stage,' Sochon commented years later, 'but at the same time the situation had given us no room for optimism'. Tama Weng's calm impassivity in the face of their arguments left them with little sense of his thinking. They had no alternative but to return to Long Akah and wait.[37]

୭ఎ

Today the village at Long Akah has gone but the abandoned fort remains, a lonely sentinel above the river. Secondary jungle is gradually reclaiming it, greedy vines encroaching through its wooden windows and floors, the rush of the river across the rapids below clearly audible from its hushed spaces. Nevertheless, the lattice-work around the tops of the fort's walls and its timber shutters imbue it with a shabby elegance and, in spite of its small size, the arrangement and proportions of its rooms convey a genteel spaciousness. To the visitor, the structure feels slightly haunted, as if Carter, Sochon and company still stalk its dusty rooms and keep watch over the river from the high bank outside. After the gruelling journey from Bario, and the torrid days of partying and talking at Long San, its quiet empty rooms must have felt to the party like a momentary paradise.

Over the preceding days they had moved their stores and weaponry into a locked room in the centre of the building's ground floor. The men themselves ate and slept on the first floor with its panoramic views across jungle and river. Outside, in a strategic spot at the top of the riverbank, they had built a Bren pit, and here one of them kept perpetual watch with the gun. Hallam had become seriously ill, in a delirious near-coma with malaria, and was being nursed devotedly by Horsnell.[38]

The morning after they left Long San the men woke feeling anxious, and as the day wore on with no sign from Tama Weng that anxiety increased. No-one was under any illusion as to the disastrous implications of a rejection. It was possible that even now Tama Weng's men were informing on them to the Japanese downriver.

At last, late in the afternoon, there came a shout from outside where Horsnell was keeping guard in the Bren pit. Carter and Sochon, along with the rest of the party, crowded to the high bank above the steps leading up from the small beach below the fort. There, advancing downriver, was a flotilla of boats, led by Tama Weng's great ceremonial canoe crammed full of his men. And at the stern, wonder of wonders, a large Union Jack – an astonishing sight given that any flags, other than Japanese, were prohibited in the territory under pain of death. The flag telegraphed for all to see the

Europeans tend to assume they know the reasons why indigenous peoples such as Dayaks support them in various theatres of war. They often understand it as tied to simple motives such as love of and loyalty towards Europeans, and/or the charisma of certain European leaders. But the reality is invariably something else. No White military leader of indigenous troops has been celebrated as much as T.E. Lawrence.

> Did the recruitment of local support depend, as the legend would have it, on Lawrence's personal diplomacy and magnetism? His charm, and his grasp of nuances of Beduin life, must indeed have been useful. But the magnet which drew men to him was, frankly, money. At a time of considerable economic difficulty for the Beduin, British gold was irresistible, and Lawrence had plenty of it to use at his own discretion.[43]

Dayak reasons for turning away from the Japanese and supporting the Allies were different: money was not a factor here. Nevertheless they generally owed more to the pragmatics of survival than a love for Whites.

For most Dayaks, regardless of their sentiments about either Japanese or Europeans, the overriding question when Semut came knocking was: which side will prove victorious? As tiny groups perennially forced to navigate between external powers competing to rule them, the overriding Dayak concern was, understandably, with survival. And lacking military and technological might, survival depended on making the right decision about whom to back.

Accordingly, the questions that Tama Weng Ajeng and his allies put to Carter were pragmatic in character, concerning his plans to defeat the Japanese, the size of the Allied forces, how their people would be protected, and so on. Their decision to support Carter's party was a considered one, made primarily on the basis not of some sentimental attachment to the British and Brookes, but rather of their assessment concerning who would win an upcoming war. Tama Weng's own intelligence was telling him that Japanese potency was failing – it was no secret that provisions were low and soldiers starving – and his friendship with Carter meant he trusted Carter's promises of an imminent Allied invasion. The Baram chiefs backed what they saw as the winning side.

Nor was this decision a token one. Indeed, as Carter himself records, from this point on, Tama Weng hardly left Carter's side. He took over the organisation of many practical aspects of the operation: drafting carriers, scouts, and working parties, arranging transport and shelter. He called for recruits to Carter's fledgling guerrilla army – his own two sons were among the first to enlist – and helped co-ordinate their training. Perhaps most importantly, his knowledge of local conditions – topography and climate, river currents, fauna, flora and so on – meant that he was indispensable when it came to mapping out future tactics and strategy. He assumed a role at the very heart of the operation.[44]

After the war, Tama Weng Ajeng was awarded an MBE by the British government for his contribution to Semut. One of the attendants who accompanied him to the dais at the presentation ceremony was Toby Carter.[45]

৩৩

It was now many days since Carter had sent a runner to Harrisson requesting Harrisson's radio generator, and he was yet to receive a response. Even though the party had moved away from the mountains to Long Akah, it was still unable to contact Bario – or anywhere else – on its ATR-4 radio. The men had been in a state of total radio silence since leaving Bario almost three weeks earlier.

But finally, a day or two after Tama Weng's decision, the party had a stroke of luck. Pare managed, quite by accident, to pick up a transmission from Harrisson's radio and so was able to establish contact with Bario. The news now relayed to Carter, however, was astounding. HQ had decreed that Harrisson should keep his generator, and would send a separate one to Carter in an upcoming stores drop.

More momentously, HQ had decided to divide the operation into three separate commands: Semut I led by Harrisson, to operate from the Kelabit Plateau north to the coast at Brunei Bay and east into Dutch territory towards Tarakan; Semut II led by Carter, to operate throughout the Baram River basin to the coast around Seria and Miri; and Semut III led by Sochon, to operate down the Rejang River as far as Sibu. Semut was no longer a single operation with Carter as its overall commander; from now on Harrisson and Sochon would each report directly to HQ Group A SRD (of which Courtney was in charge) instead of to Carter.

Having received Carter's message at Bario a week or so earlier, Harrisson had gone over his senior officer's head and appealed directly to Courtney for permission to keep his generator. His argument was reasonable: if he were to send the generator to Carter, not only would Harrisson be unable to transmit to HQ the intelligence his own party was busily collecting, but the entire operation would be off the air for the week or so it took the generator to reach its destination. Courtney accepted this argument, and undertook to send a replacement generator to Carter at Long Akah as soon as possible.

But Harrisson went a step further. He also pleaded with HQ to be allowed to run his own independent command, free of Carter's potential interference. Again his argument was fair: the distances between the three parties, and the problems of communication that had already arisen, underlined the difficulty of managing the entire operation from a single command centre as had been originally planned. In response HQ decided to gift independent commands to both Harrisson and Sochon.[46]

This was undoubtedly the correct course of action in the longer term. As Harrisson and Sochon advanced in opposite directions, it would have become impossible to co-ordinate their activities from Carter's base on the Baram River. Nevertheless there is something disquieting about this decision, not least because it appears to have rewarded Harrisson for an act of direct insubordination.

Perhaps even more disturbing is the fact that the decision was made without any consultation with Carter himself. Carter was, after all, not only one of the chief architects of the operation, not only its overall commanding officer, but also the man on the ground with by far the best knowledge of the inland terrain and its peoples, and the only one of its leaders to have had overseas war-time experience. If HQ were to be believed, his replacement radio generator, which would grant him direct contact with HQ, would be dropped to him at Long Akah very soon. It is astonishing, then, that a decision of this magnitude was made without first seeking his input.

Carter never allowed any note of chagrin over these particular decisions to creep into either his official or his personal accounts of the operation. Sochon, however, was less temperate. While he saw the sense of dividing the operation into three independent commands, he nevertheless felt that Harrisson's refusal to part with his radio generator was unconscionable. As he stated later:

> [Carter] was the senior member of all the Semut groups and
> exercised command over both Harrisson and me. It was there-
> fore to him that his superiors in Australia and Morotai would
> wish to direct their orders and from him that they would want
> to receive intelligence and operational reports. In the light of
> this normal arrangement of chain of command [. . .] the action
> taken by Carter [to ask Harrisson to send him his generator]
> was unquestionably correct. [. . .]

Carter, with the superior wisdom of experience and age, had already made his appraisal of the situation and had taken into account the fact that the whole of Semut would be off the air for the time it took to get the generator from Bario to Long Lelang. A point of fact, at this stage of the operation it would not have mattered at all provided Australia had been notified of the plan, and it would have been infinitely easier to drop a replacement machine into the wide Plain of Bah than into the very difficult DZ at Long Lelang. Harrisson's unmilitary mind did not encompass this long range viewpoint.[47]

In fact, it seems that from the start Harrisson had planned to find a way to run his own operation: the radio incident – with Carter conveniently out of the picture – simply provided the opportunity. Everyone agrees that Harrisson was an intensely competitive man. He was himself acutely aware of this character trait, writing of his own 'apparently insatiable ego, the drive to do whatever I had to do or wanted to do, either *before* or *better* than anyone else (preferably both)'.[48]

This seems to have manifested itself in a sense of competitiveness towards Carter: thus Heimann describes Carter in her account of the operation as Harrisson's 'rival', a view she can only have picked up from Harrisson himself. Harrisson acknowledged later his distaste at being forced to serve under Carter, having been given the impression when he was recruited to Semut that he would operate independently. It was for this reason, he tells us, that he 'claimed the privilege' of jumping into Borneo first, as leader of the reconnaissance party.[49]

This fits with Courtney's later comment that HQ decided to create separate commands in order to deal with 'the conflict of personalities'. But there is general consensus that Carter was not a rivalrous man – in fact, some felt he was too accommodating of others, including Harrisson – and he had had no opportunity since arriving in Sarawak to communicate with Courtney about any difficulties with Harrisson. Courtney's 'conflict of personalities' must have been based on complaints from Harrisson alone. These are likely to have been sparked by Carter's criticism of him in Bario over the way he was running the operation. But this was surely a legitimate exercise of Carter's command.[50]

Tredrea and Long, more measured commentators on Harrisson than many others who served under him, both told me later that Harrisson was obsessed from the start with having his own command. And once he had it, his intense competitiveness dictated that it be absolute. Thus Harrisson instructed Tredrea not to be in contact with any members of Semut II or Semut III, even when operating close to their territories: 'he found himself a Rajah! His command did not require of others,' Tredrea later commented drily. For his part, Sochon saw Harrisson's behaviour as inspired both by resentment over Carter's earlier reprimand to him in Bario and by a desire to maximise his role in the operation.

> It was perhaps not surprising that when [Harrisson] received Carter's order, he refused to part with his generator. Once the vital link with Australia, which he now controlled, was removed from his grasp, the recorded role that Harrisson would play in the war in Borneo would be miniscule indeed.[51]

There is undoubtedly some truth to all of this. But while Harrisson was almost certainly driven by a degree of self-interest, he also, almost equally certainly, believed the course of action he advocated would be better for the operation as a whole. And perhaps he was correct. After all, the success of special operations surely depends on the ability of operatives – including commanders – to exercise initiative when they are on their own in the field.

PART II
THE BARAM RIVER

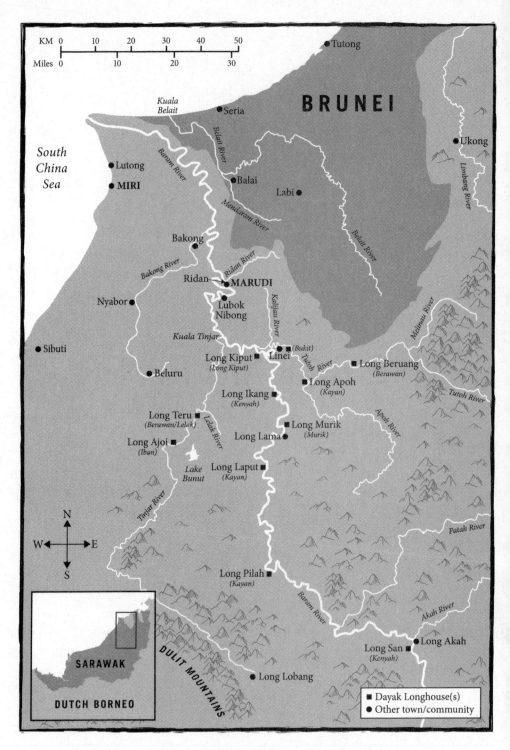

Baram River basin and environs in 1945.

6

FIRST MOVES

CARTER WAS NOT A man for rancour. He put the radio episode behind him and embraced the newly created Semut II. While the operation's focus remained the Baram River basin, including the Tinjar and Tutoh Rivers, its overall area as now defined was immense: stretching from somewhere between the Limbang and Tutoh Rivers in the north to a rough line drawn between the coastal town of Bintulu and the Dutch Borneo community of Long Nawang in the south. By contrast, the number of men in the operation was now pitifully small. With Semut III under Sochon having become a reality, Carter's own Semut II party had been reduced to five: Carter, Hallam, Horsnell, Pare and The.[1]

Nor was the party lacking only personnel. It also had few arms other than the personal ones the men had brought with them – none at all for the local recruits beginning to flock in. Unsurprisingly, Carter's first move was to request, via the tenuous connection with Semut I, a drop of reinforcements and stores: the latter to include not only the missing radio equipment but also arms and ammunition.

Together with Tama Weng Ajeng, Carter then began to organise a network of scouts and informants stretching down the Baram
River northwards to Marudi and the coast, and northwest to the
Tinjar River, Beluru, Sibuti and Miri. These were asked to supply
information on Japanese numbers, locations, movements and plans.
Carter wanted to create a detailed picture of enemy dispositions and
intentions for the entire Baram River basin.

Carter also asked his spies to find out whether there were any
European administrators from the Brooke regime left alive in the
area. The response was rapid and unequivocal. All Europeans were
either in prison (mostly in Kuching) or dead, many having been
killed under horrific circumstances at the Kenyah village of Long
Nawang, almost due south from Long Akah across the border in
Dutch Borneo.[2]

He learned that his friend Donald Hudden – the pre-war District
Officer in Marudi where Carter had spent much of his time while
working for Shell Oil – had sought safety among friendly Sa'ban not
much further up the Baram River from where Carter's own party
was now sheltering at Long Akah. However, in 1942 Hudden had
been hunted down and murdered there by a group of Ibans, two of
whom he had previously imprisoned in Marudi.[3]

Carter grieved over the loss, having hoped against hope that
Hudden and others might still be hiding out in the jungles. But grief
can be a powerful motivator. Soon he was receiving an avalanche
of intelligence about Japanese emplacements and movements in
the area. Some of it was wildly inaccurate, but taken together the
reports enabled him to build up a reliable picture. And so he began
to make his plans.

෴

The closest Japanese garrison, believed to number around twelve
men, was located at Long Lama, a tiny Chinese trading post

60 miles (96 km) further down the Baram River. Small parties of Japanese sometimes came upriver beyond Long Lama – as well as up the Tinjar River further west – seeking rice, but Long Lama was the furthest inland of the permanent forces. This was a relief to Carter, since from Long Lama it took several days' hard paddle to reach Long Akah. With his spies and scouts spread throughout the area, he would know well in advance of any Japanese movement in his direction.

Further downriver at Marudi – the Brooke government administrative centre for the area – there appeared to be surprisingly few soldiers, with estimates suggesting no more than twelve. As expected, most of the enemy forces were scattered down the coastline and throughout its immediate hinterland, close to the oilfields. In the area southwest of the Baram, from Miri and Bakong down to Bintulu, there were approximately two thousand, with fifteen hundred of them concentrated inland slightly to the west of the Baram River, around Nyabor, Bakong and Beluru. And in the area immediately northeast of the Baram, around Seria and the Belait River, there were approximately three to four hundred. While the Baram River itself was relatively free of Japanese, Carter was convinced that the planned Australian landings at Brunei Bay, slightly further northeast, would trigger a mass movement inland towards his tiny force.[4]

Supplies and reinforcements were urgently needed. And not only by Carter. Sochon's party, Semut III, could not leave for its designated operational area on the Rejang River until it had received its own stores and equipment, including a radio transmitter. In their absence the men of Semut III – Sochon, Abu Kassim and Barrie – had no option but to wait with Semut II at Long Akah.[5]

However, Semut II's only communication with the outside world was via the unreliable link with Semut I, which relayed its messages on to SRD HQ. And although Carter did not know it, Harrisson had instructed his signaller, Long, that Harrisson's own communications with HQ took precedence over those from Semut II. Indeed, he had decreed that the latter should be given low priority. Consequently, Carter's requests for men and goods were often long delayed in reaching HQ.[6]

As a result the fledgling operation was crippled from the start. Days, then weeks, went past without any sign of an aircraft bringing the necessary stores and reinforcements, not to mention the promised replacement generator for Carter's Boston radio. Young Kenyah men, recruited by Tama Weng Ajeng, were beginning to arrive at the fort, clamouring for the firearms Carter had promised. But to his shame he had none to give. Food supplies dwindled and the operatives were running out of the precious parachute silk they traded for many necessary services.

Of even greater concern to Carter were the effects of the no-show on the resolve of his new-found allies. The Dayaks of Long San and surrounding villages were now having to feed Carter's force – the operatives themselves as well as, increasingly, the new recruits beginning to arrive from throughout the area. Carter was acutely aware that this food was supplied by people – subsistence cultivators – whose economic margins were already slender.

In addition, it was now May, a busy time of year in the rice fields as a new cultivation cycle geared up. Yet, at the request of the chiefs, large numbers of local men were absenting themselves from rice field labour to work for the operation not only as guerrillas, but also as porters, guides, cooks, carriers, messengers and general labourers. Carter was scrupulous to pay all at the pre-war rates, but nevertheless the impost on small subsistence farming populations was substantial.[7]

Perhaps most importantly, the failure of either weaponry or men to materialise created a potentially dangerous loss of face. In his lengthy negotiations with Tama Weng and his lieutenants at Long San, Carter had promised that local Dayaks would be adequately armed to fight the Japanese and that Allied reinforcements would be arriving very soon to augment Carter's party. In this area, so close to the border, people knew that the Japanese had vanquished the Europeans and taken over government, and that they had killed many of them at Long Nawang in a remarkable demonstration of strength. This had undoubtedly increased local respect for Japanese spiritual potency, while correspondingly diminishing that accorded to Europeans. The inability of Carter to back up his promises could be taken as further evidence of European weakness, and so propel a change of heart about the alliance.

Of most concern in this regard was the reaction of Kebing, the senior Kayan chief in the area. The Kayan were the most numerous and powerful of the groups in the Baram River basin: there were many more of them than of Tama Weng's Kenyah. While the Kayan had given up raiding and warfare long before 1945, Carter knew of their past reputation for both: they had possessed sufficient military might to sack Brunei in 1874, an astonishing feat. Kebing's continued faith in the operation was critical.

But Carter was lucky. Having taken their time to reach a decision, neither Tama Weng nor Kebing was about to renege. Like Tama Weng, Kebing threw his personal support and considerable resources behind the operation: he was, Carter wrote to his superiors at the time, 'a tower of strength'.[8]

Together Tama Weng Ajeng and Kebing held the Kayan, Kenyah and related groups in the area behind Semut II. And in the continued absence of supplies from HQ, the operatives began to improvise. Collecting together what firearms they had, they created a firing range close to the fort, complete with homemade butts and firing rounds. Horsnell, an ex-machine gunner, was deputed to take charge of firearms training and began working with a group of thirty Kenyah warriors handpicked by Tama Weng, including his two sons.[9]

Some men in the area had owned shotguns in the past – which had since been confiscated by the Japanese – so firearms were not new to them. But the precision and power of the military weapons Semut II had in its arsenal were like nothing they had seen before: every man wanted one. Under such conditions, training was easy:

> They were apt pupils, and the mere thought of a chance to kill a few Japanese and (could they dare hope for such a wonder?) taking a head or two, drove them to heights of enthusiasm such as no regular NCO had ever dreamed he would witness. It was rewarding work on both sides.[10]

Recruits from Dayak groups other than the Kenyah were also arriving: Kayans, Penans, Berawans and Bukits among others. These were joined by two Iban pre-war members of the Sarawak Rangers, who made their way to Long Akah in response to a call put out by Carter and Sochon; more followed in the coming weeks. The numbers swelled even further with the coming of several men who had served in the Dutch East Indies Army and subsequently been conscripted by the Japanese, only to escape and make their way across the border to Long Akah.[11]

Perhaps most surprising of all, a British POW captured by the Japanese during the fall of Singapore – when he was only eighteen – turned up out of the blue. George Conleth-Smith, a Eurasian Corporal with the Royal Army Medical Corps in Singapore, had been transported in March 1942 to a POW camp at the Belait River area in Brunei, close to the mouth of the Baram River. He made three attempts to escape and each time was caught and beaten so severely that his right leg was damaged, making him partly lame.

He nevertheless escaped again, this time heading southwest through the jungle across the border into Sarawak. This time he was fortunate. He was taken in and sheltered from Japanese search parties by local Ibans who then sent him upriver to the *orang puteh* (white people) camp they had heard about at Long Akah. 'Con', as he came to be called, spoke not only fluent Malay but also some Japanese.[12]

Carter needed all the men he could get. His plan was to establish a significant guerrilla presence throughout the Baram River basin in advance of the Australian landings at Brunei Bay, which he knew must be imminent. Its main task would be to deal with the Japanese who would be moving inland away from the invading forces. But although he was now beginning to assemble a 'ragtime band' of guerrillas at Long Akah, the number of trained men at his disposal remained laughably small – especially when compared with the two thousand or so enemy soldiers in the area.[13]

The party already knew that on 1 May Australian forces had landed on Tarakan, a small island off the northeast coast of Borneo. Carter and Sochon were aware that the Brunei Bay landings would follow soon after, and they worried about the implications for their own under-manned and under-resourced operations. But in the continued absence of an air-drop, there was little they could do to prepare. Carter's frustration was amplified both by his inability to communicate with HQ directly, and by his growing suspicion that Harrisson was using his own uncontested air time to forcefully advance Semut I's competing claims.[14]

Meanwhile, the signallers picked up the occasional radio signal from Harrisson. One relayed a report that had reached Semut I suggesting a large force of Japanese were moving inland from Dutch Borneo in the direction of the upper Baram, probably in response to the landings at Tarakan. This was disturbing news since such a force could cause major difficulties for both Semut I and Semut II. Carter promptly sent Sochon and Barrie, with a force of Kenyahs, further up the Baram River to investigate. They quickly ascertained that there were no Japanese in the vicinity: the report had simply repeated one of the many rumours circulating in the wake of the Tarakan invasion.[15]

And so they waited for a drop, tormented by a frustration that now bordered on despair. To pass the time and raise spirits Sochon, a talented carver, appropriated the wooden door of the fort's toilet – a perfectly seasoned slab of timber – and carved a commemorative shield, which was mounted on the wall in the Fort. At the top, he fashioned the Sarawak coat of arms, and beneath it the words:

THIS TABLET IS TO COMMEMORATE
THE RE-OCCUPATION OF FORT LONG AKAH
AND THE RE-ESTABLISHMENT OF THE
SARAWAK GOVERNMENT BY THE FOLLOWING
PARATROOP PERSONNEL OF
HIS MAJESTY'S FORCES
MAJOR G.S. CARTER BRITISH ARMY
CAPTAIN W.L.P. SOCHON BRITISH ARMY
W.O.II D.L. HORSNELL A.I.F.
SGT C.W. PARE A.I.F.
SGT K.W. HALLAM A.I.F.
SGT J.K. BARRIE A.I.F.
SGT TEH SOEN HIN A.I.F.
SGT ABU KASSIM A.I.F.[16]

The words confirm Carter's and Sochon's view of the operation's intention to re-establish colonial government in Sarawak. They also illustrate its pecking order, with the names of the two Asian members located at the bottom.

೬೨

Finally, on 19 May – almost three weeks after the party's arrival at Long Akah – there came the unmistakeable sound of a Liberator engine. The men paddled urgently through the early morning mist to the drop zone established in the Chinese vegetable garden on the opposite side of the Baram River, and there let off the smoke signal. And at last, the exhilarating sight of parachutes, storpedoes attached, floating down through the cloud. There were fewer than Carter had hoped – the plane was carrying supplies for both Semut I and Semut II – and no weaponry or reinforcements were dropped. But at least they now had the replacement generator for the Boston radio and could look forward to direct communication with HQ. There was also an ATR-4 portable transceiver and aerial – and other necessary supplies – for Semut III.[17]

So two days later, early in the morning of 21 May, Sochon, Abu Kassim, Barrie and one of the Iban Sarawak Rangers departed Long Akah, heading for the Rejang River in the southwest. Semut III was underway, an infant operation taking its own baby steps. But its departure diminished the force at Carter's disposal even further: now he was reduced to a rump of five operatives (including himself) plus Conleth-Smith and the second Iban Ranger, in addition to the still largely untrained local guerrillas.

In the following few days the party was boosted by the arrival of 'Doc' McCallum, who had stayed in Bario on temporary loan to Harrisson as the remainder of Carter's party crossed to Long Akah. Having quickly, and furiously, fallen out with Harrisson over the issue of whether the operatives should wear boots – Harrisson insisted they go barefoot – he had followed Carter's party to the Baram.[18]

In the meantime, once Hallam had recovered from his malaria attack around mid-May, he joined Pare on radio duties. The two men arranged with Tama Weng to build a signals hut in a rubber garden around 300 yards (274 m) from the fort. They reasoned that, at this distance, if the fort came under sudden attack they would have time to destroy sets and cypher books before the Japanese discovered them. Here, throughout May, they struggled to send and receive signals to both SRD HQ and Semut I.[19]

With the arrival of the new radio generator on 19 May, hopes had been high: at last the operation would be released from its crushing dependence on Semut I. But there was no relief for Carter. In spite of the best efforts of Hallam and Pare, communication remained little better than before, still largely reliant on the fickle link with Bario. Carter was by now becoming frantic. More requests were relayed via Semut I: for weaponry, reinforcements and, especially, functioning radio equipment.

It took until 30 May – after the party had been at Long Akah for more than four weeks – for Carter's pleas for reinforcements and weapons to be answered. On that morning a Liberator arrived over the drop zone and unloaded four personnel – Lieutenant Max Wood, Sergeant Francis 'Frank' Pippen, Sergeant Denis 'Denny' Sheppard and Corporal Jack Neave – plus stores, including weaponry. Pippen was a signaller, whose expertise with wireless could now be added to that of Hallam and Pare. Neave was a medical orderly, sent expressly to complement McCallum in providing medical assistance – and so winning local support – throughout the area.

But just when it seemed that things might be looking up for Carter, he suffered another blow. After dropping its load at Long Akah, the Liberator flew back down the Baram River in search of the tiny town of Long Lama. Carter had sent a message to SRD HQ some days earlier requesting that the Japanese radio station at Long Lama be strafed, and the Liberator pilot had been directed to do this on his way back to base. Carter had provided co-ordinates and a clear description of the building. But, inexplicably, the plane instead strafed the Kayan longhouse of Long Pilah, more than 25 miles (40 km) further upriver.[20]

As if this was not bad enough, Long Pilah was the home of Kebing – the most senior Kayan chief in the region – who had thrown his wholehearted support behind Semut II. We can only imagine the mortification Carter must have felt a day or two later when the chief arrived at Long Akah with several of the injured – including a man who had lost a leg and another who had lost a hand – seeking an explanation.

As a peace offering, Carter ordered Sheppard and a number of the partly trained Kenyahs – including Tama Weng's oldest son Kalang – to accompany Kebing back to Long Pilah. Sheppard took with him a pile of newly delivered rifles, with instructions to begin training the Kayans at Long Pilah and surrounding longhouses.[21]

In the meantime Pippen added his expertise to that of Hallam and Pare, and together the three men struggled with the Boston: stringing and restringing the aerial and fiddling with the settings. But to no avail. Further stores drops – including more weapons – on 2 June and 4 June failed to solve this most intractable and disabling of Carter's problems. By early June, Semut II still lacked reliable direct communication with HQ, now in Morotai.

❦

Undeterred by his seemingly relentless run of bad luck, Carter continued to scheme. In his view the Baram River itself with its two major tributaries – the Tutoh River in the east and the Tinjar River in the west – was the key to the entire operation. The Baram was the lifeline of a large area bounded in the north and northwest by the coastal strip from Tutong to Sibuti, which included the large coastal town of Miri and the oilfields at Seria and Lutong, in the east by the rugged Tama Abu range, and in the west by the remote Dulit Mountains. Along with coastal tracks, this river system was the main avenue of commerce and administration throughout the area.

Carter's goal was to control these three main rivers, most particularly the Baram, and keep them free of Japanese. He was convinced that Japanese fleeing the Allied landings would decide to head up one or more of these rivers on their way further inland. This could spell disaster for the many Dayak longhouses along their banks.[22]

Protection of Dayak peoples from the Japanese was never explicitly included in Semut's list of formal objectives. However, the operation had been tasked with setting up spheres of influence to ease the return to civilian government, and it is obvious from his writings that Carter saw this as including the preservation of human life and civic order in the Baram area under his control; Sheppard commented later that Carter was motivated in all his actions partly by 'a compassion for the good-will of the natives'. Carter also believed that if the Japanese were to move up the Baram River and scatter into remote areas further inland, it would become impossible for the invading Australian forces to find them.[23]

In the absence of sufficient men to impede by military means any Japanese move upriver, Carter had little choice but to rely on bluff. Tama Weng and his allies were asked to spread the rumour that hundreds of Australian soldiers had arrived in the upper Baram and were organising a vast Dayak guerrilla army which was even now making its way downstream towards Marudi. The message that they hoped would soon reach Japanese ears was that not only was Marudi under threat, but there was no escape from the invading forces inland via the Baram River basin.

Carter's aim was to persuade fleeing Japanese soldiers to avoid the Baram and its tributaries at all costs. If he was successful in this, the 1500 or more Japanese concentrated in the area around Nyabor, Bakong and Beluru should instead move southwest via overland coastal tracks to Sibuti, while the 300–400 located east of the Baram in the Belait River area would probably attempt to escape through Labi or along the Belait River to the Tutoh River. It would be relatively easy for both Semut II and the invading AIF to mop up the first group, and Carter planned to have a force of trained local guerrillas waiting at the Tutoh for the second.[24]

But Carter had also set his sights on the town of Marudi itself. Marudi was the administrative and commercial centre of the Baram River basin, located around 40 miles (64 km) upriver, as the crow flies, from the river's mouth. In Carter's view, control of the town – with its easy ship access and landing sites for seaplanes – would afford control of the entire Baram River region. His own tiny party could not hope to take Marudi by force, but the small Japanese garrison there might be spooked into leaving.[25]

It was an ambitious ruse. And Carter was aware that it could only be effective if backed up with evidence. So his next move was to begin harassing Japanese forces throughout the area.

Early in June Carter sent Horsnell and The Soen Hin eastwards to the upper Tinjar River, to the old Chinese trading post at Long Lobang. Their orders were to proceed down the Tinjar, winning the support of locals as they went. While it was hoped that some would join up as guerrillas, equally as important was to encourage those who did not to kill any small groups of Japanese who entered their territories. And everywhere they went the two men were to repeat for the benefit of those who had not yet heard it (or had not believed it possible) the momentous news: Japanese heads could be taken and brought home to enhance existing longhouse collections.

Once Horsnell and The reached the area around Lake Bunut and Long Teru they were to stop and set up a permanent base. Here, and further downstream in the Bakong-Beluru-Sibuti area, were a number of Iban longhouses. Iban support for the operation was crucial and Horsnell and The were tasked with securing it.[26]

Recruitment of Ibans to the operation was fraught with risk, as Carter was only too aware. But it was a risk he was willing to take. The Iban are the most populous of Borneo's Dayak peoples. They were also, in the past, among its most aggressive, with some Sarawak Iban groups having finally relinquished headhunting only in the 1930s. And, unfortunately for Carter, there were longstanding hostilities between the Iban on the one hand and many other Dayak groups in the area, especially the Kayan, on the other.

These enmities had their origins primarily in the Brooke regime's Great Kayan Expedition of 1863, during which an estimated 15,000 Iban warriors were unleashed on the Balui River, not far south of the Baram, to loot, kill and sack Kayans and other nearby peoples with impunity. They had been exacerbated in following decades by ongoing Iban expansion into the Baram River area, often ignored by the Brookes to ensure that they could continue recruiting Iban warriors in support of their own military adventures.[27]

Carter was aware of the volatile mix he would create by adding Ibans to Semut II's guerrilla force. But he had no choice: while Kayan, Kenyah and related groups dominated the upriver areas of the Baram River basin, there were more Iban in the crucial downriver areas. Many lived around Marudi as well as in the Bakong-Beluru area where most of the Japanese were concentrated. He could only take these areas with Iban support. Carter's hope was that the Iban had been so alienated by Japanese rule – and would be so tempted by the opportunity to resume headhunting – that they would overlook old animosities and come on board.

In this he was encouraged by the generosity of Tama Weng Ajeng and Kebing. Both chiefs expressed a willingness to put aside intertribal hostilities for the sake of the operation. Indeed, Tama Weng insisted that he himself – at the head of a force of his own Kenyahs – would accompany Carter when it came time for the operation's HQ to move downriver into Iban territory.[28]

Horsnell and The Soen Hin were thus given the job of recruiting and training Ibans in the lower Tinjar River area. And not only Ibans: they were also instructed to enlist Chinese – from the many who inhabited this area – and Penans. This was dangerous work, operating, as they were, close to areas of high Japanese concentration and shadowed constantly by the threat of betrayal. Nevertheless they proved remarkably adept at it. By 8 June two local platoons had already been formed and training had begun.[29]

∞

On 4 June, a day or two after sending Horsnell and The to the Tinjar, Carter implemented the next stage of his plan. He sent Wood and Pippen, with around a dozen Kenyah guerrillas, down the Baram River. Their ultimate destination was the Tutoh River, which flows into the Baram on its true right bank, halfway between Long Lama and Marudi. Carter believed that Japanese fleeing the Australian landings were likely to head inland along the Tutoh, and he wanted trained guerrillas in place to resist them.

Wood's orders were to move up the Tutoh River to the large Berawan longhouse of Long Beruang. There he would establish a sub-HQ and begin training guerrillas from the Dayak groups found in the area, which included Kenyah, Kayan, Berawan, Penan and Bukit.[30]

But first, on its way down the Baram, Wood's party stopped at Long Pilah on 5 June. Wood had momentous orders for Sheppard. Sheppard and his force of Kenyahs, plus some of the local Kayans he had begun training, were to launch an attack on the Japanese radio station further downriver at Long Lama – the same station that had escaped its intended strafing a few days earlier. With rumours of his party's presence in the interior rife throughout the area, Carter wanted to show the Japanese that they were true.

The Japanese outpost at Long Lama was Carter's obvious first target. Not only was it (presumably) in direct wireless contact with Japanese HQ, but its strategic location – on the Baram River not far above where the Tutoh and Tinjar Rivers flow into the Baram – presented an obstacle to his plans to control all three rivers. It had to go.[31]

On receiving Carter's orders Sheppard realised at once that his chances of mounting a successful raid would be improved by making use of the additional firepower and expertise possessed by Wood's party. Wood intended to continue his own journey downriver to Long Beruang the following day, so Sheppard wasted no time.

Sheppard had been in Borneo less than a week but he already recognised that the success of any action depended on Dayak input to its planning. Dayaks could accurately predict the weather and the changing currents of the rivers. They could advise on the paths the Japanese were likely to use as well as alternative routes through seemingly trackless jungle. They were familiar with every settlement in the area, with their inhabitants and layouts. They knew where different kinds of vegetation grew and the uses to which they could be put, as well as where any of the multitude of creatures inhabiting the area – including dangerous ones such as snakes and crocodiles – would be found. And they had an intimate acquaintance with the environment: they knew where the land dipped, the path curved, the river narrowed.

Consequently, Dayak input to tactical and strategic decision-making was imperative for operational success: their expertise underpinned all calculations of the optimal timing and location for a raid or ambush, the field of fire, how long it would take to get into position, how many men should take part and how they should be placed, the risk of civilian casualties, and so on. Operatives were completely dependent on Dayak advice. As Tredrea later told me: 'I admit, I was a baby in their hands . . . I always conferred with them.'[32]

On this occasion 21-year-old Kalang – the leader of Sheppard's Kenyah force (and Tama Weng's oldest son) – was Sheppard's chief tactical advisor. After discussing the situation with him, Sheppard made the decision to attack Long Lama the next morning (6 June).[33]

Sheppard's first move was to travel down the Baram to a location closer to Long Lama, from where the strike could be launched. He took with him his platoon of Kenyahs under Kalang, and a handful of the Kayans he had begun training at Long Pilah. Wood's group accompanied them. Their destination was the Kayan longhouse of Long Laput, located only a few miles above Long Lama.[34]

∞

The anthropologist Peter Metcalf tells us that in the nineteenth and twentieth centuries it was impossible to travel along the fast-flowing rivers winding from Borneo's mountainous centre

> without remarking on the stupendous buildings that were to be found along their banks. [. . .] To travel at all in the region was to travel between longhouses, and every arrival was a surprise. After hours of seeing nothing along the riverbanks but mangroves and palms and behind them the great trees of the rainforest, the first indication was a clump of canoes drawn up around an impromptu dock made of floating logs. On the bank above was a screen of fruit trees, and behind that the looming bulk of the longhouse. From apparently empty forest, the visitor was abruptly immersed in the social density of a city.[35]

This provides some sense of how Sheppard, Wood and Pippen must have felt when they rounded a bend in the Baram River later the same afternoon and saw for the first time the longhouse at Long Laput. Built in the solid, massive Kayan architectural style, and sheltered in a long clearing cut from the jungle bordering this most beautiful of rivers, Long Laput was a staggering sight. Bending along the bank – moulding itself to the river's slow curve – for almost half a mile (800 m), it was the largest longhouse not only in the area, but in all of Sarawak. It contained close to one hundred doors and a population above six hundred people. Malcolm MacDonald, former British Governor-General, felt sufficiently moved by it during a visit in 1946 to opine that, 'What Knowle [Knole] is to England, Long Laput is to Sarawak.'[36]

The party was welcomed in the usual way by the longhouse head, Baya Lenjau, and ushered into the vast gallery. Here, surrounded by dozens of eager listeners and mournfully surveyed by Baya Lenjau's collection of blackened heads, Sheppard explained his mission. The writ of Kebing held sway here and Baya Lenjau was a willing recruit to the operation.

But before further planning could take place, the group needed to establish the size and disposition of the Japanese force in Long Lama. Carter's intelligence suggested around a dozen men, but Sheppard needed to be sure. It was agreed that Baya Lenjau would travel downriver to Long Lama – taking with him a chicken as a gift – and once there ingratiate himself with the Japanese soldiers. This would enable him to establish how many they were as well as glean some sense of their daily routines.[37]

Off went Baya Lenjau in his canoe, taking with him a number of young men to help with the paddling, as well as the chicken. Sheppard, Wood and Pippen remained at Long Laput. After setting up improvised targets, they began feverishly training local Kayan recruits – those from Long Pilah as well as some from Long Laput – in the use of firearms. Sheppard wisely believed that they should take part in the coming assault as an initiation into Semut II's operation.

The shadows of late afternoon were spreading across the river when Baya Lenjau returned. In the darkening longhouse gallery he reported that there were ten Japanese in Long Lama. One – often more – was usually found in the radio hut, and they all slept nearby in the town's wooden fort. And good news: security was lax, since they appeared to have no idea that Europeans had arrived in the interior. Baya Lenjau, Kalang, Wood and Sheppard could now thrash out the finer details of the raid.[38]

But first Baya Lenjau needed to know that the signs were favourable. He summoned his ritual specialist and asked him to consult the omens concerning the outcome of the attack. After the customary slaughter of a pig and the reading of its liver, the specialist pronounced that the signs were good: the operation would be successful. And so it was agreed: the attack would take place the next morning at first light. The men hoped that with Long Lama still in virtual darkness, they would be able to surround both the fort and the radio hut before many enemy soldiers had risen from their mats.

Instructions were relayed to all those who would take part. SRD HQ had requested a Japanese prisoner for interrogation, so Sheppard was careful to explain that at least one Japanese must be kept alive. He also confirmed the thrilling rumours circulating since Carter's announcement at Long San several weeks earlier: yes, Japanese heads could be taken. Excitement rippled through the longhouse and the men finally fell asleep to the sound of murmured stories of glorious headhunting raids from the past.[39]

෨෨

Since the completion of a bridge across the Baram River in 2019, the tiny trading town of Long Lama can be reached from Miri by car in less than three hours. The road runs through a depressingly ugly landscape littered with the detritus of felled trees and seemingly endless stretches of oil-palm.

However, in 1945 Long Lama was a remote outpost, accessible from the coast only by several days' hard paddling up the Baram River from Marudi. The town was perched in a small clearing on the true right bank of the Baram. On the other side, the tiny Lama River flowed into the larger river and all around were endless battalions of trees, marching from the riverbanks to the distant hills. The jungle here was not the mighty primary jungle found not much further upriver, but rather secondary jungle produced from generations of rice farming by local Kayans.

The landscape throughout this section of the Baram is littered with limestone stacks and cliffs which, in 1945, stood out like white sentinels from the surrounding darkness of the trees. These are riddled with caves, each of them owned by aristocratic Kayan and Kenyah families. In the caves, tens of thousands of swifts – hyperactive unpaid workers – build their tiny cup-like nests, consisting largely of the birds' glutinous saliva hardened into a kind of cement. The nests are highly prized by Chinese cooks, who still today turn them into a jelly-like soup.

Before the Japanese occupation the nests were gathered and brought to Long Lama several times a year. Here they were auctioned by the local Chinese traders to Chinese merchants who travelled upriver from Marudi. Around 40,000 to 50,000 nests were sold each year, fetching huge prices, and bestowing great wealth on both cave owners and local *towkays* (Chinese traders). But by 1945 the Allied blockade on shipping had brought this lucrative trade to a standstill. And not only this one: in keeping with their brethren elsewhere on the island, the Chinese *towkays* of Long Lama had almost nothing in their shophouses to sell.[40]

The town itself was very small: sixteen Chinese wooden shophouses stretched in a row along the top of a steep, 30-foot (9-m) high bank above the Baram River and – as so often and yet so unexpectedly in out-of-the-way parts of Sarawak at the time – a tiny wooden fort built by the Brookes. The fort was serving as living quarters for the Japanese force stationed in the town. Nearby, at the edge of the jungle, squatted a newly built hut used by the garrison as its radio station.[41]

On 6 June, well before dawn, lights glimmered down the longhouse gallery at Long Laput as men rose and readied themselves for the attack on Long Lama. The Kayans and Kenyahs secreted about their bodies and weapons certain small ritual objects believed to bestow the precious gift of *kebal* (invulnerability) – not too different in their function from the prayers that some of the Europeans may have whispered. In the darkness, with the mist like a damp blanket

across the water, Sheppard, Wood and Pippen, along with almost
two dozen Kayans and Kenyahs, filed down the notched entry logs
from the longhouse. At the river's edge they climbed into several
waiting canoes, and headed downstream.[42]

Many of the Kayans and Kenyahs carried new firearms: rifles
and American carbines. However, some were armed only with local
weaponry: *parang* (swords) and spears. But what weapons! Up until
the twentieth century many Dayak groups – including the Kayan
and Kenyah – contained supremely talented blacksmiths. They manufactured steel at least the quality of the very best found in northern
Europe, producing beautiful, highly functional blades. The British
traveller John Dalton, who spent a couple of months in Borneo in
the 1820s, tells us that their swords could cut through wrought iron
and common steel with ease:

> [O]ne day, having bet a wager of a few rupees with Selgie that
> he would not cut through an old musket barrel, he, without
> hesitation, put the end of it upon a block of wood and chopped
> it to pieces without the least turning the edge of the mandow
> [sword].[43]

A good Dayak *parang* was a highly valued object. In addition to
its blade it included a hilt – usually made from deer antler – and a
wooden scabbard, both often exquisitely carved. The best of them
were peerless fighting instruments: light, strong and wonderfully balanced. In the hands of a master warrior, protected and propelled by
his magic, they were lethal. No Dayak man would ever leave home
without his *parang*, even if he should be lucky enough to have a gun.

In spite of the darkness, the party moved quickly, hugging the
banks, soundless except for the occasional rattle of the paddles
against the boats' sides. They arrived at Long Lama just as the first
pale tremors of light appeared in the sky.[44]

7

ADVANCE DOWNRIVER

THE SHOPHOUSES OF LONG Lama loomed like a dark shadow against the sky at the top of the riverbank as the Kayans and Kenyahs in Sheppard's party carefully eased their canoes up to the town's diminutive wharf. There they were silently moored, with several men left to guard them. The remainder of the party climbed the steep wooden steps built into the cliff face, the locals soundless on their bare feet. The growing dawn gave just enough light to see by: there was no sign of movement in the town itself or the wooden fort, a deeper patch of darkness further along the riverbank. With the local Kayans leading the way, they crept towards it, weapons at the ready.

But then, disaster: sudden movement and a light not far from the fort – the radio hut! A voice sprang shockingly out of the murk, then more movement and another shout. With the element of surprise lost, Sheppard hoisted his gun and began to fire on both fort and hut. Those with him followed suit, producing a massive burst of gunfire. They were almost at the fort when a Japanese soldier ran out of its door immediately in front. Pippen shot him dead at almost point-blank range.[1]

There was now pandemonium: in the dim light it was difficult to tell who was friend and who foe. The Kayans and Kenyahs nevertheless moved quickly to surround the two buildings, in line with their instructions. As they did, another Japanese soldier appeared from the jungle behind the radio hut and went to fire his rifle at Wood, who stood several yards away at the front of the hut. The Japanese was struck down by the *parang* of one of the Kenyahs, his rifle jettisoned in the heat of the moment for a friendlier weapon. Other Japanese fell: some to gunfire, some to *parang*.

And then, quiet: profound in the wake of the noise and confusion. Two Japanese lay dead and three more were wounded, two badly. Five others were missing, presumably escaped into the jungle. As the daylight grew and Chinese began to emerge hesitantly from their shophouses, Sheppard called his troops to order on the clear ground beside the fort. It was then that he noticed: two of them held human heads.[2]

෨෧

It is all too easy for Europeans to evince horror at the idea of headhunting. But, as we have already seen, this response conveniently overlooks European fascination with, and complicity in, the practice. In Borneo, WWII came in the wake of a long history of the encouragement, and indeed recruitment, of Dayak warriors – including by the Brookes – to headhunt against the enemies of those who ruled. In spite of this, headhunting had been largely eradicated from Sarawak by the time of WWII.

In 1945 Semut operatives reintroduced the practice. Carter acknowledged this in a report written several months after the war's end:

> SRD admits to reviving the head hunting custom against the
> Japanese and many Long Houses have enriched themselves
> thereby.

The result was, Sheppard tells us, that head-taking 'became a way of
life for the guerrillas and accepted by most operatives'.[3]

While negotiating with Tama Weng Ajeng and his allies, Carter
had been explicit that headhunting against the Japanese would be
permitted. His men repeated this news in each longhouse they visited
throughout the Baram River basin, where it was met with a combination of astonishment and anticipation. Nor was Carter alone in
declaring an end to the Brooke moratorium on headhunting: both
Harrisson and Sochon did the same in the Kelabit Highlands and
the Rejang River basin respectively. However, none of them mentioned it in any official report at the time, presumably believing
that headhunting would contravene the Geneva Convention and
its reinstatement might be viewed unfavourably in some sections of
the military.[4]

Neither of these things can possibly have been a coincidence. It
suggests that the three men had discussed headhunting before they
arrived in Sarawak and agreed not only to use it as a tool for recruiting Dayaks to Semut, but also to withhold their promotion of it
from official reports. And if this is so, it is likely that at least some
of their superior officers and fellow planners in SRD knew of the
plan. Robert Wilson, Carter's second in command on Semut II, later
stated that this headhunting policy was 'laid down at a high level
planning conference in Melbourne (or possibly London) in 1944'.[5]

But Carter, Harrisson and Sochon did not stop at sanctioning
headhunting against the Japanese. All three men also offered payment for Japanese heads, especially early in the campaign when
recruitment of Dayaks was at its most urgent. Brian Walpole of
Sochon's Semut III later wrote:

[O]n arriving behind enemy lines the SRD let it be known that they would pay the Sea Dyaks [Iban] the princely bounty of one Straits Settlement dollar per Japanese head. This was about two shillings and sixpence in Australian currency at the time, or twenty-five cents. Occasionally there was trouble when we had to refuse them payment for Chinese or Malay heads, but overall the system worked quite well.[6]

Harrisson put out the word soon after arrival that he would pay for any Japanese heads brought to him at Semut I HQ; Bob Long – who as Harrisson's signaller witnessed many such transactions – explained later that Harrisson insisted on inspecting each head to make sure it was Japanese in origin. The concern to avoid reference to these arrangements in official documents led to some oddly cryptic communications in the field. Thus, Edmeades to Harrisson on 11 June 1945:

> The three men carrying [this] note have a present for you. [. . .] the head of one of the CPO [Japanese] officers [. . .] for your inspection. I have told them you will be very grateful and pleased to see them.

Other Semut I operatives were given licence to pay for heads themselves. Tredrea, who operated mostly in Dutch Borneo, was provided with Dutch guilders by Harrisson, with the rate set at five guilders per head. However, in his case the money was not needed: 'My boys were happy enough with just the heads,' he explained. 'Have sent [my Ibans] in front,' Griffiths-Marsh writes in his diary, 'and informed them $1 to the first man to bring me a nip head.'[7]

The speed with which this incentive was offered after arrival in each Semut area suggests that it too had been agreed in advance. Wilson, who took over as commanding officer of Semut II towards the end of the campaign, confirms in his final report that it had been decided before the Semut II party arrived in Borneo to pay a bounty for every Japanese head brought to it. While Semut I and Semut III appear to have paid the same amount – one Straits dollar per head in Sarawak – Hallam and Wilson both record that Semut II paid ten dollars per head. It is possible Carter believed that Kayans and Kenyahs would be reluctant to resume headhunting, and so decided to offer a larger reward.[8]

Should we condemn this policy? Perhaps. But why single out the promotion of headhunting as worthy of particular censure? As we have already seen, many other practices of war seem much crueller in both their execution and their effects. And it is hard to see how paying men to take heads home in order to honour them is any worse than paying them simply to kill. Ah yes, the Geneva Convention. But the Geneva Convention of 1929 specifies only that the dead should be protected against 'pillage and maltreatment'. And while for Europeans the removal of a dead soldier's head may be classed as a form of maltreatment, and even desecration, Dayak headhunters of the time saw it in almost the opposite terms.[9]

Ironically, many Dayaks refused to accept money for heads, believing that the honour of taking a head should be its own reward. This was true of almost all guerrillas from Kayan, Kenyah and related groups; while not all of them took heads, those who did generally found the idea of payment an affront.[10]

∽

After the attack at Long Lama, Sheppard and his men searched the Japanese radio hut, taking away documents deemed important. These were later found to include radio signals – in Japanese – sent by Hallam weeks before from Long Lellang. Although they had not made it across the mountains to their intended recipients at Bario, they had travelled westward to the Japanese garrison at Long Lama.

Astonishingly the signals appear not to have raised alarms within
the Japanese command concerning the presence of Allied forces
in the interior – it seems that no Japanese troops were despatched to
locate their source.[11]

Sheppard and his force of Kayans and Kenyahs returned trium-
phantly first to Long Laput, and then Long Pilah. They took with
them one of the wounded Japanese, whose injuries were relatively
slight. The other two were too badly hurt to move, and in fact both
died not long after. From Long Pilah, Sheppard – accompanied by the
troop of Kenyahs under Kalang – took the prisoner directly upriver
to Long Akah. Wood and Pippen, with their own group of Kenyahs,
continued downstream on their journey to the Tutoh River.

At Long Akah the prisoner was put in leg-irons unearthed in the
fort, that had at times in the past served as a jail. In a few days' time
he was joined by a second prisoner – one of the Japanese who had
escaped the Long Lama attack, now captured and brought to Long
Akah by Kayans. There, the two prisoners were confined – watched
by Kenyah guards – until a Catalina flying boat could be organised
to land on the river and collect them.[12]

While they waited for the Catalina's arrival, the operatives made
an important discovery. The Japanese prisoners were terrified at
the thought of having their heads taken, and were easily controlled
through threats of decapitation by their Kenyah guards. In fact, like
Westerners and some other peoples, most Japanese place great value
on the integrity of the body, and are horrified at the idea of body
and head being separated after death. This is almost certainly one of
the reasons why, throughout their occupation of Borneo, Japanese
soldiers were reluctant to move inland into Dayak areas.[13]

Semut II was quick to recognise the opportunity this presented
for shepherding Japanese away from the Baram River and its tributaries. Rumours about battalions of headhunters who had joined
forces with the Europeans were added to those already circulating

concerning a European advance down the Baram River. There is no doubting the effectiveness of this campaign. Wilson later commented that because of Semut II's identification with headhunting, no Japanese soldier surrendered to its forces: 'The word had gone round.' Head-taking – or at least the threat of it – was almost unmatched as a means to terrorise the enemy.[14]

◌◌

In the meantime – at last! – the party's radio issues had been resolved. On the morning of 7 June another Liberator had arrived at Long Akah and dropped stores and two personnel: Sergeant Leo Duffus, yet another signaller, and Lieutenant William 'Stan' Eadie. Eadie was a British signalling expert who had been seconded from SOE to SRD. He had been assigned to Semut II specifically to sort out its radio problems. The stores – weapons, radio equipment and food – ended up some distance away from Long Akah in virgin jungle and were not seen again, adding to Carter's already considerable trove of ill fortune. But Duffus and Eadie landed safely – albeit in the Baram River, in Duffus's case – and Eadie immediately went to work on the party's radio.

Eadie's report to Courtney on the deficiencies of the equipment provided to the party is politely worded but nevertheless excoriating. It lists a litany of equipment failures including transmitters delivered with incorrect wiring, power packs that began to smoke after a few minutes of use, hand generators too stiff to be turned, condensers that constantly shorted and chargers supplied without oil (in their desperation, some enterprising signallers had unsuccessfully attempted to substitute mosquito lotion). Some items had obviously not been tested before delivery – a shocking dereliction when men's lives might have depended on functioning radios.[15]

Not surprisingly Hallam and Pare were, Eadie noted, 'very discouraged' when he arrived, although he insisted they had done everything that could be expected of them. Part of the problem, he explained, was that Australian signallers were not receiving adequate training with respect to the more technical aspects of the role, and so ended up with little understanding of basic wireless telegraphy principles. This meant that, while they were proficient operators, if equipment failed they had no idea how to fix it.[16]

Eadie was also highly critical of both the cumbersome ciphers being used and the lack of wireless staff and equipment at HQ. The latter meant that the system was frequently overloaded, resulting in field parties being unable to get through. Eadie made a number of recommendations to improve radio communications, all of which appear to have been ignored by Courtney.[17]

Nevertheless, to Carter's intense relief, within a few days of Eadie's arrival Long Akah was finally – almost six weeks after the first party had arrived there – in reliable radio contact with HQ. Eadie also managed to get the ATR-4 intercommunication radios to talk to base to some degree, although in this terrain ATR-4 intercommunication was never reliable. Instead Carter continued to depend largely on the tried-and-true method of Dayak runners and paddlers to convey messages between different sub-parties.

Eadie's intervention occurred only just in time. On 10 June the party received, on their newly-functioning radio, the news they had been expecting for weeks. The 9th Australian Division had landed at Labuan Island and other locations in Brunei Bay, only a short distance northeast from the mouth of their own Baram River. The Australian invasion had begun.

෩

The Brunei Bay landings changed everything, and yet changed nothing. On the one hand Carter no longer needed to focus on collecting intelligence to be used during the invasion. Instead, concern now shifted to what the Japanese would do, and where they might go, in response to the advancing Allied forces. On the other hand, his primary focus remained the prevention of a Japanese retreat inland via the Baram River system.

It had been clear to Carter for some time that the Japanese did not intend to put up much resistance to the Allied invasion on the coast. His spies had been reporting since he first arrived at Long Akah that the enemy held the key coastal town of Miri only lightly, and that troop movements and preparations suggested an imminent move away from the town. While some parts of the Miri force were obviously planning a move westwards towards Bintulu and Mukah and so (hopefully) on to Sibu and, eventually, Kuching – part of a more general westward evacuation from the northeast chunk of the island indicated for some time – other parts were clearly readying themselves for a push inland.[18]

Carter was concerned about the latter group. He feared they intended to move into the fertile lands of the remote interior at the top of the Baram River and set up a 'Jap Colony'. Once there they might never be found, no matter how determined the search by the conventional Australian forces.[19]

This fear was reinforced immediately after the Australian landings by reports from his spies detailing Japanese movement inland from the coast into Semut II's area. In response, Carter sent signals to Courtney suggesting that Allied forces should be sent to the strategic points of Marudi (on the Baram), Long Teru (on the Tinjar), and Long Beruang (on the Tutoh) in order to prevent further Japanese incursions upriver. The response was discouraging. As he wrote in his later report:

> Alas for the best laid schemes of mice and men! Troops would not be available for such purposes.[20]

Nevertheless, things were finally beginning to look up. On 16 June a Liberator arrived over Long Akah and dropped more stores, including weapons, and four more personnel: Major Robert Wilson, Sergeant Bob Mason, Lance-Corporal Keith Le Guier, and Private Stewart 'Stewie' Fidler. With the departure of Sochon to the Rejang, Carter had lacked a formal second-in-command. Wilson – a 46-year-old British surgeon in civilian life, and a firearms expert who had already seen action with SOE behind enemy lines in the Netherlands and France – had been inserted to assume the role.

The arrival of the four men was a substantial boost to Carter's force, bringing the total number of fully trained soldiers to seventeen: Carter, Pare, The Soen Hin, Horsnell, Hallam, Wood, Pippen, Sheppard, Neave, Eadie, Duffus, Wilson, Mason, Le Guier, Fidler, McCallum and Conleth-Smith. Nevertheless, even including the scores of Kayan and Kenyah recruits, the numbers remained pitifully small, especially in comparison with the Japanese force the party was facing.

Lack of weapons was an even bigger problem. Eadie notes that prior to insertion at Long Akah, he left Mindoro in such a rush that the only personal weapons he brought with him were a 9mm pistol with fifty rounds of ammunition and an American jungle knife (he also had no jumpsuit or spine guard for this, his first ever parachute jump – a digger hat stuffed down his trousers substituted for the latter!). Weapons were so scarce that it was several weeks before he was able to supplement these with an American carbine. As a result, very few of the local recruits could be provided with firearms. But it would have to do.[21]

⟨⟩

Unsurprisingly, many aspects of living and working with Dayaks were proving a challenge for the European operatives, if less so for The and Abu Kassim. The strangeness and monotony of the diet during the many periods when they were relying on Dayaks for food – Dayaks ate rice for breakfast, lunch and dinner – was one of these.

'Rice, rice, rice,' Bob Long said to me seventy years later, 'you did start to long for something else.' Frank Wigzell of Semut I made a resolution before leaving Borneo to 'never, never ever touch a drop of rice for the rest of my lifetime' – a vow he kept for thirty years. Most of the vegetable accompaniments – bamboo shoots, fern fronds, cassava leaves, water spinach – were alien, as were regular meats such as monkey, turtle, venison and even snake. And then there were the chillies! 'I was afraid of the chillies,' Jack Tredrea said simply.[22]

Operatives found Dayak codes of privacy and sociability – so different from European ones – particularly difficult to deal with. Most Dayaks in 1945 prized constant close companionship and were puzzled as to why anyone might wish to spend time completely alone: 'We could never teach these people that the white man liked a little privacy,' Tom Harrisson later wrote. Waking on a longhouse gallery in the morning the operatives would find themselves surrounded by large numbers of people waiting for them to get up; going for a wash in the river in the evening they were quickly accompanied by a noisy, splashing horde. Mundane tasks such as cleaning weaponry, working over the radio, or writing in their notebooks inevitably attracted talkative throngs. In addition, Dayaks would often touch, pull, push, stroke or jostle the men in ways that could easily offend buttoned-up European sensibilities.[23]

Nevertheless, Carter reminded them constantly of the need to adapt to Dayak ways. He particularly stressed – as he had to the members of the reconnaissance party before them – the importance of treating Dayaks with respect, of never 'throwing your weight around'. Hallam later recalled an episode when in frustration he called a Kenyah a 'dopey bastard' (in English) within Carter's earshot, and was promptly told off.[24]

Operative days (and nights) were filled with Dayaks: they ate, trained, strategised, fought, slogged through jungle and laughed with them during the day, and slept beside them at night. In addition, many of the operatives had employed what they called 'personal boys' or 'right-hand boys': young men who they paid to perform such functions as carrying their weaponry and kit on jungle treks, obtaining and preparing food, building rough night shelters when needed, and teaching them Malay. These young men also filled the crucial role of acting as interpreters and go-betweens with local people: operatives were often deeply dependent on them.[25]

The more time they spent with these and other Dayaks, the more the operatives recognised their kindness, dignity and self-possession, as their personal accounts make clear. They also began to understand the wisdom of Carter's admonition to 'never throw your weight around'. Most Dayaks, they discovered, were averse to arrogance and pomposity, and adept at puncturing any sign of it in others, including Europeans. This talent appeared to be learned from an early age. Eadie:

> In the morning after I arrived at Long Akah, having posted the urgent W/T [wireless telegraphy] message and then handed over to the party W/T ops, I stood on the open ground looking up river and over the jungle and hills. It was a lovely sunny morning and I was feeling very pleased with myself, rather smug and self satisfied. A group of children had been playing jumping from the bank into the river and splashing back to the bank; but when they tired of that they came up towards me. Then a small voice said something right by my side. I smiled and nodded, not knowing what he had said. The voice a little louder piped up again and again I smiled and nodded. Then there was a tug on my trouser leg and the voice was more insistent. I smiled and patted the head of the small boy (whom I think of as wee Johnnie), but he tugged at my trouser leg again and spoke even louder. Then one of the older boys, probably about 8 or 9, burst into peals of laughter. He tried to say something but couldn't

for laughing. We all looked at him and at length, between roars of laughter and much pointing [he] said something which made all the others laugh also. The Australian weapon training sergeant was nearby and I caught sight of a smile on his face before he turned his back. So I asked him what had been said and after a bit of persuasion he told me. The older boy had said 'Isn't it funny, the big tuan [European] drops from the sky to help us fight and must know lots but he can't speak our language when even wee Johnnie (as I think of him) who is only three can speak it'. Even now when I realise I am feeling rather self important, I think of wee Johnnie.[26]

The operatives – like so many past visitors to the island – were also learning that most Dayaks love to laugh and are highly skilled at using humour to defuse potentially fraught situations. Early on during the party's stay at Long Akah, Hallam and Pare, the two signallers, had become annoyed at the number of young Kenyah men who clustered around their radio hut during every sked to watch them work. The Kenyahs' animated babble of conversation made it difficult for the signallers to hear any incoming transmissions, and they asked repeatedly for quiet. Yet they rarely got it. 'It became like a Portuguese Pub,' Hallam later ruefully noted.[27]

So the two men devised a plan. One day they connected the spare hand generator to two lengths of copper aerial wire that they then wrapped around the handrail on the landing of the radio hut. This was the same rail on which the Kenyahs sat or leaned as they smoked and chatted. They wore only bark loincloths,

leaving their bare bottoms in contact with our copper aerial wire [. . .] So on this particular evening when the noise level got too much we [. . .] changed to the other generator and gave her a good solid whirl – the result was very effective in fact

spectacular – those dyaks literally lifted off that rail like a flock
of sparrows following a 12 gauge discharge.[28]

It is difficult to see Hallam and Pare's behaviour here as anything other than highly provocative, directed towards people who
were, after all, their protectors and benefactors. In many parts of the
world – including our own – it might well have sparked a dangerous
'situation'. But not among the Kenyah.

When they realised what we had done to them they laughed
like hell – they were wonderful people with fantastic senses of
humour. & they paid us back in the form of little balls of mud
fired via their sumpits (blowpipes) into Wally and my backs as
we washed our only shirt in the Akah River the next day – big
pea shooter effect & stung like hell! But we agreed that we had
earned our treatment & they toned their chatter down while we
were trying to receive inward signals from then on.

The Kenyah response is quintessentially Dayak in its generosity and
yet refusal to be cowed: one from which many of us might learn. It is
a model in the use of laughter and play to achieve harmony.[29]

Quite independently of Carter's injunctions, the operatives –
many of them bearing the prejudices towards Asians and indigenous
peoples held by most Europeans at the time – were developing their
own surprising respect for these very different people among whom
they found themselves living. The life-saving Dayak humour was
undoubtedly key to this: almost every operative memoir comments
on it. But so too was operative recognition of the astonishing range of
skills and knowledges possessed by Dayaks, as their own deficiencies
in this most demanding of environments were increasingly laid bare.

Dayaks appeared to be familiar with every inch of the local
terrain, something that, as we have seen, operatives quickly

recognised as indispensable to any military planning. They also displayed a dazzling array of physical abilities. They could walk for hours through dense jungle at great speed without making a sound, even in the dark ('I was like a bulldozer in comparison,' Bill Beiers of Semut III told me); they could pick out a path through jungle or scrub invisible to their European counterparts; their skill with blowpipe and sword meant they rarely went without a meal during jungle journeys (unlike their gun-toting European comrades, who struggled to bag game); they could erect an overnight shelter in a matter of minutes; and they were wonderfully light and balanced in their movements.[30]

The latter not only bestowed their great dexterity with boats; it also enabled them to easily avoid obstacles on jungle paths, or to make their way across makeshift bridges. Eadie again:

> We came to a ravine which had to be crossed. The 'bridge' consisted of a round tree trunk, not very wide & devoid of branches which the locals with their bare feet and wonderful balance just walked across. I sat astride it, easing myself along it.

The image is unforgettable: the Dayaks stride across, upright and poised, while the white *tuan* is forced to pull himself across clumsily on his backside.[31]

Nor was it physical capabilities alone that impressed. 'They were intelligent people,' Bob Long told me years later, 'they caught on very quickly.' The advice Dayaks brought to military planning was considered and astute – they were 'master tacticians', wrote Walpole – as were the questions they asked in every longhouse the operatives visited as they sought support for the operation. The operatives were shocked to discover that they were already working out – through experimentation and observation – how to repair sophisticated European weapons they had never before encountered.[32]

A sea-change was occurring in operatives' attitudes. Having gone to Borneo secure in the knowledge of European superiority, they now found themselves utterly dependent on their Dayak allies not only for operational success but, indeed, for their own survival. As Tredrea told me later:

I went to Borneo thinking I'd need to teach the Dayaks how to operate and how to fight. But it turned out that it was mostly them teaching me. Without them I wouldn't have lasted a day.[33]

For their part, the Dayaks in the area were becoming accustomed to the strange *orang puteh* they had taken on as improbable allies. Years later, Dayaks from throughout Sarawak remembered the operatives with fondness. In comparison with their British colonial predecessors – whom some Dayaks saw as *sombong* or arrogant – the Semut men appeared more convivial, more accepting of local behaviours, and less concerned with status. If many Dayaks had been disappointed at the loss of potency demonstrated by their European rulers when the Japanese arrived, they were now discovering ways to appreciate *orang puteh* as allies.

In large part this can be attributed to the insistence of their party leaders that the operatives treat Dayaks with respect and work hard to accommodate local custom: 'Harrisson kept reminding us that it was their country, not ours,' Long remembered later. But it also owes much to the operatives' love of jokes and laughter – often seen as an Australian trait, but exhibited by almost all the Semut operatives, regardless of nationality. Just as most operative memoirs make mention of the Dayak sense of humour, so many Dayak accounts, even seventy years later, celebrate the same quality in the operatives. It might seem strange that this should be so important, if countless tales of war had not already made clear the key role of laughter in the creation of effective military partnerships.[34]

ᠺᠥ

On 19 June, a week after the Labuan landings, Carter received a signal from Courtney that radically altered his perception of the entire Borneo campaign.

> There will be NO rpt NO army penetration inland. You are now granted freedom of action for guerrilla forces [. . .] Good hunting.[35]

Contrary to Carter's expectations, once 9th Division forces had taken the coastal strip, they would not be moving inland. Their orders were simply to take and hold the strip. This meant that the only opposition to Japanese forces up the Baram, Tinjar and Tutoh Rivers – where Carter was convinced they would flee – would have to come from Semut forces themselves, operating with local guerrillas.

Carter was outraged and mortified. He had recruited local people to Semut II on the explicit understanding that once Allied forces invaded they would not only protect locals from reprisals, but would free the entire island of Japanese. Now he faced a situation in which thousands of Japanese troops might well move inland to escape the invasion and end up beyond 9th Division's designated sphere of operation, with only his own tiny, under-resourced force to prevent them from inflicting devastation on Dayak areas. As he saw it, if this happened, Dayaks in those inland areas would be much worse off than had 9th Division not invaded. 'Great was our disillusionment,' he commented in his later report.[36]

There was no option but for Semut II to take up the slack. The insertion of three more personnel – Sergeant Norman 'Norm'

Gilman, Corporal Neville Graham and Private Douglas 'Doug' Davey – on 20 June, plus Carter's increasing alarm at reports he was receiving about Japanese movements, galvanised him into action. On 20 June he sent a signal to Courtney at HQ: 'Essential I attack and going Marudi at once.'[37]

Carter's first move was to send Mason and signaller Duffus to the Tinjar River to reinforce Horsnell and The. He then dispatched the experienced Wilson along with Davey downstream towards Marudi, to spy out the land and carry out guerrilla attacks on Japanese in the lower Baram River area. This was an escalation of his strategy of fooling the enemy into believing the Baram was overrun with Allied soldiers. If Europeans were seen to be attacking Japanese, it would add credence to the rumours.

Wilson and Davey arrived at Lubok Nibong, a prosperous community surrounded by rubber tree plantations and market gardens 3 miles (5 km) upriver from Marudi, on 24 June. Carter had arranged for a group of the Iban and Chinese guerrillas Horsnell and The had been training on the nearby Tinjar River to join them, giving Wilson an overall party of around twenty. Wilson's first action on arrival was to send out Iban scouts to reconnoitre the area around Marudi.

The party was called into action almost immediately. The following day – 25 June – Wilson's scouts brought him news of a canoe containing Japanese soldiers travelling upstream from Marudi. Wilson hurriedly put together an ambush on the Baram River close to Lubok Nibong. It proved devastatingly effective. All on board the boat – one officer plus four other ranks – were killed. However, during the skirmish Semut II sustained its own first serious casualty: one Chinese guerrilla also died.[38]

Next day Wilson's party was reinforced by the arrival of Gilman, Fidler and Graham plus a Bren gun. But Wilson was concerned about the Japanese response to his ambush: he feared that a strong Japanese force would soon be despatched upriver. Since his own party was still very small – five operatives plus fifteen or so partly trained and poorly armed guerrillas – he decided to withdraw to a better defensive position. That night he moved upstream to Kuala Tinjar, where the Tinjar River flows into the Baram. Here the party was able to occupy a strategic position commanding both river approaches.[39]

The following morning (27 June) brought astonishing news: according to Wilson's scouts, the Japanese had quite suddenly evacuated Marudi. In fact, as Wilson was to discover later, his strike at Lubok Nibong had been an extraordinarily lucky one. The Japanese officer killed was the chief Intelligence Officer of the Miri force who had, ironically, been sent to Marudi to investigate rumours about the presence of Europeans and armed Dayaks in the interior. The loss of the party served to completely unnerve the Japanese garrison in Marudi: they fled almost immediately back to HQ, now at Nyabor. The rumours diligently spread by Carter's spies, about an advance by hundreds of Allied soldiers and Dayak headhunters, were doing their job.[40]

That night, Wilson sent Gilman and Fidler with a handful of guerrillas to reconnoitre Marudi and, if possible, to occupy it. Moving downriver in the dark, the group reached Lubok Nibong – the site of Wilson's successful ambush two days earlier – and sent scouts ahead to check whether the rumour they had heard was true. The scouts soon returned to confirm the earlier news: there were no Japanese remaining in Marudi.

The party cautiously entered the town the next morning. It was in an uproar. After the Japanese withdrawal a group of Ibans living nearby had taken advantage of the power vacuum to loot the Brooke Residency building as well as the Chinese bazaar. This had inspired some town residents to follow suit and pillage the houses of residents who had earlier fled upriver to escape the Japanese.[41]

Gilman's force put a stop to the looting and established order. However, after sizing up the situation, Gilman decided that the town would be impossible to defend if the Japanese should return at strength. He retreated back upriver to Lubok Nibong and established a command post. From there his men conducted a careful patrol of Marudi and its environs each day.[42]

∽

While Wilson's party had begun operating around Marudi, Carter himself, on 26 June, had left Long Akah. With him came Eadie and Hallam, as well as Tama Weng Ajeng leading a troop of around forty Kenyahs equipped with firearms. They travelled slowly down the Baram River, stopping at most longhouses along the way. Carter was keen to meet with longhouse heads not only to recruit men for his push downriver, but also to encourage those who stayed behind to handle – largely through the use of ambush and trickery, since they had no firearms – any small parties of Japanese who might come into the area. The acquisition of more heads was, of course, a major selling point and everywhere Carter stopped locals promised to play their part. As he advanced he also gathered intelligence about Japanese positions and movements. Sent on to Labuan, this would be used by Courtney to arrange RAAF attacks on enemy targets.

At every longhouse, enthusiastic new recruits joined the party, seemingly undeterred by the lack of firearms. Accordingly, by the time the party reached Long Lama on 29 June the party comprised a flotilla of canoes.[43]

At Long Lama, Carter established his forward HQ in the fort that had recently been taken from the Japanese by Sheppard and his men. Wilson arrived later the same day from Kuala Tinjar. The following morning – 30 June – a Catalina seaplane landed on the Baram downstream from Long Lama, on a stretch of river that the party had earlier spent hours clearing of debris. It brought not only stores and weapons, but also Carter's commanding officer, Jumbo Courtney, for a conference.[44]

Carter was anxious to advance his plan to control the Baram River basin and the first step, as he saw it, was to occupy Marudi. The town was key both for its strategic location and because of the psychological advantage its occupation would confer. The information Wilson brought concerning the chaotic scenes there after the Japanese departure only increased Carter's sense of urgency. It was agreed that he would move on to Marudi as soon as he had transferred his main HQ – consisting primarily of signallers operating the party's Boston radio, and medical personnel – downriver from Long Akah.[45]

When he left, Courtney took with him Le Guier, who had become seriously ill, as well as the two Japanese prisoners transported downriver from Long Akah: they were to be delivered to 9th Division for interrogation purposes. Courtney had hoped also to take his radio expert, Eadie. But Eadie was reluctant to return to the sterility of life at HQ and was not to be found when it came time for the plane to depart.

Over the next few days those men who had remained at Long Akah followed Carter downriver to Long Lama. Wilson, meanwhile, moved forward from Kuala Tinjar to join Gilman's patrol at Lubok Nibong, just outside Marudi. Carter himself transferred his forward HQ from Long Lama to Kuala Tinjar, less than 10 miles (16 km), as the crow flies, from the town. He was closing in on his target.[46]

ᘒ

With Carter's attention focused on Marudi, a new threat suddenly appeared elsewhere. A day or so after Wilson's return to Lubok Nibong, Iban scouts reported to him that a Japanese force had appeared on the main track due east of Lubok Nibong, around four hours march away, heading west towards the Baram River. This was too close for comfort.

Wilson promptly sent Fidler with an Iban patrol to the area, to observe the force. They caught up with its advance guard later that day and shots were exchanged, although it was unclear whether any Japanese had been hit. Next day Fidler's party followed the advance guard as it moved back eastward, eventually rejoining the main force at the Kalijau River, which flows into the Tutoh River not far southeast of Marudi. The Ibans in Fidler's party managed to cut out three enemy stragglers and take their heads.[47]

The appearance of this force served to reinforce Carter's fears concerning a possible Japanese move inland in response to the Australian invasion. The arrival of the force's advance guard on the Lubok Nibong track heading towards the Baram River suggested that it may have intended to use the Baram as an avenue to the interior. However, as a result of the skirmish with Fidler's party the force had turned away from the Baram and was now heading instead directly for the Tutoh River.

Carter had foreseen from the start of the operation that Japanese forces would attempt to escape up the Tutoh River. Consequently he had, in early June, sent Wood and Pippen with around a dozen Kenyah guerrillas – via Long Pilah, from where they went on to take part in the raid on the radio station at Long Lama – to the large Berawan longhouse at Long Beruang on the Tutoh. Their orders had been to recruit and train local Dayaks in readiness for any Japanese incursions into the area.[48]

However, Wood had misunderstood his orders. When the AIF landed at Brunei Bay on 10 June – shortly after his arrival at Long Beruang – he had removed his party from the longhouse and travelled overland to Limbang, inland from Brunei Bay, to join up with the invading 9th Division forces there. The Tutoh River, and Long Beruang, had been left unprotected and unprepared.[49]

Consequently, Carter was worried about the new enemy force. He was particularly concerned that it might still find its way to the

Baram River where it could prey on the many Dayak longhouses lining the river's banks as it moved further inland. So, on 6 July, he sent Wood – newly returned from Limbang – and Conleth-Smith, along with a small party of Bukit guerrillas from the Tutoh River, in pursuit of the force. Their orders were to guard the crossings of the lower Tutoh – where the Japanese force was soon expected – and to report any movement towards the Baram.

A day or so later, Wood sent a message to Carter requesting additional men to help him manage what appeared to be a large number of enemy troops. In response, Carter sent Graham and Davey with a party of Kenyah guerrillas from Long Ikang – an important Kenyah longhouse on the Baram River close to the mouth of the Tutoh – under the leadership of their longhouse head Gau. He also asked Courtney to arrange for the RAAF to strafe the enemy column.[50]

∞

The new threat to his east notwithstanding, Carter's primary focus remained northward, on Marudi. He was pragmatic enough to recognise that while the Japanese appeared to have abandoned the town, it might be only a few days before they realised the true size of his party and returned. He was determined to seize the town while he could. On 8 July Courtney again visited, his Catalina this time landing on the Baram River close to Kuala Tinjar where Carter now had his forward HQ.[51]

The following day, 9 July, Carter took his force downriver to Marudi.

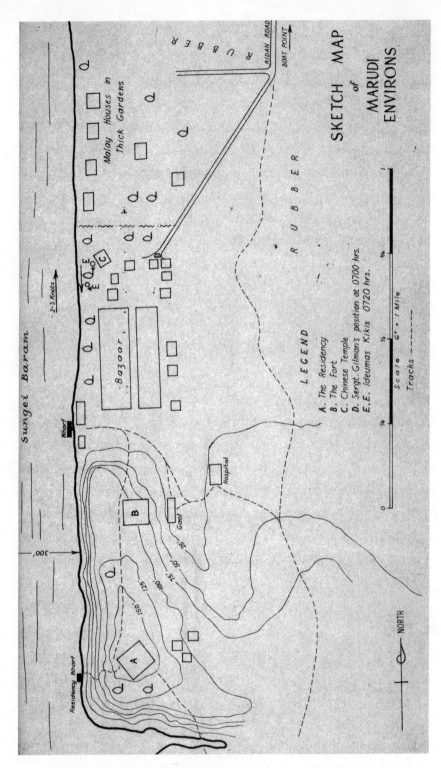

Marudi in 1945 as drawn by Robert Wilson of Semut II.

From the Australian War Memorial National Collection (ref AWM 54 619/7/79)

8

AMBUSH AT MARUDI

THE GRACIOUS OLD TOWN of Marudi nestles at the edge of the Baram River around 40 miles (64 km) as the crow flies from where it finally empties into the South China Sea. Today it is possible to drive to Marudi in around one and three quarter hours – or even to take a 20-minute flight – from Miri. But in 1945 the town was accessible only by river, or by overland tracks from Miri, Beluru, Seria and other nearby settlements. In spite of the twenty-first-century influx of motorcycles, cars and even the occasional tourist, it retains the elegance it exhibited before the war.

Marudi now contains close to 100,000 inhabitants, including substantial numbers of Kayans, Kenyahs, Penans, and related peoples, and their presence imbues it with a special character. But in 1945 its population totalled only around 1500 people, largely Chinese and Malay, although communities of Ibans and Kayans lived nearby.[1]

The town itself was focused around the Chinese bazaar, which consisted of two lines of dilapidated Chinese wooden shophouses, one behind the other, running parallel to the river. The houses were joined together in the traditional style into separate rows, each with a covered wooden walkway running down the front. The front line (closest to the river) contained thirty-one shophouses built in four rows, and the back one twenty-seven shophouses built in three rows. A Chinese temple erected in 1891 stood on the downstream side of the bazaar very close to the river (it is still there today), and slightly further downstream again was the Malay precinct of wooden houses surrounded by thick gardens.[2]

Before the war, Marudi had been the centre of administration for the entire Baram River basin. Brooke dominion over the area was spelled out in the imposing Fort Hose – a timber structure built in 1901 and named, surprisingly, after a former Resident of the Baram District rather than the more usual Brooke family member – which stood on a hill above the town overlooking the river, with the graceful Residency building nearby. Befitting the town's status as local seat of government, this was a far more impressive fort than those found at Long Akah and Long Lama, granting fine views across the Chinese bazaar and the river below. The fort burned down in 1994 but was rebuilt to the original design in 1996; today it still stands, in its current guise as the Baram Regional Museum.

Prior to the Japanese occupation, Marudi had been a flourishing commercial centre: rubber plantations and gardens for vegetables and other cash crops were located nearby, and it was a hub for trade in jungle produce collected largely by Dayaks. However, few signs of prosperity remained as Carter's force cautiously entered the town late in the morning of 9 July 1945.

Some of the Chinese shophouses had long been shuttered and empty, their owners having fled upriver, fearing persecution, when the Japanese took over. Those still open contained little to sell as a result of Japanese restrictions on trade and the effects of the Allied blockade. To make matters worse, in the preceding days the bazaar had been looted by Ibans from nearby settlements. It was a wretched town that confronted Carter's men that morning.

∾

By the time the party arrived at the wharf the word was out, and Marudi's residents had already begun to gather. Carter had by now collected so many local recruits that his retinue was very large. As an old Chinese man who was there that day told me seventy years later:

> There were many many boats – the river was full of boats. We were happy and excited – if we had any firecrackers we would have let them off! The white people had finally remembered us and come back with an army to fight the Japanese.[3]

Of the twenty men (including Conleth-Smith) who had originally comprised Carter's overall operative force, four (Horsnell, Duffus, Mason and The) had been sent to the Tinjar River, and another four (Wood, Graham, Davey and Conleth-Smith) had been despatched to the Tutoh River. Pippen had travelled to Limbang with Wood several weeks earlier, and had never returned to the operation (he later joined Semut III), and Le Guier had been invalided out to Labuan, also never to return. This left ten operatives (Carter, Wilson, McCallum, Eadie, Gilman, Hallam, Pare, Sheppard, Neave and Fidler) to take part in the occupation of Marudi.

In addition to Carter's group of ten operatives, the party contained Tama Weng and his troop of approximately forty trained Kenyahs, plus scores of new recruits – mostly Kayan – collected en route down the Baram River. There were also scouts, guides, porters, paddlers and others who worked for the operation in a range of diverse roles, including the 'personal boys' many of the operatives now employed. Dozens of canoes, including an extremely large one capable of holding one hundred people – many of them flying flags including the Union Jack and the Sarawak Banner – transported this huge congregation to the wharf under the goggle-eyed gaze of the local population.[4]

Carter immediately established his HQ in the fort – with the indomitable Tama Weng beside him – and took up quarters in the Residency. The task he faced was two-pronged: military and civil. His military role was to eliminate as many Japanese as possible from the area and prevent the remainder from heading inland up the Baram and nearby rivers. His civil role was equally as challenging: he was effectively now in charge of government in Marudi and responsible for the wellbeing of its people.

But military matters quickly took precedence. At around 8 pm the same evening two exhausted Malay men arrived at the fort after a hard, fast paddle up the Baram River. They brought urgent intelligence: Chinese spies in the pay of the *Kempei Tai* had informed the Japanese that a tiny Allied party had occupied Marudi. In response, an eighty-strong force had been sent from Bakong that morning. Its mission was to liquidate Carter's party.[5]

The information the men brought was precise. The enemy force was travelling by river: down the Bakong River to where it joins the Baram River around 10 miles (16 km), as the crow flies, downstream from Marudi, and then a longer haul up the winding Baram to the town. It was travelling in single file in five canoes, paddled by Japanese soldiers rather than locals. When questioned, the Malays estimated that if the boats maintained their present rate, they would reach Marudi around midnight. Carter calculated that he had just enough time to prepare an ambush.[6]

First he needed to establish where the Japanese normally landed when they came upstream to Marudi in local craft (as opposed to motorboats). He learnt that instead of coming to the wharf where his own party had landed they stopped at a landing point further down the Baram River. From this point, known as Ridan, the Baram embarks upon a final flamboyant loop before it eventually reaches the town wharf. The Ridan Road, on the other hand, runs straight across country for around three-quarters of a mile (1.2 km) to the Marudi bazaar, thus providing a faster – and less conspicuous – route into the town. It was certain that the enemy convoy would land at Ridan.

It was now too dark to reconnoitre the area around Ridan and further downriver, so Carter had no choice but to rely on the knowledge of locals as well as his party's rudimentary maps. After discussions with Wilson, Tama Weng and local leaders, it was agreed that the obvious location for the ambush was slightly downstream from the Ridan landing point.

It was a still, moonless night as the men left the fort, taking with them every Bren gun they had in addition to their more usual weapons. Descending the hill to the strangely empty bazaar, they entered the Ridan Road, moving as quietly as they could in the dense darkness. They were guided by Datuk Tuanku Taha, a Malay who had been the District Native Officer in Marudi during the Brooke era. Kept on – and trusted – by the Japanese, Datuk now threw his support behind Semut II. He led them along the Ridan Road – thick rubber plantations and gardens deeper sources of shadow on either side – towards the Ridan landing point on the Baram River.[7]

෨ৎ

The party totalled, in all, ten operatives and around fifty armed guerrillas. Tama Weng's Kenyahs made up the bulk of the guerrilla force, but it also included Kayans, Chinese and Ibans recruited over the preceding weeks, along with several of the former Dutch East Indies soldiers who were mostly tasked with transporting, reloading, and carrying spare barrels and magazines for the Bren guns. Shortly after leaving the fort the party was joined by a large group of the untrained Kayans recruited by Carter as he travelled downriver, plus perhaps twenty to thirty untrained Ibans. Carter estimated later that around one hundred Dayaks armed only with spears and *parangs* ended up accompanying the party.

Once they reached the river, Carter placed his men carefully. He knew that the usual Japanese pattern when travelling in convoy on rivers in the area was for smaller boats to flank any larger ones. The Malay informants had told him that the Japanese were travelling in five boats – four small and one large – and his expectation was that one of the smaller boats would be first in line, followed by the large one. Accordingly he decided to place one Bren gunner 300 yards (274 m) or so downstream from the landing point, a second around 50–100 yards (45–90 m) downstream, and three more at the landing point itself. The plan was for the gunner furthest downstream to allow the first two boats to pass by, and then open fire on the third. That would be the signal for the others to fire on the two earlier boats – one of which should be the largest – now conveniently in line with them.[8]

Guided by a local Ridan Malay, Wilson and Fidler – the latter with a Bren gun and an Iban loader – moved carefully downriver through a dense grove of rubber trees to the mouth of the tiny Ridan River, a narrow waterway which flows behind Marudi town. Here they were forced to halt and take up position. The location was not ideal: it would have been better to allow more distance between themselves and the main force stationed upstream. But it was too dangerous in the dark for them to attempt to cross the Ridan River and move further downstream.

Perhaps 200 yards (180 m) upstream from Wilson and Fidler, between the Ridan River and the landing point, Gilman was stationed with a Bren and a loader, plus eight Chinese guerrillas who were spread out in the thick rubber jungle. Fifty yards (46 m) further upstream again, in the clearing at the landing point itself, were the remainder of the force: Carter, Sheppard, Hallam, Neave, McCallum, Eadie, Pare and Tama Weng's Kenyah guerrillas. Sheppard, Hallam and Neave, each with a Bren and a man to load it, took up positions on the riverbank with the Kenyahs on each side of them, while Carter, McCallum, Eadie and Pare placed themselves nearby. The untrained Kayans and Ibans were positioned in the jungle behind.[9]

Shortly after 11 pm, every man was in place. The forty-odd burning oil wells at Seria on the coast around 40 miles (64 km) away – set on fire by the Japanese in response to the Allied landings – produced a great red glow on the northern horizon, like a scene from a grotesque medieval depiction of hell. It cast an eerie blush across the dark ribbon of the river. Otherwise, apart from a campfire that appeared further downstream around midnight, there was no light.

Midnight passed and the Japanese had not come. Nevertheless the party waited, knowing that Japanese soldiers preferred to attack at dawn. Carter had given strict orders that no-one was to make a sound until Fidler opened fire downstream, and so most spent the hours cramped and uncomfortable, shifting cautiously from one leg to the other to ease their aches as the river mist floated around them. Stiffness and damp mist were not the extent of their afflictions. As Apoi Anggang – a member of Tama Weng's Kenyah troop that night – recounted to me years later:

> We were told to keep completely quiet. No movement, no sound. It was difficult. The place was full of mosquitoes. How can you kill a mosquito without moving or making a sound?![10]

Around 5 am, Wilson, in the forward position with Fidler, heard slight sounds downriver: soft chatter and the swishes and thumps of a boat being inexpertly paddled. Ten minutes later a small canoe containing seven Japanese soldiers, all wearing steel helmets, slid in front of him, visible in the light from the fires. The Semut men later discovered that the campfire downstream had belonged to the Japanese force, which had decided to camp out for the night and attack the town at dawn. As agreed with Carter, Wilson and Fidler allowed this first boat to pass by.

Other boats could be heard approaching and five minutes later a second, larger one containing eleven men came into sight. Wilson estimated that this one was about 150–200 yards (135–185 m) behind the first: this meant that the first boat must now be close to the landing point and he could afford to wait no longer. He ordered Fidler to fire. The boat's passengers were clearly outlined against the oil-fire glow, creating a near perfect target as Fidler subjected them to a long and vicious burst from the Bren. Japanese soldiers went down in all directions and the boat overturned.[11]

Further upriver, as the first tentative glimmers of dawn arrived, Hallam could just make out the leading canoe, its black shape silhouetted against the water. But he waited for the sound of Fidler's gun:

> The wait was only a minute or so but seemed like forever as I could now hear the Japs talking quietly to each other in the 2 leading prows [prahus, i.e. boats] – then all hell broke loose & I opened up.

To Hallam's horror the river lit up brilliantly in front of him.

> It was then I realised that I had put a mix of 1 in 3 tracers in my mags and it frightened me – goodness knows what it did to those Nips who were left to see the firework display. I later thought they must have thought that they were up against at least a full infantry company.[12]

Sheppard, Neave, the Kenyahs and the other operatives also opened fire on the first boat, as did Gilman and his small Chinese force. As Wilson later commented: 'Few of them could have seen the target, but the volume of fire developed was enormous.'[13]

Several men managed to escape from the two leading boats and reach the bank, only a couple of yards away from Carter's main party. One shouted 'don't shoot', heard clearly above the ruckus. Confusion and shock set in immediately among Carter's men: had they accidentally ambushed a company from the invading 9th Australian Division?

> [B]ut then the Nip added 'I am English' so I gave him a grenade & still he stood up with a bayonet in one hand & a grenade in the other – I couldn't get another shot at him as Kenyahs came from behind dropping their -303s & drawing parangs – his head was off before his body dropped beside my Bren.[14]

All those Japanese in the leading two boats who had not disappeared into the river were rapidly discovered and dispatched, mostly by the Kenyahs and Ibans. Four heads were taken.[15]

Then absolute quiet, shocking after the deafening racket of the gunfire. For two or three minutes it held, and Carter's force began to wonder if the enemy was retreating. But it was not to be.

> I heard an old familiar New Guinea sound – a crisp bang & 20 or 30 seconds later an explosion behind me in the rubber trees – I knew Nip mortars & and that they were 'naturals' & only needed one 'sighter' so looked around for an order & saw old Toby heading up the rubber plantation's track towards Marudi – I knew what to do then OK.[16]

It seemed the Japanese had broken the mould that morning and the larger boat, containing around sixty soldiers, had been travelling towards the rear of the convoy. When the firing began it made its way to the opposite bank, around 200–300 yards (180–275 m) downriver. From there its personnel were now firing on Carter's force with their own formidable weaponry.

Carter, who had himself served in New Guinea, was no doubt also familiar with the sound of a Japanese mortar. He knew that at most twenty Japanese had been killed out of a force estimated at around eighty, and that these soldiers were, in general, vastly better-trained and better-armed than his own. While it appeared that most remaining enemy soldiers were on the opposite side of the Baram, they were likely to cross the river further downstream before too long. And once across they would have no difficulty making their way through the jungle towards Marudi. If they moved quickly enough they could cut off Carter's party from the town and fort. The result would be catastrophic.[17]

Consequently, as a second mortar followed the first and machine-gun fire spattered around the landing point, Carter ordered the party back to Marudi at speed.

ↄ◌

The men streamed down the Ridan Road towards the town. They reached Marudi just as the Chinese shops in the bazaar were beginning to unshutter. Carter posted Gilman with his Bren and two unarmed locals to act as his 'seconds' – carrying spare magazines and grenades – as a rearguard at the entrance to the bazaar. Gilman's orders were to guard the Ridan Road and nearby tracks leading into the town.[18]

Some of those in Carter's party felt sure the Japanese – following their usual pattern of dawn attacks – would not now move into Marudi until the following morning. They argued that the best course of action was to sit tight and await intelligence on the size and location of the enemy force. Others, however, were not so sure: the aggression displayed at the ambush site, and the efficiency with which the enemy force had reorganised and attacked its ambushers, suggested these were front-line troops rather than the poorly trained ones usually seen in inland areas. This, together with the size of the force, indicated that the leadership at Japanese HQ regarded Carter's party as a serious threat to its rear, and was bent on elimination. The enemy might well decide to press its advantage immediately.

The debate was rapidly resolved. Shortly after the party reached the fort not long after 7 am, they heard the frightening clatter of a Japanese Kiki machine gun from the direction of the bazaar. This was quickly followed by the equally unmistakable clamour of a responding Bren. Gilman was already in action.[19]

It was clear that the Japanese were not planning to wait before mounting an offensive. Rather, it was odds-on that they would shortly attack the fort from a different direction, probably via the jungle on the eastern side of the Residency. Carter estimated the enemy force still contained around sixty well-trained soldiers equipped with mortars and automatic weapons. Given his own lack of trained personnel and, especially, weaponry, there was no possibility of defending the town. He ordered an immediate retreat upriver.[20]

Tama Weng Ajeng rapidly organised boats – including two large ones with outboard motors – to leave from the Residency wharf slightly upstream from Marudi. By now many residents of the town had decided to join the exodus, fearing the consequences of a Japanese reoccupation. This produced a logistical nightmare, with hundreds of people scrambling down the rugged track leading from the Residency to the landing point. Carter set up a rearguard consisting of Wilson, Sheppard and fifteen to twenty Kenyah riflemen close to the Residency to guard the track's entrance from any advancing Japanese.

The main party left the wharf in a long straggle of boats at around 10.30 am. An hour or so later – with no further sign of the enemy – the rearguard followed down the path. Gilman still had not

made contact and his whereabouts were unknown. But there was no
more time to spare. On reaching the wharf the rearguard discovered
the unflappable Tama Weng waiting with the last boat.[21]

The party retreated upriver to Kuala Tinjar, scene of their optimistic departure for Marudi only the previous morning. There
Carter received news from Wood, who had been sent with a small
force to the Tutoh River some days earlier. His report shocked
Carter.

၆၅

The Tutoh emanates from the same rugged territory that Carter's
party had struggled across on its original journey to Long Lellang
and Long Akah almost three months earlier, winding its way through
a countryside of endless peaks and troughs. But in its lower reaches,
close to its union with the Baram, it flowed in 1945 through a flat
landscape – much of it boggy – covered in dense jungle that crowded
the river's banks. Wood and Conleth-Smith sensibly opted to settle
at the longhouse of their Bukit guerrillas, close to the mountainous
area of Batu Belah and slightly upstream from the small Chinese
settlement of Linei.

Wood had scouts reporting to him on the progress of the
Japanese force Carter had sent his party to observe. He knew that it
was heading across country from the Kalijau River making almost
directly for Linei. He was convinced it would attempt to cross the
Tutoh there and – while his force was not strong enough to oppose
it openly – believed he could ambush it, given sufficient men.
Accordingly he had contacted Carter several days earlier to request
reinforcements.

In response to this request, Graham and Davey had been sent,
along with a party of Kenyah guerrillas from Long Ikang under
the leadership of their longhouse head Gau. If Tama Weng was the
pre-eminent Kenyah chief on the Baram, the younger Gau – also a

penghulu – was his right-hand man, and an imposing leader in his own right. MacDonald later provided a memorable portrait of his face 'lined with wrinkles of thought and care and laughter'.[22]

On the evening of 8 July, just before dark, the Japanese advance guard – estimated at around ten to fifteen men – arrived at the bank of the Tutoh River opposite Linei and shouted for boats to cross the river. Wood, Gau and their men – having reached the area earlier – had removed all boats from the Japanese side of the river and were waiting, hidden, on the opposite bank. Conleth-Smith, who spoke some Japanese from his time as a POW, called back that there were currently no boats at Linei, but that next morning some would be available at Linei Kecil, a small Iban hamlet a mile or two further downstream.

Later that night Wood's party moved quietly downriver to Linei Kecil. Once again they removed all boats from the hamlet, taking them across the Tutoh River. An overland track ran directly to the Baram River from a point on Wood's side of the Tutoh, around 50 or 60 yards (45 or 55 m) below the hamlet; Wood was convinced the Japanese intended to use it to reach the Baram. His plan – hatched with Gau – was to ambush them as they crossed the Tutoh to the start of the track.

In keeping with the plan, Wood posted Graham, with his Bren gun, downstream from the track with instructions to sweep the river upstream. Wood, Davey, Conleth-Smith and some of their Bukit and Kenyah guerrillas lay concealed by jungle on the bank directly opposite Linei Kecil, cradling their carbines and rifles. A small boat was tied to the landing at the start of the track, in full view of the hamlet. Gau and Bakar, one of the Bukit guerrillas in the party, were clearly visible nearby.[23]

An hour after dawn several Japanese appeared out of the trees at Linei Kecil. On discovering that there were no boats in the hamlet, they called across to Gau and Bakar, asking them to bring their boat across the river. The scene played out exactly as Wood and Gau had planned. Gau and Bakar poled the boat to where the Japanese were waiting, five or six Japanese climbed in, and the two guerrillas began poling back towards the start of the track. But when they reached the deep channel in the centre of the river Gau and Bakar, in a concerted movement, capsized the boat. While they swam underwater downriver as fast as they could, the Japanese were left in the water, far from either bank, struggling under the weight of their heavy gear.

This was the signal to fire and the sound of gunshots shattered the early morning quiet. Wood, Davey and Conleth-Smith focused on those Japanese in the water with their carbines while Graham raked the opposite bank – where the remaining Japanese were clustered – with his Bren. Wood later estimated that five enemy soldiers were killed, and an unknown number injured. When Wood's party finally crossed the river to the hamlet they found no Japanese; nor was there any sign of its Iban inhabitants. But two houses had burned down (probably set alight by tracer from the Bren) and others had been looted, presumably by the Japanese.[24]

Wood was uncertain of the effect this action might have on the larger enemy force. But he was convinced that it would attempt another crossing of the Tutoh River as part of a move westwards, towards the Baram. He had no reliable intelligence about the quality of the force or its weaponry, but he knew from his scouts that he was massively outnumbered. As a result, he left Conleth-Smith with two Bukit guerrillas at the start of the track to watch the river crossing for forty-eight hours while he, with the remainder of the party, retreated downriver. Arriving at Long Kiput, a settlement on the Baram River close to the mouth of the Tutoh, he sent his report to Carter.[25]

‎§

Wood's message shook Carter. A force of what appeared to be crack enemy troops was in the process of taking Marudi on the Baram River itself, and fifteen hundred or so Japanese soldiers were close by to the west, threatening to move inland along the Baram's major tributary, the Tinjar River, where he had only a very insubstantial party in place. Now he learned that another large Japanese force had travelled inland to the Baram's other main tributary, the Tutoh River. The nightmare he had warned of all along appeared to be coming true.

Accordingly, he decided to withdraw further up the Baram River to Long Murik, not far downriver from Long Lama. A defensive position there would allow him to cover not only the main overland routes from the lower Tutoh and Tinjar Rivers to the Baram, but to defend the Baram River itself should the Japanese decide to advance up it in force.

Wood's party quickly joined him and by 13 July the entire Semut II force – with the exception of Horsnell, The, Mason and Duffus on the Tinjar River, and Gilman who had still not reappeared – were concentrated at Long Murik. Gilman arrived a day or two later. He had escaped from Marudi several hours after the rearguard and joined up with a small group of Iban guerrillas who saw him safely upriver to Carter's new HQ.[26]

The party was secure for the moment. But the retreat to Long Murik meant that the entire lower Baram River – including the area's main town and communications centre – had effectively been ceded to the enemy. This was deeply demoralising for both operatives and guerrillas. Nor did Carter's problems end there. Weapons, wireless sets, and stores – as well as code books and money locked in the fort's safe – had been left in Marudi in the party's haste to evacuate. In addition, Carter worried that the Japanese HQ to the west at Nyabor would now have precise information about the size and location of his force, and might choose to act on

this by coming upriver at strength. On top of all this, the party had
collected hundreds of refugees from Marudi who had to be fed
and housed.[27]

Nevertheless, Carter had been extraordinarily lucky: his force
had suffered almost no casualties. He later confirmed that the
Japanese party sent to Marudi not only contained many more –
better trained and armed – men than Carter's own, but was indeed
composed of first-class troops. His own men were fortunate not to
have been pinned down after the ambush, before they had time
to retreat from the town. And if the two Malays had not made the
brave trip upriver to warn them in the first place, their losses might
well have been calamitous.

But not everyone had got out. Left behind was a Chinese guerrilla who was the only Allied casualty of the ambush. He had been
shot through both knees by friendly fire and was unable to evacuate
the town. While Carter lists him as having been subsequently killed
by the Japanese, Hallam records that he hanged himself the same
night in fear of what the Japanese would do to him when they re-
entered the town.[28]

ᏉᎧ

Carter was not easily beaten. Having reported to Courtney the
results of the Marudi operation – rather optimistically declaring it
a 'modified success' – he decided to throw himself on the mercy of
the invading 9th Australian Division. In spite of the Division's stated
refusal to move inland from the coastal strip, Carter hoped – as a
reasonable man himself – that its command could be persuaded to
change its mind and help him reoccupy the town.[29]

Soon after the 9th Division landings at Brunei Bay on 10 June,
its 20th Brigade had begun pushing southwest into the coastal parts
of Semut II's territory. By 13 June it had taken Brunei Town (now
Bandar Seri Begawan) where it established its HQ. From there it had

sent troops down the coast towards the Baram River. On 21 June
the furiously burning oil town of Seria – not much more than
20 miles (32 km) east of the mouth of the Baram – was occupied by
the 2/17th Battalion.

While the 2/17th was advancing down the coast on foot, the
2/13th was approaching the key coastal town of Miri, further southwest, from the sea. Leaving Brunei Bay via landing ships on 19 June,
its men had passed the great fires at Seria around dawn on the 20th,
and landed at Lutong, just north of Miri, later that morning. Lutong
was taken without opposition and three days later, on 23 June,
Miri was entered and found to be unoccupied, just as Carter had
predicted.[30]

Since taking Miri, the 20th Brigade had advanced further into
Semut II's territory. On 24 June the 2/17th Battalion had occupied
Kuala Belait, where the Belait River meets the sea, around 15 miles
(24 km) due east of the mouth of the Baram River. On 26 June
one of its patrols arrived at the north bank of the Baram, while a
patrol of the 2/13th, which had been extending its control steadily northward from Lutong, arrived at the south bank the same day.
The Brigade's commanding officer, Brigadier Victor Windeyer, was
himself now in Kuala Belait. Carter arranged through Courtney to
fly there to meet with him.

The Long Murik position had the advantage of a cleared
Catalina landing reach. Carter – along with Eadie and Davey – was
collected from there on 13 July. Davey was sent with the two officers ostensibly because he had good on-the-ground knowledge of the
area around Marudi. However, Carter may have had other reasons
for taking him. Carter would have known about existing tensions
between SRD and 9th Division and, wily negotiator that he was,
may have felt it wise to include an Australian in the party.[31]

ᕲᕳ

Relations between 9th Division and Semut parties in the field were often fractious. In large part this appears to have resulted from an almost criminal absence of communication between their respective HQs concerning the activities of the various Semut groups. While there are few documents that cast light on this, the blame should probably be shared.

Conventional military units, like 9th Division, tend to be suspicious of special forces soldiers, often regarding them as prima donnas who make little difference to the final outcome of a war. Indeed, during WWII, 'special warfare' was not yet an accepted part of Australian military doctrine. As a result, 9th Division never fully appreciated how useful Semut might be in supporting the Brunei Bay invasion.[32]

The suspicion was likely intensified in this case by the fact of SRD's largely British leadership – in the Division's order of battle for the Labuan landings, SRD parties in the area were described as 'British units' – triggering Australian animosities towards perceived British elitism. Ironically, most Semut field operatives were in fact Australian, and some had served in regular Australian Army units (including 9th Division) before joining SRD; many shared this view of SRD and its British commanding officers. Thus David Kearney of Semut III – who had worked in staff positions at every level of the Australian Army before being recruited to SRD – later reflected:

> [B]y the time I came to Z [Special Unit], I couldn't strip a Bren, but I knew a lot about the army. And I knew bullshit when I saw it, and there was a lot of it in Z.[33]

SRD HQ, on the other hand, did itself no favours with its well-known fixation on secrecy: it seems to have frequently failed to pass on information concerning the whereabouts of its parties to 9th Division HQ. This meant that local 9th Division commanders

This illustration of Borneo jungle travel was made by a European explorer in the 1870s, but little had changed by 1945. Rather than striding across the log bridge ahead of his bearers as depicted here, the explorer almost certainly crawled across on hands and knees in their wake.

Borneo mountainous terrain in 1993. There are now few such densely jungled areas left on the island.

Many Borneo rivers are strewn with rapids, leaving locals little choice but to manhandle boats across and around the rocks.

The thickly jungled mountainous areas of inland Borneo, shown here in a photo from the 1950s, presented extraordinary challenges to travellers.

A Dayak 'bridge' across a watercourse. Several Dayak bearers carrying heavy loads (top right) have crossed safely. Like most Europeans, Semut operatives found such bridges daunting.

A famous Kayan priestess displays the elongated earlobes and tattooed arms and feet common among Kayan and Kenyah women in the 1940s.

A Kayan woman prepares leaf-wrapped bundles of rice beside her cooking hearth, in a photo from the 1950s. In many longhouses, wood for cooking was stored directly above the hearth, as here.

A Penan hunter from the upper Baram River area with a wild boar he has killed using the blowpipe in his hands. The nomadic Penan were employed by both Semut II and Semut III for their superb tracking and scouting skills.

A Kenyah man from the Baram River area performs a warrior dance in the 1950s. Semut II operatives witnessed many such dances in longhouses along the Baram.

In the past, many Dayak groups produced beautiful, highly functional, steel blades. In this photo from the 1970s an Iban man forges a *parang* blade on a stone anvil passed down through generations.

Iban women weave elaborately patterned cloths (*pua*) from cotton that, in the past, they grew, spun and dyed themselves. In a photo from the 1970s (*above*), an Iban woman weaves a *pua* using a backstrap loom while a child sleeps in a cloth hammock beside her.

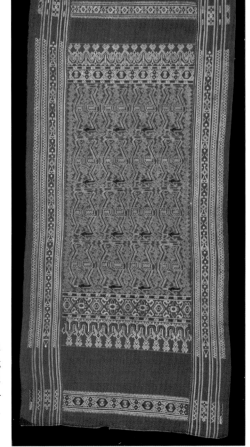

A *pua sungkit*, used in the past during headhunting ceremonies – such as that witnessed by Semut III on the Rejang River – to receive and wrap the heads.

The great Kenyah chief (and *pengulu*, later *Temenggong*) Tama Weng Ajeng, whose support for Semut was critical. In this photo, taken shortly after the war, he is wearing medals presented to him by the British, including the MBE on his right breast.

The mighty Iban leader, *Temenggong* Koh anak Jubang, in a photo from the late 1940s. He threw his weight behind Semut III and was awarded the MBE by the British after the war.

Kayan chief (and *pengulu*) Kebing in a photo taken in 1968. One of the most powerful chiefs on the Baram River in 1945, he was key to the success of Semut II.

Iban leader (and *pengulu*) Belaja anak Angkin, who was instrumental in Semut III's victories along the middle Rejang River. He carries his blowpipe (with spearhead) in his right hand. His *parang* is strapped to his left waist and his container of blowpipe darts to his right waist. Rowan Waddy, from Semut IV, stands beside him in this photo from 1945.

Young Kayan chief Baling Avun hosted the Semut III operatives in his longhouse when they first arrived at the Rejang River. In this photo, probably taken in the 1960s, he wears medals from the British and Malaysian governments, including the British Empire Medal awarded for his role in Operation Semut.

The massive bulk of a Kenyah longhouse stands out from the surrounding trees in this photo from the 1990s. The different apartment sizes reflect the differing status of longhouse residents.

The gallery (*ruai*) of an Iban longhouse on the Saribas River, Sarawak, in the early 1970s. Clusters of human heads – a common sight in longhouses in 1945 – hang from rafters down its length.

A Kenyah longhouse on the Baram River in 1951, showing extensive gallery (*usé*) and massive ironwood houseposts (*suka'*) holding up floor and roof. This longhouse was almost certainly visited by Semut II operatives in 1945.

Fort Sylvia, on the bank of the Rejang River at Kapit, served as Semut III HQ for five weeks in July and August 1945.

Ibans – some in ceremonial dress – and Europeans in front of a row of Chinese wooden shophouses. The photo is probably from late nineteenth-century Simanggang, during the rule of the second White Rajah. Similar shophouses were ubiquitous in Sarawak in 1945.

Outside the fort at Long Akah on the morning of 21 May 1945, as the men of Semut III prepare to depart for the Rejang River. Left to right: unnamed Iban ex-Sarawak constable (Semut III), Abu Kassim (Semut III), Bill Sochon (Semut III), Keith Barrie (Semut III), Toby Carter (Semut II), Wally Pare (Semut II), Kel Hallam (Semut II), George Conleth-Smith (Semut II), Don Horsnell (Semut II).

Bill Sochon with family at Buckingham Palace after the war. He is there to receive the DSO awarded for his actions during Semut III.

Tom Harrisson in Sarawak in 1946 while serving with BBCAU.

Semut II group at Labuan at the end of the war. Back row, left to right: George Conleth-Smith, Jack Neave, Don McLean, unidentified, Wally Pare, Kel Hallam, Doug Davey. Centre row, left to right: Norm Gilman, Stan Eadie, Toby Carter, Robert Wilson, 'Snowy' Middleton. Front row, left to right: Leo Duffus, Keith Le Guier, Don Horsnell, Neville Graham.

Semut III group at Labuan at the end of the war. Back row, left to right: Pip Hume, Phil Henry (Semut I), Ron Baker, 'Brick' Fowler, Brian Walpole, Eric Bell (Stallion VII), Francis Burrow, Bill Sochon, Des Foster, Bill Beiers, Ross Bradbury, Frank Pippen, Ed Spurling. Front row, left to right: Roy Campbell, Charles Heron, 'Happy' Croton, John Stokes, Keith Barrie, Arthur Astill, Gordon Phillpot, Jack Hartley.

Kayan and Kenyah troops at Long Lama after the Semut II attack on the Japanese garrison there. Denis Sheppard is top left with a former member of the Dutch East Indies army, who had absconded to Semut II, at top right. Kalang, Tama Weng Ajeng's oldest son, walks between the rows inspecting the men, who are armed with Lee–Enfield .303s and M1 carbine .30s.

A Semut II canoe, flying the British flag, during Semut II's advance down the Baram River from Long Akah to Marudi in late June 1945. In the background is the Kayan community of Long Pilah, home of the chief Kebing. Long Pilah consisted of two parallel longhouses – the lower one extending the width of the photograph – with rice granaries scattered between.

A Semut II Iban guerrilla with a Lee–Enfield .303 rifle slung over his back and a *parang* in his right hand. His *parang* sheath is strapped to his left waist.

Close-ups of intricately carved Iban (*above*) and Kayan (*below*) sword hilts from the late nineteenth/early twentieth centuries. They are made from deer antler and display powerful figures meant to assist the wielder during battle.

A photograph by 200 Flight personnel shows the fort at Long Akah used by Semut II as its HQ, and the drop zone (DZ) in the Chinese vegetable garden on the other side of the Baram River. Both are located in clearings cut from surrounding jungle.

A photograph by 200 Flight personnel shows parachutes carrying resupply storpedoes for Semut III above a jungle clearing at the edge of Kapit on the Rejang River.

Semut veteran Jack Tredrea with the author – a photo lodged at the top of her computer screen.

were often unaware of the presence of Semut operatives in their areas of operation until their men – scouting for enemy soldiers – stumbled across them by accident. It is hardly surprising that this sometimes led to conflict on the ground. And the lack of intelligence went both ways: a 20th Brigade Report notes that a Semut party encountered by its men 'had no knowledge of the tac[tical] situation or of [our] intentions or the scope of [our operation]'. The Report's author laments this failure of communication, pointing out that, had the two units been able to cooperate, 'valuable work' might have been done. [34]

The problem was exacerbated by the different – and in some respects opposed – objectives of 9th Division and SRD with respect to the Borneo campaign. With hopes high that the end of the war was in sight, the Commanding Officer of 9th Division, Major General George Wootten, was under extreme pressure from his political leaders to minimise Australian casualties. Borneo was regarded by the Australian government as something of a side-show, likely to be of little political or economic benefit once the war was over. The new Prime Minister Ben Chifley – who had only assumed the role on 13 July 1945 – emphasised the need to limit Australian commitments in Borneo, and was keen for the former colonial regimes to assume responsibility there as soon as pos-sible. Consequently, Wootten had no plan to extend 9th Division's control of Sarawak beyond its coastal strip and key centres such as Kuching.[35]

Operation Semut, on the other hand, had been driven from the start by British imperialist anxieties about its Borneo possessions. The operation was concerned almost as much with the shape of the postwar peace as it was with winning the war itself. On this basis, the Semut parties had established close relationships with local peo-ples, especially inland Dayak groups. These had been recruited to the operation on the understanding that once the Allied landings had taken place, Australian regular forces would move inland, clearing the country of remaining Japanese and paving the way for the return of the British or their vassals, the Brookes. The only problem was that SRD had forgotten to sign up the incoming Australian Army to this plan.

This already inflammatory situation had, unfortunately, been exacerbated by Harrisson. Not long after the 9th Division landings he had sent a memo to Wootten in which he lectured the General about the need to integrate regular and irregular forces and to treat the whole of Borneo as a single political entity. In Harrisson's own words, Wootten considered this 'flat impertinence'. The result was that Wootten had issued an order excluding SRD field commanders from any direct access to 9th Division HQ. Instead they were required to go through Colonel David Leach, a New Zealander seconded from SOE who had been appointed by SRD to liaise between itself and 9th Division.[36]

Carter now made the decision to throw himself directly on the mercy of 20th Brigade's commanding officer, Brigadier Windeyer, at Kuala Belait. This would allow him to avoid 9th Division HQ at Labuan, where he would likely be granted only limited access to senior officers already predisposed to dislike SRD field commanders. It was to be Carter's first face-to-face contact with the invading Australian regular forces.

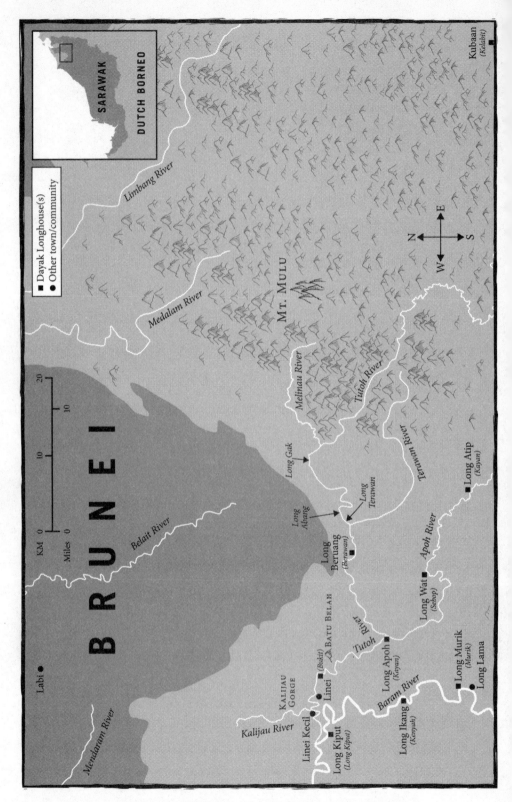

Lower/middle Tutoh River and environs in 1945.

9

TRIUMPH AND THREAT

MAJOR GENERAL WOOTTEN'S REFUSAL to allow 9th Division forces to move inland from the confines of the narrow coastal strip presented difficulties for Carter: Marudi lay beyond the Division's designated area of operation. But Carter was lucky. Windeyer – later a Justice of the High Court of Australia – was inclined to interpret his orders from Wootten with some flexibility.

Windeyer's aim for his 20th Brigade was to 'make as strong a demonstration of str[ength] as possible' throughout the area. In accordance with this, the 2/17th Battalion had already begun to patrol deeply inland from Kuala Belait, as well as up Carter's Baram River. In the two weeks preceding Carter's visit, the 2/17th had, with the help of local Dayaks, not only established a forward patrol base at Balai – inland from Kuala Belait and only 4 or 5 miles (6–8 km) east of the Baram – but had moved two platoons into the vicinity. Their orders were to keep watch for a rumoured Japanese escape route into the mountains.[1]

Carter's appearance at Kuala Belait was not, in fact, completely unexpected. On 11 July, a day after Carter had fled Marudi, Windeyer had received reports that a Japanese force had attacked an SRD party outside Marudi. As a result, one of his platoons in the Balai area – accompanied by sixteen Dayaks – had been sent on a three-day march from Balai to Ridan, where Carter's ambush had taken place. Their orders were to form a base and harass any Japanese in the area. Close to Ridan this platoon engaged in a skirmish with a well-armed Japanese party – almost certainly part of the same force Carter had attempted to ambush – and came under machine-gun and mortar fire. With a man injured, and being three days from medical help, they were forced to withdraw.[2]

To Carter's relief, Windeyer not only heard him out but agreed on the strategic importance of Marudi. He saw the sense of Carter's argument that reoccupation would enable Allied forces to control the network of rivers – all linked, in one way or another, to the Baram – throughout the area, and so disrupt Japanese communications and transport. The fact that the Japanese Command had sent a crack force to retake the town – the only offensive action by the enemy in the entire area since 25 June – served to accentuate this point. Windeyer was also moved by Carter's entreaties concerning the ill-treatment and murder of locals by Japanese soldiers.[3]

Carter's diplomatic skills – highlighted in many descriptions of the man – undoubtedly played a part in this success. But he was also likely aided by the fact that, unlike most other SRD commanders in the area, he was a New Zealander – the next best thing to an Australian – rather than a Briton. Even better: he had originally enlisted in the AIF and commanded a platoon of the 2/1st Australian Mechanical Equipment Company in New Guinea before joining SRD. Windeyer had led the 20th Brigade in New Guinea before being sent to Borneo. Carter could claim kinship.

Windeyer was unfazed by Marudi's location beyond the boundary set by Wootten for 9th Division operations. He requested permission from 9th Division HQ to send a company to Marudi for the purpose of 'investigating rubber supplies in the Baram' and establishing contact with his patrols in the Belait River/Mendaram River area. The subterfuge worked: permission was promptly granted and Windeyer assigned the job to 'D' Company from 2/17th Battalion, commanded by Major Norman Trebeck. Carter was going back to Marudi.[4]

∾

The lower Baram, below Marudi, is very different from the river's upper reaches where Carter and his men had been living for the past couple of months. Close to the coast the terrain resembles a dinner-plate – with no sign of the hills and mountains that rupture the landscape further inland – and the river spreads across it in a wide, passive corridor. The banks are fringed with palm trees and mangroves, although as one moved inland in 1945 these soon gave way to jungle, with massive trees walling the river on either side.

On 15 July, Carter, Eadie and Davey, along with Trebeck's 'D' Company, set off upriver on several large, flat LCM barges. It was a formidable force: they were armed with mortars and machine guns, and escorted by an LCM gunboat and an unarmed launch as well as a squadron of twelve Spitfires. Nothing could have been further from the makeshift and under-resourced party awaiting Carter's return at Long Murik. 'Back we went up the river,' he commented later, 'this time in more confident mood.'[5]

With them was HMAS *Tiger Snake*, a snake-class junk – small lightly armed vessels operated by the Royal Australian Navy to support special operations – in service to SRD, plus a second small armed boat also attached to SRD. *Tiger Snake* was loaded with ten tons of food for the relief of the local population of Marudi and surrounding areas. For several weeks Carter had been reporting serious food shortages to Courtney: more than three years of

Japanese occupation plus the recent looting had taken their desolate toll. Courtney had organised the relief in response to Carter's pleas for assistance. [6]

But there was still an enemy to fight. Part-way to Marudi the convoy received reports from local Dayaks that around forty Japanese – presumably from the force Carter had ambushed five days earlier – were at Ridan. Trebeck decided to engage them immediately. The Spitfires strafed and bombed the Ridan vicinity and the gunboat followed up with a barrage of rockets once it reached the area (poor Ridan). Two platoons then landed at the Ridan landing point, where Carter had set his earlier ambush.

But there were no Japanese there. Locals told them the Japanese had withdrawn to Marudi. So the Australians plodded through the steamy heat down the Ridan Road – the same route along which Carter's party had fled five days earlier – towards the town.

In the meantime, the fleet – including Carter and his men – followed the river round its final twirl to Marudi wharf. Having landed here in triumphal mode several days earlier, Carter this time expected opposition. But the town was empty of Japanese. They had withdrawn at the first sign of the Allied force and were a few hundred yards east of the bazaar, retreating eastward, when the fleet arrived. 'D' Company entered the town, from both river and road, unopposed.[7]

Five days after unceremoniously fleeing the fort, Carter now oversaw the hoisting of the Union Jack above it. To his relief he found the safe still in place – apparently unopened, although the key had disappeared (it was found several days later in the safekeeping of an ex-Brooke government official) – and the two wireless sets undamaged. The rifles and ammunition were missing but quickly located: they had been taken and hidden by Malays, with some used against the Japanese during their reoccupation of the town.[8]

Locals – those who had not fled upriver – were beginning to reappear on the streets. Carter now discovered that the Japanese reoccupation of Marudi had not taken place on 10 July, the day he and his party had fled the town, but rather a day later. On 10 July the enemy had been frightened off by Gilman, not long after the ambush at the Ridan landing point.

As the remainder of Carter's force had retreated to the fort, Gilman and his two guerrillas had been left behind in the bazaar to guard the Ridan Road. From their position they had seen ten to fifteen figures cross the road several hundred yards to the north and disappear into the thick gardens of the Malay precinct. Assuming they were Japanese, Gilman had sent one of the guerrillas to warn Carter and left the other to cover the road. He himself carefully crept – with his Bren – towards the riverbank, working his way through the handful of Chinese houses scattered between the northern edge of the bazaar and the Chinese temple. He calculated that if the figures he had seen were Japanese, this was the position they would make for.

And he was correct. A few moments later two Kiki machine guns rattled into action – the Kikis heard by Carter's party at the fort – firing on the bazaar from a position behind the temple, their operators having moved quietly there through the Malay gardens. In response Gilman left the cover of the houses and advanced alone and unsupported across the open marketplace, firing his Bren from the hip. While he could not be certain of any hits, the two Kikis immediately fell silent.[9]

We now know that immediately after Carter's ambush, a platoon of around thirty Japanese soldiers had been sent in advance of the overall force to pursue Carter's fleeing party and retake the town. However, in counterattacking at the bazaar Gilman had made a lucky strike: he had killed the platoon's commander, Second Lieutenant Ideuma. As a result, instead of moving on to the fort as ordered, the now-leaderless platoon withdrew precipitously into the Malay precinct before fleeing back to the landing point at the end of the Ridan Road. From there they had returned downriver to the main force. Carter was unaware of it at the time, but this withdrawal had gifted his party a vital reprieve: his own flight upriver was matched by his enemy's simultaneous flight downriver.[10]

However, the Japanese retreat was short-lived. The entire force returned and reoccupied Marudi – now devoid of both Carter's force and many of its residents – the following day (11 July). Some of the Malays who remained in the town had bravely attempted to resist, using rifles taken from the fort. But they were swiftly dealt with and broader reprisals carried out, with many Malays bayonetted. In all around twenty people were killed, most of them Malays. The Ridan Malay who had guided Wilson and Fidler to their position before the ambush was among those to die, along with his family. Local residents' joy at the arrival of Trebeck's force was tempered with grief over the price they had paid for Carter's earlier attempt to seize the town.[11]

But Carter's own luck had held. During its few days in Marudi the Japanese force had made no attempt to loot either fort or Residency, and had left untouched the safe, stores and radio equipment abandoned there by Carter's party. Its men had also made no effort to pursue Carter upriver, even though by then they must have had a good idea of his party's composition. Local reports suggested they had spent most of their time in the town 'gorging themselves' with food and frequenting the local brothel.[12]

After the Allies retook Marudi on 15 July, the behaviour of this Japanese force became stranger still. Instead of returning to the Bakong-Beluru area west of Marudi from whence they had come – and where the bulk of Miri force was by then concentrated – they fled in the opposite direction, eastward towards the upper Ridan River. This was so unexpected that Wilson later commented: 'It almost looks as if he [the force's CO] was told not to come back to the Bakong area in any circumstance.'[13]

In fact, this mirrors 20th Brigade's experience with Japanese soldiers throughout the larger area. With one or two exceptions – including along the Bakong River – enemy troops seemed disinclined to engage in combat, and generally avoided contact with Allied forces. The Brigade's Report notes that they were 'poorly equipped and led'. Long-term shortages of food and medicine, the daily grind of dealing with an alien, sapping environment, and growing demoralisation concerning the progress of the war were undoubtedly having their pernicious effects.[14]

Trebeck sent troops in pursuit of the Japanese force, later known as *Uchida Tai* (after its commanding officer First Lieutenant Uchida) as it fled Marudi. Several clashes occurred, during which a number of Australian soldiers – and more Japanese ones – died. But *Uchida Tai* continued to move haphazardly – and apparently aimlessly – eastward, preying on local towns and villages for food as it went. Semut II's forces harassed it along the way – attempting to turn it northward into 9th Division's coastal strip – until it moved out of Carter's operational area.

Eventually the remnants of *Uchida Tai* surrendered on 21 September to an SRD party under Lieutenant Frank Holland, close to Ukong on the Limbang River which runs into the west side of Brunei Bay. SRD HQ had sent Holland's party to the area after Semut II provided them with information as to the force's whereabouts. According to Wilson, Holland later gave Uchida's sword to Gilman, whose action in the bazaar at Marudi had been instrumental in stymying Uchida's first attack on the town and allowing Carter's party to escape upriver: 'No one in Semut II had earned it better'.[15]

࿐

The day after Carter's return to Marudi, 16 July, he travelled upriver in *Tiger Snake* accompanied by the armed SRD boat. At Long Ikang and Long Murik he rounded up his Semut force and, together with Tama Weng Ajeng, arranged for them to return to Marudi along with the evacuees. But now he faced a formidable challenge.

Trebeck's force could remain in Marudi only a few days longer before moving back to its designated area in the coastal strip. Once it was gone Carter would assume responsibility for civil affairs in the town and surrounding areas. This included finding ongoing supplies for more than fifteen hundred people, with no food in the shophouses, and rice fields which had been decimated by the Japanese.[16]

In theory, Carter should now have been able to hand over the administration of Marudi – and the provisioning of its inhabitants – to the British Borneo Civil Affairs Unit (hereafter BBCAU). BBCAU had been created in Australia – and placed under the command of 9th Division – prior to the Labuan landings. Its role was to take charge of interim civil administration throughout Sarawak, Brunei and British North Borneo as the Division recaptured towns and districts from the Japanese. Some of the old Borneo hands in BBCAU – including John Fisher and William Ditmas, both involved in early planning for Project Semut – were also members of SRD.

However, there is no mention of BBCAU in any of Carter's reports from the time. It is not hard to see why. Due largely to the now almost inevitable friction between the British and the Australians over the unit's formation, it was short of recruits – especially those with prior experience and knowledge of Borneo – and seriously under-resourced: by 6 July, for instance, it included only three medical officers. It was also beset with internal tensions as well as ongoing strains in its relationship with 9th Division.[17]

Yet the Unit was meant to assume responsibility for the entire expanse of British Borneo. Much of this had been devastated not only by more than three years of Japanese occupation, with its dolorous impact on economic activity and population health, but also by the military actions that had occurred during and since the

Australian landings. Widespread bombing and strafing by Allied planes had wreaked particular havoc. Miri, for instance, was in such a state of disrepair after Allied bombing that hundreds of its residents had to be housed at the oil company barracks while buildings and facilities were repaired.

As a result, BBCAU was overwhelmed. If not for the efforts of 9th Division commanders and ordinary Australian soldiers – who treated locals in their own hospitals and worked tirelessly to clear away rubble, clean drains, and rebuild houses, roads and bridges – the path to civil recovery in parts of Sarawak and British North Borneo would have been much harder. So thankful were locals for this assistance that when the new British Crown Colony of North Borneo was established in 1946 (replacing the previous British North Borneo), the 9th Division's insignia – a T sign – was incorporated into its coat of arms. Similarly, people living in areas down the northeast coastline of Sarawak still, in 2018, remembered the kindness of the invading Australians.[18]

Marudi had largely escaped the widespread damage meted out to other towns in the area – suffering only the bombing and strafing of Ridan, on its outskirts, by Trebeck's forces. As a result, the shortage of BBCAU personnel undoubtedly meant that no thought was given to sending anyone from the Unit to the town. However, unlike most other towns in the area, Marudi's location beyond the 9th Division limit prevented 20th Brigade troops from assisting with reconstruction there. Consequently, although SRD arranged for foodstuffs, medicines and other necessities to be supplied regularly to the town – army biscuits 'for some unaccountable reason' proving particularly popular – Carter was himself forced to assume responsibility for the town's rehabilitation, as well as the establishment of civil order and a system of public administration.[19]

Carter seems to have been happy to take on this role – clearly regarding it as entirely in keeping with the operation's key objective of smoothing the way for a return to British rule. However, it is worth noting that Harrisson and Sochon – commanding officers of Semut I and Semut III respectively – were each provided, at around this time, with a second-in-command whose main responsibility was civil affairs. As we will see, both had found the combination of military and civil responsibilities difficult to manage; Harrisson later commented that 'it was impossible to continue running all the military, civilian and liaison problems through my own head'. Although Carter's operation was smaller than either of the others it is unlikely that he found this combination much less onerous.[20]

Nevertheless, he applied himself to the task. He recruited surviving local Brooke administrators – including native officers and clerks, as well as former Brooke police – and paid them all out of SRD funds, presumably made available by Courtney. His aim was to establish a system of civil affairs as close as possible to the one in place before the war, which BBCAU – and ultimately the returning British/Brooke regime – could eventually take over.[21]

Carter also took on the urgent matter of dispensing justice, seeing himself in this role as a representative of the Brooke government. The accused were held in cells beneath the courthouse while evidence was collected, before eventually being brought to trial. Among the first to be tried were two Chinese in the pay of the *Kempei Tai* who had not only notified Japanese HQ about the first arrival of the Semut II party in Marudi, but had also informed against a number of their fellow citizens during the Japanese occupation of the town.

The two men had been captured by locals and brought to Carter. Their case elevated emotions within an angry population to fever pitch, and Sheppard was given the task – along with several local police – of guarding them. They were tried in the courthouse a couple of weeks after Semut II's reoccupation of the town, in front of Carter as president of the court and a jury consisting of leaders from local Dayak, Chinese and Malay populations.[22]

Both men were found guilty in a unanimous verdict and sentenced to death. They were taken out into the jungle beyond Marudi – with a group of Kenyah guerrillas keeping onlookers away – and shot by a squad of Tama Weng's men under the command of Sheppard. Their bodies were then turned over to their friends and families for burial.

Carter makes no mention of this episode in any of his reports on the operation and Sheppard, as late as the 1990s, asked Jim Truscott not to refer to it in the latter's book on Semut. Arguably, Carter acted lawfully in conducting the trial and prosecuting its outcome; but this is a notoriously grey area of the law. We can speculate that neither Carter nor Sheppard was prepared to take any chances on how it might be viewed by others.[23]

Marudi was getting back on its feet. But his new civil responsibilities were the least of Carter's worries. While the enemy force in Marudi itself had been dealt with, the fifteen hundred or so troops close to the Tinjar River to his west, and the Japanese force newly appeared on the Tutoh River to his east, remained in place: both of them outside 9th Division's operational zone and, as a result, unchallenged by conventional Australian forces. And each posed a potent threat not only to the wellbeing of the civilian – mostly Dayak – populations in their vicinities, but also to Carter's tiny party.

৩৩

Carter's most pressing concern was the Japanese force on the Tutoh River, known to his men – in a phrase recalling the hit movie *The Wizard of Oz* that had appeared directly before the war – as the 'Japs to the east'. As a result of Wood's attack on its advance party at Linei Kecil on 9 July, the main body of this force had turned away from the Baram River and begun to focus eastwards. According to Carter's scouts it had stayed for several days in the Linei area after the attack, taking food from local communities. During this period it had been strafed at least twice by the RAAF – once as it made its way through the Kalijau Gorge on 10 July, and a second time in the town of Linei on 13 July. These attacks had, however, failed to deflect its forward movement up the Tutoh River.[24]

In the meantime, the force's advance parties – using the labour of Javanese coolies and Indian POWs they had with them – had hacked a track southeast towards the much more sparsely populated upper Tutoh. This overland route enabled them to bypass a large southward loop of the Tutoh itself as well as to keep a good distance from the lower Baram River, which its commanders presumably now feared was controlled by Allied parties.[25]

Around 17 July, the main body of the force finally made its way along the newly cut track to the large Berawan longhouse at Long Beruang. Longhouse residents had been alert to its movements for days and had already evacuated upriver. However, Kenyah and Berawan guerrillas working with Semut II had continued to track the force after Wood and his operatives returned to the Baram River on 9 July. Seeing an opportunity to inflict serious damage, they attacked with firearms when it arrived at Long Beruang. In the ensuing skirmish three Japanese and two Kenyahs were killed, and two Kenyahs taken prisoner.

In retaliation the Japanese first looted, and then set fire to, the Long Beruang longhouse around 18 July. The building – highly flammable, as all such timber longhouses were – burned to the ground. Locals later described the residents' grief as their apartments smouldered and smoked, and the devastating loss of all food and belongings, including many precious heirlooms. Longhouse inhabitants were left in a parlous state, with no shelter and no food – Eadie reports that some died as a result, in spite of Carter arranging for blankets, food and other necessities to be dropped to them. This was exactly the scenario that Carter had warned of since first arriving in the area.[26]

The Japanese force then moved on up the Tutoh River, taking with it all the food obtained from Long Beruang. Meanwhile one of its reconnaissance parties – containing around fifteen men – appeared at the Kayan longhouse at Long Apoh, downstream from Long Beruang at the confluence of the Apoh and Tutoh Rivers. There the party was attacked by a brave group of Kayans – in fear for the safety of their own longhouse – armed only with spears and swords. In the ensuing battle three Japanese and three Kayans were killed, and four Kayans (and an unknown number of Japanese) wounded. Although the Kayans had no firearms, the intensity of their attack drove the Japanese party back east along the Tutoh. The attackers were able to capture a Japanese briefcase containing maps and papers which they handed over to Semut II a few days later.[27]

Receiving reports of these actions, Carter was especially worried about the appearance of the Japanese party at the mouth of the Apoh River. Further south this river linked with overland routes leading directly back to the Baram.

అఇ

Up to this point Carter had been handicapped by a lack of reliable intelligence about the Tutoh River enemy force: he had no idea where it had come from, how many men it contained, and how well-trained and well-armed they were. However, that dramatically changed in mid-July. At that time, the party of Kenyah and Berawan guerrillas stalking the force picked up two Indian POWs and three Javanese forced labourers who had managed to escape near Long Beruang. The escapees were in shocking condition, but – before being evacuated to Labuan – one of the POWs managed to provide vital information.[28]

Carter now learned that the force had come from Labi, not far northeast of Marudi. According to the POW it was originally around four hundred strong, and contained Japanese civilians (including ten women and six children), more than twenty Indian POWs, and about fifty Javanese forced labourers. He estimated that no more than two hundred of its Japanese members were armed with rifles, the remainder being civilians, many of them oilfield workers.

The POW also reported that the force was suffering: it was short of food and many had died from sickness since leaving Labi. He put its total strength by 18 July at under three hundred. Yet it remained capable of brutality: he told them its leader had burned alive sixteen Indian POWs in a hut behind the longhouse at Long Beruang. Wilson later examined the hut and found what appeared to be some charred bonelike material in the ashes.[29]

The force eventually came to be known as *Fujino Tai* after its senior commanding officer Lieutenant (later Captain) Fujino. It had been formed from the amalgamation of two separate companies – one of inferior, poorly-trained troops, the other a Transport Company – which had come together at Labi at the end of June, after both moving inland to escape the Australian invasion. It contained around 570 people – many more than estimated by the escaped POW – with around 450 of them being armed soldiers.

On leaving Labi, the force had first planned to cross the Baram River close to Marudi early in July, in order to link up with the large concentration of Japanese troops in the Bakong–Beluru area to Marudi's west. However, on its way to the crossing point it learned that Allied forces had taken Marudi. As a result, *Fujino Tai* turned southeast, away from the town. Shadowing the Baram along overland tracks, it straggled towards the Tutoh River.[30]

Fujino Tai was one of a number of similar Japanese 'mobs' in the region, although it later acquired special notoriety through its encounter with that incomparable publicist Tom Harrisson. In mid-July Carter knew only that it was poorly trained and led, and composed in part of civilians including women and children. A signal he sent to HQ on 25 July describes it as 'demoralised and starving'. He nevertheless recognised that it was a large force – requiring plenty of food to keep its members alive – containing at least two hundred armed soldiers. It could be expected to inflict considerable hardship on Dayak, and other, communities in its path.[31]

Carter was comforted, however, by his familiarity with the Tutoh River. He knew there were no longhouses or settlements of any consequence immediately above the now destroyed Berawan longhouse at Long Beruang. Closer to its origins in the east, the Tutoh ran through increasingly mountainous and inhospitable terrain, the same seemingly incomprehensible puzzle of steep jungle-clothed hills and valleys that Carter and his men had found so formidable on their trek to Long Lellang three months earlier. The area was inhabited mostly by nomadic Penan, highly adept at avoiding groups they had no wish to encounter.

Carter was hopeful that if the force continued eastwards along the Tutoh River, shortage of food would soon compel it to retreat back the way it had come. His plan was to have men in position along the path of the retreat to rapidly 'whittle down' the column's numbers and prevent it from moving southeast at any time towards the much more densely populated Baram River.[32]

Accordingly, as soon as Semut II had settled in Marudi, Carter despatched a force to the Tutoh River under Wilson's command. An advance party of two operatives and twenty-four Iban guerrillas under Gilman travelled there overland via Linei on 18 July, and Wilson followed with another four operatives and around fifteen more Ibans the following day. Wilson's orders were to harass the enemy column (make things 'as sticky as possible' for it), and prevent it from moving towards the Baram River either by way of the Apoh River, or back down the Tutoh itself. Instead he was to shepherd it northwest towards 9th Division's coastal zone.[33]

ᘒᘒ

Gilman's advance party reached the desolate charred skeleton of the Long Beruang longhouse around 23 July. Moving cautiously onward up the Tutoh River, they soon encountered *Fujino Tai* at Long Abang, not much further east. A skirmish ensued in which four enemy died but the Semut II party escaped unscathed. Since his force was too small to take on the column in open combat, Gilman withdrew slightly downriver to Long Terawan, close to the mouth of the Terawan River. This was an ideal defensive location from which to organise a series of harassment parties: not only did it command all reaches of the Tutoh River, but if a withdrawal were necessary the operatives could retreat up the Terawan River, cross to the Apoh River and from there make their way to the Baram River.

Wilson's party followed to Long Terawan a day or so later, and Wilson established his own HQ there. He now had a sizeable force at his disposal: seven operatives, the group of twenty or so Kenyah and Berawan guerrillas that had been tracking *Fujino Tai* for weeks, and forty Iban guerrillas. And that was not all. At Long Terawan his party quickly attracted a mass of volunteers from longhouses in the area – Tama Usun Ngo, a Kayan from Long Atip who was among them, later put their number at around eighty. Having witnessed what had happened at Long Beruang, they came – called by their chiefs and armed only with their *parang* and spears – to fight for their longhouses and livelihoods.[34]

For the next two weeks this motley force – broken up and operating in several small groups – conducted a grim war of attrition against *Fujino Tai* as it trailed slowly up the Tutoh River. Wilson and Hallam worked together with several Dayaks in one such group, Hallam keeping them in regular contact with Carter's HQ in Marudi via his ATR-4 radio. The strategy involved nothing more complicated than constant harassment: picking off stragglers, setting ambushes and leaving booby traps, the latter using three-inch mortar bombs triggered with pull- or pressure-switches (wild pigs were sometimes the unintended victims). Hallam describes surprising seven Japanese in a canoe: 'I still have the nip officer's sword (only a metal handled job but special to me).'[35]

A number of local volunteers were assigned to work with Conleth-Smith – *Tuan* [Mr] 'Con' – in another group. Many years later Tama Usun Ngo described how this group came across a party of Japanese bathing and defecating at the riverbank close to Long Terawan. During the subsequent skirmish he was hit by a bullet.

Shhhd . . . sound of the bullet! I didn't know I was hit. I just heard the sound. There was blood coming out. I touched my temple. Oh, I was hit! This is the scar I got [while showing the scar on the side of his temple]. A bit more the bullet would have hit me in the eye. Luckily it only grazed me a bit.[36]

Despite (or perhaps because of) its simplicity, Semut II's strategy had the desired effect of thinning out the Japanese column. But it did not have the hoped-for result of forcing it to retreat back down the Tutoh. Instead, *Fujino Tai* continued its inexorable slow trek eastwards towards the upper reaches of the river.

By now Wilson had begun to worry that if the column made it to the Melinau River – which flows into the Tutoh River from the northeast, some distance upstream from Long Abang – its commander might choose to turn away from the increasingly inhospitable Tutoh in favour of following the smaller river northwards. Wilson learned from local members of his force that from the Melinau River it was possible to follow overland tracks to the Limbang River further north. He was not to know it, but in the nineteenth century Kayan warriors from the Baram River area had not infrequently dragged their canoes across the watershed between the Tutoh and Limbang Rivers in order to mount headhunting raids against the Lun Bawang and Kelabit on the other side.[37]

The Limbang River was in Semut I territory so Wilson sent radio messages to Semut I (via Labuan) warning of the possible movement of the column into its area of operations. In return he received a note from Harrisson expressing concerns about any Semut II men entering Semut I's area, and requesting that in such a case his own sergeant should be in command, regardless of rank: 'Rank, on this sort of occasion, is irrelevant, I think you will agree.' This was, of course, in contravention of the usual rules of military command. We do not know how (or if) Wilson responded.[38]

By 6 August *Fujino Tai* had established a position at Long Gak, around 6 miles (9.5 km) upriver as the crow flies from Long Abang, although much further if one follows the looping Tutoh River itself. Reconnaissance parties reported to Wilson that the column's position was a strong one, enabling it to guard against possible attack from river or overland tracks, and that it had dug perimeter defences.

Wilson knew the enemy force was well supplied with rice taken from Long Beruang and he worried that it was settling in for a lengthy stay. He considered the possibility of direct assault, but the location was well chosen: he could find no good position from which to conduct a mortar bombardment. And while his own force consisted of close to 150 men, most of them were without firearms. Outright attack would be suicidal. He decided instead to request air strikes.[39]

But before these could take place Wilson was suddenly recalled to Marudi. He left on 7 August, leaving Wood in charge of the party at Long Terawan.

10

THE SACKING

WITH THE DEPARTURE OF Wilson's party to the Tutoh River, Carter was feeling more sanguine about the Japanese on his eastern flank – or at least about his ability to prevent them from preying on areas with settled populations. However, those on his western flank were an entirely different matter. The area immediately west and southwest of Marudi – centred around Bakong, Nyabor, Beluru and Sibuti – contained one of the largest concentrations of Japanese in British Borneo: fifteen hundred to two thousand in all. Carter had reported to SRD HQ weeks earlier that the enemy was preparing defensive positions in this vicinity, so it came as no surprise when large numbers of troops retreated here after the Australian landings.

Since early July Carter had been receiving reports – from both Horsnell close by on the Tinjar River and his own local spies – about the troops in this area, and had grown increasingly concerned about an impending Japanese move further inland up the Tinjar. Such a move would endanger not only the many longhouses in the vicinity but also Horsnell's tiny party located at Lake Bunut.

Carter had voiced these concerns to Courtney during his two visits. In response, Courtney had arranged RAAF airstrikes against enemy positions in the area.[1]

Windeyer, commander of the 20th Brigade, had also despatched troops inland towards this area, again presumably at Carter's behest. On 16 July – the day after the Union Jack was hoisted in Marudi – men from the 2/17th Battalion had occupied the key town of Bakong. Although only 10 miles (16 km) northwest of Marudi, Bakong was within the permitted 9th Division operational zone, so 2/17th Battalion was able to move a platoon into the town the following day. As a result, a large number of Japanese troops stationed in and around Bakong moved further inland along the Bakong River. They established a new HQ not far from Bakong at Beluru – outside the 9th Division zone – which rapidly became the epicentre of Japanese occupation in the area.[2]

Enemy troops here had plenty of stores and weaponry – including machine guns – and appeared to be well led by the commander of the Miri garrison, Colonel Aikyo. In fact, a later 20th Brigade Report notes that only in this and one other area of the Brigade's operation did Japanese soldiers seem to be 'aggressively and soundly directed': presumably because they included many well-trained men under the direct control of Aikyo. This force potentially posed a much greater threat than straggling, poorly armed and poorly led columns like *Fujino Tai*. Carter worried that it was only a matter of time before the force was compelled to move further inland in search of food.[3]

⁂

Carter had three operatives – Horsnell, Mason and signaller Duffus – in the Tinjar River area, along with one hundred and fifty trained local guerrillas, mostly Ibans. The Soen Hin had now moved further southwest to the region inland from Bintulu, where he continued to organise local Iban guerrillas. This bordered Semut III's area of operation and, on 25 July, The was transferred to Semut III, reducing Carter's force even further.[4]

Following their posting down the Tinjar River in early June, Horsnell and The had proved remarkably effective at recruiting and training locals, mostly Ibans, in the lower Tinjar region. In fact, so efficient had they been that Ibans from here were sent to join Semut II parties throughout the Baram River basin. Mason and Duffus joined Horsnell and The in late June and, in concert with their guerrillas, the party carried out a succession of raids against Japanese in the area. They had also established strong relationships with the inhabitants of local Iban longhouses, who – even when not formally joining Semut II's guerrilla force – were enthusiastic recruits to its broader opposition army.

Hallam, who visited the Tinjar area with Wilson and McCallum probably sometime in July, records the sight of eighteen Japanese heads – an entire patrol sent to search for rumoured Allied soldiers – that had been taken by the members of a single Iban longhouse. None of these Ibans had trained as guerrillas, and they had no need of such training. Instead they resorted to the core techniques of special forces warfare – guile, stealth and ambush – in which Dayaks were already supremely skilled.[5]

Under Iban customary law, it is prohibited to kill guests inside a longhouse they have entered in peace. Accordingly, when the Japanese patrol arrived seeking hospitality, the longhouse headman explained that the longhouse was under taboo – a result of an inhabitant's death – and no strangers could enter. Longhouse residents instead built a shelter for the patrol on the cleared area beside the longhouse – where the prohibition on killing did not apply – and carried food there for the soldiers' consumption. Then, while the soldiers were eating and at ease, the headman and his men killed them and took their heads.

The sole Iban casualty of this action was the headman's son. He was slashed across his right hand during the skirmish, and the sinews of his fingers sliced open. Hallam:

> The happy end to this was me watching Major R.K. Wilson (British Army) ex Harley St Lady's Doctor & Capt Ian McCallum (Medical Officer – AIF) cut a ladder up this Iban's right arm and draw the sinews down and tie them (while he was under morphia of course [. . .]) I have never seen such gratitude from one man to another as there was from that [longhouse head] and his son to Wilson & McCallum – as it was the boy's parang [sword] hand and he was the future head of that kampong [community].[6]

By mid-July, Ibans had carried out so many actions of this type in the area that the Japanese had begun to retaliate: shooting locals on sight, taking food by force and burning down longhouses. But the Japanese command decided to strike harder still. Around 18 July several large attack parties – each containing one hundred men or more – were unleashed from Japanese HQ near Beluru, to undertake a concerted push southeast through Iban territory towards the Tinjar River.[7]

Carter was appalled. He knew that once the attack parties reached the Tinjar River they would have the choice of either travelling directly up that fertile, well-populated waterway or moving eastward – across reasonably open, unprotected terrain – to the Baram River itself. This would open escape routes for the main Japanese force to follow, with potentially catastrophic consequences for Dayak populations throughout the area.[8]

With the transfer of The to Semut III, Carter's overall number of operatives (including Conleth-Smith) now stood at a paltry seventeen. Seven of these had recently been sent up the Tutoh River to deal with *Fujino Tai*. This left only seven in Marudi to man the party's main HQ and deal with the civil rehabilitation of the town and surrounding area. He had none to spare to add to the trio already on the Tinjar.

Horsnell, Mason and Duffus, along with their Iban guerrillas, did their best to harry the enemy parties and delay their push southeast. But they were no match for large groups of well-armed and well-trained Japanese soldiers, and morale began to dissipate. The Ibans had been recruited and trained specifically for guerrilla activities, and never expected to wage a war on this scale.[9]

As a result, the Japanese parties reached the Tinjar – at the time, loveliest of Sarawak rivers; today denuded and desolate – in early August, leaving a string of casualties in their wake. Perhaps news of the nuclear bombs dropped on Hiroshima on 6 August and Nagasaki on 9 August fuelled their rage. Certainly it failed to affect their forward impetus.

By 11 August the Japanese controlled the Tinjar River as far south as the Lelak River. One party had crossed country further south and burned down the Iban longhouse at Long Ajoi, perilously close to Horsnell's HQ at Lake Bunut. If they crossed to the Baram River from here, as Carter feared they would, Horsnell's men could be cut off from escape. 'This was,' Carter writes with typical understatement, 'an anxious time.'[10]

Carter pleaded repeatedly with SRD HQ for additional reinforcements: 'Just a few extra white men would make so much difference to native morale.' In his view, their very willingness to assist the operation had placed Dayaks in the Tinjar River area directly in the firing line. For this he felt deeply responsible.

All Ibans under [Japanese] immediate domination will suffer far greater hardship from now on than they did prior to the appearance of the white man. Prior to the landing of invasion

forces it had been the policy of Semut, and the logical deduc-
tion of the population, to encourage the native in the belief that
the white soldiers would help to a large extent to kill Japs. The
native role being purely guerrilla. [. . .] The Ibans have done
sterling work, so far, but they cannot be expected to wage war
on well organised Japs in fixed positions.[11]

Carter was also concerned about the broader effect on the reser-
voir of local goodwill towards the Allies that he had worked so hard
to develop. If Ibans in the area came to believe they had been misled,
this goodwill could suffer 'a serious reverse'. In this case, Semut's
larger objective – the resumption of British or Brooke rule after the
war – might itself come under threat.[12]

Courtney, however, was unmoved. Indeed, it appears that
he failed even to respond to many of Carter's signals. The only
assistance he provided was largely ineffective – and shockingly
destructive – RAAF airstrikes on towns in the area believed to be
harbouring Japanese.

Carter continued to petition for help, and Courtney continued
to rebuff – or even ignore – his entreaties. Eventually, on 9 August,
Carter flew to Labuan for talks, leaving the recalled Wilson in charge
at Marudi. The discussions continued over several days and sadly,
as with so much else of what went on in SRD, we have no record
of exactly who was present or what was said. But we do know that
on 14 August Carter was sacked by SRD HQ as the commanding
officer of Semut II.

∽

Sheppard, in an account written after the war, puts a positive spin
on Carter's removal, describing him as having been 'withdrawn'
to assist with the evacuation of civilian internees. 'Withdrawal'
was also the term used by Carter in his Semut II General Report,

obviously agreed upon by those involved to sugar-coat what had happened. Wilson – Carter's second-in-command, who took over from him as Officer Commanding Semut II – was the only one prepared to call a spade a spade. In a letter written several years after the war, he stated that Carter had been 'sacked' from the operation.[13]

Carter's General Report is the only official document we have referencing his dismissal. Here Carter states that he was not a willing party to what happened, that he was 'removed summarily', and that it came 'as a bitter blow'. It is true that he was transferred to a new position with responsibility for the evacuation of prisoners in Japanese internment camps – by no means a demotion – but his sense of shock and betrayal at the move is nevertheless on plain display. It is hard not to see this as a sacking.[14]

Carter's General Report also sets out – in his distinctive self-effacing style – exactly what he had been accused of:

> One admits to having suffered perhaps from that tropical complaint commonly known as 'jungleitis' which afflicts field men with a jaundiced outlook towards their HQ unit. One also admits to having expressed views and criticisms which taking the strictly military interpretation could be construed as 'insubordinate'.[15]

He goes on to note that his withdrawal was not welcomed by 20th Brigade – thus relieving them of any blame. And he adds:

> The success of Semut generally had helped materially to put S.R.D. on a recognised footing. One was removed by the very people whose military careers had themselves been furthered by our efforts. Granted some of them had rendered sterling service as well. Perhaps the trouble lay on a higher plane than S.R.D.[16]

It is possible that the upper echelons of 9th Division – above the leadership of 20th Brigade – were ultimately responsible for Carter's demise; he had, after all, been unhappy about their refusal to pursue the Japanese inland around Beluru. But this seems unlikely. There is no evidence that Carter had been voicing his dissatisfaction to any organisation other than SRD – he certainly made no further visits to the coast after the trip to Windeyer at Kuala Belait – and it is difficult to see why, in any case, the Division would be sufficiently exercised by the unhappiness of a middle-ranking SRD field officer to insist on his dismissal. And even if the pressure was coming from 9th Division, why would SRD not stick by Carter? Courtney had, after all, pledged to support Harrisson 'through thick and thin' in Harrisson's own fraught dealings with the Division.[17]

Carter's Report, and a later letter he wrote to the former director of SRD, make it clear that he believed the dismissal order had come from SRD HQ itself. On close inspection, it is impossible not to agree.[18]

∽

Wilson suggests that Carter was sacked in part because he was overly concerned with civil matters – including the wellbeing of locals – at the expense of pursuing necessary military action. Wilson saw the aims of the operation very differently from Carter. Carter, with his long-term friendships throughout the area and his overall objective of paving the way for an easy transition to British or Brooke rule, viewed the fostering of local goodwill as a key component of the operation.[19]

Wilson had no such scruples. As he commented at the time with respect to the occupation of Marudi:

I think to all of us the killing of Japs and the prosecution of guerrilla war with the utmost determination was of far more importance than the abandonment of a few hundred natives and a town to the enemy.

And in a report written after the war his position had hardened:

> Major Carter [. . .] felt responsible for these natives and was worried as to what could be done for them, at least as far as feeding them, if nothing else was possible. I felt no such responsibilities and recommended shooting a few of the more importunate to clear the air.[20]

We might be tempted to see this final comment as tongue-in-cheek did it not fit so well with much else that we know about Wilson. Those who fought alongside him generally agree with Hallam that he was 'a fantastic fighting officer'. However, he viewed most Borneo locals – Malays and Chinese as well as Dayaks – with contempt. Sheppard tells us that when he asked Wilson why he made no attempt to learn even rudimentary Malay, Wilson replied: 'if they wish to talk to me let them learn English.'[21]

Wilson disliked Carter – in fact, he disliked all three Semut party leaders, as he made clear in a later letter – and was deeply resentful of the man's command. There is no doubt he actively agitated against Carter during his time with Semut II, complaining especially that Carter was not sufficiently proactive on the military front and that concern with civil matters led him to ignore tactical military realities. It is likely Wilson's fame as a firearms authority – he had acted as an expert witness in murder trials at the Old Bailey – and reputation as a first-class operative while with SOE in Europe, before his transfer to SRD, carried some weight with Courtney. Wilson's background as a Cambridge-educated Harley Street surgeon can also have done him no harm in this regard.[22]

Courtney later claimed he had viewed Wilson as a 'bullshit mer-chant' who could not be taken seriously. And in this assessment he was partly correct. While much of what Wilson tells us in his various reports is accurate and even astute, both an official report written shortly after the war, and a letter he wrote to Malcolm MacDonald – former British Governor-General of Malaya and British Borneo – in 1957, contain a number of bizarre inflations of his own role in the operation, especially vis-a-vis that of Carter. These include that Wilson (not Carter) was the commanding officer of Semut II from the start (with Carter shunted to some imaginary 'Sarawak Area Command'), that in this capacity Wilson had led the raid at Long Lama (which in fact took place before he joined the operation), and that Carter's role was primarily to represent the Sarawak Government.[23]

Sheppard was so concerned about the inaccuracies in both Wilson's Report and the letter to MacDonald – including in Wilson's account, contained in the Report, of the ambush at Marudi – that he later wrote lengthy rebuttals of both. Courtney himself commented on the 'unjustified criticism' of Carter contained in the Report. Nevertheless, in defiance of this evidence of the unreliability of Wilson's claims, Courtney repeated Wilson's accusations concern-ing Carter's neglect of military priorities and ignorance of tactical realities in his own book, published in 1993.[24]

However – strangely – in the book Courtney attributes this accusation to 'some of the British officers' in Semut II. But only two British officers took part in Semut II: Wilson and Eadie. Eadie admired both Carter and his approach greatly, as is evident from his memoir. The accusation emanated from Wilson alone.[25]

Why would Courtney choose to fudge the truth about this? It can hardly have been to protect Wilson, who had died twenty years earlier. Indeed, Courtney was highly critical of Wilson in Truscott's book, *Voices from Borneo*, which appeared only a few years after

Courtney's own. We can only conclude that the evasion occurred to create the impression that the criticism of Carter was more widespread than it actually was.

In fact, it seems that Courtney shared Wilson's view of Carter as more attuned to civil than military matters. He is quite explicit about this when he describes Carter's General Report on Semut II as 'not that of a military man [. . .] It is rather that of a practical idealist and man of sensibility.' And in his later descriptions of Carter he carefully emphasises the man's idealism, concern for civilians and rapport with locals, but fails to mention any military achievement.[26]

So was this view valid? It is an odd question to pose, since from the start the operation's concern with the eventual resumption of British rule in Sarawak meant that its civil and military objectives were intertwined. Thus, its leaders were chosen because of their long-term civilian connections in the territory, and as the operation progressed there was considerable slippage between participation in BBCAU and participation in Operation Semut – John Fisher, William Ditmas and David Leach, for instance, all played simultaneous roles in both.

Carter was certainly deeply concerned about the wellbeing of local peoples, and had made the reoccupation of Marudi (a major focus of Wilson's censure) one of Semut II's main priorities. However, as Windeyer from 20th Brigade recognised, there were good military reasons to take the town. And while working to reimpose civil administration and order there, Carter nevertheless sent troops to oppose *Fujino Tai* on the Tutoh River and organised strikes in the volatile Tinjar River area – all the while pleading for more men so as to advance these military actions.

Ironically, of the three commanding officers of Semut I, II and III, Carter was the only one not to receive an adjutant with responsibility for civilian affairs, leaving him little choice but to take on himself the increasingly onerous work of civilian administration. It is also worth noting that of the three, Carter was the only one to personally engage in a direct military strike on the enemy (the Marudi ambush). It is difficult to sustain the view that he prioritised civil matters over military ones.

∾

We are left with the sobering conclusion that SRD HQ's main grievance against Carter stemmed from the latter's unrelenting demand for assistance for the peoples of the Tinjar River. In the absence of documentation it is impossible to determine the level or levels at which this grievance was felt, leaving us, unfortunately, with little option but to attribute the sacking to an undifferentiated SRD HQ. There is some evidence that Courtney did, in fact, attempt to obtain the reinforcements Carter requested. Thus a telegram Courtney sent to SRD HQ at Morotai either in early July or early August requests 'urgent reinforcement' for Semut II: 'send maximum number available up to 10 <u>fully equipped</u>.' However, these reinforcements never materialised.[27]

Looking back now, with the benefit of hindsight, it seems obvious that SRD HQ – perhaps at a level above Courtney – had decided at an early stage that Semut II was of lower priority than either Semut I or Semut III, reflected in the many fewer reinforcements ultimately committed to it. Ironically, one of the features that had initially made the Baram River attractive as the site for the overall Semut HQ – its strategic location close to the oilfields and a large Japanese presence – may have eventually sealed the fate of Carter's Semut II. Wilson later commented that the Baram was 'the most sensitive spot in the enemy "rear"' and that 'the only first-class enemy troops in Sarawak' were stationed here. The flight of hundreds more into the Bakong-Beluru-Nyabor area created a powerful Japanese force that SRD HQ probably saw as beyond the capabilities of Semut II to resist in any meaningful way.[28]

Certainly, SRD HQ's refusal to provide reinforcements to help protect the peoples of the Tinjar River did not stem from a lack of available men: Semut III received seventeen reinforcements in August alone (although nine of these were for a separate special-purpose operation). Rather it seems that, for SRD HQ, military realities dictated that SRD could do little more for the peoples of this area.

Carter, however, refused to acquiesce to SRD HQ's realities and remained implacably opposed to the abandonment of the Tinjar peoples – a view expressed in his reports and signals from the time. He argued that with extra reinforcements the enemy attack parties might be harassed to the degree that they would turn aside from their movement inland and head further southwest, away from the densely populated Baram River basin. He saw Courtney's refusal to send more operatives as a betrayal of the Tinjar, and potentially Baram, peoples and an abnegation of the promises that Carter – with SRD backing – had made to them.[29]

The AIF's 9th Division has often been criticised – including by SOA's own official historian – for its refusal to move inland to the aid of Dayak peoples during the reoccupation of Sarawak. And criticism is warranted: the Division surely had a moral obligation to protect groups threatened as a direct result of their support for Australian forces. Whether the criticism should be directed at 9th Division or the Australian Government, however, is moot. The Division was under direct instruction from its political masters to minimise its military engagement in Borneo; Courtney himself commented later that 9th Division was confined to the coastal strip and main towns 'by order of the government in Canberra'.[30]

The same cannot be said for SRD HQ: it was much less constrained by Australian Government dictate. And it seems that Courtney and his superiors had arrived at the same shameful conclusion with respect to the Tinjar River as that reached by the

Australian Government with respect to Sarawak's entire inland area: protection of its peoples was simply not worth the risk and expenditure. Here was Carter's sin, easily expressed as a favouring of civil concerns over military realities: he refused to view the peoples of the Tinjar as expendable. SRD HQ, on the other hand, clearly did.

In SRD HQ's defence we must acknowledge the widespread belief among Allied soldiers in Borneo at the time – in the wake of the dropping of the atomic bombs on Hiroshima and Nagasaki – that a Japanese surrender was imminent. By the time of Carter's dismissal, Courtney was already in receipt of a 9th Division memo discussing action to be taken at Japan's surrender, and his HQ had produced its own 'Outline Plan' to deal with such an exigency.[31]

Nevertheless, this cannot completely excuse them. Even though this belief turned out to be true, it was no certainty at the time, as the surrender memos and plans themselves are at pains to point out. Perhaps more importantly, the response of Japanese troops in the field to any capitulation by their own High Command was unpredictable; Japanese soldiers were renowned for fighting to the death rather than submitting to capture by the enemy. Indeed, as we shall see, some continued to fight on in Sarawak long after the formal Japanese surrender.

In the event, the peoples of the Tinjar River, and those of the adjoining Baram River, were lucky. While Carter was at Labuan with Courtney, around 11 August, the Japanese attack parties pushing so aggressively up the Tinjar came to a sudden halt. This quickly – and quite unexpectedly – turned into a retreat: within days they had retired back northward, to the area around Beluru from whence they came. It appeared their advance had been a punitive foray only, designed to exact revenge against Ibans in the immediate area. Nevertheless, Japanese troops in their thousands remained dug in around Beluru; Carter continued to dread what would happen when they ran out of food, as they inevitably would before too long.[32]

But then on 15 August – the day after Carter's formal withdrawal from the operation – the Japanese High Command surrendered. In the days afterwards, Wilson – now commanding officer of Semut II – increased Horsnell's force in the Tinjar River area to six men, the reinforcements taken from Marudi. Their orders were to establish a defensive perimeter south of Beluru beyond which the Japanese could not advance southwards towards the interior. In the meantime, 9th Division organised leaflets in Japanese – advising the enemy of the High Command action and seeking their surrender – to be dropped on enemy encampments.

For several weeks there was silence from Aikyo and a strange, unnerving stalemate prevailed. Horsnell reached the dreary conclusion that the enemy force would not capitulate but intended instead to fight its way out: moving either further down the coast to Bintulu, or into the interior along the Tinjar River.[33]

But Dayak spirit beings can never be discounted and, in this area at least, they were keeping watch over their human supplicants. On 18 September Japanese HQ at Sapong in British North Borneo sent a radio message to Aikyo ordering him to surrender, and on 20 September he obeyed: relinquishing his sword to Windeyer at Miri. In the following days, all those under his command rapidly and rather meekly gave up their arms. The 20th Brigade Report notes that most were glad to be captured. The starvation, illness and attacks from locals to which they had increasingly been subject had seemingly resulted in their utter demoralisation.[34]

Yet Carter was under no illusion as to the repercussions for the peoples of the Tinjar River and nearby areas if the surrender had not taken place when it did.

> The real people of the interior who had rendered us such loyal service [. . .] would have suffered increasing hardship and bewilderment, ignorant as they were of the political and military restrictions affecting their territory.[35]

In this case neither 9th Division nor the Australian Government would have been exclusively to blame. SRD HQ must have borne some of the culpability.

The situation with *Fujino Tai* was another matter altogether. When Wilson returned to the Tutoh River on 14 August – sending Wood back to Marudi to take charge of administration there in the absence of Carter – he discovered that the column had evacuated Long Gak and resumed its march eastwards into the increasingly rugged terrain of the middle Tutoh. It appeared to have no intention of surrendering – perhaps its commanders did not even know of their government's formal capitulation. Indeed, some of its forward elements had already begun to trickle northeast – as Wilson had predicted – up the Melinau River, potentially taking them into Semut I's territory.

Wilson set up his new HQ at Long Gak and his force continued its miserable war of attrition. But now, in addition to ongoing harassment designed to turn the column around, they also tried to apprise *Fujino Tai* of its government's surrender. They left notes and leaflets for its members to find; although some of these were picked up they had no effect on the column's forward momentum. The operatives even resorted to leaving radios. Hallam:

> Wilson and I personally thinned them out effectively & regularly with booby-traps and picking off stragglers – so much so that when we left an 'MCR' radio with note on it to listen to Radio Tokyo for news of their surrender etc the buggers were

too scared to touch it – walked around & Wilson & I recovered it a week later intact.[36]

In the coming days, men from Semut II picked up three Javanese forced labourers who had escaped from the column. The escapees told them that the two Kenyah guerrillas taken prisoner at Long Beruang were being forced by Fujino to act as guides. These men knew the routes from the Melinau River across to the Limbang River in Semut I's territory. And indeed, the body of the column was now moving up the Melinau. In response, Wilson sent more signals to Semut I warning of its impending arrival.[37]

If *Fujino Tai*'s commanders thought this new route promised reprieve from the hardships of the Tutoh River, they were tragically mistaken. The terrain between the Tutoh and Limbang Rivers is cruel, even today: endlessly hilly, crisscrossed with flood-prone rivers, covered with jungle and pitted with dismal leech- and mosquito-infected swamps. It was so challenging in 1945 that Semut II troops harassing *Fujino Tai* had problems establishing a supply line across it.

We can only imagine the horrors of this brutal march for the many civilians – including children – in the column. Nor was the cruelty inflicted only by the landscape or the Allies. Yonosuke Kagaya, a survivor of the march, later wrote:

> We had to walk under a blistering sun more than ten kilometres a day with very little food. One night a young man was caught stealing another's food. Next morning the head of the Unit, Lieut. Fujino, gathered everyone together and announced: 'Someone stole another's food last night. We are going to hang him as a lesson to everyone.'[38]

Conditions were so grim that mothers suffocated their children to death. As Semut II troops followed in the column's footsteps, they encountered dead Japanese bodies – including some hanging from trees – beside the track.[39]

໖໑

At the end of August Semut II received two new reinforcements, Lieutenant Percy 'Snowy' Middleton and Corporal Donald 'Don' McLean, both veterans of previous SRD operations. They were inserted specifically to bolster the force dealing with *Fujino Tai*. After weeks of resisting Carter's pleas for reinforcements for Semut II's Tinjar River party, SRD HQ now felt sufficiently moved by what was happening along the Tutoh, Melinau and Limbang Rivers to provide additional men.

There is no record anywhere of Wilson having requested reinforcements. However, his radioed warnings had caused Harrisson – by Harrisson's own admission – to kick up a fuss about the fact that *Fujino Tai* was heading in Semut I's direction. It seems not unlikely that the reinforcements were part of a desperate last-minute attempt to head off the column – and shepherd it westwards towards the coast – before it reached Semut I territory.[40]

The new reinforcements are startling for another reason. With the Japanese surrender on 15 August, 9th Division had become de facto military governor of Sarawak, British North Borneo and Brunei, and had immediately decreed that all offensive action against Japanese must cease forthwith. While the post-surrender activities of Semut II parties on the Tinjar River – which had done nothing beyond establishing a defensive perimeter around Japanese troops congregated there – could be seen as complying with this edict, the same cannot be said for Semut II's war against *Fujino Tai* on the Tutoh, Melinau and Limbang Rivers.

Nor was this the extent of the disobedience. 9th Division had also instructed that all SRD patrols be withdrawn. Had Wilson immediately obeyed this latter injunction, Semut II's dogged four-month battle to keep the Japanese out of the Baram watershed would likely have come to nought. Without the continuing presence of patrols on the Tinjar and, especially, the Tutoh Rivers it is almost certain some Japanese – most likely those in *Fujino Tai* – would have made it through to the Baram River itself.

The reinforcements sent to Wilson two weeks after the formal Japanese surrender – long after 9th Division's surrender policy had been disseminated – confirm that Wilson was not operating alone in this regard: he was doing so with Courtney's connivance. In fact, Harrisson reports that Courtney turned a blind eye to his similar subversion of the ceasefire orders further east in Semut I territory.[41]

Middleton was immediately given charge of a party of four operatives – Gilman, Conleth-Smith, Graham and McLean – along with eleven guerrillas, plus scouts and carriers. His orders were to follow the Japanese column northwards into Semut I territory. Davey, with twelve Dayak carriers, was left behind at the Tutoh River to organise ongoing supply for this party from the mouth of the Melinau River. *Fujino Tai* had long since ceased to be a single force: some members now drifted far behind the main body while others had abandoned it altogether and struck out alone or in small groups. Wilson retained a number of Semut II units in the Tutoh and lower Melinau River area to deal with these remnants.[42]

Middleton's party reached the Limbang River, via the Medalam River, around 20 September. There Middleton took command of the Semut I men in the area – including Fred Sanderson, a member of the original reconnaissance party that had landed at Bario six months earlier. We do not know what Harrisson thought of Middleton's assumption of command in Semut I territory. But we do know what Middleton thought of Harrisson: in his report written in early October he flayed Semut I's senior officers on a number of fronts, including their treatment of their own men.[43]

The remainder of the *Fujino Tai* story will be taken up in my second book. For now, we should note that Harrisson later claimed Semut II had permitted *Fujino Tai* to pass largely unmolested through its own territory en route to that of his Semut I, only mounting some (inept) resistance in response to his protests. This assertion would be comical were it not so egregious. At least two Semut II operatives, as well as a number of Dayak guerrillas and auxiliaries, were injured – some of them seriously – fighting *Fujino Tai* over several months along the Kalijau, Tutoh, Melinau, Medalam and Limbang Rivers. More heartbreakingly, several Dayak guerrillas and auxiliaries lost their lives during this bleak campaign. As a result, by the time the column reached Semut I it was much depleted from when it had first appeared at Labi in late June.[44]

Harrisson also tells us that as a result of this incompetence on the part of Semut II, he was forced to contend with the column for five months. Reader, be aware: *Fujino Tai* began to appear in Semut I's territory in late August, and finally surrendered at the end of October.[45]

Small wonder that Carter – a recurrent victim of Harrisson's mendacity – wrote wearily about him in a letter to Eadie in 1947:

> What unadulterated tripe that man puts over and apparently gets away with. I sometimes feel tempted to try and show him up but have not the time or financial backing.[46]

༄

Middleton's excursion in the Limbang area was short-lived. He, along with the other members of his party, was withdrawn to Marudi at the end of September for extraction to Labuan. With the cessation of formal hostilities the operatives were being sent home, in line with Australian military orders. Hallam continued to fight *Fujino Tai* remnants with Wilson along the Melinau River until his own recall to Marudi on 7 October. Once there he was involved in handing over to BBCAU representatives, before being evacuated by barge down the Baram River to Labuan on 16 October. Hallam and Wilson were among the last to leave.[47]

Five months after Carter's tiny band had emerged from the Akah River onto the Baram at the beginning of May, Semut II had come to an end. It had consisted of no more than twenty operatives at any one time – a total of twenty-two in all – plus around two hundred armed guerrillas. Yet it had succeeded in driving the Japanese out of the Baram River and taking over Marudi, the area's administrative and commercial heart, where it had re-established stable civil administration. And, perhaps even more remarkably, it had somehow contrived to dissuade almost two thousand enemy troops from moving inland up the Baram and Tinjar Rivers where they would have done irreparable harm to Dayak populations.[48]

This success was achieved as much through the exercise of guile – especially the cultivation of widespread rumour – as direct military action, in keeping with the logic of special operations activities. Yet for this reason it has never been fully appreciated. This can possibly be put down to the politics of the intelligence environment at the time, which saw SRD develop a strange concern with 'kill counts' – the number of Japanese killed during an operation – at the expense of other markers of operational success.

SRD was under extreme pressure in 1945 due to its poor track record: the organisation had, to date, presided over many more failures and near-misses than successes. The Borneo operations were meant to redeem this dispiriting history and produce results that would demonstrate the organisation's worth in the broader, highly politicised, Allied intelligence marketplace. In this context SRD appears to have seized on Semut's kill counts as an effective means of touting the operation's success.

Semut's kill counts appear frequently in operational reports and are provided in both the SOA Official History and Courtney's own later published account. They have been repeated so regularly since that we might almost see them – with tongues only slightly in cheeks – as the equivalent of the key performance indicators that are the despair of many modern bureaucrats. It is surely no accident that Courtney later quoted Semut's overall kill count of around fifteen hundred Japanese troops to claim the operation was thus 'cost-effective', or that Major General C.H. Finlay, SRD's former deputy director, cited it as evidence that the larger SRD effort was justified.[49]

Carter had severe misgivings about the emphasis on kill counts. He argued that other operational achievements are often far more significant than the number of enemy casualties. He also pointed out that kill counts are unreliable in their dependence on the accuracy and honesty of those doing the reporting. Dayaks at the time had a different conception of numbers from Europeans, and their counts were likely to be imprecise. And in the absence of outside scrutiny, unscrupulous operatives and commanding officers might well inflate the numbers. Indeed, the fact that Semut's kill counts were accepted without question at the time suggests their purpose was primarily advertorial.[50]

Poor Carter. As a result of these reservations he was a reluctant provider of the necessary numbers: in contrast with those of Semut I, in particular, kill counts appear rarely in his reports. In fact, it is possible that his unwillingness to embrace this practice contributed to SRD HQ's irritation with him.

Years later, Courtney agreed that kill counts were unreliable, especially for Semut I. Nevertheless, the importance accorded them in assessing the value of the Semut operations – both at the time and in the years since – cannot be underestimated. Yet it is hard not to agree with Carter that the number of enemy killed usually tells us little about the success of a special operation. Here the overall aims are often no less political than military, and the military aims themselves may be most effectively achieved with minimal loss of life.[51]

Semut's military successes, including those of Semut II, cannot be discussed piecemeal; they warrant a detailed analysis across the operation in its entirety. This will be carried out in my second book. For now, with respect to its own political objectives at least – although not, perhaps, to those of Sarawakians with a mind for independence – Semut II would have to be judged a success. Through the use of diplomacy and the careful establishment of civil order, Carter had smoothed the path, throughout the Baram River basin, for the speedy resumption of colonial rule sought by SRD's British partners. He had won his imperial peace as well as his anti-Japanese war. And in spite of their frustrations with Carter, his superiors in SRD were conscious of what he had accomplished: after the war he was awarded a Distinguished Service Order for his contribution to the operation.

Locals who served under Carter in Semut II were less fortunate. Just as the Semut II operation itself had suffered from SRD HQ's decision to concentrate resources in Semut I and Semut III, so recognition for its hundreds of local participants fell victim to Carter's sacking. At the end of the war, Carter and Wilson agreed that Wilson would be responsible for submitting award recommendations for Semut II personnel. However, while he submitted recommendations for the operatives – almost half of whom were subsequently awarded decorations for their Semut II service – Wilson appears to have made no recommendations for local recipients other than Tama Weng Ajeng.[52]

In this respect, Semut II contrasts starkly with Semut I and Semut III, both of whose local participants received a large number of awards. As a result, the names of local men who risked – and in some cases gave – their lives in the Baram River basin in 1945 have largely eluded public memory.

PART III
THE REJANG RIVER

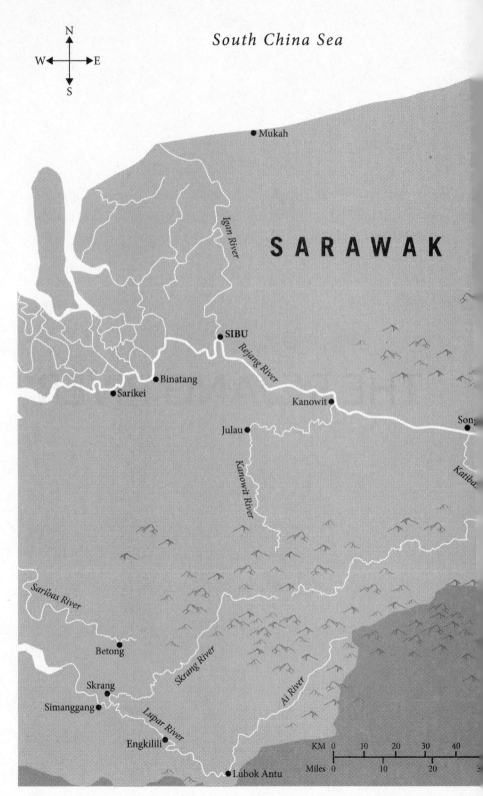

Rejang River and environs in 1945.

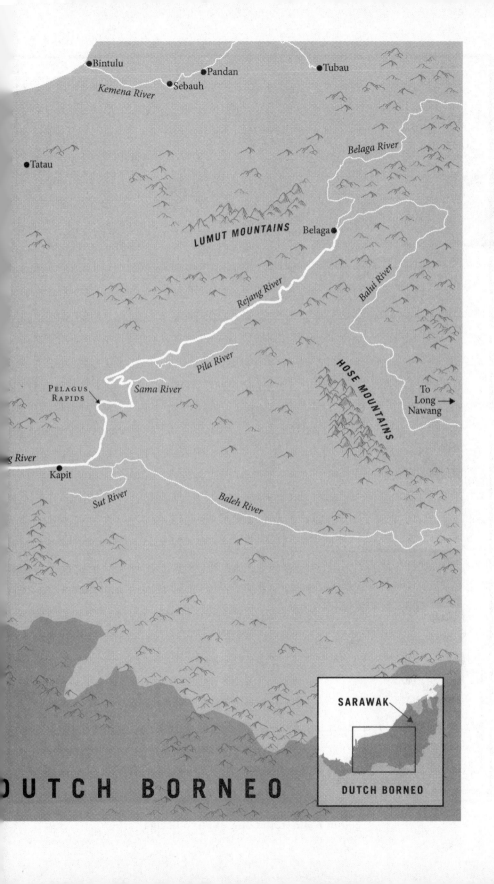

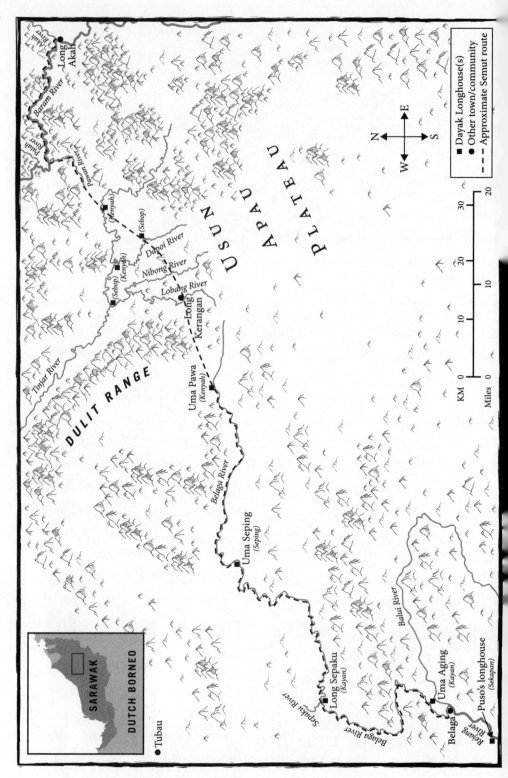

Semut route from Long Akah to Belaga.

11

TO THE REJANG

GHOSTLY TENDRILS OF MIST rose off the Baram River on the morning of 21 May as canoes carrying Captain Bill Sochon, Sergeant Abu Kassim and Sergeant Keith Barrie departed Long Akah. As the farewells of Toby Carter and his Semut II men echoed more and more faintly behind, and the great vastness of the jungle closed in on either side of the river, Sochon felt a quiet elation. At last he had command of his own operation and was leading his men into territory he knew. At the same time, he was horribly aware of the perils ahead. The party was embarking on a mission of almost inconceivable recklessness.[1]

Semut III's primary area of operation was to be the majestic Rejang River, which flows from Belaga in the remote centre of Sarawak to Sarikei on the Rejang delta in the west. The Rejang River is the longest and most important waterway in Sarawak; it was certain that the Japanese would have established encampments at key towns down its length and, in a country without roads, would be using it extensively for travel and transport. In addition, in travelling down the Rejang towards the coast, Sochon's tiny party would be moving closer and closer to the presumed Japanese head-quarters at Kuching. This was a journey into the belly of the beast.[2]

But Sochon's worries were not confined to the Japanese. He was also acutely aware that for his mission to succeed he needed to recruit guerrillas from two Dayak groups: the Kayan and related peoples living around Belaga, and the Iban living further down the Rejang River. Having spent nine years in Sarawak before the war, Sochon was under no illusion about the difficulties of this project. Both groups had been among Borneo's most voracious maraud-ers in the past, aggressively preying on neighbouring peoples. Longstanding enmities between them would create difficulties for any attempt to unite them into a single fighting force.

Yet Sochon knew that to win the Rejang he first needed to win both groups and persuade them to put aside their grievances. The strong Baram current that morning swept the Semut III party inex-orably not only towards the Japanese, but also, as Sochon saw it, towards a potential hotbed of inter-tribal animosity.

ତ∽

As the boats moved out into the current on 21 May, the party's imme-diate destination was Belaga at the top of the Rejang River. Getting there would involve a difficult journey from the Baram River basin to the Belaga River basin via the Dulit range. In 1945 this was very remote country, part of a high volcanic plateau called the Usun Apau, swathed in dense jungle and crisscrossed by countless rivers and streams. The maps the party carried were full of inaccuracies, making them heavily reliant on their Dayak guides.

In the boats with the operatives was an old Iban ex-Sarawak constable – we are never told his name, even though he stayed with the operation until its end – who had walked into Long Akah several days earlier and offered his services, as well as several Kenyah guides/porters. Packed around them, along with their personal belongings and equipment, were extra guns and ammunition, ten days supply of food, a substantial medical treatment kit, parachute silk and a generous supply of Straits dollars, most of it received in the recent storpedo drop. There was also an ATR-4 portable radio transceiver and aerial with which they intended to maintain regular contact with Semut II – which would then relay messages on to HQ. Keith Barrie carried his own MCR miniature radio, a short-wave radio receiver known as the 'biscuit tin receiver' because it came packed into a biscuit tin for use in clandestine activity.[3]

The boundary between Semut II and Semut III was to follow a rough line from Bintulu on the central coast through Belaga to Long Nawang in Dutch Borneo: anything north of this belonged to Semut II and anything south (including Belaga and Long Nawang themselves) to Semut III. In addition to the overall objectives common to all three Semut parties, Sochon – having served in the Sarawak Constabulary before the war – was tasked with recruiting ex-Sarawak Rangers and constables into Semut's auxiliary forces.[4]

The plan was that the advance party of Sochon, Abu Kassim and Barrie would recruit local guerrillas at every stage of the journey. Reinforcements to train and lead the guerrillas, plus arms, would be dropped to them by Catalina once they reached the Rejang River. Sochon had radioed Headquarters the day before Semut III's departure from Long Akah to say that he expected to arrive in Belaga around 1 June and to request the Catalina's arrival on 4, 5 or 6 June. The advantage of a Catalina landing on the river, rather than Liberators dropping parachutes and storpedoes, was that it could carry more men and equipment. It could also provide more reliable delivery, especially in heavily jungled terrain.

Sochon had arranged for the Catalina to land directly on the Rejang, somewhere between Belaga and the mouth of the Pila River. Arrangements were left deliberately vague so his party could scout the area for an appropriate location for the rendezvous, and to allow for the possibility that bad weather or other circumstances might prevent it from occurring on any particular day.[5]

Guerrillas would be recruited from those groups – especially the Kayan – inhabiting the wild region from Long Akah to Belaga, the Belaga and Balui River valleys and the upper Rejang River, as well as from the Iban further down the Rejang.

The Kayan were the largest of the Dayak groups in the upper Rejang and Balui River area. While in pre-colonial times they had generally taken fewer heads than the Iban – concerning themselves more with plunder and slaves – they had nevertheless ruthlessly expanded their territories via raiding and warfare. However, many years earlier under Brooke rule, they had largely given up raiding and headhunting. Sochon knew the Kayan from his time living in Sarawak, and admired them. But while the Baram River Kayans under Kebing had pledged themselves to Semut II some weeks earlier, the loyalties of the Rejang and Balui River Kayans in this war were as yet unknown. They were potentially a formidable foe.[6]

The Iban, on the other hand, while ruthless expansionists like the Kayan, had also been among the most ardent headhunters of all Dayak groups. Some had resisted the eradication of headhunting – as well as the taxes levied by the Brooke regime – well into the twentieth century. Indeed, as recently as 1935 – only ten years earlier – Rajah Vyner Brooke had launched a punitive expedition against Iban rebels at Kanowit, a key town on the Rejang River. And, while Sochon did not yet know it, Donald Hudden, the pre-war District Officer of the Baram region, had been murdered and had his head taken in 1942 by Ibans from the upper Rejang River area.[7]

Before he left England to join SRD in 1944, Sochon had visited Bertram Brooke, brother and heir presumptive of Rajah Vyner Brooke, and confided to him the plan to send a small group of special operatives into Sarawak. According to Sochon, Brooke had advised him to avoid the Rejang River in favour of areas populated by Kayans and Kenyahs, whom Brooke considered more trustworthy than the Iban. This accorded with Sochon's own view of the Iban as vain and unreliable.[8]

Complicating matters further were the old hostilities flickering between the Iban and the Kayan. Sochon clung to the grim hope that both groups had been so antagonised by Japanese rule they would put aside their differences and cooperate with the Allies.

Once a guerrilla force had been recruited and reinforcements arrived to train and lead it, Semut III's mission was to take it down the Rejang River towards Sibu. The ultimate goal, to be carried out by a further offshoot operation called Hippo, was to liberate those held at a large POW camp known to have been established in Kuching. Hippo was to be Sarawak's equivalent of British North Borneo's Operation Kingfisher, the latter aimed at rescuing POWs incarcerated at Sandakan.[9]

The men knew that every mile they moved away from Long Akah brought them further into the Japanese orbit. They were aware that there was a Japanese garrison at Long Lama, further downstream on the very same river along which they were so sanguinely floating that morning, as well as a very large body of Japanese closer to the coast not far west of Marudi. They had learned from Carter's spies that Japanese patrols passed regularly through the Baram and Tinjar River areas, en route to Long Nawang in the old Dutch Borneo, in search of rice and other foodstuffs. This meant they might well encounter enemy soldiers in the Baram watershed, as well as on the Belaga and Balui Rivers further southwest.

The men had also heard several days earlier the momentous news of the Australian landings on Tarakan Island on 1 May. Sochon was deeply concerned about their effects on Japanese movements along the northeast coast of Sarawak: he assumed (correctly) that the Tarakan landings heralded an imminent invasion of Australian

troops on the north coast. In his view such an invasion would inevitably push the Japanese inland into the areas where his tiny party
was operating.[10]

∽

From Long Akah, the party headed first down the swift-flowing
Baram River. Birds and monkeys skimmed through the treetops on
either side, the air was filled with the sonorous throb of cicadas,
and the men must have wondered whether they really were in a war
zone. After around 20 miles (32 km) they turned south along a small
tributary, the Pawan, and here the immense, dense mass of the jungle closed in around them as the river narrowed. Once it became
too shallow for boat travel they shared out the load, shouldered
their packs, and continued on foot, leaving the canoes behind to be
retrieved later by their Kenyah porters. For days they trekked southwest through a shadowy jungled habitat: across the Dapoi, Nibong
and Lobang River systems, and climbing to 2500 feet (760 m) to
cross the Dulit range before descending to the headwaters of the
Belaga River.[11]

The overland travel, from the Pawan River to the headwaters
of the Belaga, was gruelling. Even when following known Dayak
tracks, the men were forced to hack their way through thick
undergrowth. The jungle was dense with rattan, a sprawling thorn-
covered climber prized by locals for the ropes, twines and bindings it
produced, but loathed by the operatives for the cunning with which
it tore at their hands and clothes – shredding trousers, shirts and
boots – and clutched at their packs. To avoid it they walked as often
as possible down the slippery beds of streams and rivers, always in
the shadow of giant trees.[12]

Days of heavy rain turned the paths to mud and made them
even more treacherous. The men were never dry: boots filled with
water, and saturated clothes, and heavy packs rubbed unbearably

against sodden skin. Leeches and mosquitoes left bites – rapidly transforming into sores – all over their bodies. To make matters worse, this was hilly country, and in places the ground was rough and rocky. Stones moving underfoot were a constant danger, especially while travelling uphill. Sometimes they crossed fast-flowing rivers, transporting their gear in relays using small, unstable local canoes.

Crossing the Dulit range brought a modicum of relief. Here, the narrow Dayak jungle track unexpectedly turned into a broad cutting, with trunks laid across gullies and streams, steps cut into the steepest inclines, and handrails fitted in the most precarious places. Sochon learned that these improvements had been carried out by the Japanese just three weeks earlier, using vast amounts of both local and imported labour. The cutting stretched for 9 miles (14 km) across challenging terrain; as a result, they completed in seven hours a crossing that for government officers in the past had taken three days. But their pleasure at this discovery was tempered by gnawing unease concerning the whereabouts of the Japanese, ghostly companions at their shoulders.[13]

Arriving at the Belaga River, the party was able to obtain canoes from a local longhouse and resume the journey by river, travelling downstream for several days until it reached Belaga. This was, in many respects, preferable to travelling overland. The men were released from the oppressive humidity of the jungle and the hurts caused by vegetation, leeches and mosquitoes; they could rest weary limbs, letting the river do the work. But river travel had its own trials, rarely proving to be the languid idyll of Western romance. Dayak canoes are narrow – fashioned out of single logs – and so require the compression of large European bodies into uncomfortably small spaces. They are also unstable, demanding that the men remain in the same position for hours which induced stiffness and cramps. The build-up of water inside left the men constantly wet, and the lack of roof or shade meant they were exposed for long periods to the sun and the glare off the water. They were also terrifyingly aware of the greater likelihood of unexpectedly encountering a Japanese patrol on a river than in the jungle.[14]

∽

Nevertheless, the journey had its consolations. Barrie found himself moved by the compelling isolation of the jungle:

> The great dark forests interspersed with occasional shafts of sunlight fracturing the gloom, a tangle of undergrowth away from the beaten tracks, with a whole separate community of wild life inhabiting the canopy above.[15]

And then there was the warm welcome extended in every longhouse along the way.[16]

As we have already seen, for Dayak groups throughout this area the provision of lavish hospitality to visitors was regarded as an almost sacred duty. After each day of hot, hard travel, the party would arrive in the late afternoon at a clearing cut out of the surrounding jungle above a river, at its centre the massive wooden structure of a longhouse. They would clamber up the entry ladder to the babble of excited voices from within, and enter the cool, shadowy recesses of the longhouse gallery. They were almost certainly bidden to be seated outside the chief's apartment in the centre of the longhouse, from where they would be formally welcomed. They would be fed and, to celebrate their presence, plied with alcohol: not only *borak*, the locally produced rice wine, but also often *arak*, a lethal brew condensed in local stills. Barrie was astonished at its potency:

> real firewater! – distilled tapioca root – oh boy! – more suited for use as outboard motor fuel in my jaundiced view.[17]

Here, as with longhouse hospitality elsewhere, the local aim was undoubtedly to render the visiting Europeans drunk. With his long experience of Sarawak, Sochon had schooled his men in the importance of not refusing proffered food or drink. As a result, nights were spent imbibing copious quantity of alcohol and many days, undoubtedly, dealing with the consequences. Barrie again:

> In one longhouse on the Sungei Dapoi [Dapoi River] early on,
> I, as usual, had to imbibe for 'King and Country' a mixture of
> borak and arak well into the night. Boy – was I ill! I have a
> clear recollection even now of some bare-arsed Kayan or Iban
> holding me up against a window of the longhouse while I was
> violently ill for quite a period of time.[18]

At some point during the evening, Sochon recruited his team of porters and guides for the following day and paid off that day's crew, who returned home to the previous day's longhouse. Following Carter, he took care to pay at the rate of 50c per day per person in Straits dollars, the same rates as had been in use before the war – allowing him to highlight European generosity and call to mind the bountiful days of Brooke rule. Similarly, again drawing on lessons from Carter, the party held a medical clinic on the longhouse gallery every morning before departure.[19]

Sochon knew Dayak culture well enough to recognise that the apparent warmth of the welcomes his party received did not guarantee local support for the Allied cause. Consequently, in spite of their exhaustion, he and Abu Kassim exerted themselves each evening to persuade the locals – especially the chiefs – to come on board. Fortunately most of the chiefs in this area spoke some Malay, and communication was easy. However, winning their support was harder than Sochon had expected. At every longhouse the discussion stretched far into the night by the dim light of the flickering *damar* lamps set along the gallery, animated voices reverberating in the cavernous space.

People throughout the area were deeply unhappy about the loss of essential commodities such as cloth and sugar that had occurred under Japanese rule. They were also angry over the behaviour of Japanese soldiers, including the desecration of burial grounds and the raping of women.[20]

Nevertheless, local Dayaks accepted the Japanese prerogative to rule, gained through defeating the previous European rulers. And like those further east on the Baram River, people here knew about the Japanese massacre of Europeans close by at Long Nawang. This undoubtedly only increased local appreciation of Japanese potency while at the same time underlining the abject weakness of Europeans.

As a result, supporting the Europeans was a dangerous decision on many levels; it could lead to reprisals not only from the Japanese, but also from affronted spirits. Chiefs had to be convinced the Allies would win the war, and Sochon and Abu Kassim described in detail the Allied armies that were even now massing to invade Sarawak. The chiefs were particularly worried about weaponry: how, they asked, can we possibly fight Japanese guns with our *parang*? This was a fair question, and Sochon and Abu Kassim responded by promising the imminent arrival of an aeroplane at Belaga, loaded with firearms that would be distributed to recruits.[21]

In at least one longhouse the decision was deemed too important to be made without higher consultation, and the chief announced that the matter would be referred to the omens. Accordingly, the next morning a pig was produced. Amidst much squealing, its throat was cut with a ceremonial flourish by the local grizzled omen specialist, and its liver removed and laid on the ground. While Sochon and his men gripped their guns, terrified of the consequences should the reading go against them, he examined it minutely. But the spirits were with them: the old man finally straightened and announced that the omens were in favour of Sochon and his men.[22]

Fortunately for the mission, Sochon and Abu Kassim proved remarkably persuasive advocates. At every longhouse along the way the deliberations ended after many hours with the chiefs agreeing to support the Allies, and young men promising to travel to Belaga in the coming days to join Semut III's guerrilla force. As the weary operatives settled down to sleep each night on the hard wooden floor outside the chief's apartment, the flow of voices down the longhouse almost certainly carried the excitement of impending warfare.

Sochon requested that in the meantime locals dispose of any Japanese who arrived in the area, and suggested ways of accomplishing this. Most involved duplicity, such as locals offering to carry Japanese weaponry over difficult ground or rivers, leaving the now weaponless Japanese vulnerable to sudden attack. Invariably in these discussions it quickly emerged that Dayaks needed little coaching in this kind of warfare. A favoured strategy, already practiced against Japanese patrols, was to welcome them enthusiastically and invite them to stay overnight – presumably outside the longhouse where taboos on the killing of guests did not apply.

> After the meal and ample gourds of tuak [rice wine], the state of inebriation of their guests timed to a nicety, a fresh bunch of heads would dangle like oversized, rotten grapes from the rafters of the longhouse above the chief's quarters.[23]

In every longhouse Sochon made it clear that Japanese heads could be taken, and this was undoubtedly the main reason for the swirling excitement triggered by each Semut III visit. As Sochon told Ivor Wren years later:

I would have liked to have stopped the operations at the pre-guillotine stage, but to the Kayans this was obviously the only worthwhile part of the whole game, and we needed their cooperation. War is not an occupation for the squeamish.[24]

Longhouse dwellers were not the only people they wooed. Sochon:

We marched for a couple of hours when I gave the order to stop. I had seen nothing, heard nothing, there was just something in the atmosphere that crept under my skin; a feeling that we were being watched. Could we have stumbled on a well-hidden Japanese patrol? We stood silent for a minute or two, listening. There was nothing but the continual drip of water from the rain-soaked branches and the occasional, far-off cry of a monkey. Then I turned round. Twenty yards behind me a small, brown figure stepped out from behind a tree. Naked but for a tiny sirat [loincloth] around his loins, and clutching a blowpipe in his hand, stood a Punan. I called out to him, and his shy, worried expression changed to a grin of recognition. As he began to walk forward, almost thirty more Punans material-ised out of the jungle on all sides of us. [. . .]

Their approach had been completely wraithlike. Not by so much as a snapped twig, a cough or a broken bough had they disclosed their presence, and yet they had been following the party for the past two hours.[25]

Groups of Penan, Borneo's elusive nomadic hunter-gatherer people, roamed the area. They were ready to assist with guiding and porting, and accommodated the party in their jungle shelters for at least one night. To Sochon's relief they also agreed to support the party in its campaign against the Japanese.[26]

Western commentators have often portrayed Penan support for the Allies during WWII in terms of a simple innocent people's love for their White masters. This misrepresents the pragmatism of the local response. While Penans largely managed to avoid Japanese soldiers during the occupation, they were hit hard by the unavailability of trade goods such as sugar, salt, knives and axes. They had also suffered as a result of the cessation of the government-run markets that had been held regularly in both Brooke Sarawak and Dutch Borneo under colonial rule, at which longhouse peoples had been forced to pay fair prices for Penan products. In addition, Penan groups in the area undoubtedly knew of the alliances Sochon's party was forming with their longhouse neighbours and trade partners, and were eager not to be left out.[27]

Barrie marvelled at Penan skill with the blowpipe: 'On a couple of occasions they brought down monkeys out of the jungle canopy with these weapons.' Later, Penan tracking and scouting prowess was to prove invaluable to the operation.[28]

☙

Fear of discovery by the Japanese haunted every step. At each longhouse the operatives questioned locals closely: how far away were the Japanese? When and where had any last been seen? How regularly did Japanese come to the area? Where were the closest garrisons? Before moving in to a new area, Sochon sent trusted locals ahead to spy out the route and obtain intelligence about Japanese movements. Nevertheless they lived on their nerves, acutely aware of the massive rewards available for anyone who betrayed them. The incongruity of their situation – feasting and carousing in the heart of enemy territory – was not lost on them. At night they slept in their military webbing containing loaded revolver, hand grenades and spare ammunition, and cradled their submachine guns in their arms.[29]

Everywhere they went, Sochon impressed on locals the need to conceal the presence of *orang puteh* in the area. However, in this he reckoned without the local bush telegraph. He discovered later that people on the Rejang River had long expected the party's arrival, having been aware of Semut since the first insertions into Bario in late March. Indeed, the Iban sent riddle-messages along the Rejang to notify groups further downstream that White men had returned.

> Babi belang siko', manok bilang siko', nadai celum sarambar,
> enggau gawa' ka orang ke udah parai, enti' ngaga kereja nya' apai-
> indai aki'-ini' idup magang, pulai ka menoa tu' lalu badu' parai.
>
> One white pig and one white fowl, with no dark colours on
> them at all, are the things to redeem those who have died, when
> the rite is performed fathers and mothers, grandparents and all
> will live again and come back to this earth, risen from the dead.

Babi belang (white pig) was a common Iban term for Europeans. Similarly, Kayans and Lahanans from the Balui River southeast of Belaga remembered, seventy years later, being told that the White people were back to fight the Japanese, and that they should kill any Japanese who entered their area and hide the bodies.[30]

However, only vague rumours concerning the presence of Europeans reached the Japanese at this point, in spite of the potential rewards for anyone who betrayed the Semut III party. Nevertheless, they were concerned enough to send several patrols into the area from Bintulu. Members of these patrols became some of the earliest victims of Semut III's fledgling guerrilla force.[31]

Sochon's party only learned for certain that there were no Japanese troops stationed permanently in Belaga – their initial destination – on the last stages of the journey, travelling down the Belaga River. This came as a great relief: an enemy garrison in the town would have left them with a choice between attempting to eradicate it or finding a hiding place where they could keep their presence a secret. Neither course of action would have been easy.

The party did discover that Japanese troops passed regularly through Belaga. These either came up the Rejang River from Kapit or crossed overland from Tubau (there were permanent garrisons in both towns). They also learned that a strong force of Japanese from Sibu (close to the mouth of the Rejang) had passed through Belaga just days earlier, heading up the Balui River to Long Nawang in the old Dutch Borneo. Semut III's luck had held again.[32]

∽

On 31 May the party arrived at the large Kayan longhouse at Long Sepaku, where the Sepaku River flows into the larger Belaga River one day's journey upstream from Belaga. On the other side of the river was another wide jungle cutting made recently by the Japanese, this one running north towards Tubau. Locals told the men that the cutting had been made to assist Japanese troops travelling to Long Nawang in search of rice. However, Sochon suspected that its main purpose was to provide the large concentration of forces on the Sarawak north coast with an escape route to the interior in the event of Allied landings, which must now appear imminent.[33]

Sochon's assessment was almost identical to that of Carter: an Allied invasion would see Japanese retreat to the very remote regions around Long Nawang in Dutch Borneo. There they planned to establish settlements and farms from whence they could engage in ongoing guerrilla warfare against occupying Allied forces, a strategy they had already used in New Guinea. Sochon soon discovered that the Japanese party to have passed most recently through Belaga en route to Long Nawang had gone there to assess the feasibility of double-cropping rice using conscripted labour and POWs. This reinforced his view that the cutting at Long Sepaku, along with the newly made one his group had used to cross the Dulit range several days earlier, was intended to facilitate rapid escape inland from coastal and downriver areas.[34]

The Kayans of Long Sepaku, like many other communities in the Belaga River/Balui River area, had suffered at the hands of Japanese troops journeying to Long Nawang: rice had been taken and people threatened and manhandled. They were eager for revenge and were willing recruits to Semut III's cause. Sochon and Barrie busied themselves discussing with locals ways and means to close the escape route.

In the meantime, Abu Kassim travelled by canoe to Belaga to size up the situation there in advance of Sochon's arrival. He was accompanied by Jok Imut, a Kayan from a longhouse located further downriver who had joined the Semut party a day or two earlier.[35]

ⓖ⊙

Lim Beng Hai, a young Chinese resident of Belaga, was at his home in the early evening of 31 May when he heard his brother shouting in the distance.

> My brother Huat was seen running with all the strength he could muster down the small hill leading to our living quarters. 'Liap, the Aussies are here!' was all that he could mutter through laboured breathing.[36]

His brother Lim Beng Huat had been bathing at the wharf when Jok Imut and Abu Kassim paddled in and tied up next to him.

> For sometime past, there had been discreet whispers of allied personnels parachuting into Bario. I was taken by surprise by this unexpected intrusion. [. . .] Jok introduced us and we shook hands. Thereafter, sheer excitement overcame me. I raced up the notched logs in bounds with the Sergeant and Jok behind me. I yelled.
>   'Tan! Tan! The allies are here!'

There was dead silence and suddenly the sounds of feet pounding the *kaki lima* [walkway outside a row of Chinese shops] planks. [. . .]

The Sergeant shook hands all round and the three-and-a-half years of caged emotions while under enemy occupation escaped like a burst boiler. Free! Free! Free! Tan whooped and pounded my shoulders while I hung tenaciously to the towel wrapped round my waist.[37]

Abu Kassim called a meeting with locals. There he explained that Allied soldiers were in the area and his commanding officer would arrive tomorrow. He urged them to support the Allied cause. The response was overwhelming: everyone, it seemed, wanted to be part of Semut's operation against the Japanese.[38]

The next day, 1 June, Sochon's party moved downriver to Belaga, meeting Abu Kassim and Jok Imut en route. They arrived in Belaga early in the evening, at that moment when the stifling heat of the afternoon finally begins to leach from the air. The journey from Long Akah had taken twelve days.

လ

The tiny settlement of Belaga was huddled in a small jungle clearing at the very top of the Rejang River. Today a regular ferry service plies the route between Kapit and Belaga, but in 1945 Belaga was a remote jungle outpost, cut off from Kapit by rapids that clogged the river in several places. In particular, the notorious Pelagus Rapids, located a short distance above Kapit, imposed a formidable barrier: around 3 miles (almost 5 km) of boiling water and jagged rocks. Starting in the 1960s the rapids were progressively neutralised using explosives, but in 1945 boats and goods usually had to be portaged along the riverbank above, a process that could take from four hours to an entire day depending on conditions.[39]

Rapids on the Belaga River created an additional barrier to travellers from the north and northeast, while the surrounding countryside in all directions was hilly, densely jungled and pitted with rivers and ravines.

Today, the construction of the Bakun Dam on the Balui River upstream has rendered the Rejang a shadow of its former self. But in 1945, even 270 miles (435 km) from the sea at Belaga it was breathtaking, close to 320 feet (100 m) wide. On the high bank above the Rejang the Brookes had built in 1884 a squat timber fort – Fort Vyner, named after the then heir apparent to the position of White Rajah.

The town itself in 1945 comprised twenty-one old Chinese wooden shophouses – joined together into a single long row with its covered wooden walkway running along the front – plus a separate quarter of Malay houses. Few Dayaks lived here, but a large Kayan longhouse was located thirty minutes paddle up the Balui River. Members of many longhouses found along the Belaga, Balui and upper Rejang Rivers came regularly to the town to trade rice and jungle products in return for commodities such as cloth, salt, sugar and oil, as well as to socialise and catch up on news.[40]

Late in the afternoon of 1 June 1945 the traditional Kayan wail of triumph, OOO OOO OOO – used especially by raiders returning to the longhouse with loot, heads and/or slaves – reverberated down the Belaga River from Kayan canoes carrying the Semut III party to the town. In Belaga the sound brought scores of people to the river. Minutes later, when the canoes swept up, hordes of cheering locals were waiting, crowding the wharf and lining the riverbank. An informal guard of honour formed as the men stepped ashore; it seemed that everybody in the area had come to participate in the celebration. In an orgy of excitement, the Japanese flag was lowered and Japanese ordinances and propaganda posters ripped from the walls of the fort.[41]

Francesca Sadai, a Rejang girl around nine years old, was in Belaga that day. She described to me many years later the sense of exultation that swept through the assembled crowd at the thought that Japanese rule was soon to end. But she also recalled her terror:

> Sergeant Barrie . . . he was big, very big. And he was differ-
> ent from anyone I had ever seen before . . . different from the
> Japanese. The Japanese . . . they were like ordinary people, just
> like us. But Sergeant Barrie was different, like something out of
> a story. I was very frightened.[42]

Keith Barrie was the first European she had ever seen.

The highest-ranking chief in the Belaga area, Oyong Puso, came to meet the Semut III party as it arrived. Many accounts describe Puso as Kayan, but in fact he was Sekapan, one of the other small Dayak groups – many closely related to the Kayan – scattered throughout the area. Sochon had met him several years earlier while working in Sarawak, and was anxious to recruit him to the Semut cause. However, a Semut pre-operation briefing paper had raised doubts about Puso's loyalties, describing him as a 'poor specimen' who was very likely addicted to opium, with the paper's author fearing that this may have caused him to fall under Japanese influence 'in order to obtain his supplies'. Barrie was also unimpressed by Puso, noting that he seemed 'inclined to "the bottle" or its equivalent'. A large flabby figure, there was a slackness to his face and a passivity to his manner that Europeans sometimes found at odds with his local reputation.[43]

Perhaps those who so judged Puso had forgotten that chiefs among the Kayan, Kenyah and related groups are often restrained and modest in their personal demeanour, so that to the untrained eye extraordinary men might appear ordinary. Locals were not so fooled; Puso was a *penghulu*, and revered as both a great warrior and a shrewd leader. He was seen to have immense influence with the spirits, to the extent that men could be struck dumb at the sight of his sword, and the weapons of other men deflected away from him, indeed sometimes killing their own wielders.[44]

Importantly for Semut III's purposes, Puso's longhouse was located downstream on the Rejang River itself, close to Iban territory. He was respected and feared not only among the Kayans and other groups found around Belaga, but also among Ibans of the Rejang and Baleh Rivers. It was vital for Sochon's plan to incorporate men from both areas into his guerrilla force that he first win Puso's backing.

So it was with simple relief that he noted, on 1 June 1945, the warmth of Puso's welcome and his immediate promise of support for the operation.[45]

∾

Puso was not alone in offering Semut III his patronage. After the usual welcoming party and sequence of lengthy negotiations – during which the questions raised at every longhouse so far were again thrashed out – Baling Avun, a local Kayan chief, took the party under his wing. Baling was young, in his late twenties, and had been to school in Belaga for two years, becoming one of the first literate Kayans in the area. Later, in 1961, he produced a manuscript about Kayan religion on a typewriter provided by, of all people, Tom Harrisson.[46]

In spite of his tender years, Baling was highly respected among locals, and his support for the operation was to prove crucial. It was also brave. Belaga was frequently visited by Japanese soldiers – much more frequently than Long Akah – and like Tama Weng Ajeng and Kebing on the Baram River, Puso and Baling risked not only their own lives, but also those of many others in backing Semut. Baling took the even more courageous step of offering the men accommodation in his own large longhouse, Uma Aging, located slightly upstream from Belaga on the Balui River.[47]

The party stayed at Uma Aging over the following week, recovering from their journey. As they recuperated, they watched the town of Belaga swell with an influx of Kayan and other Dayak volunteers from surrounding jungled areas. These men were drawn by Semut III's promise of an aircraft bringing firearms, and the consequent thrilling prospect of battle – even, possibly, of headhunting. Many of the new arrivals, along with many townspeople, had never seen an aeroplane, and fewer had taken part in a headhunting expedition. Unsurprisingly, the town quivered with expectation and excitement.[48]

Sochon, however, was increasingly concerned about a possible Japanese retreat inland towards Long Nawang once the Allied assault commenced on the north coast. Such a retreat could bring large numbers of Japanese through Belaga. Accordingly, on 3 June he despatched Abu Kassim to Bintulu, the coastal town northwest of Belaga. His brief was to scout out the strength of Japanese forces there and gather intelligence about their intentions.

In the meantime, Sochon and Barrie remained at Uma Aging. There they did an inventory of their magazine and decided that they had enough spare weapons to immediately arm fourteen guerrillas. From among the many eager volunteers twelve local men, mostly Kayan, and two Chinese traders visiting from Kapit, were selected. To these they distributed .303 rifles, one or two carbines, and about one thousand rounds of ammunition before commencing basic weapons training.[49]

Sochon's main priority was to arrange for the arrival of the Catalina, scheduled for 4, 5 or 6 June. Careful preparation was vital because, since leaving Long Akah two weeks earlier, the party had failed in all attempts to make radio contact with Semut II (which, as we now know, did not gain reliable radio reception until after Eadie's arrival on 6 June). The ongoing radio silence was of considerable concern to Sochon: it meant HQ could not know that his party had reached the Rejang River. Nor had he been able to provide HQ with the location – within the large pre-designated zone – where the Catalina rendezvous would take place.

Fortunately, such a scenario had been foreseen. On Sochon's instructions Belaga locals manufactured a prearranged signal, the letter 'H', out of tree trunks lashed together. This was floated out onto the Rejang River beside the town, where it was held in position by rattan ropes fastened to the banks. Smoke grenades were also put in place, ready to be activated at the first sound of an aircraft. These crude devices were the only reliable means the party now had of alerting a Catalina to its whereabouts when the aircraft arrived over the area on the scheduled dates.[50]

On 4 June, Sochon and Barrie left Baling's longhouse early in the morning and paddled downstream, arriving at the Belaga river-bank by dawn. There they were joined by a throng of eager locals. All day they waited, ears straining for the distant throb of an engine, binoculars repeatedly scanning the sky to the north. On the follow-ing day, 5 June, they repeated the exercise. As each hour went by without the plane's arrival the sense of disappointment among the assembled locals increased. The final appointed day for the ren-dezvous was 6 June and Sochon and Barrie took up their positions beside the river with hopes high. But as hour after hour slid by with no sign of the plane, hope turned inexorably to despair. By nightfall the plane had not come.[51]

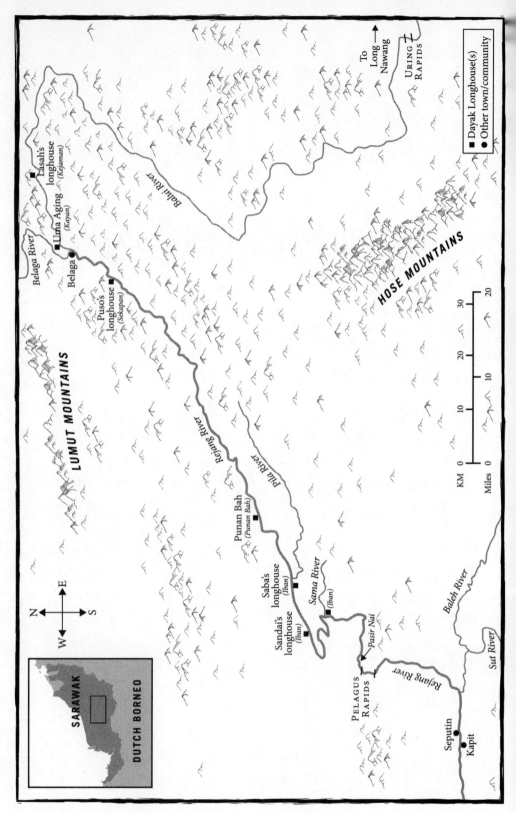

Upper Rejang River and environs in 1945.

12

MASSACRE AT PASIR NAI

THE NON-APPEARANCE OF THE Catalina was a disaster for Semut III. Over the preceding two weeks, in all their interactions with local people, the operatives had emphasised the imminent arrival of the aircraft and the subsequent distribution of the firearms it carried. Local expectations had been raised accordingly, and men from throughout the area were assembling at Belaga in the hope of joining the guerrilla force. The failure of the plane to materialise roused deep disappointment, even fury.

Worse, it was taken by many not only as a sign that the Semut III men did not keep their promises but, even more tellingly, that they suffered from the same lack of potency revealed among Europeans during the Japanese invasion. Both of these ideas radically diminished their appeal as potential allies in the eyes of local Dayaks.

Sochon and Barrie were not to know it at the time, but there had been massive disruption to the air supply program over the previous two months. Following the disappearance of the Pockley plane after the insertion of the Semut reconnaissance party, two more

200 Flight aircraft had been lost: one on Operation Sunbaker in Timor, and the other on Operation Agas in northern Borneo. In addition, many available air cover and resupply resources were being used at Tarakan and, from 10 June, Labuan. Semut III's radio silence undoubtedly intensified the problem: SRD HQ had no idea whether they had reached the Rejang River or, indeed, whether they were still alive.

As ill will within the local population grew, Baling Avun took the sensible course of action and called in his omen specialist. A pig was duly killed and its liver read. To the party's immense relief, the signs were once again good, indicating that the Allies would eventually defeat the Japanese. Over the next two harrowing weeks, as the plane obstinately refused to make an appearance, Baling ordered no less than ten pigs slaughtered in order that the omens could be read. This indicates, perhaps more clearly than anything else, the knife edge on which Semut III – and the lives of its members – balanced. Yet, whether by fortune or design on the part of Puso and Baling, the party's luck held. Every reading indicated the spirits' continued confidence in the success of the operation.[1]

The support of Puso and Baling Avun during this period was critical. Indeed, it is not too much of a stretch to say that without their sponsorship Semut III would have been stillborn. Their combined standing among local Dayak groups was immense, and together they managed to hold these behind the Semut III party. Both men were awarded the British Empire Medal after the war for their services to the operation.[2]

Local Chinese and Malays, however, were a different matter, with many becoming openly hostile and contemptuous towards the Semut III men. The animosity was unnerving, particularly in its threat of betrayal to the Japanese. Amplifying the party's concerns, the continued radio silence meant that they had no idea when, or even if, the plane might come.[3]

In response, Sochon acted decisively. On 7 June he sent a Dayak runner with a letter to Toby Carter at Long Akah. In the letter he outlined the perilous situation the party found itself in, and stressed the urgent need for arms and reinforcements. He found out later that the runner completed the trip – which on the much easier downriver leg had taken Sochon and his men twelve days – in an astonishing six days. On receipt of the letter Carter – whose radio was now, finally, functioning – immediately sent a signal to HQ. Sochon was, he told Courtney, 'sitting on top of volcano'.[4]

In the meantime, relationships with local people had deteriorated to such a degree that Sochon feared for the party's safety in Belaga. So on the night of 7 June Sochon, Barrie, the Iban policeman who had accompanied them from Long Akah, and their fourteen newly-recruited guerrillas packed their goods into several canoes and headed down the Rejang River. Semut III took the plunge and moved into Iban territory.[5]

გიდ

Under the Brooke regime the Iban, by far the most numerous of the Sarawak Dayak populations, had steadily expanded eastwards, raiding and headhunting against other Dayak groups as they went. Many of those groups had fled to increasingly remote territories to escape them. In recent years the Iban had moved inexorably up the Rejang River, encroaching further and further into the territory of the Kayan and related groups, resulting in clashes and deepening tensions.

In an effort to maintain harmony the Brookes had established a boundary at the mouth of the Pila River which flows into the Rejang not far above the Pelagus Rapids; Ibans were forbidden from settling upstream of it. The boundary was a potent reminder of the difficulties Semut III faced in endeavouring to unite Kayans and Ibans into a single guerrilla force. Indeed, the Kayans comprising

the majority of Sochon's party demonstrated remarkable commit-
ment to the operation in agreeing to move downstream into Iban
territory. [6]

Taking advice from a local Chinese trader, the Semut III party
moved away from the wide, jungled avenue of the Rejang River
itself. Instead, the men set up camp a short way up the Pila River, in
the fetid mangrove swamp that still today pervades the area. Here
they could remain unseen by Japanese parties travelling up the
Rejang while maintaining a lookout for the elusive aircraft. At this
point the Rejang River runs straight and true for over 3 miles (5 km),
providing a perfect landing site for a Catalina. A further advantage
of the position was its location between the upriver groups, including the Kayan and the Iban. This allowed the men to stay in touch
with events in Belaga two days' paddle upstream while being close
to the Iban longhouse at the furthest limit of Iban territory.[7]

The day after the party settled at Pila, Abu Kassim joined
them. He reported that the Japanese airfield at Bintulu was almost
deserted, its planes presumably being used against 9th Division in
the battle for Tarakan. This was good news as it lessened the chance
of Japanese aircraft discovering their current position.

But Abu Kassim also brought alarming news: the situation in
Belaga had degenerated still further. Some locals wanted to engage
in pre-emptive strikes against Japanese posts, while others were
holding to Puso's and Baling's position that direct action should be
postponed until Allied reinforcements and guns had arrived. Abu
Kassim urged Sochon to send arms to help Puso, who he feared
would not be able to control the situation much longer. Sochon,
a fair-minded man, felt deeply responsible.

People who have not lived under the impositions of an occupying force, and particularly one which hold [sic] human feelings
and life to be of little importance, cannot know how it is to see

impending revenge suddenly dangled so close and then, just as rapidly snatched away. Many parallel cases had been reported from the Resistance Groups in Europe.[8]

Sochon was particularly concerned about the likely outcome of any precipitous action against the Japanese: savage reprisals against the local population along with the certain discovery of the Semut III advance party. Abu Kassim was duly despatched back to Belaga, taking with him all the arms Sochon felt able to spare: one .38 Smith & Wesson pistol, one American carbine, and fifty rounds of ammunition. It was laughably meagre, but fortunately for the party, Abu Kassim was to prove a skilled administrator and negotiator. Along with Puso and Baling he managed to hold the peace in Belaga over the next crucial two weeks.[9]

In this, Abu Kassim was undoubtedly aided by the fact that at Sochon's direction Puso, during this period, organised headhunting parties to eradicate two Japanese patrols that entered the area. The first party, against a small group of Japanese travelling from Bintulu to Sibu, effected an efficient ambush, with the precious bounty of captured Japanese heads distributed among the men taking part. As a Chinese resident of Belaga later recorded:

> The distant OOO OOO OOO in unison of the Kayan voice was to rent the late afternoon air heralding the return of the ngayau [headhunting] parties in triumph over adversity. It was apparently the beginning of the end of the ominous atmosphere in Belaga and more was to follow with this first bag of human heads. [. . .]
>
> The Kayans were very thorough with their search on bodies of Japanese stragglers they had killed. Documents and firearms were handed over to the SRD and they were allowed to have such items as Swiss wristwatches, Parker pens and others of non-military nature to keep.

As a result of this operation, Semut III's tiny armoury increased by several rifles, two pistols and fifty rounds of ammunition.[10]

The second operation was against a larger group of seven Japanese, under the leadership of an officer named Imada, that had passed through Belaga days earlier en route to Long Nawang and was now returning. Puso entrusted leadership of this war party to his brother, Lasah Avun, chief of a longhouse on the Balui River, along which the Japanese party was travelling. The Japanese were persuaded to hand over some of their arms to members of Lasah's party as the Dayaks helped them to negotiate the difficult Uring Rapids. Lasah fired the first shot, which killed a Japanese soldier instantly. The headman of a local Ukit longhouse then hacked off Imada's head:

> With native dexterity, he brought down his illang parang [sword] with a quick swish onto the thick fat neck of Imada. The head was not detached but held firmly to his strong cervical vertebrae [. . .] using his old man strength, Tuai Rumah Ngoh swept his illang parang down the bloody neck cutting through and shattering the bones and sending Imada's head rolling on the shingle bank.[11]

Six Japanese were killed and one escaped; the latter was hunted down and killed a month later. Again, Semut III's armoury benefited.

These successful military forays were to be two of the few bright points for Semut III over the next two weeks. Another was the arrival at Pila of two Eurasian men. In the early days of the occupation the Japanese had killed or interned all Europeans, but had allowed many (although not all) Eurasians to remain free. Now, with the Allied forces pressing and conditions rapidly deteriorating, they had begun to round up remaining members of the Eurasian population.

Thomas 'Tom' Crocker and John Bull Douglas were fleeing possible detention when they learned of the existence of Semut III and came to offer their services. Sochon had known Douglas in the pre-war days when Douglas had worked in the fledgling timber industry. Now he was delighted to welcome both men – each with extensive contacts throughout Sarawak, and the ability to speak several local languages – to his tiny force.[12]

Nevertheless, the operation hung by a thread. The Pila swamp was a dreadful, inhospitable place: home to a range of stinging, biting creatures, including battalions of mosquitoes. The men were soaked to the skin most of the time, and the painful rashes Sochon and Barrie had gained from the chafing of equipment and clothes during the trek from Long Akah were constantly aggravated. Leech and mosquito bites gained on that trip had become infected and turned into ulcerous sores across their bodies; limbs and faces were speckled with lumps and scabs.

To make matters worse, they rapidly used up their remaining supplies of food, and having run out of Straits dollars and parachute silk, had nothing with which to barter for more. Had it not been for Teo Ah Chong, a Chinese trader who had befriended them in Belaga – he was later awarded a King's Medal for Courage in the Cause of Freedom for his assistance to the operation – they would have been completely without food apart from what they could forage. As it was, fern tops growing in the swamp formed the largest part of their diet. They lost weight at a frightening rate, indicated by the growing looseness of their clothes. They were reluctant to drink the putrid, greenish water of the swamp, and suffered perpetual thirst.[13]

The men also learned that the Japanese had heard about White soldiers in the area and had put a price on their heads of $5000 each: it seems Semut was not alone in recognising the benefit of offering payment for enemy heads. $5000 was an astronomical sum for any local individual and Sochon and Barrie were acutely aware of how

vulnerable they were with respect to both the unhappy denizens of
Belaga behind and the largely unknown Iban in front. The threat
of betrayal hung perpetually over them, intensified by the news that
the Japanese had permanent garrisons at Kapit, downriver, and
Tatau, across country to the northwest – both relatively close by. In
addition, Barrie's MCR radio brought news of the landings at Brunei
Bay to the northeast on 10 June. This fuelled Sochon's fears of an
imminent Japanese movement inland, up the Rejang River as well as
across country from Bintulu. Either of these would prove disastrous
for Semut III in its current feeble state. As Sochon told Wren later:

> It did not make for sound sleep, a luxury which, in any case, we
> had long since eschewed.[14]

Desperation drove them on. Every day, all day, Sochon and
Barrie took turns sitting among the mangroves close to the edge of
the Rejang River listening, listening, listening for the sound of an
aircraft, ready to spring into action and light the smoke grenades.
To help pass the time they worked on a training program with their
fourteen recruits. But the relentless monotony of these hours and
days of waiting served mainly to fuel a terrible anxiety. As the days
passed without the arrival of the plane they more and more came to
believe themselves abandoned.[15]

෧෧

Perhaps most depressing of all was the apparent recalcitrance
of the local Ibans. Leaders from all the nearby Iban longhouses
visited the party at its camp in the days and weeks following its
arrival. Sometimes they came singly with their own men; at others
a number of leaders, with large groups of followers, congregated
together at the camp. Of these leaders only Saba, the head of the
longhouse closest to Sochon's camp, and Sandai anak Ansi, whose

longhouse was located some distance further down the Rejang River, were prepared to offer wholehearted support.

Sandai's support, in particular, was crucial. Although still relatively young, he was already a *penghulu*, and greatly respected among Ibans in the wider area. Years later people told me of his legendary *kebal* (invulnerability) – with the power to render other men's weapons ineffective against him – and his terrifying anger, capable in itself of knocking a man down. Just as Semut III had had the good fortune to receive Puso's and Baling's patronage in Belaga, so their luck held at the Pila River with Sandai and Saba. Later both men received British Empire Medals for the assistance they provided to the operation.[16]

But Sandai and Saba were exceptions. Most other Ibans in the area appeared to be suspicious of Sochon, and reluctant to commit to Semut III. Significantly, apart from Saba and Sandai, none invited Sochon and Barrie to visit their longhouses. This indicated their concern to keep the party at arms' length.

Sochon spent interminable hours attempting to persuade his Iban visitors to join the Allied cause. While some seemed to be in favour many others were not, clearly unimpressed by Semut III's ragged, ill-resourced group, and fearing Japanese reprisals. The debate raged on for days without discernable resolution. Arguments were passionately rehearsed over and over. Decisions were arrived at only to be reversed hours later. Sochon was driven almost to distraction by the apparent difficulty of achieving a consensus on any course of action.[17]

In this he was undoubtedly influenced by the contrast between the Iban on the one hand, and the Kayan, Kenyah and related groups, among whom he had canvassed support over the previous few weeks and whose leaders had reached their decisions relatively quickly, on the other. But the Iban are different from these latter groups in crucial ways. Unlike the Kayan, Kenyah, Sekapan and so on – whose chiefs have the authority to make decisions on behalf of large groups of followers – Iban society is characterised by a 'noisy, anarchic democracy' under which every person is free to take part in discussions affecting the community as a whole. As Semut III was discovering, momentous decisions involving more than one longhouse demanded ongoing debate, with every longhouse head (along with many of his followers) airing his view. Consensus was achieved fleetingly, only to vanish again in a welter of argument and counter argument.[18]

Sochon, desperate for a resolution, was confirmed in his view of the Iban as 'unpredictable' and 'not necessarily to be counted upon'. But we surely must admire a society in which democratic principles are so in evidence, and in which conflicting views can so readily be advanced.[19]

Nor was Sochon alone in viewing the Iban unfavourably. Among Western commentators on Semut, including SOA's own official historian, the Iban have often been portrayed as opportunistic cowards who refused to provide assistance to the Allies until it was clear the Japanese were already doomed. In this, again, they are contrasted with groups such as the Kayan, Kelabit and Kenyah, who are said to have pledged support for the Allies while the war still hung in the balance.[20]

However, these critics judge Iban behaviour from a peculiarly European vantage point. Europeans glorify those who risk their lives for higher principle regardless of consequence, and understand courage partly in these terms. In this model the bravest of the brave go into battle willingly, in defence of honour and for love of country, no matter how futile or at what cost.

Many other peoples, including most Dayaks during WWII, take a different approach to warfare. For most Dayaks at the time, lives and livelihoods were more important than such abstract principles, and only the mad would risk the former for the latter. Bravery in warfare was certainly admired, but not above pragmatism and the ability to recognise when a battle could not be won. Whereas Westerners venerate those who die in unwinnable battles, Dayaks of the time generally did not. As an old man in southwest Borneo told me many years ago: 'Only a stupid man keeps fighting when he has already lost. Why would you do that? A wise man runs away.'[21]

Eadie records an occasion during Semut II's operation down the Baram River when a party of operatives and Dayaks was creeping through jungle to carry out a hit-and-run raid on a group of Japanese. As they came close to their quarry one of the Dayaks deliberately fired his rifle in the air, with the result that the attack had to be called off. When asked why he had done this, the man responded that he wanted the Japanese to run away: 'then there would be no fighting and no one would be hurt.' Eadie comments that most of the time Dayak guerrillas were prepared to 'attack bravely', so this did not indicate lack of courage. Rather, the man presumably had reason to believe the raid would not be a success – perhaps omens had warned him so. And in the face of this belief he felt no 'heroic' impulse to attack.[22]

This pragmatic approach was no less true of the Kayan, Kenyah and related groups than of the Iban, as is clear from Carter's and Sochon's accounts of the lengthy debates they engaged in at every Kayan, Kenyah, Sebop and Sekapan longhouse they visited. All of these groups needed persuasion to join Semut, and the arguments always focused around practical questions: will we be given firearms? When are the Allies coming? How will we be protected?

Further, the upriver groups from Long Lellang to Belaga that Sochon had dealt with before now – especially those in the Baram River valley – were close to the sites where European soldiers and supplies had been landed at Bario and Long Akah. They had the evidence of many local reports – if not their own eyes – and so were able to take seriously Sochon's claims about the imminent arrival of firearms and reinforcements. Crucially, when the promised plane had not arrived at Belaga, support for the operation had waned dramatically, even among Kayans and other Dayak groups in the area. Small wonder then that Rejang River Ibans – much further from the Semut landing sites – were dubious about Sochon's promises. Especially since they already knew that Semut III's much vaunted Belaga aircraft had turned out to be a mirage.

So yes, undoubtedly the Iban were opportunistic in their response to newly arrived Semut parties. But so were all Dayak groups. Caught between two powerful sets of external rulers, old and new, this was the only rational behaviour. Indeed, as we have already seen, Dayak warfare itself – with its emphasis on surprise and guile – has always been opportunistic in character, in contrast to Western conventional warfare but like Western unconventional warfare. Ironically, it was this very opportunism that made Dayak warriors, including the Iban, so valuable in the unconventional campaign being waged by the Semut parties.

Instead of criticising the Iban, we should acknowledge a singular fact: in spite of the dangers that the presence of the Semut III party posed to locals, as well as the $5000 price tag on each European head, the party was betrayed to the Japanese by no-one.

◌◌

By 16 June Sochon and Barrie were convinced that HQ had given them up for lost, and the plane would not be coming. They had also reached a point of near despair over the likelihood of persuading the Iban to cooperate with Semut. The Kayan and related upriver groups remained tenuously onside through the offices of Puso and Baling Avun, but it was unclear how long that might last. The original mission of forming a Kayan-Iban guerrilla army that would sweep down the Rejang River against Japanese positions loomed more and more as hopelessly unrealistic.

In response they hatched an audacious plan. Barrie would make the trek back to Long Akah to seek help and weaponry from Toby Carter while Sochon remained at the Pila River to continue negotiations with the Iban. When Barrie returned with whatever arms he had been able to raise, they would retreat into the remote interior and organise their own private war against the Japanese from there for as long as they could hold out.[23]

That night, as they slept in their hammocks suspended between stunted mangrove bushes, they were awakened by visitors around midnight. It was a group of Iban leaders come to warn them that a large party of Japanese, accompanied by prisoners and long rumoured to be travelling upriver, had arrived at Kapit. The Japanese party planned to continue up the Rejang River towards Belaga the next day, which would bring it very close to Semut III's camp.

Sochon was desperately worried by this news. Not only might his own group be discovered, but the people of Belaga were also in danger, given the turmoil in the town and the recent disappearance of two Japanese parties from its immediate environs. He suggested to the leaders that the Iban ambush the Japanese on their way upriver, and pointed out several locations where this might be done. After much discussion the leaders agreed to this plan, and Sochon and Barrie returned to their hammocks happier men.[24]

But their hopes were dashed yet again. Next morning the Iban leaders returned with a large contingent of followers to say that they were no longer prepared to effect an ambush. Sochon was furious. He tried to bully them into changing their minds, in part by promising that when the Rajah returned to power he would hold them personally responsible if Sochon and Barrie were to be killed. But most of the leaders were unmoved, and bitter words were spoken. The Ibans left and Semut III was on its own.[25]

Sochon and Barrie spent the day with their men planning their own ambush. After much consideration they decided to hold it at a set of rapids upriver from their camp, halfway between the Pila River and Belaga. Here they would have a clear line of fire of only 25 yards (23 m) from concealed positions on the riverbanks, and the Japanese would be significantly impeded as they moved upstream across the rapids. Sochon meanwhile sent two of his guerrillas downriver to spy on the Japanese party. Later that afternoon one returned to report that the party had landed at an Iban longhouse some distance downriver.[26]

As dusk fell, the group was back at its campsite eating a frugal meal and grimly contemplating its situation. Suddenly the evening quiet was disrupted by the unmistakeable slaps and swishes of numerous canoes travelling at speed up the Rejang River; in what must have been an instance of pure terror they heard the whoops and yells of a war party. Sochon ordered the group to scatter into the bush where they hid, gripping their weapons. In the next few moments events unfolded with horrible clarity.

> Suddenly the first Dyak burst into the clearing. We stared at him in fascination and disbelief. In his right hand he carried his long parang, the blade ominously stained dark, and in his left, held by one ear, the clearly recognisable head of a Japanese. Barrie and I came towards him, and as we approached more Dyaks came charging through the undergrowth, each carrying his gory trophy and screaming an exuberant war cry. [. . .]
>
> The less flamboyant of them had the delicacy to carry their gruesome spoils of battle in sacks, but the true object of this manoeuvre was shortly revealed not to be consideration for the European's finer sensitivities, but proof of battle prowess, as they tipped up the sacks. A cascade of heads tumbled to the ground.[27]

This was the aftermath of what came to be known as the Pasir Nai massacre. It marked the irrevocable decision of the upper

Rejang River and Baleh River Ibans to throw in their lot with the Allies.[28]

∽

It is difficult to provide a clear picture of what happened at Pasir Nai since existing accounts, whether Iban or European, vary markedly. However, it appears that a party of Japanese soldiers with their Chinese prisoners was travelling upriver to Long Nawang, where the prisoners were possibly to be used as labour in the planned rice cultivation scheme. The group was guided and portered by a party of Ibans from the Baleh River (which flows into the Rejang just above Kapit), under the leadership of Sibat anak Buyong. After crossing the Pelagus Rapids, they stopped at a small Borneo Company rest house built on higher ground above a strip of sand known as Pasir Nai.

At the rest house a large group of Ibans took the Japanese by surprise – in most renderings of the story the Japanese are tricked by one means or another – and killed them before they could draw their guns. In some versions of the story it was the Baleh River Ibans under Sibat who launched the attack; in others it was Sandai and his followers from further up the Rejang River, concerned for the safety of Sochon and Barrie should the Japanese continue upstream. In fact, it seems that both groups participated, signified by both taking heads away with them after the massacre.[29]

As a result 'Japanese' (probably mostly Chinese) heads came to adorn many Iban longhouses in the upper Rejang and Baleh River areas. The anthropologist Derek Freeman reports in his fieldnotes from 1949–51 that a Japanese head hung in the Iban longhouse on the Sut River – a tributary of the Baleh – where he was doing his fieldwork. People there told him it had been given to them by Sergeant Barrie.[30]

Twenty-nine heads were taken that day. Of those, only five appear to have been Japanese; most of the remainder were from

Chinese prisoners, with several Sikh policemen accompanying the Japanese also being killed. Garai anak Siba', who took part in the attack, later described how it went down:

> At Pasir Nai we killed Japanese, as the Iban force said. Penghulu Sandai's and Penghulu Gerinang's people all hastened to get the chance to kill Japanese. At Pasir Nai there was an office of the company, and they were brought there and climbed up, the Japanese, only three, and many Chinese who were fleeing with the Japanese. They stayed, and ate there, then Adin spoke, 'Bah!' he said, directing everyone to kill Japanese, and then the Japanese were struck by Adin. [...]
>
> The Japanese who died because of us at Pasir Nai, they were beheaded by us and their heads were smoked.[31]

Jeba anak Undit was also there:

> The Japanese asked us to put our *barang* [gear] in our boat and to load their boat as well. We were supposed to paddle them [up-river to Belaga]. When all the things had been carried down, Adin did a *ngajat* [war dance], drew his *parang* and struck one of the Japanese – too short at first and then again and again until he was killed. Another Japanese got up holding his gun and tried to swim away. Because we Ibans had been specially asked to attack the Japanese, we had to deceive them. If they weren't tricked, how were they to be killed?[32]

Two of the Chinese prisoners at Pasir Nai that day were lucky: in the melee they escaped into the surrounding jungle. From there they eventually made their way to Belaga where, ironically enough, they joined Semut III as guerrillas.[33]

◦◦

Should we be appalled at the massacre of Pasir Nai? Undoubtedly. But our anger should perhaps be directed less at the Iban perpetrators than at the horror of war. After all, Allied air attacks on towns and villages further down the Rejang River, some of them in preparation for the advance of Semut III, killed many more civilians than died at Pasir Nai. The Allied bombing of Sibu on 4 June alone is estimated to have killed at least one hundred civilians, with many more injured.[34]

From the Iban perspective, the attack at Pasir Nai was never about honour or glory, ideals not normally a feature of Dayak approaches to war at the time. Rather, the attack allowed the Ibans concerned not only to signal their shift to the Allied/Semut cause, but also to take heads. This latter motivation should not be underestimated.

Ibans have often been derided by Europeans for their love of heads. The SOA official historian describes them disparagingly as 'mainly inspired by a lust for loot and heads', while Sochon comments that their 'lust for taking heads lies very close to the surface'. Nor was it only operatives working in jungle areas who made this point. During the Allied landings on the north coast of Borneo, the Australian 20th Brigade reported difficulties in preventing Ibans from beheading Japanese POWs and Japanese dead.[35]

According to Semut operatives, the Iban desire to take heads far outstripped that of any other Dayak group. Jack Tredrea told me years later:

They all wanted heads but the Ibans wanted them most of all. They got very, very excited over the heads.

Similarly, Brian Walpole of Semut III quickly recognised the importance of headhunting within Iban culture, commenting that its promise was 'like an aphrodisiac':

The promise of more heads often made them [the Iban members of the party] literally shake in anticipation, just as someone else might have shivered from the cold.[36]

Yet for the Brooke White Rajahs, Iban love of heads – fuelled by the desire for increased potency – had been an asset, since it meant Ibans rarely refused a request to fight and head-take on the Brooke behalf, even when they were not being paid to do so. As the Semut operation progressed, some of the operatives were also – like the Brookes before them – prepared to exploit the value Ibans placed on heads. Walpole again:

> It was just beginning to get dark. Before turning in I told Bujang [an Iban member of Walpole's patrol] our intentions and fin-ished up by placing my hand on his shoulder. 'More heads, Bujang,' I said. He almost shook with delight at the prospect.[37]

Sochon had given the Ibans a license to headhunt against the Japanese. He makes no attempt to conceal this in his personal mem-oirs when describing his meetings with Iban leaders.

> We explained to them our mission; that we were here to assist in any way possible and to help them to get rid of the Japanese. They asked the usual questions, whether the Government would allow them to take heads, and I explained that this was a period of war and that as enemies of the country, Japanese heads could be taken.[38]

And crucially, when fighting for the Brooke regime, Iban soldiers had sometimes engaged in indiscriminate killing and head-taking among groups other than the designated enemy. The Brookes had often overlooked this behaviour in order to keep Iban troops onside.

Can we blame local Ibans then if, having been encouraged by Sochon to take heads, they assumed that the previous rules of engagement still applied?[39]

In fact, Sochon not only condoned headhunting against the Japanese but offered payment for Japanese heads, even though he acknowledged this in no official reports. As a result, after the Pasir Nai killings Ibans as far away as the Batang Ai (Ai River) in southwestern Sarawak, close to the border with then Dutch Borneo, knew that the European soldiers would pay money for Japanese heads. Agas anak Drahman confirmed this when he told me that Sandai had been offered money for the heads he collected at Pasir Nai but refused to take it, considering the offer insulting. Headhunting, Agas explained, should be its own reward. Sandai was not alone in this; many Ibans refused payment for heads they had taken. Others, however, were happy to claim Semut's monetary rewards.[40]

Sochon felt deeply conflicted about his new role as an advocate of headhunting, especially because of his previous position in the Sarawak Prison Service.

> I was heavily conscious of my nine years as a Police and Prisons Officer, spent in bending every effort to ensure that headhunting had been stamped out for ever. Now I was forced to give it my tacit approval, and it was an anomalous position, which I didn't enjoy.[41]

But Sochon had been charged with recruiting Ibans to the Semut operation, and the Semut leadership group obviously believed that condoning – and even paying for – headhunting against the Japanese would be an effective way of doing this. They may well have been correct. And if the Iban had not come on board when they did, things may have gone much worse for the local populations of the Rejang

River and further inland. Such are the cruel choices inevitably generated by war.

∽

Following the arrival of the Iban head-taking group at their camp, Sochon and Barrie were invited to Saba's longhouse – around 1 mile (1.6 km) further downstream – to participate in rituals to welcome home the new heads Saba and his men had taken. While they had visited Saba's longhouse previously, this was Sochon and Barrie's first entry to it as honoured guests.[42]

Iban longhouses of the time generally lacked the monumental quality characterising Kayan and Kenyah longhouses, being smaller in both height and length. Like most Iban longhouses Saba's was without the detailed carvings that adorned posts, doors and furniture in many Kayan and Kenyah houses. Nevertheless, it was an impressive structure, containing around twenty household apartments and two wide public galleries running the length of the house, one covered (*ruai*) and one uncovered (*tanju'*). And while it lacked the wooden carvings of Kayan and Kenyah houses, it made up for these with the finely woven cloths and blankets (*pua*) for which Iban women are justly famous. These softened its textures and added colour to the gloom. As in all longhouses the men had visited, the covered gallery immediately adjoining the household apartments was the hub of social and ritual life.[43]

As Sochon and Barrie climbed the entry ladder to the gallery, a headless cock was almost certainly waved over them, blood from its neck spraying liberally. Tail feathers from the creature would have been dipped in its blood and brushed against them, to the accompanying chanting of prayers. This served to purify the two men and protect them from potentially harmful forces. Ironically, this purification ceremony signified in part that they need have no fear for their own heads: it was taboo to spill the blood of visitors who came in peace, within an Iban longhouse.

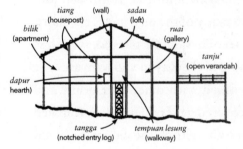

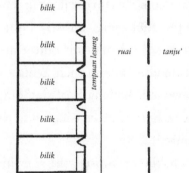

Top: As seen from the river.

Below: Cross-section (left) and floorplan (right).

IBAN LONGHOUSE[44]

Night was falling as Sochon and Barrie entered the gallery, and *damar* lamps were being set down its length. Like every other Dayak longhouse they had entered, it quivered with life and noise. Some of the women had donned their finery for the head ceremony: corsets – extending from the hip almost as far as the breast – comprising dozens of parallel rings of rattan each carrying hundreds of tiny shimmering silver clips, that nipped in the waist and torso; scores of silver bracelets on their arms; strings of glass beads around their necks; and finely woven knee-length skirts adorned with silver coins. In contrast to Kayan and Kenyah women, their bodies bore no tattoos.

Their menfolk, however, had tattoos on throats, shoulders, chests, arms, legs and the backs of hands; some sported beads around their necks and silver bracelets on their arms and legs. Both men and women wore their hair long, but on many of the men it was cut short, pudding-bowl style, around the face. Ears, while pierced, were less elongated and ornamented than those of the Kayan and Kenyah.

Sochon and Barrie were welcomed with much ceremony, and seated on mats on the floor in the covered gallery. They then watched in the flickering, ghostly light as women of the house received the newly taken heads onto elaborately woven cloths. Cradling the wrapped heads in their arms – as if beloved infants – the women traversed the length of the longhouse, up and down at a deliberate unhurried pace, singing to them all the while. This went on for hours.[45]

In the meantime, the starving men feasted and were plied with rice wine.

Unaccustomed to so bloodthirsty a ceremony, and feeling the need for some sort of stimulus to enable me to retain my composure and the content of my stomach, I gratefully, indeed eagerly, accepted a large gourd of tuak [rice wine] which I downed without hesitation.[46]

More was to come the following morning.

I awoke with a splitting head and immediately became aware of the most nauseating smell in the air. Crawling out of my jungle hammock which I had, as usual, slung in the longhouse, I groped my way to the verandah outside the ruai. A few yards away, on the open ground in front of the longhouse stood a small hut built of bamboo and attap [leaves]. From the top of this strange contraption, wisps of smoke rose into the morning air and I realised with horror that the Japanese head was being smoked preparatory to being deposited in the rafters as a permanent war souvenir.[47]

Sochon was to spend the next four days at the ceremony as the heads were progressively cured. Periodically they were brought into the longhouse to be feted anew, before being returned to the smoking hut. On the final night, curing complete, he watched young Iban women feed rice and delicacies into their gaping mouths, their spirits now valued members of the longhouse community. Over these four days a part of him had chafed at this disruption to his plans, especially in the wake of Pasir Nai. But he was acutely aware of the need to bolster the fragile alliance that had been established with the local Iban. Years later he reflected ruefully:

I wondered whether 'irregular operations against the enemy' in any other theatre of war exposed one to anything comparable to the peculiar hazards of life in a longhouse. It seemed doubtful. [. . .]

It had certainly never entered my head that my entire operation would be delayed for several days while I unwillingly participated in a ceremony which depended for its length upon the curing of a human head.[48]

Meanwhile Barrie had gone downriver on 19 June, accompanied by several Ibans, to the site of the massacre. Today, Pasir Nai is an unremarkable small beach jutting out into the waters of the Rejang. Walking its serene sand – beside a river now much depleted in both volume and force, and without the dark jungle that walled its banks in 1945 – it is difficult to imagine violent events taking place here. But in June 1945 the scene was very different.

Arriving at the jungle clearing where the rest house was located, adjacent to the strip of sand that gives Pasir Nai its name, Barrie was confronted with a scene of unspeakable carnage: twenty-nine headless bodies strewn inside and around the house. The smell was dreadful. His orders from Sochon were to dispose of the bodies in case more Japanese should travel up the river, so he tried to persuade his Iban companions to bury them. But they refused, considering it beneath them. Eventually Barrie had to be satisfied with clearing away those bodies that lay on the bank of the river, so ensuring none found their way into the current that might carry them to Japanese forces downstream.[49]

Sochon later recalled that when Barrie returned to Saba's longhouse from this mission two days later, the young sergeant's hair had turned grey.[50]

ᕲᕲ

Early in the morning on 21 June, while Sochon was still camped in Saba's longhouse, he heard, or thought he heard, the low throb of an aircraft engine. He ran along the gallery, down the slippery notched entry log, snatching his smoke flares and emergency signalling mirror, and dodging people on the way. As he reached the river an aircraft, a Catalina, loomed suddenly out of the dawn mist upstream, and flew straight towards him. He tried frantically to let off the flares, but they were by now useless and failed to light properly. In a panic he dropped the flares and attempted to signal with his mirror but too late; the plane flew over him with a roar and disappeared downstream. In that sudden desolate moment he became aware of the many Ibans who had run out of the longhouse and were lining the bank around him.[51]

And then a minute later the thrumming sound returned, it swelled, and the Catalina rushed back into view, coming towards him from the opposite direction. For what seemed an eternity he flashed desperately, in terror that it would not see him, and finally the aircraft dipped a wing in response. It circled once and its wing floats dropped. Then it settled, with almost unimaginable tranquillity, onto the river directly in front of him.[52]

Sochon seized a nearby canoe and began to paddle. As he did so the door at the side of the aircraft opened and standing in the doorway was the dapper figure of his commanding officer, Jumbo Courtney. Sochon became suddenly aware of how he must look:

> Between the thwarts of the prahu [canoe], in inches of stinking water, sat the remnants of what had once been the smart military figure which had stood in front of his [Courtney's] desk in Melbourne. The crumpled bush hat, limp and twisted out of recognition; the shirt ripped and grease stained; the gashed jungle green trousers gathered in folds around what had once been an ample waistline; the boots, their shredded soles clearly visible in the bottom of the prahu. All these outward tatters hung on a gaunt frame covered with ulcerous sores and topped by a face lined with fatigue and under nourishment.[53]

In the overwhelming, indescribable emotion of the moment, he found himself weeping.

13

BATTLE FOR KAPIT

IN THE DAYS FOLLOWING the Pasir Nai massacre, the headless corpse of a Japanese soldier – an escapee, it would seem, from Barrie's attempts to remove all bodies from the riverbank – fetched up at the wharves in Kapit, the next town down the Rejang River. When brought to the attention of Tucho, the Japanese district officer and chief of police there, he was enraged. His suspicions focused immediately on the Iban population, and he took revenge by shooting at least one Iban within the town.

Tucho was seen by local Ibans as a man of great potency and *kebal* (invulnerability): how else could he have taken Sarawak from the Europeans? As an Iban explained in the 1980s:

> He [Tucho] had already defeated the white people [. . .] the story went, and had won three big medals. He raised the flag and seized this Sarawak; Sarawak was quickly finished and all the Punjabi soldiers ran away because of him. Three white people's countries were seized by him.[1]

Nevertheless, on learning of his act of retribution, local Ibans were incensed. Leaders called for a meeting of all Ibans from throughout the region, to be held at the confluence of the Rejang and Baleh Rivers.[2]

The meeting occurred around 22 June – the day after the arrival of Courtney at Saba's longhouse further up the Rejang River – and was attended by an enormous throng of Ibans from the upper Rejang and Baleh River areas. Among those assembled that day was the great Iban leader *Temenggong* Koh anak Jubang – the *Temenggong* title, bestowed by the Rajah on individuals he wished to honour, indicated his standing – as well as the influential *penghulu* Jugah anak Barieng, and Jugah's younger brother Tedong anak Barieng. There was a long discussion, including the airing of a wide range of grievances against the Japanese. Finally, it was decided that the time had come for action.[3]

Before dawn on 24 June a vast number of Ibans, grasping their swords and spears, began to move downriver towards Kapit in an armada of canoes. Sochon later estimated that around two thousand warriors descended upon the town that day.[4]

⌒

With the arrival of the long-awaited aircraft, Semut III was transformed, overnight it seemed, from a handful of half-starved, ill-equipped men into a viable operation. Around 3000 lbs (1360 kg) of weapons (including rifles and submachine guns), ammunition and food were received in the first air-drop alone, with two more drops occurring in the following week.

Reinforcements also arrived. Along with Courtney in the plane on 21 June were new Semut III members Captain David Kearney, Lieutenant Ronald 'Ron' Baker and Sergeant Edric 'Ed' Spurling. Kearney was Sochon's new second-in-command: a 27-year-old Australian who had already served in the Middle East and

New Guinea with the AIF before being transferred to SRD several months earlier. Spurling was an experienced signaller bringing with him a Boston radio. Within three hours of his arrival the Semut III party was for the first time in radio communication with HQ.[5]

And news from outside! Sochon already knew from Barrie's MCR radio that eleven days earlier, on 10 June, Australian forces had come ashore at Brunei Bay. Now he learned that on 20 June – the previous day – a battalion had landed at the oilfield of Lutong, on the northeastern coast of Sarawak. Australian soldiers even now were advancing on the major coastal town of Miri, not too far northeast of Semut III's position.

However, the military situation was far from certain, with skirmishes still occurring and Japanese troops known to be moving inland in some areas. Perhaps more importantly, the long coastal strip from Bintulu to Kuching remained in Japanese hands, as did Kuching itself and the Batu Lintang internment camp. The urgency of Semut III's larger objective – to free those in the camp – was undiminished. Indeed, if anything, it was heightened due to fear of Japanese reprisals against their prisoners as the Allies approached.

Reports had been indicating to Sochon for some time that in the event of an Allied landing on the coast, Japanese would concentrate at Kapit, the next town down the Rejang River from Semut III's current location. From there they would attempt to withdraw into the interior and colonise the Belaga and Long Nawang areas. Kapit was obviously Semut III's first target.

Nevertheless Sochon, by nature a cautious man, was reluctant to move too quickly. Having come so far under such difficult circumstances, and acutely aware of the size of his force, he was determined to wait for further reinforcements and equipment before advancing on Kapit. In addition, local estimates varied widely as to how many Japanese were in the town: some said seven, some said forty. Sochon wanted to be certain about the number and dispositions of the enemy before he went on the attack.[6]

He was also deeply concerned about his flanks. Kearney commented years later:

> [Sochon], I think, felt pretty lost about what he was supposed to do. Mind you, it's quite possible that nobody told him what he was supposed to do. [. . .] The first day I arrived in the country, he took me into a long house, where he had about 20 maps spread out on the floor, and lectured me, using a pointer, on his strategic position in the Rajang [Rejang] valley, and told me he was concerned about his 'left flank'. We had our personal arms and 6 rusty hand grenades and I couldn't tell my left flank from a hole in the ground.[7]

Adding to Sochon's worries was the logistical nightmare of how to transport the growing mountain of equipment, weaponry and food he was accumulating from the ongoing air drops, when his force advanced downriver. The main form of local transport – the small, unstable canoe, usually fashioned from a single tree trunk – was not well adapted to this purpose.

Sochon had met with Iban leaders immediately after the Pasir Nai massacre and emphasised that for the moment no action should be taken to arouse Japanese suspicions. It had been agreed that some of the leaders, with their men, would travel to Kapit to monitor the situation there. A system of runners was established by which information could be relayed back to Sochon. In the meantime, Sochon requested an RAAF air raid on the town in the hope of striking at Japanese targets and morale.[8]

☙

The town of Kapit is set on a high bank above the Rejang River, around 125 miles (200 km) as the crow flies from the sea. Directly opposite the town, on the other side of the river, a series of low hills trail into the distance, enhancing the town's picturesque character. As elsewhere throughout Sarawak, the Brookes had felt it prudent to build here in 1880 a wooden fort, Fort Sylvia, named, rather quaintly, after the wife of the last White Rajah. This still stands on a rise overlooking the river.

Today, Kapit is a noisy thriving metropolis, its roads crammed with cars and its wharves teeming with river traffic including regular ferries from Sibu. In 1945, however, it was small (although larger than Belaga) – belying its role as the administrative and economic hub to a vast area inhabited largely by Ibans – and contained only a few streets. One of these, running parallel to the river, was made up of Chinese wooden shophouses, the commercial heart of the region, with the Chinese temple and Malay quarter both located close by. The town also contained a school, a government dispensary, a prison and several bungalows where Brooke government officers had lived before the war.

A succession of Brooke administrators had turned the area behind the fort into a beauty spot, with lush lawns, flowerbeds, an artificial lake and paths winding among the jungle-covered hills encircling it. However, the Japanese had more important things to attend to than the gardens of the European administration, and by 1945 the lake had been drained, the flower beds were full of weeds and the hill paths had been reclaimed by jungle.[9]

Before the Japanese occupation, Tedong anak Barieng had worked at the Borneo Company's timber camp located at Seputin, around 1 mile (2 km) upstream from Kapit. When the Japanese arrived they took over the camp, and recruited Tedong to work for them. As a result he came to know, and be trusted by, Japanese in the area – including Tucho.

Tedong was in the advance party of the Ibans who entered the town at dawn on 24 June. Because of his friendship with Tucho, he was seen as one of the few who might get close enough to kill him. Accordingly, he was tasked with finding Tucho and despatching him as expeditiously as possible. The advance party arrived at the government wharf and Tedong went from there to the fort, where he enlisted the help of two Iban policemen who worked for Tucho.[10]

The policemen went to Tucho's house and told him upriver Ibans were on their way to Kapit to loot the bazaar, and that some of their leaders were waiting at the fort to hold discussions with him. Tucho dressed quickly, but instead of following the policemen to the fort, he fled. Tedong's men searched for him and finally found him hiding in another house. Years later Tedong recalled what happened next:

> I asked the two of them [Tucho's escorts] to call to him that I was waiting on the *tanju'* [wooden platform] about six feet away from the top of the steps. There I heard the two of them tap the door, and I simply hid myself in case the two of them had been bribed. Having heard me, Tucho answered from within. 'Who's that?' he said. 'Tedong,' said the two of them. 'Where is he?' 'Not far from here,' they said. [. . .]
>
> Having heard me, he came out, I ran to hide at the trunk of a durian not far from Gung's house [. . .] there was high grass on the embanked path there. I reckoned he had come close and while he was turning around, I shot him. If I had struck him with a *parang* it wouldn't have succeeded because that Japanese was very tough. Then I asked Gung to behead him and although he struck five times his head was not separated and then we succeeded in paring it off. [. . .]
>
> Then the head of the Japanese killed by me was taken by my late father so that he could smoke it.[11]

Forty years later Tedong explained:

I killed Tucho, my relative [blood brother], at that time. If I had
not killed him Kapit would have been finished, because he was
very angry that the Japanese force had been killed by the people
at Pasir Nai.[12]

෨෧

Harry Buxton, a forestry officer before the war who was a friend
of Tedong's brother Jugah anak Barieng, was in the cells of Fort
Sylvia that morning. As a Eurasian he had been imprisoned by the
Japanese when they first arrived in Sarawak. He had recently been
moved to Kapit with a group of other prisoners in response to
the Allied advance: all were slated for imminent execution. From
his cell Buxton could tell that something momentous was happening: he heard war cries, a shotgun blast, and 'a general din in
the town'.[13]

Then, at around 7.30 or 8 am, there came the drone of
aircraft.

I thought, Oh, God, all this must have been so well organized,
that even Labuan – I didn't know it was Labuan at the time –
that even the planes were informed. [. . .] Then they dropped
incendiaries on Kapit town, and they gave us a blowing up as
they went scooting off.[14]

RAAF planes strafed the town, including the jail and bazaar,
with machine-gun fire: the raid ordered by Sochon. It did little harm
to Japanese targets, but considerable damage to the bazaar. One of
the prisoners sharing Buxton's cell was hit in the stomach as bullets
raked the cell, ricocheting crazily off the walls.

And then the prison door burst open, and I heard them calling my name: 'Buston! Buston!'. And two pairs of hands reached in and pulled me out – Jugah and Tedong.[15]

More than 40 years later, Buxton was overwhelmed by the unbearable emotion of that moment. As he recounted the story above to anthropologist Vinson Sutlive in 1988, he broke down in sobs.

৽৽

At Semut III headquarters beside the Pila River upstream, Sochon was receiving alarming reports that a large number of Ibans had entered Kapit and taken the town 'in a wild campaign of looting and killing'. Deeply concerned about the implications for his future plans, he despatched a patrol led by Baker, including Barrie and around ten of the Belaga guerrillas, to Kapit with orders to scout out the situation there. At the same time, Sochon ordered a second air strike on the town.[16]

The second RAAF air raid occurred the next day, 25 June. It took out the radio station, one of its main targets, but also caused civilian deaths. In addition, one of the planes dropped an auxiliary fuel tank which landed on the Customs warehouse, setting it alight. The flames, fanned by the breeze off the river, leapt across to the wooden shophouses of the nearby bazaar and soon all were razed to the ground. The only elements remaining were a row of charred ironwood posts and the concrete strong room belonging to one of the Chinese merchants.[17]

Apart from Tucho there had been three or four other Japanese in Kapit. Two were guarding the Japanese trading store in the bazaar, while at least one was at the timber company office at Seputin, slightly upriver. The Ibans had already located and killed those at Seputin, but the two in the bazaar remained at large, hiding behind one of the shophouses. As a result of the air raid and ensuing fire they were forced from their hiding place, and took refuge in an air-raid shelter. Here they were discovered by angry Ibans amid the chaos of the smouldering town centre.

Attempts were made to smoke the Japanese out of their bunker by throwing in lighted rolls of palm thatch. But this was unsuccessful, and they resisted all subsequent efforts to drive or induce them out. Eventually, an Iban leader called Nyanggau lost patience and jumped into the shelter where he stabbed one of the Japanese with a spear, but was bayoneted in return. He managed to crawl out of the bunker and died a short time later in the arms of one of his fellows.

The Ibans present were enraged at this death. So enraged that, having finally dragged both soldiers out of the bunker and killed them, they then ate the liver of one.

> True, it's really true that he was gutted. I was among those who ate his liver. The Japanese who was stabbed and killed by Nyanggau was indeed gutted. Human liver smells very strong. After that I asked Penghulu Gerinang to eat liver together with me. Gerinang shut his eyes trying to swallow the liver, and at last he could not.[18]

Cannibalism is abhorrent to most Dayaks most of the time, as it is to most Europeans. This is probably the reason why those present, including Tedong and Gerinang, had great difficulty eating the liver, so strong was the instinct to gag. Their participation undoubtedly reflects, in part, what historian Joanna Bourke refers to as the 'carnivalesque spirit' often seen in warfare, when the normal moral order becomes inverted. Just as during WWII many American soldiers collected Japanese body parts, including heads, to take home with them, and Australian operatives promoted headhunting against Japanese – both actions which in normal times would be seen as morally unacceptable – so Ibans in Kapit ate the liver of a Japanese soldier they had killed.[19]

This action also suggests – perhaps more strongly than anything else – the degree of anger Ibans in the area had come to feel towards the Japanese. The fact that the liver was consumed is significant. For the Iban, as for most Dayak peoples, the liver is seen in many respects as the repository of a person's essence, the seat of his or her emotions and drives. In eating the liver, the Iban warriors concerned were consuming the essence of the enemy himself. This is surely an expression not only of rage and a desire for revenge, but also of intense disrespect. It is yet another indication of how much the Japanese occupiers of Sarawak had alienated local peoples, including Dayaks, and of the price they paid for it.[20]

Meanwhile, Baker, Barrie and the Belaga guerrillas were hurrying down the Rejang River. They passed Pasir Nai and came to the infamous Pelagus Rapids, barrier between the upper and middle Rejang. They abandoned their canoes at the eastern end and portered their gear as rapidly as possible along a track on the jungled true right bank of the river, to the deafening roar of the seething water below. On reaching the western end several hours later, they acquired new canoes and continued downriver.

The patrol arrived in Kapit on the afternoon of 25 June, not long after the second airstrike had taken place. They found a devastated town, one not only bombed and burned by the air attacks but also looted by Ibans. They were gratefully welcomed by Malay and Chinese residents, fearful that, with all Japanese heads now procured, the Ibans might next turn their head-taking ambitions onto them.[21]

Nor, on the face of it, was this fear unreasonable. Ibans in the Kanowit area, not much further down the Rejang River from Kapit, had been subject to expeditionary reprisals by Rajah Vyner Brooke as late as 1935, in part because of their continued headhunting. And a Chinese family in the Song area – only 36 miles (58 km) downriver from Kapit – had had their heads taken in 1935, with two Ibans from Ngemah, between Song and Kanowit, executed for this crime.

As a result of these and other incidents, fear of Iban violence was widespread among non-Ibans in Sarawak at the time. Thus Lim Beng Hai, a Chinese guerrilla with Semut III, notes that like many other townspeople he was nervous in the company of Ibans. And this sentiment – whether justified or not – was not confined to Malays and Chinese. H.P.K. Jacks, the former District Officer in Kanowit, reports that as he was fleeing the Japanese invasion via Belaga to Long Nawang in January 1942, local Dayaks along the route – including Oyong Puso – expressed themselves anxious that in the absence of British and Dutch administrators they would be vulnerable to attack by Sarawak Ibans.[22]

Baker shared the population's concern. He was almost certainly aware of the operation's larger mission to establish a path to civil government after active hostilities had ceased. Consequently, although his orders were simply to gather intelligence, he decided to stay in Kapit for a day or two.

☙

Later that afternoon, around 4 pm, a Chinese and two Malays arrived at the town. They had paddled upriver from Song, returning a Japanese policeman who had travelled downstream some days earlier. When the party neared Kapit and saw the destruction of the bazaar, the Japanese man sent the paddlers on ahead to investigate while he waited on the other side of the river. However, his caution was to no avail: on hearing of his presence, Ibans crossed the river and killed him, some reports say on Baker's instructions.

The paddlers told Baker that a Japanese launch containing many soldiers was due to arrive at Kapit from Song the same night. This news alarmed Baker: he was aware of Sochon's wish to keep the presence of European soldiers in the area secret. He decided he had to prevent the launch from returning downriver with news of the situation in Kapit.[23]

Over the next few hours Baker and Barrie, in extensive consultation with locals and their party of guerrillas, devised an ambush. This would be the first offensive action taken by Semut III operatives against the Japanese.

Planning the ambush was difficult. The party was given widely varying estimates of when the launch would arrive and how many soldiers it contained. They spent a lot of time questioning locals about where the Japanese usually docked: at the government landing place, or at Japanese headquarters further upstream? Eventually, after weighing up all responses, Baker decided to set the ambush at the government wharf.[24]

Baker was shrewd: he recognised that the action presented an opportunity to draw Iban warriors in the town into the Semut ambit. Consequently he invited a large number, armed with their spears and swords, to take part. The plan, as he outlined it, was for the ambush party to straddle the path running up the steep bank from the wharf. The position was not ideal: there was little cover and the bank was behind them. However, he hoped that in the darkness, and with the element of surprise, they could inflict considerable damage before withdrawing to better defensive positions if necessary.

Baker and Barrie would be at the front of the party with Bren guns and locals to load them: perhaps 15 feet (4.5 m) from the water, concealed in the long grass that grew up the bank. Behind them, further up the bank and with a clear line of fire over their heads, were the Belaga guerrillas, all of whom had firearms. Behind them, and further up the bank again, were the Iban force armed with swords and spears. Baker instructed everyone present to take no action until he gave the signal.[25]

They waited in the deep darkness of a Borneo jungle night, ears straining to catch the sound of the launch. There was mist across the river, and visibility was low. At 11 pm or so came the pulsating echo of a diesel engine followed by faint snatches of conversation drifting on the cool evening air. The launch moved with agonising slowness, plodding towards them for what seemed like an eternity. Finally, just as they had decided it would bypass their position and head upstream to dock at Japanese headquarters, it swung into the wharf. Two spectral figures leapt ashore to tie it up.

At this moment Baker and Barrie opened up with their machine guns. The strident rat-a-tat was shocking in the night silence, and sounded the signal for the others to attack. Behind them the Belaga guerrillas strafed the boat with their rifles. Japanese in the launch quickly began to return fire.

As things heated up, Barrie decided to throw a grenade into the boat. This was almost his undoing.

> Initially I couldn't get the pin out so I applied my teeth to it, forgetting that prior to joining Semut I had had my upper teeth removed to save dental problems and was now wearing an upper denture. Result, not the grenade pin, but a tooth came out.

Eventually removing the pin, he and Baker lobbed grenades into the boat. As they did so, someone on board managed to restart the engine and the launch lurched out into the current. Later reports indicated that at least two Japanese soldiers had been killed and a Japanese woman injured. Nevertheless, the survivors got the boat back to Song.[26]

With the boat out of range and the sound of its engine fading, Baker reassembled his forces for a review. There had been no casualties among his men, but ammunition was running low. The group had come on patrol lightly armed – having not expected a confrontation with the enemy – and in addition to limited ammunition they had no more grenades. The Ibans had already dispersed, and Baker decided that his own party should follow suit and withdraw to a safe position out of town. From there they could return to head-quarters at dawn the next day.[27]

But then, twenty or thirty minutes after the first had departed, there came clearly over the water the sound of a second launch approaching from the same direction. Baker, with no idea of how many Japanese it contained, concluded that discretion was the better part of valour: he ordered his men to retreat immediately across and upriver. Under the shelter of the heavy mist they climbed in to a nearby boat and pushed out from the bank. But they quickly discovered that the boat leaked badly – one of the old derelict craft often seen abandoned by the riverside in Borneo towns. The men 'paddled like fury across river all the while bailing like mad with tin hats'.[28]

Both Baker's party and the denizens of Kapit were fortunate that night. It was later suggested that the second launch contained thirty or more Japanese soldiers, who were almost certainly fully armed. However, no doubt fearful of what was waiting in the town, the launch did not berth. Instead it cruised up and down outside the town for some time, with those on board shouting out in Malay, Iban and Japanese.[29]

Baker's group obtained replacement boats on the other side of the river and set off upstream at once. They travelled all night and most of the following day, portering their gear once again above the Pelagus Rapids. On 27 June, after an exhausting paddle upriver, they reached Sochon's party, just as it was moving from its Pila River site.

Sochon had received a second Catalina the previous day (26 June) bringing Captain Robert 'Arthur' Astill and Lieutenant Philip 'Pip' Hume to join his force, as well as another 3000 lbs (1360 kg) of stores and equipment. The continued influx of rein-forcements and supplies had jolted him into action. A flotilla of canoes carried the group's goods down the Rejang to an Iban long-house at the mouth of the Sama River, which flows into the Rejang not far above the Pelagus Rapids. Semut III was inching closer to Kapit.[30]

∞

It is easy to imagine the Iban takeover of Kapit as an anarchic affair involving thousands of warriors who, against Sochon's express advice, rampaged leaderless and uncontrolled into town. However, while thousands of warriors did descend on the town – where they killed Japanese soldiers and engaged in some looting – there is no evidence that they murdered non-Japanese civilians or destroyed much property. In fact, the destruction of buildings and burning of the bazaar in Kapit were consequences of the Allied bombing of the town, a pattern repeated throughout this region.

The Iban move on Kapit was not that of a mob suddenly deciding to take the law into its own hands. Rather it was a direct outcome of the conference of Ibans held at the confluence of the Baleh and Rejang Rivers in the days after the Pasir Nai massacre. This conference was attended by most of the Iban leaders in the upper Rejang/Baleh River area, including *Temenggong* Koh. The crucial role of Koh should not be overlooked.

Koh is often described in Western accounts as the 'paramount chief' of the Ibans, although this does not quite capture his position in a society lacking formal hereditary rank. Born in 1870, he was already an old man by the time of the Japanese occupation, but retained enormous influence. Growing up at a time when Ibans were still actively pursuing headhunting, he had a reputation as a feared headhunter.

Apart from his distinguished countenance, his most notable physical attributes were the backs of his hands. From the wrists to the finger-nails they were completely blue, as if they had been washed in ink. [. . .] In olden days when a man took a head he earned the right to have one joint of one finger tattooed. With each additional head to his credit another joint was pricked and dyed with blue-black juice. When the number of slain enemies could no longer be counted on all the joints of all the fingers and two thumbs of both hands, the pattern was continued down the back of a hand. Temenggong Koh's fingers, thumbs and hands were completely covered with these proud symbols.[31]

Unlike the Sekapan chief Puso who, as we have seen, often failed to impress Europeans, Koh appears to have been admired and respected by all. The same Semut briefing report that reckoned Puso a 'poor specimen' described Koh as 'a very fine old man. He has authority and is well liked by his junior chiefs.'[32]

Malcolm MacDonald describes Koh from a visit to his longhouse on the Baleh River in 1949, when Koh was almost 80 years of age:

His step was firm and dignified, his carriage proud, his gaze serene, sagacious and benevolent. As he moved among his people an aura of sanctity seemed to surround him. [. . .] He was the pre-eminent Iban of his time, the wisest, the best and the most honoured. If the natives wrote their racial histories and invented titles by which to remember particular heroes, he would be known as Koh the Great.[33]

There is a large dollop of 'noble savage' romanticism involved here, but these words nevertheless capture the awe with which Koh was regarded by locals and Europeans alike.

Like many other Ibans, Koh had remained relatively neutral during the Japanese occupation, annoyed at the Brooke regime's precipitous abandonment of the country without consulting the indigenous population. But the hardships suffered under Japanese rule had turned him against the Japanese, and the arrival of the Semut men – with their encouragement of Japanese head-taking – caused him to swing his support behind the Allies.[34]

In this regard Koh's influence over other Ibans in the area cannot be overestimated. We should note, for instance, that the Ibans guiding the Japanese party at Pasir Nai not only came from the Baleh River – Koh's home area – but were led by Sibat anak Buyong, Koh's grandson. We find other relatives of Koh – Gerinang, Tedong and so on – if not involved in the Pasir Nai massacre itself, at least heavily entangled in the events that followed, including accompanying Barrie to the massacre site. And although Sochon was not aware of this at the time, it is unlikely that the assault on Kapit could have happened without at least the tacit support of Koh. Ironically, while Sochon was fuming over the apparent reluctance of local Ibans to provide assistance, they were in the process of uniting throughout the area to get behind the Allied cause. Given his influence, Koh must have been instrumental in this process.

And indeed in 1947 Koh was awarded the MBE by the British Government in recognition for the part he had played during the battle for the Rejang.[35]

Sochon was livid on hearing that Ibans had taken Kapit against his strict instructions, regarding it 'as a serious embarrassment to future plans'. Yet if the thousands who assembled at the junction of the Baleh and Rejang Rivers decided to ignore his directives, how can we blame them? This was, after all, their country and they were experts – far more expert than the men of Semut III – at the kind of warfare that prevailed there. Equally as important, many had not forgotten how hastily the Europeans had abandoned them four years earlier. As Koh explained in 1955:

Not so long ago the Japanese came, making a raid of a different sort. The Japanese felt no opposition because the Tuans

> [Europeans] did not tell me anything. They did not say they
> were going to run away. If they had taken counsel with me,
> I think, they would have lived and not all died at Long Nawang.
> [. . .] But they said nothing, and ran off upriver, and so they
> were wiped out at Long Nawang.[36]

European authority and prestige had been badly damaged by the
rout suffered at Japanese hands. It is hardly surprising that local
Ibans decided the first strike in the Rejang war would be theirs.

Still today some Ibans view the battle for Kapit as a display of
Iban courage and initiative in direct contrast to the timidity and pas-
sivity exhibited by Sochon's Europeans skulking further upriver.
Koh again:

> So, for a long time, we looked after our own country, and
> there was no Tuan in Kapit; all had run away, and the Japanese
> remained. The Japanese in their turn ran away, and only then
> the Tuans came back. It was all the Ibans who defeated the
> Japanese here, and killed so many of them. The *Tuans* were
> here only for show during the fighting.[37]

It is tempting to see Kapit as yet another nail in the coffin of
European rule in Sarawak.

൭

The Japanese must now know that Allied forces were in the upper
Rejang River area. This meant there was no longer any point in
concealment. Calculating that the party was strong enough to hold
the Rejang above Kapit, Sochon sent Kearney and Astill, along
with a group of the Belaga guerrillas, downstream on 29 June to
set up a block at the junction of the Baleh and Rejang Rivers. He
had received reports of Japanese reprisals along the Katibas River

(which flows into the Rejang downstream from Kapit at Song) in response to Iban uprisings there, and was keen to avoid a repeat in the upper Rejang area. It was important, then, that this area be secured quickly, before the Japanese had time to launch an attack upriver, in retaliation for the events at Kapit.

Sochon felt some concern that Japanese patrols might circumvent the block by travelling overland: in so doing they could isolate the block party itself. However, he knew from his spies that previous attacks by Dayaks with blowpipes had left Japanese in the area with a mortal fear of the jungles: they would enter them only in large numbers. And he calculated that their awareness of an unknown number of Allied soldiers in the area would make them unwilling to deplete their garrisons at Song and Sibu to create such a force.[38]

In any case, in the unlikely event that Japanese troops moved into the jungle, their presence would soon be reported to Sochon. Following the pattern established by Carter in the Baram, one of the first tasks he had undertaken after the arrival of the aircraft was to recruit local Dayaks as spies and scouts. By the end of June he had already developed a formidable intelligence network throughout the area.[39]

Kearney and Astill's group arrived at the confluence of the Rejang and Baleh Rivers, where the multitude of Ibans had assembled five days earlier, later the same day (29 June). Selecting a position high on the riverbank with a commanding view across the junction, they began to build a block house. Sochon had received two PIATs (Projector, Infantry, Anti-Tank) – a portable anti-tank weapon only very recently developed: it fired a round capable of stopping a tank – in one of the Catalina drops, and immediately recognised their potential for attacking river traffic. These were set up as the basis of the block.[40]

The upper Rejang now seemed relatively safe from Japanese attack. However, other areas under Semut III's purview were more vulnerable. In particular, Sochon remained anxious about the situation in Belaga, given its crucial location as a communications hub between Kapit to the southwest, Long Nawang to the southeast, Bintulu to the west and the Tinjar River in Semut II's territory to the northeast, at the junction of several critical Japanese escape routes into the interior.

Accordingly, Sochon despatched the ever-dependable Keith Barrie, along with three guerrillas, to join Abu Kassim in Belaga, and arranged for a supply of arms and ammunition to be dropped there on 4 July. Barrie's brief was to gain control of the route from Bintulu to Long Nawang (which Sochon expected the Japanese to use in fleeing inland from the Allied forces), to begin training local guerrillas already enlisted by Abu Kassim (who were urgently needed to patrol this and other routes), and to work with Abu Kassim in establishing administrative order in the town. Barrie was also to build up intelligence networks among the Penans and other Dayak groups around the town, since they would be the first to know about Japanese movements into the area.[41]

Following Barrie's departure, Sochon withdrew Kearney from the river block, where he was replaced by Baker. Sochon was concerned that the Japanese retreat inland to Long Nawang might avoid Belaga altogether by crossing the Rejang south of the town, around the Pila River area. Consequently on 6 July Kearney was also sent upriver towards Belaga. His job was to visit longhouses in the upper Rejang area and establish an intelligence network there. He was also tasked – like Carter's men on the Tinjar River – with requesting help from local Iban longhouse heads in dealing with any small groups of Japanese who should enter their territories.

Sochon also arranged for newly trained guerrillas from Belaga to be sent to the Tubau district, north of Belaga, to liaise with the Semut II party working around the Tinjar River, and southeast to Long Nawang in Dutch Borneo, to seek the cooperation and assistance of Kenyahs in the vicinity. He was endeavouring to seal off the entire region north of his current location. In this way he hoped to prevent any Japanese escape inland through the area as well as any enemy attacks from that direction on his forces.[42]

Sochon's concern with Long Nawang may also have been activated by a visit from Tom Harrisson – a passenger in a Catalina delivering supplies – on 30 June. Harrisson had made the trip to discuss common strategy and cooperation now that the Japanese were being pushed inland by the advancing Australian forces. During their meeting he proposed to Sochon that he (Harrisson) broaden the area in which Semut I was operating to cover part of Semut III's territory on the Dutch side of the border where Long Nawang was located. Sochon saw this as blatant expansionism and rejected the idea out of hand. 'Harrisson left immediately after luncheon' he told Wren years later, 'and it was the last I was to see of him until after the war.'[43]

∽

While Sochon was focused on his rear and flanks, the Japanese launched a sortie directly in front. On 3 July a large launch armed with machine guns, with around eighty Japanese soldiers on board, travelled up the Rejang River from Song. It fired on every Iban longhouse it passed as well as Iban individuals on the banks and in the water. Local Ibans had been justified in their concern about the repercussions of any cooperation with Sochon's group.

On arrival in Kapit the launch continued upriver as far as Seputin, only a very few miles downstream from Semut III's river block at the Baleh River junction. But there it halted, even though those on board must have known about the presence of European soldiers further upriver. Through his growing intelligence networks Sochon – again following Carter's lead – had been carefully feeding the local rumour mill to the effect that there were approximately two hundred men in the Semut III party. It seems likely that this is why the launch went no further; the Japanese may well have been reluctant to take on a force of such size.

Instead, the launch turned back to Fort Sylvia in Kapit where the Japanese came ashore and removed every item of value. After around eighteen hours in the area they eventually returned downriver to Song.[44]

While in town the Japanese commanding officer sent for the *kapitan Cina* – the head of the local Chinese population – and interrogated him regarding the situation around Kapit. Taking a lead from Sochon's rumour mill, the *kapitan Cina* explained that the area was now under the control of a force of two hundred Australians and thousands of armed Ibans, maintained by squadrons of flying boats. This information appears to have made a strong impression, since the launch disappeared downriver and did not return. Over the next couple of days, Sochon's intelligence consistently indicated that the Japanese had abandoned Kapit in favour of Song, 36 miles (58 km) further downriver. With a garrison around one hundred strong, Song had become the new Japanese forward HQ.[45]

Emboldened by this information, Sochon decided to move again. On 5 July the party was strengthened by yet more reinforcements: Lieutenant Frank Oldham and Corporals Hubert 'Brick' Fowler, Ross Bradbury, Ronald 'Happy' Croton, Richard 'Chick' Outhwaite and Brian Walpole were inserted by Catalina along with more stores, equipment and weaponry. The following day, 6 July, the party moved from the Sama River down the Rejang to the block at the Baleh River. An armada of canoes – poled by local Dayak boatmen, both Kayan and Iban – transported the goods. At Pelagus the back-breaking task of porting them along the banks above the rapids was undertaken, again largely by local Dayaks, taking up most of the day.

On arrival at the Baleh block house Sochon discovered that the inhabitants of the nearby Iban longhouse were anxious about the possibility of Japanese reprisals in this part of the Rejang River, and wanted his party to move directly on to Kapit. So, throwing caution to the wind, he continued downriver. Arriving in Kapit around 5.30 pm, he set up his headquarters in the old Fort Sylvia, with panoramic views across the devastated town.[46]

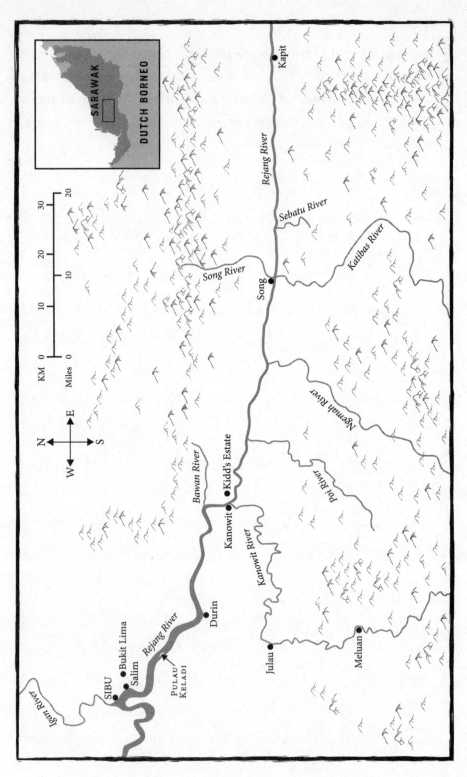

Middle and lower Rejang River and environs in 1945.

14

DOWNRIVER TO SONG

THE NEWS THAT *ORANG puteh* (white people) had returned and were seeking Japanese heads spread rapidly throughout Sarawak. It fuelled Iban inclinations towards revolt, already inflamed by perceptions of ill-treatment at the hands of the Japanese. The Iban triumph in Kapit became a catalyst for rebellion elsewhere.

In late June, immediately following the battle for Kapit, a series of uprisings took place further down the Rejang River. Ibans from the Katibas River, which flows into the Rejang at Song, broke in to the Japanese government store at Song and stole rice and other commodities, sparking further unrest in the area. In response the Japanese carried out reprisals, including occupying at least one Iban longhouse on the Katibas River. They also captured *Temenggong* Koh – whom they held partially responsible for both the Kapit and Katibas insurrections – and held him hostage at Song, pending more rebellions.[1]

The rebellious spirit was not confined to the Rejang. Around two hundred Ibans from the Batang Ai (Ai River) in southwest

Sarawak, close to the border with Dutch Borneo, descended on the Japanese post at the border town of Lubok Antu in early July. They seized confiscated shotguns; took salt, sugar and rice; and threw the government safe into the river before burning the government office to the ground. And at Engkilili, west of Lubok Antu, more than a thousand Ibans attacked the Japanese police post in early August, wielding swords and spears in the face of rifles, machine guns and hand grenades. Fifty or sixty were killed or wounded. Frustrated at their failure to take Japanese heads, some of the survivors killed and beheaded a local Chinese family.[2]

By early July Kapit was groaning at the seams with Iban and other local men who had come from outlying areas to participate in the fight against the Japanese. The town seethed with anticipation. Koh was also there, having escaped his Japanese captors. He offered his support to Sochon and, like Tama Weng Ajeng at Long Akah, he and his lieutenant Jugah anak Barieng – later also a *Temenggong* – worked to organise the new recruits. The authority they brought was critical to maintaining control over a potentially volatile situation.

Brian Walpole, newly arrived on the Rejang on 5 July, had learned a smattering of both Malay and Iban during his training on Fraser Island. Years later he described one of his first encounters with Ibans on the party's second day in Kapit.

> Quite a number of [Ibans] were hanging around the base in small groups, pointing at and discussing everything they saw. Pip Hume was showing one group how to aim a rifle. They were all dressed up in their warrior gear and holding onto their weapons tightly. [. . .]
>
> I told them my name was Brian and got them to repeat it a couple of times. Then I asked for their names, although none registered with me. I told them that I was from Australia, that I had been fighting the Japanese for ages and had taken a

lot of Japanese heads. They understood the bit about the heads.[3]

&

Semut III now entered a new phase. Since Kapit lay downstream from the Pelagus Rapids, it was much more accessible from the coast than the upper reaches of the Rejang River where Sochon and his men had previously been based. This meant the operation could expect to encounter more, and larger, Japanese river craft, including launches. The Japanese also now knew exactly where the party was located. For the first time Sochon was forced to plan against possible Japanese attacks of various types from different directions, including air sorties launched from the nearby Bintulu airfield.

On the plus side, the number of operatives had multiplied over the previous two weeks, reinforcements having been delivered piecemeal along with the supplies and equipment now regularly arriving by air. By the time Sochon moved to Kapit the original three had swelled to fourteen: Sochon, Abu Kassim, Barrie, Kearney, Baker, Spurling, Astill, Hume, Oldham, Fowler, Bradbury, Croton, Outhwaite and Walpole. Tom Crocker and John Bull Douglas – the two Eurasian men who had joined the party while it camped at the Pila River – brought the overall count to sixteen.

The number of local recruits had also increased dramatically from the original fourteen who had joined the party at Belaga (and were still with them). Ibans arriving from areas around Kapit were supplemented with Kayans and other Dayaks from the Belaga district – some of them already trained – as well as Chinese and Malays. Sochon now found himself with several hundred guerrillas, all eager to taste battle.

Nor was this the extent of the transformation: improved radio gear and an experienced signaller had generated what Barrie described as 'a quantum jump in communications'. Not only could Sochon contact SRD HQ (now on Labuan Island), but Semut III operatives in the field could communicate with Semut III HQ in Kapit via their own portable ATR-4 transceivers.[4]

And weapons! At last the long-promised guns had arrived and Sochon had enough rifles and ammunition to distribute among local recruits. The receipt of uniforms and cash meant he was also able to hand out clothing – especially much sought-after army trousers – and begin paying guerrillas a regular wage.

Last, but certainly not least, meagre meals of rice and fern fronds were now a thing of the past. Regular deliveries of canned food, rice, biscuits, chocolate, coffee, sugar and so on provided enough to feed all the recruits as well as the operatives. Indeed, Walpole reports that the food was 'like dinner at the Waldorf compared with what we'd had in New Guinea'. The change in the operation's fortunes was monumental.[5]

∞

Sochon now had two priorities. The first was to protect Semut III's new position against any possible Japanese attack. With this in mind he dismantled the block at the mouth of the Baleh River and on 10 July sent Oldham with a party, including a number of new Iban recruits, to set up a block further down the Rejang River. His plan was to move the block progressively downstream, eventually assuming control of the river as far as Sibu.

Oldham's party established the block at the mouth of the Sebatu River, not far upstream from Song. Block houses – armed with Bren guns and PIATs – were set up on either side of the Rejang River. Sochon had requested that the RAAF begin regular patrolling of this area, thereby alleviating the threat of Japanese moving upriver during the day. To combat enemy movement by night the block was equipped with spotlights and batteries placed inside bunkers on each side of the river. This allowed the party to pin down nocturnal river craft between twin beams.[6]

Meanwhile, outlying patrols were established around Kapit and defensive positions set up in the town itself to ward against attacks from jungle or river. At the same time Sochon began organising intelligence and support networks among local Iban longhouses, with the aim of extending these networks over time. As part of this strategy, local scouts were employed to patrol the jungle around Kapit, on both sides of the river. Ibans armed with blowpipes were sent to guard the riverbanks from Kapit down to the block, making infiltration by land almost impossible.[7]

As a further precaution against attack, when Kearney returned on 13 July from his reconnaissance trip in the upper Rejang, Sochon sent him with a group of guerrillas to spy out the land between Kapit and Song on the true left side of the river. Sochon had heard disturbing rumours that the Japanese planned to reach Kapit by travelling south and east from Song along the Katibas River, so bypassing his Sebatu river block. When Kearney reported back several days later, he told Sochon that local Ibans had successfully foiled any such plan.

'The Japs must have had the idea, alright' [Kearney] said. 'According to the Dyaks there've been isolated patrols around the place for the last week or so, but they've all been hacked to bits by the Iban.'[8]

Using traditional methods of jungle warfare, including ambush and blowpipes, Ibans along the Katibas instilled such fear into the Japanese that they refused to venture into the jungle, even on well-worn tracks. Many Katibas River Ibans had engaged in armed resistance against the Brooke regime in the second half of the nineteenth century, earning themselves an enduring reputation for lawlessness. As a result, an Australian military report written in

1944 warned that Ibans from this area should be treated with suspicion. Ironically, the very rebelliousness that had marked them as untrustworthy now saw the Katibas Ibans provide a crucial line of defence for Sochon's forces.[9]

∞

Sochon's second priority was to move downriver, taking Song and subsequent towns as part of an ultimate move on Sibu. This was a perilous project since Sochon's own intelligence suggested there were more than one hundred Japanese in Song alone, with another thirty stationed in Kanowit and as many as four hundred scattered around Sibu. Against this, Semut III consisted of fourteen operatives – some of them in the Belaga-Bintulu area – and several hundred local recruits divided between Belaga and Kapit. Many of the latter were still untrained.[10]

Nevertheless, it was imperative to start downriver quickly. SRD's Operation Agas in British North Borneo had by now laid bare the appalling treatment meted out to Allied POWs in the Japanese internment camp at Sandakan:

> Indeed, by May 1945, the Allies *know* the Japanese are force-marching to death hundreds of sick and starving Australian and British soldiers [. . .]
>
> Since January, the Services Reconnaissance Department and organs of military intelligence have gleaned precise information about the state of the Borneo prisoners through the special operations of AGAS, or 'sandfly' [. . .]
>
> Throughout 1945, they detail the dreadful state, and probable extermination, of hundreds of prisoners.[11]

Nothing was done to rescue the Sandakan-Ranau prisoners in part because, as Ham points out, they were seen as less important than prosecution of the larger Pacific War. However, civilians, including women and children, were believed to be held in the Batu Lintang internment camp at Kuching, and this may account for the greater concern it attracted. Whatever the reason, rescue of the Batu Lintang internees remained an urgent priority for Semut III. Sochon was tasked with reaching Sibu and launching Operation Hippo as quickly as possible.[12]

Planning for Hippo to date had been almost impossible, due to a dearth of intelligence about the camp and its inmates: the Allies were uncertain even about the number and type of prisoners held there. But this was about to change. Shortly after Sochon moved to Kapit he received information about an intelligence network in Kuching set up by a former Brooke government medical officer, Dr Marjoribanks. Initially interned in Batu Lintang by the Japanese – who had assumed he was European – Marjoribanks (a native of Madras) had been released after demonstrating he was an Indian national. He was now working as a GP in Kuching, a perfect position from which to run a network of spies.

Marjoribanks offered to provide information to Sochon about the situation in Kuching, especially at the Batu Lintang camp. He was true to his word. Over the following weeks Sochon gained a wealth of detail about not only the camp but also the disposition of Japanese soldiers in and around the town. In particular, he learned that there were few soldiers in Kuching itself; Japanese HQ was in fact located at Bau, around 30 miles (48 km) away. This information, shared with Allied HQ at Labuan, was priceless.[13]

With the emphasis on urgency, Pip Hume, a weapons expert inserted for this very purpose, got to work training the recruits flooding into Kapit. He estimated that within three to four weeks around four hundred and fifty of them would be ready for active operations.[14]

Song was the first target. Consequently, Sochon requested air raids on the town in the hope of damaging enemy emplacements.

However, the Japanese screen of security made it difficult to gain intelligence for the RAAF on gun placements, troop dispositions and activities, ammunition stores and the like. This meant that pilots had no idea what to aim at.

But Sochon's luck was in: he was not the only commander with an interest in Song. Immediately after the fall of Kapit, Iban leaders including Koh and Jugah had travelled downriver to Song, concerned about possible Iban attacks on the town. While there, Koh had been captured and held briefly by the Japanese who blamed him in part, as the highest ranking Iban leader in the area, for the uprisings in Kapit and along the Katibas River. He had managed to evade his captors and return to the upper Rejang where he linked up with Semut III.[15]

Now, in discussing Song with Koh, Sochon discovered he had a store of information from his brief time as a prisoner there.

> [He] had kept his intelligent eyes wide open whilst he was held prisoner. [. . .] He gave me a graphic description of almost every tactical position of value – but there was a drawback – a map meant nothing to the old man. Descriptions, yes – but locating a spot on a piece of paper was quite beyond him.

Like many indigenous peoples, Koh experienced the landscape around him as a material entity he moved through and was intimately connected with on many levels. The abstract representation required for map-making and map-reading involves a different apprehension of place, one with which he was not familiar.[16]

There was only one way around this problem: Koh should point out Japanese targets from the air. Accordingly, during the first RAAF attack on Song, Koh was inside a Catalina, accompanying the group of five Kittyhawk fighter-bombers that conducted the raid. He directed their attack not only on the town itself, but also on an enemy-held longhouse on the adjoining Katibas River.

In preparation for the Katibas River attack, Sochon had arranged for local Ibans to congregate in their canoes near the longhouse and ambush any fleeing Japanese. Barrie later recorded an account of this raid by Flight Lieutenant Wally Mills, captain of Koh's aircraft:

> On the river by the longhouse Wally observed there was a collection of Ibans in many prahus [canoes], positioned to attack any Japs fleeing from the longhouse. [. . .] This scene was very visible to the crew and passengers in the Catalina. Koh got very excited and was dancing around the back of the 'Cat' waving his parang over his head pleading to be put down beside his colleagues so he could join the fray.[17]

∽

Sochon hoped the air attack had weakened the enemy hold on Song, but he needed to be sure. On 16 July he sent Oldham, Outhwaite, Bradbury, Walpole, signaller Fowler and a group of Iban guides and paddlers to spy out the area around the town. For most operatives in the party this was their first taste of the countryside west of Kapit.[18]

The once-mighty Rejang River is today silted in many places, its water levels distressingly low: the bitter harvest of the massive Bakun Dam located upstream and the erosion caused by rampant logging. But in 1945 it flowed clear and high between banks whose towering trees reached out over the water, birds flickering through their canopies. Guided by the Ibans, the group paddled downstream in several small local canoes. They had no need of the protection offered by the trees and bushes at the water's edge – trusting in the block downriver – and so made good time.

Reaching the block at the Sebatu River they overnighted to a cacophony of unfamiliar sounds: 'crocodiles barking – whether angrily or not I couldn't say – fish jumping and birds screeching.' This soundscape – common at night on any Borneo jungled riverbank even forty years ago – is today confined to the island's most remote regions.[19]

The next morning the group continued downstream for a short distance, now more concerned with concealment. Close to Song, their Iban guides directed them to the riverbank, where they hid the canoes. From here they followed the guides along what Walpole describes as a 'jungle-track-that-wasn't', so invisible was it to the operatives. At last they came to a spur that afforded them a perfect view of Song.[20]

Incongruously, given all the attention it was receiving, Song was little more than a diminutive riverine trading post, much like Long Lama or Belaga. It straggled along a jungle clearing on the true right bank of the Rejang, at the point where the Song flows into the larger river. On the opposite side of the Rejang, directly facing the town, yawned the mouth of the Katibas River. Today the bustling centre that bears its name – a stopping point for ferries plying the daily route between Sibu and Kapit – is located directly across the Rejang from the town that Oldham's group surveyed that day in July 1945. Ironically, it was moved there after the war in response to the terrible destruction that the hostilities – especially RAAF bombing – had wrought.

Song contained the usual row of dilapidated Chinese wooden shophouses and a cluster of Malay dwellings. There was also a tiny wooden fort – used largely as a government office under the Brookes – located on high ground at the mouth of the Song River. Close to the fort stood a bungalow where Brooke government employees had been quartered. The town also boasted a small wooden school. Several wharves jutted out into the river, and at least one Japanese launch and a barge were berthed there, in addition to the customary haphazard collection of local craft.[21]

From their vantage point Oldham's men could see that the town was full of Japanese looking relaxed and 'as if they were there to stay'. They must also have noted that the fort had been heavily reinforced, with trenches and machine-gun emplacements at every approach. It did not look like a town that would surrender easily to a front-on attack.[22]

While they were watching, a group of local Ibans arrived and fell into friendly conversation with the Ibans in their own party. To Oldham's great good fortune, the newcomers were able to provide information about enemy movements and emplacements. The Japanese in the town, they explained, were living in the fort, the nearby employees' bungalow and the school. They also passed on the alarming news that Japanese in the area were now shooting Ibans on sight, presumably in response to the Kapit and Song uprisings.[23]

Sochon was disappointed when Oldham returned with the news that the air strike on Song appeared to have had little effect: the Japanese had dug good underground air-raid bunkers in the jungle bordering the town, and retreated there whenever they heard planes approaching. Oldham also expressed the opinion that they had enough ammunition and supplies to hold on for weeks.

Sochon dreaded such a scenario, fearing the Japanese would soon discover that the stories he had spread concerning the size of Semut III's forces were untrue. His biggest worry was that in such an event they might be sufficiently emboldened to attack Kapit. Given the futility of any full-frontal attack with the meagre forces at his disposal, he resolved instead to commence a campaign of guerrilla warfare. His plan was to progressively undermine Japanese morale in Song.[24]

❧

The first plank in this offensive was a series of air strikes on Song. Although Sochon knew the Japanese had good air-raid shelters, he reasoned that ongoing bombing and strafing would eventually sap their spirits.

Then, in the days following Oldham's return, Sochon authorised a plan proposed by one of his guerrillas. Sergeant Embah, a Malay member of the Sarawak Rangers and Constabulary for eighteen years before the war, had joined Semut III at Belaga. His plan was beautiful in its simplicity. Embah would send a local scout to Song. On arrival the scout would tell the Japanese that a strong force of Australians had gathered in the jungle outside the town, and that he could secretly lead the Japanese to their position. In the meantime, Embah would take a group of the guerrillas Hume had been training on their first action. They would set up an ambush at a prearranged point, and the scout would lead the Japanese into it.

The plan worked to perfection, its results exceeding even their wildest hopes. Embah's scout was obviously a gifted actor, since the Japanese commanding officer at Song – presumably excited at the thought of effecting such a coup – elected to himself lead twenty of his men on the sortie. Embah waited with twelve guerrillas close to the river, on the only cleared jungle path running east of Song. The Japanese walked straight into the ambush and all twenty of them were killed.[25]

At the same time, a day or so after Oldham's return, Kearney, Bradbury, Walpole, signaller Fowler and a group of several Ibans who had received Hume's basic training, were sent to Song. Their orders were to 'niggle [the Japanese] and kill a few here and there'. The group was also tasked with reconnoitring the area downriver of Song, in preparation for future plans to move on towards Sibu once the town had fallen.[26]

Kearney, the leader of the patrol, was to prove one of Sochon's most effective lieutenants. Barrie was greatly impressed by him, describing his patrolling as 'audacious, dashing and aggressive'. Unusually for SRD officers, Kearney had left school at fifteen and worked as a manual labourer before enlisting in the Australian Army on the first day of recruitment. From there he had risen to a staff position with General Blamey before transferring to SRD. Unlike most members of Semut, he had recognised early in the piece the importance of speaking Malay, and taken the time to learn the language.

> I decided that Malay would be essential if I had to depend on locals for food. I first learned the dictionary by heart then, when I got to Melbourne, I spent two hours a day with a Dutch woman [. . .] In my first week on the Rajang [Rejang] I found a young Chinese-Malay who was eager to be a batman, and I practiced with him every day for the rest of my stay in Borneo. This was probably the most sensible thing I did in Semut.[27]

The core patrol commanded by Kearney, including Bradbury and Walpole as well as a number of particularly intrepid Ibans, was formidable: Barrie later attributed much of Semut III's success along the Rejang to this one small group. Bradbury was a 23-year-old traveller (presumably a salesman) who had served with the 2/10th Australian Armoured Regiment, Walpole a 22-year-old bank officer who had spent time with the AIF in New Guinea. Both had taken part in previous SRD operations – sometimes together – and fitted perfectly the SRD 'larrikin' mould, if Walpole's later account of his wartime experiences is anything to go by.[28]

However, of perhaps greater importance were the Iban members of the party, especially the man who led them for at least some of the time. Belaja anak Angkin from the Poi River – which flows into the Rejang between Song and Kanowit – knew the area well and, although still young (twenty-eight years old), was already a *penghulu* and respected throughout the region. Sochon later commented on his 'bravery, loyalty and worth to this party', and noted that every man fortunate enough to have Belaja in his patrol had recommended him for an award. He received the British Empire Medal after the war in recognition of his services to both Semut III and Semut IV.[29]

Sochon had been careful to instruct the operatives that during interactions with locals they should make sure to demonstrate their difference from the Japanese. They must be friendly but also respectful, always offering to pay for food and work such as guiding, bearing and paddling. Like Carter, Sochon was aware of the straitened circumstances of local Dayaks and so, when moving away from HQ, his men had licence to take plenty of Straits dollars, as well as extra food to share with longhouse hosts. They also carried extra medical supplies, ready to provide medical assistance to locals when needed.

On this first trip to Song the patrol took a lot of food – the men had no idea how long they would be away – as well as Bren guns, radio equipment, and around 10,000 Australian pounds' worth of Straits dollars. Walpole also had his own miniature MCR 'biscuit tin' radio receiver. Like many other Allied soldiers in the Pacific arena he loved the broadcasts of the infamous 'Tokyo Rose': Japanese women broadcasters who transmitted (in English) details of alleged Allied losses and privations in an attempt to demoralise Allied troops. Walpole found Tokyo Rose hilarious: 'this was first class entertainment to poor bastards like us in the jungle.'[30]

The group first travelled to the block at the Sebatu River. Then, on the morning of 22 July, they set off cautiously further down the Rejang. Arriving close to Song later that day, they hid the canoes and, like Oldham's patrol several days earlier, followed their Iban members to a high, remote location overlooking the town. Here they unexpectedly found themselves spectators at an RAAF air strike.

> Suddenly we heard aircraft. An air raid warning blared out and as we watched, the Japanese raced into the jungle to hide. Two RAAF fighter bombers came into view and made three runs over Song, bombing and strafing and making a mess of things. It was thrilling to watch.[31]

The Ibans in the party, attuned to this kind of warfare, immediately saw the possibilities. Could another air strike be organised, they asked? If so, since the party now knew exactly where the Japanese took cover – just outside the town, under trees at the edge of the jungle – setting an ambush would be easy, involving nothing more than hiding close to the shelters during the raid and picking off soldiers as they emerged afterwards.

Like the operatives of Semut II before them, those of Semut III were rapidly learning to trust the skills of their Dayak comrades. As Walpole records:

> The value of having Sea Dayaks [Iban] in the lead [. . .] soon became obvious. Their inbuilt jungle radar was so strong that the risk of walking into a Japanese ambush, let alone getting lost, was next to zero. Planting AP switches at night was unnecessary. There was no way an intruder could surprise or elude a Sea Dayak sentry.

And, as on the Baram River, Dayak input to planning was increasingly seen as key to the success of any action against the enemy.[32]

Kearney thought the Ibans' proposal an excellent one. Accordingly, Fowler radioed Sochon, requesting another strike. Before long they had a response: a strike had been scheduled for nine o'clock in the morning of 24 July, two days away.

∽

Meanwhile, the group learned from local Ibans that Japanese soldiers manning a jungle outpost a short distance from Song were relieved at the same time each evening. The locals also described the path used by the replacement patrol. Again, the possibilities were obvious.[33]

So it was that late the following day (23 July) four of the Ibans in the patrol led Kearney, Bradbury and Walpole along a jungle path to an ambush position selected earlier. Here, where the path turned a sharp bend, they set their trap. Three or four men were placed in positions facing directly down the path, so the oncoming Japanese would be directly in front as they fired. A man was also positioned on each side of the path with the object of shooting any Japanese who tried to escape. Then they waited, as dusk deepened the shadows.

Before long they heard Japanese voices coming towards them. Walpole comments that unlike Semut patrols, trained to travel in silence, the Japanese often talked and laughed as they proceeded: 'Maybe they were naturally cheerful, or perhaps it gave them Dutch courage.' Whatever the reason, this played directly into Kearney's hands: the Japanese were taken completely by surprise as his men opened fire. Six dead bodies now lay on the path.[34]

The operatives searched the corpses and discovered nothing of value. They then turned to go, following standard procedure whereby ambushers depart the area as quickly as possible. But there followed a scene similar to some of those already described for Semut II on the Baram River.

> [A]s we turned to go, Bujang and his mates closed in on the bodies, whooping with delight. Hack, hack, hack – it was just like chopping wood. Next thing they were laughing and holding up their trophies by the hair, ear and nose.[35]

In contrast to many other Semut men, who were deeply disturbed by both the act of decapitation and the sight of decapitated heads, Walpole appears to have been unaffected.

> What could I say? It was their culture and, considering the way they'd been treated, I didn't blame them at all. Besides, it would have been a brave, stupid and potentially dead man who tried to

stop them. I didn't necessarily condone what they were doing, but it didn't worry me either, given what I'd seen the Japanese dish out and with my brother Denis still in their hands.[36]

The group rapidly returned the way it had come, the Ibans carrying their trophies and whooping in triumph. Once they reached base camp they displayed the heads to their fellows, while Kearney reached into his large stash of banknotes. He paid those head-takers who wanted it at the rate of one Straits dollar per head. While not mentioned in official reports, it seems likely that Kearney had brought so many banknotes with him partly for this purpose.[37]

જી∾

On the following morning (24 July) the patrol was up before daylight: the men needed to establish their ambush positions at least two hours before the air strike scheduled for 9 am. The plan was to pack up their camp and move further downriver, taking their belongings with them and carrying out the ambush on the way.

After eating, the Ibans in the party led the operatives – trying hard to make as little noise as possible – along jungle paths to the area where the Japanese had retreated during the raid two days earlier. There they hid their gear in a nearby hollow. The sun came up on a clear day, perfect for the air strike.

It was agreed the ambush itself would be carried out by Ibans in the group, since the operatives lacked the necessary skills. The Ibans went forward to the ambush positions, taking nothing with them except their *parangs*: ideal weapons for the close-combat work required. They hid in the jungle immediately around the area where they believed the Japanese would take shelter. The four operatives, much less adroit and silent in jungle conditions, took up positions further away. If the ambushers should be pursued by Japanese, they would lead them into this second ambush.[38]

Kearney's group waited anxiously, constantly checking their watches. At six minutes past nine they finally heard the thrum of aircraft engines and in Song the sirens began to wail. Japanese soldiers hurried, unarmed, into the jungle to hide in trenches dug there. Three RAAF fighter-bombers did three strafing and bombing runs, causing considerable damage to the town. Once their sound had faded away the sirens wailed again, this time giving the all-clear. And the soldiers emerged from their shelters.

They were completely unprepared for what happened next. Iban guerrillas issued silently from the trees and wielded their swords with lethal accuracy.

> The first lot of Japanese who were hacked made surprised and horrified noises. Others, seeing what was happening, ran screaming towards Song for their lives. They made no attempt to help their friends. Most of them got away, but eleven didn't.[39]

Within moments their heads were gone and the group was on its way. Eleven headless corpses lay on the path, no doubt to the further unnerving of the enemy. One of the Iban guerrillas who took part told me years later:

> I and my friends attacked the Japanese in Song. They were not expecting us and after the aeroplane noise went away we killed many of them – they weren't expecting us and we jumped out. Jumped out from the trees. We took the heads for our own longhouses.
>
> It was we Iban who were brave – the white soldiers stayed back and didn't attack. We hadn't headhunted for a long time. Kapitan Kani [Kearney] told us headhunting was now allowed.[40]

The group retreated rapidly downriver, giving the Japanese no time to organise a search. As always, the Ibans led the way – moving easily through the jungle in spite of being burdened with most of the stores and equipment – with the Europeans completely in their hands. The route traversed seemingly trackless virgin jungle, and Walpole found himself amazed at their bushcraft. As he notes, most of the Ibans came from further east and so very likely had never travelled through this area before, yet they moved 'like they walked this way every day of the week'.[41]

Meanwhile, several of the Ibans disappeared. They reappeared shortly afterwards minus the heads, having arranged with the inhabitants of a nearby longhouse to smoke them. Thus unencumbered, the group moved westwards at speed, until they finally deemed it safe to stop in a clearing. Here Fowler radioed Sochon to report their success. And Kearney took the opportunity to pay those Ibans who were receptive, at the one Straits dollar-per-head rate.[42]

After two hours the group moved on again. Kearney had a hunch that once the Japanese in Song had radioed Sibu about the attacks of the past two days, reinforcements would be sent from Kanowit. Since the RAAF now controlled the airspace along most of the Rejang River, he calculated they would travel by night. On the off-chance a Japanese launch might come upriver to Song that very night, he decided to take his patrol back to the Rejang River – this time downstream from Song – in the hope of ambushing it.[43]

As Sochon later told Ivor Wren: 'Wars have been won on wilder guesses than this.'[44]

The patrol reached the Rejang River west of Song as the sun hung low on the horizon and the jungle shadows lengthened, having seen no sign of any Japanese since the ambush. The Ibans established a camp in a secluded spot just back from the riverbank. Then, after a meal and a rest, Kearney split up the party, placing men with Bren guns at intervals of fifty yards or so along the bank. The odds that a launch would come, and that a successful ambush could be effected in the dark, were long. But Kearney was a risk-taker.

Shortly after 1 am, as they dozed over their guns after an eventful day, one of the Ibans announced suddenly that he could hear a sound. 'Motorboat,' he insisted. Sure enough, moments later they heard the throb of a launch coming upstream, accompanied by the splashes of crocodiles disturbed by its movement.[45]

As the chugging of the launch came closer, the moon – their friend tonight just as the sun had been earlier in the day for the air strike – suddenly came out from behind a cloud, lighting up the river. The party could see a large launch flying the Japanese flag travelling slowly towards them. Its top deck was crammed with soldiers. In a further stroke of astonishing luck, it was travelling close to the river-bank where the men were hidden, near enough to hear the murmur of voices.[46]

As the vessel came alongside, the Bren guns opened fire, their harsh clatter reverberating across the river. Others in the party employed rifles and grenades. They emptied magazine after magazine to the accompaniment of screams and shouts from the boat. Finally the motor stopped. The boat ran aground on the bank and caught fire. Within a few moments it had sunk into the waters of the Rejang. The river was eerily silent.

The men learned later that sixty soldiers had been on the launch, which was indeed carrying Japanese reinforcements to Song. Fifty-seven of them were killed; three somehow escaped, presumably washed to safety in the current. Semut III's only casualty was a bad burn to the hand of an Iban guerrilla acting as a Bren loader during the action. On being asked to change the gun's barrel when it overheated (spare barrels were carried for this purpose) he had forgotten to use the wooden handle provided, and instead seized it with his hand.[47]

∽

Kearney's patrol left the area directly afterwards and headed back upriver in the darkness. Their intention was to carry out yet another ambush, this time upstream of Song, in the hope of convincing Japanese in the town that they were surrounded. Walpole marvelled again at the navigational skills of the Ibans leading the party:

It was a harrowing business. Bright as it was, the moon didn't penetrate the jungle and visibility was zero. Only the sheer skill of [the Ibans] got us through.[48]

After an hour they stopped and slept, with the Europeans in the party having no idea where they were. The next morning (25 July) they moved on again. For several hours, while skirting Song, they travelled in absolute silence, a demanding exercise for the operatives. Finally, late in the afternoon, they arrived at a place overlooking both their earlier base and Song itself.[49]

There the guerrillas learned from a local Iban that following the previous day's air-raid ambush, the Japanese had dug new air-raid trenches – presumably to prevent a repeat. The trenches were narrow and located a small distance away from the jungle, on the edge of Song itself. Inspection through binoculars suggested that each trench would hold three or four men, and showed they had been covered with protective roofing to safeguard against strafing.

As before, the Ibans in the party were excited by the possibilities. Another air raid should be commissioned, they suggested, during which they would glide on to the roofs of these shelters: the noise of the raid would cover any sound. When the Japanese emerged after the raid, the Ibans would be in a perfect position to attack. Again Kearney approved. Fowler radioed Headquarters and an air raid was organised for noon on 27 July, two days' time. While they waited, the men would take a well-earned day's rest.[50]

27 July dawned clear and sunny – another perfect day for an air strike. Fowler stayed behind at the camp with his radio, while Kearney, Bradbury, Walpole and nine Iban guerrillas headed to the ambush position at around 10 am. They focused on three trenches, located a little way from the others directly in front of their previous ambush site. Once again the European members of the party waited some distance back in the trees, while the Ibans went forward to positions on the edge of the jungle directly behind the three trenches.

They waited for two hours, the increasingly familiar noise of the jungle around them:

Sometimes it sounded like animals screaming and fighting; other times I fancied they were just indignant at our presence. Then there was the creaking of overburdened trees and dead branches thumping to the ground.[51]

Finally, at 12.30, they heard the drone of aircraft. The air-raid siren sounded and the Japanese headed for their shelters. The planes appeared overhead and shot up the town: 'What a mess they made of poor little Song! [. . .] It was lovely to watch from our secure position.' As they left, vapour trails drifting across the sky, the Ibans settled securely onto the roofs of the trenches, three to each trench.[52]

In the sudden silence after the raid, Japanese began to emerge from the shelters. As they did, the Ibans fell on them from above.

Sensing something behind them, the soldiers turned to look and I saw the horror on their faces. Most of them got their first hack on the neck before they could utter a sound. The rest just took off, screaming. To my amazement, five men from an adjacent shelter – not one of our targets – came over to see what was happening just as the Sea Dyaks [Ibans] had finished attending to their first lot of victims. The visitors screamed and turned to run, but only two of them made it. [53]

A Japanese officer began organising an armed party to give chase. But too late: the raiders had already melted into the jungle.

ᕼᕼ

Before settling down to sleep that night the group discussed its next strike. They agreed it should come from a different location – perhaps somewhere closer to the river – in order to maintain the element of surprise, and the Ibans in the party began canvassing options. But the strike never came to be.

In the middle of the night the operatives were awakened from their sleep by their Iban sentries. Two local Ibans had come from Song with the news: the Japanese were loading all their men and equipment onto launches. By morning they were gone, drifting silently, engine-less, downstream under cover of darkness. Song had fallen.[54]

15

CHAOS IN KANOWIT

ON 21 JULY, WHILE Kearney's party was harassing the Japanese at Song, Sochon was taken to Labuan by Catalina for discussions with senior officers. There he met with SRD's new director, Lieutenant Colonel Jock Campbell, and the commander of 9th Division, Major-General George Wootten. Both men underlined the gravity of the situation regarding the prisoners held in the Batu Lintang camp in Kuching. As Campbell told him:

> The general is most anxious for us to get through to Kuching to release those poor devils in the POW camp before anything drastic happens to them. You know what the Japs are like when they're cornered.

By this time two of the eventual six Australian survivors from the Sandakan-Ranau POW camps in British North Borneo had managed to reach Allied forces: Dick Braithwaite on 15 June and Owen Campbell on 20 July. The stories they told about the camps were so harrowing that they were declared unsuitable for public release.[1]

As a result, Batu Lintang was on people's minds at both SRD and 9th Division, the concern only increased by intelligence coming from Dr Marjoribanks: they now knew the camp contained a substantial civilian population, including women and children. This was one of the reasons, according to Harrisson, why Allied forces – even after the landings – stayed well away from Kuching: the Allied Command was worried about 'savage and wholesale reprisals' on those interned there should their jailors come under direct threat. Sochon's clandestine Operation Hippo was still seen as the best chance of rescuing the internees unharmed.[2]

Wootten also emphasised that until Sibu was taken and Bintulu under control, it would be difficult for the Allies to press further southwest. And whoever controlled Sibu had ready access to Kuching, either by sea via Sarikei and the mouth of the Rejang River, or overland via Sarikei and Simanggang (now Bandar Sri Aman). Sibu was the key.

Yet the General added a cautionary note. While Sochon should push on towards Sibu with resolution, he must exercise even greater care to minimise casualties than he had to date. Wootten was under pressure from politicians in Australia, worried about the political ramifications of any significant loss of Australian lives so late in the war.[3]

Sochon returned to Kapit on 25 July having received one good piece of news in Labuan: he was restored to the rank of Major. Two days later, on 27 July, he received a second: the Japanese had abandoned Song.

৶৹

Semut III and its Dayak allies – Kayans and related groups in the east; Ibans in the west – now controlled a substantial area: the

Rejang River and surrounding localities from Belaga to Song, as well as areas north and east of Belaga. In addition, as luck would have it, the Japanese had appointed Abang Adang, a Senior Inspector in the Sarawak Constabulary under the Brooke regime, as chief of police in Bintulu. He knew Sochon from before the war and was busy providing Semut III with a steady stream of intelligence regarding Japanese movements in the Bintulu area.[4]

For the moment Sochon appeared to have cut off any possible Japanese escape routes from either Bintulu in the east or Sibu in the west inland to Long Nawang in Dutch Borneo. Nevertheless, the area he was attempting to control was ridiculously large: around the size of the state of Tasmania. He was acutely aware of how minuscule was his force, and thus how tenuous his hold.

In particular, the area east and southeast of Bintulu – from the coast as far as the Rejang River in the south and the Dulit range in the east – was under constant threat from the large body of Japanese located to the west of the Baram River. The area directly adjoined Semut II, and this was the same Japanese force with which Carter was now so exercised in Marudi. Sochon was worried that Japanese soldiers might move inland into this area – currently only sparsely covered by his men – to escape Australian forces moving down the coastline from the northeast.

Accordingly, at the same time as Sochon had begun planning the attacks on Song, he had sent Astill and Baker to join Barrie in Belaga. They arrived around 14 July. While Astill remained to keep peace in the town, supported by a patrol of local Dayaks, Baker moved northwest to the Bintulu-Tatau-Tubau vicinity. There he joined up with the experienced Abu Kassim who was patrolling the area along with a party of Semut III guerrillas led by John Bull Douglas, in an attempt to plug any Japanese escape routes.

Eventually the two operatives decided that for the sake of efficiency they should split up the area between them. Baker stayed on, with a group of guerrillas, around Tatau southwest of Bintulu, covering the escape route Bintulu–Tatau–Kapit. Abu Kassim moved with another patrol of locals further east along the Kemena River to the Pandan–Tubau area.[5]

An experienced Iban guerrilla named Mandau was given charge of a third patrol, also operating in the Tubau area. Like many Ibans, Mandau had been conscripted into the Japanese military after the occupation. He had been a member of the Japanese patrol under Imada ambushed by Puso's brother Lasah Avun at the Uring Rapids several weeks earlier. After the ambush Mandau had changed sides and joined the Semut III guerrillas in Belaga. Now he and Abu Kassim together covered the Bintulu–Belaga escape route. Abu Kassim also provided a vital link with Semut II, which was operating on the Tinjar and Baram Rivers not too far east of his position.[6]

When Sochon returned to Kapit from Labuan on 25 July, he brought with him two new Semut III members: Sergeant The Soen Hin, who was transferring from Semut II where he had been operating inland from Bintulu (by far the furthest south of Carter's men), and Captain John Fisher, a 34-year-old Englishman seconded from SOE. The was immediately sent back to the Bintulu area to reinforce Baker's forces, and initially deployed on patrol around Mukah. In the following weeks he took command of a group of Iban guerrillas, and this force is credited with clearing the Japanese out of Tubau, Labang and Pandan, key towns on the Kemena River inland from Bintulu.[7]

Fisher – 'Fish', as he became known among the operatives – was a member of both SRD and BBCAU, and had been involved with Semut from its earliest planning. He had been a Brooke government district officer in Sarawak before the war – based first in Kapit and then Sibu – administering the very area where Semut III was now operating. As a consequence, he spoke both Malay and Iban fluently, and was widely respected by locals along the Rejang

River from Sibu to Belaga. It was a source of much amusement to the other operatives that since most locals had difficulties pronouncing the English 'f' and 'sh' sounds, he was generally called '*Tuan* [Mr] Pisser'.

Fisher took over from Kearney as Sochon's second-in-command, with control of civil affairs in Semut III's area. His arrival freed Sochon from the increasingly onerous responsibility for civil order in towns taken from the enemy, leaving him to focus on the military part of his job. This was to prove a highly effective arrangement, one not available to Carter in Marudi.[8]

൶

Meanwhile, Sochon was receiving reports from Astill warning of a potential food shortage in Belaga. He despatched Oldham to the town around 30 July. Oldham's orders were to travel from Belaga to the Kenyah village of Long Nawang – where there were known to be abundant rice surpluses – across the border in Dutch Borneo, buy rice and send it back to Belaga. Sochon was keen to establish a presence in Long Nawang: he had heard that a large force of Japanese fleeing the Allied landings at Balikpapan on the east coast of Dutch Borneo was heading there. Having despatched the rice, Oldham was ordered to remain in the village, on guard against Japanese retreats from the east coast or through Semut III's own territory.

And Oldham was given a further brief. Rumours concerning a massacre of Europeans at Long Nawang had reached the Australian military command. Oldham was commissioned to produce a report on a possible atrocity in the area.[9]

Oldham left Belaga on 2 August, taking with him plenty of supplies and firearms, as well as a radio. Since Japanese were reported to be on the move in the area – some heading for Long Nawang – he was accompanied by a large patrol comprised mostly of Kayans, Sekapans and other local Dayaks, travelling in six longboats.

The party was guided by a Punan named Lanyieng Joo, who had travelled many times to Long Nawang and so could pick the easiest route through some of Borneo's most difficult terrain.[10]

The trip was still a gruelling one. The group first struggled up the fast-flowing and treacherous Balui River to its headwaters, porting boats and goods above seemingly endless rapids, and enduring drenching rain and flash floods along the way. At the river's source they left the boats and continued on foot, climbing the 2000-foot (610-m)-plus pass through the Iran Mountains in Borneo's central highlands to reach the Dutch border. From there they made their way to the Kayan River in Dutch Borneo, where they acquired more longboats from the Kenyahs in the area for the trip downstream to Long Nawang. They arrived on 3 September, a month after their departure from Belaga. They had kept a constant lookout along the way, but encountered no Japanese.[11]

However, on reaching Long Nawang, Oldham discovered a small Japanese patrol in place. This was ejected after a skirmish, and Oldham's men moved into the village. They held it for the next six weeks, in the face of constant radio reports suggesting the impending arrival of a large Japanese column from Balikpapan. In fact, the column never eventuated. It had turned back further south, with some of its complement holing up in caves where they were discovered years later.

Oldham also had a visit from Tom Harrisson, now styling himself as 'Commanding Guerrilla Forces, [in] Dutch Borneo and Northern Sarawak'. Sochon had already, several weeks earlier, rejected Harrisson's proposed expansion into Semut III's territory in Dutch Borneo, seeing it as naked ambition on Harrisson's part. But Harrisson was apparently unabashed. His desire to add Long Nawang to Semut I's operational area was denied only by Oldham's timely occupation of the village. Never one to be beaten, the map in Harrisson's later book incorrectly shows Long Nawang, and neighbouring localities across the border in Sarawak, as coming under Semut I's aegis.[12]

Oldham used his time in the village to uncover bodies buried after the Long Nawang massacre in 1942. He also interviewed locals about the killings. His report, written in Long Nawang on 18 September 1945, was circulated to Allied forces in the area. Despite advice that two of the main perpetrators named in the report – the commanding officer Captain Shima Mora and Lieutenant Okino – had been arrested and were being held by the Australians, neither was ever brought to trial.[13]

∞

Nevertheless, Sochon's top priority was Sibu and the subsequent launch of Operation Hippo. With the words of Campbell and Wootten ringing in his ears – and knowing that the lives of the Batu Lintang internees might rest in his hands – he could ill afford to slacken off in his push downriver. In addition, he was worried that Japanese forces travelling inland to escape the Australian landings at Balikpapan might move north into Sarawak and threaten Semut III along its vulnerable eastern flank. This increased the urgency of taking Sibu, before Japanese fleeing Dutch Borneo arrived in the upper Rejang River area.

Accordingly, Kearney's party moved into Song on 28 July, immediately following the Japanese evacuation. They came in carefully, skirting deserted sentry posts, fearing a Japanese ambush. The village itself looked strangely unfamiliar when seen close-up, without any Japanese in sight and with local people – mostly Chinese – back on the streets. Once residents spotted them, they were mobbed by a joyous crowd. The party took over a large dwelling used by the Japanese and, that night, they were treated by local Chinese to a banquet.[14]

On the same day, Oldham took a patrol and moved the river block downstream, his final action in the area before travelling to

Belaga and on to Long Nawang. The block was transferred from the junction with the Sebatu River to the junction with the Poi River, below Song and only around 12 miles (19 km) upstream from Kanowit. Having waited the conventional twenty-four hours in case of enemy return, Sochon moved his forward HQ into Song on 29 July.[15]

In the meantime, mindful of the need for haste, Sochon had ordered Kearney's party to move to a large rubber plantation colloquially known as Kidd's Estate, located slightly east of Kanowit. Kidd's Estate was occupied by an unknown number of Japanese, and Kearney's instructions were to determine how many they were and capture one for interrogation purposes. Sochon was keen to know Japanese intentions with respect to Kanowit. Would they try to hold out there? Or would they retreat to Sibu if attacked? He believed these questions could only be answered accurately by a Japanese soldier.[16]

∽

Rejang Estates Ltd was a large rubber plantation at Sengayan, on the northern bank of the Rejang River about 1.5 miles (2.4 km) east of Kanowit. Established in 1926, it was one of the largest rubber plantations in Sarawak, with around 1175 acres (475 hectares) of rubber under cultivation in 1941. Although worked largely by Ibans, the estate was owned and managed by Europeans. George Kidd was its (European) manager; hence the name by which Sochon and his men knew it. In a strange twist of irony, by the time Semut III reached the area, George Kidd and his wife were interned in Batu Lintang camp in Kuching.[17]

Early on the morning of 29 July, with the mist still lying heavily across the river, Kearney, Bradbury, Walpole and six Iban guerrillas led by Belaja, plus more Ibans to paddle the boats, set off down the Rejang from Song. Fowler and the other guerrillas stayed behind in Song with the radio, to await Sochon's arrival. The party was headed for Kidd's Estate, not much further down the Rejang from the Poi River where Belaja had his home. They travelled light, in two canoes, leaving their Brens behind: this was a job requiring stealth and speed.

After several hours on the water the party passed the new block at the entrance to the Poi River. From here they proceeded more cautiously, keeping to sheltering undergrowth along the banks wherever possible. The day was therefore already well advanced by the time they eventually arrived at the Iban longhouse Belaja was aiming for: sprawled, in the usual way, along a jungle clearing on the high bank at the edge of the Rejang River, some distance upstream from Kanowit. Belaja was well known here and the men were welcomed by the longhouse head and given food. On this and a subsequent visit Walpole was astonished at what he saw:

> Bujang showed me the workings of the longhouse and it was a
> real eye-opener. The Sea Dayaks [Ibans] were such smart and
> industrious people. They had market gardens on the sides of
> nearby hills, which they planted in seven-year cycles to rest the
> soil. Time seemed to just disappear.[18]

As always, the longhouse residents were keen to drink and talk with the visitors. It soon transpired that they knew Kidd's Estate well. As evening turned into night and lights sprang up along the gallery, they provided valuable information about Japanese activities there and elsewhere in the area. Kearney and Belaja were told that while there were quite a few Japanese at the estate, they did not appear to be on high alert. And they learned of a guard post, manned by a number of Japanese soldiers, on the estate's edge.

The minds of everyone in the party immediately turned to a raid. By the time they lay down to sleep in the longhouse gallery – following exhaustive discussions with the locals – Kearney and Belaja had a plan.[19]

At two o'clock the next morning, long before the roosters had launched into their pre-dawn cacophony, the entire party left the sleeping longhouse. They took with them two local men who had agreed to act as guides. Returning to their canoes, they continued down the Rejang River, the mass of the jungle adding a deeper shade of dark on either bank. Dayaks generally avoid river travel at night for fear of hitting dangerous obstacles such as boulders or submerged logs, which can easily capsize the small local canoes. But Kearney's run of luck continued with a bright moon above, stars huge and gleaming in the cavernous black sky, enabling them to make good time.[20]

After less than two hours, the locals guided them silently to a landing place tucked into the side of the Rejang close to Kanowit. There they left the boats under the guard of the boatmen and followed their guides along a rough jungle path. Although it was still night the moonlight allowed them to travel at speed and it was not yet dawn when they reached the guard post: a small house on the edge of the estate, beside the wide main track leading to the Kanowit river crossing. There was also a sentry box some distance from the house, to control traffic into the estate. They could see a Japanese soldier reading at a table inside the box but no sign of anyone else; the other members of the patrol were presumably asleep in the house.

One of the Iban guerrillas was sent through the jungle into the estate to glean information about Japanese numbers and emplacements there. The remainder stayed behind, close to the guard post. They knew from their longhouse information that a change of guard was due soon. Kearney decided to attack before it took place, while the enemy soldiers were still sleeping.[21]

But first they needed to secure a prisoner for Sochon. Recognising the superiority of Dayak skills for such an undertaking, Kearney agreed that Belaja should take on the job. They watched him enter the door of the sentry box behind the guard, silent as a cat. In a flash his hand was over the guard's mouth, his *parang* at his neck, and Belaja was miming graphically what he would do if the man cried out or attempted to draw his weapon. The Japanese, paralysed with shock, was quickly disarmed by a second guerrilla and bundled out of the box before he could make a sound.

Quickly the party cut the two telephone cables that ran from the box: one to the nearby house, the other into the estate. Then they crept towards the house.²²

The door was unlocked; they eased it open. There was no movement inside. They rolled in two grenades and flattened themselves on the ground. Five seconds later came a shattering explosion, the darkness fractured by vivid silver flashes. As Walpole described later

> There was enough light to see that the interior was shredded to bits. It was a large L-shaped area with a corridor leading to more rooms. No one was asleep now. A couple of Japanese lay dead, while others twitched or staggered about.²³

Some Japanese appeared from other rooms, weapons in hands, and a brief firefight ensued. Realising that he was outnumbered – there were eleven soldiers in the house according to Walpole – and that more soldiers from the estate would arrive soon to investigate the noise, Kearney quickly ordered his men back into the jungle.

Within minutes the party had disappeared, taking with them the prisoner – given the use of his hands and feet for the trek – and two Japanese heads. On the return journey to the boats they were joined by the Iban guerrilla who had left them to reconnoitre the estate. They saw no sign of pursuit and soon were back on the river.²⁴

The party arrived back at the longhouse before noon, to an uproarious welcome. The sight of the heads elicited an almost delirious excitement, and the attack was described over and over, with new embellishments added each time. Again the men were fed and overnighted in the longhouse. They kept the prisoner close by and well-guarded during the night, worried less about an escape than that a longhouse resident might be sufficiently inspired by the party's deeds to seek a Japanese head for himself.

At dawn the next morning (31 July), having paid the guides and the longhouse head, the men made their grateful goodbyes and returned to their boats for the tiresome paddle back upriver to Song. Initially, in the murkiness of a Borneo riverine dawn, the immense jungle surrounding them seemed asleep. But gradually the sun appeared, and the world came alive.

> Birds of all descriptions, screeching from the thick forest. We saw monkeys chattering and watching us from trees on the bank. Crocodiles lazed on the mud and slipped into the river at our approach.[25]

The prisoner's wrists were tied but his legs had been left free so he could clamber in to and out of the boats when necessary. As they traversed a set of rapids, he took them by surprise. With a scream, and in defiance of his bound wrists, he launched himself over the side of the canoe – which came perilously close to capsizing – into the water.

They watched him bounce from rock to rock as the current hurled him through the rapids. They dared not risk their own lives in pursuit: any attempt to turn the boats in the feverish water would have ended in disaster. They consoled themselves, as they continued upriver, with the thought that he had no chance of surviving the rip.[26]

☙

Song was now the forward HQ of Semut III, and Sochon was there when the party rather dejectedly arrived later that day. Although he had no Japanese prisoner for interrogation, Kearney was at least able to pass on intelligence gained from the Iban guerrilla's reconnaissance of Kidd's Estate. He had learned that the Japanese were worried about Allied soldiers in the area, and had a greatly inflated idea of their number. As a result, they were already withdrawing personnel and equipment to Sibu.[27]

This was encouraging news. Sochon knew that Japanese anxiety would only be amplified by the raid on Kidd's Estate, with its legacy of headless corpses. Intelligence from behind enemy lines had already revealed how distressing enemy soldiers found the discovery of comrades' headless bodies. Nevertheless, Kearney's report to his commanding officer likely also raised concerns about the headhunting the operation had brought into play.

Like Carter's men on the Baram, Sochon's operatives had for some time recognised that head-taking could play a role beyond simple recruitment of Dayaks to their cause: as a tool for terrorising and demoralising the enemy it was almost unrivalled. And yet, as Pasir Nai had shown, its resumption could also have terrible consequences for people other than Japanese soldiers. In a report written at the end of the war Carter notes that in response to Semut's reintroduction of headhunting some Ibans had 'taken the opportunity to settle scores against the Chinese'. But settling scores was only part of it. Kearney almost certainly now reported to Sochon that he had been approached by several Ibans in Song seeking payment for non-Japanese heads, presumably those of local civilians. He was horrified and refused to pay.[28]

Semut III was not alone in facing this problem. Ibans – by far the most enthusiastic adopters of the new headhunting policy – saw opportunities to profit from it in all Semut areas. Wilson (Semut II) records that Ibans of the middle Baram River brought him Chinese heads, claiming they were Japanese; he paid out 'until I got wise to their games'. Bob Long similarly told me that Harrisson's early insistence on personally vetting heads before payment stemmed from the number of non-Japanese heads being presented by Ibans.[29]

This development was not without precedent. Something similar had occurred during the eighteenth- and nineteenth-century heyday of European head-collecting, when headhunting was fostered by Europeans in some parts of the world on an almost industrial scale to feed demand back home. Thus, with a critical shortage of the tattooed chiefs' heads fetching the highest prices, some enterprising New Zealand Maori killed Europeans and tattooed their heads, before selling them to unsuspecting European buyers. In South American cities, heads of the unclaimed dead were sold by morgue officials to taxidermists to be transformed into fake Shuar shrunken heads for sale to Europeans. None of this should surprise us. After all, in our own societies the lure of wealth not uncommonly leads even apparently respectable people to unscrupulous – sometimes murderous – entrepreneurship.[30]

᳁

There was little Sochon could do other than push on. He suspected that after the attack at Kidd's Estate the remaining Japanese soldiers there would soon move into Kanowit, producing a consolidated force. As the last line of defence before Sibu itself, Sochon was convinced the Japanese would not relinquish Kanowit easily. He therefore decided to continue the strategy that had proven so effective in Song. Kearney's group – having already displayed a remarkable flair for guerrilla warfare – was now despatched to Kanowit with a general brief to harass enemy soldiers and emplacements around the town.

The party left for Kanowit the following morning (1 August). This time they took a Bren gun and extra supplies, again loading up two canoes. They travelled downriver to the same longhouse they had stayed in two days earlier, and were again received warmly – perhaps even more warmly, since the previous visit had culminated in the incomparable excitement of a harvest of Japanese heads. Evening found them talking with locals about Japanese patrols around Kanowit itself. And so they learned that every day at dawn a group of Japanese transported goods from Kidd's Estate to Kanowit, returning to the estate later in the day.[31]

The party left the longhouse at two o'clock the next morning (2 August). They took with them the Bren gun and extra supplies – they had no plan to return – as well as two local guides. They travelled once again down the Rejang, this time beyond Kidd's Estate to the outskirts of Kanowit itself.

Leaving their boats and supplies under the guard of their boatmen, they followed the guides along yet another invisible Dayak track. Walpole later commented on how arduous these night-time treks were. The jungle was pitch dark – too dense for moonlight to penetrate – but they could make no sound: agonisingly difficult for Europeans unused to jungle travel. Within an hour they had reached the well-cleared main track running from Kidd's Estate to the Kanowit river crossing. To their delight this promised, as hoped, the perfect location for an ambush.[32]

Kearney quickly placed his men in the vegetation beside the path, spacing them out in a line a metre or two apart. Walpole was placed at the end of the line closest to the estate, his job being to open fire when the last Japanese was almost level with him. The sound of Walpole's gun would be the signal for everyone else to fire on the Japanese soldier now level with him.

The men took up their positions and waited.

As we waited, the animal life seemed to stir and wake for the coming day. Rustling came from the jungle floor, birds flapped and scratched at their feathers and monkeys screeched high in the trees. Any minute. [. . .]

We heard them coming just before daylight: a dozen armed Japanese soldiers, talking and laughing as they walked and behind them five unarmed local people carrying goods. Through binoculars they looked close enough for us to reach out and touch.[33]

The ambush went exactly to plan. Six soldiers were killed, and four injured; the remainder fled into the jungle on the other side of the path. The locals, probably Malays, were rapidly questioned, and estimated that there were around sixty Japanese at Kidd's Estate. Before releasing the locals, Kearney concocted a vivid account of many more Allied soldiers in the jungle nearby, hoping they would pass this on to the Japanese. In the meantime, the Ibans took the heads of the six dead soldiers, leaving a line of headless bodies to be discovered by the enemy.[34]

Within minutes, the party was on its way back to the boats in the growing dawn light. At the river there was a sudden change of plans. Kearney had been ill over the past few days, with an increasingly debilitating skin infection and fever. He now decided to seek medical attention and departed upriver with the boatmen. The party was left in the hands of Bradbury and Walpole.[35]

∾

With Astill now ensconced in Belaga, Keith Barrie had returned to Kapit. He arrived there on 1 August and was joined, on 2 August, by three new additions to Semut III: Major John 'Ray' Wooler, Warrant Officer Class 2 Richard 'Dick' Perry and Sergeant Francis 'Frank' Pippin, the latter a signaller transferring from Semut II.

Sochon was keen to maintain the pressure on the Japanese in Kanowit, so Barrie was rapidly despatched downriver with a brief to assess their numbers, movements and intentions. He took with him a party of Iban guerrillas under the command of the experienced former Sarawak Ranger Corporal Thomas Nyandau. His departure meant there would be two patrols in the Kanowit area: one led by Barrie and one by Bradbury/Walpole.[36]

While Barrie was travelling downriver, Bradbury and Walpole's party was carefully skirting the town, gathering as much intelligence as it could about enemy positions. Arriving on 5 August at the mouth of the Bawan River – which flows into the Rejang slightly downstream from Kanowit – they took control of the area after skirmishing with a group of Dayaks working for the Japanese. The following day, still in the Bawan River vicinity, they received the first of a series of strange reports from locals. The Japanese in Kanowit, it was said, were packing all their stores and equipment onto boats. It appeared some might be about to depart Kanowit for Sibu.

This news galvanised Bradbury and Walpole. With their recent success on the river outside Song still fresh in their memories, they decided to set an ambush that night on the Rejang River just below the mouth of the Bawan. They arrived at their selected position late in the afternoon and, repeating the tactics that had proved so effective at Song, placed their men at intervals along the bank of the Rejang. Then they settled down to wait.[37]

However, in Kearney's absence they lacked his luck. As daylight faded, a pitch-black moonless night came in, making it impossible to see movement on the water. An ambush was out of the question; they were forced to abandon the idea.

On the same night (6 August) and further upstream on the riverbank directly opposite Kanowit, Barrie's group was on patrol. As they prowled cautiously through the jungle seeking a better view across the water they gradually discerned, against the heavy blackness, movement around the town. And not only movement: there was noise too. As Barrie later recorded:

In due course this resolved itself into the sound of river boat/s moving off down stream, (we could hear the familiar chonk, chonk, chonk of the engines of the river craft, which they were using, moving down towards Sibu).[38]

The Japanese in Kanowit – one hundred and fifty of them by this time according to Barrie – were retreating downriver.

Later reports confirmed that they had been drinking heavily during the evening of 6 August, having taken all remaining liquor from the bazaar. Consequently, many were intoxicated when it came time to leave. Some reports have one of them playing a banjo as they departed. Perhaps they were assuaging a sense of defeat and demoralisation, perhaps they were celebrating their departure from what probably seemed a hellish place, or perhaps they were simply letting their hair down as we all must do during even the darkest of times.[39]

Or perhaps they had already heard the unthinkable news: the US had, earlier that day, dropped an atomic bomb on Hiroshima.

Whatever their mood, by the early morning of 7 August all were gone.

ᘉ

Today, Kanowit is a bustling town full of cafes, cars and motorcycles. But in 1945, while larger than Song, it was still not much more than a village. Even then it was a busy place, since almost all trade into and out of the middle and upper Rejang River region passed through it. Indeed, large ocean-going steamers sometimes bypassed Sibu and came directly to Kanowit in search of jungle produce.

By the time WWII broke out the town contained around twelve hundred residents, three-quarters of them Chinese and the rest Malays. As with Belaga, Kapit and Song, very few Dayaks lived in the town itself. Kanowits lived upstream on the south bank of the Rejang, and many Iban longhouses were located in the surrounding area, on both the Rejang and Kanowit Rivers. Members of these groups came regularly into town to socialise and trade.[40]

The town's strategic location on a point of land at the junction of the Kanowit and Rejang Rivers, surrounded by Iban longhouses, meant it became important in the early days of Brooke rule. Here the first White Rajah, James Brooke, built a two-storey wooden fort in 1851, moved in 1859 to a bluff that commanded a view of both rivers. This was the venerable Fort Emma, the first fort built on the Rejang. Its walls were adorned with trapdoors through which cannon protruded in the earlier days of the Raj.

Following government concerns about old and unsafe Chinese shophouses, a new bazaar was built in the centre of Kanowit starting in 1927. By the time the Japanese arrived there were around forty-five two-storeyed wooden shophouses, stretching in a line from the Rejang River frontage around the bend to the Kanowit River front-age. The shops were built up off the ground on wooden piles, in blocks of around ten to twelve to reduce the risk of fire spreading. The breaks between blocks were traversed by raised boardwalks.[41]

Fort Emma, miraculously still standing, maintained a stately vigil above the men of Semut as they entered the town on 8 August 1945, the second day after the Japanese departure. They came in two sepa-rate patrols, one commanded by Kearney – who had recovered from his illness and returned to active duty – and the other by Barrie. They moved cautiously, their Iban guerrillas inevitably leading the way. They had received reports of booby traps in and around the town, and the Ibans had infinitely better instincts than their European comrades when it came to such things. Nyandau and his men from Barrie's patrol searched the area for traps and enemy soldiers, even-tually pronouncing it safe.[42]

On the previous day, Barrie's group had radioed Semut III's main HQ in Kapit with the news that the Japanese appeared to have left Kanowit. However, the group was uncertain about whether all had gone, so an air strike scheduled for later that day (7 August) had gone ahead. A Liberator had strafed the town after dropping more supplies and equipment to HQ in Kapit.

As a result, the scene that greeted Kearney's and Barrie's groups was one of devastation. The town – especially the mission compound and church where Japanese soldiers were known to be staying – had already been attacked a number of times by Allied planes, and the latest strafing added to the wreckage.[43]

Only one bungalow, which had served as the District Officer's quarters before the war, was still standing. This is where the Japanese had enjoyed their pre-departure revelry; the floor was littered with empty sake and Scotch whisky bottles. When Sochon arrived several days later he was heartbroken at the sight:

> [I]mmediately before the occupation a good many cases of liq-
> uor and other valuable supplies had been buried by the civil
> government officers. Some of these had been found by the
> Japanese, and they had made hay with their treasure trove. It
> had been a long time since I had tasted a drop of Scotch and to
> find it wasted on a bunch of saki-drinkers was too much.[44]

But the destruction of Kanowit had other, more disturbing, causes. While Kearney and Barrie did not yet know it, in the week following the ambush by Kearney's group close by at Kidd's Estate – after Japanese soldiers based there had moved into town – a group of Ibans had ransacked the Estate and taken the heads of sixteen Chinese employees. Then, when the news of the Japanese departure from Kanowit itself had spread through local longhouses, large numbers of Ibans had flocked into the town. Taking advantage of the lack of law and order, on the previous night (7 August) some had killed and taken the heads of a group of Chinese in a house behind the bazaar. Wooler reports that twenty-six heads were taken in total (presumably including those from Kidd's Estate), all of them Chinese.[45]

The bazaar itself was looted and set on fire, perhaps accidentally, by Ibans carrying torches. Tragically – or perhaps fortunately, given the murderous inclinations of the mob – most of the town's Chinese and Malay residents had fled in previous days, fearing both Allied air attacks and Iban marauders. As a result, the entire Chinese bazaar and half the Malay *kampung* [town precinct] had burned to the ground.[46]

In retrospect, none of this is surprising. The license to headhunt had drawn hundreds of Iban men to the operation, where they eventually far outnumbered operatives. But many of them came on board in a loose sense only, operating informally as scouts, runners or even participants in locally organised patrols, rather than as trained – and regularly paid – members of the operation's guerrilla force itself. These men were part of Semut III's 'army', without being subject to the day-to-day regulation and authority of its local or European commanders. It was members of this unruly force who attacked the Chinese at Kidd's Estate and Kanowit.[47]

∽

Kanowit was still in a ferment as the men of Semut III entered on 8 August 1945, and they feared further looting and loss of life. Nyandau, himself an Iban from the Kanowit area, took the lead. He set some of his men to guard the fort and other parts of the town, and he threatened to fire on any of the assembled Ibans who started trouble. As in Song, where the escalation of Iban violence was prevented by the intervention of other Ibans – Koh and Jugah who travelled there after the fall of Kapit; Jugah and Bennett Jarrow, Native Officer in the town, after the fall of Song itself – in Kanowit Ibans stared down other Ibans. Both Jugah and Nyandau later received the King's Medal for Courage in the Cause of Freedom from the British crown, in part for these actions.[48]

Given the continuing volatility, the two patrols could only wait – and hope to hold the peace – until reinforcements arrived. But while they waited, Kearney and Barrie encountered a new, terrible threat. The next day Spurling sent a radio message from Kapit:

> Labuan advises strafing Kanowit, Sibu and River today ninth. Fuck off out of Kanowit and River. Trying prevent RAAF balls up.[49]

Semut III HQ at Kapit had received a signal from Labuan to the effect that the RAAF intended to strafe Kanowit and Sibu later the same day, even though Labuan had been informed on 7 August that Kanowit was now in Semut III's hands. Sochon responded with an urgent message to Labuan asking them to keep the RAAF away from the town.[50]

However, Kearney and Barrie were faced with an imminent RAAF attack. This was not unusual: there are many reports of strafing and bombing of civilian targets in both Brunei and Sarawak by the RAAF during this period. Indeed, so indiscriminate were these attacks that Semut III members sought cover whenever they heard a plane approaching, even though the airspace was, by then, owned by the Allies. Allied troops themselves criticised the air force's 'practice of bombing conspicuous buildings even when they were unlikely to contain anything of military importance', with a 20th Brigade Report describing the destruction of civilian bazaars and shops in some areas as 'wanton'. In the week of 24–30 July alone, for instance, there were 186 Allied air sorties over North Borneo (including Sarawak), with targets including small shipping and hotels.[51]

Locals, rather than Japanese, were the main casualties of these forays, often directed at local dwellings, including longhouses.

That very day a white people's plane came and attacked our long-house for about half an hour. At that time the weather was very sunny and we were taking the opportunity to dry things, to dry *padi* [unhusked rice], and my grandfather was guarding the *padi*. The others together there all got hit by the machine gun. Many of us in the longhouse were hit and one died in the middle of the house, Ugap was his name. And our mother got hit in the thigh and the bullet buried itself in the ground. My uncle Gerantun got hit in the ankle and it was broken. My grandfather had bullets stuck in his whole body but we were able to get them out.[52]

Civilian casualties from one raid alone, the terrible attack on Sibu on 4 June, numbered over one hundred killed and many more injured.[53]

Accordingly, Kearney and Barrie were not about to take any chances. They agreed their best strategy was to indicate to the pilots of the planes that Allied forces occupied Kanowit. A few white-painted planks from a destroyed bungalow were lying on the ground, and they decided these should be used to spell out a message for the pilots. But what should it say?

Dave Kearney decided that [. . .] the message needed to be short but unambiguous. Moreover it was necessary to ensure such a message could not be misinterpreted as a Jap ruse. [. . .] It was agreed that Dave's final format would satisfy all conditions. It was set up on the riverside slope of the ridge between the District Officer's bungalow and the Kubu [fort]. It read: -
FUCK OFF[54]

Sadly, this work of art was not seen by its intended audience. The scheduled attack on the town was called off in time.

☙

Within days reinforcements had begun to arrive and Kanowit was inching towards a painful peace. Wooler came first with a patrol on 9 August and established Semut III's new forward HQ in the town. Discovering a chaotic situation and a terrified Chinese population, he set soldiers to protect the latter, including during burials of those who had died. One of his first acts was to throw sixty-three Ibans caught looting into the cells in Fort Emma.[55]

Then, on 12 August, Fisher moved to Kanowit from the Poi River area upstream where he had been settling land disputes, and took up residence in Fort Emma. He brought with him two Iban assistants.

Fisher and his team worked miracles. They immediately organised the construction of a temporary bazaar, using local paid labour. They arranged for food and other necessities, including medical supplies, to be delivered regularly from Labuan – locals told me seventy years later that these deliveries kept people alive during this terrible period. A medical dispensary was also established, supervised by Dr Chee, a local Chinese doctor, with five dressers from the Brooke era. By early September Kanowit was well on the road to recovery.[56]

Equally as important, Fisher immediately initiated a search for the Ibans who had perpetrated the looting and killing at both Kidd's Estate and Kanowit itself. Having identified them all within a few days, he had them arrested and locked in Fort Emma. They were eventually transferred to prison in Sibu and tried there after the war, being acquitted following lengthy hearings, much to the outrage of the local Chinese population.

Remarkably, Fisher was also able to recover the captured Chinese heads – perhaps a less gruesome enterprise than it might sound, since they had been smoked, and so preserved. As a result of his team's labours all of them were eventually returned to their families.[57]

16

END OF THE RIVER

SIBU, GATEWAY TO KUCHING and the Batu Lintang prisoners, was now only 27 miles (43 km) from Semut III's forward HQ. Sochon must have felt he could almost reach out desperate fingers and touch it. But once again, having come so far against so many odds, he was not to be rushed into a false move. Instead, he began methodically to weave a noose around the town.

In the first place this meant moving all Rejang River positions forward. On 9 August, the day after Kearney's and Barrie's men entered Kanowit, the river block was moved downstream by an Iban patrol led by Croton and Outhwaite. It was set up in the Durin area, around 15 miles (24 km) above Sibu. Durin's strategic location at a large bend in the Rejang made it easy for troops based there to control the true left bank of the river east of Sibu.

At the same time, Perry was sent with a group of local recruits to patrol the area opposite the block – on the true right bank of the river – from where jungle tracks led directly to Sibu. Then, on 11 August, Bradbury and Walpole took a platoon of guerrillas to

Bukit Lima on the southeastern outskirts of Sibu itself, around 3 miles (5 km) from the centre of town. Sochon's spies had told him Japanese troops in the town frequented this area, and that they had air-raid shelters there.[1]

Perhaps most important, after five weeks in Kapit the operation's main HQ moved downstream to Kanowit on 13 August. The significance of this move cannot be overstated. Finally, Sochon had emerged from hiding in the upper reaches of the river and gone on the offensive. His target was nothing less than Sarawak's third-largest town.

On arrival in Kanowit, Sochon discovered that Fisher had already taken over the fort. So he established his HQ in the bungalow of the former district officer, H.P.K. Jacks. Jacks had fled with other European Brooke administrators to Long Nawang when the Japanese invaded Sarawak at the end of 1941. However, unlike most of the others in the party, he had continued downriver and eventually escaped to Australia, thus avoiding the Long Nawang massacre. His bungalow seemed blessed with similar good fortune: it was one of the few structures left standing in the town.[2]

The operation was readying itself to pursue the same tactics in Sibu that had proved so successful in Song and Kanowit. But here the odds were greater. Not only were there more enemy soldiers in Sibu – around three to four hundred according to the party's intelligence – but they would be more desperate. Sibu was the end of the road.[3]

∾

From Sochon's new HQ at Kanowit, the operation's inexorable forward movement continued. On 12 August the river block was moved once again, this time to Pulau Keladi, a tiny island in the middle of the Rejang River around halfway between Durin and Sibu. From here it was only a hop and a skip to Sibu: around 7 miles (11 km) along jungle tracks on the true right bank of the river.

Forward HQ, under the command of Wooler, was also moved forward on 14 August, from Kanowit to Durin. There it took over the Catholic Mission building, with Wooler placing men in the church tower to cover all approaches into town. Reinforcements were streaming in from Labuan – underlining the importance of Sibu to larger planning – with nine new men inserted at Kapit by Catalina on 11 August alone.

Then on 15 August Croton and Outhwaite's platoon was sent even closer to the town, with instructions to cover its west side where the air strip was located, while local guerrillas took charge of the river block. Sochon also sent patrols led by three of the new arrivals – Lieutenant Alex McCallum, Sergeant Gordon Phillpot and Sergeant John 'Jack' Hartley – to different areas on the perimeter of Sibu. [4]

So it was that by late in the day on 15 August Sibu was effectively surrounded. Here, often operating in gardens very close to town, the patrols commenced a strategy of constant harassment. They employed classic hit-and-run tactics: firing on any Japanese they saw or setting ambushes – to kill and take captive – and then rapidly retreating into the jungle. The aim was both to damage Japanese morale and to maintain the fiction that Semut III numbered in the thousands. The tactics proved remarkably effective: Japanese casualties rose by the day and captives were regularly brought back to Semut III HQ for interrogation.

Led by Fisher, operatives continued to cultivate the support of local longhouses, encouraging their residents to act as informal scouts, guards, boatmen and so on. By now, with the Japanese clearly on the run, this was a much easier task than even four weeks earlier. In addition, the work of the Australian military and BBCAU in providing goods, including food, to residents in Kanowit and elsewhere was beginning to pay dividends. Still today, people in the area remember the Allied assistance of the time and contrast it with the privations suffered under Japanese rule.

The result was a great willingness on the part of locals to cooperate with the operation. Recruits flocked to Sochon's cause and
Hume was kept busy training. Indeed, Sochon eventually had so
many trained guerrillas at his disposal that he was able to increase
the size of patrols to as many as forty men each, and extend his network of informers until it reached into Sibu itself.[5]

Lu Ngee Jin was a Chinese policeman in Sibu under the Brooke
regime who had been kept on by the Japanese. He was able to escape
from Sibu as Sochon's forces closed in on the town, and make his
way to Semut III HQ in Kanowit.

> By this time the Allied force had moved down to Kanowit. We had
> to walk from Bawan Assan [slightly upriver from Sibu] through
> the thick jungle to reach there. We could not use the boats as the
> Japanese had set up sentries along the Rejang river. It was a tough
> journey. We started to walk just before dawn. We had to hide in
> the bushes during the day and continue our journey at night to
> avoid the Japanese sentries. At times, we had to crawl through
> padi fields and creep through fruit gardens to escape detection
> by the Japanese. On a number of occasions we met people on the
> way and asked their directions. Fortunately, we were not mis-
> taken for Japanese or the Ibans would have killed us.[6]

Like others who fled from Sibu to join the operation, Lu's knowledge of Japanese dispositions in the town was to prove invaluable to
Semut III's advance.

Intelligence reports coming to Sochon from informers within
Sibu, as well as testimony from captured Japanese prisoners, all
revealed that the harassment strategy was having the desired effect
on Japanese morale. Indeed, Sochon's information was that most
Japanese in the town were in favour of surrender. The harassment
continued.[7]

But in spite of his urgent focus ahead, Sochon continued to worry about his vulnerable flanks. With the area from Belaga to Bintulu reasonably well covered, on 11 August he sent Barrie with a patrol of six Ibans southeast along the Kanowit River (which flows into the Rejang at Kanowit) to Julau and Meluan, south of Sibu. Barrie's main brief was to prevent any possible Japanese infiltration upriver from that direction. The operation was finally expanding southward, in the direction of Kuching.[8]

☙

With Sibu directly in Sochon's sights, planning intensified for the launch of Operation Hippo. As soon as Sibu had fallen, Semut III's mission would end and Operation Hippo take its place.

On 11 August, the day before Sochon moved to Kanowit, Courtney had flown into Kapit for discussions on Operation Hippo. He had brought with him nine new reinforcements: Captain Roger Cheng, Lieutenant Alexander 'Alex' McCallum, Sergeant James Shiu, Sergeant Louis 'Louey' King, Sergeant Norman Low, Sergeant Roy Chan, Sergeant Gordon Phillpot, Corporal Desmond 'Des' Foster and Corporal Charles Heron. But these reinforcements were different from their predecessors: they were all earmarked for Operation Hippo.

Five of them (Cheng, Shiu, King, Low and Chan) were Chinese on secondment from the Canadian Army. They had been recruited by SOE in 1944, along with eight other Canadian Chinese, for a clandestine operation in China. When that failed to eventuate, the men were sent to Australia to work with SRD. As soon as they arrived in Kapit they began to mix with local Chinese in an effort to take on their dialects and behaviours. They would need to pass as locals to play their parts in Operation Hippo.[9]

Kuching lies southwest of Sibu, 115 miles (185 km) away as the crow flies, but around twice that distance if journeying overland.

The Batu Lintang internment camp was located some 3 miles (5 km) southeast of the town, close to the route the men would follow from Sibu. It was surrounded by a 5-mile (8-km) perimeter fence of barbed wire, and within its confines different categories of inmates were separated from one another, also by barbed wire. Watchtowers manned by guards were spaced at regular intervals throughout the camp.[10]

Freeing the internees would not be easy, the difficulties exacerbated by the terrible possibility that their guards might kill them during any attack on the camp. In Hippo's favour was intelligence from Dr Marjoribanks indicating there were few Japanese troops stationed in Kuching itself. The reports located most of them at Japanese military HQ at Bau, close to 30 miles (48 km) away by road.

Courtney and Sochon discussed what they knew of the situation in Kuching, and agreed on a rudimentary plan. The Hippo party, led by Sochon, would travel from Sibu to the area of the Kuap River, a couple of miles east of Kuching. Here most of the group would wait while the Canadian Chinese, led by Cheng, travelled into the city disguised as local Chinese. In this they would be aided by Dr Marjoribanks, who would arrange for the death of a Chinese elder to be faked in the town. As a result, a large traditional Chinese funerary ceremony would be organised, providing cover for the group.

In the meantime, an Australian navy frigate would travel the 22 miles (35 km) up the Sarawak River to Kuching. At the right moment Sochon's group would enter the town and a force of Australian paratroopers be dropped at Bau to contain the enemy soldiers there. Once freed, the internees would be loaded onto the waiting frigate for immediate evacuation.[11]

The details – especially key ones regarding how the Hippo group would enter the camp and release the prisoners unharmed – were still hazy, and could not be finalised until Sibu was taken.

Nevertheless, Courtney's visit was a timely prompt to Sochon that he should begin preparing for his new command.

Four days later, on 15 August, Courtney came again, this time to Sochon's new base in Kanowit. He was accompanied on this visit by Captain William Fell, a New Zealander serving with the Royal Navy. Fell later provided a colourful account of their arrival.

I took off from near Brunei in a Catalina flying-boat with Courtney and a few others, and flew over impenetrable jungle in the wildest country I had ever seen. [. . .]

At last I saw a foaming yellow strip of river far below. It seemed impossible that we should be going to land in this between its arching banks of huge trees, but down we came, circling lower, till we could clearly see the rocks and rapids and foaming water. To my horror it appeared to be full of logs, floating green islets, tree stumps and snags – none of which knew the rule of the road.

Choosing the only possible spot between snags, where the water was not actually boiling, our pilot made a perfect landing and dropped his anchor. [. . .] two dugout canoes shot out from the jungle and came racing towards us, manned by the wildest-looking crews imaginable.[12]

Their discussions were about an attack on Sibu, and how the Navy could assist. Courtney had a rough proposal for a corvette or frigate to travel up the Rejang River to Sibu and, following a strike by RAAF fighters, to pound the town from the water. Semut III would attack simultaneously from land. Fell thought the plan was workable, although there were navigation problems that needed ironing out.[13]

After they had left, Sochon began working on fresh plans for his Sibu patrols. He was interrupted by one of his radio operators carrying a new message from HQ at Labuan. The Japanese High Command had surrendered.

ⓧ

Sochon viewed the news of the surrender with intense ambivalence. On the one hand he felt pure elation that the war was won and life might, finally, return to normal. But on the other he was alarmed at the new ceasefire orders received from Labuan. He was instructed that offensive action against the Japanese must stop forthwith – the only action now permitted was defensive – and all formal patrols should be withdrawn.[14]

Sochon's dismay at these orders stemmed in part from continued reports of Japanese aggression against locals around Sibu; the orders would prevent him from providing protection. His radio message to Courtney on 21 August made this concern clear:

> Consider <u>impossible</u> withdraw forward patrols to Kanowit area. If this done natives in forward areas will be left entirely mercy of Japanese reprisals. Consider essential for protection of native population and keeping Japanese in perimeter.

But he was also deeply worried – following the Iban attacks at Kidd's Estate and Kanowit – about the repercussions of any ensuing power vacuum should his troops be withdrawn.

> As soon as they [the Japanese] laid down their arms, all hell would break loose with the Iban if the situation were not very closely watched. It was like sitting on a powder keg, with the fuse uncomfortably short and fizzing.[15]

Accordingly, he decided to defy the new orders to the degree that he could. He left all patrols in place and gave instructions that the

Japanese were to be confined within the perimeter already established around Sibu town. Any move outside this, he told his men, should be regarded as aggressive and countered immediately. And he reaffirmed to them that the security of locals was paramount. In this he almost certainly had the tacit support of Courtney: how else can we explain Courtney's continued sending of reinforcements over the following weeks? As we have already seen, Courtney overlooked similar flouting of the ceasefire orders by both Wilson and Harrisson further east.[16]

Sochon's concerns about a power vacuum – especially in towns with Chinese populations potentially at risk of Iban aggression – also led him to send patrols to more distant areas he judged particularly vulnerable. Thus Barrie, having recently (22 August) returned to Kanowit from his trip to the Julau area, was sent on 26 August with a small group of Iban guerrillas to Sarikei and Binatang (now Bintangor), two small towns in the Rejang delta southwest of Sibu. His main task was to maintain civil order in the area. However, since both towns were on the main water route from Sibu to Kuching, Sochon also believed that the patrol's presence might prevent a possible Japanese escape from Sibu.

Meanwhile, Bradbury and Walpole – along with their platoon of guerrillas – had returned from the Bukit Lima area outside Sibu, bringing two Japanese prisoners. Reunited with Kearney and signaller Fowler, the four of them were sent with a large patrol of thirty-three guerrillas to the towns of Lubok Antu and Simanggang in the far south, close to the border with Dutch Borneo. This party also left Kanowit on 26 August.[17]

At the same time, with large numbers of Japanese now in retreat, Sochon decided to shore up his defences along possible escape routes from the coast to the inland area around Long Nawang. On 24 August three more reinforcements were inserted at Kapit – Lieutenant Pierre 'Bill' Beiers with Bombardier Milton 'Jack' Felstead and Bombardier

Francis Burrow – and sent on by Sochon to join Astill in Belaga. Baker remained in Tatau, Abu Kassim in Sebauh, The Soen Hin in the Tubau area, and Oldham in Long Nawang. These men, along with the large numbers of local guerrillas now operating throughout the area, provided a solid bulwark against Japanese incursions along Sochon's eastern flank.

On 25 August Captain John Stokes and Corporal Norman Mellett – a doctor and a medical orderly respectively – arrived by Catalina, becoming Semut III's first trained medical personnel. Many of its operatives had by this time developed tropical illnesses – malaria, skin diseases and tropical ulcers being among the most common – and Stokes and Mellett were sent to Durin to provide treatment. But Stokes was worried about afflictions other than the purely tropical. Barrie later recalled the doctor inspecting all operatives for venereal disease, that great scourge of soldiers everywhere:

> So there was the Doc, seated on a box in front of the parade, shirtless and capless, holding a forked stick in front of him indicating to each of the individuals in the parade to put their equipment in it so he could turn it round for inspection without the necessity to touch the member at that stage.[18]

Stokes and Mellett quickly joined forces with the medical team already established in Kanowit and expanded their sphere of treatment to include the local population, whose health had deteriorated alarmingly during the Japanese occupation. This again highlighted the contrast between the Japanese and the Allies in the minds of locals, and further enhanced the reputation of the Allied forces.

Then on 4 September Sochon made another momentous move. He transferred his main HQ from the safety of Kanowit to an abandoned Borneo Company Ltd sawmill at Salim, less than 3 miles (5 km) upriver from the centre of Sibu. The Japanese High

Command surrender had produced no foreseeable end to his own local war. His patrols reported continuing Japanese aggression against both themselves and locals. As a result, nothing changed: the patrols stayed in place and Hume carried on training new recruits. Except that Sochon was now almost face-to-face with his enemy.[19]

∽

Another change had also occurred. With Japan's surrender, Semut III was no longer the opening act for Operation Hippo. Rather, the release of the Batu Lintang prisoners would become part of a formal surrender agreement negotiated between the Allies and the Japanese, in which Sochon would play no part. His sole focus now was the liberation of Sibu.

But this had become more complicated than originally envisaged. Given Sochon's ceasefire orders, he could no longer wrest Sibu from the occupying Japanese by force; instead he would have to persuade their commanding officer to surrender the town. Ironically, this was potentially much more difficult than taking it at the end of a gun: the Japanese commander might not yet have received formal orders relating to his country's surrender or – even if he had – he might choose to fight on. However, driven by his concern for locals, Sochon was determined to try.[20]

Wooler sent the first ultimatum on 11 August (before the Japanese government surrender of 15 August), giving the Japanese commanding officer in Sibu forty-eight hours to reply. He sent it from Kanowit, as then commander of Semut III's forward HQ. It was sent before Sochon arrived to establish the main HQ in Kanowit, and apparently without his knowledge or consent. Several days later – on 16 August – Wooler was recalled as commanding officer of Semut III's forward HQ in Durin, and on 19 August extracted to Labuan, to take no further part in the operation.

Sochon's official explanation for Wooler's withdrawal – that with the cancellation of Operation Hippo he was no longer needed – is nonsensical. All the other men who had flown in specifically to participate in Hippo, including the five Chinese Canadians, remained in situ. Barrie writes of 'personal strains' having developed between Sochon and Wooler, and of Sochon's feeling that the other man was attempting to upstage him. The unauthorised sending of the ultimatum to Sibu almost certainly reinforced this sense.[21]

Wooler had signed the ultimatum in his own name as 'Commander, British Task Forces, Rajang'. This suggests that he may, indeed, have actively coveted his party leader's command. Gavin Long notes that organisations like SRD tend to attract men

> who are not only adventurous but imaginative, individualistic
> and temperamental to an unusual degree. Such men tend also to
> [. . .] see their own chosen activity [. . .] as exerting a far greater
> effect on the progress of the war than it actually did.

They are also more likely to resent authority than regular soldiers. If Wooler felt a need to compete with his commanding officer, he was following a regrettable pattern already established among senior officers within Semut by Harrisson and Wilson.[22]

However, the ultimatum episode cannot have been the sole cause of Wooler's withdrawal, since Sochon sent him forward to Durin on 14 August, three days after the ultimatum had been sent. Reece points, instead, to something darker: an (uncorroborated) account by a Chinese member of a Semut III patrol:

> The unit had more than thirty men led by an Allied officer and
> comprised both Chinese and Ibans. On the way [to Sibu] they
> met two Japanese soldiers who jumped into the river to escape . . .
> They were eventually caught and tied to trees. The members of

the unit punched them, kicked them and even spat on them the whole night. The two Japanese kept smiling. The commanding officer at last asked them what were their last requests. They asked that their bodies be kept intact. However, the officer told them that the Ibans wanted their heads and gave permission to the Ibans to do so. The next morning, both Japanese were beheaded and their heads taken back to a nearby longhouse.

Reece suggests the patrol was led by Wooler, and that this may have been a reason for his withdrawal.[23]

Whatever Sochon's feelings about Wooler's ultimatum, its outcome was unequivocal. Wooler's Chinese messenger, a Semut III recruit called Wong Jin Chiong, was arrested, jailed and tortured on the orders of the Japanese commander in Sibu, Lieutenant Noda.[24]

Undeterred, Sochon himself sent an ultimatum to Noda on 13 August – again pre-dating the formal Japanese surrender – telling him he had until midnight on 16 August to capitulate. On 17 August – this time after the surrender of the Japanese High Command – he sent a second, again unanswered. He sent yet another on 9 September, this one 'couched in rather more peremptory terms'. By now, Sochon's intelligence networks inside Sibu were reporting the ultimatums had been received and discussed, and that most Japanese in the town were in favour of surrender. Only Noda and the town's *Kempei Tai* representatives were holding out.[25]

Sochon continued to exert pressure the only way he could. By 9 September – with Sochon himself now based at Salim, just outside the town – Sibu was surrounded by six patrols, each containing around forty local guerrillas under the command of an operative. The operation was still training – in preparation for a protracted siege – the local recruits flocking in, and Courtney was still sending reinforcements. Members of BBCAU were now also beginning to arrive. This was in accordance with SRD's recent post-surrender policy, which expressed the wish for BBCAU to assume financial responsibility for areas under SRD control by 15 September at the latest.[26]

Sochon was dumbfounded, then, by what happened next. After sending his more assertive surrender demand to Noda on 9 September, he radioed SRD HQ at Labuan to update it on his actions. But in response he was instructed to 'stop sending useless ultimatums'.

> I was ordered to 'sit tight and stay where you are'. Visualizing the rough treatment being meted out to the people of Sibu at this time and [the] probability that the enemy would be happily engaged in smashing up the place, I was anxious to take more positive action, but his orders were quite specific. Sit tight and wait.[27]

In fact, very specific surrender arrangements had come into force directly after the Japanese High Command capitulation on 15 August. In the first instance General MacArthur, commander of the SWPA force, had requested that no surrender documents be signed by Japanese field commanders until after the main surrender ceremony in Tokyo Bay on 2 September. Even after that date, restrictions concerning surrender arrangements in the field had remained in place. Thus SRD's own 'Post-Surrender Policy' stipulated: 'Parties will not accept surrender of Jap troops except as directed by local Military Commander.'[28]

Strangely, it seems that someone had forgotten to pass this on to Sochon, who had spent several weeks – in blissful ignorance of the new regulations – attempting to persuade Noda to surrender. Worse, SRD HQ appears not to have made him aware that, after the Japanese surrender on 15 August, new command arrangements had come into force: he, along with everyone else in Sarawak, now came under the direct authority of 9th Division. The 'local Military Commander' from whom he was required to seek permission to negotiate with Noda, was thus the 9th Division commander of his area.

In fact, on 29 August Courtney had drawn up an outline plan for the surrender process in SRD-controlled areas, according to which the Japanese Commander at Sibu was to surrender to Sochon at Kanowit. However, even this appears not to have been received by Sochon. Perhaps in the excitement of the period some memos were simply never sent. Or perhaps they got lost in transmission.[29]

Sochon only now began to recognise the quantum shift that had taken place with respect to SRD command structures. As he noted unhappily in his diary entry for 10 September:

> Seems that HQ should have kept me better in the picture no idea that 9Div. had taken us over to this extent – to date have received no information or orders re surrender terms or instructions. Evidently using initiative is wrong.[30]

In fact, as we have seen, in the early post-surrender period SRD HQ had managed to shelter its field commanders from 9th Division directives to some degree. This is almost certainly the reason why Sochon had been able to push on towards Sibu in the face of 9th Division orders to cease offensive action and withdraw patrols following the surrender.

But by 9 September things had changed. We now know that during a meeting with Allied negotiators on 5 September, Major General Yamamura, the commander of Japanese forces in the Kuching area, had complained that his troops were 'unsafe' at Sibu. They were, he said, 'being sniped at' by SRD in defiance of the ceasefire agreement, and he requested permission to move them to Kuching.[31]

Then, on 9 September itself, the commander of the Japanese II Army, Lieutenant General Fusataro Teshima, formally surrendered to the commander-in-chief of the Australian Military Forces, General Blamey, at Morotai Island in the Dutch East Indies. In addition, the formal surrender of Major General Yamamura was scheduled to take place on 11 September at Kuching. Amid the drama of such grand events, the struggles of a middle-ranking SRD officer to liberate the inhabitants of a small Sarawak inland town undoubtedly appeared as an irritant.

෨

Nor were the people of Sibu the only casualties of the prolonged surrender process. With Operation Hippo cancelled, the Batu Lintang prisoners – so long the focus of Sochon's planning – had become the responsibility of the newly formed Kuching Force. However, Australian forces did not occupy Kuching until 11 September, with the evacuation of prisoners commencing the following day – almost a month after the surrender of the Japanese High Command.

In place of Sochon's overland party with its group of Chinese Canadians masquerading as locals, ten aircraft were available for the eventual evacuation, as well as the ships bringing the occupation force. Ironically, instead of Bill Sochon, Toby Carter was in the vanguard of the Allied forces arriving to assist the prisoners. By 14 September, 858 of the 2024 total inmates in the camp (POWs and civil internees) had been removed.[32]

At the heart of the exercise was the 2/12th Field Ambulance. This had previously been a unit of the 8th Australian Division, the same Division to which most of the Australian POWs held in Batu Lintang belonged. The unit had earlier made a request to be part of a possible 'Burma-Singapore' force on the grounds that it belonged to the same division as the POWs held in Singapore. Now its members found themselves caring for former comrades at Kuching.

The unit's diarist wrote on 17 September that the unit performed perhaps the most strenuous work it had carried out in all its campaigns to date during those first three days in Kuching. During this period it saved the lives of up to fifty people suffering from severe fluid retention caused by starvation.[33]

Undoubtedly the time required to negotiate a complicated surrender process explains, in part, why the Batu Lintang rescue took so long. Fears that any attempt to reach the prisoners prematurely – before the local Japanese commander knew of the surrender – might lead to their massacre presumably also played a role. However as early as late August it was clear the Japanese garrison at Kuching knew of the surrender, and the Allies began dropping supplies into the camp on 30 August. Indeed, 9th Division's Outline Plan for the Japanese surrender, dated 29 August, states that the departure of the relief force for Kuching would occur 'as soon as possible after the contacting of the Japanese Commander [. . .] NOT before 0700 hours on 2 Sep 45'. Yet it did not take place until nine days after that date.[34]

Harrisson had his own take on why the liberation of Batu Lintang was so long delayed. He later claimed that 9th Division was keen to have a major photographed event of its commander, Major General Wootten, receiving the Japanese surrender from Lieutenant General Baba Masao, commander of the 37th Army, at Kuching. Until that had occurred it would not countenance any move on Kuching or the camp. Baba did not surrender (at Labuan) until 10 September, and so

> the thousands of prisoners in Kuching were held for nearly a month after the war was over. The Army would not permit anyone to relieve them.[35]

In the meantime prisoners in the camp were dying in horrifying numbers: in the final two months before Kuching Force arrived, so many were lost that their graves in the nearby cemetery were marked only with reference numbers. Between 3 September and 14 September alone – well after the Japanese High Command surrender – twenty-one British POWs died.[36]

Later reports describe a policy of 'slow starvation' implemented in the camp from mid-1944, even though adequate food resources were available; it is estimated five hundred POWs died in the camp in the seven months between January 1945 and the Japanese surrender on 15 August 1945. Of those 2024 prisoners who survived until 11 September 1945, only around half could walk to greet their liberators. Around 280 were too ill to be moved for 8–10 days, and another 850 or so had to be medically evacuated. Many of the remainder, able to be evacuated in the normal way, required hospitalisation once they reached Labuan.[37]

Nevertheless, the Batu Lintang prisoners were lucky. The final Australian and British survivors of the horrific Sandakan-Ranau POW camps in British North Borneo were killed by their Japanese captors as late as the day of the High Command surrender. Most of the Batu Lintang internees were still alive – even if only barely – four weeks afterwards.[38]

It was later established that the Japanese had been finalising preparations for the Batu Lintang prisoners' own death march – similar to those inflicted on the Sandakan-Ranau prisoners – when Kuching Force eventually arrived. On 15 July all prisoners were to be marched 18 miles (29 km) south to a new compound at Dahan. 9th Division's Prisoner of War Liaison Officer noted later that few would have survived the journey. Kuching Force came for them only just in time.[39]

෨෧

HQ's lack of enthusiasm for his 9 September ultimatum notwithstanding, Sochon finally received a response from Noda.

Late in the afternoon of the same day, Sochon was told a local canoe was approaching from downriver. On arrival it turned out to contain a Dayak messenger with a letter from Noda. This stated that all previous ultimatums had been received, and asked for further details of Sochon's authority. Sochon replied on 10 September. Mindful of his earlier rebuke, he also radioed Labuan to ask what 9th Division wanted him to do if Noda was willing to surrender.

Noda sent another message the next day, 11 September, stating that he was unable to surrender since he had not received instructions to this effect from his superiors. To Sochon's astonishment he enclosed with the letter a bag of sweets: 'On discovering the contents, I was flabbergasted, and reduced to uncontrollable fits of laughter!' Sochon responded that General Baba had formally surrendered at Labuan the previous day and asked Noda whether he had transport to shift his troops to Kuching, where they should hand themselves over to the Australian authorities.[40]

Over the next few days, messages continued to pass back and forth between the two men, and finally they agreed to meet. To Sochon's relief, 9th Division at Labuan gave its approval for both a meeting and a possible surrender. The meeting was set for the morning of 16 September at Bukit Lima, the old government rice mill and store around 3 miles (5 km) southeast of Sibu town centre. The rice store itself had been looted in the early days of the Japanese occupation and was now abandoned. However, Sochon's men had been patrolling the area closely for weeks, and knew it was heavily occupied by Japanese troops.[41]

It was agreed Noda and Sochon would each be accompanied at the meeting by four officers and that each party would carry its national flag. In anticipation of the meeting, Noda also sent Sochon a clock, taken from a Japanese aircraft:

[This] had been sent by the commander to ensure that the meeting was held at the right hour, Japanese time being an hour in advance of Allied time.[42]

Sochon had suggested that each man take four officers with him because this was the total number of officers he had available: the Medical Officer Captain Stokes, and Lieutenants Hume, Lambert and McCallum. After initiating a search among local Chinese, they acquired a small Sarawak flag, kept hidden by a Brooke loyalist during the occupation at great personal risk. This would have to do.[43]

∞

While Sochon was inching towards a possible peace on the Rejang River, Kearney's party was stirring up a hornet's nest in Simanggang, in the far south. The distance between Kanowit and Simanggang is around 75 miles (120 km) as the crow flies, and nowadays it can be covered in four hours by car following the circuitous Route 1. But in 1945 it had taken Kearney's group more than two weeks to get there over rugged, mountainous terrain: slogging first to the remote headwaters of the Skrang River, and then following the Skrang to the small town of Betong – a day or two away from Simanggang – where they finally arrived on 12 September. From Betong, Kearney sent Walpole, with twenty guerrillas, to Simanggang to call on the fifteen-strong Japanese garrison there to surrender. Kearney himself stayed in Betong to begin the work of establishing civil order in the area.[44]

Walpole's party left Betong the following morning, 13 September, heading initially for Skrang, a small village close to the confluence of the Skrang and Lupar Rivers slightly to the east of Simanggang. From Skrang, Walpole sent Iban members of his patrol ahead to spy out Simanggang. He remained in Skrang from where he telephoned the Japanese commanding officer in Simanggang to tell him of the Allied presence. According to a report written at the time, the Japanese 'refused to talk' to him.[45]

The following day, 14 September, Walpole's party crept cautiously into Simanggang along a jungle path, thereby avoiding any sentries posted on the main track. The path brought them close to a landing on the broad tidal Lupar River, which flows through Simanggang to the sea. Here they found a party of around fifteen Japanese directing a group of local labourers to load up two launches. It looked as if they were getting ready to depart.[46]

There is contention about what happened next. According to Walpole, as his party emerged from the edge of the jungle at the top of the riverbank, he called on the Japanese beside the river to surrender. But he was ignored, and soldiers in the group immediately opened fire on his party. Walpole's party scurried back into cover at the jungle's edge and a bitter battle ensued. By its end the two launches were badly damaged and all Japanese were either dead or taken prisoner.[47]

However, some of the Japanese told a different story, later lodging a complaint about the actions of Walpole's patrol. The initial complaint was laid either (or perhaps both) with the BBCAU officer, Major W.P.N.L. Ditmas, who took over control of Simanggang from Kearney's party on 20 September, or with members of 9th Division in Kuching once the Japanese prisoners were handed on to them.

Ditmas's report on the incident was later destroyed, so it is difficult to be clear on some of the details. A key accusation was that the Japanese who were at the Lupar River when Walpole's party arrived were in fact civilians, with no soldiers or *Kempei Tai* present. According to the complainants, the group of civilians was preparing to depart Simanggang for Bau, in line with the surrender agreement, when they were fired on without warning by Walpole's party. As a result, at least one civilian was killed. They further claimed that once rounded up the group was subject to mistreatment.[48]

There is no doubt Walpole arranged for punishment to be meted out to his captives.

> I had them [the Japanese prisoners] line up and couldn't help giving them a bit of a thump as they stood there. Any red-blooded Australian would've done the same after seeing the shocking way they had treated the poor local people. [. . .]
>
> I offered each of them the chance to hit me back, but none was game. I also ordered them to strip off all their clothing, which they did with some Sea Dayak [Iban] prompting. This was standard military practice. It deflated their arrogance a bit, kept them from making mischief and, best of all, brought to light any concealed weapons. Sure enough, five still had knives.

Walpole also arranged for two Ibans accused of collaboration and involvement in the murder of Europeans during the Japanese occupation to be imprisoned in the fort.[49]

Kearney and the remainder of the force arrived in Simanggang the following day. At this point there was further violence. Lena Ricketts, a Eurasian woman who had been a prisoner of the Japanese in the town, tells us:

> When the Captain from Betong [Kearney] arrived, he handed me a stick and said I could beat the prisoners if I wished. Anyway, I did not have the strength to do it, so the SRD officer, whose brother had been tortured and killed in New Guinea, and another Australian soldier, lined the Japanese up and punched each one in turn.[50]

What happened in Simanggang on 14 and 15 September 1945? We will likely never know, since most of the relevant documents were later destroyed. However, it is clear something occurred that

Walpole and Kearney subsequently felt a need to cover up. Why else would there be such a discrepancy between the number of casualties from the firefight each records? In his official report Kearney states that only one Japanese was killed, a figure he subsequently repeated during his interview with his SRD commanding officers. Walpole, on the other hand, in his book written almost sixty years later, consistently suggests that a number of Japanese died.[51]

Perhaps we can put this difference down to the failures of memory that are an inevitable consequence of old age. Walpole was, after all, 81 years old when he finished recording his account in May 2004 and, like many narratives recorded later in life, it contains inaccuracies. However, in his book Walpole also tells us he suggested to Kearney at the time that Kearney's official report not record the full story of what had happened at Simanggang, since the BBCAU officer who would be receiving it (Major Ditmas) 'isn't like us and he won't understand'. Furthermore, Brigadier Eastick's follow-up report on the incident, while finding (curiously) that no Japanese had been killed, suggests that Kearney's report had not told the truth when claiming the Japanese had been the initial aggressors.[52]

Walpole was correct in his assumption that Ditmas – although a member of SRD as well as BBCAU, and involved in the original planning of Operation Semut – would not understand. When Ditmas took over administration of the town on 20 September, he attempted to have both men court-martialled over the incident. As a result, they were rapidly transported to Labuan by SRD HQ, and from there taken back to Australia – in advance of all their Semut III comrades – to avoid questioning by 9th Division. Later, Blamey himself ordered the files relating to their offences be deleted.[53]

A story recorded in the early 1970s by anthropologist Michael Heppell among the Ibans of the Ai River, close to Simanggang, adds an intriguing coda to this story. Heppell was told that when the first group of European soldiers arrived in Simanggang at the end of

WWII, they had killed two or three Japanese soldiers there, including the Japanese commanding officer.

According to Heppell's informants, this was in retaliation for the deaths of Gilbert Arundell, the Brooke Resident – the senior administrator or governor of the area – in the nearby town of Lubok Antu, and his Iban wife and two children. Arundell and his family had escaped up the Ai River after the Japanese invasion of Sarawak, and had hidden further inland for several months under the care of local Ibans. However, in August 1942 they were tracked down, and the entire family murdered, by a group of Kanowit Ibans who had been imprisoned by Arundell in the Simanggang jail some years earlier.

Heppell was told that the Japanese commander in Simanggang had deliberately released the group of Kanowit Ibans on the understanding that they would seek out and kill Arundell and his family. According to Heppell's informants, when the European soldiers arrived in Simanggang they learned of this. So they shot the commander, and one or two other Japanese, as retribution for Arundell's murder.[54]

At SRD HQ in Labuan, Courtney had been forced to engage in considerable liaison work with 9th Division on behalf of Kearney and Walpole. The upshot was the following message sent to commanders under him on 2 October:

> From Courtney. To those whom it may have concerned in the past or may concern now or in the future. Do not rpt. not harass kill strike snub spit on or loot any Japs with whom you come in contact. Any time SRD parties hurt Jap feelings in any way, Japs complain to 9 Div who then make life difficult for your poor old colonel. Let us depart in peace.[55]

᧒

Back on the Rejang River, two days after the incident at Simanggang, Sochon was preparing for his rendezvous with Noda. He set off for

Bukit Lima early on the morning of 16 September accompanied by
Stokes, Hume, Lambert and McCallum.

> Pip Hume unfurled the Sarawak flag which now looked a
> little undersized for the important part it was to play, and we
> climbed aboard the prahu. On reaching our destination we tied
> the scruffy little craft to a tree and I marshalled our small force.
> With Lambert on one side, McCallum on the other, Hume
> acting as Standard Bearer immediately behind, and Captain
> Stokes, the medical officer, bringing up the rear, we strode
> toward the rendezvous. Now I knew exactly how Daniel felt,
> I thought to myself.[56]

After walking several hundred yards from the river towards the
meeting place, the group saw ahead of them a table which, rather
incongruously, had been placed across the track: 'Covered with a
piece of spotlessly white silk, it looked stark and unreal in the jungle setting – a bit like the Mad Hatter's tea party.' On reaching it
they found, to their alarm, that they were surrounded by armed
Japanese soldiers, with several vehicles standing nearby. Sochon was
fascinated by the immaculate presentation of the soldiers, all wearing crisp white uniforms. By contrast his own group's filthy jungle
greens, and the sores festooning their bodies, spoke graphically of
the last few months of hard jungle living.[57]

Noda spoke no English, and no-one in Sochon's party spoke
Japanese. So it was left to a young Japanese officer to interpret.
Through him Noda invited the party to Japanese HQ in Sibu where
they could discuss surrender terms in greater comfort. In spite of his
misgivings Sochon felt he had no option but to agree. Stepping away
from the path, he and his men climbed into the waiting vehicles.[58]

∽

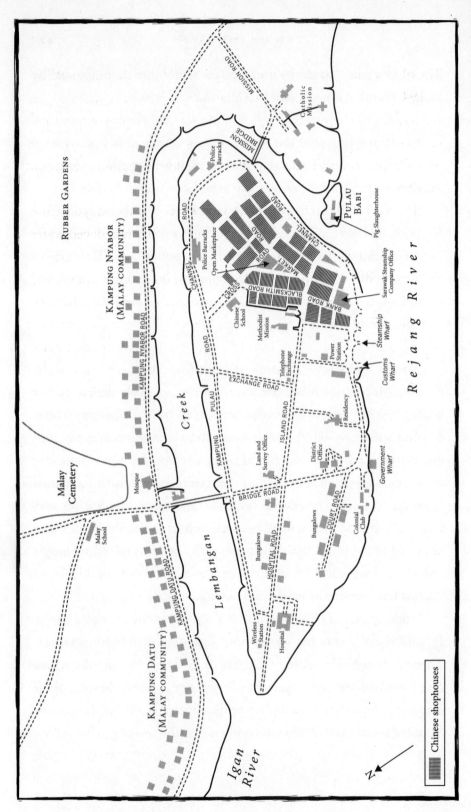

Reconstructed map of Sibu in the early 1940s.[59]

The old riverine town of Sibu as it appeared to Sochon on that day in 1945 is almost unrecognisable in today's pulsating city, with its population of close to two hundred thousand. Because of its strategic location at the junction of the Rejang and Igan Rivers, around 60 miles (97 km) from the sea, it has long been a major trading and administrative centre.

The easy navigability of the Rejang River in those days, before logging and hydro-electric schemes further upstream reduced water levels, meant that large ocean-going vessels were able to access the town. Sibu was thus a hub between areas further inland and other towns in Borneo as well as international destinations such as Singapore, Hong Kong and Shanghai. In 1945 it was Sarawak's third largest town, with a population not much less than 10,000, most of them being Chinese.[60]

Today, the centre of Sibu consists of a largely unbroken stretch of land. However, in 1945 a narrow waterway, the Lembangan Creek, enclosed the central part of town, which was thus located on a small – around three-quarters of a mile (1.2 km) long – island cut off from the surrounding land area. The mainland was reachable either by Mission Bridge or a second, longer bridge, and these were located at opposite ends of the island. Most of the town's Chinese shophouses, as well as its government buildings, were located on the island. In 1928 a fire – always the great enemy of wooden shophouses – had razed much of the old town centre, but by 1945 this had been rebuilt, partly in concrete.

The Lembangan Creek has now mostly been filled in and covered with parks, markets, roads and the other detritus of urban life. Something of the quality of the earlier town still remains in the attractive riverside walking paths, with their grand old trees and hedges, as well as in the wharves – for both ocean-going vessels and small local boats – lining the Rejang River at the centre of town. In the early 1940s it was a charming town to the European eye, with grassy banks lining the river, fine trees, immaculately kept roadsides, and gardens surrounding large wooden bungalows.[61]

Sochon had spent time in the town before the war, and liked it. However, his entry on 16 September 1945 was shocking. The Japanese had allowed the roads and verges to fall into disrepair, but worse was the impact of bombing. Sibu had first been briefly bombed by the Japanese on Christmas Day 1941, but this had caused minimal damage and the loss of only four lives. Almost all the damage Sochon was now witnessing had been caused by Allied bombing in 1945, in futile attacks on the Japanese forces garrisoned in the town.[62]

The first raid occurred on the morning of 9 March and was followed over the months by others. The town and suburbs were badly hit, with many shophouses and government buildings destroyed as well as schools and a church. The worst raid occurred on 4 June when there was heavy bombing of the town centre including the crowded marketplace. This and the shophouses lining the surrounding roads were completely destroyed.

As in Song and Kanowit, none of the raids had resulted in enemy casualties: the Japanese had long since moved most of their offices out into the suburbs from whence they retreated to air-raid shelters on the edge of the town when they heard aircraft approaching. Around one hundred civilians were killed during the 4 June attack and many more were injured. The moans of the injured could be heard from the rubble for many days afterwards.[63]

Many of Sibu's residents had fled to neighbouring longhouses and villages to escape the bombing. Sochon's sense of disconnect on arriving in the town undoubtedly emanated in part from its strange sense of emptiness.

The Japanese HQ was located in the Sarawak Steamship Company's office building, remarkably still standing. Once the party was inside, with weapons left at the door and using the Japanese interpreter, Noda asked what procedures he should follow to effect a formal surrender. After weeks of stubborn resistance he had finally, and quite suddenly, capitulated.[64]

Sochon had already given Noda's question a great deal of thought and decided that Sibu Island itself could easily be turned into an effective POW camp. With guards placed on both bridges, and a patrol armed with machine guns located on the opposite bank of the creek, it would be almost impossible for Japanese soldiers assembled there to escape. He instructed Noda that all troops under his command must leave their mainland positions and be on the island by 4 pm the same afternoon. Sochon's soldiers would take over the town and the Japanese would leave by boat for Kuching the following morning (17 September), leaving 90 per cent of their arms behind. He arranged for a formal surrender document to be typed up in English and for copies to be signed by both himself and Noda. Mission accomplished, he and his men then left to look around the town.[65]

Later that day, at 4 pm, Sochon arrived at Mission Bridge to watch as the last of the Japanese troops moved onto the island as per his instructions. Everything appeared to be going to plan. But then, as Lieutenant Lambert led in the first group of local guerrillas to take up their posts guarding the bridge, the accord almost fell apart.

As Noda saw the young officer lead this motley crew to take over their duties, he flew into a towering rage. In a wild fit of temper he demanded to know how he had been tricked. Looking at this ragged, unkempt and ill-equipped force he must have been stunned to think that his ample garrison had lain down their arms to this bunch of half naked savages. They certainly didn't look very impressive, for some were wearing shorts only; some had shirts while a few were dressed in sirats [loincloths]. Nearly all were grubby and dishevelled.[66]

But it was too late for Noda. His men were imprisoned on the island, under the guard of Sochon's unorthodox army.

Sochon and his officers were turning to go when there came the sound of gunfire from the bridge. Reaching for their pistols they spun round, expecting to see the infuriated Japanese attempting a break. But the noise was not from Japanese weapons. Instead, jubilant Chinese onlookers were pelting their erstwhile captors with firecrackers.[67]

Next morning (17 September) at 9 am, Sochon and his officers presented themselves at Mission Bridge. Searches among the local population had still failed to locate a sizeable Sarawak flag. So finally, the owner of the house where they were staying had sat up at his sewing machine through the night and manufactured a decent replica. This now hung from the flagpole beside the wharf.[68]

To their delight, the men discovered that on hearing the news of Noda's surrender, many of the town's residents had flooded back. From the ruins of shopfronts hung flags of all kinds – the Union Jack, the Stars and Stripes, the Chinese flag and the Sarawak banner – like brightly coloured lights in the midst of the devastation. Since possession of any kind of Allied flag was punishable by death under Japanese rule, it was astonishing – and deeply moving – to discover so many had survived.

On arrival at Mission Bridge, the men were joined by Noda and two of his officers, and together they walked through the wreckage of the streets to the steamship wharf. There they found that the last of the Japanese soldiers had already boarded the remaining Japanese launches, ready to set off for Kuching.[69]

Four months after the original Semut III force of four men (including the Iban constable) had left Long Akah, its mission was over. Against all the odds Sochon had united Kayans and Ibans – as

well as Chinese and Malays – into a guerrilla army that had progressively taken the entire Rejang River from the enemy – starting
at Belaga in the east and ending at Sibu and the Rejang delta town
of Sarikei in the west. By the end of the operation, Semut III also
had control of a much larger surrounding area: from Bintulu east
to Tubau and south to the Rejang, from Kanowit and Sibu south
to Simanggang, from Belaga southeast along the Balui River to the
border with Dutch Borneo, and even extending to Long Nawang
across the border.

This was an astonishing achievement by any measure. Sochon's
meagre force of thirty-seven SRD operatives and approximately
four hundred and fifty local guerrillas had, by his reckoning, recaptured approximately 25,000 square miles (65,000 square km) of
territory – an area roughly the size of Tasmania and equating to
around half of Sarawak's total land mass. And that was not all:
through clever juggling of available personnel, including locals, it
had subsequently prevented Japanese troops from moving across
that territory to inland areas where they could have wreaked
havoc with remote communities and created a headache for the
incoming civilian administration. Perhaps most importantly, it
had taken a string of towns – including Sarawak's third-largest –
from the enemy, and established there the basis for a return to
civilian rule.[70]

Operation Semut's overall military accomplishments – including its contribution to the Labuan landings and the defeat of the
Japanese throughout British Borneo – will be discussed in the second book. For now, there can be little doubt about the success of
Semut III with respect to the operation's political aims. Like Carter
on the Baram, Sochon had worked hard to foster goodwill among
Rejang River locals towards the Allied forces, and highlight differences between Europeans and Japanese. The efforts of Fisher and
subsequent BBCAU men added to this European lustre; the historian

Bob Reece notes that some locals viewed *Bikau* (BBCAU) as the best government Sarawak could have.[71]

Ironically, as Australia was beginning to assert a fledgling independence from Britain, its Semut operatives were helping, largely unwittingly, to protect British interests in Sarawak. This was the price of British control over SRD. By the operation's end British rule in the territory – whether by the Brookes or as a Crown Colony – was secure, at least for the moment. We can only wonder how the mostly Australian operatives – many of them resentful about British command within the operation – might have felt about this hidden goal had they been aware of it.

Within Sarawak itself, the prevention of wholesale killings of Chinese by Ibans along the Rejang River – in the face of a yawning power vacuum following Japanese withdrawals – has often been seen as Semut III's most important success. And Sarawakians are right to celebrate this, for the area could easily have descended into chaos. We should note, however, that potential carnage was arrested as much by Iban leaders along with local members of Sochon's force – setting themselves in the paths of other Ibans – as by Semut III's European operatives. As with so much else during Operation Semut, it is unlikely that the operatives could have put an end to the turmoil on their own.

Furthermore, this success was double-edged: it was Semut's licensing of headhunting against Japanese soldiers that had opened the way for the killings to occur in the first place. Indeed, once Carter, Harrisson and Sochon had advertised the new headhunting policy, the deadly outcome – especially in the Semut III area with its majority Iban population – was not unexpected to anyone with an appreciation of Sarawak's past or the history of European payment for heads elsewhere. Sochon was alive to the antinomies here:

> To the Dyaks it must have seemed all very confusing. The
> Brooke officers had rapped their knuckles and told them that

headhunting was not to be indulged in, so they'd more or less obeyed this injunction. Then comes Tuan Sochon and Semut III who says that headhunting is on again, declaring open season on Japanese heads, so away we go on an orgy we haven't seen since the 'good' old days. Now, just as we're beginning to have some fun [. . .] we're thrown in the cooler! And they talk about the inscrutable oriental!![72]

This is the other, dark, side of Semut's success, especially that of Semut III. Along the Rejang River the new headhunting policy saw around fifty Chinese killed at Pasir Nai, Kidd's Estate and Kanowit – not including the non-Japanese heads presented to Kearney and other operatives elsewhere. The outcome was lasting friction between Ibans and Chinese in the area: 'a heightening of racial tension not seen in Sarawak since the Chinese rebellion of 1857'. It took years for relations between the two groups to return to normal.[73]

We are right to be horrified at these deaths. And yet, without the reintroduction of headhunting, fewer Ibans are likely to have joined Semut III's ranks. In this case, Japanese columns like Semut II's *Fujino Tai* may well have formed in the Rejang River area and travelled inland, resulting in widespread devastation for local communities, including Chinese. In warfare there are sometimes no acceptable options.

And if we are horrified at the civilian deaths caused by headhunting, we should be no less appalled by the number of civilians who were killed – well over one hundred in the Rejang River area alone, with hundreds more injured and massive destruction of buildings and infrastructure – by futile RAAF bombing and strafing raids. We can only imagine the desolation and grief experienced within communities affected by these raids – many of them, again, Chinese. It is hard to see why Iban headhunting of civilians should be condemned while these deaths are treated as acceptable 'collateral damage'.

Sochon was acutely aware of how reliant his operation was on local contribution; more than a dozen locals who worked with Semut III were recognised with awards after the war. A number of Semut III operatives also received decorations, including Sochon himself. He, like Carter, was awarded the Distinguished Service Order in acknowledgement of Semut III's extraordinary feats along the Rejang.

But this was not all Sochon received: in Sibu, on the morning of 17 September 1945, he was presented with something perhaps almost as precious. Before boarding the boat, Noda turned, saluted and, palms upstretched and outward in a gesture of surrender, handed Sochon his Samurai sword. He then climbed onto the boat and ordered it to cast off. Sochon watched it head downriver, before it disappeared finally around a bend.[74]

EPILOGUE

IN A RAMBLING WOODEN house on the outskirts of Lawas in 2015 I listened for two hours as an old Lun Bawang man – gaze drifting inward as he sifted through his memories – told me his WWII story. Initially forced to porter for the Japanese, Basar Paru ended the war fighting against them in Tom Harrisson's Semut I army. Despite his great age – well into his nineties – his face was unlined, his memory keen, his observations acute. As shadows from neighbouring trees lengthened across the house and the interview slid reluctantly to a close, he suddenly looked straight into my eyes and said:

> The white soldiers came. They were good, brave. But we were also brave. I hope that white people's stories remember us too.[1]

Basar Paru died three years later. I hope he never knew about the Dayak absence from official Semut reports, as it would have grieved him. However, he would have been warmed by the enduring admiration and friendship towards Dayak peoples exhibited by Semut operatives themselves. Few of them ever forgot, even as the decades passed and fading memories might have excused them.

Eadie, writing forty years later, remembered 'the unpleasant; the misery and discomfort of lying for hours in the damp brush at the side of a river in ambush [. . .] But the happy times are much more vivid with the genuine, warm hospitality of the Kenyahs and Kayans who were such delightful people.' For Frank Wigzell fifty-five years later, 'my encounter with the Ibans, Dayaks, Dusans, Ponans, Kelabits, Tagals, Muruts and the Orang Sungai people of Borneo [. . .] has given me the greatest experience of my life'. 'I never saw any of them again,' wrote Brian Walpole sixty years later, 'but Bujang has remained in my thoughts to this day.'

> I'd lost a true, trustworthy friend. [. . .] The long war years had made me almost immune to becoming upset, but I must admit I found Bujang's departure somewhat traumatic after what we had been through together. What a marvellous people the Sea Dayaks [Iban] were.[2]

Jack Tredrea told me seventy years later of the lump that still 'catches in my throat' when he remembered his Dayak 'boys': 'the finest bunch of people I had the privilege of fighting with.'[3]

Some operatives stayed on temporarily in Sarawak at the end of hostilities as members of BBCAU. Others established or resumed more permanent connections: Toby Carter returned to his job with Shell Oil, Tom Harrisson was appointed Curator of the Sarawak Museum in 1947, and Bill Sochon took up a position reforming the Sarawak prison system before, in 1953, becoming Commissioner for Prisons in Singapore, a short hop across the South China Sea.

Most, however, returned to Australia and attempted to resume the rhythms and habits of pre-war civilian life. All SRD men I spoke with told me how difficult this had been, especially in the early days – tormented by sleepless nights, terrible dreams, sudden rages, unexpected rushes of fear, as well as ongoing battles with malaria, hookworm, hepatitis, amoebic dysentery and other tropical illnesses. For many the distress was exacerbated by their inability to talk about their experiences, even to their families, because of the vows of silence they had taken when recruited to SRD.

SRD operations remained under a strict security embargo until 1981 when the organisation's files were finally declassified, and some operatives – perhaps many – were forbidden from speaking about the organisation for much of that period. Tredrea was one of those ordered at his postwar debriefing not to mention his SRD activities to anyone for thirty years, under pain of serious legal consequences. Others were ordered to keep silent for the remainder of their lives. Others again were banned from speaking for much shorter periods or even given no secrecy instructions at all.

These variations are not surprising. Special operations forces were in their infancy during WWII and SRD commanders, like their men, were inventing many of the rules as they went along – 'flying by the seat of their pants' as one operative put it. As a result, SRD was a chaotic organisation at the best of times, as is demonstrated again and again throughout this book. In the overwhelming confusion of the immediate postwar period, it appears that its leadership failed to formulate a consistent policy regarding ongoing security.[4]

The consequence was that while some SRD veterans were little concerned with postwar secrecy – publishing books and articles and even establishing veterans' associations in some towns soon after the war – for others, probably most, the immediate postwar decades were an exercise in forgetting. Like Tredrea, many Semut operatives remained silent about their Borneo experiences until at least the mid-1970s. Some never spoke of them at all, their families only learning of their service after their deaths, via their military records.

But from the 1980s on, there was a flowering of written accounts about Semut, especially among men from below the ranks of commissioned officers. Through the lonely years of forgetting, they had remembered. Some began to revisit Borneo from this time, retracing their footsteps to areas where they had operated during the war and searching out old friends. And their families, enthralled by the vivid stories brought back, often accompanied them. Still today, children and grandchildren of Semut veterans return regularly to Borneo, to honour not only their fathers and grandfathers, but also the Dayak people they fought beside.

As we have seen, some of those in Allied senior command positions in Borneo – whether with 9th Division or SRD – ultimately viewed their Dayak allies as expendable: a disgraceful betrayal that could easily have had terrible consequences for local communities. Operatives, on the other hand, never forgot the debt they owed. The same sense of gratitude that saw Carter and Sochon refuse to abandon Dayaks when ordered to do so, continued to suffuse operative memories long after the war was over.

Thus Keith Barrie went to work writing letters to Australian newspapers in the 1990s, when he was aged in his eighties, opposing the Bakun Dam Project on the beautiful Balui River along which men from his Semut III had fought. In describing the 'help, generosity and kindness' shown to Semut operatives by local Kayans he implicitly pointed to the debt Australians had thereby incurred. Elsewhere he wrote of his 'sense of shame' on learning in 1990 about the threat posed to the forests in which the Penan lived, a shame that derived from the failure of Australian governments to support the Penan in their struggle, thereby denying the debt they owed.[5]

In the last years of his life Jack Tredrea returned to Bario every year in March to commemorate the Semut reconnaissance party's landing there on 25 March 1945. When I asked why he did this, given how gruelling these trips to the centre of Borneo were for someone of his age, he said simply: 'they're wonderful people and I owe them. We all owe them.' His last visit was in March 2017, aged 96.[6]

∾

Most Semut operatives were anxious in 1945 when presented with the option of going to Borneo: frightened of its jungles and Dayak peoples. And who can blame them? For in the popular imagination of the time, Borneo was a terrifying place. Nevertheless they bravely put aside their fears and went. For many, the jungles turned out to be even worse than imagined: dark, hellish places that haunted their nightmares for years afterwards.

But the Dayaks were not at all as expected. Rather than the savage headhunters of their fevered imaginations, the operatives found dignified peoples who treated them with astounding generosity. It cannot have been easy for Dayak communities to host operatives given the heavy drain on already scarce resources (including manpower lost to Semut's armies) and the daily demands and irritations of looking after a horde of hopelessly at-sea strangers, not to mention the ever-present threat of Japanese reprisals. They came on board not out of any deep love for Europeans and European rule – as some have wanted to claim – but rather out of strategic considerations fuelled by a wish to survive. Nevertheless, once they did they treated the operatives with unflagging kindness.

Before arriving in Borneo most operatives were prey to the prejudices and fears about Asians and indigenous peoples common among Europeans at a time when their own legal systems still classed many such peoples as inferior. Yet, as Harrisson tells us, Dayaks found a way to disarm such prejudices 'quickly, gently, invisibly, unfelt'. Eadie wrote years later of his first night in a Dayak longhouse – at Long Beruang on the Tutoh River. He had been in Sarawak only a few days, spoke no local language and had arrived at Long Beruang to find that the operatives he was meant to be joining there had moved on. He was the sole European in the longhouse, days away from his comrades at Long Akah. And he was afraid.

> I had to take my turn [at dancing] & managed a kind of highland fling, finishing with a somersault. It was quite an evening – completely dark outside, lighting inside by oil lamps which gave off little light but quite a bit of smoke & smell; the men in loin cloths looking pretty fierce, the ladies in sarongs with their elongated ear lobes weighed down by heavy rings. After my dance I realised that my revolver, my only weapon, was not in its holster. I began to wonder if their idea was to get me sozzled & then add my head to the others hanging in the longhouse. However after a short time the revolver was quietly handed back to me – it had probably fallen out during the dance.[7]

This quiet – but inexorable – dismantling of prejudice runs implicitly through many operative accounts: from Hallam's summation of the Long Akah electrocution incident ('we agreed that we had earned our treatment'), to Beiers' look of incredulity as he recalled an Iban child helping him up the slippery entry ladder into a longhouse, to Walpole's astonishment at the organised industry of an Iban garden. A number of operatives record their amazement at how quickly Dayaks learned from them – 'something to startle anyone', as Harrisson later put it:

> Their capacity for mastering the handling of a Bren gun would put almost any white soldier to shame. They were even able to carry out difficult repairs, and learned to make replacements for broken parts on Bren guns, carbines, Sten guns, entirely by observation, experiment and experience.[8]

Others were shocked at Dayak concern with broader political affairs.

> I had expected such apparently rather primitive people to have no interest in the world outside their longhouse, but this was not so. They were interested in the war in Europe, and in what the situation would be after the war when Sarawak would no longer be run by Rajah Brooke.[9]

That operatives should be surprised by such Dayak capabilities and interests tells us more about European preconceptions at the time than about Dayaks themselves. But it is also testament to the remarkable capacity of Dayak peoples to puncture even the most obdurate European prejudices, a capacity reflected in many European accounts over the centuries. The second of these two books – which tells the stories of Semut I and Semut IV – focuses less on relationships between operatives and Dayaks than on those among the operatives themselves, especially between the (largely British) command and the (largely Australian) other ranks. We will see there that many operatives ended up liking and respecting their Dayak allies far more than their own commanding officers.

∽

But finally the war was over and these improbable allies, having fought a remarkable campaign together, had to go their separate ways. There was still mopping up to be done – firearms to be retrieved from reluctant locals, workers to be paid off, BBCAU officers to be briefed. But by mid-October 1945 most Semut operatives had been ferried to Labuan for eventual transport back to Australia. Home! 'I just felt lucky to have survived,' Bill Beiers told me 70 years later, 'when so many others hadn't.'[10]

Beiers – and all other Semut operatives – were indeed lucky: of the one hundred and twenty or so who took part in the overall operation, not one died – a remarkable statistic. By contrast, of the two thousand or so locals who fought as part of Operation Semut – most of them Dayaks – at least thirty lost their lives. Many more were injured.[11]

But the unlikely survival of every operative cannot be put down to luck alone, as the operatives themselves were at pains to point out. 'Bujang did everything he could to look after me and protect me and I was grateful,' wrote Walpole. 'I was lucky to have him.' Frank Wigzell tells us:

It was at this time [. . .] that I noticed I had three warriors at my side twenty-four hours a day. Where I went they went. [. . .] When we were on patrol or in action they were but an arm's length away.[12]

Charles Hardy records that a local chief sent his son

and fifteen or twenty warriors to be my bodyguard, stay with me and protect me wherever I went in Borneo. That saved my life, of that I am certain.[13]

We can now begin to appreciate Jack Tredrea's plea that this book foreground Dayak contribution to the operation, and the truth of his repeated claim: 'None of us would have survived more than a day or two without them.'

To recognise their dependence on their Dayak allies is in no way to detract from the extraordinary courage and achievements of the operatives themselves. It is rather to acknowledge, finally, a simple reality: Operation Semut could not have succeeded – or even got off the ground – without the skills, knowledge and labour of its

Dayak participants. Its planners knew this from the start, and the recruitment of Dayaks was thus one of the operation's key objectives. It was also one of its greatest achievements. It is time to follow the operatives and recognise the debts we owe.

Bob Long put it most simply – and most powerfully. 'The Dayaks were our saviours, really' he told me during our first meeting in 2014. Although this claim may seem extravagantly Biblical, it is not inaccurate. The Dayaks took the operatives in, cared for them, fed them, advised, carried and guided for them, and taught them how to survive a seemingly deathly environment. They also ate, slept, fought and died beside them. And finally, they ensured that every one of them returned home.[14]

APPENDIX

SEMUT II NOMINAL ROLL
SOA/SRD Operatives*

Surname	Given Names	Rank	Service No./ AK No.	Nationality	Decorations**
Abu Kassim bin Marah	Unknown	Corporal; promoted to Lance Sergeant 26/04/45	WX36796	Malayan	Nil
Barrie	John 'Keith'	Sergeant	QX19782; AK168	Australian	MM
Carter	Gordon Senior 'Toby'	Major	VB336939/ QX48608; AK247	New Zealander	DSO

---

* Abu Kassim, Barrie and Sochon were not formal members of Semut II; they were assigned to Semut III immediately when the original unified Semut operation was divided into three parts in early May 1945. I have included them here because they stayed with Semut II at Long Akah, under Carter's command, for more than two weeks while waiting for Semut III to get under way.

It has not been possible to confirm some individual details, including full names and decorations, due to missing and/or inaccessible service records.

** Includes only decorations received for actions carried out during Operation Semut.

Surname	Given Names	Rank	Service No./ AK No.	Nationality	Decorations**
Conleth-Smith	George	Corporal	7532653	Singaporean (British Subject)	Unknown
Davey	Douglas 'Doug' Wilfred	Private	VX92910; AK193	Australian	Nil
Duffus	Leo Herbert	Sergeant	VX35706; AK26	Australian	Nil
Eadie	William Stanley 'Stan'	Lieutenant	VB314859; AK112	British	MID
Fidler	Stewart 'Stewie' Heritage	Private	VX128451; AK194	Australian	MM
Gilman	Norman 'Norm' Ellis Rusden	Sergeant	NX15749; AK269	Australian	MID
Graham	Neville Bruce	Corporal	NX42041; AK266	Australian	Nil
Hallam	Kelvin 'Kel' Walter	Sergeant	TX16283; AKS25	Australian	Nil
Horsnell	Donald 'Don' Leslie	Warrant Officer II	SX3396; AK204	Australian	MID
Le Guier	Keith Allan	Lance Corporal	VX93198; AK179	Australian	Nil
Mason	Bob R.	Sergeant	VB1872767; AKV112	British	Unknown
McCallum	Ian Archibald Neil 'Doc'	Captain; promoted to temporary Major (11/06/45)	VX63314; AKV28	Australian	MID
McLean	Donald 'Don' James	Corporal	NX130199; AK187	Australian	Nil
Middleton	Percy Vine 'Snowy'	Lieutenant	VX6649; AK103	Australian	Nil
Neave	Jack	Corporal	VX93557; AK137	Australian	Nil
Pare	Charles Walter 'Wally'	Sergeant	NX164342; AK192	British	MID
Pippen	Francis 'Frank' Vincent	Sergeant	NX114963; AKS32	Australian	Nil
Sheppard	Denis 'Denny' Michael	Sergeant	NX137521; AK219	Australian	MID

Surname	Given Names	Rank	Service No./ AK No.	Nationality	Decorations**
Sochon	William 'Bill' Lomas Philipe	Captain; promoted to Major 22/07/45	VB325984; AK240	British	DSO
The	Soen Hin	Acting Sergeant; confirmed as Sergeant 20/04/45	WX36793	Timorese	Nil
Wilson	Robert Kenneth	Major	VB40055; AK249	British	MID
Wood	Max Holbrook	Lieutenant	VX3459; AKV15	Australian	Nil

Guerrillas (irregular local forces)

Around 200 guerrillas equipped with and trained in the use of firearms served as part of Semut II. Other locals joined them for particular actions, armed only with swords and spears. An unknown number died and more were injured.

The names of only a very few have survived, mostly those who received postwar awards. They are acknowledged elsewhere in the text.

If we had the names of all Semut II guerrillas and spaced them as we have operative names, the list would fill ten pages.

The following two pages are left blank in recognition of those whose names have been lost. Each blank page represents around 100 unknown guerrillas.

In memory of the unknown Semut II guerrillas.

In memory of the unknown Semut II guerrillas.

SEMUT III NOMINAL ROLL
SOA/SRD Operatives*

Surname	Given Names	Rank	Service No./ Ak No.	Nationality	Decorations**
Abu Kassim bin Marah	Unknown	Corporal; promoted to Lance Sergeant 26/04/45	WX36796	Malayan	Nil
Astill	Robert 'Arthur'	Captain	WX36583; AK49	Australian	Nil
Baker	Ronald 'Ron' James	Lieutenant	SX993; AKV20	Australian	Nil
Barrie	John 'Keith'	Sergeant	QX19782; AK168	Australian	MM
Beiers	Pierre William 'Bill'	Lieutenant	NX136161; AK23	Australian	Nil
bin Lansi	Eusop	Corporal	W15805; AK173	Malayan	Nil
Bradbury	Ross William	Corporal	WX17377; AK211	Australian	Nil
Burrow	Francis Wallis	Bombardier	SX25881; AK274	Australian	Nil
Campbell	Royston 'Roy' Harold	Signalman	WX16899	Australian	Nil
Chan	Roy Sin Twe	Sergeant	VCK69908; AKO376	Canadian	MM
Cheng	Roger Kee	Captain	AKO366	Canadian	Nil
Croton	Ronald James 'Happy'	Corporal	NX35662; AK148	Australian	Nil
Felstead	Milton 'Jack'	Bombardier	SX30453; AK273	Australian	Nil

---

*   Many lists of Semut personnel are highly inaccurate. The list of Semut III personnel found in the SOA 'Official History', for instance, includes a large number of men who served with Semut I or Semut II but not with Semut III; possibly they were originally assigned to Semut III but never sent to it.

It has not been possible to confirm some individual details, including full names and decorations, due to missing and/or inaccessible service records.

**   Includes only decorations received for actions carried out during Operation Semut.

Surname	Given Names	Rank	Service No./ Ak No.	Nationality	Decorations**
Fisher	John Cartwright Braddon 'Fish'	Captain	VB246500; AK238	British	Nil
Foster	Desmond 'Des' Lionel	Corporal	NX73768; AK267	New Zealander	Nil
Fowler	Hubert Norman 'Brick'	Corporal	WX16232; AK212	Australian	Nil
Hartley	John Frederick 'Jack'	Sergeant	NX78025; AK181	Australian	Nil
Heron	Charles Edward	Acting Corporal; confirmed as Corporal 30/10/45	VX71000; AK96	Australian	Nil
Hume	Philip 'Pip' William	Lieutenant	VB325730; AK234	British	Nil
Kearney	David 'Dave' John	Captain	VX1631; AK293	Australian	MC
King	Louis 'Louey'	Sergeant	VCK50207; AKO371	Canadian	MM
Lambert	Frederick	Lieutenant	WX34366; AK299	Australian	Nil
Low	Norman Mon	Sergeant	VCK49895; AKO378	Canadian	MM
McCallum	Alexander 'Alex' James Hugh	Lieutenant	WX40745; AK301	Australian	Nil
Mellett	Norman Robert Ross	Acting Corporal; confirmed as Corporal 20/09/45	SX26223; AK138	Australian	Nil
Oldham	Frank Rassendale	Lieutenant	VX31289; AK45	Australian	Nil
Outhwaite	Richard Martin 'Chick'	Acting Corporal; confirmed as Corporal 20/09/45	VX75967; AK209	Australian	Nil
Perry	Richard 'Dick' Charles	Warrant Officer II	VX4918; AK169	Australian	Nil
Phillpot	Gordon Henry	Acting Sergeant; confirmed as Sergeant 30/09/45	NX144227; AKO394	Australian	Nil

Surname	Given Names	Rank	Service No./ Ak No.	Nationality	Decorations**
Pippen	Francis 'Frank' Vincent	Sergeant	NX114963; AKS32	Australian	Nil
Shiu	James	Sergeant	VCK69286; AKO375	Canadian	MM
Sochon	William 'Bill' Lomas Philipe	Captain; promoted to Major 22/07/45	VB325984; AK240	British	DSO
Spurling	Edric 'Ed' Ray	Sergeant	WX16848; AKS187	Australian	Nil
Stokes	John Lewis	Captain	SX22304; AKV633	Australian	Nil
The	Soen Hin	Acting Sergeant; confirmed as Sergeant 20/04/45	WX36793	Timorese	Nil
Walpole	Brian Blayney	Acting Corporal; confirmed as Corporal 20/09/45	VX95325; AK202	Australian	Nil
Wooler	John Raymond 'Ray'	Major	VB117768; AKO313	Canadian	Nil

Guerrillas (irregular local forces)

Around 450 guerrillas equipped with and trained in the use of firearms served as part of Semut III. Other locals joined them for particular actions, armed only with swords and spears. An unknown number died and more were injured.

The names of only a very few have survived, mostly those who received postwar awards. They are acknowledged elsewhere in the text.

If we knew the names of all Semut III guerrillas and spaced them as we have operative names, the list would fill twenty-three pages.

The following four pages are left blank in recognition of those whose names have been lost. Each blank page represents more than 100 unknown guerrillas.

In memory of the unknown Semut III guerrillas.

In memory of the unknown Semut III guerrillas.

In memory of the unknown Semut III guerrillas.

In memory of the unknown Semut III guerrillas.

ENDNOTES

CHAPTER 1: 'THIS EDEN OF MIXED BLESSINGS'

1   Author, interviews with Siran Ida and Adteh Kediah Aran, Bario Asal (Bario), 22 March 2015, 25 March 2015; author, Bario interviews, March 2015; author, interviews with Jack Tredrea, Adelaide, 30 September 2016, 1 October 2016. Among many Dayak peoples, an individual's name changes when certain key life events, such as becoming a parent or grandparent, take place. Keling Langit's name had changed to Siran Ida by the time I interviewed her in 2015.

2   On Operation Semut as 'successful' see e.g. 'The Official History of the Operations and Administration of Special Operations – Australia', Vol. 2, Part III, p. 1, A3269, 08/A, NAA; Ooi, 'Prelude to invasion' in *J. of the Australian War Memorial* 37, pp. 13–15. 'Consistently over-glamorised [. . .] puerile and [. . .] unnecessary' from Letter, R.K. Wilson to Rt. Hon. Malcolm MacDonald, 21 April 1957, p. 7, 101/4/1–67, GB–0033–MAC, Durham University Library; 'lack of control and accountability' from Braithwaite, *Fighting Monsters*, p. 318.

3   Headhunting as Dayak 'sport' from Australian Military Forces, *Borneo Book for Servicemen*, p. 20; 'It was hard to know' from author, interview with Bob Long, Perth, 17 September 2014.

4   'The most beautiful place' from author, interview with Jack Tredrea, Adelaide, 15 September 2014; 'The energy-sapping heat' from Griffiths-Marsh, *Sixpenny Soldier*, pp. 2–3.

5   'Implacable force' from Conrad, *Heart of Darkness*, pp. 48–9; 'The nastiest noise' from Harrisson, *World Within*, p. 215, emphasis in original.

6 Dower, *War Without Mercy*; Friend, *Blue-Eyed Enemy*; 'mad dogs' etc. from Larson, *Severed*, pp. 57–8.

7 'Kill or be killed' from Dower, *War Without Mercy*, p. 10; Bourke, *Intimate History of Killing*, pp. 25–31.

8 *Sixpenny Soldier*, p. 3.

9 *My War*, pp. 167–8.

10 Spencer Chapman, *Jungle is Neutral*.

11 'This Eden of mixed blessings' from Wren, *Down-Stream Twice*, unpublished manuscript, p. 153.

12 Report, Major R.K. Wilson to Officer Commanding SRD, n.d., p. 2, AWM54, 619/7/79, AWM.

13 'July 10th (Tuesday) – I left' from Hardy, 'Chapter 15', in Long (ed.), *Operation Semut 1*, p. 451.

14 'None of us would have survived' from author, interview with Jack Tredrea, Adelaide, 16 September 2014. On local support in special operations philosophy see e.g. US Army Field Manual *Army Special Operations Forces Unconventional Warfare*, pp. 4–8, 5–3.

15 'I just learned to sit down' from author, interview with Jack Tredrea, Adelaide, 5 October 2016.

16 Cit. King, *Peoples of Borneo*, p. 237.

17 Heimann, *Airmen and the Headhunters*, p. 139.

18 'The victim died to old relationships' from Sutlive, *Iban of Sarawak*, p. 30; Davison and Sutlive, 'The children of *Nising*', in Sutlive (ed.), *Female and Male in Borneo*; Sellato, *Hornbill and Dragon*, p. 34.

19 'I wanted to retch' from Griffiths-Marsh, *Sixpenny Soldier*, pp. 292–3; 'The atavistic scene' from Wren, *Down-Stream Twice*, unpublished manuscript, p. 213.

20 Bynum, *Fragmentation and Redemption*.

21 Larson, *Severed*, pp. 17–21, 40–3, 61ff.

22 Pringle, *Rajahs and Rebels*; Wadley, 'Punitive expeditions' in *Ethnohistory* 1; Walker, *Power and Prowess*, Ch. 4; Edwards and Stevens, *Short Histories*, pp. 120–6; Davison and Sutlive, 'The children of *Nising*', in Sutlive (ed.), *Female and Male in Borneo*, p. 169.

23 Published books containing lengthy detailed accounts of Operation Semut include Harrisson, *World Within*; Wigzell, *New Zealand Army Involvement*; B. Long (ed.), *Operation Semut 1*; Griffiths-Marsh, *Sixpenny Soldier*; Walpole, *My War*; Lightner, *All Elevations Unknown*; Malone, *Kill the Major*. None of these covers all four parts of the operation. Truscott et al's unpublished account does, but is less a description of the operation itself than of participant perspectives on it. Briefer published accounts of the operation (whole or

part) are also found in Carter, 'Sarawak Adventure', in *N.Z. Surveyor* XIX(3); Horton, *Ring of Fire*; McDonald, *New Zealand's Secret Heroes*; Powell, *War by Stealth*; Courtney, *Silent Feet*; Heimann, *Most Offending Soul*; Campbell, *Z-Special: Desert–Jungle–Sabotage*; Feuer, *Australian Commandos*; Smith, *They Came Unseen*; among others.

24 Carter, 'Sarawak adventure' in *N.Z. Surveyor* XIX(3); Report, 'Semut III Party Report', Major W.L. Sochon, n.d., p. 3, 38/1/1-67, GB-0033-MAC, Durham University Library.

25 Personal published accounts of Semut I are found in Harrisson, *World Within*; Wigzell, *New Zealand Army Involvement*; Griffiths-Marsh, *Sixpenny Soldier*; B. Long (ed.), *Operation Semut 1*, which contains contributions from twenty operatives.

26 'About the only thing' from Morrison, *Fair Land Sarawak*, pp. 97–8.

27 'Sniffing the ground' from Stanley, 'Sniffing the ground', in *J. of the Australian War Memorial* 25.

CHAPTER 2: THE JAPANESE OCCUPATION

1 Reece, *Masa Jepun*, p. 31.

2 Ibid.

3 'unlikely that the Japanese' from Wong Tze Ken, *Historical Sabah*, p. 13.

4 'The Japs took Kuching' from Keith, *Three Came Home*, p. 28.

5 Pringle, *Rajahs and Rebels*; Wadley, 'Punitive expeditions', in *Ethnohistory* 1.

6 Walker, *Power and Prowess*, Ch. 4; Pringle, *Rajahs and Rebels*, pp. 104, 126, 132, 240; Wadley, 'Punitive expeditions', in *Ethnohistory* 1; Davison and Sutlive, 'The children of *Nising*', in Sutlive (ed.), *Female and Male in Borneo*, p. 169; Rousseau, *Central Borneo*, pp. 32–5; King, *Peoples of Borneo*, pp. 144–5.

7 Hua, *Pussy's in the Well*, p. 7.

8 Ooi, *Japanese Occupation of Borneo*, p. 6; King, *Peoples of Borneo*, p. 148.

9 Keith, *Three Came Home*, pp. 16–17.

10 Reece, *Masa Jepun*, p. 123. Whites murdered by Dayaks in Sarawak after the Japanese occupation include Gilbert Arundell, Resident of the Second Division, and Donald Hudden, District Officer at Marudi: both were hunted down by Ibans in 1942. Similarly, Lieutenant Davijd of the Royal Netherlands East Indies Army and a small group of Dutch civilians were killed by Punan in Dutch Borneo in 1942. See Reece, *Masa Jepun*, pp. 44–8; Clayre, 'The fate of Donald Hudden', in *Borneo Research Bulletin* 30; Sellato, 'Crime scene', in *Borneo Research Bulletin* 32, pp. 226–7; Horton, *Ring of Fire*, p. 72.

11 Ooi, *Japanese Occupation of Borneo*, pp. 28–9, 36; Reece, *Masa Jepun*, p. 30.

12 Reece, *Masa Jepun*, p. 24.

13 Ooi, *Japanese Occupation of Borneo*, pp. 30–1; Talib, *Development of the Sarawak Administrative Service*, PhD thesis, p. 150; Wong Tze Ken, *Historical Sabah*, p. 28; Silver, *Blood Brothers*.

14 Ooi, *Japanese Occupation of Borneo*, pp. 38–9; Reece, *Masa Jepun*, p. 79.

15 Reece, *Masa Jepun*, pp. 27, 147–8; Ooi, *Japanese Occupation of Borneo*, pp. 55–6, 75; Stanley, *Tarakan*, pp. 8–9.

16 'The very sight of a KP man' from Reece, *Masa Jepun*, p. 79.

17 'Author's preface', testimony of Maarof bin Abdullah, translated and edited by Major R.K. Hardwick, 16 August 1944, Folder 1, PR00534, AWM.

18 Ibid.

19 Reece, *Name of Brooke*, p. 147; Reece, *Masa Jepun*, p. 123; Ooi, *Japanese Empire Vol. I*, pp. 161–2; Ritchie, *Life Story of Temenggong Koh*, p. 237.

20 Reece, *Name of Brooke*, pp. 146–7.

21 Friend, *Blue-Eyed Enemy*, p. 73; 'For the first time' from p. 11; 'there was often doubt' from Cruickshank, *SOE in the Far East*, p. 5, emphasis in original.

22 Ooi, *Rising Sun Over Borneo*, pp. 33–4; Koh, 'Temenggong Koh: Reminiscences', in *Borneo Research Bulletin 25*, pp. 162–3.

23 Cit. Ritchie, *Life Story of Temenggong Koh*, p. 236.

24 Reece, *Masa Jepun*, pp. 117–8.

25 Ooi, *Japanese Occupation of Borneo*, pp. 57–9, 76; Reece, *Masa Jepun*, p. 141; Hall, *Kinabalu Guerrillas*, p. 33.

26 'Blue-eyed enemy' from Friend, *Blue-Eyed Enemy*, p. 59; also p. 60.

27 Ooi *Japanese Occupation of Borneo*, pp. 120–1; Reece, *Masa Jepun*, Ch 8; 'If you didn't bow' from personal communication, Akei' Lus, Gerai, 9 October 1986.

28 A1066, IC45/95/8, NAA; Sutlive, *Tun Jugah of Sarawak*, p. 116–7; author, interview with Ngang Tingang, Long Dungan (Belaga), 23 May 2015.

29 On the Sandakan POW camp and the Sandakan-Ranau death marches see especially Ham, *Sandakan*; Silver, *Sandakan*; Smith, *Borneo*; Braithwaite, *Fighting Monsters*.

30 Heidhues, *Golddiggers, Farmers and Traders*, p. 207; Ooi, *Japanese Occupation of Borneo*, pp. 109, 112.

31 On the Jesselton/Kinabalu Uprising see Ooi, *Japanese Occupation of Borneo*, pp. 98–9; Silver, *Blood Brothers*, pp. 173–82; Hall, *Kinabalu Guerrillas*; Wong Tze Ken, *Historical Sabah*, pp. 95–102; Russell, *Knights of Bushido*, pp. 261–4; Reece, *Masa Jepun*, pp. 162–3; Horton, *Ring of Fire*, pp. 47–72.

32 'This broken land' from Ham, *Sandakan*, p. 451; Stanley, 'Sniffing the ground', in *J. of the Australian War Memorial 25*, p. 39.

33 Harrisson, 'Chinese in Borneo', in *International Affairs* 26(3), p. 357.

34 Reece, *Masa Jepun*, pp. 150–1; Stanley, *Tarakan*, pp. 8–9.

35 Braithwaite, *Fighting Monsters*.

36 Personal communication (email), Clifford Sather, 22 July 2015; Reece, *Masa Jepun*, p. 215.

37 'After the morning manoeuvre' from Lim and Tan, *Sarawak Under the Throes*, p. 157, also pp. 157–162; Tan, *William Tan of Sarawak*, pp. 39–40, 134–6.

38 Barrie, *Borneo Story*, unpublished manuscript, MSS1532, AWM, p. 107; Ham, *Sandakan*, p. 474.

39 Reece, *Masa Jepun*, pp. 151, 160, 165.

40 Reece, *Masa Jepun*, p. 170; Powell, *War by Stealth*, p. 279; 'Notes on Interrogation of Major General Kuroda, Chief of Staff to Lieutenant General Baba, Commander 37 Japanese Army Held at HQ 9 Aust Div 11 Sep 45', n.d., AWM54, 627/4/7, AWM; 'Notes on Conference between Maj Gen Kuroda, Chief of Staff to Lt Gen Baba and Staff of HQ 9 Aust Div 10 Sep 45', n.d., AWM54, 627/4/7, AWM.

41 Reece, *Masa Jepun*, p. 167; Ooi, *Japanese Occupation of Borneo*, pp. 57–8, 100.

42 Author, interview with Lipang Munan, Long Tengoa (Lawas), 11 April 2015.

43 Reece, *Masa Jepun*, pp. 84, 131; Helliwell, 'Japanese Malay', in *Bijdragen* 170.

44 'Shiningly moon-white men' from Harrisson, *World Within*, p. 11. For a WWII example of Dayaks stroking white skin see Heimann, *Airmen and the Headhunters*, p. 84. Dayak people still admired and stroked the author's pale skin in southwest Borneo in the 1980s.

45 Sellato, 'Crime scene', in *Borneo Research Bulletin* 32; personal communication, Bernard Sellato, Canberra, 21 October 2016.

46 See e.g. Rooney, *Khabar Gembira*, p. 118 on the Kenyah.

47 Hansen, *Stranger in the Forest*, p. 45; King, 'Editor's Introduction' in Tillema, *A Journey Among the Peoples of Central Borneo*, p. 12.

48 'It's true we had the same skin' from personal communication, Akei' Lus, Gerai, 9 October 1986.

49 Bob Reece, interview with Garai anak Siba', Nanga Benin, January 1994.

50 Hall, *Kinabalu Guerrillas*, p. 32.

CHAPTER 3: PLANNING

1 Stanley, *Tarakan*, pp. 14–25; Horner, *High Command*, pp. 394–7; Ooi, 'Prelude to invasion', in *J. of the Australian War Memorial* 37, pp. 2–3.

2 'The Official History of the Operations and Administration of Special Operations – Australia', Vol. 1, Part I, A3269, O7/A, NAA; Powell, *War by Stealth*, pp. 19–20, 23–7, 72–5, 188–95; Moor, 'Abbreviated history'.

3 '[E]ither whilst you are a member' from 'Z Special Unit', declaration by G.S. Carter, 24 March 1944, HS 9/274/2, NAUK. I could find no secrecy declarations on the service records kept in Australia for SRD personnel, even though every operative I interviewed remembered signing one and they are mentioned in written accounts. This is probably because of the destruction of SRD files in Australia after the war. Some declarations survive on SRD personnel files kept in the NAUK, as in the example above.

4 'Nothing but a wooden cross' from Powell, *War by Stealth*, p. 349; 'I reckoned I could not ask' from Barrie, *Borneo Story*, unpublished manuscript, MSS1532, AWM, p. 18.

5 'Applications are requested' from Campbell, *Z–Special*, p. 161; McDonald, *New Zealand's Secret Heroes*, p. 94.

6 Powell, *War by Stealth*, p. 348.

7 'Lost property' from Powell, *War by Stealth*, p. 267, also pp. 273, 275; Sligo, *Backroom Boys*, pp. 186–93; 'Borneo', WO 208/1053, NAUK.

8 Powell, *War by Stealth*, pp. 19, 187, 189, 191.

9 'A branch of SOE' from Harrisson, 'Chinese in Borneo', in *International Affairs* 26(3), p. 358; 'save some of the face' from Harrisson, *World Within*, p. 173. For an example of constant conflation of SRD and SOE see Howarth, *Undercover*.

10 'A British Trojan horse' from interview with Lieutenant Colonel Courtney in Pratten and Harper, *Still the Same*, p. 129; Powell, *War by Stealth*, pp. 273–5; Fahey, *Australia's First Spies*, p. 175; 'Save England's Asiatic Colonies', from Howarth, *Undercover*, p. 288.

11 'The Colonial Office' from Powell, *War by Stealth*, p. 267; Sligo, *Backroom Boys*, pp. 187–8.

12 Report, 'Semut II – General Report', Major G.S. Carter, 5 October 1945, p. 2, A3269, A14/A, NAA.

13 Meeting notes, 'Project Semut', 16 February 1944, AWM54, 627/4/15 Part 1, AWM.

14 Powell, *War by Stealth*, pp. 270–3; Courtney, *Silent Feet*, pp. 17–30; Harrisson, 'Chinese in Borneo', in *International Affairs* 26(3), p. 357.

15 Report, 'SRD Intelligence Branch internal conditions in British North Borneo and Sarawak under Japanese occupation', 3 February 1945, AWM54, 627/4/15 Part 2, AWM.

16 Memo, 'Semut Project', 13 June 1944, AWM54, 627/4/15 Part 1, AWM; Memo, '"Semut" Project. Phase 1', 14 August 1944, AWM54, 627/4/15 Part 1, AWM.

17 'Semut Project Outline Plan', 16 September 1944, AWM54, 627/4/15 Part 1, AWM.

18 'The real [. . .] objects' from Note, AD4/2348 to CD, 18 November 1944, HS1/239, NAUK.

19 'contribute effectively' from Courtney, *Silent Feet*, p. 16.

20 'Semut 1st. Phase Plan', n.d., AWM54, 627/4/15 Part 1, AWM; 'Semut Project Outline Plan', 16 September 1944, AWM54, 627/4/15 Part 1, AWM.

21 Jack Tredrea and Bob Long both told me that Harrisson had little Malay at the start of the operation. 'Harrisson's Malay was not a lot better than mine at the start, and mine was very poor', from personal communication (telephone), Bob Long, 2 June 2016. See also Morrison, *Fair Land Sarawak*, p. 98.

22 'I never knew a man' from Morrison, *Fair Land Sarawak*, p. 98; 'ravenous ego' from Heimann, *Most Offending Soul*, p. 4.

23 'A rougher diamond' from Letter, K.W. Hallam to Allan Wood, 19 June 1984, p. 37, PR84/247, AWM; 'an "Englishman"' from ibid.

24 Memo, 'E.T.D. Semut Phase 1', 12 October 1944, AWM54, 627/4/15 Part 1, AWM; Memo, 'S.R.D. Projects / Agas and Semut', 13 October 1944, AWM54, 627/4/15 Part 1, AWM.

25 'Project Semut Summary', 11 November 1944, AWM54, 627/4/15 Part 1, AWM.

26 '"H" Section Master Plan (Borneo – SWPA)', n.d., AWM54, 627/4/15 Part 1, AWM; '"H" Section. Outline of General Operational Plan', n.d., AWM54, 627/4/15 Part 1, AWM; Harrisson, *World Within*, p. 177; Wren, *Down-Stream Twice*, unpublished manuscript, p. 110.

27 Report, 'Semut II – General Report', Major G.S. Carter, 5 October 1945, pp. 2–3, A3269, A14/A, NAA; 'The Official History of the Operations and Administration of Special Operations – Australia', Vol. 2, Part III, p. 25, A3269, O8/A, NAA; Wren, *Down-Stream Twice*, unpublished manuscript, pp. 110–1. Harrisson, in his *World Within* pp. 176ff – and following him other commentators – claims that he was the chief opponent of the submarine entry method and that Carter was in favour of it. This is incorrect. The sources listed above and the more general planning documents make clear that Carter, Harrisson, Sochon and possibly other members of the planning group with experience in Borneo all opposed submarine entry.

28 'Project Semut Summary.', 11 November 1944, AWM54, 627/4/15 Part 1, AWM.

29 Ibid.

30 'Project Semut Summary', 11 November 1944, AWM54, 627/4/15 Part 1, AWM; Report, 'Semut III Party Report', Major W.L. Sochon, n.d., p. 1, 38/1/1-67, GB-0033-MAC, Durham University Library; Wren, *Down-Stream Twice*, unpublished manuscript, pp. 89, 116–7.

31 Harrisson, *World Within*, pp. 179–84; Heimann, *Most Offending Soul*, pp. 177–8.

32 'Project Semut Summary', 11 November 1944, AWM54, 627/4/15 Part 1, AWM.

33 'Go in first' from Harrisson, *World Within*, p. 180.

34 'Semut II', Major G.S. Carter, n.d., p. 4, 'S.O.A. Vol. 2 South China Sea Area', Papers of G.B. Courtney, SASR Historical Archives; 'Project Semut Summary', 11 November 1944, AWM54, 627/4/15 Part 1, AWM.

35 Memorandum, 'Air Reconnaissance – Sarawak (British Borneo)', 17 October 1944, AWM54, 627/4/15 Part 1, AWM; Report, 'Report on Preparations and Reconnaissance for "Semut"', Captain T. Harrisson, 18–20 January 1945, A3269, A13A, NAA; 'several large clear places' from Harrisson, *World Within*, p. 151, emphasis in original.

36 Harrisson, *World Within*, pp. 148–50.

37 Report, 'Semut II – General Report', Major G.S. Carter, 5 October 1945, p. 2, A3269, A14/A, NAA.

38 Report, 'Semut II – General Report', Major G.S. Carter, 5 October 1945, p. 2, A3269, A14/A, NAA. See also 'The Official History of the Operations and Administration of Special Operations – Australia', Vol. 2, Part III, p. 66, A3269, O8/A, NAA; Courtney, 'Obituary', in Barrie, *Borneo Story*, unpublished manuscript, MSS1532, AWM, p. 153.

39 Interview with Lieutenant Colonel Courtney in Pratten and Harper, *Still the Same*, p. 130.

40 Long, *Final Campaigns*, p. 621; Powell, *War by Stealth*, pp. 208–11; Dynes, *Leyburn's Liberators*; interview with Lieutenant Colonel Courtney in Pratten and Harper, *Still the Same*, p. 131.

41 Personal communication (telephone), Jack Tredrea, 7 March 2016.

42 Sanderson, 'Chapter 4', in Long (ed.), *Operation Semut 1*, p. 46.

43 Author, interview with Jack Tredrea, Adelaide, 1 October 2016.

44 Author, interview with Bob Long, Perth, 17 September 2014.

45 Tredrea, 'Chapter 5', in Long (ed.), *Operation Semut 1*, p. 94.

46 'Could only have known' from Sanderson, 'Chapter 4', in Long (ed.) *Operation Semut 1*, p. 46; 'Departing from Leyburn' from Dynes, *Leyburn's Liberators*, p. 13; 'I already had a sense' from author, interview with Jack Tredrea, Adelaide, 1 October 2016.

47 Untitled account, n.d., p. 2, Wallet 22, 3DRL/6502, AWM.

48 'The strain on my nerves' from Sanderson, 'Chapter 4', in Long (ed.), *Operation Semut 1*, p. 48.

49 Different authors give different dates for the third insertion attempt, ranging from 22 March to 25 March. Harrisson's official reports say 23 March as

does the SOA 'Official History'. However, the flight logs and most operative accounts say 25 March, and this is the date on which the insertion is officially commemorated in Sarawak. See Dynes, *Leyburn's Liberators*, p. 129; Long (ed.), *Operation Semut 1*, pp. 525–8.

50 Author, interview with Jack Tredrea, Adelaide, 30 September 2016.

51 Dynes, *Leyburn's Liberators*, pp. 12–3; Barrie, *Borneo Story*, unpublished manuscript, MSS1532, AWM, p. 49; Harrisson, *World Within*, pp. 137–8, 191–2; Hallam, 'Chapter 6', in Long (ed.), *Operation Semut 1*, p. 103; author, interview with Jack Tredrea, Adelaide, 30 September 2016.

52 Edmeades, 'Chapter 2', in Long (ed.), *Operation Semut 1*, pp. 27–8; Hallam, 'Chapter 6', in Long (ed.), *Operation Semut 1*, pp. 103–4; Tredrea, 'Chapter 5', in Long (ed.), *Operation Semut 1*, p. 94; author, interview with Jack Tredrea, Adelaide, 30 September 2016.

CHAPTER 4: ARRIVAL

1 Author, interviews with Siran Ida and Adteh Kediah Aran, Bario Asal (Bario), 22 March 2015, 25 March 2015; author, Bario interviews, March 2015.

2 Author, Bario interviews, March 2015.

3 Harrisson, *World Within*, pp. 114–5, 194; author, interview with Siran Ida and Adteh Kediah Aran, Bario Asal (Bario), 22 March 2015; Janowski, *Rice, Work and Community*, PhD thesis, p. 346.

4 'Sogged and swooshed' from Harrisson, *World Within*, p. 192.

5 'Bad luck if the Japs' from author, interview with Jack Tredrea, Adelaide, 30 September 2016; 'I did an express trip' from Hallam, 'Chapter 6', in Long (ed.), *Operation Semut 1*, p. 104.

6 Letter, K.W. Hallam to Allan Wood, 19 June 1984, pp. 21–2, PR84/247, AWM; Tredrea, 'Chapter 5', in Long (ed.), *Operation Semut 1*, pp. 94–5; Hallam, 'Chapter 6', in Long (ed.), *Operation Semut 1*, p. 104; Edmeades, 'Chapter 2', in Long (ed.), *Operation Semut 1*, pp. 28, 30.

7 Harrisson, *World Within*, pp. 193–4.

8 Author, interviews with Siran Ida and Adteh Kediah Aran, Bario Asal (Bario), 22 March 2015, 25 March 2015.

9 Author, Bario interviews, March 2015; Harrisson, *World Within*, pp. 10, 196.

10 Harrisson, *World Within*, pp. 22–3; Harrisson, 'Eight men dropped from the skies – Part 1', in *Commando 2*, 2020, p. 41.

11 'In no uncertain terms' from author, interview with Jack Tredrea, Adelaide, 15 September 2014; author, interview with Bob Long, Perth, 17 September 2014; Letter, K.W. Hallam to Allan Wood, 19 June 1984, pp. 31–2, PR84/247, AWM.

12 'Never throw your weight around' from author, interview with Jack Tredrea, Adelaide, 15 September 2014; 'When dealing with natives' from 'SRD Intelligence Branch, Semut – Phase II, Infm Summary No. 3', 23 January 1945, p. 4, A3269, A16/A, NAA.

13 Barrie, *Borneo Story*, unpublished manuscript, MSS1532, AWM, p. 129.

14 Author, interview with Maran Talla, Bario, 25 March 2015.

15 'On the Army socks' and 'One pair sprang a hole' both from 'Socks', 16 November 1944, AWM54, 627/4/15 Part 2, AWM.

16 '2 lbs. Horlicks tablets', '4 lbs. curry powder' and '4 lbs. Vegemite' all from 'Requirements for "Recce" Party (Semut)', n.d. AWM54, 627/4/15 Part 2, AWM; 'comforts', '12 lbs. Havelock Fine Cut Tobacco', '100 pkts. Cigarette Papers' and '2 boxes Chewing Gum' all from 'List No. 1, Semut Phase One', 11 November 1944, AWM54, 627/4/15 Part 1, AWM; see also 'Requirements for Recce Party (Semut)', 2 May 1944, AWM54, 627/4/15 Part 2, AWM.

17 'Ingeniously arranged' from Harrisson, *World Within*, p. 186.

18 Harrisson, *World Within*, p. 199.

19 Author, Bario interviews, March 2015; Harrisson, *World Within*, pp. 199–200.

20 Author, interview with Siran Ida and Adteh Kediah Aran, Bario Asal (Bario), 22 March 2015; author, interview with Maran Talla, Bario, 25 March 2015.

21 Author, Bario interviews, March 2015; author, interviews with Jack Tredrea, Adelaide, 30 September and 1 October 2016; Report, 'Semut 1', Major T. Harrisson, 4 September 1945, pp. 2–3, A3269, A13/A, NAA.

22 Barrie, *Borneo Story*, unpublished manuscript, MSS1532, AWM, p. 52.

23 Barrie, *Borneo Story*, unpublished manuscript, MSS1532, AWM, p. 53.

24 'I said to Keith Barrie' from author, interview with Jack Tredrea, Adelaide, 15 September 2014; 'All my security training' from Edmeades cit. Harrisson, *World Within*, p. 203.

25 Harrisson, *World Within*, p. 202.

26 'After drinking their Borak' from Tredrea, 'Chapter 5', in Long (ed.), *Operation Semut 1*, p. 95.

27 Harrisson, *World Within*, p. 207, emphasis in original.

28 'I began to realise' from Harrisson, *World Within*, p. 207.

29 Hallam, 'Chapter 6', in Long (ed.), *Operation Semut 1*, p. 105; Harrisson, *World Within*, pp. 203, 207; author, interview with Jack Tredrea, Adelaide, 16 September 2014; author, Bario interviews, March 2015.

30 'Project Semut Summary', 11 November 1944, AWM54, 627/4/15 Part 1, AWM. Harrisson, *World Within*, pp. 210–1, states that he sent only Edmeades and Barrie to Long Lellang, and that Hallam stayed in Bario to work on the

radio. This is incorrect: Hallam accompanied Edmeades and Barrie on the trip, as accounts by all three men – and other documents – make clear.

31 On the ATR-4 transceiver, see Holmes, *Wendell Fertig and his Guerrilla Forces*, p. 66.

32 English text from Harrisson, *World Within*, p. 20; Kelabit translation by Datu Ose Murang.

33 Letter, K.W. Hallam to Allan Wood, 19 June 1984, pp. 22–5, PR84/247, AWM; Wren, *Down-Stream Twice*, unpublished manuscript, pp. 155–7; Harrisson, *World Within*, pp. 19–20.

34 'Jungle boots' from Barrie, *Borneo Story*, unpublished manuscript, MSS1532, AWM, p. 56.

35 Wren, *Down-Stream Twice*, unpublished manuscript, pp. 155–6; Southwell, *Uncharted Waters*, p. 199.

36 'The tiger leeches in this country' and 'That night at Kubaan' both from Letter, K.W. Hallam to Allan Wood, 19 June 1984, pp. 23, 24, PR84/247, AWM.

37 Spencer Chapman, *The Jungle is Neutral*, pp. 56–7.

38 Letter, K.W. Hallam to Allan Wood, 19 June 1984, pp. 24–5, PR84/247, AWM.

39 Barrie, *Borneo Story*, unpublished manuscript, MSS1532, AWM, p. 56.

40 Letter, K.W. Hallam to Allan Wood, 19 June 1984, p. 29, PR84/247, AWM; Edmeades, 'Chapter 2', in Long (ed.), *Operation Semut 1*, p. 31; Barrie, *Borneo Story*, unpublished manuscript, MSS1532, AWM, p. 57.

41 Carter cit. Barrie, *Borneo Story*, unpublished manuscript, MSS1532, AWM, p. 63.

42 Barrie, *Borneo Story*, unpublished manuscript, MSS1532, AWM, p. 57; Hallam, 'Chapter 6', in Long (ed.), *Operation Semut 1*, p. 106; Letter, K.W. Hallam to Allan Wood, 19 June 1984, p. 26, PR84/247, AWM; Wren, *Down-Stream Twice*, unpublished manuscript, p. 159.

43 Hallam, 'Chapter 6', in Long (ed.), *Operation Semut 1*, p. 105; Letter, K.W. Hallam to Allan Wood, 19 June 1984, p. 6, PR84/247, AWM.

44 Barrie, *Borneo Story*, unpublished manuscript, MSS1532, AWM, p. 57.

45 Letter, K.W. Hallam to Allan Wood, 19 June 1984, p. 27, PR84/247, AWM.

46 Hallam, 'Chapter 6', in Long (ed.), *Operation Semut 1*, pp. 105–6; Letter, K.W. Hallam to Allan Wood, 19 June 1984, pp. 26–7, PR84/247, AWM.

47 For the first letter see: Letter, J.K. Barrie to Major Harrison [sic], 9 April 1945, Wallet 13, 3DRL/6502, AWM. For descriptions of the second letter see: Letter, K.W. Hallam to Allan Wood, 19 June 1984, p. 1, PR84/247, AWM; Hallam, 'Chapter 6', in Long (ed.), *Operation Semut 1*, p. 106.

48 Harrisson, *World Within*, pp. 211–2.

49 Harrisson, *World Within*, pp. 212–3, 222; Report, 'Semut 1', Major T. Harrisson, 4 September 1945, p. 2, A3269, A13/A, NAA; Barrie, *Borneo Story*, unpublished manuscript, MSS1532, AWM, p. 61; Report, 'Semut III Party Report', Major W.L. Sochon, n.d., p. 1, 38/1/1-67, GB-0033-MAC, Durham University Library; author, personal communication (telephone), Bob Long, 2 June 2016.

50 'The war suddenly seemed' from Wren, *Down-Stream Twice*, unpublished manuscript, p. 124.

51 Long, 'Chapter 7', in Long (ed.), *Operation Semut 1*, p. 127; personal communication (telephone), Bob Long, 2 June 2016; Dynes, *Leyburn's Liberators*, p. 22.

CHAPTER 5: TO THE BARAM

1 'Semut II', Major G.S. Carter, n.d., pp. 5–6, 'S.O.A. Vol. 2 South China Sea Area', Papers of G.B. Courtney, SASR Historical Archives; Carter, 'Sarawak adventure', in *NZ Surveyor* XIX(3), p. 249; Wren, *Down-Stream Twice*, unpublished manuscript, pp. 130–1.

2 'Semut II', Major G.S. Carter, n.d., p. 6, 'S.O.A. Vol. 2 South China Sea Area', Papers of G.B. Courtney, SASR Historical Archives; Carter, 'Sarawak adventure', in *NZ Surveyor* XIX(3), pp. 249–50; Wren, *Down-Stream Twice*, unpublished manuscript, pp. 130–2.

3 'Semut II', Major G.S. Carter, n.d., pp. 6–7, 'S.O.A. Vol. 2 South China Sea Area', Papers of G.B. Courtney, SASR Historical Archives; Carter, 'Sarawak adventure', in *NZ Surveyor* XIX(3), p. 250; Wren, *Down-Stream Twice*, unpublished manuscript, pp. 131–2.

4 'The sky seemed full' from 'Semut II', Major G.S. Carter, n.d., p. 7, 'S.O.A. Vol. 2 South China Sea Area', Papers of G.B. Courtney, SASR Historical Archives; 'And then quite clearly' from Wren, *Down-Stream Twice*, unpublished manuscript, pp. 132–3.

5 Long, 'Chapter 7', in Long (ed.), *Operation Semut 1*, p. 130.

6 Barrie, *Borneo Story*, unpublished manuscript, MSS1532, AWM, p. 58; Letter, K.W. Hallam to Allan Wood, 19 June 1984, p. 28, PR84/247, AWM; Report, 'Semut II – General Report', Major G.S. Carter, 5 October 1945, p. 3, A3269, A14/A, NAA; 'Semut II', Major G.S. Carter, n.d., p. 6, 'S.O.A. Vol. 2 South China Sea Area', Papers of G.B. Courtney, SASR Historical Archives; personal communication (email), Valerie Mashman, 17 November 2015.

7 The name is sometimes recorded as Teh Soen Hin, but more often as The Soen Hin. Although the former seems more correct, the name is spelt The not only in his official military file, but also in several letters he wrote after the war.

8 Pare's date of birth is given on his service record as 13 August 1923. However, he had lied about his age on enlistment; his date of birth was in fact 13 August 1924 (Vanessa Haw, personal communication [email], 31 August 2020).

9 Sanderson cit. Long, 'Chapter 7', in Long (ed.), *Operation Semut 1*, p. 130; Wren, *Down-Stream Twice*, unpublished manuscript, p. 154.

10 Wren, *Down-Stream Twice*, unpublished manuscript, p. 133; Harrisson, *World Within*, pp. 223–4, 226–7; Long, 'Chapter 7', in Long (ed.), *Operation Semut 1*, p. 129.

11 Wren, *Down-Stream Twice*, unpublished manuscript, pp. 135–6; Harrisson, *World Within*, pp. 213–4, 227; personal communication (telephone), Bob Long, 2 June 2016.

12 'Visibly displeased' from Harrisson, *World Within*, p. 228; 'unbusinesslike attitude' and 'perhaps rather more accent' both from Wren, *Down-Stream Twice*, unpublished manuscript, p. 155; 'there was an air of playing' from Wren, *Down-Stream Twice*, unpublished manuscript, p. 160.

13 Harrisson, *World Within*, pp. 208–9, 228–9; Wren, *Down-Stream Twice*, unpublished manuscript, pp. 136, 160.

14 Letter, K.W. Hallam to Allan Wood, 19 June 1984, pp. 33–4, PR84/247, AWM.

15 Report, 'Semut II – General Report', Major G.S. Carter, 5 October 1945, p. 3, A3269, A14/A, NAA.

16 Long, 'Chapter 7', in Long (ed.), *Operation Semut 1*, p. 136; personal communication (telephone), Bob Long, 2 June 2016.

17 Wren, *Down-Stream Twice*, unpublished manuscript, p. 165.

18 'Semut II', Major G.S. Carter, n.d., pp. 10–11, 'S.O.A. Vol. 2 South China Sea Area', Papers of G.B. Courtney, SASR Historical Archives; Report, 'Semut II – General Report', Major G.S. Carter, 5 October 1945, pp. 3–4, A3269, A14/A, NAA; Barrie, *Borneo Story*, unpublished manuscript, MSS1532, AWM, pp. 65–6.

19 'Godsend' from 'Semut II', Major G.S. Carter, n.d., p. 8, 'S.O.A. Vol. 2 South China Sea Area', Papers of G.B. Courtney, SASR Historical Archives; also from Carter, 'Sarawak adventure', in *NZ Surveyor* XIX(3), p. 251.

20 'Semut II', Major G.S. Carter, n.d., pp. 8, 10, 11, 'S.O.A. Vol. 2 South China Sea Area', Papers of G.B. Courtney, SASR Historical Archives; Carter, 'Sarawak adventure', in *NZ Surveyor* XIX(3), p. 251; author, Long San interviews, August 2018.

21 'Semut II', Major G.S. Carter, n.d., p. 11, 'S.O.A. Vol. 2 South China Sea Area', Papers of G.B. Courtney, SASR Historical Archives; Report, 'Semut II – General Report', Major G.S. Carter, 5 October 1945, p. 4, A3269, A14/A, NAA.

22 Author, interview with William Lusing, Long San, 14 August 2018; 'Semut II', Major G.S. Carter, n.d., p. 11, 'S.O.A. Vol. 2 South China Sea Area', Papers of

G.B. Courtney, SASR Historical Archives; Report, 'Semut II – General Report', Major G.S. Carter, 5 October 1945, p. 4, A3269, A14/A, NAA.

23 On activism against the Baram River dam see https://web.archive.org/web/20150103214605if_/http://www.sarawakreport.org/baram/. On the staggering degree of corruption underlying this and other Sarawak dam and logging projects see Rewcastle Brown, *Sarawak Project*; Straumann, *Money Logging*.

24 In 1955 Tama Weng Ajeng, following the death of his oldest son, changed his name to Oyong Lawai Jau as per Kenyah custom. Publications appearing after 1955 refer to him by the latter name.

25 '[His] features' from MacDonald, *Borneo People*, p. 262; 'Born and bred' from p. 261.

26 'Every arrival took on the quality' from Metcalf, *Life of the Longhouse*, p. 38; Morrison, *Fair Land Sarawak*, p. 78.

27 'Semut II', Major G.S. Carter, n.d., p. 11, 'S.O.A. Vol. 2 South China Sea Area', Papers of G.B. Courtney, SASR Historical Archives; Carter, 'Sarawak adventure', in *NZ Surveyor* XIX(3), p. 253; author, interview with Laran Along, Tanjung Tepalit (Long San), 15 August 2018.

28 Author, interview with Laran Along, Tanjung Tepalit (Long San), 15 August 2018.

29 See Winzeler, *Architecture of Life and Death*, p. 72.

30 Metcalf, *Life of the Longhouse*, p. 38; Morrison, *Fair Land Sarawak*, p. 78.

31 Author, interview with Anthony Lawai Karing, Long San, 14 August 2018.

32 Letter, K.W. Hallam to Allan Wood, 19 June 1984, p. 9, PR84/247, AWM.

33 'Semut II', Major G.S. Carter, n.d., p. 11, 'S.O.A. Vol. 2 South China Sea Area', Papers of G.B. Courtney, SASR Historical Archives; Report, 'Semut II – General Report', Major G.S. Carter, 5 October 1945, p. 4, A3269, A14/A, NAA; author, interview with Anthony Lawai Karing, Long San, 14 August 2018.

34 'Extremely astute' from Report, 'Operation – Semut, Intelligence Report No. 4', 26 June 1945, p. 1, A3269, A16/A, NAA; author, Long San interviews, August 2018.

35 'Jap heads only' from 'Semut II', Major G.S. Carter, n.d., p, 14, 'S.O.A. Vol. 2 South China Sea Area', Papers of G.B. Courtney, SASR Historical Archives; Carter, 'Sarawak adventure', in *NZ Surveyor* XIX(3), p. 254; author, Long San interviews, August 2018.

36 Author, interview with Anthony Lawai Karing, Long San, 14 August 2018.

37 'We were not unduly alarmed' from Wren, *Down-Stream Twice*, unpublished manuscript, p. 167.

38 Letter, K.W. Hallam to Allan Wood, 19 June 1984, pp. 1, 3, PR84/247, AWM; 'Diary –1945', Sgt K. Hallam, Wallet 10, 3DRL/6502, AWM; Barrie, *Borneo*

Story, unpublished manuscript, MSS1532, AWM, photo following p. 66; author, Long San interviews, August 2018.

39 Barrie, *Borneo Story*, unpublished manuscript, MSS1532, AWM, pp. 66ff; Wren, *Down-Stream Twice*, unpublished manuscript, pp. 167–8; author, interview with William Lusing, Long San, 14 August 2018.

40 'Tears of welcome', 'like timid wild animals' and 'came shyly out to meet us' from 'Semut II', Major G.S. Carter, n.d., pp. 10, 12, 'S.O.A. Vol. 2 South China Sea Area', Papers of G.B. Courtney, SASR Historical Archives; Carter, 'Sarawak adventure', in *NZ Surveyor* XIX(3), p. 252.

41 Metcalf, *Life of the Longhouse*, pp. 80–5; Pringle, *Rajahs and Rebels*, pp. 130–4, 267–9.

42 Ibid.

43 'Did the recruitment' from Calder, 'Introduction' in Lawrence, *Seven Pillars of Wisdom*, p. xv.

44 'Semut II', Major G.S. Carter, n.d., pp. 11–12, 'S.O.A. Vol. 2 South China Sea Area', Papers of G.B. Courtney, SASR Historical Archives; Letter, Denis Sheppard to Major J. Truscott, 2 April 1997, Q. 26, Truscott Papers; 'Borneo Story', Denis M. Sheppard, 18 November 1997, p. 3, Truscott Papers; author, interview with Apoi Anggang, Tanjung Tepalit (Long San), 16 August 2018.

45 *Sarawak Gazette* 1067, p. 25; MacDonald, *Borneo People*, p. 262.

46 Personal communication (telephone), Bob Long, 2 June 2016, 15 June 2016; Harrisson, *World Within*, p. 229; Report, 'Semut II – General Report', Major G.S. Carter, 5 October 1945, p. 8, A3269, A14/A, NAA; Wren, *Down-Stream Twice*, unpublished manuscript, pp. 160–1.

47 Wren, *Down-Stream Twice*, unpublished manuscript, p. 160.

48 Harrisson, *World Within*, p. 187, emphasis in original.

49 'Rival' from Heimann, *Airmen and Headhunters*, pp. 209, 212; 'claimed the privilege' from Harrisson, *World Within*, p. 180.

50 'The conflict of personalities' from Courtney, *Silent Feet*, p. 58.

51 Personal communication (telephone), Bob Long, 2 June 2016; author, interviews with Jack Tredrea, Adelaide, 30 September 2016, 1 October 2016; 'he found himself a Rajah!' from Truscott, *Voices from Borneo*, p. 20; 'It was perhaps not surprising' from Wren, *Down-Stream Twice*, unpublished manuscript, p. 160.

52 '[We] treated Harrisson as an uncontrollable force' from Truscott, *Voices from Borneo*, p. 16.

CHAPTER 6: FIRST MOVES

1 It is difficult to be certain of the boundary between Semut I and Semut II. We know that the Limbang River fell within Semut I territory and the Tutoh River

within Semut II territory. The boundary between Semut II and Semut III, on the other hand, was clearly described by Sochon in his Party Report. See 'The Official History of the Operations and Administration of Special Operations – Australia', Vol. 2, Part III, pp. 27, 37, A3269, O8/A, NAA; Report, 'Semut III Party Report', Major W.L. Sochon, n.d., p. 2, 38/1/1-67, GB-0033-MAC, Durham University Library; Report, 'Operations Semut II 9 August – 8 October 1945', Major R.K. Wilson, 20 October 1945, p. 4, A3269, A14/A, NAA.

2   Report, 'Semut II – General Report', Major G.S. Carter, 5 October 1945, pp. 6–8, A3269, A14/A, NAA; 'Semut II', Major G.S. Carter, n.d., p. 13, 'S.O.A. Vol. 2 South China Sea Area', Papers of G.B. Courtney, SASR Historical Archives; author, Long San interviews, August 2018.

3   'Semut II', Major G.S. Carter, n.d., p. 13, 'S.O.A. Vol. 2 South China Sea Area', Papers of G.B. Courtney, SASR Historical Archives. On what happened to Donald Hudden see Clayre, 'The fate of Donald Hudden', in *Borneo Research Bulletin* 30; Reece, *Masa Jepun*, pp. 47–8; author, interview with Tama Sihan, Long Banga, 16 March 2015.

4   Report, 'Semut II – General Report', Major G.S. Carter, 5 October 1945, pp. 8–11, A3269, A14/A, NAA; Memorandum, 'SRD Intelligence Report No. 155', 24 May 1945, A3269, A16/A, NAA; 'Semut II', Major G.S. Carter, n.d., p. 14, 'S.O.A. Vol. 2 South China Sea Area', Papers of G.B. Courtney, SASR Historical Archives; Report, 'Operation – Semut, Intelligence Report No. 1', 7 June 1945, p. 2, A3269, A16/A, NAA.

5   Report, 'Semut III Party Report', Major W.L. Sochon, n.d., pp. 1–2, 38/1/1-67, GB-0033-MAC, Durham University Library; Barrie, *Borneo Story*, unpublished manuscript, MSS1532, AWM, p. 67.

6   Personal communication (telephone), Bob Long, 2 June 2016; Letter, K.W. Hallam to Allan Wood, 19 June 1984, p. 36, PR84/247, AWM.

7   Author, interview with Apoi Anggang, Tanjung Tepalit (Long San), 16 August 2018; author, interview with Laran Along, Tanjung Tepalit (Long San), 15 August 2018.

8   'Tower of strength' from Report, 'Operation – Semut, Intelligence Report No. 4', 26 June 1945, p. 3, A3269, A16/A, NAA.

9   Barrie, *Borneo Story*, unpublished manuscript, MSS1532, AWM, p. 67; Wren, *Down-Stream Twice*, unpublished manuscript, p. 169.

10 Sochon cit. Wren, *Down-Stream Twice*, unpublished manuscript, p. 169; author, Long San interviews, August 2018.

11 Report, 'Operation – Semut, Intelligence Report No. 4', 26 June 1945, p. 3, A3269, A16/A, NAA; Wren, *Down-Stream Twice*, unpublished manuscript, p. 171; Barrie, *Borneo Story*, unpublished manuscript, MSS1532, AWM, p. 67; author, Long San interviews, August 2018.

12 Report, 'Operation – Semut, Intelligence Report No. 6', 28 June 1945, pp. 1–2, A3269, A16/A, NAA; Letter, K.W. Hallam to Allan Wood, 19 June 1984, p. 2, PR84/247, AWM.

13 'Ragtime band' from Report, 'Semut II – General Report', Major G.S. Carter, 5 October 1945, p. 8, A3269, A14/A, NAA.

14 Report, 'Semut II – General Report', Major G.S. Carter, 5 October 1945, p. 6, A3269, A14/A, NAA.

15 Barrie, *Borneo Story*, unpublished manuscript, MSS1532, AWM, p. 68; Wren, *Down-Stream Twice*, unpublished manuscript, pp. 168–9.

16 Wren, *Down-Stream Twice*, unpublished manuscript, p. 170. A photograph of the shield can be seen in Barrie, *Borneo Story*, between pages 68 and 69. In 2018 it was no longer in the Long Akah fort; its current whereabouts is a mystery.

17 Wren, *Down-Stream Twice*, unpublished manuscript, p. 170; Dynes, *Leyburn's Liberators*, p. 127; author, interview with Apoi Anggang, Tanjung Tepalit (Long San), 16 August 2018.

18 Harrisson, *World Within*, p. 231; Long, 'Chapter 7', in Long (ed.), *Operation Semut 1*, p. 133; Heimann, *Most Offending Soul*, p. 192.

19 Letter, K.W. Hallam to Allan Wood, 19 June 1984, pp. 3–4, PR84/247, AWM; 'Diary – 1945', Sergeant K. Hallam, Wallet 10, 3DRL/6502, AWM.

20 'Monograph, Corrections & Additional Comments', Denis M. Sheppard, n.d., p. 3, Truscott Papers; Memorandum, Director SRD to Controller AIB, 24 May 1945, A3269, A16/A, NAA.

21 Truscott, *Voices from Borneo*, pp. 44–5; 'Monograph, Corrections & Additional Comments', Denis M. Sheppard, n.d., p. 3, Truscott Papers; author, interview with Apoi Anggang, Tanjung Tepalit (Long San), 16 August 2018.

22 Report, 'Semut II – General Report', Major G.S. Carter, 5 October 1945, pp. 8–10, A3269, A14/A, NAA.

23 'A compassion for the good-will' from Letter, Denis Sheppard to Major J. Truscott, 2 April 1997, Q. 51, Truscott Papers.

24 Report, 'Semut II – General Report', Major G.S. Carter, 5 October 1945, pp. 9–10, A3269, A14/A, NAA; 'Semut II', Major G.S. Carter, n.d., pp. 14–15, 'S.O.A. Vol. 2 South China Sea Area', Papers of G.B. Courtney, SASR Historical Archives; Carter, 'Sarawak adventure', in *NZ Surveyor* XIX(3), p. 255.

25 Report, 'Semut II – General Report', Major G.S. Carter, 5 October 1945, pp. 9–10, A3269, A14/A, NAA.

26 Ibid.

27 Metcalf, *Life of the Longhouse*, pp. 80–5, 283; Pringle, *Rajahs and Rebels*, pp. 130–4, 268–9, 328; Rousseau, *Central Borneo*, p. 12.

28 Report, 'Semut II – General Report', Major G.S. Carter, 5 October 1945, p. 10, A3269, A14/A, NAA.

29 Telegram, Semut II, No. SE 24, n.d., A3269, A14/A, NAA.

30 Report, 'Semut II – General Report', Major G.S. Carter, 5 October 1945, p. 9, A3269, A14/A, NAA; Report, 'Semut Project Interim Report to 7 June 45', n.d., p. 4, A3269, A14/A, NAA.

31 'Monograph, Corrections & Additional Comments', Denis M. Sheppard, n.d., p. 3, Truscott Papers; Letter, K.W. Hallam to Allan Wood, 19 June 1984, p. 7, PR84/247, AWM.

32 From author, interview with Jack Tredrea, Adelaide, 15 September 2014.

33 'Borneo Story', Denis M. Sheppard, 18 November 1997, p. 2, Truscott Papers; Letter, Denis Sheppard to Major J. Truscott, 2 April 1997, Q. 26, Truscott Papers.

34 'Borneo Story', Denis M. Sheppard, 18 November 1997, p. 2, Truscott Papers; 'Monograph, Corrections & Additional Comments', Denis M. Sheppard, n.d., p. 3, Truscott Papers; author, interview with Apoi Anggang, Tanjung Tepalit (Long San), 16 August 2018.

35 Metcalf, *Life of the Longhouse*, p. 1.

36 Metcalf, *Life of the Longhouse*, p. 291; Fong, *A History of the Development of Baram River Basin*, p. 111; 'What Knowle [Knole] is' from MacDonald, *Borneo People*, p. 243.

37 'Monograph, Corrections & Additional Comments', Denis M. Sheppard, n.d., p. 3, Truscott Papers; Truscott, *Voices From Borneo*, pp. 44–5.

38 'Monograph, Corrections & Additional Comments', Denis M. Sheppard, n.d., p. 3, Truscott Papers; Truscott, *Voices From Borneo*, pp. 44–5; author, interview with Apoi Anggang, Tanjung Tepalit (Long San), 16 August 2018.

39 Author, Long San interviews, August 2018.

40 Macdonald, *Borneo People*, pp. 241–2.

41 Fong, *A History of the Development of Baram River Basin*, p. 218; author, interview with Apoi Anggang, Tanjung Tepalit (Long San), 16 August 2018.

42 Author, interview with Apoi Anggang, Tanjung Tepalit (Long San), 16 August 2018.

43 Heppell, 'Two curators', in *Sarawak Museum Journal* 89, p. 30.

44 Author, interview with Apoi Anggang, Tanjung Tepalit (Long San), 16 August 2018.

CHAPTER 7: ADVANCE DOWNRIVER

1 Author, interview with Apoi Anggang, Tanjung Tepalit (Long San), 16 August 2018; 'Monograph, Corrections & Additional Comments', Denis M. Sheppard, n.d., p. 2, Truscott Papers; Truscott, *Voices from Borneo*, p. 29.

2   Author, Long San interviews, August 2018; 'Monograph, Corrections & Additional Comments', Denis M. Sheppard, n.d., p. 3, Truscott Papers; Letter, Denis Sheppard to Major J. Truscott, 2 April 1997, Q. 42, Truscott Papers; Telegram, Semut II, No. SE 30, n.d., A3269, A14/A, NAA; Report, 'Semut II – General Report', Major G.S. Carter, 5 October 1945, p. 10, A3269, A14/A, NAA; 'Appendix 2. Extracts from a Diary kept by Superior Private Kawamoto', p. 1, A3269, A14/A, NAA.

3   'SRD admits to reviving' from Report, 'Conditions within Sarawak 1945', Major G.S. Carter, 10 November 1945, p. 6, HS 8/951, NAUK; 'became a way of life' from 'Borneo Story', Denis M. Sheppard, 18 November 1997, p. 4, Truscott Papers.

4   As well as the report by Carter mentioned above, both Carter and Sochon allude to their reintroduction of headhunting in later unofficial accounts. See e.g. 'Semut II', Major G.S. Carter, n.d., p. 14, 'S.O.A. Vol. 2 South China Sea Area', Papers of G.B. Courtney, SASR Historical Archives; Carter, 'Sarawak adventure', in *NZ Surveyor* XIX(3), p. 254; Untitled memoir, n.d., [p. 20], Wallet 22, 3DRL/6502, AWM; Wren, *Down-Stream Twice*, unpublished manuscript, pp. 214, 257. While Harrisson never acknowledged his sanctioning of headhunting in print, both Tredrea and Long later confirmed it to me (author, interviews with Jack Tredrea, Adelaide, 30 September 2016, 1 October 2016; personal communication [telephone], Bob Long, 15 June 2016), as did family members of several deceased Semut I operatives.

5   Letter, R.K. Wilson to Rt. Hon. Malcolm MacDonald, 21 April 1957, p. 8, 101/4/1-67, GB-0033-MAC, Durham University Library. As we will see below, some of Wilson's claims in this letter – particularly those relating to his own role in the operation and the actions and command of Carter – are obviously untrue. Others, however, are accurate. Sheppard later wrote a detailed critique of the letter, but did not dismiss the claim quoted here. See 'Borneo Story', Denis M. Sheppard, 18 November 1997, Truscott Papers.

6   Walpole, *My War*, p. 130. See also Reece, *Masa Jepun*, p. 212; Reece, *Name of Brooke*, p. 149.

7   Personal communication (telephone), Bob Long, 15 June 2016; 'The three men carrying [this] note' from Letter, E3 [Edmeades] to A1 [Harrisson], 11 June 1945, Wallet 14a, 3DRL/6502, AWM; 'My boys were happy enough' from author, interview with Jack Tredrea, Adelaide, 1 October 2016; 'Have sent [my Ibans] in front' from Diary, PR85/036, AWM, p. 74.

8   Report, Major R.K. Wilson to Officer Commanding SRD, n.d., p. 38, AWM54, 619/7/79, AWM. For Semut I, Tredrea reports five Dutch guilders and one Straits dollar per head (Questionnaire, Q. 42, Truscott Papers; author, interviews

with Jack Tredrea, Adelaide, 30 September 2016, 1 October 2016); Long one Straits dollar (personal communication [telephone], Bob Long, 15 June 2016); Griffiths-Marsh one dollar (Diary, PR85/036, AWM, p. 74). For Semut III, Walpole reports one Straits dollar (*My War*, p. 130); King one Sarawak (Straits) dollar (http://www.ccmms.ca/veteran-stories/army/louey-king/). For Semut II Hallam reports ten dollars (Letter, K.W. Hallam to Allan Wood, 19 June 1984, p. 8, PR84/247, AWM), as does Wilson (Report, Major R.K. Wilson to Officer Commanding SRD, n.d., p. 38, AWM54, 619/7/79, AWM).

9   Geneva Convention for Amelioration of the Condition of Wounded and Sick 1929, Article 3. See also Wels, *Dead Body Management in Armed Conflict*, p. 4.

10 See e.g. Letter, K.W. Hallam to Allan Wood, 19 June 1984, pp. 8–9, PR84/247, AWM; author, Long San interviews, August 2018.

11 Letter, K.W. Hallam to Allan Wood, 19 June 1984, p. 6, PR84/247, AWM.

12 Letter, K.W. Hallam to Allan Wood, 19 June 1984, pp. 6–8, PR84/247, AWM; 'Monograph, Corrections & Additional Comments', Denis M. Sheppard, n.d., p. 3, Truscott Papers; 'Borneo Story', Denis M. Sheppard, 18 November 1997, p. 4, Truscott Papers.

13 Letter, K.W. Hallam to Allan Wood, 19 June 1984, pp. 8–9, PR84/247, AWM. On Japanese views regarding the integrity of the body after death see Ohnuki-Tierney, 'Brain death and organ transplantation', in *Current Anthropology* 35(3), pp. 235–6; Lock, *Twice Dead*, pp. 223–4.

14 Letter, K.W. Hallam to Allan Wood, 19 June 1984, p. 8, PR84/247, AWM; Report, Major R.K. Wilson to Officer Commanding SRD, n.d., p. 38, AWM54, 619/7/79, AWM; 'the word had gone round' from Report, 'Operations – Semut II – 14 July 1945', Major R.K. Wilson, n.d., p. 24, A3269, A14/A, NAA. The first of Wilson's reports referred to here – written after the war and now lodged in the AWM – needs to be treated with considerable caution. Like Wilson's letter to Malcolm MacDonald cited earlier, many of the claims in this report – especially those relating to Wilson's own role in the operation and the actions and command of Carter – are obviously untrue, and contradict statements made in Wilson's earlier reports. Sheppard was so concerned about the many inaccuracies in this report that he provided Jim Truscott with a lengthy corrective of it, supported by an exchange of letters with Carter dating from the 1980s (sadly, both corrective and letters are now lost) – see Truscott, *Voices from Borneo*, p. 30. However, as with Wilson's letter to MacDonald, there is also much in the report that is accurate and, indeed, perceptive.

15 Report, 'Semut II – Signals', Lt W.S. Eadie, 5 September 1945, 'Semut Documents and Photographs', Docs. 16752, IWM.

16 'Very discouraged' from Memo, Lt Eadie to OC A Group, 18 September 1945, 'Semut Documents and Photographs', Docs. 16752, IWM; Report,

'Semut II – Signals', Lt W.S. Eadie, 5 September 1945, 'Semut Documents and Photographs', Docs. 16752, IWM.

17 Report, 'Semut II – Signals', Lt W.S. Eadie, 5 September 1945, 'Semut Documents and Photographs', Docs. 16752, IWM; Report, 'Semut II – General Report', Major G.S. Carter, 5 October 1945, p. 6, A3269, A14/A, NAA.

18 Report, 'Semut II – General Report', Major G.S. Carter, 5 October 1945, pp. 7–9, A3269, A14/A, NAA; 'Semut II', Major G.S. Carter, n.d., p. 14, 'S.O.A. Vol. 2 South China Sea Area', Papers of G.B. Courtney, SASR Historical Archives; Long, *Final Campaigns*, p. 456.

19 'Jap colony' from 'Semut II', Major G.S. Carter, n.d., p. 14, 'S.O.A. Vol. 2 South China Sea Area', Papers of G.B. Courtney, SASR Historical Archives.

20 Report, 'Semut II – General Report', Major G.S. Carter, 5 October 1945, p. 9, A3269, A14/A, NAA.

21 'Semut II – Sarawak, Borneo', W.S. Eadie, 4 April 1987, pp. 1–2, 11, 'Accounts', Docs. 16752, IWM.

22 'Rice, rice, rice' from author, interview with Bob Long, Perth, 17 September 2014; 'never, never ever touch' from Wigzell, *New Zealand Army Involvement*, p. 233; 'I was afraid' from author, interview with Jack Tredrea, Adelaide, 15 September 2014.

23 'We could never teach' from Harrisson, 'Eight men dropped from the skies' in *Commando* 2020, p. 41.

24 'A dopey bastard' from Letter, K.W. Hallam to Allan Wood, 19 June 1984, p. 32, PR84/247, AWM.

25 Operatives generally make little or no reference to 'personal boys' – which they refer to by a variety of terms – in their written accounts. Wilson mentions them several times in official reports, making it clear that a significant number of Semut II operatives employed them, e.g. Report, Major R.K. Wilson to Officer Commanding SRD, n.d., p. 24, AWM54, 619/7/79, AWM; Report, 'Operations – Semut II – 14 July 1945', Major R.K. Wilson, n.d., p. 15, A3269, A14/A, NAA; Report, 'Operations Semut II 9 August – 8 October, 1945', Major R.K. Wilson, 20 October 1945, p. 7, A3269, A14/A, NAA. They are also referred to in some personal accounts. E.g. Hardy of Semut I refers to 'my boy Sungian', Hallam of Semut II writes of 'my "Kenyah boy" Tom-Kechil', Kearney of Semut III mentions his 'batman', Walpole of Semut III refers repeatedly to his 'friend' Bujang, and Chan of Semut III speaks of his 'Chinese boy' who spoke 'Chinese, Cantonese, Mandarin, Malayan and English so I depend on him all the time'. See Hardy, Chapter 15, in Long (ed.), *Operation Semut 1*, p. 446; Letter, K.W. Hallam to Allan Wood, 19 June 1984, p. 7, PR84/247, AWM; Letter, David Kearney to Jim Truscott, 28 December 1997, Truscott Papers; Walpole, *My War*;

Wesley Lowe, interview with Roy Chan, Heroes Remember – Canadian Chinese Veterans, Veterans Affairs Canada. Dayaks throughout Borneo also told me that many operatives employed local men to carry out these tasks. Not all 'personal boys' were Dayaks – some were Chinese or Malays – but most were, especially in the inland areas where the Semut parties were primarily based.

26 'Semut II – Sarawak, Borneo', W.S. Eadie, 4 April 1987, pp. 16–17, 'Accounts', Docs. 16752, IWM.

27 'It became like a Portuguese pub' from Letter, K.W. Hallam to Allan Wood, 19 June 1984, p. 4, PR84/247, AWM.

28 Letter, K.W. Hallam to Allan Wood, 19 June 1984, pp. 4–5, PR84/247, AWM.

29 'When they realised' from Letter, K.W. Hallam to Allan Wood, 19 June 1984, pp. 5–6, PR84/247, AWM.

30 'I was like a bulldozer' from author, interview with Bill Beiers, Melbourne, 21 November 2016.

31 'We came to a ravine' from 'Semut II – Sarawak, Borneo', W.S. Eadie, 4 April 1987, p. 7, 'Accounts', Docs. 16752, IWM.

32 'They were intelligent people' from author, interview with Bob Long, Perth, 18 September 2014; 'master tacticians' from Walpole, *My War*, p. 149. On repairing European weaponry see Harrisson, *World Within*, p. 279; author, interview with Sigar Berauk, Lawas, 10 April 2015; author, interview with Basar Paru, Long Tuma (Lawas), 12 April 2015.

33 Author, interview with Jack Tredrea, Adelaide, 16 September 2014.

34 'Harrisson kept reminding us' from author, interview with Bob Long, Perth, 18 September 2014.

35 Telegram, S.F. to Semut, No. 6, n.d., A3269, A14/A, NAA.

36 'Great was our disillusionment' from Report, 'Semut II – General Report', Major G.S. Carter, 5 October 1945, p. 9, A3269, A14/A, NAA.

37 Telegram, Semut II, No. SE 40, n.d., A3269, A14/A, NAA.

38 Report, 'Semut II – General Report', Major G.S. Carter, 5 October 1945, pp. 9–10, A3269, A14/A, NAA; 'Operations – Semut II – 14 July 1945', Major R.K. Wilson, n.d., p. 2, A3269, A14/A, NAA; Report, Major R.K. Wilson to Officer Commanding SRD, n.d., p. 2, AWM54, 619/7/79, AWM.

39 Report, Major R.K. Wilson to Officer Commanding SRD, n.d., p. 3, AWM54, 619/7/79, AWM.

40 'Appendix 3. Extracts from an Interrogation of General Aikyo', 27 September 1945, A3269, A14/A, NAA; Report, 'Semut II – General Report', Major G.S. Carter, 5 October 1945, p. 10, A3269, A14/A, NAA.

41 'Operations – Semut II – 14 July 1945', Major R.K. Wilson, n.d., p. 3, A3269, A14/A, NAA; Report, Major R.K. Wilson to Officer Commanding SRD, n.d., p. 3, AWM54, 619/7/79, AWM.

42 Ibid.

43 'Semut II – Sarawak, Borneo', W.S. Eadie, 4 April 1987, pp. 10–11, 'Accounts', Docs. 16752, IWM; author, interview with Apoi Anggang, Tanjung Tepalit (Long San), 16 August 2018.

44 'Notes on the visit of O.C. Group A to Semut II by Catalina on 30 June 45', Major G. Courtney, n.d., A3269, A14/A, NAA; 'Semut II – Sarawak, Borneo', W.S. Eadie, 4 April 1987, p. 10, 'Accounts', Docs. 16752, IWM.

45 'Semut II – Sarawak, Borneo', W.S. Eadie, 4 April 1987, p. 11, 'Accounts', Docs. 16752, IWM; 'Operations – Semut II – 14 July 1945', Major R.K. Wilson, n.d., p. 3, A3269, A14/A, NAA; Report, Major R.K. Wilson to Officer Commanding SRD, n.d., p. 3, AWM54, 619/7/79, AWM.

46 Report, Major R.K. Wilson to Officer Commanding SRD, n.d., p. 3, AWM54, 619/7/79, AWM; 'Operations – Semut II – 14 July 1945', Major R.K. Wilson, n.d., p. 3, A3269, A14/A, NAA; author, interview with Apoi Anggang, Tanjung Tepalit (Long San), 16 August 2018.

47 Report, 'Operations Semut II 9 August – 8 October, 1945', Major R.K. Wilson, 20 October 1945, p. 2, A3269, A14/A, NAA; Report, Major R.K. Wilson to Officer Commanding SRD, n.d., p. 4, AWM54, 619/7/79, AWM.

48 Report, 'Semut II – General Report', Major G.S. Carter, 5 October 1945, pp. 9–10, A3269, A14/A, NAA.

49 Report, 'Semut II – General Report', Major G.S. Carter, 5 October 1945, p. 10, A3269, A14/A, NAA; 'Notes on the visit of O.C. Group A to Semut II by Catalina on 30 June 45', Major G. Courtney, n.d., A3269, A14/A, NAA; Report, Major R.K. Wilson to Officer Commanding SRD, n.d., p. 2, AWM54, 619/7/79, AWM.

50 Report, 'Operations Semut II 9 August – 8 October, 1945', Major R.K. Wilson, 20 October 1945, p. 2, A3269, A14/A, NAA; Report, Major R.K. Wilson to Officer Commanding SRD, n.d., p. 24, AWM54, 619/7/79, AWM.

51 Telegram, Gp A, No. CM 143, n.d., A3269, A14/A, NAA; Signal, Gp A, No. CM 131, n.d., A3269, A14/A, NAA.

CHAPTER 8: AMBUSH AT MARUDI

1 Chee, *Population of Sarawak*, PhD thesis, p. 81; Report, 'Report by Party Leader – Semut II', O.C. Group 'A' Adv HQ S.R.D., 29 July 1945, A3269, A14/A, NAA.

2 Fong, *History of Development of Baram River Basin*, pp. 173–4, 181.

3 Personal communication, unknown Chinese man, Marudi bazaar, 10 August 2018.

4 'Semut II – Sarawak, Borneo', W.S. Eadie, 4 April 1987, p. 11, 'Accounts', Docs. 16752, IWM; author, interview with Apoi Anggang, Tanjung Tepalit (Long San), 16 August 2018.

5   Report, 'Semut II – General Report', Major G.S. Carter, 5 October 1945, p. 10,
    A3269, A14/A, NAA; 'Appendix 3. Extracts from an Interrogation of General
    Aikyo', 27 September 1945, A3269, A14/A, NAA; 'Semut II', Major G.S. Carter,
    n.d., p. 15, 'S.O.A. Vol. 2 South China Sea Area', Papers of G.B. Courtney, SASR
    Historical Archives; Carter, 'Sarawak adventure', in *NZ Surveyor* XIX(3), p. 255.

6   'Operations – Semut II – 14 July 1945', Major R.K. Wilson, n.d., p. 4,
    A3269, A14/A, NAA; 'Appendix 1. Interrogation of 2/Lieut Kuroki', 28
    November 1945, A3269, A14/A, NAA; Report, Major R.K. Wilson to Officer
    Commanding SRD, n.d., p. 5, AWM54, 619/7/79, AWM; 'Semut II – Sarawak,
    Borneo', W.S. Eadie, 4 April 1987, p. 11, 'Accounts', Docs. 16752, IWM.

7   Report, 'Operations – Semut II – 14 July 1945', Major R.K. Wilson, n.d.,
    pp. 4–6, A3269, A14/A, NAA; Report, Major R.K. Wilson to Officer
    Commanding SRD, n.d., pp. 5–8, AWM54, 619/7/79, AWM; Letter, K.W.
    Hallam to Allan Wood, 19 June 1984, p. 35, PR84/247, AWM; author, inter-
    view with Apoi Anggang, Tanjung Tepalit (Long San), 16 August 2018.

    The descriptions of the Ridan ambush found in Wilson's two reports ref-
    erenced above, while containing much important detail, must be treated with
    great care. Both reports were written after the war with the explicit intention
    of having them included in an SRD 'Unit War History'. As well as contra-
    dicting one another at certain points, both inflate Wilson's position within
    Semut II at the expense of Carter; the AWM report, particularly, seriously mis-
    represents the nature of Semut II's command arrangements, as I will discuss in
    Chapter 10. Sheppard, who was present at the Ridan ambush, was so concerned
    about the inaccuracies in Wilson's portrayal of it that he later wrote a detailed
    rebuttal of this portrayal for Jim Truscott, supported by correspondence with
    Carter himself – see Chapter 7 Footnote 48 and also 'Borneo Story', Denis M.
    Sheppard, 18 November 1997, p. 2, Truscott papers. Even in the absence of this
    rebuttal (since lost) it is possible to pick out errors in Wilson's descriptions. For
    example, he locates Carter at a 'command post' to one side of the action. Other
    written accounts make no mention of this. More importantly, Apoi Anggang –
    who took part in the action – spontaneously recalled Carter being in the party at
    the landing point itself, and in command of the overall action (author, interview
    with Apoi Anggang, Tanjung Tepalit (Long San), 16 August 2018). In drawing
    on Wilson's reports I have cross-checked them constantly with other accounts,
    including those of present-day Marudi and Ridan residents.

8   Report, 'Semut II – General Report', Major G.S. Carter, 5 October 1945,
    p. 10, A3269, A14/A, NAA; Report, 'Operations – Semut II – 14 July 1945',
    Major R.K. Wilson, n.d., pp. 6–7, A3269, A14/A, NAA; Report, Major R.K.
    Wilson to Officer Commanding SRD, n.d., p. 8, AWM54, 619/7/79, AWM; Letter,

K.W. Hallam to Allan Wood, 19 June 1984, p. 12, PR84/247, AWM; author, interview with Apoi Anggang, Tanjung Tepalit (Long San), 16 August 2018.

9 Report, 'Operations – Semut II – 14 July 1945', Major R.K. Wilson, n.d., pp. 6–7, A3269, A14/A, NAA; Report, Major R.K. Wilson to Officer Commanding SRD, n.d., pp. 8–10, AWM54, 619/7/79, AWM; Letter, K.W. Hallam to Allan Wood, 19 June 1984, p. 12, PR84/247, AWM; author, interview with Apoi Anggang, Tanjung Tepalit (Long San), 16 August 2018.

10 Author, interview with Apoi Anggang, Tanjung Tepalit (Long San), 16 August 2018; Report, Major R.K. Wilson to Officer Commanding SRD, n.d., pp. 10–11, AWM54, 619/7/79, AWM; Report, 'Operations – Semut II – 14 July 1945', Major R.K. Wilson, n.d., p. 8, A3269, A14/A, NAA; Letter, K.W. Hallam to Allan Wood, 19 June 1984, pp. 12–13, PR84/247, AWM.

11 Report, 'Operations – Semut II – 14 July 1945', Major R.K. Wilson, n.d., pp. 8–9, A3269, A14/A, NAA; 'Appendix 1. Interrogation of 2/Lieut Kuroki', 28 November 1945, pp. 4–6, A3269, A14/A, NAA; Report, Major R.K. Wilson to Officer Commanding SRD, n.d., pp. 11–12, AWM54, 619/7/79, AWM; Letter, K.W. Hallam to Allan Wood, 19 June 1984, p. 13, PR84/247, AWM; 'Semut II', Major G.S. Carter, n.d., p. 15, 'S.O.A. Vol. 2 South China Sea Area', Papers of G.B. Courtney, SASR Historical Archives; Carter, 'Sarawak adventure', in *NZ Surveyor* XIX(3), p. 255.

12 'The wait was only a minute' and 'It was then I realised' both from Letter, K.W. Hallam to Allan Wood, 19 June 1984, p. 13, PR84/247, AWM.

13 Report, 'Operations – Semut II – 14 July 1945', Major R.K. Wilson, n.d., p. 10, A3269, A14/A, NAA.

14 '[B]ut then the Nip added' from Letter, K.W. Hallam to Allan Wood, 19 June 1984, pp. 14–15, PR84/247, AWM.

15 Report, 'Operations – Semut II – 14 July 1945', Major R.K. Wilson, n.d., p. 10, A3269, A14/A, NAA; Report, Major R.K. Wilson to Officer Commanding SRD, n.d., pp. 12–13, AWM54, 619/7/79, AWM; author, interview with Apoi Anggang, Tanjung Tepalit (Long San), 16 August 2018.

16 Letter, K.W. Hallam to Allan Wood, 19 June 1984, p. 15, PR84/247, AWM.

17 'Semut II – Sarawak, Borneo', W.S. Eadie, 4 April 1987, p. 11, 'Accounts', Docs. 16752, IWM; Report, 'Operations – Semut II – 14 July 1945', Major R.K. Wilson, n.d., pp. 11–12, A3269, A14/A, NAA; Report, Major R.K. Wilson to Officer Commanding SRD, n.d., pp. 13–15, AWM54, 619/7/79, AWM; 'Semut II', Major G.S. Carter, n.d., p. 15, 'S.O.A. Vol. 2 South China Sea Area', Papers of G.B. Courtney, SASR Historical Archives; Letter, K.W. Hallam to Allan Wood, 19 June 1984, pp. 15–16, PR84/247, AWM; author, interview with Apoi Anggang, Tanjung Tepalit (Long San), 16 August 2018.

18 Letter, K.W. Hallam to Allan Wood, 19 June 1984, pp. 15–16, PR84/247, AWM; Report, 'Operations – Semut II – 14 July 1945', Major R.K. Wilson, n.d., pp. 11–12, A3269, A14/A, NAA; Report, Major R.K. Wilson to Officer Commanding SRD, n.d., p. 16, AWM54, 619/7/79, AWM.

19 Report, 'Operations – Semut II – 14 July 1945', Major R.K. Wilson, n.d., p. 13, A3269, A14/A, NAA; Letter, K.W. Hallam to Allan Wood, 19 June 1984, pp. 15–16, PR84/247, AWM; 'Semut II – Sarawak, Borneo', W.S. Eadie, 4 April 1987, p. 11, 'Accounts', Docs. 16752, IWM; author, interview with Apoi Anggang, Tanjung Tepalit (Long San), 16 August 2018.

20 Carter, 'Sarawak adventure', in *NZ Surveyor* XIX(3), p. 255; 'Semut II', Major G.S. Carter, n.d., p. 15, 'S.O.A. Vol. 2 South China Sea Area', Papers of G.B. Courtney, SASR Historical Archives; 'Semut II – Sarawak, Borneo', W.S. Eadie, 4 April 1987, p. 11, 'Accounts', Docs. 16752, IWM.

21 Report, 'Operations – Semut II – 14 July 1945', Major R.K. Wilson, n.d., pp. 15–16, A3269, A14/A, NAA; Report, Major R.K. Wilson to Officer Commanding SRD, n.d., pp. 18–19, AWM54, 619/7/79, AWM; Letter, K.W. Hallam to Allan Wood, 19 June 1984, p. 16, PR84/247, AWM; author, interview with Apoi Anggang, Tanjung Tepalit (Long San), 16 August 2018.

22 Report, 'Operations Semut II 9 August – 8 October, 1945', Major R.K. Wilson, 20 October 1945, p. 2, A3269, A14/A, NAA; Report, Major R.K. Wilson to Officer Commanding SRD, n.d., pp. 24–5, AWM54, 619/7/79, AWM; 'lined with wrinkles' from MacDonald, *Borneo People*, p. 280, also pp. 268–9.

23 Report, 'Operations Semut II 9 August – 8 October, 1945', Major R.K. Wilson, 20 October 1945, p. 2, A3269, A14/A, NAA; Report, Major R.K. Wilson to Officer Commanding SRD, n.d., pp. 25–6, AWM54, 619/7/79, AWM.

24 Report, Major R.K. Wilson to Officer Commanding SRD, n.d., pp. 26–7, AWM54, 619/7/79, AWM.

25 Report, Major R.K. Wilson to Officer Commanding SRD, n.d., pp. 27–8, AWM54, 619/7/79, AWM; Report, 'Operations – Semut II – 14 July 1945', Major R.K. Wilson, n.d., p. 16, A3269, A14/A, NAA; Report, 'Operations Semut II 9 August – 8 October, 1945', Major R.K. Wilson, 20 October 1945, p. 2, A3269, A14/A, NAA.

26 Report, 'Operations – Semut II – 14 July 1945', Major R.K. Wilson, n.d., pp. 16–17, A3269, A14/A, NAA; author, interview with Apoi Anggang, Tanjung Tepalit (Long San), 16 August 2018.

27 Report, 'Operations – Semut II – 14 July 1945', Major R.K. Wilson, n.d., pp. 16–18, 20–1, A3269, A14/A, NAA; Carter, 'Sarawak adventure', in *NZ Surveyor* XIX(3), p. 255.

28 Report, 'Semut II – General Report', Major G.S. Carter, 5 October 1945, pp. 10–11, A3269, A14/A, NAA; Report, 'Operations – Semut II – 14 July 1945', Major R.K. Wilson, n.d., pp. 22–3, A3269, A14/A, NAA; Carter, 'Sarawak adventure', in *NZ Surveyor* XIX(3), p. 255; Letter, K.W. Hallam to Allan Wood, 19 June 1984, p. 35, PR84/247, AWM. Author conversations in Marudi confirmed that Hallam's report on the fate of the Chinese guerrilla who died in Marudi was correct.

29 'Modified success' from Report, 'Semut II – General Report', Major G.S. Carter, 5 October 1945, p. 11, A3269, A14/A, NAA.

30 Long, *Final Campaigns*, pp. 484–9.

31 Long, *Final Campaigns*, p. 488; Report, 'Semut II – General Report', Major G.S. Carter, 5 October 1945, p. 11, A3269, A14/A, NAA; 'Semut II – Sarawak, Borneo', W.S. Eadie, 4 April 1987, p. 12, 'Accounts', Docs. 16752, IWM; Report, 'Operations – Semut II – 14 July 1945', Major R.K. Wilson, n.d., pp. 22–3, A3269, A14/A, NAA; Report, Major R.K. Wilson to Officer Commanding SRD, n.d., p. 21, AWM54, 619/7/79, AWM; 'Semut II', Major G.S. Carter, n.d., p. 15, 'S.O.A. Vol. 2 South China Sea Area', Papers of G.B. Courtney, SASR Historical Archives.

32 Courtney, *Silent Feet*, p. 55; 'The Official History of the Operations and Administration of Special Operations – Australia', Vol. 2, Part III, pp. 67, 70, A3269, O8/A, NAA.

33 'British units' from Long, *Final Campaigns*, p. 459; '[B]y the time I came to Z' from Letter, David [Kearney] to Brad [Ross Bradbury], 5 September 1997, Truscott Papers.

34 Harrisson, *World Within*, pp. 141–2, 260, 269; Letter, David [Kearney] to Brad [Ross Bradbury], 5 September 1997, Truscott Papers; Powell, *War By Stealth*, pp. 362–3; Report, '20 Aust Inf Bde – Report on Operation Oboe Six', 16 August 1945, pp. 31–2, AWM357, 7, AWM, 'had no knowledge' and 'valuable work' both from p. 32.

35 Sligo, *Backroom Boys*, pp. 218–9; Courtney, *Silent Feet*, p. 54; Powell, *War by Stealth*, p. 291; Long, *Final Campaigns*, p. 491.

36 'Flat impertinence' from Harrisson, *World Within*, p. 269; Letter, Frank Wigzell to Major J. Truscott, 25 May 1997, Q. 4, Truscott Papers.

CHAPTER 9: TRIUMPH AND THREAT

1 'Make as strong a demonstration' from Report, '20 Aust Inf Bde – Report on Operation Oboe Six', 16 August 1945, p. 19, AWM357, 7, AWM; Long, *Final Campaigns*, pp. 489, 491–2.

2 Long, *Final Campaigns*, p. 492; Report, '20 Aust Inf Bde – Report on Operation Oboe Six', 16 August 1945, p. 21, AWM357, 7, AWM.

3 Report, '20 Aust Inf Bde – Report on Operation Oboe Six', 16 August 1945, pp. 21–2, AWM357, 7, AWM; Long, *Final Campaigns*, p. 492.

4 'Investigating rubber supplies in the Baram' from Report, 'Semut II – General Report', Major G.S. Carter, 5 October 1945, p. 11, A3269, A14/A, NAA; Report, '20 Aust Inf Bde – Report on Operation Oboe Six', 16 August 1945, p. 22, AWM357, 7, AWM; Long, *Final Campaigns*, p. 492.

5 Report, '20 Aust Inf Bde – Report on Operation Oboe Six', 16 August 1945, p. 22, AWM357, 7, AWM; Long, *Final Campaigns*, p. 492; 'Back we went' from 'Semut II', Major G.S. Carter, n.d., p. 16, 'S.O.A. Vol. 2 South China Sea Area', Papers of G.B. Courtney, SASR Historical Archives.

6 Report, 'Report by Party Leader – Semut II', O.C. Group 'A' Adv HQ S.R.D., 29 July 1945, A3269, A14/A, NAA; Telegram, Group A, No. GM 152, n.d., A3269, A14/A, NAA; Signal, Gp A, No. CM 131, n.d., A3269, A14/A, NAA.

7 Report, 'Semut II – General Report', Major G.S. Carter, 5 October 1945, p. 11, A3269, A14/A, NAA; Long, *Final Campaigns*, p. 492; Report, 'Operations – Semut II – 14 July 1945', Major R.K. Wilson, n.d., p. 19, A3269, A14/A, NAA; 'Semut II', Major G.S. Carter, n.d., p. 16, 'S.O.A. Vol. 2 South China Sea Area', Papers of G.B. Courtney, SASR Historical Archives.

8 Long, *Final Campaigns*, p. 492; Report, 'Operations – Semut II – 14 July 1945', Major R.K. Wilson, n.d., p. 18, A3269, A14/A, NAA.

9 Report, 'Operations – Semut II – 14 July 1945', Major R.K. Wilson, n.d., p. 13, A3269, A14/A, NAA; Report, Major R.K. Wilson to Officer Commanding SRD, n.d., pp. 16–17, 28–9, AWM54, 619/7/79, AWM.

10 Report, 'Operations – Semut II – 14 July 1945', Major R.K. Wilson, n.d., pp. 22–3, A3269, A14/A, NAA; Report, Major R.K. Wilson to Officer Commanding SRD, n.d., pp. 29, 36–7, AWM54, 619/7/79, AWM; 'Appendix 1. Interrogation of 2/Lieut Kuroki', 28 November 1945, p. 8, A3269, A14/A, NAA; 'Semut II – Sarawak, Borneo', W.S. Eadie, 4 April 1987, pp. 11–12, 'Accounts', Docs. 16752, IWM.

11 Report, 'Semut II – General Report', Major G.S. Carter, 5 October 1945, p. 11, A3269, A14/A, NAA; Report, 'Operations – Semut II – 14 July 1945', Major R.K. Wilson, n.d., pp. 7, 18, A3269, A14/A, NAA; Report, 'Report by Party Leader – Semut II', O.C. Group 'A' Adv HQ S.R.D., 29 July 1945, A3269, A14/A, NAA; Report, Major R.K. Wilson to Officer Commanding SRD, n.d., pp. 29–30, AWM54, 619/7/79, AWM.

12 Report, 'Operations – Semut II – 14 July 1945', Major R.K. Wilson, n.d., pp. 18–19, A3269, A14/A, NAA, 'gorging themselves' from p. 19.

13 'It almost looks as if' from Report, 'Operations – Semut II – 14 July 1945', Major R.K. Wilson, n.d., p. 22, A3269, A14/A, NAA.

14 'Poorly equipped and led' from Report, '20 Aust Inf Bde – Report on Operation Oboe Six', 16 August 1945, p. 26, AWM357, 7, AWM.

15 Report, '20 Aust Inf Bde – Report on Operation Oboe Six', 16 August 1945, p. 22, AWM357, 7, AWM; Long, *Final Campaigns*, pp. 492–3; Report, 'Report on the taking of 27 P.O.W. by Lt. Holland and Cpl. Rawlings', 22 September 1945, Wallet 10, 3DRL/6502, AWM; Report, 'Operations – Semut II – 14 July 1945', Major R.K. Wilson, n.d., pp. 19–20, A3269, A14/A, NAA; Report, 'Operations Semut II 9 August – 8 October, 1945', Major R.K. Wilson, 20 October 1945, p. 3, A3269, A14/A, NAA; Report, Major R.K. Wilson to Officer Commanding SRD, n.d., pp. 31–2, AWM54, 619/7/79, AWM, 'No one in Semut II' from p. 32.

16 Report, 'Report by Party Leader – Semut II', O.C. Group 'A' Adv HQ S.R.D., 29 July 1945, A3269, A14/A, NAA; 'Semut II – Sarawak, Borneo', W.S. Eadie, 4 April 1987, p. 12, 'Accounts', Docs. 16752, IWM; author, interview with Apoi Anggang, Tanjung Tepalit (Long San), 16 August 2018.

17 Sligo, *Backroom Boys*, Ch. 9, Ch. 10; Long, *Final Campaigns*, pp. 401–5, 496–8.

18 Report, '20 Aust Inf Bde – Report on Operation Oboe Six', 16 August 1945, p. 28, AWM357, 7, AWM; Long, *Final Campaigns*, pp. 496–7; Sligo, *Backroom Boys*, p. 232; Donnison, *British Military Administration*, p. 196.

19 'For some unaccountable reason' from Report, 'Report by Party Leader – Semut II', O.C. Group 'A' Adv HQ S.R.D., 29 July 1945, A3269, A14/A, NAA.

20 'It was impossible to continue running' from Harrisson, *World Within*, p. 282.

21 Report, 'Report by Party Leader – Semut II', O.C. Group 'A' Adv HQ S.R.D., 29 July 1945, A3269, A14/A, NAA; Report, 'Semut II – General Report', Major G.S. Carter, 5 October 1945, p. 13, A3269, A14/A, NAA; Powell, *War by Stealth*, p. 297.

22 'Monograph, Corrections & Additional Comments', Denis M. Sheppard, n.d., p. 2, Truscott Papers; Report, 'Semut II – General Report', Major G.S. Carter, 5 October 1945, p. 13, A3269, A14/A, NAA; Letter, K.W. Hallam to Allan Wood, 19 June 1984, p. 35, PR84/247, AWM.

23 Letter, K.W. Hallam to Allan Wood, 19 June 1984, p. 35, PR84/247, AWM; 'Monograph, Corrections & Additional Comments', Denis M. Sheppard, n.d., p. 2, Truscott Papers.

24 Report, Major R.K. Wilson to Officer Commanding SRD, n.d., p. 28, AWM54, 619/7/79, AWM, 'Japs to the east' from p. 21; Report, 'Operations Semut II 9 August – 8 October, 1945', Major R.K. Wilson, 20 October 1945, p. 2, A3269, A14/A, NAA; Telegram, Group A, No. GM 152, n.d., A3269, A14/A, NAA; 'SRD Information Report No. 307', Director S.R.D., July 1945,

A3269, A16/A, NAA; Inward Signal, 'A' Group to Adv HQ, No. CM 152, n.d., A3269, A14/A, NAA.

25 Report, 'Operations Semut II 9 August – 8 October, 1945', Major R.K. Wilson, 20 October 1945, p. 2, A3269, A14/A, NAA.

26 Report, 'Operations Semut II 9 August – 8 October, 1945', Major R.K. Wilson, 20 October 1945, p. 2, A3269, A14/A, NAA; 'Semut II – Sarawak, Borneo', W.S. Eadie, 4 April 1987, p. 12, 'Accounts', Docs. 16752, IWM; author, interview with Apoi Anggang, Tanjung Tepalit (Long San), 16 August 2018.

27 Report, 'Operations Semut II 9 August – 8 October, 1945', Major R.K. Wilson, 20 October 1945, p. 2, A3269, A14/A, NAA.

28 Report, 'Operations Semut II 9 August – 8 October, 1945', Major R.K. Wilson, 20 October 1945, p. 3, A3269, A14/A, NAA; 'Semut II – Sarawak, Borneo', W.S. Eadie, 4 April 1987, p. 18, 'Accounts', Docs. 16752, IWM.

29 Ibid.

30 Report, 'Semut II – General Report', Major G.S. Carter, 5 October 1945, p. 10, A3269, A14/A, NAA; Report, 'Operations Semut II 9 August – 8 October, 1945', Major R.K. Wilson, 20 October 1945, pp. 1–3, A3269, A14/A, NAA; 'Interrogation of Capt. Fujino and 1st Lieut. Kamimura by Major Wilson and F/Lt Bartram of SRD at Labuan on the 1st December 1945', n.d., AWM54, 41/4/35, AWM; Bartram, 'Chapter 17', in Long (ed.), *Operation Semut 1*, pp. 491–2.

31 'Demoralised and starving' from Signal, Group A to HQ SRD C M 259, n.d., A3269, A14/A, NAA.

32 Report, 'Report by Party Leader – Semut II', O.C. Group 'A' Adv HQ S.R.D., 29 July 1945, A3269, A14/A, NAA, 'whittle down' from p. 2.

33 Report, 'Report by Party Leader – Semut II', O.C. Group 'A' Adv HQ S.R.D., 29 July 1945, A3269, A14/A, NAA, 'as sticky as possible' from p. 2; Report, 'Operations Semut II 9 August – 8 October, 1945', Major R.K. Wilson, 20 October 1945, p. 3, A3269, A14/A, NAA.

34 Report, 'Operations Semut II 9 August – 8 October, 1945', Major R.K. Wilson, 20 October 1945, p. 3, A3269, A14/A, NAA; Report, 'Report by Party Leader – Semut II', O.C. Group 'A' Adv HQ S.R.D., 29 July 1945, p. 2, A3269, A14/A, NAA; Pustaka Negeri Sarawak, *Unsung Heroes*, pp. 46–9.

35 Letter, K.W. Hallam to Allan Wood, 12 July 1984, pp. 2–4, PR84/247, AWM, 'I still have the nip officer's sword' from p. 3; Letter, K.W. Hallam to Allan Wood, 19 June 1984, p. 16, PR84/247, AWM.

36 'Shhhd . . . sound of the bullet!' from Pustaka Negeri Sarawak, *Unsung Heroes*, p. 49.

37 Report, 'Operations Semut II 9 August – 8 October, 1945', Major R.K. Wilson, 20 October 1945, p. 4, A3269, A14/A, NAA; Harrisson, *World Within*, p. 274.

38 Report, 'Operations Semut II 9 August – 8 October, 1945', Major R.K. Wilson, 20 October 1945, p. 4, A3269, A14/A, NAA; Bartram, 'Chapter 17', in Long (ed.), *Operation Semut 1*, pp. 492–3; 'Rank, on this sort of occasion' from Letter, (CO) Semut I to Wilson, 3 August 1945, Wallet 7, 3DRL/6502, AWM.

39 Report, 'Operations Semut II 9 August – 8 October, 1945', Major R.K. Wilson, 20 October 1945, p. 3, A3269, A14/A, NAA.

CHAPTER 10: THE SACKING

1 Telegram, Gp A, No. CM 143, n.d., A3269, A14/A, NAA.

2 Report, '20 Aust Inf Bde – Report on Operation Oboe Six', 16 August 1945, p. 22, AWM357, 7, AWM; Report, 'Report by Party Leader – Semut II', O.C. Group 'A' Adv HQ S.R.D., 29 July 1945, A3269, A14/A, NAA; Report, 'Semut II – General Report', Major G.S. Carter, 5 October 1945, pp. 11–12, A3269, A14/A, NAA; Long, *Final Campaigns*, p. 493.

3 Report, 'Semut II – General Report', Major G.S. Carter, 5 October 1945, pp. 11–12, A3269, A14/A, NAA; Report, 'Report by Party Leader – Semut II', O.C. Group 'A' Adv HQ S.R.D., 29 July 1945, A3269, A14/A, NAA; 'aggressively and soundly directed' from Report, '20 Aust Inf Bde – Report on Operation Oboe Six', 16 August 1945, p. 26, AWM357, 7, AWM.

4 Report, 'Semut II – General Report', Major G.S. Carter, 5 October 1945, p. 11, A3269, A14/A, NAA.

5 Letter, K.W. Hallam to Allan Wood, 19 June 1984, pp. 10–11, PR84/247, AWM; Report, 'Semut II – General Report', Major G.S. Carter, 5 October 1945, pp. 11–12, A3269, A14/A, NAA.

6 Letter, K.W. Hallam to Allan Wood, 19 June 1984, pp. 11–12, PR84/247, AWM.

7 Report, 'Semut II – General Report', Major G.S. Carter, 5 October 1945, pp. 11–12, A3269, A14/A, NAA; Report, 'Report by Party Leader – Semut II', O.C. Group 'A' Adv HQ S.R.D., 29 July 1945, A3269, A14/A, NAA.

8 Report, 'Semut II – General Report', Major G.S. Carter, 5 October 1945, p. 12, A3269, A14/A, NAA; Report, 'Operations Semut II 9 August – 8 October, 1945', Major R.K. Wilson, 20 October 1945, p. 1, A3269, A14/A, NAA.

9 Report, 'Semut II – General Report', Major G.S. Carter, 5 October 1945, p. 12, A3269, A14/A, NAA; 'Information Report No. (AIB) 515', 11 August 1945, A3269, A16/A, NAA.

10 'Information Report No. (AIB) 534', 22 August 1945, A3269, A16/A, NAA; Report, 'Operations Semut II 9 August – 8 October, 1945', Major R.K. Wilson,

20 October 1945, p. 1, A3269, A14/A, NAA; 'This was an anxious time' from Report, 'Semut II – General Report', Major G.S. Carter, 5 October 1945, p. 12, A3269, A14/A, NAA.

11 'Just a few extra white men' from Report, 'Semut II – General Report', Major G.S. Carter, 5 October 1945, p. 12, A3269, A14/A, NAA; 'All Ibans under [Japanese] immediate domination' from Report, 'Report by Party Leader – Semut II', O.C. Group 'A' Adv HQ S.R.D., 29 July 1945, pp. 2–3, A3269, A14/A, NAA.

12 'A serious reverse' from Report, 'Report by Party Leader – Semut II', O.C. Group 'A' Adv HQ S.R.D., 29 July 1945, p. 3, A3269, A14/A, NAA.

13 'Borneo Story', Denis M. Sheppard, 18 November 1997, p. 3, Truscott Papers; Report, 'Semut II – General Report', Major G.S. Carter, 5 October 1945, p. 13, A3269, A14/A, NAA; Letter, R.K. Wilson to Rt. Hon. Malcolm MacDonald, 21 April 1957, p. 5, 101/4/1-67, GB-0033-MAC, Durham University Library.

14 'Removed summarily' and 'as a bitter blow' both from Report, 'Semut II – General Report', Major G.S. Carter, 5 October 1945, p. 13, A3269, A14/A, NAA.

15 Ibid.

16 Ibid.

17 'Through thick and thin' from Truscott, *Voices from Borneo*, p. 16.

18 Report, 'Semut II – General Report', Major G.S. Carter, 5 October 1945, pp. 13–14, A3269, A14/A, NAA; Letter, G.S. Carter to Chapman-Walker, 22 September 1947, 'Correspondence re SRD Association War Memorial ('47–'57)', Docs. 16406, IWM.

19 Letter, R.K. Wilson to Rt. Hon. Malcolm MacDonald, 21 April 1957, pp. 4–5, 101/4/1-67, GB-0033-MAC, Durham University Library; Report, Major R.K. Wilson to Officer Commanding SRD, n.d., pp. 19, 32–3, AWM54, 619/7/79, AWM.

20 'I think to all of us' and 'Major Carter [. . .] felt responsible' both from Report, Major R.K. Wilson to Officer Commanding SRD, n.d., pp. 33, 19, AWM54, 619/7/79, AWM.

21 Letter, K.W. Hallam to Allan Wood, 19 June 1984, pp. 41–2, PR84/247, AWM, 'a fantastic fighting officer' from p. 36; Letter, R.K. Wilson to Rt. Hon. Malcolm MacDonald, 21 April 1957, p. 6, 101/4/1-67, GB-0033-MAC, Durham University Library; 'if they wish to talk to me' from 'Borneo Story', Denis M. Sheppard, 18 November 1997, p. 3, Truscott Papers.

22 Letter, R.K. Wilson to Rt. Hon. Malcolm MacDonald, 21 April 1957, p. 6, 101/4/1-67, GB-0033-MAC, Durham University Library; Courtney, *Silent Feet*, p. 59; Truscott, *Voices from Borneo*, p. 30; Watters, 'Loch Ness, Special Operations Executive and the first surgeon in paradise', in *ANZ Journal of Surgery* 77.

23 'Bullshit merchant' from Truscott, *Voices from Borneo*, p. 30; Report, Major R.K. Wilson to Officer Commanding SRD, n.d., AWM54, 619/7/79, AWM; Letter, R.K. Wilson to Rt. Hon. Malcolm MacDonald, 21 April 1957, 101/4/1-67, GB-0033-MAC, Durham University Library.

24 Truscott, *Voices from Borneo*, p. 30; 'Borneo Story', Denis M. Sheppard, 18 November 1997, Truscott Papers; 'unjustified criticism' from Courtney, *Silent Feet*, p. 70.

25 'Some of the British officers' from Courtney, *Silent Feet*, p. 59; 'Semut II – Sarawak, Borneo', W.S. Eadie, 4 April 1987, p. 18, 'Accounts', Docs. 16752, IWM.

26 'Not that of a military man' from Barrie, *Borneo Story*, unpublished manuscript, MSS1532, AWM, p. 153; Courtney, *Silent Feet*, p. 59.

27 Signal, Group 'A', No. CM 338, n.d., A3269, A14/A, NAA, emphasis in original.

28 'The most sensitive spot' and 'the only first-class enemy troops' both from Letter, R.K. Wilson to Rt. Hon. Malcolm MacDonald, 21 April 1957, p. 7, 101/4/1-67, GB-0033-MAC, Durham University Library.

29 Report, 'Semut II – General Report', Major G.S. Carter, 5 October 1945, pp. 12–13, A3269, A14/A, NAA; Report, 'Report by Party Leader – Semut II', O.C. Group 'A' Adv HQ S.R.D., 29 July 1945, pp. 2–3, A3269, A14/A, NAA.

30 'The Official History of the Operations and Administration of Special Operations – Australia', Vol. 2, Part III, pp. 67, A3269, O8/A, NAA; 'by order of the government' from Courtney, 'Z Special Unit operations' in *U.S.I. News Victoria* 2(94).

31 Stanley, *Tarakan*, pp. 180–1; Bartram, 'Chapter 17', in Long (ed.), *Operation Semut 1*, p. 483; 'Memorandum on Action to be Taken on Surrender of Japan', Colonel A.G. Wilson, 9 August 1945, AWM54, 627/4/7, AWM; 'SRD Outline Plan – Surrender of Japan', Lt Col G.S. Courtney, 12 August 1945, AWM 54, 627/4/7, AWM.

32 Report, 'Semut II – General Report', Major G.S. Carter, 5 October 1945, p. 12, A3269, A14/A, NAA; Report, 'Operations Semut II 9 August – 8 October, 1945', Major R.K. Wilson, 20 October 1945, p. 1, A3269, A14/A, NAA.

33 'Information Report No. (AIB) 575', 11 September 1945, p. 2, A3269, A16A, NAA.

34 'Interrogation of Colonel Aikyo at HQ 20 Aust Inf Bde on 20 Sep 45', 21 September 1945, AWM54, 41/4/35, AWM; Report, '20 Aust Inf Bde – Report on Operation Oboe Six', 16 August 1945, p. 31, AWM357, 7, AWM.

35 'The real people of the interior' from Report, 'Semut II – General Report', Major G.S. Carter, 5 October 1945, p. 13, A3269, A14/A, NAA.

36   Report, 'Operations Semut II 9 August – 8 October, 1945', Major R.K. Wilson,
      20 October 1945, pp. 4–5, A3269, A14/A, NAA; 'Wilson and I personally'
      from Letter, K.W. Hallam to Allan Wood, 12 July 1984, p. 2, PR84/247, AWM.

37   Report, 'Operations Semut II 9 August – 8 October, 1945', Major R.K. Wilson,
      20 October 1945, p. 4, A3269, A14/A, NAA.

38   Reece, *Masa Jepun*, pp. 200–2, 'We had to walk under' from p. 201.

39   Report, 'Patrol Report Melinau – Limbang Area', Lt P.V. Middleton,
      6 October 1945, A3269, A14/A, NAA.

40   Harrisson, *World Within*, pp. 274–5.

41   Harrisson, *World Within*, p. 307; see also Bartram, 'Chapter 17', in Long (ed.),
      Operation Semut 1, p. 483.

42   Report, 'Operations Semut II 9 August – 8 October, 1945', Major R.K. Wilson,
      20 October 1945, p. 5, A3269, A14/A, NAA; Report, 'Patrol Report Melinau –
      Limbang Area', Lt P.V. Middleton, 6 October 1945, A3269, A14/A, NAA.

43   Report, 'Patrol Report Melinau – Limbang Area', Lt P.V. Middleton,
      6 October 1945, A3269, A14/A, NAA.

44   Wilson later estimated that Semut II had already killed 46 members of *Fujino
      Tai* (which he here calls 'Kamamura Tai') before it got far up the Melinau
      River; we know that more were killed further on. This figure also leaves out
      the number of injured. See Report, 'Operations Semut II 9 August – 8 October,
      1945', Major R.K. Wilson, 20 October 1945, p. 10, A3269, A14/A, NAA.

45   Harrisson, *World Within*, pp. 274–5. In a later report Harrisson states that
      Fujino Tai arrived at the Limbang River system on 24 July. This is incorrect.
      In the same narrative Harrisson correctly places the column at Linei, close to
      the mouth of the Tutoh River, on 13 July, and it is impossible that it could have
      got from there to the Limbang River system – a journey of several weeks – in
      eleven days. The dates Sanderson provides for *Fujino Tai*'s movements are also
      incorrect. For example, he dates orders from Harrisson regarding the pres-
      ence of *Fujino Tai* in the upper Tutoh River to 2 July, when we know *Fujino
      Tai* did not begin its journey from Labi until the start of July. In the later part
      of his account Sanderson appears to have dated every event a month earlier
      than it actually occurred – e.g. he writes 3 August for an event that occurred
      in early September. See Report, 'Report on Fujino Force', Major T. Harrisson,
      31 October 1945, AWM54, 41/4/35, AWM; Sanderson, 'Chapter 7', in Long
      (ed.), *Operation Semut 1*.

46   Letter, Toby Carter to Stan [Eadie], 8 April 1947, p. 2, 'Semut Documents and
      Photographs', Docs. 16752, IWM.

47   Report, 'Patrol Report Melinau – Limbang Area', Lt P.V. Middleton,
      6 October 1945, A3269, A14/A, NAA; Report, 'Operations Semut II 9 August –

8 October, 1945', Major R.K. Wilson, 20 October 1945, p. 5, A3269, A14/A, NAA; 'Diary –1945', Sgt. K. Hallam, Wallet 10, 3DRL/6502, AWM. Some *Fujino Tai* remnants made it as far as Long Lellang in the upper Tutoh; local Kelabits, 70 years later, reported transporting a handful of starving Japanese downriver to Marudi after the surrender. See personal communication (email), Valerie Mashman, 17 November 2015; 'Evacuation of Fujino Force', Major T. Harrisson, 8 November 1945, AWM54, 41/4/35, AWM.

48 The SOA Official History lists Semut II as having 25 operatives. However, this includes Sochon, Abu Kassim and Barrie who were not formal members of Semut II, as discussed in the Appendix. It also includes Leach, who was never formally a part of Semut II. I have included Conleth-Smith, who underwent a vetting process and was treated by both Carter and Wilson as a member of the operation. See 'The Official History of the Operations and Administration of Special Operations – Australia', Vol. 2, Part III, p. 38, A3269, O8/A, NAA; Report, 'Operation – Semut, Intelligence Report No. 6', 28 June 1945, pp. 1–2, A3269, A16/A, NAA.

49 'The Official History of the Operations and Administration of Special Operations – Australia', Vol. 2, Part III, p. 68, A3269, O8/A, NAA; Courtney, *Silent Feet*, p. 117; 'cost-effective' from Courtney, 'Z Special Unit operations', in *U.S.I. News Victoria* 2(94); Finlay comment from Courtney, *Silent Feet*, pp. 244–5. In his comment Finlay refers to 'guerrilla operations in British Borneo' rather than specifically to Semut. However, the number of casualties and operatives provided are those of Semut alone.

50 Report, 'Semut II – General Report', Major G.S. Carter, 5 October 1945, pp. 83, 86, A3269, A14/A, NAA. See also Heimann, *Most Offending Soul*, p. 429.

51 Courtney, *Silent Feet*, p. 117.

52 Letter, R.K. Wilson to Tom [Harrisson], 19 March 1947, Wallet 21, 3DRL/6502, AWM.

CHAPTER 11: TO THE REJANG

1 Report, 'Semut III Party Report', Major W.L. Sochon, n.d., p. 2, 38/1/1-67, GB-0033-MAC, Durham University Library; Wren, *Down-Stream Twice*, unpublished manuscript, pp. 173–4; author, Long San interviews, August 2018. There are five separate accounts by Sochon relating to Operation Semut: the official Semut III final report, a set of notes (without title or author's name, but recognisably by Sochon) now located in the Harrisson Collection at the AWM, two distinct narratives in Ivor Wren's *Down-Stream Twice* (formally authored by Wren but mostly written in the first person in Sochon's own words), and a set of diary entries appendiced to Barrie's *Borneo Story*. They

were produced at different times and are sometimes at odds. Nevertheless, taken together, they provide perhaps our most important body of information about Semut III.

2 There is contention about where the Rejang (Rajang) River begins and the Balui (Baluy) River ends. In this book I treat Belaga as the cut-off point: the Rejang River is downstream from Belaga and the Balui River is upstream. The phrase 'upper Rejang River' as used here refers to the stretch of river between the Pelagus Rapids and Belaga.

3 Wren, *Down-Stream Twice*, unpublished manuscript, p. 171; Report, 'Semut III Party Report', Major W.L. Sochon, n.d., p. 2, 38/1/1-67, GB-0033-MAC, Durham University Library; Barrie, *Borneo Story*, unpublished manuscript, MSS1532, AWM, p. 83.

4 Report, 'Semut III Party Report', Major W.L. Sochon, n.d., pp. 1–2, 38/1/1-67, GB-0033-MAC, Durham University Library; 'Project Semut Summary', 11 November 1944, AWM54, 627/4/15 Part 1, AWM; Wren, *Down-Stream Twice*, unpublished manuscript, pp. 89, 116–7. In reality, Semut III personnel operated north of the line described here: as far as the Dulit range, which provided a more natural boundary between Semut II and Semut III than the artificial one set down on paper. As a result Semut II and Semut III operational areas overlapped to some degree, as shown in the map of operational areas at the start of the book.

5 Untitled account, n.d., p. 12, Wallet 22, 3DRL/6502, AWM; Report, 'Semut III Party Report', Major W.L. Sochon, n.d., p. 2, 38/1/1-67, GB-0033-MAC, Durham University Library; Wren, *Down-Stream Twice*, unpublished manuscript, pp. 172–3.

6 Metcalf, *Life of the Longhouse*, pp. 93–4, 128, 133; Pringle, *Rajahs and Rebels*, pp. 130, 327–8; Wren, *Down-Stream Twice*, unpublished manuscript, pp. 143–5.

7 The last Kanowit punitive expedition has often been dated to 1934; Pringle, however, tells us that it most likely occurred in 1935. See Pringle, *Rajahs and Rebels*, p. 245; Edwards and Stevens, *Short Histories*, pp. 152–4.

8 Wren, *Down-Stream Twice*, unpublished manuscript, pp. 90, 146–7.

9 Report, 'Semut III Party Report', Major W.L. Sochon, n.d., p. 1, 38/1/1-67, GB-0033-MAC, Durham University Library; Wren, *Down-Stream Twice*, unpublished manuscript, pp. 10, 117.

10 Wren, *Down-Stream Twice*, unpublished manuscript, pp. 170–1; Barrie, *Borneo Story*, unpublished manuscript, MSS1532, AWM, p. 83.

11 Untitled account, n.d., pp. 12–14, Wallet 22, 3DRL/6502, AWM; Report, 'Semut III Party Report', Major W.L. Sochon, n.d., p. 2, 38/1/1-67, GB-0033-MAC, Durham University Library; Wren, *Down-Stream Twice*, unpublished

manuscript, pp. 174–81; Barrie, *Borneo Story*, unpublished manuscript, MSS1532, AWM, pp. 157–8; author, Long San interviews, August 2018.

12 Untitled account, n.d., p. 13, Wallet 22, 3DRL/6502, AWM; Wren, *Down-Stream Twice*, unpublished manuscript, pp. 179, 181.

13 Untitled account, n.d., pp. 13–14, Wallet 22, 3DRL/6502, AWM; Report, 'Semut III Party Report', Major W.L. Sochon, n.d., p. 2, 38/1/1-67, GB-0033-MAC, Durham University Library; Wren, *Down-Stream Twice*, unpublished manuscript, pp. 179–80; Barrie, *Borneo Story*, unpublished manuscript, MSS1532, AWM, p. 72.

14 Wren, *Down-Stream Twice*, unpublished manuscript, pp. 181–2.

15 Barrie, *Borneo Story*, unpublished manuscript, MSS1532, AWM, p. 72.

16 Due to the mobility of local Dayak populations and the lack of accurate ethnographic maps for the period, it is difficult to be certain about the identity of the Dayak groups in whose longhouses the party stayed. The problem is exacerbated by Sochon's and Barrie's umbrella use of the term 'Kayan' to refer to almost any non-Iban Dayak group; Sochon also labels some groups 'Kalamantan', a term that is no longer considered useful. My guess is that in the Dapoi River area the group stayed mostly with Sebop and Kenyah, and on the Belaga River with a variety of groups. See Rousseau, *Central Borneo*, pp. 324, 326–7; Metcalf, *Life of the Longhouse*, pp. 323–6. I have also drawn on hand-drawn maps of the Belaga and Balui River areas provided by Jérôme Rousseau.

17 'Real firewater!' from Barrie, *Borneo Story*, unpublished manuscript, MSS1532, AWM, p. 71.

18 'In one longhouse' from Barrie, *Borneo Story*, unpublished manuscript, MSS1532, AWM, p. 71.

19 Wren, *Down-Stream Twice*, unpublished manuscript, pp. 178, 180, 183.

20 Author, Long San interviews, August 2018; author, Sungai Asap interviews, May 2015; author, Belaga interviews, May 2015.

21 Report, 'Semut III Party Report', Major W.L. Sochon, n.d., pp. 2–3, 38/1/1-67, GB-0033-MAC, Durham University Library; Barrie, *Borneo Story*, unpublished manuscript, MSS1532, AWM, p. 73.

22 Wren, *Down-Stream Twice*, unpublished manuscript, pp. 175–6.

23 Untitled account, n.d., pp. 14–15, Wallet 22, 3DRL/6502, AWM; Wren, *Down-Stream Twice*, unpublished manuscript, pp. 183–4, 'After the meal' from p. 184.

24 'I would have liked' from Wren, *Down-Stream Twice*, unpublished manuscript, p. 184.

25 Wren, *Down-Stream Twice*, unpublished manuscript, p. 177. Sochon and/or Wren are here confusing Punan and Penan, as many commentators did at the time. The people the party encountered were Penan, not Punan.

26 Wren, *Down-Stream Twice*, unpublished manuscript, pp. 177–8; Barrie, *Borneo Story*, unpublished manuscript, MSS1532, AWM, pp. 72–3.

27 Author, interview with Ving Lawing, Marudi, 11 August 2018; author, interview with Uda Limau and Ganet Nyato, Kuching, 28 February 2015.

28 'On a couple of occasions' from Barrie, *Borneo Story*, unpublished manuscript, MSS1532, AWM, p. 73.

29 Barrie, *Borneo Story*, unpublished manuscript, MSS1532, AWM, p. 71; author, Long San interviews, August 2018.

30 Report, 'Semut III Party Report', Major W.L. Sochon, n.d., p. 3, 38/1/1-67, GB-0033-MAC, Durham University Library; Untitled account, n.d., p. 16, Wallet 22, 3DRL/6502, AWM; 'Babi belang siko" from Reece, *Masa Jepun*, p. 204; Richards, *Iban–English Dictionary*, p 37; author, Sungai Asap interviews, May 2015.

31 Author, Sungai Asap interviews, May 2015; untitled account, n.d., p. 15, Wallet 22, 3DRL/6502, AWM.

32 Report, 'Semut III Party Report', Major W.L. Sochon, n.d., p. 2, 38/1/1-67, GB-0033-MAC, Durham University Library; Untitled account, n.d., p. 14, Wallet 22, 3DRL/6502, AWM.

33 Report, 'Semut III Party Report', Major W.L. Sochon, n.d., p. 2, 38/1/1-67, GB-0033-MAC, Durham University Library; Untitled account, n.d., p. 14, Wallet 22, 3DRL/6502, AWM; Wren, *Down-Stream Twice*, unpublished manuscript, p. 185.

34 Wren, *Down-Stream Twice*, unpublished manuscript, p. 180; Untitled account, n.d., p. 16, Wallet 22, 3DRL/6502, AWM. See also Lim and Tan, *Sarawak Under the Throes*, pp. 50–1.

35 Report, 'Semut III Party Report', Major W.L. Sochon, n.d., p. 2, 38/1/1-67, GB-0033-MAC, Durham University Library; Untitled account, n.d., pp. 14–15, Wallet 22, 3DRL/6502, AWM; Wren, *Down-Stream Twice*, unpublished manuscript, p. 185; author, Sungai Asap interviews, May 2015.

36 Lim and Tan, *Sarawak Under the Throes*, pp. 43–4.

37 Lim, *Chaos at Lubok Belaga*, p. 3.

38 Ibid, pp. 4–8; author, interview with Francesca Sadai, Kanowit, 2 December 2015.

39 Barrie, *Borneo Story*, unpublished manuscript, MSS1532, AWM, pp. 91–2; Report, 'Report on the Safe Areas in the 3rd. Division, Sarawak', Captain John Fisher, 9 August 1944, pp. 5–6, AWM54, 619/2/2, AWM.

40 Lim, *Chaos at Lubok Belaga*, pp. 1–3.

41 Lim and Tan, *Sarawak Under the Throes*, pp. 45–7; Wren, *Down-Stream Twice*, unpublished manuscript, pp. 186–7; Untitled account, n.d., p. 15, Wallet 22, 3DRL/6502, AWM; Lim, *Chaos at Lubok Belaga*, p. 17.

42 Author, interview with Francesca Sadai, Rumah Benjamin Angki Kuboy (Kanowit), 2 December 2015.

43 'Poor specimen' and 'in order to obtain' from Report, 'Report on the Safe Areas in the 3rd. Division, Sarawak', Captain John Fisher, 9 August 1944, p. 8, AWM54, 619/2/2, AWM; 'inclined to "the bottle"' from Barrie, *Borneo Story*, unpublished manuscript, MSS1532, AWM, p. 74; MacDonald, *Borneo People*, p. 224.

44 Author, interview with Jau Lutun and Sait Senyum, Rumah Sekapan Panjang (Belaga), 22 May 2015; author, interview with Itu Lassa, Punan Bah, 10 December 2015.

45 Untitled account, n.d., p. 15, Wallet 22, 3DRL/6502, AWM; Wren, *Down-Stream Twice*, unpublished manuscript, pp. 185–6.

46 Personal communications (email), Jérôme Rousseau, 27 February 2019 and 2 March 2019. Baling's name is often misspelled as Baleng Abun, including in Sochon's accounts.

47 Untitled account, n.d., p. 16, Wallet 22, 3DRL/6502, AWM; Barrie, *Borneo Story*, unpublished manuscript, MSS1532, AWM, pp. 73–4.

48 Author, interview with Igang Igo, Uma Belor (Sungai Asap), 26 May 2015; author, interview with Levo Ugang, Uma Lahanan (Sungai Asap), 26 May 2015.

49 Untitled account, n.d., pp. 16–17, Wallet 22, 3DRL/6502, AWM; Wren, *Down-Stream Twice*, unpublished manuscript, pp. 188–9, 194–5.

50 Untitled account, n.d., p. 17, Wallet 22, 3DRL/6502, AWM; Wren, *Down-Stream Twice*, unpublished manuscript, pp. 188–9.

51 Untitled account, n.d., p. 17, Wallet 22, 3DRL/6502, AWM; Wren, *Down-Stream Twice*, unpublished manuscript, p. 189.

CHAPTER 12: MASSACRE AT PASIR NAI

1 Untitled account, n.d., p. 18, Wallet 22, 3DRL/6502, AWM.

2 *Sarawak Gazette* 1075, p. 182; 'Honours and Awards – Loyal Service Medallion', Semut III Party Report, 38/1/1-67, GB-0033-MAC, Durham University Library. See also Barrie, *Borneo Story*, unpublished manuscript, MSS1532, AWM, p. 74.

3 Untitled account, n.d., p. 18, Wallet 22, 3DRL/6502, AWM; Wren, *Down-Stream Twice*, unpublished manuscript, pp. 191, 194–6, 200.

4 Untitled account, n.d., pp. 18–19, Wallet 22, 3DRL/6502, AWM; Wren, *Down-Stream Twice*, unpublished manuscript, pp. 190–1; Barrie, *Borneo Story*, unpublished manuscript, MSS1532, AWM, p. 76; 'sitting on top of volcano' from Telegram, Semut II, No. SE 33, n.d., A3269, A14/A, NAA.

5 Report, 'Semut III Party Report', Major W.L. Sochon, n.d., p. 3, 38/1/1-67, GB-0033-MAC, Durham University Library; Wren, *Down-Stream Twice*, unpublished manuscript, p. 173; Barrie, *Borneo Story*, unpublished manuscript, MSS1532, AWM, p. 76.

6 MacDonald, *Borneo People*, p. 223.

7 Report, 'Semut III Party Report', Major W.L. Sochon, n.d., p. 3, 38/1/1-67, GB-0033-MAC, Durham University Library; Wren, *Down-Stream Twice*, unpublished manuscript, pp. 193–4; Barrie, *Borneo Story*, unpublished manuscript, MSS1532, AWM, p. 76.

8 Wren, *Down-Stream Twice*, unpublished manuscript, pp. 194–5, 'People who have not lived' from p. 195.

9 Report, 'Semut III Party Report', Major W.L. Sochon, n.d., p. 3, 38/1/1-67, GB-0033-MAC, Durham University Library; Wren, *Down-Stream Twice*, unpublished manuscript, p. 195.

10 Report, 'Semut III Party Report', Major W.L. Sochon, n.d., p. 4, 38/1/1-67, GB-0033-MAC, Durham University Library; Wren, *Down-Stream Twice*, unpublished manuscript, pp. 201–2; Untitled account, n.d., [pp. 20–1], Wallet 22, 3DRL/6502, AWM; Lim and Tan, *Sarawak Under the Throes*, pp. 123–5, 'The distant OOO' from p. 124.

11 Lim and Tan, *Sarawak Under the Throes*, pp. 143–5, 'With native dexterity' from p. 144; Lim, *Chaos at Lubok Belaga*, pp. 31–4; Report, 'Semut III Party Report', Major W.L. Sochon, n.d., p. 4, 38/1/1-67, GB-0033-MAC, Durham University Library; Wren, *Down-Stream Twice*, unpublished manuscript, p. 206; author, interview with Levo Ugang, Uma Lahanan (Sungai Asap), 26 May 2015. Lasah Avun was awarded a British Empire Medal after the war for this and other actions he took on behalf of Semut III. See *Sarawak Gazette* 1067, p. 25.

12 Wren, *Down-Stream Twice*, unpublished manuscript, pp. 180, 204; Untitled account, n.d., p. 14, Wallet 22, 3DRL/6502, AWM; Barrie, *Borneo Story*, unpublished manuscript, MSS1532, AWM, p. 84; Lim and Tan, *Sarawak Under the Throes*, p. 44.

13 Wren, *Down-Stream Twice*, unpublished manuscript, pp. 196–7; *Sarawak Gazette* 1075, p. 183; 'Honours and Awards – Loyal Service Medallion', Semut III Party Report, 38/1/1-67, GB-0033-MAC, Durham University Library.

14 Wren, *Down-Stream Twice*, unpublished manuscript, pp. 194, 200–1, 'It did not make' from p. 201; Untitled account, n.d., [p. 22], Wallet 22, 3DRL/6502, AWM.

15 Untitled account, n.d., [p. 27], Wallet 22, 3DRL/6502, AWM; Wren, *Down-Stream Twice*, unpublished manuscript, pp. 197–200.

16 Author, interviews with Setepan anak Jaweng, Nanga Pila (Upper Rejang River), 7 October 2015, 8 October 2015; *Sarawak Gazette* 1067, p. 25; Reece, *Masa Jepun*, p. 175; author, Nanga Merit (Upper Rejang River) interviews, December 2015.

17 Report, 'Semut III Party Report', Major W.L. Sochon, n.d., p. 4, 38/1/1-67, GB-0033-MAC, Durham University Library; Wren, *Down-Stream Twice*, unpublished manuscript, pp. 203–7, 146–7; Untitled account, n.d., [pp. 20–3], Wallet 22, 3DRL/6502, AWM; Barrie, *Borneo Story*, unpublished manuscript, MSS1532, AWM, pp. 76–7; author, interview with Agas anak Drahman, Nanga Merit (Upper Rejang River), 12 December 2015; author, Nanga Pila (Upper Rejang River) interviews, December 2015.

18 'Noisy, anarchic democracy' from Pringle, *Rajahs and Rebels*, p. 328.

19 'Unpredictable' and 'not necessarily to be counted upon' from Wren, *Down-Stream Twice*, unpublished manuscript, p. 147.

20 See e.g., MacDonald, *Borneo People*, p. 222; 'The Official History of the Operations and Administration of Special Operations – Australia', Vol. 2, Part III, p. 69, A3269, O8/A, NAA.

21 'Only a stupid man' from personal communication, Akei' Budi, Gerai, 7 July 1986.

22 'Then there would be' and 'attack bravely' both from 'Semut II – Sarawak, Borneo', W.S. Eadie, 4 April 1987, p. 18, 'Accounts', Docs. 16752, IWM.

23 Untitled account, n.d., [p. 22], Wallet 22, 3DRL/6502, AWM.

24 Report, 'Semut III Party Report', Major W.L. Sochon, n.d., p. 4, 38/1/1-67, GB-0033-MAC, Durham University Library; Wren, *Down-Stream Twice*, unpublished manuscript, p. 203; Untitled account, n.d., [p. 22], Wallet 22, 3DRL/6502, AWM.

25 Report, 'Semut III Party Report', Major W.L. Sochon, n.d., p. 5, 38/1/1-67, GB-0033-MAC, Durham University Library; Wren, *Down-Stream Twice*, unpublished manuscript, p. 207; Untitled account, n.d., [p. 23], Wallet 22, 3DRL/6502, AWM.

26 Wren, *Down-Stream Twice*, unpublished manuscript, pp. 210–1; Untitled account, n.d., [pp. 23–4], Wallet 22, 3DRL/6502, AWM.

27 Wren, *Down-Stream Twice*, unpublished manuscript, pp. 211–2, 'Suddenly the first Dyak' from p. 211; Untitled account, n.d., [pp. 24–5], Wallet 22, 3DRL/6502, AWM; Report, 'Semut III Party Report', Major W.L. Sochon, n.d., p. 5, 38/1/1-67, GB-0033-MAC, Durham University Library; Barrie, *Borneo Story*, unpublished manuscript, MSS1532, AWM, p. 77; author, interviews with Setepan anak Jaweng, Nanga Pila (Upper Rejang River), 7 October 2015, 8 October 2015.

28 My account here of events leading up to the Pasir Nai massacre is based on later
    descriptions by Sochon (Wren, *Down-Stream Twice*, unpublished manuscript,
    pp. 210–1; Untitled account, n.d., [pp. 22–5], Wallet 22, 3DRL/6502, AWM),
    and differs in certain respects from the earlier accounts found in his official report
    (Report, 'Semut III Party Report', Major W.L. Sochon, n.d., pp. 4–5, 38/1/1-67,
    GB-0033-MAC, Durham University Library) and, following that, SOA's official
    history ('The Official History of the Operations and Administration of Special
    Operations – Australia', Vol. 2, Part III, p. 52, A3269, O8/A, NAA). The later
    accounts accord more closely with those provided by locals; it seems that Sochon
    slightly doctored the account contained in the official report.

29 Report, 'Semut III Party Report', Major W.L. Sochon, n.d., p. 5, 38/1/1-67,
    GB-0033-MAC, Durham University Library; Wren, *Down-Stream Twice*,
    unpublished manuscript, pp. 213–4; Untitled account, n.d., [p. 24], Wallet 22,
    3DRL/6502, AWM; Barrie, *Borneo Story*, unpublished manuscript, MSS1532,
    AWM, p. 77; Reece, *Masa Jepun*, pp. 204–5; Lim, *Chaos at Lubok Belaga*,
    pp. 48–52; MacDonald, *Borneo People*, p. 101; Bob Reece, interview with Garai
    anak Siba', Nanga Benin, January 1994; Bob Reece, interview with Jeba anak
    Undit, Nanga Sejunggur, January 1994; author, interviews with Setepan
    anak Jaweng, Nanga Pila (Upper Rejang River), 7 October 2015, 8 October 2015.

30 Fieldnotes of Derek Freeman, Tun Jugah Foundation, Kuching.

31 'At Pasir Nai we killed' from Bob Reece, interview with Garai anak Siba',
    Nanga Benin, January 1994. There is consistency across most accounts
    that five Japanese were killed, and most record the total number of deaths
    as twenty-nine. See Wren, *Down-Stream Twice*, unpublished manuscript,
    p. 212; Untitled account, n.d., [p. 24], Wallet 22, 3DRL/6502, AWM; Reece,
    Masa Jepun, p. 205. Barrie and Sochon (in his diary) both give the total num-
    ber of deaths as twenty-four: five Japanese and nineteen Chinese. However,
    these overlook the Sikh police also killed. See Barrie, *Borneo Story*, unpub-
    lished manuscript, MSS1532, AWM, p. 77; Bill Sochon, 'Semut Diary – 1945',
    in Barrie, *Borneo Story*, unpublished manuscript, MSS1532, AWM, p. 159.

    There are important variations between Sochon's different accounts of the
    massacre. In his official report he gives the impression that most of those killed
    were Japanese, with 'a number' of Chinese also having their heads taken. In
    a later account he asserts that all those killed were Japanese with the excep-
    tion of several Sikhs; this version was later replicated in Courtney's account.
    See Report, 'Semut III Party Report', Major W.L. Sochon, n.d., p. 5, 38/1/1-
    67, GB-0033-MAC, Durham University Library; Wren, *Down-Stream Twice*,
    unpublished manuscript, p. 212; Courtney, *Silent Feet*, p. 96; also Reece, *Masa
    Jepun*, p. 216, Footnote 6.

32 Bob Reece, interview with Jeba anak Undit, Nanga Sejunggur, January 1994.

33 Lim and Tan, *Sarawak Under the Throes*, p. 149.

34 Reece, *Masa Jepun*, p. 180.

35 'Mainly inspired by' from 'The Official History of the Operations and Administration of Special Operations – Australia', Vol. 2, Part III, p. 69, A3269, O8/A, NAA; 'lust for taking heads' from Wren, *Down-Stream Twice*, unpublished manuscript, p. 147; Report, '20 Aust Inf Bde – Report on Operation Oboe Six', 16 August 1945, p. 23, AWM357, 7, AWM.

36 'They all wanted heads' from author, interview with Jack Tredrea, Adelaide, 16 September 2014; 'Like an aphrodisiac' from Walpole, *My War*, p. 205; 'The promise of more heads' from Walpole, *My War*, p. 215. See Davison and Sutlive, 'The children of *Nising*', in Sutlive (ed.), *Female and Male in Borneo*, pp. 165–8.

37 'It was just beginning' from Walpole, *My War*, p. 153. See also Griffiths-Marsh: Diary, pp. 73–4, PR85/036, AWM.

38 Untitled account, n.d., [p. 20], Wallet 22, 3DRL/6502, AWM.

39 Pringle, *Rajahs and Rebels*; Edwards and Stevens, *Short Histories*, pp. 153–4.

40 Reece, *Masa Jepun*, p. 212; Reece, *Name of Brooke*, p. 149; Walpole, *My War*, p. 130; author, interview with Agas anak Drahman, Nanga Merit (Upper Rejang River), 12 December 2015.

41 Wren, *Down-Stream Twice*, unpublished manuscript, p. 214.

42 Some accounts state that Sochon and Barrie participated in these headhunting rituals at Sandai's longhouse. This is incorrect: Sandai's longhouse lay further downriver, at Nanga Merit. See Barrie, *Borneo Story*, unpublished manuscript, MSS1532, AWM, p. 83; Reece, *Masa Jepun*, p. 205.

43 Author, Nanga Pila (Upper Rejang River) interviews, December 2015.

44 See Freeman, *Report on the Iban*, p. 8; Winzeler, *Architecture of Life and Death*, p. 51.

45 Wren, *Down-Stream Twice*, unpublished manuscript, pp. 216–7; Untitled account, n.d., [p. 25], Wallet 22, 3DRL/6502, AWM; Barrie, *Borneo Story*, unpublished manuscript, MSS1532, AWM, p. 78.

46 Wren, *Down-Stream Twice*, unpublished manuscript, pp. 217–8.

47 Wren, *Down-Stream Twice*, unpublished manuscript, p. 218; see also untitled account, n.d., [p. 25], Wallet 22, 3DRL/6502, AWM.

48 Wren, *Down-Stream Twice*, unpublished manuscript, pp. 219–20, 'I wondered whether' from p. 219; Untitled account, n.d., [pp. 25–6], Wallet 22, 3DRL/6502, AWM.

49 Barrie, *Borneo Story*, unpublished manuscript, MSS1532, AWM, pp. 78–9; Wren, *Down-Stream Twice*, unpublished manuscript, pp. 222–3; Untitled account, n.d., [p. 27], Wallet 22, 3DRL/6502, AWM.

50 Wren, *Down-Stream Twice*, unpublished manuscript, p. 226.

51 Different accounts give different dates for the arrival of the Catalina. Barrie, for instance, says 22 June and tells us that others say 23 June (Barrie, *Borneo Story*, unpublished manuscript, MSS1532, AWM, p. 83). However, both Sochon's official report and the SOA history give the date as 21 June and this is consistent with the known dates of events that followed. See Report, 'Semut III Party Report', Major W.L. Sochon, n.d., p. 5, 38/1/1-67, GB-0033-MAC, Durham University Library; 'The Official History of the Operations and Administration of Special Operations – Australia', Vol. 2, Part III, p. 53, A3269, O8/A, NAA.

52 Wren, *Down-Stream Twice*, unpublished manuscript, pp. 223–4; Untitled account, n.d., [p. 27], Wallet 22, 3DRL/6502, AWM.

53 'Between the thwarts' from Wren, *Down-Stream Twice*, unpublished manuscript, p. 224–5.

CHAPTER 13: BATTLE FOR KAPIT

1 Vinson Sutlive, interview with Tedong anak Barieng, Kapit, 30 June 1988.

2 Ibid; author, Nanga Pila (Upper Rejang River) interviews, December 2015.

3 Vinson Sutlive, interview with Tedong anak Barieng, Kapit, 30 June 1988; Ritchie, *Life Story of Temenggong Koh*, p. 128; Sutlive, *Tun Jugah of Sarawak*, pp. 110–11. Flight Lieutenant Reid, commander of the Catalina that brought Courtney to Nanga Pila on 21 June, saw around a dozen Dayak canoes, each containing many occupants, on the river close to Kapit that afternoon. See Memo, ALO to Group 'A', 25 June 1945, A3269, A15/A, NAA.

4 Report, 'Semut III Party Report', Major W.L. Sochon, n.d., pp. 5–6, 38/1/1-67, GB-0033-MAC, Durham University Library; Reece, *Masa Jepun*, p. 207. There are many conflicting stories, including conflicting dates, concerning what happened in Kapit, sometimes within a single account. I have produced the narrative here after sifting through all existing accounts – including those from Iban and Chinese locals – and other related materials.

5 Wren, *Down-Stream Twice*, unpublished manuscript, p. 225; Untitled account, n.d., [p. 27], Wallet 22, 3DRL/6502, AWM; Barrie, *Borneo Story*, unpublished manuscript, MSS1532, AWM, p. 83.

6 Wren, *Down-Stream Twice*, unpublished manuscript, p. 225; Report, 'Semut III Party Report', Major W.L. Sochon, n.d., p. 5, 38/1/1-67, GB-0033-MAC, Durham University Library.

7 Letter, David [Kearney] to Brad [Ross Bradbury], 5 September 1997, Truscott Papers.

8 Report, 'Semut III Party Report', Major W.L. Sochon, n.d., p. 5, 38/1/1-67, GB-0033-MAC, Durham University Library; Wren, *Down-Stream Twice*,

unpublished manuscript, pp. 226–7; Untitled account, n.d., [p. 27], Wallet 22, 3DRL/6502, AWM.

9 MacDonald, *Borneo People*, p. 84; Yao, 'Those momentous days in Kapit', in *Sarawak Gazette* 1166, pp. 92–4; Sutlive, *Tun Jugah*, p. 109.

10 Vinson Sutlive, interview with Tedong anak Barieng, Kapit, 30 June 1988.

11 Ibid, 'I asked the two of them' from this source; Sutlive, *Tun Jugah*, p. 111; Reece, *Masa Jepun*, pp. 207–10; Yao, 'Those momentous days in Kapit', in *Sarawak Gazette* 1166; author, interviews with Binit anak Langai, Nanga Pila (Upper Rejang River), 7 December 2015, 8 December 2015; author, interview with Agas anak Drahman, Nanga Merit (Upper Rejang River), 12 December 2015.

12 Vinson Sutlive, interview with Tedong anak Barieng, Kapit, 30 June 1988.

13 Sutlive, *Tun Jugah*, p. 112.

14 'I thought, Oh, God' from Sutlive, *Tun Jugah*, pp. 112–3.

15 Reece, *Masa Jepun*, p. 210; Yao, 'Those momentous days in Kapit', in *Sarawak Gazette* 1166, p. 94; 'And then the prison door' from Sutlive, *Tun Jugah*, p. 113; Vinson Sutlive, interview with Harry Buxton, Kuching, 12 July 1988.

16 'In a wild campaign of looting' from Wren, *Down-Stream Twice*, unpublished manuscript, p. 228; Report, 'Semut III Party Report', Major W.L. Sochon, n.d., p. 5, 38/1/1-67, GB-0033-MAC, Durham University Library; Barrie, *Borneo Story*, unpublished manuscript, MSS1532, AWM, pp. 84–5.

17 Yao, 'Those momentous days in Kapit', in *Sarawak Gazette* 1166, p. 95; Lim and Tan, *Sarawak Under the Throes*, pp. 24–5; Untitled account, n.d., [p. 28], Wallet 22, 3DRL/6502, AWM; Wren, *Down-Stream Twice*, unpublished manuscript, p. 228.

18 Vinson Sutlive, interview with Tedong anak Barieng, Kapit, 30 June 1988, 'True, it's really true' from this source; Yao, 'Those momentous days in Kapit', in *Sarawak Gazette* 1166, p. 95; Sutlive, *Tun Jugah*, p. 113; Ritchie, *Life Story of Temenggong Koh*, pp. 129–30; Reece, *Masa Jepun*, pp. 207, 210.

19 Bourke, *Intimate History*, pp. 25–31, 'carnivalesque spirit' from p. 25; Larson, *Severed*, pp. 54ff.

20 Personal communication (telephone), Michael Heppell, 22 November 2018; personal communication (email), Clifford Sather, 26 June 2019, 27 June 2019; Sutlive, *Tun Jugah*, p. 113.

21 Barrie, *Borneo Story*, unpublished manuscript, MSS1532, AWM, pp. 84–5; Wren, *Down-Stream Twice*, unpublished manuscript, pp. 228–9; Yao, 'Those momentous days in Kapit', in *Sarawak Gazette* 1166, p. 95; Untitled account, n.d., [p. 28], Wallet 22, 3DRL/6502, AWM.

22 Edwards and Stevens, *Short Histories*, pp. 155–7; Lim and Tan, *Sarawak Under the Throes*, pp. 261–2; Report, 'Report by H.P.K. Jacks', H.P.K. Jacks, 27 March 1942, FCO 141/12402, NAUK.

23 Yao, 'Those momentous days in Kapit', in *Sarawak Gazette* 1166, p. 96; Report, 'Semut III Party Report', Major W.L. Sochon, n.d., p. 6, 38/1/1-67, GB-0033-MAC, Durham University Library; Wren, *Down-Stream Twice*, unpublished manuscript, p. 229.

24 Wren, *Down-Stream Twice*, unpublished manuscript, p. 229; Barrie, *Borneo Story*, unpublished manuscript, MSS1532, AWM, p. 85; Untitled account, n.d., [p. 28], Wallet 22, 3DRL/6502, AWM.

25 Wren, *Down-Stream Twice*, unpublished manuscript, pp. 229–30; Barrie, *Borneo Story*, unpublished manuscript, MSS1532, AWM, pp. 85–6; Untitled account, n.d., [p. 28], Wallet 22, 3DRL/6502, AWM; Bill Sochon, 'Semut Diary – 1945', in Barrie, *Borneo Story*, unpublished manuscript, MSS1532, AWM, p. 159.

26 'Initially I couldn't' from Barrie, *Borneo Story*, unpublished manuscript, MSS1532, AWM, p. 86; Wren, *Down-Stream Twice*, unpublished manuscript, pp. 230–1; Untitled account, n.d., [p. 28], Wallet 22, 3DRL/6502, AWM.

27 Barrie, *Borneo Story*, unpublished manuscript, MSS1532, AWM, p. 86; Report, 'Semut III Party Report', Major W.L. Sochon, n.d., p. 6, 38/1/1-67, GB-0033-MAC, Durham University Library; Wren, *Down-Stream Twice*, unpublished manuscript, pp. 230–1; Untitled account, n.d., [p. 28], Wallet 22, 3DRL/6502, AWM; Reece, *Masa Jepun*, p. 210.

28 'Paddled like fury' from Barrie, *Borneo Story*, unpublished manuscript, MSS1532, AWM, p. 86.

29 Report, 'Semut III Party Report', Major W.L. Sochon, n.d., p. 6, 38/1/1-67, GB-0033-MAC, Durham University Library; Barrie, *Borneo Story*, unpublished manuscript, MSS1532, AWM, pp. 86–7; Wren, *Down-Stream Twice*, unpublished manuscript, p. 231; Untitled account, n.d., [p. 28], Wallet 22, 3DRL/6502, AWM; Yao, 'Those momentous days in Kapit', in *Sarawak Gazette* 1166, p. 96.

30 Report, 'Semut III Party Report', Major W.L. Sochon, n.d., p. 6, 38/1/1-67, GB-0033-MAC, Durham University Library; Barrie, *Borneo Story*, unpublished manuscript, MSS1532, AWM, p. 86; Untitled account, n.d., [p. 27], Wallet 22, 3DRL/6502, AWM; Wren, *Down-Stream Twice*, unpublished manuscript, p. 231.

31 'Apart from his distinguished' from MacDonald, *Borneo People*, p. 85; Wren, *Down-Stream Twice*, unpublished manuscript, p. 239; Tan, *William Tan of Sarawak*, p. 70.

32 Report, 'Report on the Safe Areas in the 3rd. Division, Sarawak', Captain John Fisher, 9 August 1944, p. 3, AWM54, 619/2/2, AWM.

33 MacDonald, *Borneo People*, p. 128.

34 Koh, 'Temenggong Koh: Reminiscences', in *Borneo Research Bulletin* 25, pp. 162–3.

35 *Sarawak Gazette* 1075, p. 182.

36 'As a serious embarrassment' from Wren, *Down-Stream Twice*, unpublished manuscript, p. 228; 'Not so long ago' from Koh, 'Temenggong Koh: Reminiscences', in *Borneo Research Bulletin* 25, pp. 162–3; see also Ooi, *Rising Sun Over Borneo*, pp. 33–4.

37 Koh, 'Temenggong Koh: Reminiscences', in *Borneo Research Bulletin* 25, p. 163.

38 Report, 'Semut III Party Report', Major W.L. Sochon, n.d., p. 6, 38/1/1-67, GB-0033-MAC, Durham University Library; Wren, *Down-Stream Twice*, unpublished manuscript, pp. 232–3.

39 Author, interviews with Binit anak Langai, Nanga Pila (Upper Rejang River), 7 December 2015, 8 December 2015; author, interview with Agas anak Drahman, Nanga Merit (Upper Rejang River), 12 December 2015.

40 Report, 'Semut III Party Report', Major W.L. Sochon, n.d., p. 6, 38/1/1-67, GB-0033-MAC, Durham University Library; Wren, *Down-Stream Twice*, unpublished manuscript, pp. 232–3.

41 Report, 'Semut III Party Report', Major W.L. Sochon, n.d., p. 6, 38/1/1-67, GB-0033-MAC, Durham University Library; Barrie, *Borneo Story*, unpublished manuscript, MSS1532, AWM, pp. 87–9; Wren, *Down-Stream Twice*, unpublished manuscript, p. 234.

42 Report, 'Semut III Party Report', Major W.L. Sochon, n.d., pp. 6–7, 38/1/1-67, GB-0033-MAC, Durham University Library; author, interviews with Binit anak Langai, Nanga Pila (Upper Rejang River), 7 December 2015, 8 December 2015.

43 Telegram, S.F., No. CM 66, n.d., A3269, A15/A, NAA; 'Harrisson left immediately' from Wren, *Down-Stream Twice*, unpublished manuscript, p. 227; Untitled account, n.d., [p. 27], Wallet 22, 3DRL/6502, AWM; Harrisson, *World Within*, p. 273. In his two memoirs referenced above, Sochon dates the visit at around 26 June; however, the telegram referenced above makes clear it took place on 30 June.

44 Report, 'Semut III Party Report', Major W.L. Sochon, n.d., pp. 6–7, 38/1/1-67, GB-0033-MAC, Durham University Library; Wren, *Down-Stream Twice*, unpublished manuscript, p. 235; Untitled account, n.d., [p. 29], Wallet 22, 3DRL/6502, AWM; Reece, *Masa Jepun*, p. 210.

45 Report, 'Semut III Party Report', Major W.L. Sochon, n.d., p. 7, 38/1/1-67, GB-0033-MAC, Durham University Library; Wren, *Down-Stream Twice*, unpublished manuscript, pp. 235–6.

46 Report, 'Semut III Party Report', Major W.L. Sochon, n.d., p. 7, 38/1/1-67, GB-0033-MAC, Durham University Library; Wren, *Down-Stream Twice*,

unpublished manuscript, p. 236; Untitled account, n.d., [p. 29], Wallet 22, 3DRL/6502, AWM; author, interview with Agas anak Drahman, Nanga Merit (Upper Rejang River), 12 December 2015.

CHAPTER 14: DOWNRIVER TO SONG

1   Report, 'Semut III Party Report', Major W.L. Sochon, n.d., p. 6, 38/1/1-67, GB-0033-MAC, Durham University Library; Reece, *Masa Jepun*, p. 211; Barrie, *Borneo Story*, unpublished manuscript, MSS1532, AWM, p. 93; Wren, *Down-Stream Twice*, unpublished manuscript, p. 239; Untitled account, n.d., [p. 28], Wallet 22, 3DRL/6502, AWM.

2   Reece, *Masa Jepun*, p. 212; Reece, *Name of Brooke*, p. 149.

3   Walpole, *My War*, pp. 132–3. Walpole's account, written almost 60 years later, is prone to exaggerate his own role in the operation and sometimes muddles the order in which events occurred. Nevertheless, handled carefully, it is an invaluable source of information about Semut III's activities along the middle and lower Rejang River

4   'A quantum jump in communications' from Barrie, *Borneo Story*, unpublished manuscript, MSS1532, AWM, p. 83.

5   'Guerrillas', Semut III Party Report, 38/1/1-67, GB-0033-MAC, Durham University Library; Walpole, *My War*, pp.138, 141, 'like dinner at the Waldorf' from p. 141.

6   Report, 'Semut III Party Report', Major W.L. Sochon, n.d., p. 7, 38/1/1-67, GB-0033-MAC, Durham University Library; Wren, *Down-Stream Twice*, unpublished manuscript, pp. 236–7; Untitled account, n.d., [p. 29], Wallet 22, 3DRL/6502, AWM.

7   Report, 'Semut III Party Report', Major W.L. Sochon, n.d., pp. 7–8, 38/1/1-67, GB-0033-MAC, Durham University Library; Wren, *Down-Stream Twice*, unpublished manuscript, p. 237; Untitled account, n.d., [p. 29], Wallet 22, 3DRL/6502, AWM.

8   Report, 'Semut III Party Report', Major W.L. Sochon, n.d., p. 8, 38/1/1-67, GB-0033-MAC, Durham University Library; 'The Japs must have had' from Wren, *Down-Stream Twice*, unpublished manuscript, pp. 242–3.

9   Report, 'Semut III Party Report', Major W.L. Sochon, n.d., p. 8, 38/1/1-67, GB-0033-MAC, Durham University Library; Edwards and Stevens, *Short Histories*, pp. 120–36; Pringle, *Rajahs and Rebels*, pp. 132, 216, 254; Report, 'Report on the Safe Areas in the 3rd. Division, Sarawak', Captain John Fisher, 9 August 1944, p. 4, AWM54, 619/2/2, AWM.

10 Report, 'Operation Semut III – Intelligence Report No. 7', Services Reconnaissance Department, 25 July 1945, AWM54, 619/7/69, AWM; Report, 'Semut III Party

Report', Major W.L. Sochon, n.d., pp. 8–9, 38/1/1-67, GB-0033-MAC, Durham University Library; Wren, *Down-Stream Twice*, unpublished manuscript, pp. 237–8; Untitled account, n.d., [p. 29], Wallet 22, 3DRL/6502, AWM.

11   Ham, *Sandakan*, pp. 328–9, emphasis in original.

12   Ham, *Sandakan*, Ch. 28; Powell, *War by Stealth*, pp. 282–3.

13   Cipher Telegram, L.H.Q. Melbourne to C. in C. India, 22 June 1945, WO 208/1055, NAUK; 'Report on Investigations – Aust and Allied Prisoners of War – 9 Aust Div Area', n.d., WO 361/1761, NAUK, p. 6; Wren, *Down-Stream Twice*, unpublished manuscript, pp. 238–9; Reece, *Masa Jepun*, p. 188; Courtney, *Silent Feet*, pp. 102–3.

14   Report, 'Semut III Party Report', Major W.L. Sochon, n.d., p. 8, 38/1/1-67, GB-0033-MAC, Durham University Library; Wren, *Down-Stream Twice*, unpublished manuscript, p. 237.

15   'Honours and Awards – Loyal Service Medallion', Semut III Party Report, 38/1/1-67, GB-0033-MAC, Durham University Library; Wren, *Down-Stream Twice*, unpublished manuscript, pp. 239–40; Untitled account, n.d., [p. 29], Wallet 22, 3DRL/6502, AWM; Sutlive, *Tun Jugah*, pp. 113–4; Reece, *Masa Jepun*, p. 211; Barrie, *Borneo Story*, unpublished manuscript, MSS1532, AWM, pp. 92–3. In his later narratives – the Wren account and the manuscript in the AWM – Sochon provides a different version of Koh's escape from the Japanese. According to this later version he (Sochon) caused the Japanese to release Koh by sending them a note to the effect that Koh needed to return home as his wife and other village members were ill. This story is repeated by both Barrie and Reece. Apart from its intrinsic implausibility, it is contradicted by local accounts as well as Sochon's own report from the time, according to which Koh 'evaded' the Japanese much earlier (with no mention of any assistance from Sochon) and made his own way to the Baleh River, before Sochon had reached Kapit.

16   '[He] had kept his intelligent eyes' from Wren, *Down-Stream Twice*, unpublished manuscript, p. 240.

17   Wren, *Down-Stream Twice*, unpublished manuscript, pp. 240–1; Barrie, *Borneo Story*, unpublished manuscript, MSS1532, AWM, pp. 92–3, 'On the river' from p. 93; Reece, *Masa Jepun*, p. 211.

18   Report, 'Semut III Party Report', Major W.L. Sochon, n.d., p. 8, 38/1/1-67, GB-0033-MAC, Durham University Library; Wren, *Down-Stream Twice*, unpublished manuscript, p. 242; Courtney, *Silent Feet*, p. 102.

19   'Crocodiles barking' from Walpole, *My War*, p. 135.

20   'Jungle-track-that-wasn't' from Walpole, *My War*, p. 135.

21   Report, 'Operation Semut III – Intelligence Report No. 7', Services Reconnaissance Department, 25 July 1945, AWM54, 619/7/69, AWM; Lim and

Tan, *Sarawak Under the Throes*, pp. 17–18; author, interview with Uba anak Ungka and Jubin anak Ugap, Song, 4 December 2015.

22 'As if they were there to stay' from Walpole, *My War*, p. 135; Report, 'Operation Semut III – Intelligence Report No. 7', Services Reconnaissance Department, 25 July 1945, AWM54, 619/7/69, AWM; Lim and Tan, *Sarawak Under the Throes*, pp. 17–18.

23 Walpole, *My War*, pp. 135–6; Lim and Tan, *Sarawak Under the Throes*, p. 18; author, interview with Uba anak Ungka and Jubin anak Ugap, Song, 4 December 2015.

24 Report, 'Semut III Party Report', Major W.L. Sochon, n.d., p. 8, 38/1/1-67, GB-0033-MAC, Durham University Library; Wren, *Down-Stream Twice*, unpublished manuscript, p. 242.

25 Report, 'Semut III Party Report', Major W.L. Sochon, n.d., p. 8, 38/1/1-67, GB-0033-MAC, Durham University Library; 'Honours and Awards – Loyal Service Medallion', Semut III Party Report, 38/1/1-67, GB-0033-MAC, Durham University Library; Wren, *Down-Stream Twice*, unpublished manuscript, p. 244.

26 Report, 'Semut III Party Report', Major W.L. Sochon, n.d., p. 8, 38/1/1-67, GB-0033-MAC, Durham University Library; Walpole, *My War*, pp. 137–8, 'niggle [the Japanese]' from p. 142.

27 'Audacious, dashing and aggressive' from Barrie, *Borneo Story*, unpublished manuscript, MSS1532, AWM, p. 84; Letter, David Kearney to Jim Truscott, 28 December 1997, Truscott Papers, 'I decided that Malay' from this source; Truscott, *Voices from Borneo*, unpublished manuscript, p. 28. Walpole gives the impression throughout *My War* that he was the only member of the patrol who spoke Malay. This is incorrect.

28 Barrie, *Borneo Story*, unpublished manuscript, MSS1532, AWM, p. 84; Walpole, *My War*.

29 Waddy, 'An Adventure in Sarawak – Borneo', p. 23, in Waddy, *On Operations with Z Special Unit – WWII*, unpublished manuscript; 'bravery, loyalty and worth' from 'Honours and Awards – Loyal Service Medallion', Semut III Party Report, 38/1/1-67, GB-0033-MAC, Durham University Library; *Sarawak Gazette* 1067, p. 25. Key information about the activities of Kearney's patrol, including Belaja, in the middle Rejang, was obtained from several conversations with two of its Iban members on my first visit to Kapit in August 1990, long before I had heard of Operation Semut. It was only in 2015, on reading through my notes of these conversations, that I discovered they related to Semut III. Because the conversations were informal – and I did not record the full names of my interlocutors – I have not included them in the

list of interviews contained in the Bibliography and have referenced them as 'personal communications'.

30 Walpole, *My War*, pp. 138, 141, 'this was first class' from p. 164.

31 Report, 'Semut III Party Report', Major W.L. Sochon, n.d., p. 8, 38/1/1-67, GB-0033-MAC, Durham University Library; Walpole, *My War*, pp. 138–9, 'Suddenly we heard' from p. 139.

32 Walpole, *My War*, pp. 138–9, 'The value of having' from p. 138; Letter, David Kearney to Jim Truscott, 28 December 1997, Truscott Papers; author, interviews with Binit anak Langai, Nanga Pila (Upper Rejang River), 7 December 2015, 8 December 2015.

33 Personal communication, two unknown Iban men, Kapit bazaar, August 1990.

34 Walpole, *My War*, pp. 139–40, 'Maybe they were naturally cheerful' from p. 140; personal communication, two unknown Iban men, Kapit bazaar, August 1990.

35 '[A]s we turned' from Walpole, *My War*, p. 140.

36 'What could I say?' from Walpole, *My War*, p. 140.

37 Walpole, *My War*, pp. 141, 153.

38 Walpole, *My War*, pp. 142–3; personal communication, two unknown Iban men, Kapit bazaar, August 1990.

39 'The first lot' from Walpole, *My War*, p. 143; Courtney, *Silent Feet*, p. 102.

40 Personal communication, two unknown Iban men, Kapit bazaar, August 1990.

41 Ibid; 'like they walked this way' from Walpole, *My War*, p. 143.

42 Walpole, *My War*, pp. 143–4.

43 Wren, *Down-Stream Twice*, unpublished manuscript, p. 245; Letter, David Kearney to Jim Truscott, 28 December 1997, Truscott Papers.

44 Wren, *Down-Stream Twice*, unpublished manuscript, p. 245.

45 'Motor boat' from Walpole, *My War*, p. 146; Wren, *Down-Stream Twice*, unpublished manuscript, p. 245.

46 Walpole, *My War*, pp. 146–7; Wren, *Down-Stream Twice*, unpublished manuscript, p. 245; personal communication, two unknown Iban men, Kapit bazaar, August 1990.

47 Report, 'Semut III Party Report', Major W.L. Sochon, n.d., pp. 8–9, 38/1/1-67, GB-0033-MAC, Durham University Library; Walpole, *My War*, pp. 147, 193; Wren, *Down-Stream Twice*, unpublished manuscript, pp. 245–6; author, personal communication, two unknown Iban men, Kapit bazaar, August 1990. Walpole (p. 193) places the burning of the hand during another later action. However, he is mistaken. There was no later action of the type he describes – he has confused it with the ambush outside Song described here. Conversations with Ibans in Kapit in 1990 made clear that the hand was burnt during this Song action.

48 Walpole, *My War*, pp. 147–8, 'It was a harrowing business' from p. 148.

49 Ibid.

50 Walpole, *My War*, p. 149; Courtney, *Silent Feet*, p. 102; personal communication, two unknown Iban men, Kapit bazaar, August 1990.

51 Walpole, *My War*, pp. 150–1, 'Sometimes it sounded' from p. 151.

52 'What a mess they made' from Walpole, *My War*, p. 151; Report, 'Semut III Party Report', Major W.L. Sochon, n.d., pp. 8–9, 38/1/1-67, GB-0033-MAC, Durham University Library.

53 Walpole, *My War*, pp. 152–3, 'Sensing something behind' from p. 152; Courtney, *Silent Feet*, p. 102.

54 Walpole, *My War*, p. 154; Wren, *Down-Stream Twice*, unpublished manuscript, p. 246; Courtney, *Silent Feet*, p. 102; Report, 'Semut III Party Report', Major W.L. Sochon, n.d., pp. 8–9, 38/1/1-67, GB-0033-MAC, Durham University Library; personal communication, two unknown Iban men, Kapit bazaar, August 1990.

CHAPTER 15: CHAOS IN KANOWIT

1 Report, 'Semut III Party Report', Major W.L. Sochon, n.d., pp. 8–9, 38/1/1-67, GB-0033-MAC, Durham University Library; Wren, *Down-Stream Twice*, unpublished manuscript, pp. 248–50, 'The general is most anxious' from p. 248; Ham, *Sandakan*, pp. 363, 370.

2 Wren, *Down-Stream Twice*, unpublished manuscript, pp. 248–9, 261; 'savage and wholesale reprisals' from Harrisson, *World Within*, p. 298.

3 Wren, *Down-Stream Twice*, unpublished manuscript, pp. 249, 253–4, 259–60.

4 Wren, *Down-Stream Twice*, unpublished manuscript, p. 243.

5 Report, 'Semut III Party Report', Major W.L. Sochon, n.d., pp. 7–8, 38/1/1-67, GB-0033-MAC, Durham University Library; Wren, *Down-Stream Twice*, unpublished manuscript, p. 259; Barrie, *Borneo Story*, unpublished manuscript, MSS1532, AWM, p. 94; author, Sungai Asap interviews, May 2015.

6 Report, 'Semut III Party Report', Major W.L. Sochon, n.d., pp. 7–8, 38/1/1-67, GB-0033-MAC, Durham University Library; Wren, *Down-Stream Twice*, unpublished manuscript, p. 259; Lim and Tan, *Sarawak Under the Throes*, pp. 121–2, 149; author, Sungai Asap interviews, May 2015.

7 Report, 'Semut III Party Report', Major W.L. Sochon, n.d., p. 9, 38/1/1-67, GB-0033-MAC, Durham University Library; Wren, *Down-Stream Twice*, unpublished manuscript, pp. 250–1; Lim and Tan, *Sarawak Under the Throes*, pp. 121–2, 149; Bill Sochon, 'Semut Diary – 1945', in Barrie, *Borneo Story*, unpublished manuscript, MSS1532, AWM, p. 161.

8 Wren, *Down-Stream Twice*, unpublished manuscript, pp. 250–2; Barrie, *Borneo Story*, unpublished manuscript, MSS1532, AWM, pp. 94, 115;

personal communication (email), Annabel Venning, 27 January 2019; Venning, *To War with the Walkers*, pp. 33–4, 249–50; Reece, *Masa Jepun*, p. 186.

9   Report, 'Semut III Party Report', Major W.L. Sochon, n.d., p. 9, 38/1/1-67, GB-0033-MAC, Durham University Library; Wren, *Down-Stream Twice*, unpublished manuscript, p. 258; Bill Sochon, 'Semut Diary – 1945', in Barrie, *Borneo Story*, unpublished manuscript, MSS1532, AWM, p. 160.

10 Lanyieng was later awarded a British Empire Medal for his work with Semut III. See *Sarawak Gazette* 1067, p. 25.

11 Lim and Tan, *Sarawak Under the Throes*, p. 169, 183ff; Truscott, *Voices from Borneo*, unpublished manuscript, p. 31; author, Sungai Asap interviews, May 2015.

12 Lim and Tan, *Sarawak Under the Throes*, p. 169, 256ff; Truscott, *Voices from Borneo*, unpublished manuscript, p. 31; 'Commanding Guerrilla forces' from 'Semut I', Major T. Harrisson, 2 October 1945, A3269, A13/A, NAA; Harrisson, *World Within*, pp. 189, 280, 320. On Harrisson's assumption of grandiose titles see also Letter, K.W. Hallam to Allan Wood, 19 June 1984, p. 30, PR84/247, AWM.

13 'Internees – Allied Abroad Massacre of Allied Nationals at Longnawang, Borneo', A1066, IC45/95/8, NAA; Ooi, *Japanese Occupation of Borneo*, p. 91.

14 Report, 'Semut III Party Report', Major W.L. Sochon, n.d., p. 9, 38/1/1-67, GB-0033-MAC, Durham University Library; Walpole, *My War*, pp. 155–9.

15 Barrie, *Borneo Story*, unpublished manuscript, MSS1532, AWM, p. 94; Bill Sochon, 'Semut Diary – 1945', in Barrie, *Borneo Story*, unpublished manuscript, MSS1532, AWM, p. 160; Wren, *Down-Stream Twice*, unpublished manuscript, p. 246.

16 Wren, *Down-Stream Twice*, unpublished manuscript, p. 251; Walpole, *My War*, p. 161.

17 Edwards and Stevens, *Short Histories*, p. 139.

18 Walpole, *My War*, pp. 161–2, 165–6, 'Bujang showed me' from p. 185.

19 Walpole, *My War*, p. 166, 183–4; personal communication, two unknown Iban men, Kapit bazaar, August 1990. Walpole mixes up the detail of this and a subsequent ambush carried out at Kanowit. Both Sochon, in his Party Report, and locals were clear that the attack on the guard post took place at Kidd's Estate and the later ambush much closer to Kanowit. The Iban guerrilla reconnoitred Kidd's Estate, not Kanowit as in Walpole's account.

20 Walpole, *My War*, pp. 169–70. According to Walpole, Kearney was paralytic when they left the longhouse after drinking too much the night before; as a result he (Walpole) was forced to organise the attack. This is not how

local Iban participants remembered it: they told me that Kearney and Belaja together were responsible for the attack's planning and implementation.

21 Walpole, *My War*, pp. 186–7, 190; personal communication, two unknown Iban men, Kapit bazaar, August 1990.

22 Walpole, *My War*, pp. 187–8; personal communication, two unknown Iban men, Kapit bazaar, August 1990. In his recommendation for Belaja's decoration, Sochon makes special mention of Belaja's actions during this attack. See 'Honours and Awards – Loyal Service Medallion', Semut III Party Report, 38/1/1-67, GB-0033-MAC, Durham University Library.

23 Walpole, *My War*, p. 188.

24 Walpole, *My War*, pp. 174–5; personal communication, two unknown Iban men, Kapit bazaar, August 1990.

25 Walpole, *My War*, pp. 175–8, 'birds of all descriptions' from p. 178.

26 Walpole, *My War*, p. 178; Report, 'Semut III Party Report', Major W.L. Sochon, n.d., p. 9, 38/1/1-67, GB-0033-MAC, Durham University Library; Wren, *Down-Stream Twice*, unpublished manuscript, pp. 251–2; personal communication, two unknown Iban men, Kapit bazaar, August 1990.

27 Report, 'Semut III Party Report', Major W.L. Sochon, n.d., p. 9, 38/1/1-67, GB-0033-MAC, Durham University Library.

28 'Taken the opportunity to settle' from Report, 'Conditions within Sarawak 1945', Major G.S. Carter, 10 November 1945, p. 6, HS 8/951, NAUK; Walpole, *My War*, p. 163.

29 'Until I got wise' from Letter, R.K. Wilson to Rt. Hon. Malcolm MacDonald, 21 April 1957, p. 8, 101/4/1-67, GB-0033-MAC, Durham University Library; personal communication (telephone), Bob Long, 15 June 2016.

30 Larson, *Severed*, pp. 21–8, 36–9.

31 Walpole, *My War*, pp. 182–3, 166.

32 Walpole, *My War*, pp. 184–6, 166–7, 171.

33 Walpole, *My War*, pp. 171–3, 'As we waited' from pp. 172–3; personal communication, two unknown Iban men, Kapit bazaar, August 1990.

34 Walpole, *My War*, pp. 171–5; Report, 'Semut III Party Report', Major W.L. Sochon, n.d., p. 9, 38/1/1-67, GB-0033-MAC, Durham University Library; personal communication, two unknown Iban men, Kapit bazaar, August 1990.

35 Report, 'Semut III Party Report', Major W.L. Sochon, n.d., p. 9, 38/1/1-67, GB-0033-MAC, Durham University Library; Letter, David [Kearney] to Brad [Ross Bradbury], 5 September 1997, Truscott Papers; Walpole, *My War*, p. 189.

36 Report, 'Semut III Party Report', Major W.L. Sochon, n.d., p. 9, 38/1/1-67, GB-0033-MAC, Durham University Library; 'Honours and Awards – Loyal Service Medallion', Semut III Party Report, 38/1/1-67, GB-0033-MAC,

Durham University Library; Barrie, *Borneo Story*, unpublished manuscript, MSS1532, AWM, p. 95.

37 Report, 'Semut III Party Report', Major W.L. Sochon, n.d., p. 10, 38/1/1-67, GB-0033-MAC, Durham University Library; Wren, *Down-Stream Twice*, unpublished manuscript, pp. 23–4; author, Kanowit interviews, December 2015.

38 Barrie, *Borneo Story*, unpublished manuscript, MSS1532, AWM, pp. 95–6, 'In due course this resolved' from p. 96.

39 Report, 'Semut III Party Report', Major W.L. Sochon, n.d., p. 10, 38/1/1-67, GB-0033-MAC, Durham University Library; Report, 'Semut III Activities – Aug 2-Aug 18, 1945', Major J.R. Wooler, 23 August 194[5], p. 2, A3269, A15/B, NAA; Wren, *Down-Stream Twice*, unpublished manuscript, pp. 254–5; Barrie, *Borneo Story*, unpublished manuscript, MSS1532, AWM, p. 96.

40 Edwards and Stevens, *Short Histories*, pp. 140–2; MacDonald, *Borneo People*, p. 78; Chee, *Population of Sarawak*, PhD thesis, pp. 81–2.

41 Edwards and Stevens, *Short Histories*, pp. 140–2; author, Kanowit interviews, December 2015.

42 Report, 'Semut III Party Report', Major W.L. Sochon, n.d., p. 10, 38/1/1-67, GB-0033-MAC, Durham University Library; 'Honours and Awards – Loyal Service Medallion', Semut III Party Report, 38/1/1-67, GB-0033-MAC, Durham University Library; Barrie, *Borneo Story*, unpublished manuscript, MSS1532, AWM, p. 96.

43 Report, 'Semut III Party Report', Major W.L. Sochon, n.d., p. 10, 38/1/1-67, GB-0033-MAC, Durham University Library; Bill Sochon, 'Semut Diary – 1945', in Barrie, *Borneo Story*, unpublished manuscript, MSS1532, AWM, p. 161; Report, 'Semut III Activities – Aug 2-Aug 18, 1945', Major J.R. Wooler, 23 August 194[5], p. 1, A3269, A15/B, NAA; Courtney, *Silent Feet*, p. 103; Edwards and Stevens, *Short Histories*, p. 163.

44 '[I]mmediately before the occupation' from Wren, *Down-Stream Twice*, unpublished manuscript, p. 256.

45 Edwards and Stevens, *Short Histories*, pp. 163–4; Report, 'Semut III Activities – Aug 2-Aug 18, 1945', Major J.R. Wooler, 23 August 194[5], pp. 1–2, A3269, A15/B, NAA; Ooi, *Japanese Occupation of Borneo*, pp. 127, 146; author, interview with Lawrence Ato, Julau (Kanowit), 1 December 2015; author, interview with Jarit anak Bujai, Kanowit, 3 December 2015.

46 Edwards and Stevens, *Short Histories*, p. 164; Wren, *Down-Stream Twice*, unpublished manuscript, p. 256; Courtney, *Silent Feet*, p. 103; author, interview with Jarit anak Bujai, Kanowit, 3 December 2015.

47 Edwards and Stevens, *Short Histories*, p. 163; Sutlive, *Tun Jugah*, pp. 113–4.

48 'Honours and Awards – Loyal Service Medallion', Semut III Party Report, 38/1/1-67, GB-0033-MAC, Durham University Library; Reece, *Name of*

Brooke, p. 150; *Sarawak Gazette* 1075, p. 183; author, interview with Lawrence Ato, Julau (Kanowit), 1 December 2015; author, interview with Jarit anak Bujai, Kanowit, 3 December 2015.

49   Barrie, *Borneo Story*, unpublished manuscript, MSS1532, AWM, p. 97.

50   Bill Sochon, 'Semut Diary – 1945', in Barrie, *Borneo Story*, unpublished manuscript, MSS1532, AWM, p. 161.

51   Reece, *Masa Jepun*, p. 182; 'practice of bombing' from Long, *Final Campaigns*, p. 484; 'wanton' from Report, '20 Aust Inf Bde – Report on Operation Oboe Six', 16 August 1945, p. 46, AWM357, 7, AWM; 'HQ UK Base – Incoming Message', Airintel Brisbane, 2 August 1945, WO 208/1055, NAUK.

52   Nichol anak Ragan, interview with Listen Baling anak Luang, Kapit, 14 June 1995.

53   Reece, *Masa Jepun*, p. 180.

54   'Dave Kearney decided' from Barrie, *Borneo Story*, unpublished manuscript, MSS1532, AWM, p. 97; Reece, *Masa Jepun*, p. 182; Bill Sochon, 'Semut Diary – 1945', in Barrie, *Borneo Story*, unpublished manuscript, MSS1532, AWM, p. 161. According to Reece, Ross Bradbury told him that this event occurred on 28 July. However, Semut III were not yet in occupation of Kanowit on 28 July. Barrie dates it to the morning of 9 August, which accords with Sochon's account of when the strafing raid was timed to occur.

55   Report, 'Semut III Activities – Aug 2-Aug 18, 1945', Major J.R. Wooler, 23 August 194[5], pp. 1–2, A3269, A15/B, NAA; Report, 'Semut III Party Report', Major W.L. Sochon, n.d., p. 10, 38/1/1-67, GB-0033-MAC, Durham University Library.

56   Report, 'Semut III Party Report', Major W.L. Sochon, n.d., p. 10, 38/1/1-67, GB-0033-MAC, Durham University Library; Report, 'Sarawak – Rajang Valley', Captain Stokes, n.d., A3269, A15/A, NAA; Report, 'Semut III Activities – Aug 2-Aug 18, 1945', Major J.R. Wooler, 23 August 194[5], pp. 1–2, A3269, A15/B, NAA; Wren, *Down-Stream Twice*, unpublished manuscript, pp. 261–2.

57   Wren, *Down-Stream Twice*, unpublished manuscript, p. 257; Edwards and Stevens, *Short Histories*, p. 164; Ooi, *Rising Sun over Borneo*, p. 99; Barrie, *Borneo Story*, unpublished manuscript, MSS1532, AWM, p. 98.

CHAPTER 16: END OF THE RIVER

1   Report, 'Semut III Party Report', Major W.L. Sochon, n.d., pp. 10–11, 38/1/1-67, GB-0033-MAC, Durham University Library; Wren, *Down-Stream Twice*, unpublished manuscript, pp. 25, 258, 260.

2   Report, 'Semut III Activities – Aug 2–Aug 18, 1945', Major J.R. Wooler, 23 August 194[5], p. 2, A3269, A15/B, NAA; Bill Sochon, 'Semut

Diary – 1945', in Barrie, *Borneo Story*, unpublished manuscript, MSS1532, AWM, p. 162; Report, 'Report by H.P.K. Jacks', H.P.K. Jacks, 27 March 1942, FCO 141/12402, NAUK; Talib, *Development of the Sarawak Administrative Service*, PhD thesis, p. 154.

3 Report, 'Operation Semut III – Intelligence Report No. 7', Services Reconnaissance Department, 25 July 1945, AWM54, 619/7/69, AWM.

4 Report, 'Semut III Party Report', Major W.L. Sochon, n.d., p. 11, 38/1/1-67, GB-0033-MAC, Durham University Library; Report, 'Semut III Activities – Aug 2–Aug 18, 1945', Major J.R. Wooler, 23 August 194[5], p. 2, A3269, A15/B, NAA.

5 Report, 'Semut III Party Report', Major W.L. Sochon, n.d., p. 11, 38/1/1-67, GB-0033-MAC, Durham University Library; Reece, *Masa Jepun*, p. 184; author, Sibu interviews, November 2015.

6 Reece, *Masa Jepun*, pp. 182–4, 'By this time' from p. 183.

7 Report, 'Semut III Party Report', Major W.L. Sochon, n.d., pp. 11–12, 38/1/1-67, GB-0033-MAC, Durham University Library; Report, 'Semut III Activities – Aug 2–Aug 18, 1945', Major J.R. Wooler, 23 August 194[5], p. 2, A3269, A15/B, NAA.

8 Report, 'Semut III Party Report', Major W.L. Sochon, n.d., p. 10, 38/1/1-67, GB-0033-MAC, Durham University Library; Wren, *Down-Stream Twice*, unpublished manuscript, pp. 259–60; Barrie, *Borneo Story*, unpublished manuscript, MSS1532, AWM, p. 99.

9 Report, 'Semut III Party Report', Major W.L. Sochon, n.d., p. 11, 38/1/1-67, GB-0033-MAC, Durham University Library; Wren, *Down-Stream Twice*, unpublished manuscript, pp. 260–1; Reginald H. Roy, interview with Roger Cheng, 22 February 1971, University of Victoria Digital Collections.

10 Ooi, *Japanese Occupation of Borneo*, p. 69; 'Report on Investigations – Aust and Allied Prisoners of War – 9 Aust Div Area', n.d., WO 361/1761, NAUK, p. 8.

11 Wren, *Down-Stream Twice*, unpublished manuscript, p. 261; Reginald H. Roy, interview with Roger Cheng, 22 February 1971, University of Victoria Digital Collections.

12 Fell, *Sea Our Shield*, p. 224.

13 Report, 'Semut III Party Report', Major W.L. Sochon, n.d., p. 11, 38/1/1-67, GB-0033-MAC, Durham University Library; Wren, *Down-Stream Twice*, unpublished manuscript, pp. 262–3.

14 Report, 'Semut III Party Report', Major W.L. Sochon, n.d., p. 12, 38/1/1-67, GB-0033-MAC, Durham University Library; Wren, *Down-Stream Twice*, unpublished manuscript, pp. 263–5; Report, 'Semut III Activities – Aug 2–Aug 18,

1945', Major J.R. Wooler, 23 August 194[5], p. 2, A3269, A15/B, NAA. See also Bartram, 'Chapter 17', in Long (ed.), *Operation Semut 1*, pp. 483–4.

15 'Consider <u>impossible</u>' from Message, Semut 3 to Morotai, [21 August 1945], A3269, A15/B, NAA, emphasis in original; Report, 'Semut III Party Report', Major W.L. Sochon, n.d., p. 13, 38/1/1-67, GB-0033-MAC, Durham University Library; 'As soon as they' from Wren, *Down-Stream Twice*, unpublished manuscript, p. 265; Bill Sochon, 'Semut Diary – 1945', in Barrie, *Borneo Story*, unpublished manuscript, MSS1532, AWM, p. 163.

16 Report, 'Semut III Party Report', Major W.L. Sochon, n.d., p. 12, 38/1/1-67, GB-0033-MAC, Durham University Library; Wren, *Down-Stream Twice*, unpublished manuscript, pp. 263–4.

17 Report, 'Semut III Party Report', Major W.L. Sochon, n.d., p. 12, 38/1/1-67, GB-0033-MAC, Durham University Library; Barrie, *Borneo Story*, unpublished manuscript, MSS1532, AWM, pp. 100, 105–6; Walpole, *My War*, pp. 228–30; Reece, *Masa Jepun*, p. 186.

18 Report, 'Semut III Party Report', Major W.L. Sochon, n.d., p. 13, 38/1/1-67, GB-0033-MAC, Durham University Library; 'So there was the Doc' from Barrie, *Borneo Story*, unpublished manuscript, MSS1532, AWM, p. 115; Report, 'Sarawak – Rajang Valley', Captain Stokes, n.d., A3269, A15/A, NAA.

19 Report, 'Semut III Party Report', Major W.L. Sochon, n.d., p. 12, 38/1/1-67, GB-0033-MAC, Durham University Library; Wren, *Down-Stream Twice*, unpublished manuscript, p. 264.

20 Wren, *Down-Stream Twice*, unpublished manuscript, p. 263.

21 'Ultimatum', R.J. Wooler, 11 August 1945, A3269, A15/B, NAA; Report, 'Semut III Activities – Aug 2–Aug 18, 1945', Major J.R. Wooler, 23 August 194[5], p. 2, A3269, A15/B, NAA; Report, 'Semut III Party Report', Major W.L. Sochon, n.d., pp. 11–12, 38/1/1-67, GB-0033-MAC, Durham University Library; 'personal strains' from Barrie, *Borneo Story*, unpublished manuscript, MSS1532, AWM, p. 98.

22 'Commander, British Task Forces, Rajang' from 'Ultimatum', R.J. Wooler, 11 August 1945, A3269, A15/B, NAA; 'who are not only adventurous' from Long, *Final Campaigns*, p. 622. See also Powell, *War by Stealth*, pp. 347–50.

23 Reece, *Masa Jepun*, pp. 184, 203, 'The unit had more' from p. 184.

24 Report, 'Semut III Party Report', Major W.L. Sochon, n.d., p. 11, 38/1/1-67, GB-0033-MAC, Durham University Library; Reece, *Masa Jepun*, p. 184.

25 Report, 'Semut III Party Report', Major W.L. Sochon, n.d., pp. 11–12, 38/1/1-67, GB-0033-MAC, Durham University Library; Wren, *Down-Stream Twice*, unpublished manuscript, pp. 263–5.

26 Report, 'Semut III Party Report', Major W.L. Sochon, n.d., pp. 12–13, 38/1/1-67, GB-0033-MAC, Durham University Library; Reece, *Masa Jepun*, p. 184;

Bill Sochon, 'Semut Diary – 1945', in Barrie, *Borneo Story*, unpublished manuscript, MSS1532, AWM, pp. 163–5; 'Notes on Meeting held at HQ BBCAU 22 Aug 45', n.d., AWM54, 627/4/7, AWM.

27 'Stop sending useless ultimatums' and 'I was ordered' both from Wren, *Down-Stream Twice*, unpublished manuscript, p. 265.

28 Long, *Final Campaigns*, p. 553; 'Notes on S.R.D. Policy – Post Surrender', 20 August 1945, AWM54, 627/4/7, AWM.

29 'SRD Outline Plan: Surrender of Japan', O.C. Group 'A', 29 August 1945, AWM54, 627/4/7, AWM.

30 Bill Sochon, 'Semut Diary – 1945', in Barrie, *Borneo Story*, unpublished manuscript, MSS1532, AWM, p. 165; see also Wren, *Down-Stream Twice*, unpublished manuscript, p. 264.

31 'Unsafe' and 'sniped at' both from Untitled transcript, Interrogation of Major General Yamamura, 5 September 1945, p. 9, AWM54, 41/4/35, AWM.

32 Long, *Final Campaigns*, p. 563; 'Report on Investigations – Aust and Allied Prisoners of War – 9 Aust Div Area', n.d., WO 361/1761, NAUK, p. 8; Ooi, *Japanese Occupation of Borneo*, p. 69; Harrisson, *World Within*, p. 307; 'Borneo Story', Denis M. Sheppard, 18 November 1997, p. 3, Truscott Papers.

33 Long, *Final Campaigns*, p. 563.

34 'Report on Investigations – Aust and Allied Prisoners of War – 9 Aust Div Area', n.d., WO 361/1761, NAUK, p. 8; 'as soon as possible' from 'Surrender of Japan – 9 Aust Div Outline Plan', 29 August 1945, p. 3, AWM54, 627/4/7, AWM, emphasis in original.

35 Harrisson, *World Within*, pp. 306–7.

36 'Report on Investigations – Aust and Allied Prisoners of War – 9 Aust Div Area', n.d., WO 361/1761, NAUK, pp. 117–9.

37 'Report on Investigations – Aust and Allied Prisoners of War – 9 Aust Div Area', n.d., WO 361/1761, NAUK, pp. 109–20, 'slow starvation' from p. 112.

38 Ham, *Sandakan*, p. 432.

39 'Report on Investigations – Aust and Allied Prisoners of War – 9 Aust Div Area', n.d., WO 361/1761, NAUK, pp. 113, 118; see also Ooi, *Japanese Occupation of Borneo*, p. 122.

40 Wren, *Down-Stream Twice*, unpublished manuscript, pp. 264–5, 'On discovering the contents' from p. 265; Bill Sochon, 'Semut Diary – 1945', in Barrie, *Borneo Story*, unpublished manuscript, MSS1532, AWM, p. 165.

41 Report, 'Semut III Party Report', Major W.L. Sochon, n.d., p. 13, 38/1/1-67, GB-0033-MAC, Durham University Library; Wren, *Down-Stream Twice*, unpublished manuscript, p. 265; Bill Sochon, 'Semut Diary – 1945', in Barrie, *Borneo Story*, unpublished manuscript, MSS1532, AWM, pp. 165–6; Reece, *Masa Jepun*, pp. 36–7; Hua, *Pussy's in the Well*, p. 144.

42 Wren, *Down-Stream Twice*, unpublished manuscript, pp. 265–6.

43 Wren, *Down-Stream Twice*, unpublished manuscript, p. 266.

44 Report, 'Report on occupation of Simanggang', D. Kearney, 21 September 1945, Truscott Papers; 'Notes on visit of GSOI to Kuching dated 5 October 1945', Lt Col G.S. Courtney, 9 October 1945, AWM54, 627/4/17, AWM; Walpole, *My War*, pp. 230–3; Reece, *Masa Jepun*, p. 186.

45 Walpole, *My War*, pp. 234–7; Letter, Brian Walpole to Major Jim Truscott, 31 January 1998, Truscott Papers; 'refused to talk' from 'Notes on visit of GSOI to Kuching dated 5 October 1945', Lt Col G.S. Courtney, 9 October 1945, AWM54, 627/4/17, AWM.

46 Walpole, *My War*, pp. 240–1; Letter, Brian Walpole to Major Jim Truscott, 31 January 1998, Truscott Papers; 'Notes on visit of GSOI to Kuching dated 5 October 1945', Lt Col G.S. Courtney, 9 October 1945, AWM54, 627/4/17, AWM; Report, 'Report on occupation of Simanggang', D. Kearney, 21 September 1945, Truscott Papers.

47 Report, 'Report on occupation of Simanggang', D. Kearney, 21 September 1945, Truscott Papers; Walpole, *My War*, p. 241; Letter, Brian Walpole to Major Jim Truscott, 31 January 1998, Truscott Papers.

48 Report, 'Report on clash between SRD and Japanese at Simanggang', Brig T.C. Eastick, 12 October 1945, AWM54, 627/4/17, AWM; 'Notes on visit of GSOI to Kuching dated 5 October 1945', Lt Col G.S. Courtney, 9 October 1945, AWM54, 627/4/17, AWM.

49 Walpole, *My War*, pp. 243, 253, 'I had them' from p. 243; Reece, *Masa Jepun*, pp. 186–7.

50 Report, 'Report on occupation of Simanggang', D. Kearney, 21 September 1945, Truscott Papers; 'When the Captain from Betong' from Porritt, 'More bitter than sweet', in *Sarawak Gazette* 1531, p. 53.

51 Report, 'Report on occupation of Simanggang', D. Kearney, 21 September 1945, Truscott Papers; 'Notes on visit of GSOI to Kuching dated 5 October 1945', Lt Col G.S. Courtney, 9 October 1945, AWM54, 627/4/17, AWM; Walpole, *My War*, pp. 241, 283; see also Letter, Brian Walpole to Major Jim Truscott, 31 January 1998, Truscott Papers.

52 'Isn't like us' from Walpole, *My War*, p. 261; Report, 'Report on clash between SRD and Japanese at Simanggang', Brig T.C. Eastick, 12 October 1945, AWM54, 627/4/17, AWM.

53 Walpole, *My War*, pp. 264–7, 270–3; Letter, David [Kearney] to Brad [Ross Bradbury], 5 September 1997, Truscott Papers.

54 Personal communication, Michael Heppell, Melbourne, 18 Feb 2019. A slightly different account of the killing of Arundell and his family can be found in Reece, *Masa Jepun*, pp. 44–6.

55 'To all parties from Courtney', 2 October 1945, PR90/172, AWM.

56 Report, 'Semut III Party Report', Major W.L. Sochon, n.d., p. 13, 38/1/1-67, GB-0033-MAC, Durham University Library; 'Pip Hume unfurled' from Wren, *Down-Stream Twice*, unpublished manuscript, p. 266; Bill Sochon, 'Semut Diary – 1945', in Barrie, *Borneo Story*, unpublished manuscript, MSS1532, AWM, p. 166.

57 Wren, *Down-Stream Twice*, unpublished manuscript, pp. 266–7, 'Covered with a piece' from p. 267.

58 Wren, *Down-Stream Twice*, unpublished manuscript, pp. 267–8; Bill Sochon, 'Semut Diary – 1945', in Barrie, *Borneo Story*, unpublished manuscript, MSS1532, AWM, p. 166.

59 See Ting et al, *Sibu of Yesterday*, p. 63; Ting, *Precarious Power, Forts and Outstations*, PhD thesis, p. 209.

60 Chee, *Population of Sarawak*, PhD thesis, p. 81.

61 MacDonald, *Borneo People*, p. 76; Wren, *Down-Stream Twice*, unpublished manuscript, p. 268.

62 Wren, *Down-Stream Twice*, unpublished manuscript, p. 268; Reece, *Masa Jepun*, p. 36; Hua, *Pussy's in the Well*, pp. 143–4; author, interview with Haji Ibrahim Manjat bin Uyau, Kuching, 25 November 2015.

63 Reece, *Masa Jepun*, pp. 180–1.

64 Wren, *Down-Stream Twice*, unpublished manuscript, pp. 268–9.

65 Report, 'Semut III Party Report', Major W.L. Sochon, n.d., p. 13, 38/1/1-67, GB-0033-MAC, Durham University Library; Wren, *Down-Stream Twice*, unpublished manuscript, pp. 269–70; Bill Sochon, 'Semut Diary – 1945', in Barrie, *Borneo Story*, unpublished manuscript, MSS1532, AWM, p. 166.

66 Wren, *Down-Stream Twice*, unpublished manuscript, pp. 272–3, 'As Noda saw' from p. 273.

67 Wren, *Down-Stream Twice*, unpublished manuscript, p. 273.

68 Wren, *Down-Stream Twice*, unpublished manuscript, p. 275. Sochon later donated this flag to the Sarawak Museum (ibid).

69 Report, 'Semut III Party Report', Major W.L. Sochon, n.d., p. 13, 38/1/1-67, GB-0033-MAC, Durham University Library; Wren, *Down-Stream Twice*, unpublished manuscript, pp. 275–6; Bill Sochon, 'Semut Diary – 1945', in Barrie, *Borneo Story*, unpublished manuscript, MSS1532, AWM, p. 166.

70 The SOA Official History lists 47 operatives as having taken part in Semut III. However, the list contains many errors – some of those included, for instance, were members of Semut I rather than Semut III. See 'The Official History of the Operations and Administration of Special Operations – Australia', Vol. 2, Part III, pp. 48–9, A3269, O8/A, NAA. On the number of guerrillas, see Report, 'Semut III Party Report', Major W.L. Sochon, n.d., 38/1/1-67,

GB-0033-MAC, Durham University Library; on square miles of territory, see Wren, *Down-Stream Twice*, unpublished manuscript, p. 276.

71 Reece, *Name of Brooke*, p. 150.

72 'To the Dyaks it must' from Wren, *Down-Stream Twice*, unpublished manuscript, p. 257.

73 Ooi, *Rising Sun over Borneo*, pp. 96–101; 'a heightening of racial tension' from Reece, *Name of Brooke*, p. 150; Edwards and Stevens, *Short Histories*, p. 164.

74 Sochon's family later donated Noda's sword to the Australian War Memorial.

EPILOGUE

1 Author, interview with Basar Paru, Long Tuma (Lawas), 12 April 2015.

2 'The unpleasant; the misery' from 'Semut II – Sarawak, Borneo', W.S. Eadie, 4 April 1987, p. 19, 'Accounts', Docs. 16752, IWM; 'my encounter with the Ibans' from Wigzell, *New Zealand Army Involvement*, p. 232; 'I never saw any of them' from Walpole, *My War*, pp. 260–1.

3 'Catches in my throat' from author, interview with Jack Tredrea, Adelaide, 1 October 2016; 'the finest bunch of people' from Tredrea, *Army Career*, unpublished manuscript, p. 11.

4 Campbell, *Z-Special*, p. 246; Macintyre, *SAS*; 'flying by the seat of their pants' from personal communication (telephone), anonymous SRD operative, 9 October 2018. For an example of the chaos in SRD at war's end see Bartram, 'Chapter 17', in Long (ed.), *Operation Semut 1*, p. 483.

5 Letter, Keith Barrie to *Sydney Morning Herald*, in *Z Special Unit Association (Victoria) Inc., Newsletter* No. 25, November 1996, 'help, generosity and kindness' from this source; 'sense of shame' from Barrie, *Borneo Story*, unpublished manuscript, MSS1532, AWM, p. 72.

6 'they're wonderful people' from author, interview with Jack Tredrea, Adelaide, 16 September 2014.

7 'Quickly, gently, invisibly' from Harrisson, *World Within*, p. 279; 'I had to take my turn' from 'Semut II – Sarawak, Borneo', W.S. Eadie, 4 April 1987, p. 8, 'Accounts', Docs. 16752, IWM.

8 'We agreed that we had earned' from Letter, K.W. Hallam to Allan Wood, 19 June 1984, p. 6, PR84/247, AWM; author, interview with Bill Beiers, Mornington (Melbourne), 21 November 2016; Walpole, *My War*, p. 185; 'something to startle anyone' from Harrisson, *World Within*, p. 279.

9 'I had expected' from 'Semut II – Sarawak, Borneo', W.S. Eadie, 4 April 1987, p. 16, 'Accounts', Docs. 16752, IWM.

10 'I just felt lucky' from author, interview with Bill Beiers, Mornington (Melbourne), 21 November 2016.

11 'The Official History of the Operations and Administration of Special Operations – Australia', Vol. 2, Part III, p. 68, A3269, O8/A, NAA. The number of dead locals given in the Official History includes only those killed up until 15 August 1945. It is almost certain that others died after that date.

12 'Bujang did everything' from Walpole, *My War*, p. 138; 'It was at this time' from Wigzell, *New Zealand Army Involvement*, pp. 207–8.

13 Hardy, 'Chapter 15', in Long (ed.), *Operation Semut 1*, p. 449.

14 'The Dayaks were our saviours' from author, interview with Bob Long, Perth, 17 September 2014.

BIBLIOGRAPHY

EXTENSIVE ETHNOGRAPHIC FIELDWORK AMONG Dayak peoples throughout Borneo between 1985 and the present provides the bedrock upon which this book is built. This fieldwork has involved living in Dayak communities, immersing myself in daily life, and engaging in tens of thousands of hours of conversation on every conceivable topic, including WWII. Since 2015 I have also travelled extensively throughout Sarawak and parts of Sabah, visiting almost all the places mentioned in this book and talking to the people there specifically about their WWII experiences. The result is thousands of recordings, photographs and pages of fieldnotes, providing me with an intimate, detailed knowledge of Borneo and its Dayak peoples, including their histories of WWII. On occasion when writing the book I needed information about a Dayak group with which I am less familiar; in these cases I called on the knowledge, fieldnotes and published accounts of other Borneo ethnographers.

The book also draws heavily on more than one hundred and twenty formal recorded interviews I conducted in both Borneo and Australia on the topic of WWII in Borneo, some focusing specifically on Operation Semut. Most of these were conducted between 2015 and 2018 and were around 1.5–2 hours in length.

As noted in the Preface, archival sources on SRD, including Operation Semut, are thin and unreliable. In writing this account I have made use of all relevant archival material I could unearth in Australia and the United Kingdom, as well as private records to which I was granted access by generous individuals and families. Much important information was available only in secondary sources, and I have made extensive use of these as well.

The Bibliography below gives details of all sources, other than the ethnographic fieldwork, I have drawn on in writing this book.

FORMAL INTERVIEWS CONDUCTED BY AUTHOR (AUTHOR'S COLLECTION)

Interviews are grouped according to where they were conducted and then by date.

In the Endnotes I mostly refer to a single interview; however, when several interviewees at the same location made similar points, I refer to the entire group of interviews carried out at that location (e.g. 'Bario interviews' or 'Long San' interviews).

My Sarawak Research Associate, Valerie Mashman, participated in those interviews marked*.

Australia
Adelaide
Jack Tredrea (Australian): 15 September 2014 (twice), 16 September 2014, 30 September 2016 (twice), 1 October 2014 (three times), 5 October 2016.
Language: English.
An abridged version of the first of these interviews is held at the AWM: PAFU2014/371.01
Mornington
Bill Beiers (Australian): 21 November 2016.
Language: English.

Naracoorte
Barney Schinckel (Australian): 4 October 2016.
Language: English.
Perth
Bob Long (Australian): 17 September 2014 (twice), 18 September 2014.
Language: English.
An abridged version of the first of these interviews is held at the AWM: PAFU2014/372.01
Sydney
Allan Russell (Australian): 5 July 2017.
Language: English

Sabah, Malaysian Borneo
Padas River and environs
Lokowon bin Antahai (Murut): 19 August 2018 at Kampung Alutok.
Language: Murut and Malay. Interpreter: Ricky Ganang.
Tongon bin Angie (Murut): 19 August 2018 at Kampung Malutut.
Language: Murut and Malay. Interpreter: Ricky Ganang.
Unggi Malinau (Murut): 20 August 2018 at Tenambong.
Language: Murut and Malay. Interpreter: Ricky Ganang.
Langub Padan (Lun Bawang): 20 August 2018 at Kampung Baru Jumpa.
Language: Lun Bawang. Interpreter: Ricky Ganang.

Sarawak, Malaysian Borneo
Ba'Kelalan
Padan Ubung Labo (Lun Bawang): 30 March 2015* at Budok Nor.
Language: Lun Bawang. Interpreter: Sang Sigar.
Balang Paran (Lun Bawang): 31 March 2015* at Budok Nor.
Language: Lun Bawang. Interpreter: Sang Sigar.
Rigo Bareh (Lun Bawang): 31 March 2015* at Budok Nor.
Language: Lun Bawang. Interpreter: Sang Sigar.
Kaya Meru (Lun Bawang): 31 March 2015* at Budok Nor.
Language: English.
Paran Padan (Lun Bawang): 1 April 2015* at Budok Nor.
Language: Malay.
Ngilo Sigar (Lun Bawang): 1 April 2015* at Budok Nor.
Language: Malay.
Tagal Paran (Lun Bawang): 2 April 2015* at Budok Nor.
Language: Malay.
Rinai Sakai (Lun Bawang): 2 April 2015* at Long Lungai.

Language: Lun Bawang. Interpreter: David Pengiran.
Sakai Bangau (Lun Bawang): 2 April 2015* at Long Lungai.
Language: Lun Bawang. Interpreter: David Pengiran.

Bario and environs
Maran Ayu, Balang Lugun and Sina Maran Ayu (Kelabit): 18 March 2015* at Arur Dalan.
Language: Malay.
Litah Ayu (Kelabit): 20 March 2015* at Pa Lungan.
Language: Kelabit. Interpreter: Supang Galih.
Uun Paran (Kelabit): 20 March 2015* at Pa Lungan.
Language: Kelabit. Interpreter: Supang Galih.
Siran Ida and Adteh Kediah Aran (Kelabit): 22 March 2015*, 25 March 2015 at Bario Asal.
Language: Kelabit (1st interview); Malay (2nd interview). Interpreter: Diane Kapong Rajah.
Ngalinuh Karuh (Kelabit): 22 March 2015* at Bario Asal.
Language: Kelabit. Interpreter: Panai Aran.
Sina Paran Matu (Kelabit): 22 March 2015* at Bario Asal.
Language: Kelabit. Interpreter: Panai Aran.
Sina Balang Radu (Kelabit): 22 March 2015* at Bario Asal.
Language: Kelabit. Interpreter: Panai Aran.
Gala Raut (Kelabit): 23 March 2015* at Bario.
Language: Kelabit. Interpreter: Florence Apu.
Maran Lugung (Kelabit): 24 March 2015* at Bario Asal.
Language: Kelabit. Interpreter: Florence Apu.
Maran Talla (Kelabit): 25 March 2015* at Bario.
Language: Kelabit. Interpreter: Florence Apu.

Belaga and environs
Lato Juman (Kayan): 22 May 2015* at Long Amo.
Language: Kayan and Malay. Interpreter: Non Ding.
Jau Lutun and Sait Senyum (Sekapan): 22 May 2015* at Rumah Sekapan Panjang.
Language: Malay.
Kuleh Emang (Lahanan): 23 May 2015* at Belaga.
Language: Malay.
Ngang Tingang (Kenyah): 23 May 2015* at Long Dungan.
Language: Malay.
Surieng Leguey (Kejaman): 24 May 2015* at Belaga.
Language: Kejaman and Malay. Interpreter: Paul Kivai.
Teo Ahtong (Chinese): 24 May 2015* at Belaga.
Language: Malay.

Data Kakus
Lenchau Bilong and Angun Bilong (Kenyah): 29 May 2015*.
Language: Kenyah. Interpreter: Jawa Tusau.
Ubong Bilong, Jan Ngau and Tingang Engan (Kenyah): 29 May 2015*.
Language: Kenyah. Interpreter: Jawa Tusau.
Ilong Lesut, Tugong Bilong and Ongan Jau (Kenyah): 29 May 2015*.
Language: Kenyah. Interpreter: Jawa Tusau.
Tanyit Bayak (Kenyah): 29 May 2015*.
Language: Kenyah. Interpreter: Jawa Tusau.
Urai Lawing (Kenyah): 30 May 2015*.
Language: Kenyah. Interpreter: Jawa Tusau.
Lisim Along, Empang Tading and Usun Bayak (Kenyah): 30 May 2015*.
Language: Kenyah. Interpreter: Jawa Tusau.
Liling Jok (Kenyah): 30 May 2015*.
Language: Kenyah. Interpreter: Jawa Tusau.
Tet Along and Ann Along (Kenyah): 30 May 2015*.
Language: Kenyah. Interpreter: Jawa Tusau.
Atuk Ukung (Kenyah): 30 May 2015*.
Language: Malay.

Kanowit and environs
Lawrence Ato (Iban): 1 December 2015* at Julau.
Language: English.
Lenya bin Jaro and Ti binti Pagang (Rejang): 2 December 2015* at Kampung Bedil.
Language: Malay.
Jantan anak Besi (Iban): 2 December 2015* at Nanga Latong.
Language: Malay.
Benjamin Angki Kuboy (Rejang): 2 December 2015* at Rumah Benjamin Angki Kuboy.
Language: English.
Francesca Sadai (Rejang): 2 December 2015* at Rumah Benjamin Angki Kuboy.
Language: Malay.
Jarit anak Bujai (Iban): 3 December 2015* at Kanowit.
Language: Malay.

Kapit
Engin anak Nyipa (Iban): 15 May 2015*.
Language: Malay.
Wilfred Billy Pangau (Iban): 18 May 2015*.
Language: English.
Jeffery Kumbong anak Laja (Iban): 18 May 2015*.
Language: English.

Tan Kien Wi (Chinese): 14 December 2015*.
Language: English.

Kuching
Uda Limau and Ganet Nyato (Penan): 28 February 2015*.
Language: Malay and Penan. Interpreter: Ose Murang.
Richard Labung (Lun Bawang): 3 March 2015*.
Language: English.
Patrick Sigar (Lun Bawang): 4 March 2015*.
Language: English.
Morris Kapong Senap (Kelabit): 9 March 2015*.
Language: English.
Maran Lugun (Kelabit): 10 March 2015*.
Language: Malay.
Bo' Tajang Laing (Kayan): 6 May 2015*.
Language: Kayan. Interpreter: Mebang Tajang Bato.
Sidi Munan (Iban): 7 May 2015*.
Language: English.
Edward Lakin Mansel (Bidayuh/English/Japanese): 7 May 2015*.
Language: English.
Vera Ng Meng Ngo @ Vera Badong anak Anggie (Iban): 9 May 2015*.
Language: English.
Joseph Koh Sibat (Iban): 10 May 2015*.
Language: English.
Albert Rumpang Kedit (Iban): 12 May 2015*.
Language: English.
Stephen Wan Ullok (Kenyah): 4 June 2015*.
Language: English.
Taran Saging (Kenyah): 4 June 2015*.
Language: Malay.
Rufus Nangang (Iban): 25 November 2015*.
Language: English.
Haji Ibrahim Manjat bin Uyau (Melanau): 25 November 2015*.
Language: Malay.

Lawas and environs
Udan Rangat (Lun Bawang): 27 March 2015*, 9 April 2015 at Long Tuma.
Language: English (1st interview); Lun Bawang (2nd interview). Interpreter: Ricky Ganang.
Monica Pantulusang (Lun Bawang): 9 April 2015 at Lawas.
Language: English.

John Sigar (Lun Bawang): 10 April 2015 at Lawas.
Language: English.
David Matthew Baru (Lun Bawang): 10 April 2015 at Lawas.
Language: English.
Sigar Berauk (Lun Bawang): 10 April 2015 at Lawas.
Language: Lun Bawang. Interpreter: Ricky Ganang.
Sali Lupung (Tagal): 11 April 2015 at Long Tengoa.
Language: Lun Bawang. Interpreter: Ricky Ganang.
Lipang Munan (Tagal): 11 April 2015 at Long Tengoa.
Language: Lun Bawang. Interpreter: Ricky Ganang.
Basar Paru (Lun Bawang): 12 April 2015 at Long Tuma.
Language: Lun Bawang. Interpreter: Ricky Ganang.
Upai Baru (Lun Bawang): 13 April 2015 at Pengalih.
Language: Lun Bawang. Interpreter: Ricky Ganang.
Usop bin Brahim (Kedayan): 13 April 2015 at Lawas.
Language: Malay.

Long Banga and environs
Tama Sihan (Sa'ban): 14 March 2015* at Long Banga.
Language: Sa'ban. Interpreter: Elis Belare.
Ulan Yii (Sa'ban): 15 March 2015* at Long Peluan.
Language: Sa'ban. Interpreter: Anye Yii.
Laki Tawan (Penan): 15 March 2015* at Long Peluan.
Language: Penan. Interpreter: Elis Belare.
Balang Tauh (Kelabit): 16 March 2015* at Long Peluan.
Language: English.
Selon Buleng (Sa'ban): 16 March 2015* at Long Puak.
Language: Sa'ban. Interpreter: Elis Belare.

Long San and environs
William Lusing (Kenyah): 14 August 2018 at Long San.
Language: Malay and Kenyah. Interpreter: Thomas Jalong.
Anthony Lawai Karing (Kenyah): 14 August 2018 at Long San.
Language: Malay and Kenyah. Interpreter: Thomas Jalong.
Laran Along (Kenyah): 15 August 2018 at Tanjung Tepalit.
Language: Kenyah. Interpreter: Thomas Jalong.
Apoi Anggang (Kenyah): 16 August 2018 at Tanjung Tepalit.
Language: Kenyah. Interpreter: Thomas Jalong.

Long Semadoh
Padan Ating (Lun Bawang): 4 April 2015*.
Language: Lun Bawang. Interpreter: Mike Ukab Palong.

Semali Panai (Lun Bawang): 4 April 2015*.
Language: Lun Bawang. Interpreter: Mike Ukab Palong.

Marudi
Ren Keso (Penan): 11 August 2018.
Language: Penan. Interpreter: Joseph Darius Lajo.
Lajo Tiun and Singin Lawing (Penan): 11 August 2018.
Language: Penan. Interpreter: Joseph Darius Lajo.
Ving Lawing (Penan): 11 August 2018.
Language: Penan. Interpreter: Joseph Darius Lajo.

Miri
Nelson Balang Rining (Lun Bawang): 11 March 2015*.
Language: English.
Maran Raja (Kelabit): 12 March 2015*.
Language: Kelabit. Interpreter: Joseph Raja.
Larry Siga (Tabun): 12 March 2015*.
Language: English.
Peter Liling (Kelabit): 13 March 2015*.
Language: Malay.

Sibu and environs
Adrian anak Ringgau (Iban): 13 May 2015* at Sibu.
Language: English and Malay.
Juki anak Tawi (Iban): 28 November 2015* at Tanjung Penasu Batang Igan
Language: Malay and Iban. Interpreter: Simon Sawing.
Tadon anak Liang (Iban): 29 November 2015* at Rumah Catherine anak Liom.
Language: Malay and Iban. Interpreter: Catherine anak Liom.
Saleh anak Saong (Iban): 29 November 2015* at Bawang Assan.
Language: Malay.
Igey anak Tamin (Iban): 29 November 2015* at Bawang Assan.
Language: Malay.
John Ting (Chinese): 30 November 2015* at Sibu.
Language: English.
Tiong Pick Lan (Chinese): 30 November 2015* at Sibu.
Language: English and Foochow. Interpreter: John Ting.

Song
Uba Anak Ungka and Jubin anak Ugap (Iban): 4 December 2015.
Language: Malay.

Sungai Asap Resettlement Scheme

Lating Abun (Kayan): 25 May 2015* at Uma Balui Ukap.
Language: Malay and English.
Huirang Jok and Imang Jok (Kayan): 25 May 2015* at Uma Bawang.
Language: Kayan. Interpreter: Tony Kuleh.
Jok Laeng (Kayan): 25 May 2015* at Uma Juman.
Language: Kayan. Interpreter: Luhat Tugau.
Igang Igo (Kayan): 26 May 2015* at Uma Belor.
Language: Kayan. Interpreter: Luhat Tugau.
Hiroh Ului (Kayan): 26 May 2015* at Uma Belor.
Language: Kayan. Interpreter: Luhat Tugau.
Elli Sawang (Lahanan): 26 May 2015* at Uma Lahanan.
Language: Kayan. Interpreter: Luhat Tugau.
Levo Ugang (Lahanan): 26 May 2015* at Uma Lahanan.
Language: Kayan. Interpreter: Luhat Tugau.
Ubang Lawai (Kayan): 26 May 2015* at Uma Belor.
Language: Kayan. Interpreter: Luhat Tugau.

Upper Rejang River

Sawing anak Tek (Iban): 20 May 2015* at Nanga Benin.
Language: Iban. Interpreter: Milang Jawing.
Anam anak Bunggang (Iban): 20 May 2015* at Nanga Benin.
Language: Iban. Interpreter: Milang Jawing.
Binit anak Langai (Iban): 7 December 2015*, 8 December 2015 at Nanga Pila.
Language: Iban and Malay. Interpreter: Setepan anak Jaweng.
Setepan anak Jaweng (Iban): 7 December 2015*, 8 December 2015* at Nanga Pila.
Language: Malay.
Brain Mering (Punan): 9 December 2015* at Punan Bah.
Language: English.
Boi Kesai (Punan): 9 December 2015* at Punan Bah.
Language: Malay.
Bujang Belulok (Punan): 9 December 2015* at Punan Bah.
Language: Punan. Interpreter: Brain Mering.
Itu Lassa (Punan): 10 December 2015* at Punan Bah.
Language: Malay.
Sabing Belari (Punan): 10 December 2015* at Punan Bah.
Language: Malay.
Satty anak Berasap (Iban): 12 December 2015 at Nanga Merit.
Language: Iban. Interpreter: Megong anak Legang and Lorraimmie anak Megong.
Agas anak Drahman (Iban): 12 December 2015 at Nanga Merit.
Language: Iban. Interpreter: Megong anak Legang and Lorraimmie anak Megong.

Rena anak Ringkai (Iban): 12 December 2015 at Nanga Merit.
Language: Iban. Interpreter: Megong anak Legang and Lorraimmie anak Megong.

FORMAL INTERVIEWS CONDUCTED BY OTHERS (AUTHOR'S COLLECTION)

By Vinson Sutlive
Tedong anak Barieng (Iban): 30 June 1988 at Kapit.
Language: Iban. Written translation: Otto Steinmayer.
Harry Buxton (Eurasian): 12 July 1988 at Kuching.
Language: English.

By Bob Reece
Garai anak Siba' (Iban): January 1994 at Nanga Benin.
Language: Iban. Written translation: Otto Steinmayer.
Jeba anak Undit (Iban): January 1994 at Nanga Sejunggur.
Language: Iban. Written translation: Otto Steinmayer.

By Nichol anak Ragan
Listen Baling anak Luang (Iban): 14 June 1995 at Kapit.
Language: Iban. Written translation: Otto Steinmayer.

ARCHIVAL SOURCES

Arafura Research Archive, Charles Darwin University
14-003, Alan Powell Collection.

Australian War Memorial, Canberra (AWM)
AWM52 (War diaries, AMF, Second World War)
   1/5/62, Headquarters RAA 9 Aust Div and HQ Kuching Force, September – December 1945.
AWM54 (Written Records, 1939–45 War)
   41/4/35, 'Surrender of Japan – Interrogations of Japanese Commanders and Staffs, Conference Notes'.
   376/5/13, 'Report on Kuching to Headquarters, British Borneo Civil Administration Unit'.
   376/5/17, 'Policy of Civil Administration for the information and guidance of the Military upon liberation of Sarawak, North Borneo, Brunei and Labuan, May 1945'.
   376/5/31, 'British Borneo Civil Affairs Unit – Notes on discussion between Lieutenant Colonel Leach, BBCAU, Major Jinkins SRD and Colonel Wilson, GSO1 9 Australian Division, 1945'.

619/2/2, 'Report on the Sarawak Area'.

619/7/49, 'Movement Report No. 1 on British North Borneo Area'.

619/7/68, 'Allied Intelligence Bureau Information Reports, Services Reconnaissance Department Project – Semut – 1945'.

619/7/69, 'Allied Intelligence Bureau Information Report 500 – Services Reconnaissance Department – Sarawak'.

619/7/70 Part 1, 'Semut Operations – Reports by Lieutenant R.E. Waddy – Stores – Summaries, 1945'.

619/7/70 Part 2, 'Semut Operations – Reports by Lieutenant R.E. Waddy – Stores – Summaries, 1945'.

619/7/70 Part 3, 'Semut Operations, Patrols in British Borneo Area, Report by Lieutenant R.E. Waddy, 1945'.

619/7/79, 'Reports: Operation Semut II, 25 June – 14 July 1945'.

621/2/15 Part 1, 'Topographical Information, Borneo'.

621/2/15 Part 2, 'Topographical Information, North Borneo including Sandakan'.

621/2/15 Part 3, 'Topographical and General Information, Miri-Sarawak'.

621/2/15 Part 4, 'Topographical Information, Brunei – North Borneo, Jan 1945'.

621/2/15 Part 5, 'Topographical Information, Jesselton and Vicinity and Kudat North Borneo'.

621/2/15 Part 6, 'SRD Intelligence Branch, Information Summaries, Borneo'.

621/2/15 Part 7, 'HQ 1 Australian Corps – 3 Australian Aerial Photographic Interpretation Unit Photo Interpretation Reports, Sandakan – Berhala Island, Sandakan Airfield Area, Tawao Town and Airfield Area'.

627/4/1, 'SRD – British North Borneo, Activities, Narratives and Reports from April 1944 to August 1945'.

627/4/2, 'SRD – British and Dutch Borneo – Notes on meeting held at BBCAU 22/8/1945. Policy Post Surrender'.

627/4/3, 'SRD – Borneo Area, Operational Reports, Nos 1 to 9, 1945'.

627/4/4, 'SRD – Dutch Borneo, Distribution of Arms to Native Population in the Netherlands, 1945'.

627/4/6, 'SRD – Correspondence and Reports concerning operational parties in Borneo and Northern Territory Force – Participation in SRD Projects, 1945'.

627/4/7, 'SRD Policy – Surrender plans, post-surrender plans'.

627/4/8, 'Operation instructions issued by Group "A" Advanced HQ SRD'.

627/4/12, 'SRD – British North Borneo'.

627/4/15 Part 1, 'Semut Project Administrative – Stores and Supplies Procedure'.

627/4/15 Part 2, 'Semut Project Administrative – Stores and Supplies Procedure'.

627/4/16 Part 1, 'SRD Intelligence Reports, XIII-1 Tarakan'.

627/4/16 Part 4, 'SRD Intelligence Reports, XIII-6 Sinkawang, 1944'.

627/4/16 Part 5, 'SRD Intelligence Reports, XIII-7 Pontianak, 1944'.

627/4/16 Part 7, 'SRD Intelligence Reports, XIII Sarawak, Brunei, Labuan, 1945'.

627/4/16 Part 8, 'SRD Intelligence Reports, XIII Dutch Borneo, 1945'.

627/4/16 Part 10, 'SRD Intelligence Reports, XIII Sarawak, 1945'.

627/4/16 Part 11, 'SRD Intelligence Reports, XIII-8 Balikpapan'.

627/4/16 Part 15, 'SRD Intelligence Reports, XIII-25 Jesselton, 1944'.

627/4/16 Part 17, 'SRD Intelligence Reports, XIII-26 Kudat'.

627/4/16 Part 18, 'SRD Intelligence Reports, XIII-28 Sandakan'.

627/4/16 Part 21, 'SRD Intelligence Reports, XIII-50 Kuching Area, 1944'.

627/4/16 Part 22, 'SRD Intelligence Reports, XIII-51 Labuan, 1943'.

627/4/16 Part 23, 'SRD Intelligence Reports, XIII-52 Miri, 1944'.

627/4/16 Part 24, 'SRD Intelligence Reports, XIII-53 Bintulu A/F Sarawak'.

627/4/16 Part 25, 'SRD Intelligence Reports, XIII-54 Lutong, 1944'.

627/4/16 Part 26, 'SRD Intelligence Reports, XIII-55 Brunei, 1944'.

627/4/17, 'SRD – Report on clash between SRD and Japanese at Simanggang – Disposal of enemy equipment, Handover by SRD to BBCAU'.

627/4/18, 'SRD General Staff Intelligence, Special Report No. 6, Condition in British North Borneo and Sarawak 4/8/1945'.

627/5/1 Part 1, 'SRC – XV – Malaya, 1945'.

627/5/1 Part 2, 'SRC – Reports – Singapore, 1945'.

627/5/1 Part 10, 'SRC – Reports – XV-12 Sembawang, 1944'.

627/5/1 Part 13, 'SRC – Reports – XV-14 Singapore (Harbour and Naval Base)'.

627/10/1 Part 13, 'Swatow [Part 13 of 16]'.

779/1/17, 'Report on Allied prisoners of war in Brunei, Miri, Kuching Area'.

779/2/16, 'Prisoners of War Reception Group, Labuan – Reports and messages'.

779/3/82, 'Information – Allied Prisoners of War [. .] Detailed report on Allied PW in the Brunei – Miri Area between March/June 1945. Summary of information concerning Prisoners and Civilian internees Borneo'.

AWM192 (Honours and Awards, Second World War)

301, Box 6, Figgis P.E. – Graves J.E.

303, Box 9, Joshua R. – Loder G.B.

304, Box 7, Gray A.C. – Hill W.C.

307, Box 17, Wear R.W.N. – Zupp I.C.

309, Box 1, Abadee S. – Belson W.A.

310, Box 14, Robino P. – Smith E.S.

311, Box 5, Dhu H.R. – Fietz W.H.

316, Box 13, Perret L. – Robin J.W.D.

317, Box 10, Lodge E.B. – McWilliam J.M.

318, Box 12, Mulroney R. – Perren W.A.

AWM357 (Records of NX396 Brigadier Sir Victor Windeyer, Commanding Officer, 20th Australian Infantry Brigade)

7, '20 Aust Inf Bde – Report on Operation Oboe Six'.

14, 'Report on investigations – Australian and Allied prisoners of war – 9 Aust Div Area – 15 Aug 1945 to 27 Nov 1945'.

3DRL6502, Papers of Tom Harnett Harrisson.

PR00534, Papers of William Stanner.

PR84/247, Papers of Kelvin Hallam.

PR85/036, Papers of Roland Griffiths-Marsh.

PR85/325, Papers of Alan Wood.

PR90/172, Papers relating to Services Reconnaissance Department (SRD) AIF.

National Archives of Australia, Canberra (NAA)

A1066 (Department of External Affairs)

IC45/95/8, 'Internees – Allied Abroad Massacre of allied nationals at Longnawan, Borneo'.

A3269 (Department of the Army)

J4, 'Group "A" SRD – Distribution of Arms (Netherlands Borneo Natives)'.

O7/A, 'Official History of the Operations and Administration of Special Operations – Australia (SOA), also known as [. . .] Services Reconnaissance Department (SRD), Volume 1 – Organisation – Copy no 1'.

O8/A, 'Official History of the Operations and Administration of Special Operations – Australia (SOA), also known as [. . .] Services Reconnaissance Department (SRD), Volume 2 – Operations – Copy no 1'.

O8/B, 'Official History of the Operations and Administration of Special Operations – Australia (SOA), also known as [. . .] Services Reconnaissance Department (SRD), Volume 2 – Operations – Copy no 4 [. . .] abridged version of copy no 1'.

Q1/A, 'Official History of the Operations and Administration of Special Operations Australia (SOA), also known as [. . .] Services Reconnaissance Department (SRD) – Volume 4 – Training Syllabi – Part 1 – Appendix F'.

Q1/B, 'Official History of the Operations and Administration of Special Operations – Australia (SOA), also known as [. . .] Services Reconnaissance Department (SRD) – Volume 4 – Training Syllabi – Part 1'.

Q2, 'Official History of the Operations and Administration of Special Operations – Australia (SOA), also known as [. . .] Services Reconnaissance Department (SRD) – Volume 4 – Training Syllabi – Part 2'.

Q11, 'Official History of the Operations and Administration of Special Operations – Australia (SOA), also known as [. . .] Services Reconnaissance Department (SRD) – Volume 5 – Photographs – Copy no 2'.

A13/A, 'Semut I, copy I (British North Borneo, March – September 1945), Contents different from copy II'.

A14/A, 'Semut II, copy I (British North Borneo, March – September 1945), Contents different from copy II'.

A15/A, 'Semut III, copy I (British North Borneo, March – September 1945), Contents different from copy II'.

A15/B, 'Semut III, copy II (British North Borneo, March – September 1945), Contents different from copy I'.

A16/A, 'Intelligence and Information Reports – Semut (British North Borneo, March – September 1945'.

A16/B, 'Semut IV, copy I (British North Borneo, March – September 1945), Contents different from copy II'.

A16/C, 'Semut IV, copy II (British North Borneo, March – September 1945), Contents different from copy I'.

A10851 (Directorate of Military Intelligence)

10, 'Mr Ivan Southall's Notes for a book on the history of SRD – Services Reconnaissance Department in World War Two'.

B883 (Army Headquarters)

NX114963, Pippen, Francis Vincent.

NX130199, McLean, Donald James.

NX136161, Beiers, Pierre William.

NX144227, Phillpot, Gordon Henry.

NX15749, Gilman, Norman Ellis Rusden.

NX164342, Pare, Charles Walter.

NX35662, Croton, Ronald James.

NX42041, Graham, Neville Bruce.

NX73768, Foster, Desmond Lionel.

NX78025, Hartley, John Frederick.

QX11361, Sanderson, Charles Frederick.

QX19782, Barrie, John Keith.

QX35742, Cusack, Roderick Douglas Clive.

QX48608, Carter, Gordon Senior.

SX11095, Edmeades, Eric Arthur.

SX18853, Tredrea, Jonathan.

SX22304, Stokes, John Lewis.

SX25881, Burrow, Francis Wallis.

SX26223, Mellett, Norman Robert Ross.

SX30453, Felstead, Milton.

SX3396, Horsnell, Donald Leslie.

SX993, Baker, Ronald James.

TX16283, Hallam, Kelvin Walter.

VX128451, Fidler, Stewart Heritage.

VX1631, Kearney, David John.

VX31289, Oldham, Frank Rassendale.

VX3459, Wood, Max Holbrook.

VX35706, Duffus, Leo Herbert.

VX4918, Perry, Richard Charles.

VX63314, McCallum, Ian Archibald Neil.
VX6649, Middleton, Percy Vince.
VX71000, Heron, Charles Edward.
VX75967, Outhwaite, Richard Martin.
VX92910, Davey, Douglas Wilfred.
VX93198, Le Guier, Keith Allan.
VX93557, Neave, Jack.
VX95325, Walpole, Brian Blayney.
WX16232, Fowler, Hubert Norman.
WX16705, Long, Bertram Charles.
WX16848, Spurling, Edric Ray.
WX17377, Bradbury, Ross William.
WX36583, Astill, Robert Arthur.
WX36793, The Soen Hin.
WX36796, Abu Kassim.
B884 (Army Headquarters)
W15805, Lansi bin Eusop.

Special Air Service Regiment (SASR) Historical Archives, Perth
Papers of G.B. Courtney.

Durham University Library Archives
GB-0033-MAC, Malcolm MacDonald Papers.

Imperial War Museum, London (IWM)
16406, Papers of Lieutenant Colonel J.E.B. Finlay.
16752, Papers of Lieutenant W.S. Eadie.
16755, Papers of Major J. Truscott.
16756, Operation Semut documents, 1945.

National Archives, London (NAUK)
CAB 84/70/48, 'Operations in Borneo. Note by Secretary'.
CAB 84/71/32, 'Operations in Borneo. Note by Secretary'.
CAB 121/717, Operations in Borneo, March 1945 – August 1946.
DEFE 2/1171, Operations in Borneo: Report.
FCO 141/12402, Sarawak: military use of Dayaks in Malaya; reports by officers who escaped Sarawak at time of invasion.
FO 916/1422, British subjects in Borneo – welfare.
HS 1/239, Special Operations Executive – Australia – Personnel.
HS 1/244, Monthly situation report Sarawak and Borneo; SWPA monthly report; SRD operations quarterly; weekly sitreps and SRD operations; Melbourne sitreps; summary of operations Aug 1944 – May 1945.

HS 1/251, SRD operations in Borneo in support of Oboe; Robin/Platypus and others.
HS 1/253, SRD operations 1942–1945; miscellaneous alphabetical . . . memorandum on SRD operations in British Borneo.
HS 7/93, Summary of Services Reconnaissance Department projects, 1942–1945.
HS 7/94, Summary of Services Reconnaissance Department projects, 1942–1945.
HS 8/951, Colonial Office: Special Operations Australia (SOA) in Borneo and Sarawak.
HS 9/274/2, Gordon Senior Carter.
HS 9/377/5, Alfred Dudley Crowther.
WO 208/1053, Borneo.
WO 208/1054, Borneo.
WO 208/1055, Borneo.
WO 252/514, Special report: Labuan, Sandakan and Tarakan areas of North Borneo.
WO 361/1761, Report on investigations in British Borneo (British North Borneo, Labuan, Brunei, Sarawak) concerning Australian and Allied prisoners of war, 9th Australian Division Area, 15 August to 27 November 1945.
WO 373/65/2011, Recommendation for Award for Carter, Gordon Senior.
WO 373/65/2013, Recommendation for Award for Sochon, William Lomas Philip.
WO 373/65/2255, Recommendation for Award for Bower, Douglas Norman.
WO 373/65/2466, Recommendation for Award for Harrisson, Tom Harnett.
WO 373/93/116, Recommendation for Award for Courtney, Godfrey Basil.

The University of Victoria Digital Collections, Victoria, Canada
Roger Cheng, interview by Reginald H. Roy, 22 February 1971, SC104_CR_215, The University of Victoria, Digital Collections.

Tun Jugah Foundation, Kuching
Fieldnotes of Derek Freeman.

PRIVATELY HELD COLLECTIONS
Papers and other resources of Bob Reece (Perth).

Papers of Major J. Truscott (Perth).

PUBLISHED WORKS
Books
Avun, Baling, *The Old Kayan Religion and the Bungan Religious Reform* (translated and annotated by Jérôme Rousseau), Institute of East Asian Studies, UNIMAS, Kuching, 2003.
Bala, Sagau Batu, *Kelabit's Story: The Great Transition*, Trafford, Singapore, 2013.

Bartram, Flight Lieutenant Paul, 'Chapter 17' in Bob Long (ed.), *Operation Semut 1: Soldiering with the Head-Hunters of Borneo*, B. Long Publications, Bayswater, W.A., 1989.

Bock, Carl, *The Head-hunters of Borneo: a Narrative of Travel Up the Mahakkam and Down the Barito*, Oxford University Press, Singapore and Oxford, 1985 [1881].

Bourke, Joanna, *An Intimate History of Killing: Face-to-Face Killing in Twentieth-Century Warfare*, Basic Books, New York, 1999.

Braithwaite, Richard Wallace, *Fighting Monsters: An Intimate History of the Sandakan Tragedy*, Australian Scholarly, North Melbourne, 2016.

Bynum, Caroline Walker, *Fragmentation and Redemption: Essays on Gender and the Human Body in Medieval Religion*, Zone Books, New York, 1992.

Calder, Angus, 'Introduction to T.E. Lawrence' in *Seven Pillars of Wisdom*, Wordsworth, Ware, 1997.

Campbell, Lloyd, *Z-Special: Desert–Jungle–Sabotage*, Australian Military History Publications, Loftus, 2006.

Conrad, Joseph, *Heart of Darkness*, Penguin, Harmondsworth, 1973 [1902].

Courtney, G.B., *Silent Feet: The History of 'Z' Special Operations 1942–1945*, Slouch Hat Publications, McCrae, 1993.

Cruickshank, Charles, *SOE in the Far East*, Oxford University Press, Oxford and New York, 1983.

Davison, Julian and Vinson Sutlive, 'The children of *Nising*: images of headhunting and male sexuality in Iban ritual and oral literature', in Vinson H. Sutlive, Jr (ed.), *Female and Male in Borneo: Contributions and Challenges to Gender Studies*, Borneo Research Council, Williamsburg, Virginia, 1991.

Donnison, F.S.V., *British Military Administration in the Far East 1943–46*, H.M.S.O., London, 1956.

Dower, John W., *War Without Mercy: Race and Power in the Pacific War*, Pantheon, New York, 1986.

Dynes, Phil, *Leyburn's Liberators: and those Lonely Special Duties Air Operations*, P. Dynes, Gloucester, NSW, 1999.

Edmeades, Captain E.A., 'Chapter 2', in Bob Long (ed.) *Operation Semut 1: Soldiering with the Head-Hunters of Borneo*, B. Long Publications, Bayswater, WA, 1989.

Edwards, Leonard and Peter W. Stevens, *Short Histories of the Lawas and Kanowit Districts*, Borneo Literature Review, Kuching, 1971.

Evans, Stephen R., *Sabah Under the Rising Sun Government*, Opus Publications, Kota Kinabalu, 2007 [1990].

Fahey, John, *Australia's First Spies: The Remarkable Story of Australia's Intelligence Operations, 1901–45*, Allen & Unwin, Sydney, 2018.

Fell, Captain W.R., *The Sea Our Shield*, Cassell, London, 1966.

Feuer, A.B., *Australian Commandos: Their Secret War Against the Japanese in WWII*, Stackpole Books, Mechanicsburg, Pennsylvania, 2006 [1996].

Fong Hon Kah, *A History of the Development of Baram River Basin in Sarawak*, Julitta Lim, Kuching, 2008.

Freeman, Derek, *Report on the Iban*, Athlone Press, London, 1970.

Friend, Theodore, *The Blue-Eyed Enemy: Japan Against the West in Java and Luzon, 1942–1945*, Princeton University Press, Princeton, New Jersey, 1988.

Geddes, W.R., *Nine Dayak Nights*, Oxford University Press, Melbourne, 1957.

Griffiths-Marsh, Roland, *The Sixpenny Soldier*, Angus & Robertson, Sydney, 1990.

Hall, Maxwell, *Kinabalu Guerrillas*, Borneo Literature Bureau, Jesselton, 1965 [1962].

Hallam, Sergeant K.W., 'Chapter 6' in Bob Long (ed.), *Operation Semut 1: Soldiering with the Head-Hunters of Borneo*, B. Long Publications, Bayswater, WA, 1989.

Ham, Paul, *Sandakan: The Untold Story of the Sandakan Death Marches*, William Heinemann, Sydney, 2012.

Hansen, Eric, *Stranger in the Forest: On Foot Across Borneo*, Houghton Mifflin Company, Boston, 1988.

Hardy, Charles, 'Chapter 15', in Bob Long (ed.), *Operation Semut 1: Soldiering with the Head-Hunters of Borneo*, B. Long Publications, Bayswater, WA, 1989.

Harrisson, Tom, *World Within: A Borneo Story*, Cresset Press, London, 1959.

Harrisson, Tom (ed.), *Borneo Jungle: An Account of the Oxford University Expedition of 1932*, Oxford University Press, Singapore, 1988.

Heidhues, Mary Somers, *Golddiggers, Farmers, and Traders in the 'Chinese Districts' of West Kalimantan, Indonesia*, Cornell Southeast Asia Program, Ithaca, New York, 2003.

Heimann, Judith, *The Most Offending Soul Alive: Tom Harrisson and his Remarkable Life*, University of Hawai'i Press, Honolulu, 1997.

Heimann, Judith, *The Airmen and the Headhunters*, Harcourt, Orlando, 2007.

Holmes, Kent, *Wendell Fertig and his Guerrilla Forces in the Philippines: Fighting the Japanese Occupation, 1942–1945*, McFarland and Co., Jefferson, North Carolina, 2015.

Horner, David, *High Command: Australia's Struggle for an Independent War Strategy 1939–1945*, Allen & Unwin, Sydney, 1992.

Horton, D.C., *Ring of Fire: Australian Guerrilla Operations Against the Japanese in World War II*, Macmillan, Melbourne and Crows Nest, 1983.

Hose, Charles, *Natural Man: A Record from Borneo*, Oxford University Press, Singapore and New York, 1988 [1926].

Howarth, Patrick, *Undercover: The Men and Women of the Special Operations Executive*, Arrow Books, London, 1990.

Hua, Julitta Lim Shau, *Pussy's in the Well: Japanese Occupation of Sarawak 1941–1945*, Research and Resource Centre, SUPP Headquarters, Kuching, 2005.

Jones, L.W., *The Population of Borneo: A Study of the Peoples of Sarawak, Sabah and Brunei*, Opus Publications, Kota Kinabalu, 2007 [1966].

Keith, Agnes, *Three Came Home*, Eland, London, 2002 [1948].

King, Victor T., 'Editor's introduction to H.F. Tillema' in *A Journey Among the Peoples of Central Borneo in Word and Picture*, Oxford University Press, Singapore, 1990.

King, Victor T., *The Peoples of Borneo*, Blackwell, Oxford and Cambridge, 1993.

Larson, Frances, *Severed: A History of Heads Lost and Heads Found*, Granta, London, 2014.

Lightner, Sam Jnr, *All Elevations Unknown: An Adventure in the Heart of Borneo*, Broadway Books, New York, 2001.

Lim Beng Hai and Gabriel Tan, *Sarawak Under the Throes of War: Reflection of a 'Z' Special Force Operative*, Penerbitan Sehati Sdn Bhd, Kuching, 2010.

Lim Beng Huat, *Chaos at Lubok Belaga*, Borneo Literature Bureau, Kuching, 1977.

Lock, Margaret, *Twice Dead: Organ Transplants and the Reinvention of Death*, University of California Press, Berkeley, 2002.

Long, Bob (ed.), *Operation Semut 1: Soldiering with the Head-Hunters of Borneo*, B. Long Publications, Bayswater, WA, 1989.

Long, W.O.II B.C., 'Chapter 7', in Bob Long (ed.), *Operation Semut 1: Soldiering with the Head-Hunters of Borneo*, B. Long Publications, Bayswater, WA, 1989.

Long, Gavin, *The Final Campaigns*, Australian War Memorial, Canberra, 1963.

MacDonald, Malcolm, *Borneo People*, Jonathan Cape, London, 1956.

Macintyre, Ben, *SAS: Rogue Heroes. The Authorized Wartime History*, Penguin, London, 2017.

Malone, Paul, *Kill the Major: The True Story of the Most Successful Allied Guerrilla War in Borneo*, Strategic Information and Research Development Centre, Selangor, 2020.

McDonald, Gabrielle, *New Zealand's Secret Heroes: Don Stott and the 'Z' Special Unit*, Reed, Auckland, 1991.

McDonald, Gabrielle Kirk and Olivia Swaak-Goldman (eds), *Substantive and Procedural Aspects of International Criminal Law: The Experience of International and National Courts*, Kluwer Law International, The Hague and Boston, 2000.

Metcalf, Peter, *They Lie, We Lie: Getting on with Anthropology*, Routledge, London and New York, 2002.

Metcalf, Peter, *The Life of the Longhouse: An Archaeology of Ethnicity*, Cambridge University Press, New York, 2010.

Morrison, Alastair, *Fair Land Sarawak: Some Recollections of an Expatriate Official*, Studies on Southeast Asia, Southeast Asia Program, Cornell University, Ithaca, New York, 1993.

Morrison, Hedda, *Sarawak*, MacGibbon and Kee, London, 1957.

Ooi Keat Gin (ed.), *Japanese Empire in the Tropics, Volumes I and II*, Ohio University for International Studies, Athens, 1998.

Ooi Keat Gin, *Rising Sun Over Borneo: the Japanese Occupation of Sarawak, 1941–1945*, Macmillan, Basingstoke and London, 1999.

Ooi Keat Gin, *The Japanese Occupation of Borneo, 1941–1945*, Routledge, London and New York, 2011.

Powell, Alan, *War by Stealth: Australians and the Allied Intelligence Bureau 1942–1945*, Melbourne University Press, Carlton South, Victoria, 1996.

Pratten, Garth and Glyn Harper, *Still the Same: Reflections on Active Service from Bardia to Baidoa*, Army Doctrine Centre, Georges Heights, NSW, 1996.

Pringle, Robert, *Rajahs and Rebels: The Ibans of Sarawak Under Brooke Rule, 1841–1941*, Cornell University Press, Ithaca, New York, 1970.

Pustaka Negeri Sarawak, *The Unsung Heroes: Voices of the Sarawakian Guerrillas of 'Z' Special Unit*, Pustaka Negeri Sarawak, Kuching, 2013.

Reece, Bob, *Masa Jepun: Sarawak under the Japanese 1941–1945*, Sarawak Literary Society, Kuching, 1998.

Reece, R.H.W., *The Name of Brooke: The End of White Rajah Rule in Sarawak*, Oxford University Press, Kuala Lumpur, 1982.

Rewcastle Brown, Claire, *The Sarawak Report: The Inside Story of the 1MDB Exposé*, Lost World Press, London, 2018.

Richards, Anthony, *An Iban–English Dictionary*, Oxford University Press, Petaling Jaya, 1988.

Richardson, Hal, *One-Man War: The Jock McLaren Story*, Angus & Robertson, Sydney, 1957.

Ritchie, James, *Temenggong Oyong Lawai Jau: A Paramount Chief in Borneo: The Legacy*, James Ritchie, Kuching, 2006.

Ritchie, James, *The Life Story of Temenggong Koh (1870–1956)*, Kaca Holdings Sdn Bhd, Sarawak, n.d.

Rooney, John, *Khabar Gembira (The Good News): A History of the Catholic Church in East Malaysia and Brunei 1880–1976*, Burns and Oates/Mill Hill Missionaries, London and Kota Kinabalu, 1981.

Rousseau, Jérôme, *Central Borneo: Ethnic Identity and Social Life in a Stratified Society*, Clarendon Press, Oxford, 1990.

Russell, Lord of Liverpool, *The Knights of Bushido: A Short History of Japanese War Crimes*, Cassell and Co., London, 1958.

Sanderson, Sergeant Charles Frederick, 'Chapter 4', in Bob Long (ed.), *Operation Semut 1: Soldiering with the Head-Hunters of Borneo*, B. Long Publications, Bayswater, WA, 1989.

Saunders, Graham, *Bishops and Brookes: The Anglican Mission and the Brooke Raj in Sarawak 1848–1941*, Oxford University Press, Singapore, 1992.

Sellato, Bernard, *Hornbill and Dragon*, Elf Aquitaine Indonésie/Elf Aquitaine Malaysia, Jakarta and Kuala Lumpur, 1989.

Silver, Lynette Ramsay, *Sandakan: A Conspiracy of Silence*, Sally Milner, Binda, NSW, 1998.

Silver, Lynette Ramsay, *Blood Brothers: Sabah and Australia 1942–1945*, Opus Publications, Kota Kinabalu, 2010.

Sligo, Graeme, *The Backroom Boys: Alfred Conlon and Army's Directorate of Research and Civil Affairs, 1942–46*, Big Sky Publishing, Moss Vale, NSW, 2013.

Smith, Kevin, *Borneo: Australia's Proud but Tragic Heritage*, K.R. & H. Smith, Armidale, 1999.

Smith, Neil C. Lieutenant Colonel, *They Came Unseen: The Men and Women of Z Special Unit*, Mostly Unsung Military History, Brighton, Victoria, 2010.

Southwell, C. Hudson, *Uncharted Waters*, Astana Publishing, Calgary, 1999.

Spencer Chapman, F., *The Jungle is Neutral*, Chatto & Windus, London, 1949.

Stanley, Peter, *Tarakan: An Australian Tragedy*, Allen & Unwin, Sydney, 1997.

Straumann, Lukas, *Money Logging: On the Trail of the Asian Timber Mafia*, Bergli Books, Basel, 2014.

Sutlive, Vinson H. Jr., *The Iban of Sarawak: Chronicle of a Vanishing World*, Waveland Press, Prospect Heights, Illinois, 1978.

Sutlive, Vinson H. Jr., *Tun Jugah of Sarawak: Colonialism and Iban Response*, Sarawak Literary Society, Kuching, 1992.

Tan, William, *William Tan of Sarawak: Architect, Politician, Social Worker*, s.n., Kuching, 1997.

Tillema, H.F., *A Journey Among the Peoples of Central Borneo in Word and Picture* (edited by Victor T. King), Oxford University Press, Singapore, 1990 [1938].

Ting, John H.S. *The History of Architecture in Sarawak Before Malaysia*, Pertubuhan Akitek Malaysia Sarawak Chapter, Kuching, 2018.

Ting, John Sik Kang, Chua Cheen Choon and Wee Kok Poh, *Sibu of Yesterday*, Sarawak Chinese Cultural Association, Sibu, 2002.

Tredrea, Jack, 'Chapter 5', in Bob Long (ed.), *Operation Semut 1: Soldiering with the Head-Hunters of Borneo*, B. Long Publications, Bayswater, WA, 1989.

Venning, Annabel, *To War with the Walkers: One Family's Extraordinary Story of Survival in the Second World War*, Hodder & Stoughton, London, 2019.

Wagner, Ulla, *Colonialism and Iban Warfare*, OBE-Tryck Sthim, Stockholm, 1972.

Walker, J.H., *Power and Prowess: The Origins of Brooke Kingship in Sarawak*, Allen & Unwin/ University of Hawai'i Press, Sydney and Honolulu, 2002.

Walpole, Brian (with David Levell), *My War*, ABC Books, Sydney, 2004.

Wels, Welmoet, *Dead Body Management in Armed Conflict: Paradoxes in Trying to do Justice to the Dead*, Jongbloed, The Hague and Leiden, 2016.

Wigzell, Francis Alexander, *New Zealand Army Involvement: Special Operations Australia South-West Pacific World War II*, Pentland Press, Durham, 2001.

Winzeler, Robert L., *The Architecture of Life and Death in Borneo*, University of Hawai'i Press, Honolulu, 2004.

Wong, Marjorie, *The Dragon and the Maple Leaf*, Pirie Publications, London, Ontario, 1994.

Wong Tze Ken, Danny, *Historical Sabah: The War*, Opus Publications, Kota Kinabalu, 2010.

Yong, Tan Sri Stephen, *A Life Lived Twice: A Memoir*, Estate of Stephen Yong, Sarawak, 2010.

Journals, Magazines and Newspapers

Carter, G.S., 'Sarawak adventure', *The N.Z. Surveyor* XIX(3), 1946, pp. 246–57.

Clayre, Beatrice, 'The fate of Donald Hudden', *Borneo Research Bulletin* 30, 1999, pp. 140–2.

Courtney, G.B., 'Z Special Unit operations from Australia, 1942–1945', in *U.S.I. News Victoria*, 2(94), 1989.

Harrisson, Tom, 'The Chinese in Borneo 1942–1946', *International Affairs (Royal Institute of International Affairs 1944–)*, 26(3), 1950, pp. 354–62.

Harrisson, Tom, 'Eight men dropped from the skies – Part 1', *Commando: The Magazine of the Australian Commando Association*, Edition 2 2020, 2020.

Helliwell, Christine, 'The Japanese Malay: ethnic categorisation in southwest Borneo', *Bijdragen tot de Taal-, Land- en Volkenkunde* 170, 2014, pp. 191–214.

Heppell, Michael, 'Two curators, a classification of Borneo swords and some swords in the Sarawak Museum collection', *Sarawak Museum Journal* 89, 2011, pp. 1–40.

Koh, Temenggong, 'Temenggong Koh: reminiscences', *Borneo Research Bulletin* 25, 1993, pp. 153–65.

Ohnuki-Tierney, Emiko, 'Brain death and organ transplantation: cultural bases of medical technology', *Current Anthropology* 35(3), 1994, pp. 233–54.

Ooi Keat Gin, 'Prelude to invasion: covert operations before the re-occupation of Northwest Borneo, 1944–45', *Journal of the Australian War Memorial* 37, 2002, pp. 1–31.

Porritt, V.L., 'More bitter than sweet: Lena Ricketts' experiences during the Japanese occupation of Sarawak 1941–1945', *Sarawak Gazette* 1531, March 1995, pp. 46–53.

Sandin, Benedict, 'Sources of Iban traditional history', *Sarawak Museum Journal* 67 (Special Monograph No. 7), 1994.

Sellato, Bernard, 'Crime scene: the Müller Mountains region in Japanese times', *Borneo Research Bulletin* 32, 2001, pp. 225–7.

Stanley, Peter, '"Sniffing the ground": Australians and Borneo – 1945', *Journal of the Australian War Memorial* 25, 1994, pp. 37–43.

Tillema, H.F., 'Apo-Kayan, the heart of Borneo', *The Nederland Mail* 1, 1934, pp. 1–4.

Wadley, Reed L., 'Punitive expeditions and divine revenge: oral and colonial histories of rebellion and pacification in Western Borneo, 1886–1902', *Ethnohistory* 51(3), 2004, pp. 609–36.

Watters, David A.K., 'Loch Ness, Special Operations Executive and the first surgeon in paradise: Robert Kenneth Wilson (26.1.1899 – 6.6.1969)', *ANZ Journal of Surgery* 77, 2007, pp. 1053–7.

Wong, Tony, 'Operation Oblivion unknown piece of Canada's war history', *The Star*, https://www.thestar.com/entertainment/television/2014/01/24/operation_oblivion_unknown_piece_of_canadas_war_history.html, 24 January 2014.

Yao Ping Hua, 'Those momentous days in Kapit', *Sarawak Gazette* 1166, 30 April 1956, pp. 92–6.

UNPUBLISHED MANUSCRIPTS AND THESES

Barrie, Keith, *Borneo Story*, unpublished manuscript, MSS1532, AWM, 1992.

Chee K. Lam, *The Population of Sarawak*, PhD Thesis, The Australian National University, 1983.

Janowski, Monica, *Rice, Work and Community among the Kelabit of Sarawak, East Malaysia*, PhD Thesis, London School of Economics, 1991.

Moor, Rick, *Abbreviated history of special operations forces operating from Australia in WW2*, unpublished manuscript, author's collection, n.d..

Sochon, Bill, 'Semut Diary – 1945', in Keith Barrie, *Borneo Story*, unpublished manuscript, MSS1532, AWM, n.d.

Talib, Naimah bte Said, *The Development of the Sarawak Administrative Service from its Inception (1840s) to 1963*, PhD Thesis, University of Hull, 1993.

Ting, John Hwa Seng, *Precarious Power, Forts and Outstations: Indigenisation, Institutional Architecture and Settlement Patterns in Sarawak, 1841–1917*, PhD Thesis, University of Melbourne, 2014.

Tredrea, Jonathan, *Army Career of Jonathan Tredrea*, unpublished manuscript, author's collection, n.d.

Truscott, Major Jim et al., *Voices from Borneo: The Japanese War*, unpublished manuscript, https://pdfslide.net/documents/voices-from-borneo.html, n.d.

Waddy, Rowan E., *On Operations with Z Special Unit – WWII*, unpublished manuscript, author's collection, 1995.

Wren, Ivor, *Down-Stream Twice: A Sarawak Saga*, unpublished manuscript, author's collection, 1968.

MILITARY MANUALS

The Borneo Book for Servicemen, Australian Military Forces, author's collection, n.d.

Army Special Operations Forces Unconventional Warfare (Field Manual 3-05.130), Headquarters, Department of the Army (US), https://fas.org/irp/doddir/army/fm3-05-130.pdf, 2008.

GOVERNMENT GAZETTES

Supplement to the *London Gazette*, 25 October 1938.

Supplement to the *London Gazette*, 26 October 1943.

Supplement to the *London Gazette*, 11 November 1943.

Supplement to the *London Gazette*, 26 April 1946.

Supplement to the *London Gazette*, 7 November 1946.

Supplement to the *London Gazette*, 26 October 1948.

Supplement to the *London Gazette*, 30 March 1951.

Sarawak Gazette 1059, 1 November 1941.

Sarawak Gazette 1067, 1 February 1947.

Sarawak Gazette 1075, 1 October 1947.

CONVENTIONS AND TREATIES

Convention for the Amelioration of the Condition of the Wounded and Sick in Armies in the Field, Geneva, 27 July 1929.

ONLINE RESOURCES

Chinese Canadian Military Museum, 'Norman Mon Low', http://www.ccmms.ca/veteran-stories/army/norman-mon-low/

Chinese Canadian Military Museum, 'James Shiu', http://www.ccmms.ca/veteran-stories/army/james-shiu/

Chinese Canadian Military Museum, 'Roger Cheng', http://www.ccmms.ca/veteran-stories/army/roger-cheng/

Chinese Canadian Military Museum, 'Louey King', http://www.ccmms.ca/veteran-stories/army/louey-king/

Chinese Canadian Military Museum, 'Roy Chan', https://www.ccmms.ca/veteran-stories/army/roy-chan/

Sarawak Report, Baram Dam Blockade, https://web.archive.org/web/20150103214605if_/http://www.sarawakreport.org/baram/

Veterans' Affairs Canada, 'Heroes Remember – Canadian Chinese Veterans: Roy Chan', https://www.veterans.gc.ca/eng/remembrance/those-who-served/chinese-canadian-veterans/profile/chanr#transcript

PICTURE CREDITS

Page 1

Illustration: from Bock, *Head-hunters of Borneo*.

Photograph: Bernard Sellato. Courtesy of Bernard Sellato.

Page 2

Top photograph: Jean Subra OMI. Courtesy of Bernard Sellato.

Bottom photograph: from Morrison, *Sarawak*.

Page 3

Photograph: from Sellato, *Hornbill and Dragon*. Courtesy of Bernard Sellato.

Page 4

Top left photograph: Mering Ngo. Courtesy of Mering Ngo.

Top right photograph: from Morrison, *Sarawak*.

Bottom photograph: from Sellato, *Hornbill and Dragon*. Courtesy of Bernard Sellato.

Page 5

Top photograph: from Morrison, *Sarawak*.

Bottom photograph: Michael Heppell.

Page 6

Top photograph: Bernard Sellato. Courtesy of Bernard Sellato.

Photograph of *pua*: John Gollings.

Page 7

Photograph: from Truscott et al, *Voices from Borneo*. Courtesy of Jim Truscott.

Page 8

Photograph: from MacDonald, *Borneo People*.

Page 9

Top photograph: Christine Horn. Source: Sarawak Museum, Kuching.

Bottom left photograph: from Waddy, *On Operations with Z Special Unit*. Courtesy of Jill Waddy.

Bottom right photograph: from Avun, *The Old Kayan Religion*. Courtesy of Edward Usa.

Page 10

Top photograph: Bernard Sellato. Courtesy of Bernard Sellato.

Middle photograph: Michael Heppell.

Bottom photograph: from Winzeler, *Architecture of Life and Death*.

Page 11

Top photograph: source: Ho Ah Chon's Photographs, Special Collection, Pustaka Negeri Sarawak. Courtesy of Pustaka Negeri Sarawak.

Bottom photograph: source: The Bodleian Libraries, University of Oxford, MSS. Pac. 83, Vol. 11, Photo 34. By permission The Brooke Heritage Trust.

Page 12

Top photograph: from Barrie, *Borneo Story*. Courtesy of Keith Barrie's family.

Bottom left photograph: from Harrisson, *World Within*.

Bottom right photograph: source: Sarawak Museum, Kuching.

Page 13

Top and bottom photographs: from Barrie, *Borneo Story*. Courtesy of Keith Barrie's family.

Page 14

Top and bottom photographs: from Barrie, *Borneo Story*. Courtesy of Keith Barrie's family.

Page 15

Photograph of guerrilla: from the collection of the National Archives of Australia, Special Operations Australia (SOA) – Services Reconnaissance Department (SRD – Operations – SEMUT 2, A3269, Q11/76(D), Iban armed with rifle and *parang*.

Photographs of hilts: Michael Heppell.

Page 16

Top left photograph: from the collection of the National Archives of Australia, Special Operations Australia (SOA) – Services Reconnaissance Department (SRD) – Operations – SEMUT 2, A3269, Q11/78(D), [location of drop zone, SEMUT II headquarters in Long Akah, Baram River, and, Akah River].

Top right photograph: source: collection of the National Archives of Australia, Special Operations Australia (SOA) – Services Reconnaissance Department (SRD) – Operations – SEMUT 2, A3269, Q11/88(C), Supply Dropping – verification by photograph – re-supply SEMUT 3, 8 July 1945.

Bottom photograph: Colin Behn. Courtesy of Colin Behn.

ACKNOWLEDGEMENTS

WRITING A BOOK OF this kind demands astounding generosity from strangers as well as friends. It is impossible to compile an exhaustive list of the many people who have helped during its long gestation. Nevertheless, some have been so important that they cannot escape acknowledgement.

The Australian Research Council and the Australian War Memorial (AWM) both provided funding for the broader research project in which this book originated. Paul Pickering from the Australian National University (ANU) and Tim Sullivan of the AWM lent crucial support during the project's early days. The School of Archaeology and Anthropology in the College of Arts and Social Sciences at the ANU has been my academic home since the 1990s. I am grateful to the many colleagues there with whom I have discussed the project.

Thanks to staff at the AWM Research Centre, the National Archives of Australia, the National Archives (UK) and the Imperial War Museum (UK) for their unfailing professionalism. Robyn van Dyk, Head of the AWM's Research Centre and Partner Investigator on our joint ARC Linkage Grant, has provided endless assistance and support. I also thank Greg Mawkes at the Special Air Service Regiment Historical Archives in Perth, Mary Paton at the Arafura Research Archive at Charles Darwin University, Peter Knight, editor of *New Zealand Surveyor*, and Jan Knight of Survey and Spatial New Zealand, all of whom helped me track down relevant documents.

In Sarawak, Ipoi Datan, then Director of the Sarawak Museum, sponsored the research. Datu Aloysius Dris, Dato Lim Kian Hock, Tan Sri Datuk Amar Leonard Linggi anak Jugah, Tan Sri Datuk Amar Leo Moggie anak Irok and Puan Sri Datin Amar Elizabeth Moggie, Datu Ose Murang and John Ting Sik Kang all helped identify and locate potential interviewees. Datu Ose Murang and Datu Robert Lian Balangalibun both provided crucial assistance with translation and clarification of detail during the writing process. My thanks to them all.

Without Jayl Langub's extensive networks some of the fieldwork would not have been possible, and without his boundless kindness many seemingly intractable problems would not have been solved. I am grateful to scores of *kepala kampung* throughout Sarawak and Sabah who provided hospitality and assistance during my field trips in 2015 and 2018, as well as to the many interpreters used during the interviews (their names are listed in the Bibliography). Thanks to Joseph Darius Lajo, Thomas Jalong and Ricky Ganang who all travelled with, and interpreted for, me at different times. I owe a special debt to Valerie Mashman, who worked as a research associate with the project in its early stages, journeying with me during part of 2015 and later supporting the project in every way she could. Without her perspicacity, enthusiasm and talent for organisation the project may never have got off the ground.

The book would not have come into being without the insight, energy and kindness of my agent Margaret Gee. After a lifetime of academic publishing, working with the folks at Penguin Random House has been a revelation: thanks especially to the warm professionalism of my publisher, Alison Urquhart, and the thoughtful brilliance of my editor, Clive Hebard. My osteopath, Tom Eastman, and gardener, David Rosser, kept my body and garden healthy during months of ten-hour days at the computer. Shamim Homayun did a sterling job at short notice sorting out place names. Alicia Freile demonstrated extraordinary fortitude and creative flair to produce the beautiful maps. I cannot convey how much I owe my research assistant, Nicole Townsend. She displayed a genius for ferreting out documents key to the Semut story as well as unlimited patience while teaching me the arcane intricacies of military history referencing systems.

Garth Pratten and Peter Stanley patiently helped this neophyte find her way in the unfamiliar discipline of military history; I am especially grateful to Garth for providing detailed commentary on several pages of the manuscript. John Ting gave crucial assistance with maps and photographs. Others who generously shared their expertise in a range of areas include Rita Armstrong, Jinap Ato, Jamie Coates, Andrea De Antoni, Mark Fletcher, David Horner, Doug Knight, Jayl Langub, Paul Malone, Valerie Mashman, Narrelle Morris, Alan Powell, James Ritchie, Chris Roberts, Neil Smith, Neil Spackman, Ting Ing Kiet and John Walker.

Information from an earlier generation of anthropologists – who carried out fieldwork in Borneo as early as the 1960s – has been critical to the accuracy of my account. Michael Heppell, Jérôme Rousseau, Clifford Sather, and Vinson Sutlive have searched through old fieldnotes, dug out and scanned fieldwork maps, and called on their vast knowledge of various Borneo peoples to answer a multitude of impossible questions: they make me proud to call myself an anthropologist. Vinson also sent me an invaluable collection of interviews he recorded in Sarawak in the 1980s, while

Michael kindly contributed some beautiful photographs for repro-
duction in the book.

Jim Truscott and Bob Reece – whose own books charted the way
for so much that I write here – are each owed a huge debt. They
made available to me their private collections of documents, interview transcripts, notes and tapes relating to Operation Semut and
WWII in Borneo more generally. Without these materials this book
would have been considerably poorer. Jim also assisted in numerous
other ways, including drawing my attention to previously unrecog-
nised sources and tracking down hard-to-find documents.

Many family members of SRD veterans helped bring this pro-
ject to fruition: some sent me written material and photographs,
others met and/or talked with me over the phone. I am grateful to
Margaret Archibald, Vona Beiers, John Bower, Jenny Coats and
Donald Schinckel, Stephen Ellis, Warwick Giblin and Belinda Kerr,
Andrew Greenwood, Mayken Griffiths-Marsh, Stephen Halgren,
Vanessa Haw, Donn Leckie, Judi Millar, Bill Nibbs, Barbara Royle,
David Sanderson, Kim and Peter Sterelny, and Jill Waddy and
Lindall Watson. I owe special thanks to Anne Barrie, who allowed
me to borrow precious original memoirs, and Annabel Venning,
who has contributed to this project in more ways than she realises.
Finally, I can never adequately repay Colin and Lynnette Behn for
the unflagging openhearted generosity they have shown me on so
many fronts since I first met them in 2014.

The bedrock of the book is the years of participant observation
fieldwork I have carried out in Borneo since the 1980s; I thank from
the bottom of my heart all those local people – mostly Dayaks – who
took me into their homes and lives during that time. I also conducted more than one hundred and twenty formal interviews for the
book in Sarawak and among SRD veterans in Australia; I am deeply
grateful to all those who allowed themselves to be interviewed
(listed in the Bibliography). My friendships and many conversations

with three SRD Borneo veterans – Bob Long, Allan Russell and, especially, Jack Tredrea – informed the narrative in multiple ways.

Heartfelt thanks to Hannah Bulloch and Peter McCarthy, who made time to read and provide valuable comments on the complete manuscript while under extreme work pressure of their own. Rick Moor and Bernard Sellato – retired military officer and eminent scholar of Borneo respectively – not only fielded incessant questions on points of detail but also read every chapter in draft – some chapters over and over – and still found time to go through the entire manuscript once it was completed. Their copious comments and suggestions saved me from many errors and pointed me towards crucial themes I otherwise might not have seen. Bernard also generously supplied a number of the photographs reproduced in the book. They both showed me the meaning of friendship.

A number of exceptionally kind and forbearing friends overlooked my relentless denial of sociality, listened patiently to my obsessive retellings of the Semut story, kept the home fires burning while I was doing fieldwork and helped in innumerable other ways over the years I worked on this project. Thanks to Fiona Allen, Hannah Bulloch, Shona Elliott, Mark Fletcher, Ken George, Alastair Greig, Michael Heppell, Martha Macintyre, Annie McCarthy, Peter McCarthy, Eileen McNally, Elizabeth Minchin, Helen Moore, Kirin Narayan, Susie Russell, Affrica Taylor, Robyn van Dyk, John Walker, Ryan Walter, Cathy Wylie and Rose Zobec. The last period of the writing coincided with the COVID-19 lockdown; I owe more than I can say to Eileen and Susie – my Canberra COVID 'family' – who ensured that body and soul remained nourished during that period.

Finally, this book is dedicated to two remarkable men who died during its writing. Jack Tredrea inspired me to write it, and his optimistic spirit animates it. Barry Hindess never understood why I wanted to write it, but he knew that it made me happy. And that was enough.

INDEX

Note: Page locators in italics denote maps and/or illustrations. Dayak and Asian surnames are not inverted.